REVOLUTIONARIES
WITHOUT REVOLUTION

Revolutionaries Without Revolution

ANDRÉ THIRION

Translated by Joachim Neugroschel

MACMILLAN PUBLISHING CO., INC.
New York

© Editions Robert Laffont, S.A., 1972

English Translation Copyright © 1975 by
Macmillan Publishing Co., Inc.

Macmillan Publishing Co., Inc.
866 Third Avenue, New York, N. Y. 10022
Collier-Macmillan Canada Ltd.

Library of Congress Cataloging in Publication Data

Thirion, André, 1907–
    Revolutionaries without revolution.
    1. Thirion, André, 1907–   —Biography.
I. Title.
PQ2639.H368Z513 1975   322.4'2'0924 [B]   74-9859
ISBN 0–02-617400–6

Originally published in France under the title
Révolutionnaires sans Révolution.

FIRST AMERICAN EDITION 1975

Printed in the United States of America

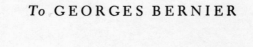

To GEORGES BERNIER

CONTENTS

1
BACCARAT

BACCARAT IS A SMALL INDUSTRIAL TOWN ON the edge of an unattractive plateau. It is agreeably situated at the very point where the valley of the Meurthe passes into the Vosges, From the wooded hilltops overlooking the town and the valley on the west, you can see both the plateau and the Vosges. At the time of my birth, the Meurthe, upstream from Baccarat, forked into two arms that converge again downstream. The smaller of the arms, which has recently silted up, flowed along the foot of the rocky ridge on which the village of Deneuvre was built. This ridge, towering some hundred and fifty feet above the valley, is sheer on all sides. Deneuvre was an ancient Gallic settlement that the Romans fortified. The castrum, whose ruins are still extensive, was built in the third or fourth century. Part of the outer wall is intact, and the moat is quite distinct. The remnants of a turretlike structure look like a trained bear standing on his hind legs. This is the oldest construction in the entire area.

Throughout the High Middle Ages, Deneuvre's solid walls prevented any number of pillages. At the other end of the ridge, opposite the Roman castrum, stood a fortified castle. At that time, Baccarat was merely a suburb of Deneuvre, leading to the bridge across the Meurthe. In the late thirteenth century, Baccarat was separated from Deneuvre, and the Counts de Blamont constructed a small fortress there. Situated on a rock that was lower than the one in Deneuvre, this new fortress, within crossbow-shot, was meant to billet their men. Some of its very high walls are still standing, as are a watchtower that looks like a seashell and the large tower of the Voués, in lovely rose and yellow stones. My grandmother had seen that tower still intact, with its roof surging up more than a hundred feet over the town. After it was ignited by a bolt of lightning, the alarmed town aldermen had a stonework landing demolished.

The vicissitudes of laws and conquests awarded Baccarat to the bishops of Metz, who built a castle next to the fortress. In 1552, the town and the castle became French, while Deneuvre remained Lorrainese. These subtle distinctions did not disturb the lansquenets of the Thirty Years' War. In 1636 the Swedes, allies of Louis XIII, stormed Deneuvre, killing everyone who fell into their hands and setting fire to the town and its castle. For good measure, they also destroyed the castle of Blamont and Baccarat. After these invaders came the Plague, and by the end of the war nearly all the inhabitants were dead. Deneuvre was ruined forever.

On the wreckage of the surrounding walls, the survivors built the farms and the houses that are still there today, except for those that were burned down in 1914. One noble edifice bears the date 1660. In the middle of the eighteenth century, King Stanislas' administrative skill and the absence of war brought back prosperity. A church was erected on the ruins of the castle of Deneuvre; its bulbous clocktower gives the entire structure a foreign look. A bishop of Metz founded the celebrated crystal works, which were originally intended to manufacture glass. By the end of the century, using the excellent sand from the Meurthe, the ashes of bracken and fir trees, and the lead of the high valleys in the Vosges, they began producing crystal. A few years before the French Revolution, a stone bridge with seven arches was built across the larger arm of the Meurthe.

In 1914, Baccarat had seven thousand inhabitants and a garrison of nearly three thousand men. The crystal factory employed two thousand workers and covered dozens of acres on the right bank of the Meurthe. A brewery and a plant manufacturing metal poles employed two hundred workers. There were two stonework shops, a lemonade maker, two sawmills, a printing plant, three or four small embroidery businesses handling the homemade goods of the villagers, artisans in all the specialties, two doctors, a church, a chapel, a synagogue, a hospital, a brothel, the notaries and bailiffs necessary for the handling of properties in the area, and a private bank, the Banque Crépin. Although Baccarat had never been a farming center, as Deneuvre was, almost a dozen farm families lived either in town or on the hills. Richest of all were the Steffs, who lived above Humbepaire, at the Bingottes, an imitation stronghold with machicolated battlements.

A good third of the crystal workers and all the management, except for the chief engineer, lived within the factory enclosure, whose doors were locked every evening. Those men who were not lodged by the boss hurried twice a day through the main streets, which echoed with the clopping of wooden shoes and the clinking of tin bowls. After each meal, the streets belonged to the soldiers in their colorful uniforms. The commanders regularly held parades and reviews. Each battalion had a band, with big and small drums, bugles, and hunting horns. The band of the Twentieth was excellent, thanks to a certain Captain Médard, a fine musician who made sure that good instrumentalists were detailed to his battalion. Médard greatly admired my father, who gave him lessons in harmony. Every Sunday the Captain's men would play in double time at the bandstand on Promenade du Patis, which runs along the left bank of the Meurthe, opposite the crystal works. Whenever the band would march down our street, Médard would order his musicians to halt under our windows, if he knew my father was at home, and serenade him with a sort of morning concert. The horsemen used trumpets of the kind used during the First Empire; their sharp blare was rather cheerful.

On the right bank of the Meurthe, Baccarat was built around a long street that stretched for more than a mile alongside the river. This street is commercial at the center, lower-class to the south, and middle-class to the north. The center of town, in 1914, was Rue des Ponts on the left bank, it ran perpendicular to the two arms of the Meurthe, which cut it off at either end. In those days, the street level was at least three feet lower, and the overall appearance was more coherent and less pretentious than it is today. The backdrop to the west was the sober and harmonious façade of the Gondrecourt boarding school, with its triangular frontal, and, further up, the church of Deneuvre, which was perched on a terrace of the old castle. To the east, the street opened wide upon the Meurthe. The river itself remained out of sight, however, because, in order to build the bridge and the church, a kind of knoll had been raised upon the bank. No doubt Roman ruins may still be found underneath it. The church of 1914, which was done in Gothic style by a contemporary of Viollet-le-Duc, did not withstand the Second World War. On the other side of the street, lower down, almost at water level, stood a small but rather boastful castle of modest classical appearance, which belonged to the owners of the crystal works. Its façade had the distinguished look of houses built in the eighteenth century by architects who had been trained before the Revolution. The views of the right bank were the same as today: the terrace of the crystal works with its lovely trees and, just half a mile away, the open forests of Grammont, which ran perpendicular to the large bridge and parallel to the backdrop formed by Gondrecourt on the other bank.

Most of the houses on Rue des Ponts were built between 1780 and 1850 in the simple and noble style that had been fashionable in Lorraine since the late seventeenth century. The first-floor windows have basket-handle arches and freestone architraves; those on the next story are smaller, but their form is the same. At times, they are replaced by a row of rectangular or circular dormer windows, which let light into the attic. The red-tile roofs are flatter than the housetops in Alsace or Burgundy, a tradition that probably dates back to Roman times. The street was adorned with two bronze fountains like those that can still be found in Raon-l'Etape. The larger fountain, which had a circular basin, ennobled the sidewalk in front of the home of our cousins, the Guébourgs. The smaller, surmounted by a lion, ornamented the other side of the street, up at the Banque Crépin.

I was born at No. 20 Rue des Ponts, in the house that my father had purchased for his marriage. To judge by the arrangement of the cellars and my memory of the façade and the gardens, the house constituted half of a two-story mansion constructed around 1880. There were five windows facing the street and two wings at an angle. Our entrance door opened upon an outside stairway of seven or eight steps. On the ground floor there was a tobacco shop kept by a highly dignified, white-bearded gentleman who was nonreligious, a supporter of the Republic, and head of the local Freemasons.

The staircase from the street floor to the next landing was a wide single flight that led into an antechamber which served as a waiting room for my father's pupils. With the exception of my grandmother's apartment on the third story, where Louis-Philippe reigned, the house

was "modern" in each single detail. Following designs by Tony Selmersheim (to whom we owe the monumental wrought-iron gate of
the Petit Palais) and with the help of a carpenter from Deneuvre—
an intelligent and capable man who had been converted to the art
of his time—it was decorated in turn-of-the-century style. Doors,
windows, paneling, open beams, coffered ceilings—everything was
decked out with the sharp, twisted molding that was then fashionable. On the second floor, the pink parlor and my father's library
faced the street. The pale mahogany and tulip-wood furnishings of
the pink parlor were by Selmersheim, and the curtains were by Tif-
fany, as was the upholstery of the armchairs and the sofa. The back
of the room was filled by a Steinway grand piano, on which a plaster
cast from the Louvre—a small-scale reproduction of the Nike of
Samothrace—was perched. The pink parlor was usually off limits for
me, either because my father was composing or because my mother
was playing bridge. Adjoining it, my father's library, with furniture
by Majorelle, occupied a long, narrow room whose walls were lined
with thousands of volumes. We would sometimes stay there in the
winter because there was a divan and a continuously burning heater.
The library opened into the green parlor, less sophisticated, and appointed with large and comfortable upholstered armchairs, a "modern" bookcase with special sections for music and periodicals, and
two pianos, one of which had a pedal board, like an organ. Music lessons were given in the green parlor.

On the other side of the landing, a sort of pantry led into the kitch-
en and into the extraordinary dining room. I called this highly successful creation by Tony Selmersheim Mélisande's dining room. On
the wallpaper depicting vistas of trees full of autumn leaves, the
trees in the foreground reached all the way up to the ceiling. They
stood along paths that were strewn with dead leaves, and the carpet was also littered with dead leaves. A gigantic and complicated
buffet had three upper doors with panes showing the trails in a forest.

The children's room was included in my grandmother's apartment.
It was the only room of no artistic interest in the entire house!

The house was lit by means of municipal gas and kerosene lamps.
Electricity didn't reach Baccarat until 1920. The crystal factory had
harnessed a natural waterfall up river on the Meurthe to provide the
power for its rudimentary machinery. The gas produced a hot, white
light that was both luxurious and abundant. But people tended to
make greater use of kerosene lamps, which created huge zones of

shadow and mystery. My parents' lamps were copper or bronze and decorated with writhing water nymphs, flowers, and creepers. The most popular was the Pigeon lamp, which is sold today in flea markets and antique shops. Its cylindrical reservoir of white or yellow metal, which could hold at best a half-pint of coal oil, had a handle surmounted by a spherical globe of transparent glass covering a wick, which often smoked. The height of the wick was adjusted by means of a button. During the war, the Pigeon lamp was the most widely used lighting device in Lorraine. I did homework by its light, which was weaker than that of a candle.

The roads were white, and in dry weather a vehicle of any kind would raise a cloud of dust. The town rang with the shouts of knife-and-scissors grinders, peddlers, glaziers, and basket weavers, who also made cane-bottomed chairs. Marriages, deaths, public auctions, and market days were announced by the town crier, whose drum could be heard from far off. Friday was market day. Before 1914, the market was in our street. Peasant women brought one-pound hunks of butter with geometrical designs carved with a fork or simple flowers printed with a mold. Enveloped in cabbage or lettuce leaves, the hunks were arranged in pretty black wicker baskets that the women carried on their arms. (Today these baskets would look marvelous in Saint-Tropez.) On some Fridays, I encountered in the kitchen a gaunt old man who sold contraband salt and matches wrapped in thick blue paper. My grandmothers bought only smuggled salt. They felt that robbing the government was not robbing, a notion that scandalized their sons.

Occasionally on a Sunday in summer, my father would borrow my uncle Albert's buggy and Mignon, the placid white horse. The buggy looked like a Rousseau painting. We never got farther than two or three miles from Baccarat. Usually we drove out to a farm near Thiaville, which we reached via a shady road along the Meurthe. The farm was hidden at the entrance to a dale, through which the Saint-Pierre creek flowed. There we would have a luncheon of home-made bread, butter, and cream with excellent Sainte-Laudy lemonade served in black corked bottles that looked like champagne bottles and bore a large yellow label proudly reproducing all the medals won at contests and exhibitions. During the last prewar year, when my father was ill, Dr. Schmitt, our family physician, would take his daughter and my mother, who were good friends, along on his rounds of visits. Dr. Schmitt had an open-topped automobile. On days when there was no school, I had to join them. I really hated those boring trips through the horrible villages of the plateau, interrupted by endless stops during which I had to endure the chatter of the two young women.

The crystal works belonged to the Michauts, an old Catholic family of reactionaries who had integrated themselves little by little into the French aristocracy. In 1912, the head of the family, Adrien Michaut, was a middle-aged man with polite and distant manners. Accustomed to being in command, he was a patronizing authoritarian, a real Simon Legree. A mayor of the town and district councilor, he did a fine job representing the people who had come to power with the Duke de Broglie and the industrial barons.

The crystal factory was a realm of moral order, and through its influence the entire town was austere and right-minded. Liberalism was the privilege of men who were independent of the crystal works, such as government officials, or Rauch the brewer, or my uncle Albert. It is very audacious, however, to characterize the opinions of those Republicans as liberal.

There was never the least mention of strikes or unions or socialism at the crystal works. And the brewer or the manufacturer of metal poles would have been no more tolerant of such talk than Adrien Michaut. They were separated from the lord of the manor only by their manners, their social background, their life style, their more familiar ways, and, above all, by a dash of anticlericalism. These members of the opposition never went to mass, and they accused Adrien Michaut of running a virtual inquisition in his plant with the aid of the clergy. But they would never have allowed their wives to miss a service, and their daughters had to attend the Gondrecourt boarding school. My father's situation in this regard was peculiar: he voted for the Republicains, he was a freethinker, but he attended mass every Sunday. He was the titular organist of the church, and he could use the grand thirty-two-stop organ to work on his interpretations. The entire clergy of the diocese used to consult him in matters of music, and the aristocrats in the area sent their children to him for piano lessons.

Adrien Michaut's principles were based on a sort of feudal Christian paternalism. His whole family, and he himself, exemplified simplicity and all the other virtues. For the Michauts, the population of Baccarat was divided into castes, and individuals were equal only before God and the law; elsewhere, the hierarchies had to be maintained, with Adrien Michaut at the top. But, although this system was founded on the inequality of wealth and position and assumed that deference to higher stations was the absolute rule of conduct, it also imposed certain unavoidable duties on the upper classes. First of all, one had to live unostentatiously, eschewing any lavish expense. The Michauts might live in castles, never lose touch with absolute luxury, deal with royalty, and entertain the princes of the world, but, in a virtual tour de force, they managed to make this seem like an episodic and strictly professional aspect of their life. The wives and daughters had their hats and clothes made by the milliners and dressmakers of the little town and they were not distinguished by their elegance or the richness of their wardrobe. The master's wife made a strict rule of receiving during her weekly "at home" the wives of the notables, and she would return visits. In a sewing group over which she presided the local housewives knitted for the poor. In fact, she was up to her ears in charity work. Joined by the wives of her husband's associates and a few young ladies of good breeding including my mother, she visited the poor and the sick, bringing them meat and other food and helping to make a birth or a death more bearable. In return for all of this, each person was expected to remain in his or her place and be right-thinking.

The clergy and the various nuns played an important part in the social life. Although religious groups of high-school students, girls, women, men, and old people brought together a part of the population for healthy exercises, the common people were virtually excluded from such associations. The church gave life in town a rhythm, with its baptisms, weddings, burials, first communions, masses, vespers, complines, and processions. Nearly all these ceremonies were announced by long tollings and pealings, and since Deneuvre did not want to be left behind, the town was regularly a-jingle and a-clatter. Spiritual nourishment was dispensed by sermons, home visits by the priests, and the Catholic press.

Despite his political successes, Adrien Michaut wanted to make his crystal works a town within the town, where he could fortify the social hierarchy as far as possible. He worried about private lives, would not tolerate bad habits, and always had something to say about marriages: each person was expected to choose someone of his own station. Thus, the son of a clerk, or the clerk himself (this modest title was applied to heads of departments), could not marry the daughter of a café owner or a simple worker. This solicitude extended even to the master glaziers and to masters of cutting or engraving. On the other hand, Michaut never abandoned anyone. As long as they could stand on their feet, the old could work in the factory. Dozens of men who were practically useless were charitably employed at jobs invented to give the illusion of activity and as a pretext for a salary. For old-timers who were really in a bad way, there was the home, which, of course, was run by nuns.

Since its reorganization in the early nineteenth century, the Baccarat crystal works had never experienced any strikes or layoffs. When the great depression of 1930 hit France, Adrien Michaut at first wanted to buck it. He insisted on manufacturing wares that never sold, then paid some of his personnel to do nothing. But as the situation continued, his reserves began to drain away, and he had to reduce working hours and lay off some hundred workers. Once there were unemployed men in Baccarat, the unions went into action. Adrien Michaut was an old man. He did not survive the challenge to his entire system. For the first time, the workers of the *Cristallerie* joined a union.

During Michaut's lifetime, Baccarat crystal had enjoyed a worldwide reputation for the quality of the material and the technical perfection of its manufacture. But the inspiration was lost. The conservative spirit of its owner as well as the taste of its clientele, (royalty and the solidly established bourgeoisie) deprived Baccarat of the originality and imagination sometimes seen in other, albeit lesser-known, French crystal works. The factory had been managed so parsimoniously that costs of technical or artistic research had been reduced to an absolute minimum. At the turn of the century, Gallé and Daum posed no threat to the management of the Baccarat *Cristallerie,* who adapted the "modern" style with prudence and moderation. But the work of the glaziers was miserable; in 1914, the methods were still those of 1830. Glassblowers never lived to a ripe old age, and the beauty of the product depended largely on the quality of the manpower. There had already been several generations of glass workers and specialists in cutting and engraving, but by 1919 the exodus of both male and female labor to Nancy and the Paris area was apparent. The salaries at the new crystal factories were very high.

2
FAMILY AFFAIRS

"FAMILY" MEANT THE THIRIONS, THE GEYERS, the Sainte-Laudys, and, secondarily, the Guébourgs. Only the Thirions were of Lorrainese stock. They originally came from Harreberg, a forest village near Dabo, and had been sawyers for generations. All of them left soon after the Revolution for the swampy area around Vic, especially Vergaville, where they had bought property. My great-grandfather was a musician. One of his sons settled in Baccarat before 1870. Not only was he head of music at the crystal factory, but he also took care of the harmonium at church and composed waltzes in Second Empire style.

My grandfather married a Geyer, whose family came from Alsace and had settled in Baccarat some twenty years earlier. My grand-mother had been a beauty. It was she who brought me up. Widowed at fifty, she died at a very old age. I have never been able to decide whether she was stupid or had just given up hope. She played the piano rather badly, adored Beethoven and the operas of her time—Meyerbeer, Ambroise Thomas, Gounod—but she bewailed her son's music. There was no melody in it. She made the best of an evolution that inflicted Fauré, Debussy, Ravel, and Stravinsky on her.

She read a good deal, disliked Anatole France, but was enraptured by Balzac, whom she plunged into over and over again. "He saw everything," she would say, "and understood everything, and I always find something new in him." She was very pious, and incapable of doing almost anything with her hands except embroidery and mending. The dishes she cooked became more and more inedible. She knew nothing of scandalmongering or maliciousness.

The Geyers were rather quaint. The great-grandfather, a cousin to my grandmother, was an eccentric who ran a draper's shop after squandering a part of his old bourgeois fortune. In the silverware that the Geyers owned and that the Germans seized in our cellar in 1914, there were a great number of pieces from a Strasbourg bishop who died during the first few years after the Restoration. In the Geyer mansion, an absurd combination of a department store and ready-to-wear shop, the vast, badly kept, humid rooms, were full of ancient armchairs, multicolored wooden saints, and small, precious bits of furniture in marquetry or Martin varnish. Window mannequins, their busts covered with black filoselle, stood among the Louis XVI easy chairs and dressing tables. Grandfather Geyer's wife, née Didio, apparently thought of herself as an empress. She was a drug addict, but that never prevented her from being very amorous. In 1912 or 1913, her husband, who was over seventy-five, was attacked by a swarm of bees and brought home dying. The widow gazed for a long time at her husband's corpse in deeply restrained sorrow. Finally, between two polite tears, she sighed, "And to think that just this morning . . ."

The son inherited the father's temperament. He spent most of his life in bed with his wife (my mother's sister). Sometimes, when the two of them had company, say a family dinner, the guests would have to wait because at the last moment my uncle had been unable to resist pouncing on her.

When my father was young, the Geyer home was very gay. Costumes were donned on any pretext; there were theatricals and masked dinners. During vacation time, distant cousins, who were far from uninteresting, would arrive. The brother of my uncle Emile Geyer was a young and greatly promising psychiatrist. He had written his dissertation on Ibsen's plays. Around 1905, he committed suicide—a gesture that definitively prevented my uncle from doing any sustained work.

The Didios played a large role in my childhood. Uncle Léon, as the Geyers said, was an infantry general. His career had been terminated by a duel he had fought in Nancy with a delightful Bohemian, an expert swordsman and worshipful master of a Masonic lodge, Gouthière-Vergnolle, who later, around 1925, was to help me a great deal with my artistic undertakings. Uncle Léon was a handsome man with a large mustache and he was as tall as my father. He had a gift for anecdotes, and for hours on end he would tell the story of his life in a terrible Alsatian accent. His brother Oscar built railroads in Russian Poland, so the family owned stacks of Russian railway bonds. "Don't lend the Tsars any money," he would say. "They're going to go bankrupt. But with railroads you can rest easy." He failed to foresee nationalization and knew nothing about the theory of imperialism.

When the Franco-Prussian War was announced in 1870, Oscar hopped the first train back to France to defend his country. That was before Sedan. The day he arrived in Paris, his brother Léon was already on duty. Léon sent a buddy to meet him at the station.

"But I don't know your brother. Does he look like you?"

"No, but you can't miss him."

When the train chugged in, a young man wrapped up in a gigantic tricolor stepped down from a first-class compartment. It was Oscar! He threw a huge patriotic party, and then he bought a company of pontifical zouaves and fought on the Loire with d'Aurelle de Paladines.

The Sainte-Laudys weren't from Lorraine either. They came from Béarn. The family had broken up early in the Second Empire and left their native region. One boy went to South America; my grandfather came to Baccarat. He married a Vosgian farmer's daughter who owned a bit of property; then he started a lemonade factory and a liquor store, whose reputation spread for miles around. "He was a gentleman, your grandfather Sainte-Laudy was," my father would often tell me. He earned a pile of money. His wife bore him eleven children, seven of whom survived despite medieval hygienic conditions.

The Sainte-Laudys were true Gascons, proud and individualistic. Some of them had a bent for mysticism and adventure. The most remarkable of them were Victor and his sister Jeanne, my mother, who were very close to one another. Victor entered the Dominican order and became a missionary in Van, Armenia. But the most colorful Sainte-Laudy and the one I liked the most was my uncle Albert, the father of my cousins Simone and Marguerite. He was loud and as hotheaded as a musketeer, fearless and above reproach, upright, authoritarian, impartial and muddling, and fidgety. His mere presence livened things up. His three Lunéville nephews, the sons of the eldest brother, resembled him in various degrees. Two of them were in German concentration camps during the war.

The Guébourgs were more distant connections, apparently on the Geyer side. We saw a lot of them because they had an important position in our little town. Older than my father, but younger than my grandmother, they constituted one of the pillars of Catholicism in Baccarat. The family consisted of René, his sister Marie, and their old mother Adeline. My cousin René Guébourg, a former seminarian, then a lay-order dignitary, limped, wore a goatee, had a fine presence, and was ascetic, severe, and harsh. He had kept his sister Marie single, although she—a lovely, distinguished, and slightly affected lady —would gladly have taken the plunge. To their great shame, their father had been a butcher, and it was imperative to forget such a rude heritage. They had enough money not to have to work and to be able to finance all sorts of charities. Two or three times a year, they would give grand family dinner parties, with a couple of archpriests and church deacons in the places of honor. I was dragged along to these after I was ten; bored stiff, I would always manage to say or do something improper. My mother dreaded this but my aunt Louise cheerfully looked forward to it, because I always said things that people didn't.

I liked my cousin Marie, and I liked the house she lived in before 1914 because it was full of things I never saw at home—old tapestries, crystal balls, a harp. I didn't much care for my cousin René. He taught me the rudiments of Latin, and the lessons were hours of torture.

My great joy was René Guébourg's relationship with the Crouziers. Désiré Crouzier was his closest relative and the town drunk: he was never sober. Any meeting of the two was a spectacle. Whether he was flopped down on a stoop, half-conscious, or staggering through the street singing at the top of his lungs, Désiré could sense that his cousin was coming. René, mortified, would try to avoid his scandalous relative. But it was wasted effort. As soon as he caught sight of René Guébourg, no matter how far away, Désiré Crouzier would gather his last ounce of strength and hail the goateed ascetic, reeling toward him as fast as he could and yelling: "Hi, René. C'mon, say hello. Be nice, René." Anyone who witnessed the scene found it funny.

But we had to be careful because René Guébourg was one of the town authorities, and he was far from easygoing. I always cracked up, but when I turned around to enjoy my old cousin's embarrassment, I'd get a slap or two.

The town drunk interested me not because he put my cousin in a ludicrous position, but because he was the grandson of Balafré. Old Mother Crouzier was *the* senior citizen of Baccarat. She was over ninety-five in 1912 and still trotted off to mass every Sunday. Her eyes were bloodshot and almost burnt out, but even though she couldn't see much, she enjoyed the respect paid to her age and to her father's exploits. My cousin Marie and my grandmother would often tell me a story that I would have gladly heard twenty times over because I wanted to be surrounded by heroes. The little old lady's father had joined the Consulate's army at the age of fifteen. In order to look bigger and older, he had stuck a pack of cards in his boots. He fought in seventeen campaigns and was wounded fourteen times, or vice versa. A saber slash across his face had scarred him forever; hence his nickname, Balafré, Scarface. In 1815, he was demobilized, and the arrival of the cossacks rubbed him the wrong way. To avoid paying any forced military contribution, he hid all his valuables—a few jewels, the cross, some silver, and a pair of pistols—under a dung heap. The cossacks discovered everything, and Balafré, who was also suspected of working with the partisans, was sentenced to a flogging. The punishment was inflicted in front of his house, and but for the intervention of a chivalrous officer, who was touched by this courageous veteran's scars, he would have been flogged to death. Every time I ran into the old red-eyed witch, I respectfully greeted the daughter of a soldier of Napoleon.

My father was no kind of soldier, but he was a very handsome man, with a pointed beard, pepper-and-salt like his hair (in our family, hair began to gray at twenty). He was always very correctly dressed, rather like a professor. He rarely laughed; he was anything but intimate, avoided confidences, and didn't like to be contradicted. I only saw him get a bit sociable at functions where a few young women were present. But he did radiate a reassuring self-confidence, and his mere presence was warming. Before 1914, he would go to Nancy three times a week to do his shopping and give lessons at the Conservatory. He spent an entire day at Lunéville, where he had pupils in the garrison and where he played a bit of chamber music.

Our home was entirely devoted to music. It was understood that my father was a very important figure in that art. Hours of silence were imposed upon us, and we were periodically forbidden to go upstairs. At an early age, Louis Thirion had revaled such exceptional gifts that he had gained the respect of his own father and of everyone else who played for fifteen leagues around. He was still a boy when he entered the Nancy Conservatoire, but he was already a talented violinist and pianist, and he became an excellent organist. The richness, firmness, skill, and originality of his musical works are still widely praised. The Schola Cantorum had reached its peak, and it was in Vincent d'Indy's milieu that he became friends with Gustave Samazeuilh and got to know Albert Roussel. Except for Roussel's compositions, however, he didn't much care for the music of the Schola. His closest friend was Florent Schmitt, also a native of Lorraine, born in Blamont and ten years his senior. The two of them went on pilgrimages to Bayreuth, but it was the music of the Russian Five, especially Rimski-Korsakov and Borodin, that really made their personalities blossom. In his youth, my father was a fervent worshipper of Paul Dukas, to whom he dedicated his first symphony; he considered Dukas his true teacher. He loved the rigor and modesty of the composer of *La Péri*. But he was more attracted to Debussy and Ravel. More than anything, he revered the pianistic style, the inspiration of the *Preludes*, and Ravel's harmony and orchestration. Like all musicians of his time, he regarded the premières of *Petrouchka* and *The Rite of Spring* in 1912 and 1913 as major events. Among the classical masters, he preferred Bach and Schumann.

He made a strict rule of playing piano two hours a day, and my adolescence proceeded among Bach's fugues, Schumann's *Carnaval*, Fauré's barcarolles, the two books of the preludes, and *The Children's Corner* suite, *Gaspard de la nuit*, *Iberia*, the *Goyescas*, and *Petrouchka*. From 1904 to 1913, my father devoted all his summers to composing; several sonatas of his were performed, as well as a trio, a string quartet, and two symphonies that gained him a certain renown in France and Germany. He never spoke about his music and made no particular effort to have it presented.

He had married my mother at twenty-three. Jeanne Sainte-Laudy was his childhood sweetheart. He apparently had qualms about making her his wife, however; my mother—a native of Béarn, black-haired, and richer, more ambitious, and more decisive than he—more or less forced him into marriage.

Their conjugal bliss did not last. My father, radiant with his success in Paris, was attractive to women and not insensitive to them.

My mother was soon betrayed and took refuge in piety and duty. When her brother, the Dominican, settled in Van, she organized what amounted to a committee for the support of his mission and for the benefit of little Armenians. She was in touch with dozens of charitable souls who helped to sell Armenian lace everywhere for the benefit of Uncle Victor's schools and dispensaries.

Things took a turn for the worse around 1910, soon after my sister was born. The family doctor had advised my mother against having another child. My father fell madly in love with the attractive and elegant wife of a guardsman-general (which was what the forestry officials were called). This passion soon became the talk and almost the scandal of the town. Madame R. was also madly in love with my father. Whenever they couldn't meet socially—which was actually quite easy, since their families were on good terms—the lovers contrived lengthy and useless walks in front of their houses, but their pretense of strolling never fooled anyone. My mother ignored Madame R., who strode up and down Rue des Ponts under the most futile pretexts, while my father, interrupting his work, openly stationed himself at his office window. In fine weather, my father would take me walking through the woods behind the railroad station, which he was very fond of. But he would suddenly cut our excursion short, send me home, and head straight for Madame R.'s house. I wasn't at all happy about this, because Madame R. had a small daughter, scarcely younger than myself, whom I liked. And when I got back and told my grandmother, "Father's over on Rue de Frouard," she would shrug, warning me not to tell my mother about it. Although I was proud to be in on a secret whose full significance I did not understand, I was as subtly and unwittingly naughty as any child and soon forgot my grandmother's instructions. I never suspected how much harm my indiscreet remarks did to my poor mother. Not until later did I come to appreciate her coolness and self-control in the face of such wounding information: I was betraying my father in reporting to my mother that he had gone to Rue de Frouard.

However, that romance overwhelmed my father and his mistress so powerfully that it became impossible for Monsieur R. and my mother to remain near them, or even in the same town. There was talk of transferring the guardsman-general. He may even have gone away from Baccarat, leaving his wife and his daughter behind temporarily. Both parties seemed to be heading toward a separation, or even a divorce. After composing a very beautiful sonata for piano and cello—in which one has no trouble hearing highly vivid and yet melancholy feelings—my father started a second symphony. He wanted to finish it by autumn 1913. But he never did; when all he had left to do was orchestrate the andante and the finale, he fell gravely ill. His nervous depression was aggravated by overexertion, which had begun when the R.'s moved away, and his troubled mind impaired the quality of his musical inspiration. My father stopped everything for a few months. He didn't fully recover until halfway through the lovely spring of 1914.

One sunny day, my mother took me for a long walk down the Promenade du Patis. She told me that we would be spending the summer in Switzerland, that my father would not be coming with us, and that I might not even see him when we came home because I would be going to school in Lausanne. "We shall leave your sister here, and your grandmother and your father. I need rest very badly. My health would get worse very quickly if I stayed in Baccarat." I had no clear idea of what was going on, except that I would be separated from my sister, of whom I was very fond. On the other hand, I would be seeing lakes and glaciers. The thought of being alone with my mother in a foreign land made me feel bigger, older, more important.

My mother was supposed to meet a friend of hers. She left me alone for a few moments. I remember that I saw Charles Crépin on the Promenade, a twenty-five-year-old dandy and banker's son. I greeted him like an adult and talked with him like one, passing along the news about my father's health as though we were talking about a mutual friend. My solemnity was reported at home by Charles Crépin, who was astonished and amused by my self-confidence and tone of voice during the conversation.

The war upset all these plans. Monsieur R. was killed in one of the earliest battles. Nearly forty years later, I told the story to Lady Mendl when we were talking about our parents. "How funny," said Yvonne. "Do you realize that I knew Madame R. and her daughter very well? We were living in Saint-Quay-Portrieux. Madame R., her daughter, and their maid settled very near us. Madame R. was a beautiful woman, who always seemed to be somewhere else: we assumed she was despondent because she had lost her husband so recently, but we found out the truth from the servants. 'Not at all!' said Madame R.'s chambermaid. 'She's not sad because she's a widow. Madame has been living loosely!' " I was very much in love with Yvonne Mendl; I told her that I envied my father and that if she and I were ever to have a parting of ways, I could wish for nothing better than such an homage from her chambermaid.

At vacation time, we would entertain relatives from the area of Dieuze, Lorraine, which was then German. They would stay in my grandmother's apartment for a few days. Then my father, my mother, and the Geyers would spend two or three days on the other side of the border. Everyone spoke French, because German has never been the language of the people in the swamp region. These visits and our trips to Dieuze led to conversations that intrigued me greatly because they were totally inconsistent with what our teachers told us about Alsace-Lorraine. The Baccarat family argued that the Germanization of the annexed provinces was moving right along. Although my grandmother's generation was still emotionally attached to France, some members of the younger generation, especially the men, were rallying to Prussia, despite very anti-German remarks at home. My great-aunt Maria entertained German officers from the Dieuze garrison at her own table. Sometimes, my father, or my uncle Geyer, would be dining at that very same table. When the officers didn't understand French, my aunt would openly make fun of them; her remarks, such as "Look at the way they're guzzling, those pigs," were famous throughout the family. When they spoke about Auguste, Aunt Maria's son, however, my uncles would say, "He's a Prussian, and if things keep on like this for a while longer, they'll all end up like him."

In 1913, Florent Schmitt rented a house in Petite Fosse, near Saint-Dié, for the holidays. My parents went to visit him, and since the Schmitts had a boy my age, I was taken along. Before we left, my parents gave me a long lecture. "Madame Schmitt doesn't pronounce her r's, just like in the days of the Directory; for instance, she says, 'Pa'is' and 'Ba'ets Usses' instead of 'Paris' and 'Ballets Russes.' Just make sure you don't seem to notice it." "As for Florent," my father added, "he's liable to have sudden and violent tantrums during some trivial conversation about an orchestra leader or a journalist. Even at dinner, he may take his wife aside—she can't help it, but she's not afraid—and throw dishes and plates out the window. You mustn't pay attention and above all you mustn't be scared; you mustn't laugh. Everyone stays calm. Madame Schmitt will ask the maid to clear the table; once the dishes have been replaced, everything will be peaceful again."

Sure enough, while they were talking, I think, about the Ballets Russes (it was the first time that I heard the name Stravinsky, whom my father and Schmitt so greatly admired), Schmitt had a violent outburst. A couple of dishes, glasses, and napkins flew out the window, which faced a small garden on the same level as the dining room. "C'mon André," said Raton Schmitt, and we went out on the grass to collect the results of his father's anger.

The Schmitts would then stay in our house for a few days. Patriotic frenzy was at its height because of some army maneuvers in the area. Baccarat was full of red trousers from somewhere or other, belonging to artillerymen and dazzling horseman. The whole point of the operations seemed to be the recapture of the Baccarat bridge, and since the assault would be taking place almost directly beneath our windows, nobody wanted to miss it. Unfortunately for me, it was scheduled very early in the morning, and my parents didn't think it was right to awaken the children. Nevertheless, I did hear the fusillade in my half-sleep; the following year, I had the same impressions, but this time they were real. I think a rainfall spoiled the whole spectacle. Late in the morning, my father took me to see another warlike scene that attracted the curious. At the far end of town, a few hundred yards from the edge of the Rappe Forest, the artillerymen had set up a 75-millimeter gun and were shooting a round every minute. I recently passed along that road, and a few yards away I found the original gun pit. What was the target of their fierceness? The road to Merviller or the steeple of the church? In those days, most of the firing was on a flat trajectory. The climax was to be a maneuver on the garrison's small drill ground. Two Farman biplanes had managed to land there, but now they couldn't take off again because of the deluge. Under the whirling rain that quashed the cavalry charge and the action that the public floundering about in the mud, was waiting for, I was able to admire the martial bearing and the green and gray uniforms of several Russian generals. Supposedly, there was even a grand duke in this glittering but stoic group.

During July 1914, the tension soon became intolerable for everyone. I noticed the very same anxiety in 1938 and 1939. Ultimately, people were wishing for war. Future operations were pictured with what seemed astonishing realism, because we knew the numbers of the units that would oppose our valiant infantry. We even knew the names of many of the German officers; the lieutenants spoke of them as though they were dueling rivals, though subsequent events made it clear that they would never meet face to face.

At home, we held a council of war to decide the measures to be taken in case all the reservists were called up. It was agreed that if things went badly, the family would seek refuge in our cellars, which were solidly vaulted and, we thought, artillery-proof. The whole family consigned their most cherished possessions to my father's care, since he was the least exposed; the Geyers brought their silverware, stacked up in champagne baskets, which were stowed away in the wine cellar facing the street.

There was no more talk of divorce, or of a trip to Switzerland. All the men were mobilized. My father was detailed to the auxiliary service and remained in town. Since he couldn't find an infantry uniform that fit him, he had to be content with a Red Cross armband and a kepi, which wasn't particularly martial. Edmond Crépin, the banker, stored the manuscript of the second symphony in the bank vault along with the securities and the deeds. Overnight, the class structure was demolished, and social ladders were gone. Professors and business leaders, simple soldiers or junior officers, were all one before the stripes. I would have liked my father to be a captain of the dragoons or the hussars. I was slightly consoled by the fact that, during the early days of the war, he often met with the garrison officers or other officers who, passing through Baccarat, dropped by to say hello to my mother; those visits gave him some status.

I settled happily into the war. Nothing would have displeased me more than the prospect of spending the rest of my life in peace and calm. I was quite proud to be personally living the History of France.

3
THE BAPTISM
OF FIRE

THE INITIAL VICTORIES IN ALSACE WERE GREETED
enthusiastically, but one morning we heard the cannon: the 20th Infantry Battalion was taking a stand against a Bavarian regiment at Badonviller. To everyone's amazement (for the 20th had a reputation for invincibility), we learned that night that the battle had not gone well. The infantrymen had fought courageously, but they were outnumbered. I escorted my aunt Louise and my mother to the station, where they were unloading the first casualties. The wounded were carried on stretchers from the station to a field hospital set up in the crystal-works school, some two hundred yards away. That was my first experience with blood. The mildly wounded led the way. We knew them all, and they told us who had died. Women were sobbing. Then the stretcher bearers brought the seriously wounded, wrapped in freshly bloodstained bandages, their faces white as sheets. Little Lorenceau's leg had been hacked to shreds. Young and handsome, his jet-black hair longer than the regulation cut, he lay absolutely prone upon his stretcher, making a theatrical entrance into the school. His beauty and the seriousness of his wound crowned all the horror. The boy lost the leg and throughout the entire war he remained the only young man in Baccarat; the other males in town were all old men or children.

We soon forgot this skirmish because the whole French army eventually passed through Baccarat. French troops recaptured Badonviller, and they marched across the border of 1871. The army was magnificent, like my tin soldiers. The march through town lasted five days. Sometimes an airplane with a black cross flew two or three hundred yards over the mass of resplendent uniforms. It was said that the gendarmes had discharged their heavy revolvers in the direction of the *Täuben,* which caused a good deal of amusement.

Around the fifteenth of August, my mother's health took a sudden turn for the worse. Dr. Schmitt's diagnosis was otitis; an immediate operation was necessary. My father obtained a permit to take my mother to the polyclinic of a military hospital in Nancy. The only people left in our home were my paternal grandmother—the good Alsatian—my sister, and I. Grandmother Sainte-Laudy joined us as a reinforcement.

We could hear cannon and we managed to discern some smoke from burning houses on the horizon. There was a succession of triumphant communiqués. The French were advancing everywhere, gradually liberating the annexed province of Lorraine; victory was taking the war away from our little town. Suddenly, on August 21, the military convoys began rolling back in the same stream as when they had sped toward the enemy. They were joined by pitiful retinues of refugees, peasants from Sainte-Pôle, Montigny, Domèvre, Blamont, with all the carts in creation. Rumor had it that the armies had been beaten before Saarburg and were now retreating. We quickly guessed the extent of the defeat when we saw the rows of hay wagons coming from Lorraine, all of them crowded with casualties. The entire 13th Corps ebbed back on foot, exactly as it had advanced. But now the regiments hurried through town in ranks of eight, with little discipline. The uniforms were dirty and torn, and the men were dying of thirst; all the children drew water nonstop from the bronze fountains and handed jugs and pails to the soldiers, who sometimes drank without halting. My grandmother decided to give the officers a glass of wine, and our neighbors did the same.

The convoys and the soldiers kept coming. Between them came the herds of animals evacuated by the border farmers. Those old men or ageless women in black were steering hay wagons full of furniture, children, and cripples. We heard the cannon again. The optimists believed it was the booming of the heavy artillery at the fort of Manonviller, but the dull sound, at first muffled and intermittent but tenacious, gradually became more distinct and more resonant. There was no longer any doubt about the development of the fighting.

On August 22, the little town began to empty. My aunts packed their bags like most of our neighbors. I must admit that the retreat was more and more depressing to watch; everything seemed confused, there were wounded men in the ranks, and even the horses were sometimes covered with blood. But, despite everything, the discipline remained intact. The grave officers and soldiers, absolutely exhausted and mortified by the retreat, kept marching by. To the civilian populace, which had grown accustomed to brass bands and the quick step of parades, it was absolute downfall. Whenever a fresher-looking group arrived, we took heart; but the next hour brought a new mob of dismal foot soldiers, new files of wagons full of casualties, and farmers terrorized by the battle.

At home, we were wondering what we ought to do. My grandmother kept receiving friends and relatives who had made up their minds to leave town. There was much talk about German atrocities. The newspapers were full of tales of the abominations in Belgium, but there were examples closer at hand. After the first battle, in Badonviller, the conquering Germans had shot a dozen civilians, both men and women; we knew some of them.

By the evening of August 22, no more trains were running on the Nancy line, and the station was open only to members of the military.

On August 23, the town was half empty. The cannons were at the gates, and the smoke of burning houses was rising everywhere along the skyline. One of my uncle Albert's clerks, too old to be mobilized, came to notify my grandmother that he too was leaving Baccarat with the carriage and Mignon the horse. He suggested that we all go along to Rambervillers. People were frightened because there was talk of defending the town. The engineers had mined an arch of the Great Bridge, and the soldiers were preparing retrenchments along the Meurthe. I had a violent and childish bit of temper at the thought of fleeing like the others. My grandmother refused flatly and haughtily: she was in charge of her son's house, his manuscripts, his paintings, his books, his silverware, and everything else. Grandmother Sainte-Laudy had also experienced the German occupation in 1870; remembering the defeat of the French at Nompatelize, she seconded my paternal grandmother's refusal. They sent the carriage away and prepared for the worst by furnishing one of the cellars with mattresses and provisions.

The retreating soldiers said that the Germans were approaching. We began to hear rifle fire in between the cannon. The ebb of French troops was an uninterrupted procession, but after an enormous traffic jam that lasted most of the day, there were long periods when there were no troops or convoys in the street. The evening was calm; the cannon fire had stopped. I even saw one or two mounted squadrons riding toward the enemy; their horses were trotting as though on parade, their uniforms were not covered with dust, and they looked as though they had just stepped out of a toy box. "The retreat's over," I said to my old cousin René Guébourg, who had come to consult with my grandmothers. He explained that they were merely reconnoitering and that there was no hope that these two hundred horsemen could possibly stop the German army. On the contrary, their riding toward the front was a sign that the enemy was not far off.

All our talk gravitated around the possibility of a departure, which became more and more improbable as the battle drew closer. There were no authorities left in Baccarat. The Republican mayor, a man named Tisserand, had left. So had the priest and the principal of the public school. My cousin Guébourg, who was of a clerical and reactionary persuasion, made scornful remarks about all these departures, even that of the priest, whom everyone loved and respected. The Germans had an annoying habit of shooting mayors and town priests, of course, but danger did not exclude duty! Quite naturally, but not without a certain selfish satisfaction, the onetime alderman René Guébourg was preparing to take over the relief. In the same way, the former mayor, Michaut, a district councilor as well as the owner and manager of the crystal works, also remained at his post. These were the people the unit leaders met with when they billeted in the town. But if the French were going to defend Baccarat, as they had apparently been ordered to do, they would have to blow up the Great Bridge. And the firing line would pass a hundred yards from the house. Should we run the risk of finding ourselves smack in the middle of the fighting, even in a solid cellar?

The morning of August 24 was sunny and hot (the evening before it had rained a bit). The news was even worse. The cannon fire had resumed very early and very close by. The rifle fire had reached all the hills of the right bank. The battle had come too near for us to entertain any reasonable thought of evacuating. Besides, my cousin Guébourg announced that the soldiers who were supposed to defend the bridge were also leaving. For my grandmother, this was a general defeat, a repetition of 1870. Once again, there would be no fighting in Baccarat. Then the Germans occupying the town had been scrupulously correct. Everyone had gone back to the habits of everyday life. My grandparents had entertained Prussian officers who loved music. "They play Beethoven very well," my grandmother was fond of saying. All we could do now was wait until the last French people had left.

But things didn't go quite as they had in 1870. The French of 1914 were apparently not willing to give in as easily as their grandfathers. To the north and east of the town, there was a great deal of shooting and booming. Whenever there were no retreating soldiers, Baccarat was deserted. All the shopkeepers had closed up, the streets were deserted, and a good many houses were empty.

W took in a panicky couple, the Lhotes. The man was seriously ill and had been discharged. His wife, a native of Lorraine, tall, blonde, and sanctimonious, was a born bearer of ill tidings, demoralized and demoralizing. Her only interests in life were prayer and misfortune—and perhaps, although she never admitted it to herself, men.

The Lhotes lived on the right bank, at the northern end of town. The shooting from a French battery installed just outside their windows had led them to ask us for shelter. The approach of the battle finally stopped that stupid woman's endless chatter. Since we could hear the cannon on all sides and the shells whistling overhead, all conversation was limited to furtive exchanges of banal impressions. In the morning, there were more troop movements, more hurried and less frequent than the day before. They struck us as somewhat contradictory. We saw ambulances and munitions wagons passing, but the climax seemed at hand. After a quick lunch—no one was hungry—we all returned to our observation posts in the pink parlor. Troops and convoys were becoming rarer and rarer; we no longer heard the dull thumping of French batteries, shells were bursting closer but not very often, the fusillade was less intense to the north.

We were glued to the closed windows. The blinds had been folded back to the walls, so that nothing interfered with our vision. My grandmother said that that was how it had to be for the arrival of the Germans, who would be worrying about treachery. The silence of the street, with nothing and no one passing, was disturbingly solemn and dangerous. It was very hot. Around three o'clock, when we were expecting to see the Germans and assuming that there were no French troops left on the right bank, several sections of a colonial infantry regiment appeared, in disorder and confusion. I had tin soldiers just like them, and they also looked like the color illustrations of the militia of 1871 in schoolbooks. These men were much wearier and dirtier than all the preceding troops; they were literally white with dust. Seven or eight of them left ranks and stretched out in the shade along houses or sat down on the steps of the small outside stairway at the drugstore across the street. Noncommissioned officers stopped the column and harangued the laggards, but, with tired gestures, they refused to fall back in. The officers did not insist, and the troop marched off. The laggards took off their packs and rifles; evidently they wanted to sleep. A few moments later, an automobile stopped in front of the exhausted soldiers. Out stepped a general, who spoke to them very gently: "C'mon, boys, just a little more effort; the Germans are coming and you'll all be captured." The soldiers replied with a volley of oaths. The general asked two or three men to get in with him, and the car went off. I was stunned by this overwhelming evidence, right before my eyes, of the defeat: soldiers at the end of their strength, refusing to fight or even to obey. How powerful the enemy must be if it had met the beautiful army (which had so blithely marched off to battle a week ago) and so quickly torn it to shreds. I was wondering what would happen to those soldiers lying on the sidewalk if a party of Germans were to loom up in the street. Then, on the roof of the drugstore, in a crash of thunder, a dazzling sharp orange light suddenly produced a thick white smoke. I could make out the soldiers scrambling to their feet and grabbing up their equipment in flight. That was the first shell that fell upon the town. Others followed.

We all tumbled down into the cellar. And I never found the floor in my father's library to be as slippery as it was that day.

The cellar we took refuge in faced the courtyard of the house, underneath the inside staircase. A path separated it from the wine cellar, which was under the curb of the street and now sheltered all the family silverware in champagne baskets. A large path perpendicular to the other one led to the street and to the yard. As soon as they were settled on their mattresses, the Lhotes and the grandmothers started telling their beads aloud. The town was undergoing a light artillery attack. We could hear the shells coming; the bursts were spaced fairly far apart. Once the rhythm of the firing was clearly in her head, Grandmother Thirion could no longer stand it: she had to see. After each explosion, she would scramble up to the first floor, into the pink parlor, dragging the other grandmother along. The two old ladies would return with a whole collection of useless information, "It dropped on the Such-and-such house. . . . A direct hit on the parlor of the So-and-so's. . . . Well, that crystal they were so proud of must be in a fine state. . . . This time it's the Crépin maid's room. . . . There's a fire at the crystal-works school." And so on. This chronicle of local destruction fed their backbiting conversation in between the Lord's Prayers and the Ave Marias. The Lhotes, trembling with fear, tried to keep the grandmothers from going upstairs, but the two old women were intrepid. Sometimes they miscalculated; if they had misread a whistling, an explosion very nearby would surprise them at the very door of the cellar. They would then drop back a few steps, listening attentively for the next shell, and we would hear Grandmother Thirion say to her crony, "Let's go."

Around five or six o'clock, the bombing of the immediate neighborhood came to a stop. With nothing more to see, the grandmothers decided to get everyone to come back upstairs. For a good long time, we stayed on the main floor, in the vestibule between the courtyard and the cellar, listening to the departing gunfire, the clatter of discharges, and the whistles, which varied widely according to the calibers. Some shells roared by like locomotives. The explosions were now rather far away.

Then the shooting stopped. It may have been around seven. My Guébourg cousins, whose house was a few hundred yards down the street, came for news. Nothing had been touched in our place. My old cousin and I walked as far as the Great Bridge, returning by way of the parish house and what looked like a small square in front of the town hall. It was a true war setting: several houses had been hit and had gaping holes in front or on top. The slashed telegraph lines were sprawling on the pavements. The streets were littered with all sorts of debris, pieces of tile, equipment, and huge shell splinters. But the destruction was not on the scale of the racket that we had heard. The bridge was obstructed by an enormous barricade of wagons filled with hay. The crystal-factory schools were burning. Not a soldier was to be seen, French *or* German, and the noise of battle had stopped.

As we were finishing our tour of town and rejoining the grandmothers, who were waiting on our doorstoop, two or three women who had ventured toward the bridge came running back. "It's the Germans!" they were yelling. We returned to the windows in the pink parlor. Outside, it was already growing dark. Lower-class women, in shawls and work jackets, were clustering at the entrance of Rue du Bréchon almost across from us. They watched the bridge but were careful to stay in the small street, which provided a sort of shelter and a good line of retreat. We could tell from their motions that they could see the Germans on the bridge, probably busy taking down the barricade. The municipal beadle and town crier, an old man with a medal from 1870, came out of the Jardins d'Espagne grocery store with a hunting rifle. He looked positively fearful. The women in work jackets dashed over to disarm him. The old crier gave in, threw the rifle in the gutter, and sheepishly disappeared down the small street. Now everyone disappeared. From the direction opposite the Great Bridge, two German horsemen, of the light cavalry, slowly trotted into our street; they were flanking a prisoner in red trousers. Their arrival at the bridge set off the forward movement of the foot soldiers. Cautiously advancing along the houses, holding one finger on the triggers of their rifles, stopping occasionally to take aim at a window without shooting (one of them aimed his weapon on our windows, and we were sensible enough not to move), a few German soldiers took over our street. They were exactly as in pictures, dressed in gray-green, with pointed helmets and tawny boots. Unlike the French, they didn't seem tired.

It was a relief. The battle was over. We were German, and the thought of any kind of reversal in favor of the French was inconceivable after what we had just seen.

Night had fallen, and everyone was very hungry. We were about to sit down in the Mélisande dining room to eat an enormous bacon omelet—which I can still smell—when someone rang the doorbell. The maid came to my grandmother: "It's the Germans," she said. My grandmother instantly went down, and we followed her to see what it was all about. I can still hear that extraordinary conversation: later on, my grandmother repeated it twenty times, so I can guarantee the authenticity of every detail.

In the entrance hall stood an officer, a few German soldiers, and a French prisoner from the 17th Light Infantry Battalion. The officer saluted, clicking his heels, which did not surprise my grandmother, who felt forty-four years younger.

"Major X., I am in command of the battalion occupying Baccarat. Madame, you have a tobacco shop in your house. I need tobacco for my men."

"But, sir, that shop doesn't belong to me. It is the property of our tenant, who went away a few days ago and didn't leave me the keys."

"I'm sorry, madame. With your permission, I will break down the door."

"Sir, I don't see what good that would do. I am not authorized to sell you my tenant's tobacco. Besides, in France tobacco belongs to the government, and my tenant has to render accounts to the state."

The major was visibly amused.

"Madame, do not forget that we are at war; we are at war with the French state. My men need tobacco; they have gone without it for four days. I will authorize them to take whatever they find in the store, but I will make sure that they do as little damage as possible to what belongs to you."

"Sir, you are putting me in an awkward position. The house itself belongs to my son, who is mobilized, and I feel that my responsibility is involved."

The major put an end to this untimely conversation by making out a small requisition order, which he handed to my grandmother.

A soldier cautiously forced open the door of the tobacco shop and pulled up the iron curtain that protected the window. The men accompanying him removed the packages of tobacco. The major himself supervised the operation.

"Are there any French people left in town?" he asked my grandmother.

"Goodness," she said, "I don't think so. We saw the very last ones pass by in the late afternoon. But I haven't left the house—my daughter-in-law's mother and my two grandchildren are also here—and I only know what I have seen myself."

"In that case," replied the major, "you can sleep without fear. The French are beaten, and I hope that the war will move away from you."

He saluted, clicked his heels, and ordered the outside door of the shop carefully closed again.

My grandmother was completely at ease. She deplored the pillage of the store, but she had again found the victorious Prussians deferential and polite, albeit with a slight tendency to seize other people's property. But the comparison with 1870 stopped there, because the armies of the Republic appeared to be tougher than those of Napoleon III. The fires reddening the horizon did not presage anything good. So we took new precautions. We brought canned food, chocolate, and sugar down to the cellar, and the children were put to bed fully dressed. My sister and I took off only our shoes.

I had trouble falling asleep. I was utterly crushed by the French defeat; I just couldn't believe it. In any event, if the bombardment were to start in again, I would go down to the cellar with my tin soldiers, beginning with the lovely box of the capture of Madagascar, a Christmas gift from 1913, which I had been forbidden to touch and which I had put up on the table in front of my bed. I could see the three stacked compartments in which colonial soldiers in white helmets were pursuing the Madagascans.

Half asleep, I could hear the familiar noises of Sunday. Every Sunday morning at eight, after leaving mass, the crystalry children would amuse themselves by raking canes up and down the corrugated-iron screens protecting the window of a draper's shop next to the Klein Pharmacy. No matter how much the riverside dwellers complained, the kids started in again every Sunday. Sure enough, I heard the clackety-clack clackety-clack, but much louder—as though a whole mob of children had come. I was wide awake by now and realized it was something else. Besides, my grandmother burst into the room. "Get up, children, get down to the cellar; the French are here." While she got my sister up, I went to peep out the window. Hundreds of French soldiers were trotting and shouting along the houses; bugles were blaring the charge. Toward the bridge, there was an enormous fusillade dominated by the steady clackety-clack of German machine guns. It might have been around 4 A.M.

The Guébourgs came back to our cellar via Rue du Presbytère and the gardens. We could hear the hurried steps of a large troop shifting along the house toward the bridge. The soldiers were yelling, calling to one another, halting, starting up again, shooting. Strange noises were mixed in; it sounded like wet objects, with attached pots and pans, were falling. This time, there was no question of my grandmother's watching, because swarms of bullets were whistling through the street, flattening against the walls of houses, smashing the windows. There was nothing we could do but keep reciting the Lord's Prayer and the Ave Maria and strain our ears to try and follow the ins and outs of the battle. We heard orders, and the fusillade, which had seemed to be slowing down, started off again, harder than ever. The German machine guns occasionally halted, leading us to think that the bridge had been taken. Once their firing resumed, however, we had to admit that the French were not succeeding. The bombardment began again. This time, our street was directly under fire.

It all lasted for three hours. And then we once again heard the quick hurried steps of a large troop. We couldn't be mistaken: the French were going away. The fusillade stopped and then resumed farther off, toward Deneuvre, but more raggedly. The German machine guns stopped, and artillery fire grew longer and slower. There was a moment of relative silence, a rifle shot very close, somewhere around the gardens, and then new footsteps on the sidewalk. This time, the orders were in German. There was no doubt about the outcome of the battle. My grandmother plucked up courage and went back up to her observation post. She returned very grave and nervous. "The battle is over around here," she announced. "There are a lot of casualties, and the other end of the street is all in flames. The town hall is burning." She climbed back up several times to follow the progress of the conflagration. My cousin René Guébourg wanted to find out what had happened to his house. He hurried back. "The ground floor is a shambles," he reported. "A Frenchman was killed right on our stoop. The Germans drove away the firemen who wanted to fight the fire in the town hall, and our neighbor's house is about to burn. The fire is not going to stop." Nobody knew what to do! We were all still in the cellar because of the fighting in the direction of Deneuvre. From time to time, the grandmothers went to survey the advance of the flames. Overhead there was a terrifying din of broken glass and shouts. German soldiers were using their rifle butts to smash in the window of the tobacco shop. We went up to the ground floor, and in the hallway I found myself facing German foot soldiers with fixed bayonets. Two of them were mounting the stairway leading to the second floor. In the street, a German officer was waiting for my grandmother. It was the major who had come yesterday.

"Madame," he said to my grandmother as soon as he caught sight of her, "you'll have to leave your home immediately. Our men have repulsed the attack of your soldiers, but this is"—and he pointed at the bayonet-wielding foot soldiers—"are our relief force. I cannot answer for them; they are not under my command. They're going to burn down your house. This officer here will accompany you to the station so you will be safe."

We all left the house immediately, like robots, without even thinking of taking a handkerchief or an extra shirt. I marched along next to the officer; then came the grandmothers, the little maid

Thérèse, who pushed my sister's carriage, the Lhotes, my cousin René Guébourg, who clumped along on his old mother's arm, and my cousin Marie, who always moved at top speed, no matter what the situation. The Guébourgs did not accompany us up to the depot; I think they made their way to the presbyterium. The fire was devouring their home. What I saw was infernally beautiful. The entire southern part of the street, the town hall, the houses on the small square, and a lot of others were burning and roaring like a forge. An enormous cloud of black smoke obscured the flames and clustered at the entrances to cross streets. German soldiers with fixed bayonets were ransacking the houses; presumably, they also set fire to anything that wasn't already burning. On the street and the pavements there were corpses in red trousers—more of them the closer we got to the bridge. The church steeple was jagged from the shells. Nearly all the burning houses were already pierced. The bridge was literally covered with dead bodies and wounded men from the 86th Infantry Regiment; the injured were propping themselves up on their elbows, asking for something to drink: "Water, little boy," they said as I passed beside them. It was very hot. There were no German corpses to be seen; they had already been carried away. And I assume that the wounded soldiers who remained were those who could not be helped by the medical knowledge of that era.

I was slightly ahead of the rest of the troop. I halted. Over the entire length of the bridge, there arose a very soft concert of laments and weak calls. I was surprised to hear men wailing like children. I was ashamed. I would have been happier if they had not cried in front of the victorious enemy. I didn't realize they had fallen in a battle of insane heroism. I merely thought they had clumsily lost. The burning of the street was truly terrible, like a divine punishment. The battle was continuing toward the south, where we could see the white smoke of explosions. German soldiers were stripping the French corpses even while several badly wounded men begged for help. I was revolted by this looting, which might well have been merely a routine military activity.

The major's dragoons were still occupying their combat positions. Soldiers lying on the walls were aiming their guns at the bridge. The crystal-works school had stopped burning. The station was full of refugees.

Behind the railroad tracks, the battery of the 77th, which had come out at the end of the attack and begun to burn the houses, was still shooting a few rounds at the Glonville woods. Then they held fire, probably because there were no more targets. In mid-afternoon, the Germans harnessed the pieces and began moving to the south. The battle, which was gradually moving away, manifested itself in irregular cannonades full of crescendos and pauses. At times it suddenly stretched along the entire horizon. Grandmother Thirion was about to reach a major decision. She explained her motives to the unhappy spectators whose houses were blazing. "I don't want to see any more fighting," she said, "especially with my grandchildren. The entire city is going to be destroyed. And the French may want to recapture that damned bridge again! If we stay here, it will be certain death. We must go behind the German lines. Our family will go to Dieuze, to my sister-in-law, and have some peace."

This was an insane idea. We had no means of transportation, and Dieuze is seventy miles from Baccarat. But my grandmother's audience found her reasoning luminous, a godsend. We left the station around six in the evening. The first stop would be Merviller, where we would spend the night in the presbyterium. Our group of wanderers was typical of all exoduses. The two grandmothers with their maid, the perambulator, and a boy were joined by a half-dozen homeless people; a babbling old woman, a young and pretty dressmaker pushing a delivery van in which her paralyzed father was lying, and others. The road to Merviller bore traces of the previous day's fighting. In the ditches, there were corpses of the colonial infantry, enormous and so black that I thought they were Negroes. Trees had been dented by the shells. Here and there throughout the fields, we could make out the corpses of men and horses. The beasts were elephantine, their stiff legs sticking up toward the sky, and they gave off a terrible stench.

Beyond the hamlet of Criviller, we could climb up a slope to a summit from which Merviller could be seen. Merviller was burning. "Out of the frying pan into the fire," said my grandmother. I had never heard this expression before, but I guessed what it meant. We halted, and the men had the reasonable idea of returning to the hamlet of Criviller, which was undamaged, to spend the night. The inhabitants had fled. The door to the inn was standing wide open. Someone went to look for mattresses in the bedrooms, and we stretched them out on the floor of the bar. There were hens in the chicken roosts and food in the kitchens. We could dine comfortably. Ever since we had left the depot, I had been admiring the young dressmaker. I found her fresh and pretty—her blouse was nicely filled—clean and neat. I knew her even though I had never spoken to her before. She was the darling of the noncommissioned officers. She would often walk before our house, completely surrounded. Her reputation wasn't very good. I wanted to sleep next to her, and I imagined that I could bury my head in her blouse. I had already arranged it all, and she was willing. But my old and ugly grandmother Sainte-Laudy ordered me to sleep next to her, to protect me against everything, perhaps even impure dreams!

The next morning, there was a lot of difficult explaining to do to a German officer who asked us what we were doing there. He could tell we weren't spies, however, and let us go. My grandmother's ideas no longer fooled anyone. Everyone else returned to Baccarat, and we were the only ones who went on to Merviller, where the fire had reached only a few houses. My grandmother unsuccessfully looked about for a vehicle to carry us to Dieuze, but she had to bow to facts: only the Germans could furnish such transportation, and there was absolutely no possibility of their taking French people onto Imperial soil on the pretext that they were visiting their family! A deluge was pouring down. The third night, I ran a high temperature; I was sitting up in bed and, says my grandmother, calling to arms, mounting an attack on the whole of Germany while singing the Marseillaise. There was no physician in Merviller. They put me in a small reed carriage and the old woman, the Lhotes, the little maid, and the two perambulators went back along the road to Baccarat. We knew that only the center of town had been burned; the other houses of the family were undamaged. We were going to my maternal grandmother's home.

My fever had dropped. On the way back, at the very same spots, I saw the corpses of colonials which I had seen three days earlier. Our arrival in Rue des Ponts was dreadful. The street was nothing but a succession of blackened house fronts, toppled walls, and debris, which was still smoldering. The façade of our house was standing; a bit later it would be torn down. The door to the cellar was wide open and German soldiers were divvying up the family silverware and the three thousand bottles in my father's reserve.

For the first time, my grandmother lost heart. This was too much;

she passed by wordlessly. She was giving up. As soon as she reached the house on Grande Rue and entered my uncle Albert's bedroom, which was to be ours for a time, she sat down on the bed, and although she did not ordinarily show her emotions, she silently and stiffly wept a few tears as she stroked my forehead.

4
COLD, SEX, AND SPRINGTIME

THE FIRST FEW DAYS OF THE GERMAN OCCUPA-
tion brought calm to the small town. The center was in ruins. The
bells no longer rang, except for those in Deneuvre. The church
steeple in Baccarat was still standing despite the loss of a few chunks.
The people who had stayed in town were mainly occupied with finding food. There was no water: sewers had been smashed, and we
were afraid that the corpses lying about almost everywhere in the
countryside had contaminated the wells. My cousin René Guébourg
bustled about. Adrien Michaut obtained some German fatigue men
to re-establish a supply of drinking water, which interested the conquerors even more than the conquered, and he made sure the
wounded horses who were dying on parish territory were killed and
that the dead were buried.

The Germans were no longer advancing. Here and there, they had
even been driven back. The firing line, which lay some five or six miles
to the south, was almost stable. The lemonade factory, its annexes,

and a part of the house in which we had taken shelter were requisitioned for a company of the 113th Infantry and its general staff.
These Baden troops were good-humored and not noisy. I inherited
a lovely flat drum with a broken skin, full of red triangles. The five
officers were civil and courteous, almost apologetic about being there.
One of them was greatly interested in Thérèse, our maid, an Alsatian
from Chatenois, who found the conquerors irresistible. She very
quickly abandoned us to go home; my grandmother didn't dare give
her any more orders. Almost all the officers knew a little French.
They managed to make the life of the two old ladies and the two
children less difficult. Every day the captain sent men over to the
Rauch brewery to get beer for his lieutenants and milk for the children.

We could still hear the cannon booming toward the west and the
south. From time to time, the din became louder and thicker; it
would start very early in the morning. The nights were generally silent. During the day, we mostly saw artillery convoys passing by.
The German artillerymen wore spherical helmets, while the foot
soldiers wore pointed helmets.

In the afternoons, the convoys returning from the line of fire would
come along the road to Rambervillers, which went past my uncle's
house. The wagons, piled high with equipment and weapons, among
which some French gear stood out, occasionally bore traces of the
battle. There were files of ambulances full of wounded men, with
badly injured soldiers with bloodstained bandages marching next to
them, and French prisoners who looked like convicts. One morning
I was crossing the street when a half-dozen delivery vans stopped.
The drivers were trying to find their way. A dreadful smell wafted
over from the vehicles. In one of the vans, behind some loose curtains, I could make out a pile of human corpses. The Germans didn't
always bury their dead on the spot. Presumably they cremated them.

We had no war news. All we knew was that the whole of Belgium
had been taken, and that there was fighting just outside Paris. The
fall of Paris was announced; the officers read out victory communiqués, which the soldiers received with the traditional *Hoch*'s. But
none of this was convincing, because the front at Rambervillers did
not yield, and the Germans were marking time before Nancy. One
very sunny afternoon, an automobile stopped before the house. Out
came a second lieutenant, who dashed up four stairs steps at a
time and called out to his aunt. It was my cousin Auguste. He threw

himself into my grandmother's arms. She was glad to see him, even though she would have preferred him in a different uniform. There was a long conversation in my uncle Albert's parlor. I only listened to part of it, primarily because it bored me, but also because I didn't care for Auguste as a German officer. He was enthusiastic. "We're much stronger than I thought," he said. "We have enormous cannon that nothing can resist. The war's almost over. You'll be German like us, and you'll see that everything will be better!"

My grandmother wasn't all that delighted at the thought of becoming German. She hadn't forgotten the burned-down house and particularly the pillage of the cellars. She told her nephew all about it. "But Auntie," replied Auguste, "why didn't you complain to an officer? He would have stopped the pillage right away, and you would have gotten everything back. Our regiments are highly disciplined. They're not like the French." My cousin belonged to a general staff; he had been given leave to visit his family. At the time, he was engaged to a girl from Berlin. After the Marne, he had himself transferred to the Russian front. In 1920, he married a Parisian.

My grandmother dreaded a surprise like that of August 25. She made us sleep fully dressed, one at the head and the other at the foot of the bed. Sometimes the booming came dangerously near. We were frighteningly dirty.

Around the third or fourth of September, the company was mustered and left. It was a melancholy departure. At dawn, the regiment attacked near Sainte-Barbe. The following night, the soldiers returned. They weren't the same men. Now they were dead tired. The captain took my grandmother aside. "The regiment lost eight hundred men today," he said. "Fortunately, my company wasn't in the front ranks; we didn't even advance by one kilometer; two more attacks like this one, and there will be nothing left of the 113th. Your soldiers fight well," he added. "We barely penetrated their positions." The 113th marched off to another attack the next day; their losses were dreadful. One of the lieutenants came to pick up his buddies' personal effects. He was the only officer in our house who hadn't been injured; the rest had been killed or wounded, and the captain was badly wounded.

This news evoked a good deal of comment, for it chimed with what the neighbors had heard. "All the German attacks have failed," they said, "and the French are advancing." The Baden troops were relieved by Bavarians, who were much less pleasant. Their officers

were the authentic brutes of patriotic French stories. We inherited
an arrogant and irascible major with a nasty face, who addressed his
men as though they were dogs. One afternoon, he came to the
quarters, issued some orders, then some counterorders, had all the
men fall in, then stand at ease, only to return a bit later, nervous
and worried. "Make me a soup," he ordered my grandmother.

"With what?" she replied.

He ferreted out a few bouillon cubes, and while the water was
heating he confided to my grandmother that his regiment was about
to leave Baccarat: "You'll soon see the French again," he added.

Indeed, there were larger and larger troop movements toward the
east, all of which did look like a German retreat. The general staff
was withdrawing two Bavarian divisions from Lorraine and sending
them toward the Yser, where Hitler, a recruit in the 16th, was to
receive his baptism of fire. As soon as the major had swallowed his
soup, he planted himself at the very top of the stairway leading into
the courtyard of the lemonade factory and roared out orders as
though he, all by himself, were representing the whole wrath of
heaven. His sergeants dashed off in all directions and roared in turn.
The soldiers left the barns, the lemonade factory, the nearby synagogue, and fell in on Grand Rue. They marched off toward the
bridge in an irreproachable formation. But not all the Germans were
marching so well. The cannon were coming closer: we could distinguish the noise of the musketry and the shooting of the machine
guns. None of us had forgotten those days in August: the battle was
returning. The weather was unsettled and cheerless. It started to rain;
German convoys, cannon, mud-covered foot soldiers who were worn
out and dreary gave us a new image of defeat.

The grandmothers were worried. We were told that the Germans
were retrenching in the hills on the right bank, that they were pointing their cannon at Baccarat, that they were going to blow up two
arches of the Great Bridge, both the one that the French had mined
in August and a second one to outdo them. The Sainte-Laudy cellars
were not safe. A house with good shelters across the street offered
us refuge. It was pouring. Small formations of Germans were still
passing. We were put to sleep in a large bed, then taken down to
the cellar. A thunderstorm had come, so we could barely discern
the booming of the cannon. In the cellar there were about twenty
people, mostly women. All of us had been suffering from dysentery
for several days now. Two barrels had been brought down, and people

relieved themselves as best they could. We expected new street fighting. The bridge exploded shortly before dawn. Then came the trampling of hurried rear guards. They stopped in front of the house, where a few horsemen were stationed, directing the latecomers toward the forest on the slope; the German engineers had thrown a makeshift bridge across the Meurthe. Then silence enveloped the twelfth of September 1914.

In the morning, we went back to my uncle's house. There were no German soldiers left in town. The sky brightened, and a timid sun appeared among frayed clouds. My grandmother saw that we were very dirty and still in our summer clothes. So she decided to buy us some stockings and coats. It was still before noon when we went to a well-stocked clothing store next to the Gondrecourt boarding school, across from the ruins of the castle of the Counts de Blamont. An enormous shout, "The French are here!" brought us out of the store. Two cavalrymen, waving their sabers, had stopped in the middle of the street, slightly taken aback by the uproar they had aroused. "Here it comes again," said my grandmother. "Quick. Let's get back!" And leaving behind her purchases and the salesgirl, she grabbed our hands and made us scurry to my uncle's house. Once home, she was a bit embarrassed about her panic because the arrival of the French riders had not elicited any German reaction. The Germans were at least five hours ahead of their adversaries. Other cavalrymen came riding up; they galloped around the town, questioning any townspeople they met, and they waded across the Meurthe. I saw foot soldiers coming; they marched slowly, with drawn bayonets, along the houses. The commanding officer stopped his detachment of some fifty men right in front of our house. "Where are the Germans?" asked the officer, a very young lieutenant. I told him everything I knew: that the Great Bridge had been blown up, that there might be a pontoon bridge by the forest, that cannon were pointing at the town all around the Steff mansion—in short, everything I had heard since that morning. I added that the Germans billeted at my uncle's place had left Baccarat the day before. "You're quite sure there are none left? We'll see; show us the way."

The officer took out his revolver and pushed me ahead of him: a dozen men followed him, poising their bayonets. I led him to the lemonade factory. The soldiers poked at the straw with their bayonets and climbed up into the barns. "What's that?" said one of the men when he saw my drum. "It's mine; a German gave it to me."

"You don't need it, kid. You're too young." And he carried off my drum as a trophy. I was revolted by his conduct. Since the Germans had gone, I knew I wasn't risking anything by taking the soldiers to the barns, but the Frenchmen themselves didn't realize it. I found it outrageous that my countrymen could force a kid of my age to march before their bayonets.

With Baccarat recaptured, hundreds of civilians could come home. They returned in the euphoria of victory. All traces of defeatism had disappeared. The refugees of August 24, who were most numerous, hadn't been very far off, and they had run the worst risks. Most of them had remained in the middle of the battle, waiting in the ditches until the outcome of the struggle permitted them to reach the back areas of one of the two camps, where they had then been enjoined not to move. They told horrible stories about the hundreds of corpses strewn throughout the woods and the famous breach of Charmes. Although the fighting in the east had played its part in the general strategy and the German army in Lorraine had often been beaten on the terrain, everyone knew that the day had been carried at the Marne, not before Rozelieures or Rambervillers, and that the victory had been hard-won. There was no touch of heroism in the stories. On the contrary, people had seen French soldiers turning tail. We were amazed at a war that barely resembled the epics in history books. People attributed the successes to technology and described the devastating power of mysterious explosives shot by 75-millimeter guns.

After a few days, public services functioned as before. Everyone could count on food, and the dysentery abated. As soon as the road from Nancy was negotiable, my father came to Baccarat, which he knew was partially destroyed. I saw him arrive, pale, running like a madman across the street because some idiot had told him that his mother and his children had died when his house burned down. He was still in civilian clothes. I instantly recovered my love and admiration for him because our life immediately changed. We were washed and dressed in new clothes, and things went forward in an organized way. My father's position in the army was still unclear. He was assigned to run a hospital, but it was nearly empty because there was no fighting on the new and uncertain line that was being established east of the town. Crépin the banker also returned. The bank had been reduced to ashes, along with the rest of Rue des Ponts, but the vault was still intact, half buried in rubble. I accompanied my father when Edmond Crépin pressed the secret spring. The entire contents had withstood the fire, only the edges of the bundles of papers had been charred by the heat. The manuscript of the second symphony was undamaged. It was in a huge red folder, which we took with us at every alarm throughout the war.

The front was some six miles from Baccarat. The sector was calm. After the battle of Verdun, there were more and more reliefs. We saw famous divisions marching past. Each relief evoked aerial reconnoitering by the enemy. Until 1917, these were routine flights; the release of a few small bombs now and then caused no damage. The alarm was sounded by a permanent bugler stationed next to a machine gun that was being used by territorial soldiers on a terrace overlooking the city, at the foot of the church of Deneuvre.

On a clear day, the line of fire, toward the north, was staked out by observation balloons, "sausages." The two adversaries would leave them in place for several weeks and then, one day when they became angry, they would both take their balloons down. The task of pulling them down was generally assigned to skillful aviators. It was like a fair. It sometimes took place within sight because one of our favorite promenades was along the edge of the Glonville forest and the Rappe, from which we could plainly see the line of balloons. We could also make out the roads at which the German artillery was shooting. The smoke from the explosions was very distinct, but the noise often vanished before reaching us.

The winter climate of Baccarat is severe: the cold settles in December and lasts for a long time. The winters in the First World War were exceptionally hard. Throughout February 1916 there was a north wind, and the nights were freezing cold. We learned about the battle of Verdun from an uninterrupted rumbling that made the windowpanes quiver. It wouldn't stop; we could hear it all day long. In nights of heavy frost, this dramatic rumbling, which frightened everyone, could become intense enough to wake people up. Old women who couldn't fall back to sleep would pray for the rest of the night. The first accounts of the battle confirmed the fears of the townspeople. In late March, we saw divisions arriving from that inferno. Regiments would often take the road to Rambervillers and march past our house. The men looked as though they were dressed in dry mud; they never spoke. We watched them in terror and pity.

Rationing stamps were issued for bread, sugar, and coal. The butchers were closed twice a week. Food prices went up. In late 1917, the Russian bankruptcy brought sudden financial difficulties to families who had thought themselves secure. Lower-class people got along on the allowances for families of servicemen and on the salary raises. My mother, being too proud to ask the mayor's office for anything, lived off her capital and had a hard time making ends meet.

The winter of 1917–18 was exceptionally long and hard. The thermometer stayed just above freezing for several weeks and sometimes sank even lower. The Meurthe froze over, and the ice was solid enough for the passage of horse-drawn 75-millimeter guns and their shell-filled caissons. The sewers burst; the drains were sealed by the ice. Only a few fountains in town had drinking water. Piles of garbage accumulated in front of the houses. But these miseries were nothing compared with the unrelenting massacre of men. We were constantly hearing about new casualties. The anxiety would increase during offensives. Families who hadn't heard any news from their soldiers for a long while would ask everyone what regiments were involved, whether the losses were heavy, which units were still in the line. I was preparing for my first communion and therefore attended all the masses. As a choir boy, I was needed for requiems and prayers of intercession for the deceased. The church was filled with women in black, those most recently in mourning veiled in crepe. Whenever the priest intoned the *Dies Irae* or, in low masses, the *Libera Me,* sudden sobs from the whole crowd would accompany the funeral chants. At times they even drowned them out as the celebrant's voice choked with emotion.

It seemed as though that winter would never end. But finally the cold yielded; we could clean the houses and the streets. The barracks and billets emptied. Americans relieved the French. In late March, some towering model-T's brought a few soldiers dressed in khaki and sporting large Boy Scout hats. They installed themselves at all the crossroads with orderlies on motorcycles and arranged a new invasion. New, luxuriously equipped soldiers arrived from everywhere—at the small depot, in trucks, or even on foot. Beneath our windows, along the narrow street which had already seen so many soldiers marching past, huge caterpillar tractors dragged heavy cannon behind them. It was the 42nd U.S., the Rainbow Division, in which a young general served who was marked for a great future, Douglas MacArthur.

In a couple of days, Baccarat became another town in another world. Young, solid, well-dressed, optimistic men were quartered everywhere, at a loss as to where they might store their enormous amount of matériel, which seemed to be increasing constantly: trucks, cars, machine guns, cannon, munitions, and all kinds of food. They played baseball on the Patis and set up huts and pitched tents all over the place. There was a field hospital in the park of the crystal works, with fresh, pretty nurses and whole lines of ambulances that were very different from the animal-drawn vans of 1914. Along came huge cans of lard, salted butter, white bread, and heaps of sugar. Rationing cards were almost beside the point.

We inherited a "field mess" of surgeons. Three of them were quartered in our home. Along with their pale tobacco, their cars, and their ordnance, these officers brought a sense of security and confidence which we badly needed. Ludendorff's attacks were shaking the Allied front; new names were endlessly extending the list of those who had fallen on the field of honor. But none of this really mattered. The health, wealth, and vitality of the Americans wiped away all the bad news. With such impressive reinforcements, France was sure of winning the war. We would soon witness the end. The populace took the 42nd Division unto its bosom. Those young guys from Pennsylvania and Ohio filled in the vacuums, eased the sufferings of absence, and brought back joy. They helped us forget the French army. The town shook with new rhythms, ragtime. The most famous song, "Alexander's Ragtime Band," was played everywhere, all day long, in cafés, houses, with "Roses of Picardy," and on all sorts of instruments. We saw the army surplus arrive—dungarees, sweaters, and particularly the plaited uniform belts with copper buckles, which were instantly adopted by all the kids, who bawled out ditties, warping them with their Lorraine accents and their French pronunciation. At school the usual insults and curses gave way to "sonofabitch," used constantly by everyone, from the five-year-olds to the seniors.

Everything was astir. The 42nd Division was there to be trained. There were more and more raids; the cannon fire became more frequent. The doughboys soon paid for their derring-do and their inexperience: a middling skirmish of patrols cost them twenty men. We treated these first casualties with great love. They were brought to Baccarat and buried with great pomp in a new cemetery that was especially opened for the occasion. The procession was led by a slow-stepping infantry band playing Chopin's *Funeral March*, the first time I ever heard it. When the losses began to multiply, the army created cemeteries near the front for soldiers killed there. On Thanksgiving Day, several of the kids, including myself, were given enormous masses of flowers to place on the graves while all the newsreel cameras focused on them. MacArthur kissed us all before the regulation three volleys.

I was supposed to have my first communion in late April. My mother turned me into a veritable saint. She gave me a notebook for jotting down every day, not the good things I did (that would have been too simple), but the deprivations and mortifications that I imposed upon myself. Every evening, my mother would review these insane accounts. Prayers were lengthened for the sake of the fatherland, to obtain my father's return to the Catholic faith, and so on; any pretext would do.

After the great day, I discarded the little notebook, but this excess of piety and the various prohibitions had separated me from my playmates. I was at the head of the class, so I enjoyed a certain prestige, but I remained an outsider. All the other kids hung around the American barracks, begging biscuits, candy, chocolate, chewing gum, Colt cartridges, and a thousand other treasures to which I had no access. I joined in on only one of their astounding Thursday expeditions toward the front to bring back some stock plates of yellow powder, which we kept in cigar boxes, and some flares. When I came home, I was severely punished. Everyone was studying for the junior-high-school certificate. But since I ostensibly was supposed to start lycée the following year and shortly thereafter take the scholarship exams, I didn't have to take the finals. The other children knew they would soon be learning a trade, whereas I would be continuing my studies. And then, more than anything else, I was hesitant in approaching girls because of our family austerity and my lack of freedom. All my schoolmates had girl friends; they were starting to kiss them. They talked about things I didn't understand. The only females I associated with were my cousins; I liked Simone, the older one, but she always acted superior. I never dreamed of having a date with her. Besides, she was as carefully chaperoned as I, whereas my schoolmates could meet the elementary-school girls, who turned their heads every time one of their favorites passed by.

I went to school on the day of the Armistice. Old man Juliac had not received any official instructions and opened the doors. My mother refused to let me take the day off. Nearly all the kids stayed out; no one saw any sense in coming. After a foggy morning, the afternoon was warm and a bit sunny. I knew that all the kids had taken off for Montigny, where there were a few batteries and where the army had been setting up more and more depots for some time. They were only minimally guarded and contained all sorts of matériel. The kids brought back flares, signal rockets, and powder, and made beautiful fireworks. The garrison soldiers didn't want to be outdone, but apparently their stock wasn't as good as the stuff the kids had picked up with the help of the military convoys.

Baccarat, which had been inhabited by battalions ready for revenge, which had been devastated by battle and had quartered soldiers from all continents, now slipped into a tranquil sleep from which it was never to wake. The most active and ambitious of its citizens could sense this and were preparing to leave for wider horizons.

We moved to Nancy, and it was intoxicating. We had a huge apartment facing the Forestry School. Our house was the only one on the street that hadn't been built under Louis XIV. The beauty of this neighborhood has always represented in my mind extraordinary intellectual comfort. Our whole family lent us furniture until my father could acquire the decoration he liked. He asked my advice before making his choices, which made me feel proud and important. He took me along to the stores in Majorelle and the workshops of Gauthier Poinsignon, who had adopted a sober and dry style. Guy Ropartz had been named to direct the Strasbourg Conservatory. My father succeeded him in Nancy, but his position wasn't confirmed, which was a major disappointment. His candidacy was supported by the right wing, but the left wing attacked him for his friendship with Ropartz and his good relations with the church. The left carried the day. In 1920, Alfred Bachelet, a good theater musician at the Opera, obtained the coveted directorship. Bachelet and my father had mutual friends, and their relationship improved even more because Bachelet greatly respected his symphonic music.

During the war, I had suffered from our degrading situation. In Nancy, I once again enjoyed the status and comfort accorded to the son of an esteemed and well-known man. Everything in Nancy was much bigger, and I liked this new dimension. Ours was the cathedral parish, and my father gave a concert on the ancient and monumental organ there. My mother and I resumed our pious habits in a setting that was much more exalting than the neo-Gothic one in Baccarat. Dominicans used to shower attentions on my mother because my uncle, who was killed in 1915, was still remembered in his order. My mother decided to present me to the lycée chaplain in order to have me repeat my first communion in the chapel. The chaplain, Father Constantin, was a tall, thin, ascetic old man and a great scholar. He lived in the old part of the lycée, next to the chapel, in an apartment made up of a series of small rooms on different levels. The thought of being presented to him pleased me greatly. Wasn't I a good Catholic? My mother's connections assured her in advance of an excellent welcome. The conversation was commonplace. Then I said something—I can't remember what, something very appropriate and natural, or so I thought—and Father Constantin rose to his feet, backed up a few paces, mounted the two steps separating a kind of study from the room we were sitting in, raised a forefinger of anathema at me, and flatulently declared: "Madame, this child will cause you a great deal of sorrow!" My mother didn't argue; she didn't understand the whole thing any more than I did. All we could do was leave.

I never lost a desire for revenge. During the retreat preceding the ceremony, I showed more interest in the lovely blond hair of the administrator's daughter, the only female amid the boys, than in the chaplain's homilies. In my compositions for religious instruction, I brazenly copied Father Constantin's lectures, which did not prevent me from being low in class. Two years later, when filling out a form, I joyously wrote "None" in reply to the question: "What is your religion?"

The Henri Poincaré Lycée did not disappoint me. It had been slightly damaged by bombs, and even though the class hours were announced by drums, as under Napoleon I, the discipline had become much less strict because of the war. Furthermore, the preparatory classes were made up largely of young veterans. Some of them came straight from the front, and they introduced manners much freer than those of the professors in swallowtails. I liked my school chums, and I soon gained a certain influence. I started a club, and since there was no room for sociocultural centers, we met in front of the lycée, around the statue of Mathieu de Dombasle, a famous agriculturist. One of our aims was to organize a collective resistance against an English teacher, a young woman we didn't much care for.

I became interested in sexual matters, and wondered where babies came from. Watching dogs mating wasn't very helpful because sometimes both partners were of the same sex. My chums didn't seem to know any more than I did. I spent a few days of vacation in Dieuze to celebrate the repatriation of the entire family to the motherland. My grandmother's sister had a hardware store with offices useful for all sorts of games. Her clerk, thirteen or fourteen years old, was better informed than I was, but I had the advantage of living in a big town and being the owner's nephew. The conversation quite naturally drifted to the subject that was closest to my heart. I asked the clerk, "Where do babies come from?"

"Why, they come out through the cunt."

I was even more puzzled.

"Come out into the shed," he said. "We'll get Angèle and I'll show you."

We had a good excuse to go into the shed; there was scrap iron to put away. Angèle was working in a nearby shed, probably doing laundry. She looked about thirteen, big and gawky, with a ruddy face, towlike hair, and a rather pointed budding chest. She didn't seem very smart, but there was something slightly depraved about her.

"C'mon, Angèle, show us your butt. He's never seen one."

"If I feel like," said the girl. The clerk pulled her braids. "Show us your butt, I said."

She lifted her dress and looked at me. She had no pants on and she was just barely pubescent.

"Take a closer look," said the clerk. "There it is. Just put your finger on it. C'mon, do what I say."

I hesitatingly touched Angèle's vagina. It was pleasant, it yielded to the touch, but there was no hole. My finger was probably too high. I got up enough nerve to touch one of her breasts as well. She snickered, "He dunno nuttin'."

"Shit," said the clerk, "I'll show you. Angèle likes a finger there but nothing else. It's still a lot of fun."

He took out his penis. Angèle still had her dress up. He pressed against her, and they masturbated one another. "See if anyone's coming," the clerk told me.

I strained my ears and glanced at the door of the shed, but I tried not to miss anything of this new and interesting sight. I couldn't tell what they were after. The clerk ejaculated. I think Angèle sighed; anyway, she kissed the boy very hard. He was happy to show me his sperm. "See, that's jism; that's where babies come from. But you have to stick your dick in the hole. It's your turn if you like."

I went over to Angèle, who kissed me and put her head on my trousers. But someone called out, "Angèle! Angèle!"

"Shit," said Angèle, "I have to go."

We waited a while. She came running back. "I can't stay," she said. "I've gotta help." I still didn't understand it all, but I finally knew where the famous hole began.

"Hell, that's what they piss through," the clerk had said.

The ejaculation explained the delicious feeling that I had had while climbing a tree a few months earlier. I had wet my pants. It wasn't very difficult.

I hung around the house until I caught sight of Angèle, who must have worked in a nearby grocery store. She smiled at me. I would have liked to take a lesson from her, but the clerk was less cooperative and I left Dieuze. I made up my mind to try it as soon as possible with my cousin Madeleine, who used to show her thighs with native ease. I tried once during a game of hide-and-seek, but Madeleine didn't understand what I was after. She got scared and ran away. A few years later, she jokingly reproached me for not having been more insistent.

5
NANCY IN 1920

THE SCHOOL OF NANCY HAD EXHAUSTED ALL OF its creative powers by 1914, but no one realized it. In 1909, at the very moment when this group of artists was in full triumph (except for Gallé, who had died in 1904) at the Eastern Regional Fair, the tide of fashion was turning, and the younger generation was beginning to find Art Nouveau a joke. Most members of the School were skillful craftsmen, especially of domestic products, and were hardly disturbed by the aesthetics of the Ballets Russes—for the good reason that none of them had ever attended a performance. Furthermore, none of them could change techniques overnight. The Munich Exhibit of 1911 had strengthened their feelings that they alone possessed the truth and represented French taste, whose grace and poetry were imperiled by Germanic heaviness and the barbaric simplicity of crude materials and plain contours.

By 1920 Munich taste and Arabian Nights Orientalism had carried the day. Abstract art had also begun, borrowing its vocabulary from Cubism. The leaders of the School of Nancy, most of them mature by 1910, had survived the war, and nearly all of them had found secure positions. Their president, Victor Prouvé, had just been named director of the School of Fine Arts of Nancy, though that institution no longer had any raison d'être. Its creations were old-fashioned and provincial, and even the people of Nancy were no longer interested in ordering Art Nouveau furnishings or objects. Prouvé himself, strongly aware of the new aesthetic trend, renounced the wild arabesques, roots, liana, and twisting water nymphs that still dazzle today, and he concentrated instead on academic painting à la Rubens. Afraid to risk the divine follies which customers no longer wanted, the cabinet-makers, architects, glass blowers, typographers, bookbinders, and wall-paper manufacturers simplified their ornamentation but still preserved the characteristic modulations of the noodle style. All they managed to produce, however, were wretched objects that were as old-fashioned as they were ugly. Everything in Nancy—shop signs, typefaces, vases, ashtrays—was now "modern," ad nauseam. Five years after the war, arts and crafts in Lorraine had lost all their originality. Only the crystal works were assured of a clientele because of the quality of their products, their worldwide renown, and a prudent adjustment to public taste.

Even my father had developed a dislike for the style in which he had furnished our home in Baccarat. Now he admired the Théâtre des Champs-Elysées, the furniture of Francis Jourdain, and the architecture of Frank Lloyd Wright. Though he was aware of the disintegration of the School of Nancy, he did not, as a good Lorrainer, want to break with tradition in one move. So he bought two soberly "modern" bedroom sets, with English tapestries designed around 1910, furnished two other rooms with Majorelle furniture—in a style very close to the one that was to triumph in 1925 at the Exhibition of Decorative Arts, but which, despite everything, still smacks of 1900—and ordered the dining room from Francis Jourdain. Since the house that had burned down in 1914 had to be rebuilt, my father bought some land in the former domain of the Commandery of St. John of Jerusalem, overlooking the pond on whose shore they had found the corpse of Charles the Bold, and in 1923 had a house built there. Designed by Parisian architects, the house is in the soft, fanciful style of the era and shows the influence of Poiret and the Munich school. The grillwork of the gate and the balconies was forged by Edgar Brandt, a blacksmith and cannon manufacturer who designed the gate to the Bayonet Trench, a monument that was greatly admired at the time. The Nancy School, which in 1904 had exhibited embroideries devised by my mother, was quite dead.

Our lively family discussions about the choice of furniture, wall-paper, architecture, woodwork, cast iron, and what not made me realize the extent to which Nancy had become a city devoid of artistic resources and creative spirit. After leaving Baccarat, which had had nothing, I had been dazzled by the capital of Lorraine, by the turn-of-the-century houses as well as Stanislas Square. But I soon recognized that nothing much was happening amid all this sublime architecture; the entire populace was living in another age. Nothing seemed modern in this town, and the mustiness of the Nancy School was really oppressive. My growing admiration for the grand creations of the eighteenth century in Lorraine ultimately made me despise anything that had been built in Nancy during the nineteenth and twentieth centuries, with the exception of two or three turn-of-the-century façades by Vallin. I associated them with Scandinavia, with Ibsen's dramas, the mysterious poetry of enormous industrial land-scapes immersed in a blue mist. I developed an aversion toward the ten or twenty poignant floral constructions, with harp-shaped windows and tulip-shaped chimneys, that can fortunately still be seen in neighborhoods dating from the 1900's. I came to understand the value and charm of these dream houses a few years later when I reacted against the impoverished projects of Le Corbusier and André Lurçat, which I viewed with great distaste.

My father was the only person to whom I could confide my thoughts, because none of my schoolmates had the least interest in art. Spurred by the need to convert others, which I have felt throughout my life, I had founded the group that became the Stanislas Club a year later. Its purposes were literary, artistic, philatelic, athletic, and its journal, which I dubbed *En Avant*, published novels, verse, criticism, and drawings by the select few, all pseudonymous. The journal was handwritten, and its two or three copies circulated from hand to hand. When a certain Schmitt brought out a similar periodical, put together with the help of newspaper clippings, I decided that freedom of the press was not applicable to high schools and determined to force my competitors out of business. Liking nothing better than a good fight, the four supporters of the Stanislas Club harmonized their literary admirations and their urge for excitement by reincarnating the Three Musketeers. When school was dismissed, we pursued our antagonists through the streets at top speed, converging by agreement under the arcades of Immanuel Héré's Arch of Triumph. Dropping our bookbags and portfolios, we fought in pairs; the winner had to force both his opponent's shoulders against the ground.

Though these exercises interfered with the regular publication of *En Avant*, it nevertheless managed to survive the Musketeer era. The final issue, which came out when we were in our last year at the lycée, brought me into contact with Jean Ferry, who contributed a poem and a Danse Macabre inspired by Saint-Saëns. With Jean I could talk about literature and music. My new friend, a large fellow with very fuzzy hair and glasses, was a pronounced Oriental type, with a curious square head. I was mad about Symbolist poetry and loved Mallarmé and Verlaine, but Ferry knew only the classics and, among the moderns, Anatole France. He had already made deep inroads into nineteenth-century English literature, however, and greatly admired Jerome K. Jerome's *Three Men in a Boat*. He was always at the head of the class with French compositions, whereas I was barely in the middle. This grading struck me as unfair because my writings were much more original than Ferry's and I resented the pedantic professor. But Ferry's essays were probably better constructed and written than my own.

During the final term, we were supposed to write on a bucolic subject, which I enjoyed. I decided to suggest the contrast between heat and coolness by describing, in a sort of rhythmic prose, first desert landscapes and then greenery and lakes. I used a kind of refrain that began, "The glaucous noise of the waves," and was very proud of this device. The teacher, after heaping praise on Ferry's essay and reading much of it in class, came to mine. "All I can say about this," he declared, "is that it is a good example of the kind of composition one should not write. The theme is absurdly handled, and the style is pretentious and hazy. 'The glaucous noise of the waves.' I assume that Thirion wanted to write 'the noise of the glaucous waves,' but he may have wanted to imitate the decadent poets, especially Mallarmé, who sometimes associates sounds with colors, which is of course completely gratuitous."

Ferry's success made me slightly jealous, a shabby feeling that came back to me much later when I reread *The Social Tiger*. Breton's fulsome praise had annoyed me, and I was prepared to denounce the text as simply a pastiche of Kafka, when I recalled the affair of our high-school compositions and recognized the sources of my irritation. I instantly felt very ashamed and had a good laugh thinking that, after all, the *Tiger* was the sort of book that would terrorize our pedant.

Jean Ferry's father was a banker. He was also a bibliophile, and his son was proud of the limited editions, the illustrated books, and the bindings in his father's library. The walls of the banker's apartment were hung with objects that were either ugly or stupid, and the literature he liked didn't strike me as very interesting, at least in the form of luxurious editions.

That year I was starting to get very interested in girls. My interest extended far and wide. For example, there were the two brunettes at Joan of Arc Lycée. They were sisters, always dressed in sky blue, and I pestered them with my leers every time we met. I made Jean Ferry join me in complicated and exhausting maneuvers merely to cross the path of the two sisters several times as they tranquilly made their way home.

Ferry told me that there were anti-Semites in France and that the condition of Jews throughout Eastern Europe was not very enviable. I couldn't believe it. For me, Jews were adherents of a particular religion, like Catholics or Protestants. Even when Ferry got me to read a novel by Israel Zangwill, I wasn't convinced. After all, Wallachia and Armenia hadn't yet made it out of the era of tribal feuds and massacres. Nevertheless, Gyp's horrible pastiche in *A la Manière de* did disturb me. The Dreyfus Affair had not been forgotten. Little by little, I was forced to agree: Ferry's fears were not as groundless as I would have liked them to be. This realization was extremely unpleasant, and at heart I reproached Ferry for dwelling so much on things I would have preferred to remain unaware of.

Jean Ferry was more deliberate, more prudent, more studious than I was. Mathematics bored him and science left him cold. I was passionately fond of discussing metaphysics or politics. Ferry was something of a conformist, and his lack of enthusiasm for challenging God's existence, free choice, and Poincaré got on my nerves. I wanted to dance, fall in love, comprehend natural phenomena, achieve elegance, engage in endless discussions about the great problems of the origins of worlds, causality, ultimate ends, social processes. I stopped seeing Jean Ferry and started publishing a literary review in order to gather some traditional friends enamored of mechanics, preparing for university, and fond of mathematics and general ideas. When I ran into Ferry three years later, he had met Sadoul, who got him into the Nancy-Paris Committee. But my concerns were different, and my aspirations and tastes had become more clearly delineated. This change was another reason, I think, why I drifted away from Ferry.

Sadoul was a soldier at Mont Valérien. On leave in Nancy, he had brought back the first issue of *The Surrealist Revolution*. This was a great event for both of us. Sitting in a beerhall on Rue Saint-Jean, I was scrutinizing the glossy red, violently anti-"modern" cover, in the style of medical pamphlets, when along came Ferry and a friend.

Ferry leafed about in the review and said that Sadoul had already shown it to him. "Didn't you notice anything?" he asked. "I think you'll agree with me."

I didn't understand what he was getting at; his question sounded like an oral exam. "What are you talking about?" I replied. "There are so many things in here." I was thinking about the homage of the Surrealists to Germaine Berton, the anarchist who killed one of the Royalists connected with L'Action Française. This was the essential point of the review, as far as I was concerned. At last we had intellectuals whose talent and originality I could admire and who were spitting at Barrès, Péguy, the Unknown Soldier, Montherlant, L'Action Française, etc. I said as much to Ferry.

"No," he said, "I don't mean that. I mean the texts. What do you think of the texts?"

I had read them all, and I particularly liked Desnos. "The North Star sends the South Star this telegram: Behead Instantly your Red Comet and your Violet Comet who are Betraying you." I told Ferry, but my answer displeased him.

He became insistent: "But what's important, you do agree, is that they're dreams, stories of dreams?"

"It's not only obvious," I answered, "it also says so." I couldn't understand Ferry's amazement. Or, rather, I credited it to his respect for the most conventional forms of writing (which I recalled from our days in high school). I attached no importance to this incident, and the few conversations I subsequently had with him during the activities of the Nancy-Paris Committee reinforced my conviction that he wasn't really in touch, that Pierre MacOrlan or Joseph Conrad was of greater interest to him than Surrealism.

Ferry, who must have been a rather unhappy teen-ager, suddenly left Nancy and signed up as a sailor or radio operator on a tramp steamer which took him around the world. I saw him again after his

odyssey in 1930 or 1931, I think—when I was visiting my father
in Nancy. I was at the height of my revolutionary intransigence and
Communist faith. We hiked across the Malzéville plateau and through
several villages together. Ferry had found the sailor's life exalting.
He loved the sea, exotic countries, ports of call, all that "local color"
of allegedly modern literature which made me sick to my stomach.
I lectured him about political commitment. I tried to show him that
adventures and voyages were meaningless, that strikes, the destruction of the middle classes, violence, revolution, and terror were the
only landscapes worth knowing. They were the marvelous harbors
we had to reach at any cost. I blasted the things he worshipped.
Modern literature was made up entirely of Breton, Aragon, a couple
of their friends; older writing boiled down to a small number of seers
and forerunners. Jean Ferry awkwardly attempted to save a few names
from the holocaust. I felt like a whirlwind, and even now I feel as
though I acted like one that day. Ferry mentioned Lewis Carroll,
whom he knew better than the Surrealists, except perhaps for Aragon.
"But *Alice in Wonderland* is also a dialectical phenomenon," I
explained. Nothing fell outside my system, except for the things I had
totally demolished. We parted, anathematizing one another, and I
had a feeling I would never see him again. He had become a person
I deemed unsalvageable.

Two or three years passed before I ran into him once more. He
had either come to know Breton through his uncle José Corti (who
published the Surrealists) or appeared at the Café Cyrano with
some people from the *Revue du Cinéma*. In any case, one evening in
1933, to my great surprise, he showed up at the daily apéritif on
Place Blanche. His arrival coincided with a growth in the Surrealist
following, an increase in the faithful. I was on the verge of leaving,
but Ferry was a steady customer until the war. He became a deeply
poignant interpreter of Raymond Roussel, tenderly guiding disoriented
readers through that monumentally beautiful and frenzied *oeuvre*
(though, all in all, such explication and orientation may have been
unnecessary). Ferry wrote insipid scenarios and film scripts, even
during the war. His wife was intelligent and as bedizened and painted
as a carnival; she had previously lived with Georges Hugnet and
André Breton. He continued to reveal a certain conformism in regard
to regimes and rulers, as if the whole matter didn't concern him,
but he also wrote a few rather brief and forceful texts, masterpieces
of gray humor which never diverged from a serene pessimism that

nothing could shake. Rereading them, I came to realize the slow, grave, and prudent evolution that my old schoolmate had gone through. Jean Ferry bears witness to the contradictions of Surrealism and the ambiguity of its successive positions, which both reflected and stood outside the times. He entered through the doorway of creativity rather than furor and revolution, and that door, thank goodness, is the one that has always stood open; it was used by the bearers of new fuel. Although Artraud and Soupault were theoretically banished from the group for excessive trust in the exemplary value of their writings, Francis Ponge, Georges Hugnet, Pieyre de Mandiargues, Julien Gracq, and Joyce Mansour—to name but a few—came to Surrealism precisely because they bore within themselves an exemplary literature.

In comparison with that new wave, Artaud and Soupault were revolutionaries. The writings of Ponge and Ferry skillfully express their authors' feelings about the illusory nature of such action, the frequency of the deviations, and the preposterousness of the results of that movement. Our pedantic teacher was right: Jean Ferry was a born writer, and his works deserve to be read aloud in class.

6
GEORGES SADOUL AND NANCY–PARIS

CHARLES SADOUL WAS A SMALL, SWARTHY MAN. Lively and always on the go, he had devoted his youth to Lorraine and revenge. After the victory, far from disarming and seeking ways to break through the infernal cycle of Franco-German wars, he, like so many others, had moved toward a militant hostility to anything German. The founding publisher of the regionalist monthly *Le Pays Lorrain*, he had been elected counselor-general of the Vosges by the canton of Raon-l'Etape. He became curator of the marvelous Lorraine Museum.

With a personal fortune, he could live off his private income with no trouble. Charles Sadoul dedicated nearly all his time to his collections and his vocation as a Lorraine patriot. In Nancy, he enjoyed an indisputable prestige, shored up by that of his brother, who was a presiding judge. Charles Sadoul lived in a simple and austere house on Rue des Carmes that had been built in the eighteenth century. It was full of Lorrainese objects and furnishings, and its huge library was well supplied with works on witchcraft. He would spend his summers in Raon-l'Etape, on an estate that was also chock-full of Lorrainese furniture and books. He was a friend of Maurice Barrès and the historian Louis Madelin and entertained them whenever they made a trip to the East.

In the early part of the century, Charles Sadoul wanted to collect everything that could be known about folksongs of Lorraine. He dragged my father along into the villages and hamlets in quest of lullabies, plaintive ballads, and dance tunes. The two men would ask old women to sing for them while they jotted down the words and music. Nothing is left of this worthy undertaking except the few items that were published sporadically in the local press. The original notes vanished in the burning of Baccarat in 1914; the texts and the definitive manuscript were consumed in the fire that destroyed the Sadoul house in Raon-l'Etape in 1944. Such were the occasional ravages of Teutonism.

In 1922, Georges, the eldest of the four Sadoul children, was a first-year law student while I was still a junior at the lycée. I hardly knew him. He struck me as uncommunicative, distant, extremely caustic, pretentious. I had acquired a certain renown at the Henri Poincaré Lycée because of a composition that was actually a credit to my teacher, an intelligent and modern man whose attitude toward the antiquated and boring programs imposed upon lycée students, allegedly to teach them their mother tongue and familiarize them with their literature, was one of ironic deference. He strongly hinted that there were other things to read. The subject of the assignment had been: "What maxim or watchword would you adopt for governing your life?" I selected "Don't Worry," more out of sassiness than conviction. It was also a fashionable homage to one of the songs from the operetta *Dédé*, which was all the rage at the *Bouffes Parisiens*. It might also have reflected the current philosophy. My essay received the highest grade. The teacher read it aloud to the entire class. My chums weren't particularly astounded at my nonconformism; what surprised the prudent stick-in-the-muds of Lorraine was the fact that my audacity could be praised and honored. The story made the rounds of the entire school and even circulated in town. It greatly pleased Georges Sadoul.

Shortly before summer vacation of that year, 1922, my father asked me if I knew Georges Sadoul and what I thought of him. I had never thought of him. "Charles Sadoul," my father went on, "feels that his son and you have similar ambitions and tastes. The Sadoul family is spending the holidays five miles from Baccarat. We agreed that the two of you could visit one another whenever you like. Until you get your own bicycle, you can borrow your uncle Albert's or the one that belongs to Grandmother Sainte-Laudy's roomer." This arrangement began a very close friendship, which turned into a collaboration and did not end until 1932 with the break-up of the Surrealist group.

Massive and stocky, Georges Sadoul had an extraordinary physical resistance, which enabled him to buck fatigue at all times. At twenty, he could walk thirty miles in a day and start all over again in the morning. Blond, with blue eyes, thin lips, and an undershot jaw, he had strangler's hands—at least, according to Cora, his ecstatic German girl friend of 1929—but his hands also had a worker's skill. He walked like a duck, with a characteristic lurch which one could recognize a hundred yards away. Rather disorderly and careless, he had a truly natural bent for drawing. He would always illustrate his letters with nudes and animals delineated with a skillful and personal touch. He read a great deal and had the memory of an elephant. People liked him, and he was always a good friend. Though thrifty and prudent in matters of money, like so many Lorrainese, he was hospitable and generous. Willful, tough, obdurate, scrupulously diligent in anything he did, he nevertheless had no backbone. He disliked head-on attacks; a brutal offensive confused him. He needed to move in an organized, respectable, and circumspect atmosphere, from which he himself might gain regard and esteem. Indulgence and respect were assured to the members of the clan who observed the rituals with the proper precision and deference, and a good conscience resulted from the fact that one had come to rely, once and for all, on a superior moral authority that defines the rules of decorum. Nevertheless, a certain liberty of action derived from the overall sum of accepted hypocrisies and of rule observed. Georges Sadoul found such surroundings, successively, in his parental home, the Surrealist group, and the Communist Party. In 1922, he felt ill at ease in a province where nothing, apart from bourgeois mores, struck him as worthy of respect or esteem. He yearned to travel; he craved foreign beauties, English suits and ties, and conversation partners who were less narrow-minded than provincial intellectuals. He wanted to be part of his era, was interested, although a bit snobbishly, in art, and had a sense of the ridiculous as well as a feeling for quality; for the art world of Lorraine he could feel only pity, scorn, and annoyance. He was familiar with the most recent books, whose authors and titles I knew only by name—Gide, Paul Morand, Valéry, Giraudoux, Cocteau, Max Jacob, Martin du Gard, Larbaud.

My father, claiming I had everything I needed at home, never gave me an allowance. He subscribed to *Mercure de France, Revue Musicale, Art et Décoration,* and *Comoedia.* There were more than two thousand volumes in his library, but all the works or authors, except for two or three, had been part of the library that had gone up in smoke in 1914. Yet in the course of eight years, the literary world had been transformed from top to bottom. I was intrigued by the fascinating publications in new typefaces that I could leaf through at the Victor Berger bookshop, where the whole town bought its books: *La Nouvelle Revue Française, L'Esprit Nouveau,* the fly-by-night magazines of young poets. I had discovered the Dada writings that the Parisians found so funny, and I had done imitations of them.

Georges Sadoul had pocket money, and because he was prudent—he didn't smoke, drink, or go out with girls—he could buy books and new magazines. He knew and loved Proust, whom I discovered through him. Reading *Swann in Love* was all the more exalting because I was in love with a girl named Odette. Sadoul had bought the first translations of Freud. He lent them to me, and became involved in passionate discussions because I felt that I had to integrate psycho-analysis into my budding Marxism. I myself brought nothing but a very faded Symbolism, Rimbaud, Verlaine, Charles Cros, Tristan Corbière—none of whom, except for Rimbaud, were enjoying more than a succès d'estime—and Guillaume Apollinaire. Apollinaire was in our home library too, and my admiration for anything he wrote —*Alcohols, Calligrams, The Decaying Sorcerer, The Seated Woman*— was unbounded.

Our exchanges of books and ideas reinforced our mutual feeling of confinement in Nancy. Our hikes through the Vosges, which sometimes went on for days, were something of a flight. We certainly loved the somber and romantic fir forests, but more than anything we preferred the easy climbs around the peaks. Our enthusiasm, which was fenced in by our provincial town, would unfurl violently over endless stretches, and if it sometimes got lost there, it left us with a clear field: the world lay before us.

My prejudices rapidly fell away. First, Sadoul occupied the terrain. We saw one another nearly every day, and we talked about everything: girls, art, nature, philosophy, religion, and even politics. Sadoul wasn't interested in philosophy or in metaphysics or politics. He found his father's nationalism tiresome but he didn't mind it. My antimilitarism and my sympathies with revolutionary movements seemed to him on a higher level than simple vituperation of Germany. He believed himself—or tried to be—Catholic. That was, incidentally, the era of conversions; Cocteau's, for instance, caused a lot of talk. Mauriac and Maritain occupied the literary press and defended Christianity less stupidly than Henry Bordeaux or René Bazin. It all got on my nerves, but Sadoul was not insensitive to the influence in Nancy of an association of Catholic students animated by a subtle and active Jesuit. I accompanied him every Sunday to the cathedral, where we arrived late for the eleven-o'clock mass. I loved that majestic edifice, whose façade is an example of success in shocking proportions. I would search out the faces or silhouettes of girls I knew among the faithful. Sadoul didn't even pretend to pray, but at the elevation of the Host he would assume a posture of humble respect, whereas I would make fun of him and pointedly refuse to bow.

Our literary conversations were more concerned with narrative excitement than with the quality of the writing. Besides, Sadoul was insensitive to form. Because of his natural sense of humor, however, he took great pleasure in the distortions of banal reality by grotesque tales. He could condense them marvelously, stressing their humor or preposterousness and, if necessary, taking some liberties with objective reporting. This gift for storytelling was one of the delights of his conversation. Even though problems of style and composition always caught my attention in literary works, Georges Sadoul's interest in plot seemed extremely valid, and I was converted to his approach. In the house at Raon-l'Etape, Sadoul had found all the back issues of *Fantômas*, with the marvelous illustrated covers of the period, as well as *Orlando Furioso* and *Jerusalem Delivered*. I set much store in our reading between 1922 and 1924 because it contributed to the definitive ruin of all "modern" literature in our minds and because those splendid wonders prepared us for the salvation we found in *The Surrealist Manifesto*.

Sadoul displayed innate good taste for the plastic arts. Painting interested him more than writing, but music left him cold; he used to say complacently that concerts bored him. Nancy has a well-stocked art museum, and we would often go there. We particularly studied the so-called primitive painters and works of the Italian Renaissance. It was during these visits that I grew to like Baroque painting, especially Simon Vouet, who was then out of favor. Sadoul didn't share my opinions in this regard. He found me eclectic and criticized my weakness for Mannerism and Flamboyant Gothic, failing to understand that I could also love the Romanesque churches that he admired exclusively. Later he changed. When Bellange was discovered, Sadoul published an extremely lucid article on him in his father's magazine, and he terminated his life's work with a big book on Jacques Callot.

In their relations with painters, the provinces are very far from Paris. The market is in Paris, and there seems to be little hope that this will ever change. The competition is in Paris too, and even the most dazzling success in the provinces is never taken seriously in the capital. The advocates of decentralization won't accomplish a thing until they bring back the princely patronage of the Court of Burgundy. As early as the seventeenth century, the great painters of Lorraine —Callot, Bellange, Georges de la Tour, Claude Gelée—had to go to Paris or Rome for advice, inspiration, and clients, even with the relative generosity of the dukes of Lorraine. In 1922, the population of Lorraine, shut off from the times, had even forgotten Impressionism (if they ever knew it at all) to such an extent that no one exhibited the delicate and sensitive paintings done in the days of the School of Nancy by Charles de Meixmoron. The most gifted local neo-Impressionist, Michel Colle, gave up dissolving forms in light before Breton landscapes, although around 1900 he had established certain formulas that Bonnard was to employ a bit later. Nancy did have galleries and an artistic circle, which favored the awful products of backward academicism. Nevertheless, Victor Prouvé's liberal and enthusiastic teaching had inspired a number of young painters who more or less clumsily reflected certain aspects of the School of Paris. The most widely respected was Paul Colin, a very mediocre easel painter who was destined to become a well-known poster designer. A happy-go-lucky sort, he lived in Paris, which brought him prestige and buyers. He would sometimes come back to his province and dazzle his old friends with his free-and-easy ways, his chatter, and his gumption: he drank, kissed girls right in front of a few local bohemians, who were dumb with admiration, and left a few drawings and plants to Nancy.

Jean Lurçat's visits were more discreet. Lurçat was a reserved young man, as proper as an Englishman, distinguished from the common run by a natural and intimidating nonchalance. He had nothing of the ways of the roaring twenties, but he did smell of pale tobacco and whiskey, and he brought a sort of new spirit with him. His paintings at the time were very close to Cubism. They were reminiscent of Survage, with the same slightly soft elegance. All sorts of influences were evident in them, as in a mirror, but the colors were lively, fresh, and youthful. Sadoul was fond of Lurçat, who had already made a name for himself in Paris. The older generation in Nancy considered him a fraud despite his bourgeois background and the esteem of Victor Prouvé, who always said that Lurçat was his most talented student. Exhibitions of works by Colin, Lurçat, and other sons of Nancy slightly aware that they were living in the golden age of French painting were unfortunately rather rare. They were pale reflections of the prodigious efflorescence in Paris, emphasizing things that had been shown ten years earlier. But they never ushered anything in.

Both Sadoul and I were more interested in what was going to be painted than in what had been painted. We looked for the sources of future art in the old masters. My daily exposure to Signac, Bonnard, Matisse, Ravel, and Debussy evoked excessive admiration for the large bathing women and the academic portraits that Picasso was painting and led to some firm conclusions about the birth of a neo-Classical art. Sadoul didn't have to change scenes because the Lorraine objects and furniture from before 1830, which filled his parents' home, were neutral enough to accommodate anything, except Impressionism. Sadoul despised Monet's cathedrals and the water lilies; he wanted painting to develop toward a greater formal rigor in forms, a direction it seemed to have been following for a number of years. Georges Seurat, whose *Grande Jatte* I marveled at in Wiesbaden in 1921, struck him, along with Cézanne, as the only French painter before the Cubists worthy of mention. His trip to Italy in 1923 fixed his taste for some time. He returned home completely won over by Florence, the cathedral of Assisi, the towers of San Gimignano, and the frescoes of Piero della Francesca and Paolo Uccello. He devised a theory of painting which discriminated works whose surface is smooth with clear outlines from those in which a concern for material and the effects of light is more important. He cast aside Rubens, Rembrandt, Fragonard, and Delacroix, even Dürer, making no exception for the late-fifteenth-century Germans (such as Grünewald). The truth, according to him, lay totally with the Quattrocento painters.

Despite these bizarre standards, Sadoul's ideas about painting largely coincided with my own conclusions. I shared his admiration for the frescoes at Arezzo as soon as he showed me photographs of them. I already knew and liked Uccello. But I did not abandon sixteenth-century German painting, Delacroix, *Jupiter and Thetis,* or Ingres' *Turkish Bath.* Our discussions, which were sometimes very brutal, focused on details or nuances, but we would have been hard put to find better instruction. In 1924 I realized that the absolute we sought, when all else failed, in a return to classical rules, had been attained thirteen years earlier by Braque and Picasso in *Ma Jolie,* the *papiers collés,* and the sublime brown and beige Cubist mono-chromes, which captured light and mystery with the weapons that Poussin had employed. By liberating themselves from servile depiction of objects and the notion of perspective, Braque and Picasso revealed a new world of forms. It was as though the limits of the visible and the perceptible had been enlarged. I had to admit that the broadening of the limits of the visible was as attractive as, if not more so than, the painterly ideal. But, even while I admired Braque and Poussin, I was not insensitive to the different world of Grünewald, Cranach, and the Fontainebleau School. The discovery of Surrealism a few months later enabled me to find my bearings within such diversity, which was irritating only to the prisoners of a system.

Sadoul shared my opinion on Braque and Picasso of 1912, but his dogmatism lasted longer than my neo-Classicism. Either he was more susceptible to dogmas than I or he had realized that dogmatism is not always a bad frame of reference. For example, he didn't care for Braque's new manner in *The Canéphores.* His judgment was certainly too severe, but it became cruelly judicious as soon as people began to compare the canéphores to the firm and heavy young women in the Arezzo frescoes.

Sadoul and I agreed about most of the simplistic but clear ideas expressed by Ozenfant and Le Corbusier in the books that were all the rage then: *Towards an Architecture* and *The New Spirit.* Perhaps in reaction to the aesthetic of the School of Nancy, we tended to endorse the celebration of industrial beauty. Only a blind man could fail to be moved by the grandeur of the Solvay works in Dombasle, which we passed several times a year en route to our country houses, or the infernal power of the high furnaces of

Pompey, which set the entire northern sky of Nancy aglow in wintertime. Today, these factories of 1920, bristling with girders and traveling cranes and with their high brick chimneys, are as touchingly out of date as Ferdinand Barbedienne's bronzes and the department-store catalogues that Le Corbusier made such fun of. The "functional" beauty of the Voisin automobiles and the Farman biplanes on the Paris–London line, which Ozenfant and his colleague praised to the skies, obviously expressed a notion that also led to Lanvin's frocks or Molyneux's hats, just as the lofty chimneys of locomotives and the calash railroad coaches during the 1860's are closely related to the opera hats and crinolines. It took us three years to realize the value of the aesthetics course for primary schools in *The New Spirit*, which argues in favor of a pre-established order with a helter-skelter jumble of maunderings on the golden section, the reduction of cathedrals to isosceles triangles and semicircles, and the fight against slums. But such books did influence their contemporaries; they vouchsafed aesthetic pleasure and domestic comfort by means of a few simple rules. This was to be our way too. Although I resisted Le Corbusier's cubes slightly, Sadoul was won over. This, paradoxically, resulted in hastening our entry into the Surrealist group.

Sadoul went to Paris more and more often. He came to realize how badly informed the provinces were—the only intellectual exchanges were those between conservative or backward minds—and devised the idea of livening up Nancy with visits by avant-garde Parisians. The original impetus was probably the desire of young people in Lorraine to put on plays, the eternal demon of the provinces. Nancy-Paris, a committee of literary and artistic action, was founded, and Victor Guillaume was wise enough to make Georges Sadoul its head. Victor Guillaume looked like a small apostle. He had the necessary receding hairline, tonsorial halo, serious and glowing eyes, slow gestures, and Newgate frill. He started at the turn of the century as a carver of furniture, but he eventually began to paint. Laboriously he sought his way through Cézanne and gradually found it in a combination of small luminous surfaces that, with the growing maturity of his work, ultimately absorbed the contours of objects and individuals. Obstinately faithful to his province, modest to a fault, Victor Guillaume had no reputation in Paris. He lived out his life at the foot of the ruined castle of the Vaudémonts, in the poverty that he had always known.

The Nancy-Paris Committee was made up of a painter, an antique dealer, three journalists, a police draftsman who wanted to write, and a law student. They were joined by a lycée pupil (myself) a few days before the first lecture in a cultural program organized by Georges Sadoul under the aegis of the *Nouvelle Revue Française.* The theme of this lecture was movies, though Sadoul did not then realize that he would devote the major part of his life to that subject. Jean Epstein, supposedly a "new wave" filmmaker, was asked to speak. Hundreds of people come, and the success of that evening instantly launched Nancy-Paris. The next lecture was given by Henri Prunières, head of the *Revue Musicale,* a world-renowned monthly that devoted a lot of space to the most modern music. For the first time, I heard characteristic works of the Six. I was extremely anxious to get to know more of them.

My father had been at the première of *The Ox on the Roof.* He had often spoken about the show, which had amused him, but he hadn't found the music very interesting. Prunières' lecture and the enthusiasm it aroused in me roused him from a sort of lethargy brought about by disappointments and health problems. Overnight, works by young musicians appeared in our library and piled up on the pianos. The simple style, the fresh inspiration, the sense of humor, the sober development in these compositions contrasted with the heaviness of the pupils of Franck, the starchy refinements of Fauré's and Debussy's disciples. The harmonies were new, and sometimes sour. These were refugees from previous systems that ultimately looked like prisons. I started deciphering as much of that music as I could.

Georges Sadoul prepared the second season of Nancy-Paris (1924–25) before he left Nancy to do his hitch in the service. Because of his father's good connections with the general staff, he was assigned to an idle unit in the Paris region. I took charge of the committee's musical activities and organized concerts of the music that I wanted to hear. I loved planning programs and hiring performers. Composers, sopranos, and virtuosos were amused at dealing with a seventeen-year-old kid who was studying for the Polytechnical School. I got Henri Sauguet, generally considered a great white hope of French music, to come. He was brilliant and illustrated his talk with excerpts from the music he loved. Suzanne Peignot, the favorite interpreter of young composers, sang them with her gracefully intelligent voice.

Sauguet got me to share his admiration for the *Gymnopédies* and

Idylle. However, I instantly recognized that these strange, dreamlike pieces were outside the usual style of their respective composers, Satie and Chabrier, and I have never changed my mind.

Sauguet and I wrote to one another regularly for several months. We stopped when we realized that we couldn't agree on anything. His great intellectual honesty and the firmness of his convictions are reflected in the austere compositions anticipated by the melancholy of the early ballets. Even the twelve-tone wave of the sixties may not have eroded their value.

Sauguet's concert was one of the last to be put on by Nancy-Paris, which did not survive after I moved to the capital. That year, the people of Nancy listened to works by Stravinsky, Béla Bartók, and Anton Webern, whom they had never even heard of. Earlier I had invited Darius Milhaud and Francis Poulenc. In 1926, Poulenc himself played the piano part in his trio for oboe, piano, and bassoon. The rehearsals took place in my father's mansion on Rue Girardet. There I discovered how rigorous the execution of a musical work could be, an ideal that the Nancy concerts were ultimately far from achieving. Stravinsky had made fashionable a sophisticated return to Baroque music as a source of inspiration and a model of structure. This manner was exploited for about a dozen years by almost every musician in France. Poulenc's *Trio* was one of the finest compositions in that vein. It had, for me, the mystery of a meeting of masks, and I rather gratuitously compared it to the Chirico of the great metaphysical period. I wrote Poulenc several perfectly stupid letters to that effect, trying to get him to break off with Cocteau, one of his best friends, in order to remain true to his genius!

I felt a great admiration for Darius Milhaud. At the time, all I knew by him was his chamber music and piano versions of his theater works. He himself did not disappoint me. He came to Nancy in 1925 with his wife during a great frost, but since he had taken a trip to Russia shortly before, the climate of Lorraine seemed almost mild by comparison. On the eve of his concert, he was kind enough to accompany me to a private session of the Artistic Circle of the East, where they were playing (and very badly at that) my father's sonata for piano and cello. "I know your father's music," said Milhaud. "When I was a young Conservatory student before the war, I heard his first symphony. I don't know what I'd think of it today, but I liked it then. It was different from the languid affectations of the Impressionists."

Milhaud asked me what I liked: "Ah, so you like Schumann! I
hate him almost as much as Wagner. It's all bowler-hat music.
I could much more readily understand your liking Schubert's quartets
and lieder." At the symphonic concerts in Nancy, I had greatly
enjoyed Ernest Bloch's symphonic poem *Schelomo*. When I told
Milhaud about this discovery and asked him about the composer, I
was forced to listen to a tirade: "Well, you know, our personalities
are incompatible. Both of us are Jews. The Diaspora has divided Jews
into Sephardim and Ashkenazis, who are dissimilar in both their
physical appearance and their character. I'm Provençal and Sephardic.
Bloch is an Ashkenazi; he comes from a country where there's
practically nothing but fog and mist."

Far more than the man and the musician, it was the traveler
returning from the U.S.S.R. that fascinated me in Milhaud. He had
been the guest of the Soviet government. I showered him with questions: What was it like? How were the people? First Milhaud
described the touching triumphal arch of streamers and timber that
welcomed the traveler at the border station. But he left my curiosity
unsatisfied because, even though he spoke at length about his trip
and his sympathies for the Bolsheviks, nothing that he said corresponded to my notion of a new world. Back then, there were
still a few traces of liberalism left in Russia, thanks to the New
Economic Policy. Party members were still having real political
discussions, and deep within them appeared the oppositions that
Stalin was preparing to wipe out with concentration camps, torture,
and death. Trotsky was being challenged, which came as a surprise to
the outside world, where his name was associated with Lenin's, but,
paradoxically, the attacks on the leaders of the Revolution and the
Civil War were interpreted as a sign of democratic ways rather than
as dynastic quarreling. Trotsky could still be heard and published.
The French, brought up on the history of their own revolution, were
not particularly surprised that the Russian leaders were fighting among
themselves. As long as they were not killing one another, their
discussion methods seemed to constitute a perceptible progress over
that of the Convention. Their efforts to fend off famine and to struggle
against poverty aroused sympathy. The goals were gigantic; what more
could one ask? Milhaud wasn't very interested in the power struggles
raging within the Russian Communist Party. He was uninformed and
could only say that they were not disturbing everyday life. "The
revolutionary city," he said, "is Leningrad. Moscow is conservative

and played only a secondary part in October 1917. In Leningrad, you feel that things are still hot. Any Russian who's doing anything new lives in Leningrad. By the way, the Hermitage has a collection of modern French painting that far surpasses Paris. They're doing astonishing experiments in Leningrad. I heard orchestras without conductors, and their cooperation amazed me. But don't think that modernism in art has won out. A lot of ancient institutions are still there, and their staffs are outmoded. Old Glazunov is still the director of the Leningrad Conservatory. He represents the Academy, defends his ideas, and enjoys a great deal of prestige, but he makes sure that his school offers a liberal instruction. I've met some astonishingly gifted young men: you'll soon be hearing about Kabalevsky and Shostakovitch."

As both an organizer of concerts and a music critic for *Le Pays Lorrain*, I had to hear everything being played in Nancy. Thus, I met Ravel and Enesco. I was annoyed at my father, who had known both of them for a long time yet never invited them over. I considered Enesco a virtuoso who had dabbled in musical composition, for I was unfamiliar with the richness and newness of his works. On the other hand, I was bowled over by a luncheon invitation from Eugène Isaye. The illustrious violinist was past eighty, but he stood as straight as a man of forty. His romantic countenance, his giant stature, and his noble, tranquil, and self-confident bearing, like that of an old idol, were admirable. Watching him, I felt as though I were defying time. The man speaking to me was the one to whom César Franck had dedicated his famous sonata. "I also knew Franz Liszt!" he told me, amused by my stupefaction.

The year 1925 was decisive for my development and for Georges Sadoul's. I had opted for the Revolution and, after a good deal of thought, joined the Communist Party. Like every young person, I was trying to group all my admirations in a coherent bundle in order to find a new but clear definition of good and evil. In 1925, Soviet Russia still had her place in modern art: the French were translating Babel, Yessenin, Pilniak; the specialized critics hailed Alexander Blok and Mayakovsky as great poets; Blok's alleged influence on the Revolution, Mayakovsky's militant part in the Civil War, expressed realms above Péguy or Claudel. Meyerhold's and Stanislavsky's theaters were praised as the foremost vanguard. The Constructivists, who had developed a new architecture and decorative art in the spirit of Cubism, seemed to be honored in Russia. Didn't the Soviet

Pavilion at the Exhibition of Decorative Arts outclass all the others, including Le Corbusier's, simply through its modernism?

A new, modern-minded bookdealer greatly sympathized with the activities of Nancy-Paris. My father opened a charge account for me and authorized me to buy books. This came at exactly the right moment. I devoured the tales and novels of young Soviet writers. The only thing that really interested me about them was a certain uprootedness, for this was really conventional literature. But it was different with Breton's *Soluble Fish* or *Les Pas Perdus*. I didn't understand the full significance of the latter because of its allusions to things I knew nothing about. Yet I was gripped by a force of mind, a rigor, and a fixity of purpose that I had never encountered anywhere else. The tone and style seemed to be part of the greater tradition of French prose writers of the 1700's and yet totally modern. Wasn't this absolute beauty?

I have already mentioned the effect that the first few issues of *The Surrealist Revolution* had on me. Eluard's poems, the writings of Artaud and Desnos, attained, for me, the heights of poetic expression, surpassing in originality anything I had ever read before. Contrary to all the other French writers, Surrealists supported the Revolution. In the *Last Strike*, Breton declared his solidarity with the proletarian struggles; he suggested going even further. If Aragon still had qualms about the importance of the Russian Revolution, several of his friends were already Communists by 1924. The two movements seemed bound together by the very force of History. In October 1925, when the Surrealists loudly rallied to the Comintern, I had no further reasons to curb my attraction to what they wrote or painted. I was happy and confident in the feeling that everything I admired was on the same side of the fence.

Sadoul's progress was rather different. Political problems did not as yet interest him (if they ever have); nor did the Revolution, except for its colorful aspects. He had read a good deal of Max Jacob and, at his very first contact, exactly measured the quality and newness of the Surrealist writings. The challenge to established reputations— Barrès, Gide, France—won him over because it agreed with his general thoughts on their works. Finally, the importance the Surrealists attached to dreams and the unconscious was consistent with his own experiences.

At *La Nouvelle Revue Française* he had learned how much the heads of the house admired and feared Aragon and Breton—especially

Aragon, who was gaining a "brilliant" reputation. Sadoul read *Anicet*, then *Télémaque's Voyage* with transports of delight. I was dazzled by the stories in the *Libertinage*. The breeziness, the ease, the effectiveness, and the humor struck me as unique and unprecedented. These epithets fail to describe all the richness of that book. Drieu La Rochelle, during the only and very long conversation that we had in 1926, made a statement which I have never forgotten because it shocked me (at the time, I took it for backbiting): "I prefer *The French Woman* to anything else that Aragon wrote—and believe me, I like everything of his. I consider these fifteen pages one of the major works of our literature. They anticipate novels that will assure their author's reputation!"

Reading the *Songs of Maldoror* had not hastened Sadoul's or my progress toward Surrealism. It was the works of Aragon and Breton that made us realize the importance of Lautréamont. Whn I had read *Maldoror* at fourteen, I had simply classed it as wild romanticism, like *The Last of Satan* and *Caspar of the Night*. On the other hand, certain movies had led us to reject the everyday reality that disgusted us: all the Charlie Chaplin and Mack Sennett films in 1923, *The Cabinet of Doctor Caligari* a bit later, and, as far as I'm concerned, two other German movies: *The Three Lights* and especially *Nosferatu*. The vision of *Potemkin* in 1926 probably removed Sadoul's final objections to Russian Communism.

Thus, by the end of 1925, Sadoul and I had made up our minds. The Surrealists were offering everything that we asked of literary expression and much more. We had to get in touch with them as soon as possible. I urged Sadoul to do it. He temporized, probably because of timidity. He couldn't quite see how he might go about it, and he was even more discouraged because everything he heard about Aragon's and Breton's exacting personalities was frightening. Why didn't we ask them to come and give a few lectures in Nancy? I was ready to assume the risks of a scandal, but Sadoul doubted that our idols would accept.

The secretary-general of the Nancy-Paris Committee was Maurice Boissais, a Protestant functionary, a sentimental bon vivant, and a would-be writer. His models were Lacretelle and Jules Romains, and he continued to admire Paul Morand and Dunoyer de Segonzac. Sadoul's relations with Boissais were tense, but I managed to maintain a certain unity within the group. Sadoul wanted to achieve a great coup in 1926 by showing Nancy all the painting and architecture of the time. He was on good terms with both Lurçats, the painter and the architect. His support of Le Corbusier's ideas led him to give architecture a large place in his project. He invited Theo van Doesburg and the Stijl group, Walter Gropius, Mies van der Rohe and the Bauhaus, Americans, and the most modern French architects. Ozenfant agreed to give a lecture in the same room in which Sadoul gathered an exhibition of works by the best-known painters and sculptors of the School of Paris: Braque, Picasso, Léger, Matisse, Chagall, Derain, Marcoussis, Lurçat, Zadkine, Lipchitz, Laurens. The show was to take place in the largest gallery in Nancy, which was also the most official, and all the publicity was to focus on the commercial value of the works shown: a million francs, which seemed a great deal to all of us.

We had some problems with Boissais because Sadoul obstinately refused to include the painters of the Salon d'Automne. His only concession, which turned out to be highly profitable, was to invite four or five Lorrainese painters of modern tendencies and to include Victor Prouvé, the former head of the School of Nancy. As it happened, all the material organization in Nancy fell on my shoulders, partly because of Boissais' laziness, so that, despite the dispute, things went smoothly.

The Galerie Pierre, which used to be on Rue Bonaparte in Paris, lent us some of the Parisian paintings. While there, Sadoul was introduced to Aragon, an old friend of the gallery owner. The contact with the Surrealists we had been seeking for so long had finally been achieved. With his acute sense of opportunity, Aragon suggested that we also show some Surrealist painters. A letter from Sadoul two or three days later informed me that we were to add the names of Arp, Max Ernst, Chirico, Masson, and Miró to the list of artists. All their paintings, Sadoul wrote, would be shown together as a separate group. Nancy would thus have the privilege of being the scene of the second Surrealist exhibit in the world.

I was overjoyed, but our troubles were only just beginning. France was fighting a war in the Riff, and the Surrealists had wholeheartedly endorsed the catch phrases of the Communist Party: fraternization with the rebels and disobedience of orders from the military leaders. There had been indignant stories in the newspapers. At the Saint Pol Roux banquet, Desnos, clinging to a chandelier and kicking out at the diners, had yelled "Long live Germany!" while Breton and the others started a free-for-all. This scandal and a number of violent antipatriotic demonstrations had aroused brutal reactions. Newspapers were calling for a boycott of Surrealist publications and demonstrations.

I had a supplement printed for the catalogue, and Sadoul brought the paintings. When we started hanging them, Boissais burst into the gallery and declared that his honor as a functionary would not permit him to condone the inclusion in this exhibit of paintings by apologists for military disobedience. The situation was actually funny, but voices soon were raised. Sadoul was in a quandary. He felt that the show was ruined and wanted to call it off. "The paintings will be hung," I said to Boissais, "and the exhibit will open as planned."

"Well, then I'll resign. And I won't be alone. I'll explain why; you'll have the entire press and all of Nancy against you."

"Tough!"

Boissais did resign, and so did the journalists and the antique dealer. There was a slight hullabaloo in town. The paper on which our journalists worked ran a confused explanation of the resignations: the Surrealists were relegated to a minor part because they were still obscure and incidental figures totally unknown in the provinces. Indignation mainly centered on the fact that eight years after the armistice, an honorable position was being granted in Nancy to photographs, drawings, and projects by German architects. Sadoul wasn't ready to fight. He immediately departed for Paris, leaving the whole matter to me. I have never been one to scuttle back from something, and I adroitly tried to open the show on the date set. I replaced the four dissidents with five young men who were sympathetic to our action but had both reputation and prestige in Nancy because of their talents and their family backgrounds. I had myself elected secretary-general of the committee and used other maneuvers to alleviate the situation: more posters, handbills, personal invitations. Victor Prouvé, the very respectable director of the School of Fine Arts, opened the exhibition with his customary good will. It was a grand success.

7
THE MIRAGE OF
THE REVOLUTION

IT ALL STARTED IN 1920, AROUND THE FIRST OF
May. Strikes and unemployment were everywhere. Hundreds of workers
paraded through the streets of Nancy with signs and red flags. Severe,
resolute, a bit sad, they didn't look evil, yet they inspired fear. France's
victory hadn't solved a thing. At the time, I was getting out the first
issue of *En Avant*. I included a sort of editorial favorable to the workers'
marches and to the May First celebration of a Labor Holiday. My
mother, who was to die a few weeks later, didn't want *En Avant* to
circulate in school before she had read it through. She disapproved of
what I had written about the First of May. "You're going to cause
trouble for your father," she said. "People will think we're Socialists.
Besides, you're too young to understand what's going on." I pasted a
white page over the indicted article and replaced it with something or
other.

I had obeyed, but I was not convinced. Such condemnation was
motivated only by a fear of what people would say. She seemed to be

seriously contradicting all the Christian teachings—equality, charity, brotherly love—as well as the great principles of the Rights of Man, the moral foundations of the secular school. Could adults be hypocrites and liars? In 1920, I was very pious, very patriotic, and a strong supporter of the Republic. Throughout the war, I had never doubted our ultimate victory because the cause of France was that of Justice, and God could only be on the side of Justice.

Besides, the Germans, who were guilty of atrocities, had been punished and wicked old Wilhelm II had lost his imperial throne. His punishment followed the laws of progress, because a republic was the best possible form of government. Among its other virtues, the republic protected its citizens against arbitrary treatment, gave each person a chance, and so on. But both my mother's prohibition of the article and the workers' signs indicated that there were faults in the sublime truths that I had learned and in the society that claimed to cherish them.

My mother's death, as great as my grief may have been, did not justify her prohibition. On the contrary, when she was no longer there, she could no longer exercise the intellectual oppression that might have crushed my doubts and shifted the focus of my attention. I was deeply disturbed by the many contradictions between everyday reality and dogmas and principles I was taught. Reality, no longer shining in the heroic glow of the war, gradually revealed its defects and lies to me, including the structures and laws that catechism and school ignored or deformed. I wanted to learn about and understand these. My friends and I had endless discussions about the Bible, the Gospels, and the existence of God. Is the universe God, or does it proceed from God? How can an omnipotent and infinitely good God tolerate and even encourage human misery? How can we believe in a revelation and in miracles when there have been no examples ever since such phenomena have been open to even superficial scientific testing. If truth is in revelation, how can we tell the real God from the false gods, truth from trickery? Wasn't it more reasonable to admit that God is a human concept? The hypothesis of a primal force, supernatural and almighty, creative and uncreated, struck me as displacing but not resolving the riddle of Life and the World. I saw it as an argument in favor of atheism, and I stopped going to mass. But although the dogma may have been wrecked, I still had very deep traces left of Christian philosophy and morality. The absolute equality of men before God, the total leveling of talents, privileges, chance, and success at the moment when souls are weighed, are, for any Westerner, the source of the notion of justice—even if he doesn't believe in the immortality of the soul or the Last Judgment. The Western idea that all men are born free and equal has generated all the Socialist systems, with the sole exception of Fourier's. It may not even be wrong to believe that the revisions of reformers and theologians in regard to the universal distribution of grace, the notion of predestination, and the concept of a chosen people gave the zealots of racism or of a salvation by a social class their first weapons.

I had always sided with the righters of wrongs. I had suffered when I learned that Don Quixote is someone people make fun of. I was thus a ready-made recruit for Socialism. But I was not led to this new church by the feelings of sympathy and charity that emerge in sensitive souls when slumming.

As a petty-bourgeois lycée pupil, I did not suffer a boss's exploitation; nor did those near and dear to me. There was no blatant poverty in Baccarat, nor in Pompey or Neuves-Maisons. The bosses were paternalistic, hostile in principle and out of selfishness to the labor unions, but fairly human. Workers were decently housed almost everywhere. Charities and benevolent societies vied to regulate, within the social structure, the gravest social problems. Firm restrictions, with no mechanism for appeal, took care of the rest. Workers contented themselves with little and lived decently: salaries were low, each person cultivated his garden, careful budgeting helped make both ends meet, and money was deposited in savings accounts. Besides, no one ever wanted to change his job or trade, because that would have involved a good deal of trouble. The condition of shop employees or waitresses in Nancy was hardly more enviable than that of the metallurgists in Frouard or the winders in the electrical works. There were still enough soldiers around to support honest prostitution. I was not bewailing anyone's particular lot. But the overall conditions of these proletarian lives aroused in me the same malaise as the confining countryside or the horizonless villages. Everything there seemed determined once and for all, until death, in poverty and monotony. It was easy enough to see that such immobility congealed society as a whole, except for the tiny, wealthy fringe of glamorous spendthrifts in Paris, Deauville, or Monte Carlo. Luxury, travel, pleasure, and power gave the life of these privileged few dimensions that were unknown elsewhere.

The lot of the people I knew in Lorraine—intellectuals, tradesmen, industrialists—did not strike me as very enviable. Mediocrity prevailed everywhere, mingled with stupidity and ugliness. The moral order that had followed the refusal to yield to German arms and the determination to win the war disgusted me more and more each day. For forty years, Nancy had been planning to avenge and reconquer Metz and Strasbourg. Once victory had been achieved, we had to pay its price, and accounts could not be settled with the disappearance of a quarter of our young men. The border no longer ran along the blue line of the Vosges; it was now the course of the Rhine. The symbol of the fatherland was no longer Nancy, but Strasbourg. Furthermore, Strasbourg was larger than Nancy, and more active as well. The mines and metallurgy of Metz were much bigger and richer than those of the Nancy basin.

In short, everything had changed: life went on in melancholy resignation, and people realized that Nancy had lost the privileged position it had gained after the defeat of 1870. But they refused either to comprehend or to adjust to the situation. The soldiers who had been killed (the best ones no doubt) might have had a different perspective on the present and the future. The survivors plunged into a disgusting celebration of the massacres, which expressed a yearning for the years of warlike exaltation rather than a commemoration of the missing. They sought refuge in a cult of the dead, with grotesque monuments and massive parades of pitiful and embittered invalids. A whole people was reverting to its past. What a curious throwback of national ambition, compared with the parades of red trousers and the cavalry charges!

The clergy happily participated in this exploitation of cemeteries and tried to regain an influence over the general populace and the younger generation that the secular school had severely dented. They generally had the support of industry, which saw the priests and their good works as a solid rampart against the expansion of the Reds. Minor priests took advantage of all the feasts of devotion in Alsace and Lorraine (Sainte Odile, Joan of Arc, and other medieval heroines hardly prepared to patronize children of Mary, but transformed long ago into chaste little dullards with the Pope's approval) to organize noisy trips with sausage feasts banderoles, rural masses, pilgrimages to relics, and sheaves on the military monuments. Each year, these jingoistic processions became more and more anachronistic.

Historical research, defensive arguments, memoirs, and apologias kept challenging the received ideas on the origins of the war and the prestige of the great leaders. The governments had lied so much that the official theses on the causes of the conflict and the history of the battles were almost totally discredited. The Communist thesis that an imperialist war had been fomented by finance capital to settle, by force of arms, conflicts between banking or industrial interests added new explanations that were enticingly simple and apparently rigorous.

All the pacifists used them, with more or less distortion. The theory that attributed the war to the cannon manufacturers acquired a considerable popularity. This immense myth, which is still inspiring politics today, had particular strength in Lorraine, an area of heavy industry where the Wendel family owned factories on both sides of the 1914 border.

Thus everything at once managed to belittle patriotism, society, and religion. I could find no moral rule that wasn't spoiled by hypocrisy or money, by force or lies. Awakening to sex, I realized that the austere rules of the Lorraine bourgeoisie and the Church's prohibitions were merely particular forms of oppression—and the least justifiable at that. The free ways of the working class were to my mind more in keeping with the times than the prudishness of my social milieu.

Everything led me to believe that true liberty was still to be won. High-school history says that liberty is won by force. My favorite period in French history was the Revolution of 1789. Who, after all, hasn't been mad about Mirabeau, Danton, Saint-Just, and Robespierre? In those days, things had moved swiftly; society was transformed in the twinkling of an eye and, according to the history books, become more just. I was particularly attracted to the attitudes or speeches that reverse situations, to violent acts of liberation, to the heroism of the French Revolutionary armies. Revolution and putsches were rumbling at our doors, in Italy, Germany, Central Europe, and the Baltic. In any other circumstances, I would probably have been drawn to the army, but by 1923 the defense of the fatherland had become a meaningless concept. The occupation of the Ruhr seemed more like brigandage, and the colonial operations in Syria, Indochina, and Morocco wrecked the image of a France supposedly bringing peace, civilization, and freedom to the natives. The most violent voice of traditional nationalism was L'Action Française, whose influence on young men in the petty and middle bourgeoisie, whether Royalists or not, and on future officers, grew in proportion to the mental confusion of French political leaders and their inability to govern except by improvisation. I found Maurras' articles stupid and full of hatred. The very thought that this gross and narrow-minded man could have given thousands of young French people the illusion of an ideology and a morality speaks tellingly of readers' ability to comprehend a text. Léon Daudet, sometimes funny and often ignoble, had the style of another age.

The industrial strides of the reconstruction years were profitable to a number of adults, but young intellectuals realized all the more acutely the wide gap between the potential energy of a nation like France, the conservative spirit of its elites, and the growing incoherence of its political leadership. In spite of my sympathies with Socialist ideas and my growing attraction to the revolutionary movement, I reacted no differently than my right-wing fellow students to the mediocrity of ambitions and results. We all wanted to be as proud of our country as we had been in 1918; but all we were offered was ministerial crises. The right-wing students filled the classes preparing for the Saint-Cyr military academy, which accepted precisely those we considered the dumbest, who could never succeed in either literature or science. Along with them came the sons of families that traditionally produced officers. They all knew that entering Saint-Cyr meant knuckling under to obedience, discipline, and duty, but it did not mean learning to fight a war in order to win. No conversation about tactics or strategy was possible with the Cyrians or Cyrians-to-be: they would learn it all later on. Perhaps they would never even know how to lead a battle. Their business was to fight. But who in the world with? Where was the enemy in 1923? Who was threatening France? Was the French army destined to act as a police force in Cilicia, to march against awkward and no doubt useless demonstrations on the Rhine, to employ cannon and machine guns against Syrians or Moroccans armed with scrap rifles they had got from traffickers?

The devaluation of the franc and the rent laws came as blows to small property owners, who blamed the left wing in 1925, when radicals and Socialists showed that they were incapable of pursuing a realistic financial policy. In 1922 and 1923, it had been the right wing's turn to prove its financial inability and clumsiness. France was on the Rhine, Germany was apparently on the verge of revolution, and nothing seemed likely to reinforce the influence of aggressive nationalism or the enemies of democracy. L'Action Française was slowing down. The success of the march on Rome and Mussolini's takeover at first had no effect on my friends. But when, two or three years later, the Fascist regained control, the new assertion of Italian ambition and the publicity given to its minor successes, such as the punctuality of Italian railroads, were echoed by more and more students in the high schools and universities. This response reached its peak during the university incidents of 1926, which showed the administrative incompetence of the left-wing cartel. L'Action Française attracted a new set of young people by openly adopting pro-Fascist positions. I doubt that those of my friends who sympathized with Maurras' arguments and Mussolini's prestige took their reactionary stance in full knowledge of the facts. I doubted it in 1925 too. They wanted an authoritarian and active state that would accomplish great things. I tried to show them that the right wing was no better than the left and that the creative order they hoped to establish could rise only upon the ruins of obsolete social and political structures which we would have to destroy (and which Mussolini hadn't destroyed); but they replied that if the Socialists came to power, we would have a regime of garrulous dreamers. The far left had no men who inspired confidence: in Russia, Lenin and Trotsky were no doubt bloody terrorists but strong, energetic men. France, however, had no revolutionaries, only dishonest politicians. I was struck by how little these people cared about maintaining or suppressing fundamental liberties: freedom of press, assembly, association. They didn't need these rights and, if necessary, would glady exchange them for authority. Even though I was a Communist by 1925, a partisan of dictatorship by the proletariat, and an advocate of suppressing liberties for my opponents, I was terribly disturbed by the ease with which students were prepared to forego all the gains of democracy. The Mussolinism of L'Action Française bothered me just as much. Italian expansion could occur only at the expense of France, whether in Africa or elsewhere. In 1925, the workings of Fascism were not as clear as ten years later (when Italy publicly demanded Nice, Savoy, and Tunisia), but no one could fail to understand it. At the very heart of integral nationalism appeared the old defeatism of the émigrés of 1792. Basically, Maurras and his friends were less interested in assuring the greatness and prosperity of France and in changing her political orientations, even if this diminished her. This ideology, based on the defense of the social order rather than on nationalism, reinforced my Marxist convictions: the class struggle, which involves the international solidarity of friends or enemies, was quite obviously the prime mover of history!

It was my discovery of class struggle that made me a Marxist. I was searching for a base for my intuitive Socialism and my revolutionary will, a doctrine that would explain the latter through the former. I had charged at random through Saint-Simon, Victor Considérant, Fourier, and Proud'hon. All of them wanted a redistribution of wealth and privilege, but none of them seemed truly revolutionary. Saint-Simon bored me; I found Fourier funny but delirious; Proud'hon was closer to what I was looking for. In 1932, leafing through Mallet and Isaac's *History of France* during my final year of school, I came upon a small note in which the authors state that Marx explains the entire history of humanity through the class struggle. Well, that was obvious. At last, all the wars that the teachers had been drumming into me became meaningful as rational undertakings in a world endowed with a logical structure. I dashed over to the town library, where I found the first few volumes of *Das Kapital* in Deville's translation. The concept of surplus value and its appropriation by the capitalists was as brilliant, to me, as that of the class struggle. Scientific Socialism certainly deserved its name. A perusal of the *Communist Manifesto*, and of the most important parts of Friedrich Engels' *Anti-Dühring*, published in the famous pamphlet *Utopian Socialism and Scientific Socialism*, completed my conversion.

Thus, the social revolution was ineluctably inherent in the development of the modern world. A kind of determinism encompassed all my opinions and arranged them in a coherent order that represented the highest consciousness that man could reach in regard to his destiny. For some time I had already been regularly buying *L'Humanité*. Not all the newsdealers carried it, so I had a copy saved for me every day at a stand on Rue des Carmes, near the lycée. I would call for it at noon. The salesgirl was very pretty, which didn't hurt matters any. In 1924, I had been bowled over by the news of Lenin's death. At election time, I acquired a card as a sympathizer of the Communist Party. In 1926, I organized my first political demonstration. The Action Française students had staged single-file processions through the streets, condemning the left-wing coalition then in power and Georges Scelle, an unfortunate Sorbonne professor who wasn't with them. Here and there, workers were heckling the demonstrators. I convinced a small group of workers to follow me and found myself at the head of a retinue that kept growing. I moved through the principal streets of Nancy. A few students had joined us. Now and then, I would stop the procession and harangue the crowd, making sure that I seemed to be supporting the coalition government so that the police wouldn't bother me. We tried unsuccessfully to intercept the Royalists. The demonstration ended in front of the central police headquarters, and I believe I demanded the release of a worker who had been arrested during the right-wing demonstration. I was just in the midst of my last harangue, leaning against the gate of a firehouse, when a small man elbowed his way through my audience and literally pounced upon me in absolute fury. It was Charles Sadoul, Georges' father. "Aha! Are you happy with what you're doing?" he said, livid with rage. "You're stirring up Frenchmen against one another without realizing that the Germans are watching." He swept his hand toward the east. "The Germans, do you hear, the Germans—they're applauding you and laughing at you. I forbid you to ever darken my door again."

My audience and I were dumbstruck by that insane outburst (it was 1926). I made sure that Charles Sadoul wasn't mistreated by the demonstrators, who didn't exactly like his diatribe. From that day on, the doors of the Sadoul home were closed to me. Finally, at Georges' insistence, they authorized the elderly maid to let me in. But I was not allowed anywhere except in Georges' room on the second floor, which I reached through a maze of staircases and corridors. If I happened to run into anyone else, he or she would pointedly turn away and utter a few unpleasant noises. At Raon-l'Etape, it was worse. They would make me wait in the garden, and my coming would have to coincide with the siesta of the Counselor-General of the Vosges, for fear that he might see me!

Many years later, the Sadoul family allowed its son Georges to make his career in the Communist Party. The French middle classes had become tolerant.

The success of the counterdemonstration that I had organized inspired me to found an Alliance of Anti-Fascist Students. I wrote a leaflet, had it printed at the Union House, and distributed it with a couple of my friends in all the faculties. There were less than ten students in my Alliance, and it was hard for us to pay the printer's bill. I had an altercation in the street with a Royalist, who hit me with his cane, albeit lightly. The right-wing students felt that I had played the game and done a good job of it. The unionists of the People's House considered me one of their own. As a young member of the Communist Party, I became secretary of my cell: Communist workers had taken part in the demonstration, and they said that I had done what the organizations of the Party had failed to do.

8
RUE DU CHATEAU
IN 1927

THE SCHOOL YEAR OF 1927 ENDED BADLY, AT least for me. The two years before, in the special mathematics class, had been deplorable. Louis Longchambon, who was then a professor on the Faculty of Sciences in Nancy, had easily persuaded me that I wasn't right for the Polytechnical School, and he added that the Ecole Normale Superieure was waiting for me—which came as a slight surprise. In his opinion, I ought to start preparing for the admission examination through the section of natural sciences, which was not very popular. So I registered for the S.P.C.N. (the Certificate of Higher Science Studies) and general mathematics. The first semester had been successful; then I had cut all my classes. Failures in July and October had penalized my self-confidence.

There were many reasons for this. Naturally, my meeting Katia, the dazzling passion of my twentieth year, meant that much time intended for studying had been spent on love. Katia lived in a seventeenth-century mansion on Rue Saint-Nicolas. She brought the mystery and charm of the East to a boy who, as a member of the Communist Party for two years and secretary of the Nancy chapter, was ready to receive them as a message. My political responsibilities in themselves were a powerful motive for my scholarly desertion, for they were accompanied by a great craving for Marxism and Leninism. But there was still another focus of my energy, and a very powerful one at that: Surrealism and my activities as a "cultural animator" in the Nancy-Paris Committee. None of these concerns were compatible with a study of mathematics and natural sciences.

Besides, I had made up my mind. I would leave Nancy in November 1927 and move to Paris, taking my pretty Katia along. I would register at the Sorbonne, though no studies interested me because I wanted to become a professional revolutionary. The myth of revolution had totally absorbed me. I wanted to be at hand to deliver the final blows to a rotten and decadent capitalism that would soon be submerged by the proletarian uprising.

My solitary and liberal father, alien to any political concern, lived amid his books, his paintings, and his musical scores. He left his apartment only to give his courses at the Conservatory or to hear a concert. I had had no trouble coming into contact with the literature of my time: Apollinaire, Rimbaud, Lautréamont, all the Symbolists, were in my father's library next to Stendhal, Balzac, Edgar Allan Poe, and Shakespeare. The art on our walls was signed by Bonnard, Vuillard, K. X. Roussel, Matisse, Odilon Redon, Picasso, and Signac. What did my father think of his undisciplined, turbulent, and violent son? I must have been terrifying. He accepted without protest the idea of my departure, granting me a monthly five hundred francs, which he was soon to reduce and ultimately terminate. But my plans had been hatched with Georges Sadoul, who was working for Gallimard. Sadoul had got me a job as editor with Madame Jeanne Tachard, the owner and director of the Suzanne Talbot fashion house. I was succeeding Aragon, Breton, and several others. My salary was to be four hundred francs a month for a weekly editorial session and perhaps a few cultural excursions. Katia had her private means. So all we had to do was get on the train.

By November 1927, Sadoul, Katia and I were staying at the Studio Hotel in Vanves. I had matriculated at the Sorbonne but hardly ever went to classes; I was entirely dedicated to the Party. At the time, I was one of the leaders of the Fifth Chapter, which covered half the southern suburbs; the other half, the Fourth Chapter, was the domain of Maurice Thorez. Georges Sadoul had joined the Surrealist group. We had, incidentally, planned all this around 1925. For my part, I had been in less of a hurry because I had made up my mind to devote my life to political action.

In 1926, I had been an editor on the Communist weekly in Nancy, *La Lorraine Ouvrière et Paysanne,* and had used various pseudonyms. There, I had serialized a novel, whose title evokes all its content: *The Black Mass.* In it, I paid homage to every rite: love, violence, revolt, anticlericalism, sacrilege, unhappy fates, kidnappings, apparitions, coincidences, etc. But within a year, I had turned my back on artistic creation, and on all intellectual restlessness. I lived only for action. I wanted to become an integral part of the life of the working class. The problems of immediate tactics, Party organization, and trade unions were the only objects worthy of my energy, together with a profound study of the Marxist-Leninist teachings. Strange as it may seem, all these things separated me a bit more every day from Sadoul, who was almost a Trotskyite. If it hadn't been for our old friendship, the discovery of Paris, a continual curiosity about everything concerning the Surrealists, an obvious need to proselytize, and the constraints of living together, we would have gone our separate ways by the summer of 1928. I had nevertheless reported to the café the moment I arrived in Paris. Twice a day, Surrealism held its meetings around André Breton at the Cyrano, then at the Radio on Place Blanche, with many apéritifs. I dropped by four or five times. I visited the Surrealist Gallery on Rue Jacques Callot several times, especially for the extraordinary Chirico show in March 1928.

Sadoul would often dine in Montmartre with Breton and a few others after the daily meeting at the Cyrano. En route to Vanves, Rue du Château was a natural stopover. Sadoul spoke enthusiastically about that weird place where people lived at night and which looked as though it were turning into a second Surrealist center, where one could meet other people who hardly ever came to the Cyrano.

Around 1900, a tiny, wretched pavilion had been built at 54 Rue du Château, facing Rue Bourgeois, slightly back from the sidewalk, from which it was separated by a low wall and iron bars. The ground floor was covered with glass toward the street, like the locksmith shops you can still come across in the suburbs. It consisted of a rather large main room, and a small courtyard that ran back to a huge factory wall. The construction had a second landing, the façade was brick, with a plastering effect inspired by Louis XIII clampings. Having become a ragpickers' house, it was abandoned soon after the First World War.

The neighborhood was dreary, proletarian, and unhealthy; it in-cluded a few countryish remnants that were more disturbing than rural. Built at the edge of the former villages of Montrouge and Vaugirard, it had been dubbed Plaisance (pleasure), no doubt de-risively, because its streets were dark and cramped, and it contained a good number of dead ends, alleys, and shady hotels. A few feet from the house, Rue du Château crossed a bridge over the Western railroad line and sloped down a grade to Boulevard Pasteur, a setting virtually designed for crime.

Rue du Château was the obligatory passage point for caravans of animal-drawn milk trucks, wobbling enormous empty jugs over the highly uneven cobblestones as they rolled over to the Western freight station on the other side of the bridge. The racket they made heralded the approach of dawn or the first subway train.

In 1924, Rue du Château lured several young men who were mainly concerned with cinema: Marcel Duhamel, Jacques Prévert, Yves Tanguy. Duhamel had a bit of money. He rented the abandoned pavilion for four thousand francs a year. The house was repaired from top to bottom. The courtyard was covered over and transformed into a livable room, with light coming through two skylights. Running water was piped in everywhere, and an impressive electrical system was installed.

The street door opened directly into the main room. To the right of the entrance, a small kiosk on the courtyard contained the toilets; the dormer window, about six feet high, was very convenient for anyone who had forgotten his keys.

Tanguy had decorated the pavilion to surprise and disturb. The entrance door had the ambiguous character that such openings often assume in dreams in which outside and inside get muddled up. After crossing the threshold, the visitor confronted a stairway whose seven steps led up to another house. If he took another step, a trapeziform mirror, inspired by the decors of *Doctor Caligari*, reflected his image from eight yards away. He then found himself in a sort of theater yard that was furnished like a small garden. High above his head, along the side wall to the right, there was a loggia on pilings, with two windows with small panes. Benjamin Péret once lived in the loggia for several months. Sadoul set up an office there.

The furniture of this fantasy courtyard consisted of two chests, on which one could sit, a massive rectangular wooden table, with square feet, for meals (the two narrow benches for guests were kept underneath), an armchair and a rocking chair, both in rattan, an iron folding table, and a teatable on wheels, for drinks. Everything was painted in green, the color of public benches. A high narrow bookcase holding books, objects, and an aquarium stood against the left-hand wall across from the loggia, between the table and one of the chests, on a sort of cupboard, in which the record collection was kept. On top of this cupboard stood the turntable of an abominable but ingenious phonograph in which records were turned through the friction of a rubber wheel run by the motor of a windshield wiper.

The floor was covered with a mottled linoleum that was nearly black. The walls were hung with unbleached canvas, framed with green-painted wooden sticks; this lining followed an angular route echoing that of the large mirror downstairs. The area beneath the pilings of the loggia formed a retreat that pleasantly extended the room, even though one couldn't stand up straight. Its walls were entirely covered with a lovely collage of movie posters, and on the floor four black-leather mattresses awaited tired visitors or pretty girls. It also looked like an opium den, though poppyseed burned very rarely, if ever, on Rue du Château. An immense green and grayish-brown curtain full of Cubist designs could hide the glass casing. At the back of the large room, a steep staircase with a wooden banister led to the upper landing; facing the stairs was a kitchenette with a gas hot plate, a sink, a cupboard, and dishes.

The three bedrooms gave an impression of comfort and intimacy not to be found in the banal, if unusual room I have just described. A thick velvet pile, beige, covered the floors, muffling noise and suggesting a comfortable informality. Each of the bedrooms had a very wide bed, a sink with running water, a screen, a wardrobe, and small walnut-stained deal tables. The walls had been coated with a grainy, cream-colored mortar, which framed Jean Lurçat wallpaper pasted along a wide slanting stripe unevenly drawn. The wallpaper was very cheerful and extremely effective, as were the folding screens, which were covered with a sophisticated assemblage of letters, portraits, and phrases snipped out of movie posters. The three bedrooms were lit by bracket lamps and bedside lamps in alabaster, very lovely creations by Pierre Charreau. The ground-floor bedroom, the former courtyard, was simpler than the other two; its walls were covered with unbleached canvas. Its only decoration was a leather-lined ancestral figure from the Gabon.

All the doors were decorated with sign plates: *Mining Society of the Feroe Islands* on the door of the kitchenette, *Counsel of the Board, Secretariat General,* and *General Management* on the bedroom doors. And, last but not least, a huge strip of calico, the first trophy of expeditions that were to become more and more frequent: *Every Saturday, wild fowl.*

The most extraordinary object was a kind of tabernacle wrapped in striped fur and dotted with a vertical line of glass eyes. On top of it, there was a human-sized head in fur, with glass eyes, a leather nose, and real teeth; perhaps it was a mummy's head wrapped in fur. On either side of the tabernacle hung an arm of light in gilded bronze, à la Louis XV. This disturbing piece of furniture came from the Flea Market, I think. It was reproduced on the cover of the special *Variétés* issue on *Surrealism in 1929.* Sadoul gave it a place of honor under the loggia.

The big room had a very high ceiling, and a main beam carried an electric spotlight. Ultimately, we were so worried about its power consumption that we controlled it with a partial switch. At night, after drawing the Cubist curtain, you were hundreds of miles away from Plaisance.

In December 1927, the pavilion on Rue du Château housed Jacques Prévert and Simone, Yves Tanguy and Jeanette, and, off and on, Marcel Duhamel and ravishing Gazelle, as well as various passers-through. One could meet Roland Tual, Raymond Queneau, Max Morise, André Masson, Michel Leiris, Marcel Noll, Malkine, Jacques Baron, Pierre Unik, Pierre Prévert, Péret, and Desnos. My first visit was deeply impressive, provincial that I was.

One knocked on the door, stepped inside, had a drink, and departed with grave and mysterious feelings. It was like a secret assignation with strangely disturbing persons. One would bring tidings that stopped conversation, provoked Queneau's cavernous and sarcastic laughter, and aroused abrupt judgments. There was a bit of all this at the Cyrano, but away from Breton, everyone, although each maintained a personal way of speaking and remained habitually on guard, was warmer, more genuine, less strained. These people, slightly older than me, seemed elegant, relaxed, and self-confident. The English clothes, the carefully chosen neckties, the ease of the young women contrasted with the dreary garments worn in the provinces and the awkwardness of my little schoolmates. Familiarity did not exclude a certain reserve. The language was straightforward but never gross or off-color. Drunkenness was never comic, maudlin, or exhibitionistic; it was violent or tragic. Marcel Duhamel, who, to my eyes, looked like the Prince of Wales, seemed to embody, in his clothes and bearing, an Anglo-Saxon ideal of elegance that I had often drawn upon in Lorraine to exorcise the sight of teen-agers in leggings, priests in berets, and artists in floppy *lavallière* neckties. Max Morise, Roland Tual, and Michel Leiris also seemed to come straight out of the seductive international set that my imagination had conjured up from my readings of Paul Morand and Valéry Larbaud. But the most extraordinary personality in the group was Jacques Prévert, who looked more perceptibly Parisian than most of his friends.

I don't know what the future will do with Prévert's written works. His books enjoyed a tremendous success just after the First World War. Do young people still read them today? I really hope so. While writing this book, I open at random a copy of *Paroles*; it is the 177th printing, a number ordinarily reserved for Sagan-like best sellers. With the same pleasure as twenty-five years ago, I read: "An old man of gold and a watch in mourning—a queen of pain and a man from England," and so on. I have no doubt that this *Procession*, capable, once it is under way, of widening the horizons of my scene, changing its material and proportions, will not be able to preserve its imaginative power against the appeal of the next street, the news in the evening paper, or television. Given this knack of transfiguring the most banal reality by means of the simplest devices, Prévert's remarkably keen eyes under drooping lids, his irresistible aptness of expression, and an infectious liveliness, made his conversation, or rather his monologues, into a stunning experience. I shall probably never find even a near equivalent of it. It may have been a new phenomenon. People have abundantly quoted the slightly funny remarks of such *boulevardiers* as Tristan Bernard. With Prévert, it was wit rather than humor, and we respected almost everything he said. At a certain point of intoxication, he would become even funnier, and, aided by an inimitable gravity (he never laughed), he would create the most unexpected situations at the expense of everything and everyone.

Yves Tanguy was a man of few words. He always looked as though he were dressed in a trenchcoat (even after he'd taken it off), and his demeanor was modest but assured. He never spoke about his painting —in contrast to contemporaries who are so careful to keep us informed about their "investigations" or "experiments." He was almost apologetic about his work and never aspired to any success. He sold next to nothing and readily gave away his drawings and canvases to the shrewd people who asked for them. He was poor, downed an amazing amount of beer, and got nasty when he was drunk, as though stricken by a kind of self-destructiveness. Prévert claimed that Tanguy had a particular grudge against mailboxes and that after the twelfth bottle of beer he would smash his head against one and batter it to smithereens.

To a superficial observer, Yves seemed to be moving in a simplified universe, within which he distinguished between good and evil, friends and pigs, with the help of touchingly childish little tests. But his simplifications reflected merely his modesty and preference for clarity. They were the result of a great discernment, an abhorrence of lies and ramshackle compromises. Tanguy read more than the rest, was interested in everything, and his judgment was very fine. He quickly saw through the games people played and the disguises they used for appearances' sake or to encourage helpful misunderstandings. As a friend, he was loyal, discreet, and bewildering. Ultimately, he came to realize that what he was creating was far more important than professions of faith or anathemas. And he acted accordingly.

Historians have tried to distinguish the Rue du Château group in 1926–27 from everything that was discussed or planned at Breton's place on Rue Fontaine or in the Café Cyrano. The regrettable pamphlet of 1929, entitled *A Corpse* and signed by most of the regular frequenters of the Rue du Château pavilion in Prévert's day might substantiate this idea of opposition. But it is more accurate to talk about degrees of mental development and particular angles of vision than differences in nature. It was their growing awareness of their own personalities that prompted certain individuals to emancipate themselves. On Rue du Château, we played all the Surrealist games, and perhaps we made more exquisite corpses there than anywhere else, but our true interest focused on more popular means of expression. This led to the creation, a bit later, of the Black Series, Prévert's movies, *Paroles*, Queneau's novels. Breton's place was a laboratory, where various and frequent contributions (as long as they didn't simply evaporate, leaving no traces) might produce blinding flashes of lightning, storms, strange crystallizations. One of the facets of Breton's genius was to maintain an almost constant sense of revelation around himself and to set up tests and combats to distinguish the better from the worse. Nevertheless, Breton's dominating personality, his intransigence, his love of glamour, his penchant for true and loyal human relationships, his haughty delight in ruptures, were scarcely favorable to the autonomous development of the forces whose flowering he prompted or favored. In the atmosphere on the Rue du Château, which was freer, more open, and more accommodating, the seeds sown on the Rue Fontaine shot up and ripened. Anything that grew needed further nourishment, for harvests do not come from permanent seeding.

Both Rue du Château and Rue Fontaine abhorred the licentiousness of the artistic Bohemia that surrounded them. Drugs and homosexuality were condemned, with two or three exceptions, such as Malkine and Crevel, because of their basic honesty and human qualities. Sleeping around was just not done, and dirty jokes were forbidden. The golden rule was passionate love, preferably faithful, between two individuals of opposite sex. And once passionate love had been exalted as the supreme good, unique love imposed itself as the ideal. One could love only once. Any other possibility would open the door to libertinage, with the complacencies that involved for oneself and others. Such complete lack of realism had implacable consequences. It was scandalous to covet your neighbor's wife if she was loved. The beloved woman became an object of total veneration. One might kill oneself, perhaps even betray the Revolution, for love. The state of love produced an outburst of solidarity and affection toward its victim. Brief flings, always suspect, could be excused only by unusual circumstances, sometimes invented out of whole cloth to rationalize a passing fancy. Yet the prostitution of women was not condemned, and brothels had their avowed defenders: Aragon, Eluard, and even Breton. These narrow and slightly contradictory rules were often broken by the force of life, but, all in all, most of the Surrealists remained fairly faithful to them.

The moral rigor on Rue Fontaine, which grew tougher and tougher, tended to preserve the solipsism of each individual and the purity of the whole group. Nearly all material support was condemned: work was scorned, and journalistic or quasi-artistic activities amounted to treason. Everyone's associations were closely examined, and trouble-makers, spies, or pigs were found everywhere. Max Ernst and Miró were insulted for agreeing to do ballet sets. Artaud was reproached for being an actor, and Vitrac for writing and producing plays, a privilege accorded only to Raymond Roussel. Surrealism closed itself off in a world of poverty. The only commercial operations were the episodic dealings for artworks and for the publication of one's own works. Buyers and publishers had to offer guarantees of morality. The publisher, for instance, agreed never to put out works by authors considered scandalous, or at least didn't advertise them on the back of a Surrealist book. This somewhat infantile sensitivity doomed anything that men like Duhamel, Prévert, and Queneau set out to do.

Rue du Château was less severe, more objective, and also more eclectic. I cannot say for certain whether the intransigence of one set and the compromises of the other were always as useful to them as they deserved. In contrast to Rue Fontaine, Rue du Château focused little of its intellectual activity on the plastic arts. We did, however, contribute more than anyone else to modern definitions of Beauty. Yves Tanguy did paint, of course, though no one at that time realized how significant he was. His presence as a "dauber" (*his* term) had little influence on the conversations in the house, although some of us were already collectors, because Tanguy was a Surrealist first and a painter second. Masson, whose drawings and paintings were highly admired, dropped by mainly because his studio was in the neighborhood. He would talk more about his myths than his pictorial technique. Man Ray paid neighborly visits, more as a photographer, as a filmmaker, as a fabricator of astonishing objects, and as a link to the American colony in Paris, than as a painter. The men on Rue du Château were in many ways more of their time than those on Rue Fontaine. Jazz and American films, horror movies, newspaper features and crimes, the stupidities of everyday life, insubordination, the melancholy poetry of penny machines, and the deadly boredom of the industrial suburbs were assimilated for the use of the next two generations. The films *Port of Shadows* and *A Rare Bird*, the novel *The Skin of Dreams*, are fine testimonies to at least part of this shift.

On Rue Fontaine, André Breton's personal collection—the Chiricos, Picassos, Max Ernsts, Duchamps, Picabias, and what not, and the primitive objects from Oceania—made the place look like one big museum. Of course, every painting, every object sent out an exceptionally powerful emanation, a hallucination, which adhered to it like a shadow wherever it was put. Anyone who arrived even slightly late could not escape unscathed. But there was something timeless, or better yet a sort of natural *void*, about that studio, whose door bore the copper date 1713 and the initials of the Master of the House. The presence of human beings was not taken for granted there; meeting people from another era would probably have come as no surprise.

Rue du Château was a setting for an improvised play. Because the actors brought the latest edition of *Paris-Soir,* the action had to take place around 1927.

Nor was Rue du Château haunted by the metaphysical and political concerns of Rue Fontaine. Yet we were very open to the influence of a person of great stature, a true loner, whose work was shaped by a coherent philosophy: Georges Bataille. I am tempted to believe that the high place that Bataille assigned to eroticism in one's efforts to explore the world and oneself and in fulfilling one's destiny has had a vast influence on people under thirty-five (an effect that cannot be measured in terms of his book sales). In 1927, Bataille was soon to publish an admirable text that had to be sold clandestinely, *The Story of the Eye,* and it was mainly in that guise that he appeared to young tourists like myself. Sex was highly regarded on both Rue du Château and Rue Fontaine, but only as an intellectual category and a subject of artistic inspiration. Nevertheless, the voice of the divine Marquis de Sade would have been out of place on Rue du Château, whereas on Rue Fontaine it resounded with all the force it must have had in medieval bastilles. On the other hand, activities like those of Sargeant Bertrand, who profaned the dead girls buried in the Montparnasse Cemetery were prodigiously conjured up on Rue du Château. I suspect that Bataille harshly criticized the superficiality of philosophical discussions at Breton's home and the focus on magic, Freud, and Marx. His objections probably relieved the consciences of the writers of the pamphlet *A Corpse,* by furnishing them with what is known in far-left jargon as an ideological foundation. But apart from an implicit reference to Bataille's thought and judgment as an antidote to the politicizing of Rue Fontaine, it was with humor that Rue du Château damaged the fits and starts of Breton's philosophizing. The general conversation always took an absurd turn at the prompting of Prévert, who when Berkeley was exerting a huge fascination on Breton, applied immaterialism to letterboxes and the Paris Fair. The whole grandiose affair was the kind of madness on which my Marxist orthodoxy thrived.

Nevertheless, Rue du Château had a political mission. In 1926, the discussions with Pierre Naville after the publication of the brochure *The Revolution and the Intellectuals* took place in the pavilion. It would be amusing to explain that Tanguy, Prévert, and Duhamel thereby felt uncomfortable and cramped for space. They separated. During the first few weeks of 1928, Georges Sadoul took over

Duhamel's lease, and he, Katia, and I moved in immediately. We kept the furnishings of the former tenants, and everything stayed as it was. Marcel Duhamel also left us his marvelous collection of American jazz records, which specialists now grab up at skyrocketing prices. I would soon be adding everything that came out by Armstrong, Duke Ellington, and Sophie Tucker. Sadoul settled in the second-floor bedroom with the southern exposure, Katia and I in the adjacent bedroom formerly occupied by Tanguy; the door was decorated with one of the painter's earliest compositions, a smoky horizon. Under the velvet pile of his room, Sadoul discovered several notebooks filled with writings by Prévert. We were very surprised. We had never realized that Prévert wrote, and we may have been the first to read him. The notebooks included the first draft of a novel whose main character was Onoto, a bird with feathers that grew in instead of out.

9
BECOMING A PROFESSIONAL REVOLUTIONARY

IN 1926, THE COMMUNIST PARTY OFFICE AT
Nancy was on Rue Saint-Nicolas, in a narrow house that was falling
apart. The entrance was a dusty bookshop, where you could buy the
earliest French translations of Lenin's works. Behind the store, there
was an inadequate damp meeting hall with no rear exit. One flight up,
behind an anteroom poorly lit by a window facing a sort of chimney,
was the fairly large office of the standing committee. It contained
the mimeograph machine for leaflets and the typewriter. The regional
secretary lived on the next floor, but his kitchen, or a kind of pantry,
was next to the anteroom. In summertime, his stout wife would wash
and iron there, while gossiping with a friend, usually criticizing her
husband heavily because he was neglecting her more and more.

The regional structure had just been enlarged and renewed. The
top man was Vuillemin, a metallurgy worker who had become regional
secretary after a brief course at a Party school. Next in command
was Perrouault, Vuillemin's scapegoat and leader of the United Trade

Unions. Vuillemin had a seat on the Central Committee of the Party. A bit later on, they were joined by a third person, Fougerolles, a tall construction worker with a mustache, corduroy pants, and a resounding voice; he came from the South of France and spoke Italian. He had been sent to Longwy to revolutionize and organize the foreign manpower, but he soon sold himself to the bosses and the police. I ran across him again in December 1940 in disturbing conditions. These three men were appointed by the Party and drew the same salary as a qualified worker.

The "Eastern Region," a product of the Bolshevization in 1924, had taken over the former federations of the three departments of Lorraine. This administrative regrouping fulfilled an idea of the technocrats; the experiment was unsuccessful, however, and a few years later they went back to the departmental structure. In 1926, the department of the Vosges had a certain autonomy; the Party was headed by a teacher at the Epinal Lycée, Pierre Laurent, known as Darnar, now the editor of the *Dauphiné Libéré*. Darnar was dismissed by the government, for in those days the Republic would not allow its teachers to take any open political stance, especially when such propaganda was revolutionary. Darnar moved from Epinal to Nancy and became more and more important in the regional secretariat. He edited the Party weekly, *La Lorraine Ouvrière et Paysanne*. Intelligent, active, and ambitious, he was sentenced to prison during the great repression of 1929–30. While he was in the House of Detention, he ran into Maurice Thorez; the two prisoners got along famously, and Thorez, after his release, encouraged Darnar's rise through the Party ranks.

All these men were young and very earnest. They soon took on the habits of bureaucrats, however, especially the workers. Vuillemin did not lack authority, but he particularly valued his position. Except for Darnar, they were self-educated, and all they knew about the doctrine was what they read in *L'Humanité* or *Les Cahiers du Bolchevisme*, the Party's theoretical monthly. Even Darnar, who was more responsive to concrete political problems than to the patient analysis of causes and to reflection on teachings, was not very well versed in Marxism.

The Party had little influence on the "masses." The hazards of the split of Tours had left two mayoralties to the Communists: Plainfaing in the Vosges and Chaligny in the mining basin of Nancy. Although the two mayors affected a certain independence from the regional secretariat, it was better not to offend them, for the sake of the Party.

Perrouault imposed the sectarian policies of the era on his unions. The nearby C.G.T. had a larger following among workers than the "United" did. The heads of the departmental United, a relatively leftist "reformist" group, were quite aware of the part they had to play to keep the proletariat from always being the loser, but the behavior of the United group was always inflammatory and irresponsible. Even in massively conservative Lorraine, a united action of all the partisans of progress seemed a matter of simple common sense, but the United people were annoying. Their insults, their systematically accelerated demonstrations, their Paris-imposed stirrings of the mob brought the workers nothing but resounding failures. Strikes led to greater repression from the bosses. Needless to say, any advantages obtained for the workers by the "reformists" were greeted with sarcasm by the United people. The closer they got to the assembly line, the slacker the tension between the two factions became, because they were confronted at every moment with the brutal facts of production. Behind a desk on Rue Saint-Nicolas in Nancy, however, the brutal fact looked like Party orders.

One of the major responsibilities of the Eastern Regional secretariat was to infiltrate the army, creating and maintaining regimental cells in metropolitan garrisons and in the Rhineland. The Comintern held to this line of action as a means of setting up a network of Russian espionage. The "antiwork" (antimilitarist) campaign was organized with methods of undercover struggle; the French Police and the Deuxième Bureau (the French F.B.I.) made a particular point of getting to know it and dismantling its structures. The men in charge were generally recruited among the leaders of the Communist Youth, and the ability they showed in this work made for prompt advancement. This underground activity was linked with more overt propaganda directed at reservists when they were called up for duty. The results were sometimes spectacular.

The Eastern Region comprised a certain number of chapters, whose administrative jurisdiction could cover as much as a precinct. The cell meetings were bleak. Members commented on the decisions of the Party and the articles in *L'Humanité*, or on daily life in the factory. Things would pick up as soon as the meeting turned to practical tasks: pasting up posters, distributing leaflets, setting up small meetings for sympathizers. At this point, the participants used various excuses to slip away. It was always the same people who did the work. In the whole Nancy chapter, there were no more than three or four cells, with about thirty members, mostly workers employed in small enterprises.

Union problems were handled first within the union groups. All the Communists in the same union, or even in the cells, might meet. Since the majority of the United people were either Communists or sympathizers, these sessions were a repetition of the general union meetings; the same speakers would be talking on the same topic twice to the same audience. Thus, a great deal of time was spent in debate, to the detriment of any action. The Party was always right, everything was explained by the treason of the "reformists" or repression from employers, and analyses or "self-criticism" dealt only with form or means; any facts contradicting what was believed to be doctrine or Party line were simply brushed aside. Such cocksureness enabled the leaders to accept any mishaps lightly, and they could keep small bands of committed workers in a complacent state of moral euphoria. As the general political line grew firmer and firmer, the Party collapsed more and more. Out of pride or blindness, it generally remained passive in regard to outside incidents; each responsible person awaited orders, which often failed to come. On the other hand, the Party offered plenty of random insults and calls to a curiously vague action, though the latter rarely got beyond the state of printer's ink or oratorical flights at public meetings.

At the time, the government had lost all patience with the Russians' negative attitude toward France, the Soviet campaign against French imperialism, and Communist infiltration in barracks and colonies. In preparing the legislative elections of 1928, its goal was to break the left-wing coalition definitively by separating the Communist electorate from the Socialist Party and reducing the parliamentary importance of Léon Blum's friends. Some radicals also had a personal interest in their positions, which could be nibbled away by Socalists who could get the most votes of any left-wing candidate on the first ballot and receive the help of Communist votes on the second. When the Minister of the Interior, Albert Sarraut, declared in a resounding speech (paraphrasing a famous comment of Gambetta's), "Communism is the enemy," the Communists were caught off guard and did not react. Under the influence of their parliamentary leaders, they decided to laugh it off, and they continued with their little Leninist cookbook as though nothing had happened. This deliberate scorn of the adversary's plans, this refusal to attempt any serious political examination, this conscious choice of passivity, disturbed me deeply. I began to lose my blind faith in the Party leaders.

Vuillemin and the others had little to teach me, except for a few committee or public-meeting tricks. On the other hand, I learned a lot from the most unusual Communist in all Lorraine, Charles Hainchelin, a French teacher in a technical school. Hainchelin never got involved with the regional apparatus. He was tall, thin, delicate in health, with a nose like a rudder, and married to a tiny woman. He was still under thirty when I met him. An indefatigable worker, he read voraciously, and corresponded with forty people, writing letters like school papers, often on the pages of class notebooks. Intuitive, cultivated, lucid, modest, but suspicious, and totally unambitious, he usually did his best to stand aside and utter only objective and sensible judgments. Marx and particularly Lenin were his frames of reference, but, unlike most Communist theoreticians, he preferred to go back to the sources in order to grasp the thoughts of the great models in all their richness and complexity. Their ideas bristle with contradictions, which he refused to sidestep. He favored a sort of middle-line orthodoxy and invoked the authority of the work done at the Marx-Engels Institute, which old Riazanov headed. He could read Russian well, and he would practice translating, for friends, any texts that he felt were essential.

A native of the North, Hainchelin had witnessed the birth of the Communist Party in the mining and textile centers. He had spent a militant period in the Communist Youth Organizations, along with a number of people who were destined to lead the Party during the coming twenty years. His political finesse, his doctrinal knowledge, his scrupulous honesty, and his absolute disinterest, as well as his unconditional loyalty to the Soviet Union, won him solid friendships in the Comintern. But, except perhaps for a few discreet tasks, he had detached himself from all his responsibilities in the apparatus. He was disgusted with the stupidity, the incongruous ambition, and the self-importance he had encountered in all the Party authorities. He was afraid that the system per se and its organizational principles would lead to nothing but a mediocre staff incapable of handling events. Despite these qualms, he had not joined any of the groups opposing the general line because he was convinced that they were doomed to an absolute and definitive revolutionary ineffectiveness. His distrust of French Communists led him to see the Soviet Union as the guarantee and hope of the world revolution.

Hainchelin cared little for meetings and public discussions. His preference for secrecy and conspiracy is understandable, but I wonder whether, by wanting to play the power behind the throne, by believing only in the value of discreet and personal pressures, he wasn't edging himself out more and more. Yet he was not one of those dreamers or intellectuals who feared that action would distort pure doctrine or thwart principles. In the Resistance, he died with weapons in his hands while fighting for the liberation of the little town of Thiers.

As an out-and-out materialist, Hainchelin felt that Marx had turned the page of philosophy. Engels had proved in *Anti-Dühring* that the dialectical method, once restored, would supply answers for everything. He regarded Lenin's laborious opus *Materialism and Empiriocriticism* as the major testament of a philosophical orientation that was beyond reproach. His orthodox rigor impressed me greatly, and I tried to be loyal. Never having been a believer, however, I acknowledged all the strokes against dogma from facts and readings, whereas Hainchelin, with commendable stubbornness, resisted any doubts and innovations, at least during the time we knew each other.

By 1926, he no longer set foot in the office. Nevertheless, people kept him informed, came to see him, asked his advice. He seemed to be involved in several secret networks. As a neophyte, I felt that this proximity to suspected undercover work, this mysterious closeness to the holders of supreme truth, gave Hainchelin immense prestige, which added to our mutual liking. In talking with him, I felt as though I were approaching the arcana of the revolution. I thought I could discern behind his words the wisdom, the lucidity, the prudent determination, and the irresistible force of the Comintern. The first book he gave me to read was, quite intentionally, Lenin's *The Childhood Disease of Communism.*

In November 1927, I arrived in Paris with the prestige I had won in Nancy as well as some luster gained from the publication of a few pages on Party organization in *Les Cahiers du Bolchevisme.* Concerns of this sort pleased the Russians and the Germans and graduates of the Moscow schools. I instantly became second in rank at the Fifth Chapter, and I devoted nearly all my time to the Party.

The chapter secretary was an extraordinary person, a German called Barmotte, whose true identity I never learned. He was supposedly handed over to the Nazis by Vichy in 1940.

Barmotte, a former construction worker was short, robust, and blond, with a small mustache like Hitler's. He seemed to me to possess the major qualities of a professional revolutionary. Prudent, patient, courageous, in perfect control of himself, aware that all problems have to be solved by analysis and action, an enemy of discouragement and passivity, a stickler for the truth because he knew that self-importance and boasting will always trip you up, he guided his chapter like the skipper of a boat. He was everywhere, knew everything, checked the way his orders were carried out. When necessary, he would modify methods, the way a captain changes course to allow for shifts in the currents or winds, or for fatigue among the crew. He had no tolerance for failure, but he knew how to suggest excuses or explanations, if necessary, that avoided hurting a person's pride and permitted an easy and fruitful self-criticism. He moved so often that his closest fellow workers never knew how to get hold of him, apart from the appointments he made with them. He had no respite, no relaxation, no personal life.

Barmotte had been one of the Communist leaders of Westphalia. An excellent organizer, he played a major role in the uprisings of 1923, and their collapse had forced him to take refuge in France. After he was sentenced to a long prison term, he had continued his political work in secret until he was informed that his own and other people's safety depended on his leaving Germany. I have always assumed that they wanted to get rid of him, although he would have remained neutral during the conflicts that rocked the German Communist Party in 1924 and 1925.

In the summer of 1923 the central government of the Reich was collapsing in impotence and scorn. It was clear that Germany was ripe for the revolution, although the chances of a successful proletarian uprising were fairly uncertain: the right had the weapons and the strongest cadres. Eventually, Zinoviev, and particularly Trotsky, decided to let the German Communist Party prepare an insurrection. Stalin, wavering and cautious, went along with it. The Russians furnished a few military specialists.

The workers had to be armed, and Barmotte led several raids. He spoke about his extraordinary adventures dispassionately, emphasizing the causes of his failures and successes. He refused to blame the failure of the revolution on the leaders of the right wing of the German Communist Party. They had submitted everything to a vote by the Congress of Business Committees. Everyone knew that the Communists formed a very small minority at that Congress, while the trade unionists (nearly five-sixths of the delegates) had no taste for insurrection. "That was the finest example," said Barmotte, "of what Lenin called parliamentary stupidity. If in 1917 the Bolsheviks had waited for a favorable vote by the Constituent Assembly, in which they did not have a majority, they would never have taken power."

In retrospect, it is clear that the Germany of 1923 could never have been the scene of a victorious Communist revolution. The German proletariat, or at least its far-left organizations, might have seized power in 1919, but their chances diminished steadily after the assassination of Liebknecht and Rosa Luxemburg. There may have been another fleeting opportunity in 1932, which I'll come to later. However, as the Bolshevik virus—whether of a Trotskyist or Stalinist strain—settled into the bodies of German workers, their combativeness and their political sense lessened. The revolutionary will of the German proletariat was far weaker in 1923 than in 1919. By 1933, it was a mere memory.

In 1927, my only impression of the history of working-class struggles in Germany was the image of a series of opportunities missed because of Socialist treason or the incompetence of "opportunists." In the language of the Comintern, this term defined and condemned those Communists who set exaggerated store by legal forms and parliamentary action, or who were incapable of using any extralegal means, when necessary, to advance toward a takeover and ready the masses for it.

Barmotte saw a new example of "opportunistic" deviation in the reaction of the French Communist Party to Albert Sarraut's attacks. I fully shared his opinion. At the news of the execution of Sacco and Vanzetti, tens of thousands of Parisians invaded the big boulevards and started rioting. Barmotte and I both attached an inordinate importance to these disturbances. Though they had no future, their timing convinced us that the "radicalization of the masses," which we had long been awaiting, was finally under way. There was much talk about Party politics in the Paris region. The cells were authorized to make criticisms and to vote on motions. In reality, this outburst of inner democracy was supposed to obtain a massive condemnation of the Trotskyite opposition. The undertaking presented no difficulties, since the polemical excesses of the Trotskyites assured their defeat. According to them, Thermidor was imperiling the Russian Revolution. Assertions like this antagonized the rank and file because they seemed so unlikely. Metaphysical debates on Socialism in a single country did not interest the workers. It was at the very least paradoxical to induce them to fight for a power that would get them nowhere. All in all, it was better to vote for the Socialist-Radicals.

The other problems that were brought up irresistibly recalled early Christian heresies. For some time now, the anti-Communist about-face of the Kuomintang had troubled the intellectuals in the Party. The "oppositional" point of view on the Comintern policy regarding Chiang Kai-shek had been skillfully and maliciously set forth in *Clarte*, a magazine edited by Pierre Naville and Marcel Fourrier. But after the Communist uprising in Canton had been bloodily crushed, how could one avoid condemning Trotsky's "leftism" despite the brilliant sarcasm with which the theoretician of the permanent Revolution had greeted that adventure? Although a militant could find no dogma or daily political action in André Malraux's *The Conquerors*, that novel at least restored the human reality of the conflict. It brought no arguments to Trotskyism; quite the contrary, it inspired confidence in the methods of the apparatus.

The members of the Party were preparing to place their confidence in Stalin, whose apparent modesty and diffidence were reassuring and who had the overwhelming majority of the Russian Communist Party behind him. Only a few initiates in France, perhaps including Boris Souvarin, knew that Stalin was capable of anything. As for the horrors that had already been perpetrated by the system, Trotsky had to his credit the massacre of the sailors of Kronstadt. All his talk about the workers' democracy never convinced anyone of his sincerity.

The issue in Russia was power, not doctrines or tactics. The same problem was about to arise in the Communist parties of the West. The Trotskyites' only success was their imposition of leftist tactics on men who wanted to insure their personal power—especially Stalin, whose utter brutality unfolded in the harsh politics demanded by the opposition. With all the energy he had, Stalin, in 1929, started Russia off on the forced collectivization and authoritarian industrialization that was to turn that immense country into one gigantic dungeon. In imitation, the International followed the famous policy of class warfare and was hoist with its own petard. Since most of the leaders of the Communist parties were unwilling to let themselves blithely be inoculated with such obvious madness, the Comintern encouraged the irrelevant ambition of intransigent young members blinded by doctrine.

But, in fact, everything cannot be blamed on a manipulation of the Communists by a few specialists. A good many militants wanted to pursue much harsher policies in their own countries. The Trotskyite opposition had too many recent failures on its record, and the Party members were offended and embarrassed. In the pseudo-scientific but blindly faithful world of the Communists, the only possible cause of failure was a misunderstanding or neglect of the fundamental principles. To ward off disaster, it was crucial to restore true faith in all its rigor. More than a perusal of *The Childhood Disease* was necessary to effect a permanent cure of the leftism spontaneously produced by young people and neophytes, however, and the denunciation of "opportunistic" errors and the revolutionary rhetoric continued to stir up the Communist International until Adolf Hitler put everything back in place. Like many militants, including me, Barmotte hoped that the discussion would lead to what we called a rectification of the Party. Back in Nancy, Charles Hainchelin had insinuated that the International wasn't all that satisfied with the French leaders.

I hurled myself into the thick of the quarrel. First, I drew up a voluminous list of the opportunistic errors committed since the last Party congress, together with recommendations for developing a vague sort of revolutionary activism anywhere and any time. The title was *The Platform of the Fifth Chapter*. Its political content was a highly orthodox development of the incredible line that could be plucked out of the latest official publications of the Comintern. Capitalism was supposed to be in a state of general crisis that was manifestly getting worse and worse; this also held true for the imperialist contradictions. But in 1928 the capitalist world had reached a peak of prosperity. For the past four years, while Germany had been laboring, producing, paying her debts, its citizens had stopped fighting with one another and fomenting putsches. France had not been so well off since 1913. The Italian economy was undergoing spectacular improvement thanks to Fascism. The United States was experiencing a gigantic boom. Nothing hinted at the great depression of 1929, and the Comintern specialists were no better prophets than the bourgeois economists. (Except for a few episodic remarks by Eugène Varga, the most sensible economist in the Communist world, to whom no one paid any attention.) As for imperialist contradictions, they expressed themselves in a general reduction of military budgets.

Our platform also denounced the heightening of any danger of war. Imperialist threats against the U.S.S.R., we asserted, had become more precise! Faced with this catastrophe, the "radicalization" of the working masses—a cliché meaning that the proletariat was more and more clearly expressing its desire for revolutionary change—became a major fact that forced the Communist parties to adopt an intransigent and aggressive stance in the warfare between the classes.

All of this verged on delirium. The war psychosis, Stalin had discovered, could be used to terrify the Russians and justify the definitive transformation of a proletarian dictatorship into a police dictatorship —with the expulsions, concentration camps, trials, and massacres that were to follow. Actually, the Soviet Union had never been so secure. Her relations with Germany were those of an accomplice. Even though the Comintern financed subversion wherever it could, the imperialists had long since given up promoting even the slightest attempt to change the Soviet regime. As for the radicalization of the masses, it was manifest everywhere in the electoral defeats of Communist parties and their declining influence in trade unions.

First we prepared the scenarios of imaginary dramas; then we tried to decide how the Communists could play the leads. We advocated increased antigovernment activity, a refusal to appear before any bourgeois court whatsoever (hence the illegal situation of a growing number of comrades), the politicizing of strikes, the creation of armed groups for protection, the development of antimilitarist propaganda, agitation in favor of independence for colonial peoples —a mélange of tasty recipes gleaned from Lenin's works. We condemned any electoral alliances with the middle-class parties and put unacceptable but reassuring conditions on any possible agreement with the Socialists: those were the tactics of class warfare. This platform may have been a good exercise in political sectarianism and blindness, but it nevertheless kept within the established limits of Leninism. Ill-disposed as we were toward the Socialist Party and its leaders, we would never have dreamed or lumping them with the Fascists, as the Stalinists, shortly thereafter, did.

The political ideas of the Fifth Chapter were largely shared by many militants, by the cadres returning from the Moscow schools, and by the Communist Youth groups. What made our platform original and a bit disturbing was its demand for changes in the makeup of the Party's Political Bureau. It was thought that we had gone too far. The same question was being asked in high places, but we should not even admit this, much less proclaim it. Our section voted overwhelmingly in favor of the platform in the presence of two representatives of the Party leadership: Alfred Costes, one of the most honest dignitaries of the Federation of Metal Workers, and François Chasseigne, a former secretary of the Communist Youth. Barmotte and I thought that we stood a good chance of getting our point of view across at the coming Regional Conference because our success had been favorably commented upon in the cells. There were various signs that we would have support of representatives from the International.

Since I was a good orator, it devolved upon me to present the theses of the Fifth Chapter to the delegates of the "Paris Region." I was very convincing. My "opportunistic" adversaries were visibly stunned. Privately, the delegates guaranteed that we would win. A night session had been foreseen for the closing discussion and vote. At 7 P.M., the Party secretariat directed me, at a moment's notice, to replace an important speaker at a public meeting in the suburbs. During my absence, Chasseigne publicly accused me of conspiring against the Party leadership and especially of trying to get André Marty into the Political Bureau (which he actually did enter a few years later). Barmotte, caught off guard, had no answer ready. Our opponents took advantage of the situation to table the theses of the Fifth Chapter and obtained an almost unanimous vote in favor of the proposals developed by the Communist Youth Federation, which were virtually identical to ours. This seemed to be a total condemnation of any challenge to the Party leaders. By the end of 1928, however, the makeup of the untouchable Political Bureau was profoundly modified. In early 1929, the prime posts were taken over by leaders of the Communist Youth.

Throughout 1928, I had been leading almost a worker's life, spending most of the day between Issy-les-Moulineaux and Villejuif, Antony and Malakoff, proletarian quarters of Paris. In the morning, I was at the gates of factories, handing out leaflets, trying to deliver a brief harangue, or making contacts. The focal points were Issy-le-Moulineaux and Montrouge and the Meter Company. Here the Party had few members, for in the big businesses salaries were better, workers did overtime, and the bosses were more vigilant. During the day, I had to prepare leaflets, posters, and notices of meetings, distribute the material, evaluate, with Barmotte and two or three others, various activities, plan future operations, and draw up the weekly schedule we shared with the Fourth Chapter. At night, there were cell meetings or committees, the trade-union conferences, the many work sessions at 120 Rue La Fayette, the Party seat, and public assemblies. In our two districts, we had to direct the election campaign. Every evening, I had to strengthen two public meetings and often settle a contradiction, because our candidates for Parliament were rather awful. We lost, but the results were no worse than anywhere else.

I soon learned that a revolutionary militant loses his entire personality and all contact with reality. He has once and for all accepted an ideology that forms his entire *Weltanschauung*. He will never again question it, first of all because he doesn't have the time; secondly, because the information that might get him to change his mind will never reach him; and finally, because he doesn't have the right to. His role is to repeat what he has learned, to make others accept it. If he fails to accomplish this, he will no longer be a militant revolutionary; he will be nothing, with a huge void inside himself. Little by little, the outside world becomes what one has read in books, what one tells other people day after day the militant turns into a robot who would never dream of confronting words with reality. In the name of discipline, the higher interests of the Party, or the Revolution, the Communist represses all qualms, all misgivings, even in the deepest recesses of his unconscious. With no evil intentions, he must contradict himself whenever higher authority (and no one else is entitled to do so) changes the official position and authorizes him temporarily to see the world "as it really is." The Communist reads hardly anything, even the works of the Party. He subsists mainly on summaries and digests, and if he comes across a heretical text he is instantly on the alert, not because he has unveiled a heresy but because the language doesn't conform to prototypes.

The militant lives in a world of abstractions and formulas: the bourgeoisie, capitalism, imperialism, and the like. He believes in the existence of the middle class as an entity or a person; it listens, registers, reflects, and decides. This simplistic world is comfortable because it is convenient. There is nothing mysterious about it; it is familiar and consistent. A militant's intellectual activity is always concerned with details. The quality and results of certain Communist operations generally surprise people unfamiliar with this singular world. On the scale of strategy, Communists base their decisions on data that are usually phantasmagorical, following the instructions of the mythomaniacal foreign policy of the Soviet Union. Unless exceptional circumstances come to their rescue, failure is certain: Communists will save appearances as best they can by lying openly and by immediately changing the subject. But on a tactical level, all operations, even absurd ones, are worked out with such loving detail that only the mammoth business concerns and advertising agencies can offer a valid analogy. In some specific place and circumstances the goal to be attained from some populace or group may be absurd, but the militants will nevertheless carefully study the ways in which that absurdity can be "sold"—who will buy it, how can it best be presented to the consumer?—and each good or bad result will be the object of meticulous analyses on which the militants will lavish an enormous wealth of intelligence, shrewdness, and patience. They will see and imagine all sorts of things, but they will never manage to realize that the absurdity won't sell because it's absurd or because there are no buyers.

In 1928, my militant activity had virtually confined me, outside of a few sallies, to the Fifth Chapter. I might have been forever lost, absorbed in the small caricatured world of militant activity, if a success of the Fifth Chapter platform had, say, landed me a regional agitprop job. I would then have remained in Paris instead of spending vacations with my family, and I wouldn't have been able to put a halt to things, thereby preserving my clearheadedness. A very serious event in my private life forced me to make a decision. The small allowance that my father was sending me would have been too little to live on if Katia hadn't had some resources of her own. She had been married in Bulgaria before coming to France. On her wedding night, she had fled back home to her parents. Subsequently, she had worked out a bizarre arrangement with her husband. She would go to Nancy and study medicine. Her husband would pay for it, and then they would see. However, her medical studies annoyed me, and I had led her to drop out of school. In 1927, rather than returning to Bulgaria for the holidays, she, together with a girl friend, had moved to Saint-Dié in the Vosges.

In 1928, Katia's husband lost patience and informed her that she had to come home. I was about to do eighteen months of military service; the most reasonable thing she could do was to go back to her parents in Bulgaria and start divorce proceedings. This separation was cruel because my material future was so insecure; it seemed that all our dreams were to be scattered in a rude awakening. My induction was three months away. I resigned from all my responsibilities in the Fifth Chapter and passed instructions on to my successor. As of October, politics for me would be undercover antimilitary work. I would make the necessary contacts in Nancy before going to our vacation house in Baccarat.

Any brutal interruption in the flow of a life leads to reflection and useful stock-taking. I was a disciplined Communist but I didn't want to be blind. I was convinced that the quest for truth could not possibly compromise my adherence to Marxism or my attachment to the Party. The year 1928 had been marked by action that was consistent with a whole side of myself. But I had read only doctrine: Marx, whose complete works were being published by Editions Costes, Bukharin, Trotsky, Lenin, whose complete works were slowly being issued by Les Editions Sociales Internationales. There was so much more to know. For example, I was unfamiliar with Hegel.

And then there was the well-known problem of superstructures. This convenient, vague, and vivid term is used by Marxists (especially Russians) to encompass anything that does not fall under production or exchange of merchandise or another of the great social categories. Art, religion, philosophy, war, sex (to the extent that it is not reproduction of the species), everything having to do with the psyche, any social phenomena more complex than employers and employees, and what not, are all part of the superstructure. It encompasses quite a load of things on the deck of the capitalist ship! For instance, nothing in Marxism allows for an explanation of top hats. Yet both Marx and Engels wore them. And this young professional revolutionary was soon to go astray in the tangle of superstructures!

10
TROTSKY COMES
BACK TO
MONTPARNASSE

KATIA'S ABSENCE WAS VERY HARD ON ME. I spent long periods nourishing my melancholy with regrets and memories. But I did not experience it as a definitive separation. It was a long voyage; each of us had gone home for a vacation that went on and on. Helped by the lightness of youth and the lust for life of a twenty-year-old, these holidays were merrier than any others. I had converted my father to the gramophone. We enjoyed listening to records on the most recent portable gadget, which sounded astonishingly faithful and precise. I had bought a few of the jazz discs that could be found on the French market: Jack Hilton, Paul Whiteman, Ted Lewis, the Revellers. In fact, these were more like classical concerts than true jazz sessions. I danced every evening with my cousins, my sister, and their friends. I also flirted of course: isn't true fidelity the fidelity of the heart? At least that was what I told myself. I discovered that, according to the double standard, a man can maintain a clear conscience even in difficult and ticklish situations. This realization surprised me a bit: faithful to traditional logic, I held to the principle of the excluded middle and Hegelian dialectics. Freud's theories on the ego, the id, and the superego struck me, wrongly, as purely clinical; in any event, the mechanism of such psychology never seemed to invalidate Descartes or Hegel. And here I was, allowing myself to move about in a milieu of contradictions which I was fully aware of. I was thriving. It was fun to think that the middle isn't always excluded, that there are opposites that get along with one another and lack sufficient internal energy to let the negation be denied yet nevertheless do not impose an unpleasant tension. To alleviate my surprise and fully reassure myself, I would imagine a succession of planes or levels endowed with a meaning or a hierarchy. I used this geometrical model to explain how apparently contradictory impulses, mutually exclusive in principle, could coexist without disturbing the fine balance of the individual or turning him inside out. Since I didn't stop to linger on these episodes; since I had no intention whatsoever of undertaking a serious analysis of my feelings and desires, viewing them all as givens; and since I admitted that they weren't truly contradictory, that such oddities might be the result of a poor statement of the problem, I hastily flipped the page. In any case, my spatial model permitted me to define a quality in the contradictory and the identical; it made logic more supple and complicated. Although I paid little attention to these affective details, my focus nevertheless formed a reference point to which I subsequently returned. It allowed me to expose the trace of a first crack in the lovely doctrinal construction from which I drew the strength of my convictions and the guidelines of my thought.

As usual, Georges Sadoul spent the summer holidays in Raon-l'Etape. We exchanged visits. We remained on our guard warily. Sadoul's sympathies with Trotskyism had become clear but were not based on anything serious. They mainly echoed Breton and the approving chorus at the Café Cyrano. The Communist Party had welcomed the Surrealists as warmly as possible, considering its own habits, the social make-up of its cadres, and the average intellectual level of its leaders. But the Surrealists of 1926–27 had everything that was necessary to shock or wound the people in the cells. The Surrealists were young bourgeois whose only contact with workers had been in the army, except when they needed a house painter or a plumber. In uniform, both workers and intellectuals are primarily soldiers, adjusting with greater or lesser ease to discipline, collective life, the military mind, and

danger. Men from a middle-class background more quickly acquire the
rank or office that separates them from the mass. In a cell, the workers
are in their own element; their occupation gives them a title that the
bourgeois will never be able to acquire. This title is worth much more
than any knowledge of dogma or general education. For young intellectuals who joined the Revolution, the usual grind of Communist
cells, with their confused discussions about practical tasks, their impoverished commentaries on articles in *L'Humanité*, their lack of spontaneous reactions to sensational news or great problems, all wrecked
several months of illusory exaltation. The Surrealists were too well-
dressed, they were too excited, and they spoke a language that was
hard to understand. If you wrote a leaflet, the intellectual would introduce a tone or words that weren't current in factories. Just what was
Surrealism anyway? The sight of a single issue of *The Surrealist Revolution* would inject suspicions in the minds of nearly all the militants.
Any attempt to defend Surrealism triggered dreadful emotional fric-
tions: on one side, the representatives of everything that would be
accepted, admired, and imitated forty years later, and, on the other
side, individuals who voted red but adhered to the most reactionary
forms of art. These defenders of a Victorian morality were shocked by
any challenge to forms, modes of representation, ways of living and
speaking. Perhaps the Surrealists, if they didn't belong to a world of
madmen, could be viewed as revolutionaries in their own way, but no
one wanted that kind of revolution.

Man sticks first and foremost to his habitual ways of seeing and
understanding. In 1927, the members of the Communist Party pasted
up antimilitaristic posters; some of them may have been capable of
sacrificing their lives to the proletarian revolution, but they disapproved
of blasphemy and sex. For them, family life, the artwork on French
banknotes, movie serials, and modesty were as sacred as the verses of
the International.

The intellectuals in the Party were much more fearful, with very
few exceptions. They were often failures and, knowing little of Marxism, had turned Communist in the enthusiasm of youth, or out of
bitterness toward a society that gave them no foothold, or because they
had been seriously wounded by some injustice. Then there were the
teachers of bourgeois culture, pushed toward the Party by their hatred
of war or money. The best of the Communist intellectuals in the late
twenties, those for whom Marx and Lenin were not mere names, had
mostly adopted, or were about to adopt, the theses of the Trotskyite

opposition. These men were the first Party members that Aragon and Breton met. Marcel Fourrier, one of the head editors of *Clarté* was one of them. Breton had instantly liked his modesty, his kindness, his common sense. Fourrier was very quickly won over to Surrealism and bought its paintings and savage objects. In 1926, he became a moderate Trotskyite, maintaining contact with the Party but unshakably hostile to Stalinism. He introduced Boris Souvarin to Breton. That brilliant man, one of the founders of the French Communist Party, who had had personal relations with all the great October revolutionaries, was expelled in 1923. He founded and edited the *Bulletin Communiste*, the best-written and most widely read organ of the opposition. Before his expulsion, it was the French Communist Party's sole official publication on theory; not until 1924 was it replaced with the *Cahiers du Bolchevisme*. Souvarin's influence was a powerful factor in turning the Surrealists toward Trotsky. His intelligence, cultural background, and character captivated Breton. Souvarin warned him against the Party and against the International, and during his brief stint in the organization Breton had to concede that his warnings were well-founded. Nor did Victor Serge, meeting with the *Clarté* people, express any support of Stalin. A former anarchist, a friend of Bonnot, Garnier, and the others, he had been prosecuted with the whole bunch in the famous trial. This episode gave him a certain prestige in the eyes of the Surrealists, especially because his unselfishness had received the rousing sanction of the court. The testimony of such opposition figures weighed heavier than *L'Humanité's* official commentaries on the Soviet crisis. But in 1926, the Trotskyites were all still in the party that was considered the center of revolution. When Aragon, Breton, and a few others solemnly joined in late 1926, they did so under the tutelage of Hegel, Marx, Lenin, and Trotsky. Their entrance into cells was often accompanied by foolish incidents. Breton had to undergo interrogations by a committee of inquiry that was very embarrassed about its responsibilities. Ultimately, most of the Surrealists lacked the leisure necessary for a militant life: girls, movies, outings for a young bourgeois during the wild twenties, competed dangerously with political meetings. Thus everything helped to justify the honorable discharge that occurred in the spring of 1927.

The events immediately preceding Breton's request for Party membership greatly determined the road I was to choose at the end of 1928 and to follow for over four years. I have already said that, despite blunders, misunderstandings, and incompatibilities, the Communist effort to absorb the Surrealists was real. Henri Barbusse, because of hypocrisy or prudence or at the request of political advsiers, devoted one or two features in *L'Humanité* to the problem of language, the role that words play in literary works. Reading the articles, I felt that he was accomplishing something worthwhile; in forcing himself to focus on a world that had been totally alien to him, he was extending a kind of welcome to young comrades. His understanding of Surrealism was both touching and stupid. Breton was furious. The issue arose just in time for him to kick up a fuss exactly like those created later on, in other areas, by certain press conferences by General de Gaulle. Each side had to justify a doctrinal position or a mode of behavior in a situation where the balance of forces could become favorable only if the people involved cast off and grotesquely caricatured the opponent. That was how the pamphlet *Legitimate Defense* came about in October 1927. It treated Pierre Naville roughly, piled up qualms about the policies of the Party, slung mud at Barbusse and *L'Humanité*, and mentioned all the "ideological differences separating him from doctrine" as though Breton wanted to set up the basis of possible later debates by assuming all his responsibilities at the outset.

Many observers felt that *Legitimate Defense* was a break with Communism. The Communists, of course, didn't at all appreciate an attack on their press, even for the best reasons, from outside the Party. Soon any criticism even within the Party would become impossible. And the terms used by Breton were extremely offensive.

However, things didn't move so simply. Benjamin Péret began writing for *L'Humanité*, so for several months it ran articles that were frantically anticlerical. Jacques Doriot, very powerful at the time, admitted to an interest in the violence of the Surrealistic diatribe. A couple of weeks after publishing *Legitimate Defense*, Breton registered with the Communist Party. Nevertheless, it presented problems because Breton was inevitably destined to occupy an eminent position in relation to literature and art, which did not fail to wreck a few comfortable situations within the ranks. There was nothing inherently absurd or insulting about the procedure of the inquiry committee; some of the Party leaders were even counting on its verdict to win over the Surrealists. But it turned out to be naïve and stupid. The heavy apparatus of the committee led, according to the rules of the organization, to a mechanism of rejection and ran the risk of angering the person under inquiry. For all the uncustomary humility he assumed, Breton was cognizant of his moral strength and the ludicrousness of the situation.

None of the Communists understood or wanted to understand that the publication of the pamphlet prior to his joining the Party had implicitly committed the author to accept discipline for anything that couldn't be derived from or accepted in the pamphlet. Wasn't this essentially what the Party wanted? Permeated with all the bourgeois values, the Communist appartus felt that Breton and Surrealism were not well-known enough to warrant a red-carpet treatment. The petty rodents on several levels couldn't resist the opportunity to pounce on an alien body and tear it to shreds. It was in this framework of disappointments and bureaucratic arguments that the "opposition" ferment sprang up among the Surrealists. Breton admired Trotsky. Stalin's treatment of the opposition, the expulsions and deportations to Siberia, no doubt hastened the withdrawal of the Surrealists from their initial position. That act was justified when the Comintern, so disagreeable and inhospitable, appeared to be amputating its purest revolutionaries.

International politics, from 1914 to the present, has been mostly irrational, paranoid, and violent. In this context, one can wonder what might have happened if there had been a conjunction of one of the Communist big-mouths of 1927 (Doriot, say, rather than Thorez) and the Surrealists at the head of a mass party that was theoretically revolutionary. But Stalinism was to hurl Doriot toward Fascism and confine the Surrealists to the realm of disasters. In May 1968, most of the graffiti on Paris walls quoted Breton rather than Lenin.

Later on, there were temporary successes in the attempts at a match between Surrealists and Communists. The most durable was that of the Czech Surrealists, who for several years carried on under the official stamp of the Communist Party—until Stalinism put things in proper order. In Yugoslavia, the Surrealists furnished cadres to the Communist Party and to Tito's government, but as of 1933 nearly all of them wanted to be professional revolutionaries. Their enthusiasm left nothing of their Surrealism.

In 1927, the French Communist Party didn't know what to do with the intellectuals who were coming to it. It reserved for itself the use of sympathetic celebrities intended for a solemn role as voices of universal conscience. Romain Rolland, whose petty-bourgeois pacifism was criticized, was the ultimate resort. The Party still hadn't understood the effects it could gain from the membership of actors, filmmakers, and journalists. There was nothing to attract them with because all, or nearly all, means of expression were in the hands of the enemy. The state, now a major distributor of jobs, at that time disposed only of the Opera and the Comédie-Française, which were colonized by the parties in power. The Communists needed propagandists and found excellent ones in the working class. Entrusting intellectuals with this task presented the risk of unforeseeable deviations; perhaps they would even erect a barrier of language and manners between the Party and the masses. The Communists, however, were far from the strongest group within the proletariat. Except in the Paris region, most of the workers interested in politics turned, out of sentiment and prudence, to the Socialists or to the Socialist Radicals. What could the Party do with Max Ernst or André Breton to win the miners of Lens whose novels could sentimentally describe the crushing life of laborers or the sorrows of unwed mothers in the spinning mills? Intellectuals, led to believe they could be useful by creating Marxist study groups for either workers or their own edification, were merely deluding themselves even more, but no one realized it. This wasn't the era of Lafargue, Kautsky, or Lenin. Dogma was well established, and its interpretation was left to the elders. Soon it would become the monopoly of Stalin; the subject matter in such groups would be limited to comments on Stalin or paraphrases of Trotsky. One could also force the latest scientific discoveries into dialectical materialism, though that operation tempted no one in France because the "Marxists" were ignorant of all contemporary physics.

People claimed that the history of the French Communist Party since its founding could easily be summed up: each year, the old-timers were expelled by the newcomers. There was an element of truth in this sally. The Comintern encouraged the ambition and naïveté of the younger members in order to accelerate "Bolshevization." I did not escape that law. Pierre Naville had taken the rather peculiar step of joining the Party in order to become an opposition spokesman. Eliminated by Breton from the board of *The Surrealist Revolution,* where he had promoted a lyrical sympathy for the Orient and "tradition," Naville had become a Communist before the others. Fascinated by Trotskyism, he was more familiar with Marxism than either Aragon or Breton. He was thoughtful and hard-working, but a sectarian and probably a hard-liner, like all sectarians. He embraced the Communist ideology like a religious belief, at the same time adopting the most rigid interpretations of dogma. I am inclined to think that the references to Thermidor, which recurred so often in Trotsky's invectives against Stalin and his supporters, were the major factor inducing Pierre Naville to fall in with the "opposition." He thereby became the defender of the true faith.

In 1926, the editors of *Clarté*, Marcel Fourrier, Victor Crastre, Jean Bernier, and the Surrealists had tried to come to an agreement on the material for a new periodical, *La Guerre Civile*, which would replace *Clarté*. This would have been a good way to resolve the problems caused by Breton's rallying to the principles of the Third International, but they might as well have tried to square the circle, for in order to absorb Surrealism in all its richness and not limit it to literary contributions, they would have had to permit a philosophical liberalism which not a single Communist found congenial. Naville was not one of the more accommodating. He became the champion of a mental discipline which eventually resulted in his expulsion from the Party. In his brochure *The Revolution and the Intellectuals: What Can the Surrealists do?*, published in 1926, he ably called the Surrealists to account for their tendencies and intentions (a tactic that the Stalinists were later to adopt), and he was a worse stickler for doctrine and more severe than the committee of inquiry that harassed Breton a year later within the Communist Party. Naville questioned Breton's acquiescence to historical materialism, and accused the Surrealists of advocating a vague notion of revolution, possibly quite remote from the proletarian revolution. He was worried by their individualism and their interest in subjective idealism.

These highly perfidious criticisms had the rigor of articles of faith. At first they won me over, but then my conviction was shaken by Breton's reply, *Legitimate Defense*. Orthodoxy was certainly on Naville's side: the distinction that Breton made, in his own defense, between historical materialism, to which he subscribed, and "dogmatic" materialism, which he seemed to condemn by wrongly claiming that historical materialism is its formal negation, does not in any way represent Engels' thought. On the contrary, since that distinction had no other goal than to prepare the reader to allow for a sort of equivalence between subjective idealism and historical materialism, it reinforced the weight of Naville's indictments of the Surrealists. But in Breton's argumentation, in the things protected by his dialectics, there was a wondrous world that Pierre Naville's dry orthodoxy could never attain. Without attempting to get at the bottom of things for now, and admitting that my decision was based more on intuition than a reasoned conviction, although by no means did I approve of all the

devious twists of *Legitimate Defense*, I had to agree that Naville's
animadversions, as well-founded as they may have looked at first sight,
had little relevance. They were more akin to traditional discussion
procedures than to an exhaustive view of the subject. After all, was it
such a threat to the Revolution for the Surrealists to worry about
coincidences or psychic phenomena if these were merely subject matter
for artistic creation or an excuse for exploring the unconscious? And
even if the Surrealist writings contained a few "errors," could they
possibly lead the proletariat astray from its historical mission? Weren't
they by reason of those very "errors" a power for inciting revolution?
Wasn't their nonconformity more valid than that of the official
tartuffisms?

After the publication of the letters contained in *Au Grand Jour*,
which put a dignified and decent end to the pitiful escapade of the
five signatories (Aragon, Breton, Eluard, Unik, and Péret) in Communist cells, Naville took a step backward. He admitted that Berkeley,
Locke, and Hegel might be seen in a different light than that of the
schools for Party cadres. He constructed a curious theory of militant
pessimism in order to give credit to a kind of organic complicity that
allegedly existed among all the Surrealists—Communists and non-
Communists alike. This time it wasn't a matter of principles, or even
a concurrence on objectives, but a frame of refrence sought at the very
core of each individual's behavior, a way of seeing things. This neb-
ulous proposition, which implied profound discords, for it let the
previous injunctions stand, is stated in the article *Better and Less Well*,
written in 1927 and published in *The Surrealist Revolution*. It was
then printed as a separate brochure.

All things considered, what I retained from Naville's text was his
definitive rejection of Surrealism. And, despite our jointly held Marxist
convictions, his rejection was not mine. This was extremely important
because I was afraid that Naville might have enough influence on the
Surrealists to win them all to Trotskyism.

In 1928, Pierre Naville, although only a bit older than me, was far
more mature. He knew exactly where he was headed. His knowledge
of Marxism was no better than mine, but his philosophical background, partly because of his education, was wider and more thorough.
He had economic means that I didn't have and a self-assurance that
absolutely showed me up. I made up for this lack with a great unawareness and a total scorn for the future. The difference between us
really bore on the social milieux in which we were developing. Naville

had remained a bourgeois intellecual; I was almost completely integrated into the working class. And the workers were not Trotskyites. For them, Thermidor signified a return to capitalism: there was no perceptible indication that the U.S.S.R. was about to embark on the same road. Clumsily, or foolishly, as you like, Russian Communists remained attached to the idea of a world revolution. The proletarian dictatorship was assuming an exemplary value: there was one country, and only one in the world, in which property relations had been upset, and that country was the Soviet Union. The quarrels of the opposition surpassed popular common sense, and I imagine that it was more or less the same in Russia. The opposition's variations on Thermidor, especially Trotsky's, were of such a disconcerting range that no one could take them seriously, except by attaching more importance to brilliance of style and polemical talent than to the facts themselves. Intellectuals are always more open to argumentation than to reason; Naville was no exception.

For Breton, ideas were what counted. The substance of criticism relevant to events interested him even less than Naville. On the other hand, the philosophical bearing of remarks, viewpoints, the train of ideas were a powerful stimulus on his imagination and sensitivity. Trotsky was admirable. Breton was rarely mistaken in his judgments. Stalin differed so little from the dozens of politicians in office almost everywhere. Trotsky was an exceptional writer and thinker. The unjust fate of Trotsky, the genius, the angel, condemned by assemblies of cowards and mediocrities, predisposed Breton's pessimism in his favor. All this joined with the bullying of the inquiry committee to underscore Breton's conviction that it was wise and honorable to quit the French Communist Party, but it never sufficed to prompt Breton to join the Trotskyite opposition. This distinction was of major importance to me as soon as I fully comprehended it.

Like almost all the members of the Party, like all the Communist voters, I felt that Stalin was right. He had so much to do, building socialism and defending the U.S.S.R., that he should not be handicapped with ideological anxieties. As for the extension of the revolutionary movements, that was first and foremost the task of each national party. Lenin had not come to seek the French in 1917 in order to seize power. In the growing deluge of invectives crashing down upon Trotsky, I took polemics into account. I preserved intact my admiration for the organizer of the Red Army; but didn't the history of Bolshevism show that it had sometimes been necessary to exclude some of its best men? When a convoy speeds up again, some of its passengers, who got off while it was slowing down, will be unable to return to their trucks. That was what happened to Kautsky, Plekhanov, and even Rosa Luxemburg.

During the publication of *What Can the Surrealists Do?* in 1926–27, I exchanged several letters with Naville. This correspondence was of little use to me. My own letters were probably confused and contradictory, Naville's reflected the serene optimism of believers: truth will be triumphant; men and ideas will gradually take the place assigned to them by revolutionary determinism. "You have to let the revolutionaries revolutionize themselves," Naville once said to me when I had defended the thesis that a progressive awareness of the correct line was attained through daily political action.

After my last conversation with Naville, probably early in 1928, I felt as though I had been visiting a heretic who was primarily concerned with the pureness of his heresy and fully resolved to omit anything that might ruffle the calm surface of his lovely tranquil lake. It didn't much matter to him whether his heresy won out or not. Pierre Naville had become a Marxist and Trotskyist for himself alone, and possibly for the glory of his master.

In 1928, Stalinists and heretics were blind. They all draped history in cheap finery that they chose according to secret and unacknowledged preferences, but they were also incapable of understanding and explaining what was happening under their very eyes. In the quarrel between the Trotskyites and Stalin over evolution of the U.S.S.R. (was Russia building socialism or capitalism?), neither of the parties really knew what it was all about. They should have first defined socialism and used something beyond two or three little esoteric or contradictory phrases piously gleaned from the complete works of Marx. They ought to have had some knowledge of the capitalist economies of their time. On the advice of Naville, who set very great store by it, I took along on my summer vacation Trotsky's brochure of 1925, *Toward Capitalism or Toward Socialism*, which had recently been translated into French. Naville saw it as a scientific comparison of the Russian and American economies. He couldn't have been more wrong. Today, one can't help being very hard on that text: the great man, like all the Bolsheviks of his time, knew nothing about Soviet economy and the direction it was taking. His ignorance of the modern structures of capitalism was equally great. Historians of 1970 view that work as Trotsky's rather laborious act of courtesy toward the conceptions of the majority to which he no longer belonged. In point of fact, no one reading it could find any challenge to Stalinist theses and to the general line that the Russian Communist Party was following. And yet, on the eve of the great collectivization, the die was largely cast. No hope was allowed; the mechanisms were in place and they were about to run under Stalin's iron rod. Much much later, Trotsky used the term "bureaucratic collectivism" to describe the society that was being built in Russia around 1928. Without falling into fatalism may we not wonder whether there really was any other possibility?

To see clearly in the confusion of doctrinal quarrels and the Russian reality, all of us would have had to abandon our unconditional admiration for Lenin and our Marxist faith. Trotsky wasn't much help; a prisoner, like Stalin, of a system that was also his own, he was doomed to use his prodigious intellect for solving very peripheral problems of tactics or methods. Trotsky was the copilot of the Soviet Union. If circumstances were to become very unfavorable to Stalin, even the bureaucrats would call back Trotsky, well aware that he would retain them in their jobs. Stalin knew this; he had his rival assassinated as soon as the circumstances made Trotsky's return sufficiently probable to worry him.

The development of Russian affairs in 1928 and 1929 enabled the partisans of Stalin, myself among them, to chalk up constant points against the opposition. The more Stalin stressed his left-wing politics, stepping up the pace of industrialization, dispossessing the rich peasants, and the more precisely the International pursued its so-called Third Period strategy, announcing new revolutionary waves—which of course never arrived—the less effective Trotsky's arguments became. Now no one dared regard Stalin as a traitor, a bankrupt, or a revisionist. Wasn't he a prudent but able revolutionary, resolute, skillful, and inflexible? At least that was everyone's image of him in 1928. It was incomplete, and highly exaggerated, but not so false. The problem was not whether Stalin would go on with the building of socialism or strangle the Revolution, but whether it was worth it all. No Communist would ask himself such a question. In any event, Trotsky's partisans, who had shouted so loudly for Thermidor and surrender, didn't look very good. The opposition members capitulated one after another, admitting their mistakes, acknowledging the cogency of the Party's general line, endorsing Stalin.

Nor did the politicians and economists of capitalist countries comprehend anything. They were incapable of being canny observers of their own system of production. A few Anglo-Saxon theoreticians turned out to be the worthy successors of Adam Smith, Ricardo, and Marx, but in 1928 they had no audience. It was five years before certain governments successfully palliated the effects of an anarchy that the Marxists considered irremediable. The Communists themselves could make no progress in political economy, because theoretically Marx had already said everything. The abundance of false statistics produced by the Russians didn't help at all. Only a few founders of the Third International could discern the truth. But since all of them had been expelled, they were doomed to offer testimony that the believers impugned in advance.

At the end of September 1928, my father moved from the tranquil and austere Rue Girardet to a mid-twenties house that he had had built on Avenue Foch. The two of us had a wonderful time selecting the wallpaper and arranging the furniture. My father would often take my advice, which he felt was based on a more modern aesthetic. The house was very cheerful. My sister Françoise, who had become very beautiful, would bring over a swarm of friends her own age, whom she dominated with her personality and self-assurance. These girls were rather different from the boarding-school refugees that I had known a few years earlier. They were discovering summer vacations and travel, and adopting an independent style that amazed Nancy. Françoise had made astonishing strides at the piano. She had always been gifted. At fourteen, she had presented herself without warning at my father's class in the Conservatory. She was admitted, and a year later she won the First Prize. She had begun working with Cortot, who predicted a career for her, but we were all worried about her health. Even though she looked robust, she still suffered from the aftereffects of a bout with tuberculosis. We thought it had been overcome, but it was soon to have a dramatic sequel.

To get into the swing of things, I attended meetings of regimental cells. I also traveled to Metz, where I distributed an allegedly subversive issue of *L'Avant-Garde* to the garrison soldiers. There was a notice in my pocket ordering me to join the 18th Engineering Corps in Mayence, but a recent law had reduced the length of military service by six months in order to tighten the budget. The government decided to put this measure into effect immediately. The men who were supposed to be called up in 1928 were told to wait until May 1929. So I decided to return to Paris.

The conditions of my return weren't very pleasant. My father had decided to reduce my allowance to two hundred francs a month. So what! I would move to Rue du Château, where I wouldn't have to pay any rent, and I'd go to work in a factory. Still, I was sensible enough to ask my father for the large slow-combustion stove that he used to heat his classroom in Rue Girardet. Since he no longer needed it, he agreed to send it to Rue du Château. This efficient device was to make our life comfortable through the long, cold winters of 1928 and 1929 and allow for interminable nighttime conversations with Aragon.

No one met me when I arrived in Paris at dusk. As usual, I found the key hanging on a nail by the toilet near the fanlight. I expected to find the large room on the ground floor more of a mess. Blatantly looming up on one of the wall sofas, an unexpected object revealed an unwonted visitor or perhaps a new tenant: the half-length photograph, life-sized, of an unfamiliar young woman, her arms sheathed in enormous ivory bracelets up to the elbows. It was enlarged from a Man Ray photograph subsequently reproduced in the August 15, 1929, issue of *Varietés*. I immediately assumed that the woman in bracelets was Nancy Cunard, whose affair with Aragon was the talk of the town. A good many Surrealists were disturbed because of Nancy's fortune.

Someone had moved into my room. I could tell by the leather suitcases covered with worldwide travel stickers and by the hundred-odd neckties hanging in the closet that Aragon was the new occupant. Rather amused by this surprise, I settled in the third bedroom, the one on the ground floor, whose only windows were small skylights. I had brought new records along, "Ol' Man River" and other songs from *Showboat*, which I tried out on the phonograph. In walked Margolies, a student of architecture at the School of Fine Arts and a classmate of Maurice Blech, whose family was friendly with the Sadouls. Maurice Blech had gone to Paris ahead of us to finish his studies. He was handsome, well dressed, intelligent, and a good friend, but his successes with women were the strength of his prestige, especially his audacious coup of being Josephine Baker's first lover in Paris. Although the idyll had been very short-lived, we were all still full of admiration and pride two years later. Margolies confirmed the fact that Aragon was living in the pavilion. But the big news was that Sadoul was madly, irremissibly, unhappily, and passionately in love.

Around 1924, two girls, spunky and dazzlingly beautiful, ambitious and penniless, had come to Paris from Aubervilliers. Many young people still do this when they are sixteen or so and are sick and tired of factories, Arabs, and their friends' motorcycles, but in 1924 it was quite a trip. The two Suzannes (they both had the same first name) had sworn never to set foot in Aubervilliers again and never to be content with mediocre adventures. Yet what else could they do in order to live? Suzanne I was petite, with an expressive Parisian face, very beautiful eyes, and a smile like a greedy angel's. Suzanne II was tall, slender, gracefully shaped, with regular, slightly Nordic features. There was something naturally distinguished about her; she looked like a movie star. She was supposedly of Dutch descent. Very flirtatious and very attractive, both loved love and luxury. They wanted to experience everything; one of them even stayed in a brothel for a while, using her friend's identity. By 1928, they had both become elegant, sophisticated women, but, despite unquestionable successes, they were still as ambitious as ever.

After various ups and downs, Suzanne II had naturally been drawn to the Latin Quarter. She had been Vitrac's girl friend and claimed to have inspired one of his plays; next she lived with a young American who was studying at the Sorbonne. He had a bit more money than the others but he still had to be careful with it. Very taken with Suzanne, he had rented her a hotel room near Montparnasse station. In 1926, he suddenly had to leave for the States. He was gone a rather long time, but he had left her enough to live on decently. When he returned, he was more in love with her than ever. She had been unfaithful because she was nervous about their future and was wondering whether it wasn't time for her to look elsewhere. When he announced his return, she was only half waiting for him, uncertain about how to act because he wasn't much of a letter writer. He looked prosperous, busy, and mysterious. In fact, the young American had just come into a huge fortune. He had become some kind of rubber king. He married Suzanne II and took her back to America.

Stricken with homesickness, Suzanne II had come back to Montparnasse all alone in October 1928, with money, clothes, and jewels. She was fully intent on having fun. Maurice Blech picked her up and, out of vanity or egged on by some demon, brought her around to Rue du Château, where Sadoul was living in total boredom. Just the night before, Sadoul had had his fortune told, and the cards had prophesied that the love of his life would be visiting him at home. That was almost all that was needed to make Suzanne's entrance seem as natural as the postman's visit. Sadoul and Suzanne went night-clubbing until dawn, and by then he had fallen madly in love with the ravishing young woman.

What made Sadoul's love even more intense was the presence of Suzanne I at André Breton's side. The Surrealists set great store by coincidences. The other beauty from Aubervilliers, who had stayed in Paris, had forged ahead in banking, industry, and the fine arts and was wavering between security and the quest for absolute love. She had temporarily moved in with Breton at 42 Rue Fontaine, slightly redecorating his studio by designing a large bookcase and shifting the objects and paintings around. For three years, interrupted by disagreements, separations, returns, and, if memory serves me, a marriage with a mediocre but rich and well-known writer, Suzanne I made Breton's life an alternation of heaven and hell. Her own instability was coupled with his unfortunate economic difficulties.

As soon as Sadoul described the object of his passion, Suzanne I recognized her old friend. Her real name was Hélène, but she had changed it out of affection and admiration. The things we learned about Hélène/Suzanne's character weren't very reassuring. It soon became evident that she had come to Paris to take advantage of her freedom, that she was toying with Sadoul's passion for her. It seemed clear she would make her admirer the unhappiest of men.

Georges Sadoul had had little experience with women. In 1928 he was still an editor at Gallimard, spending several hours there every day. Twice a day, he sat down at the Café Cyrano, wandered around Montparnasse or at the Bal Nègre, saw a lot of movies, but never had any affairs. The storm broke suddenly: all he thought about was Suzanne, all he talked about was Suzanne. As unprepared as one could be to confront a person as sophisticated as she was, he was awkward, infatuated, stubborn, and up to his ears in disappointment.

This fateful passion wiped away the misunderstandings and quarrels that had drawn us apart. Sadoul needed me; we became friends again as though Trotsky had never existed. I did all I could to help and distract him. I devised complicated maneuvers for him to meet Suzanne and lower her resistance. I did manage to get him to endure his suffering patiently until he could find some relief.

11
ENTER ARAGON

WITH THE PUBLICATION OF HIS TREATISE ON STYLE
in 1928, Aragon increased his notoriety. Although it had not yet
reached the "greater public," his reputation had already spread beyond
the small world of writing and art. The book scandalized a few people, but even they had to agree that the author was something of a
genius. The antipatriotic, antimilitaristic, and antireligious content of
the *Treatise on Style* widened Aragon's audience among young people
and leftists.

Elegant, dandyish, romantic, handsome, caustic, evanescent, dazzling,
Aragon intrigued men, who feared his intelligence, his vivacity, his
biting repartee, and captivated women, who doted on his aura of
mystery. To keep his distance, he magisterially exuded a kind of
icy politeness in the best eighteenth-century tone, though that didn't
prevent him from being sensitive and fraternal with his friends. He
knew how to arouse trust, and then he would talk on and on. And
he spoke the way he wrote; the style, the tone, the phrases of his books
calmed and cheered his listeners as much as the dexterity of his
words.

Nancy Cunard was roughly the same age as Aragon. Her mother,
Lady Cunard, was one of the grand ladies of British society. A patroness

of the arts and an intrepid traveler, Nancy was said to be on very intimate terms with Sir Thomas Beecham, and her name was very famous on the high seas. People claimed she wasn't very easygoing. Nancy, at eighteen, had married a handsome cavalry officer who had gone out of her life rather quickly: he had been either killed in Flanders or kicked out by his wife, who wasn't meant for army life. She was attractive, deceptively thin, of medium height, slender, with the gaze of a serpent, lovely walnut-colored hair, and freckled skin. Aristocratic and British, like the heroine of a novel, she moved with the self-assurance of women who are used to receiving and being received. She dressed extremely well, with an eccentric touch that, late in life, she gradually emphasized until it was eventually overdone. She spoke a polished French with no accent, occasionally using funny or picturesque anglicisms, and her voice was as melodious as a siren's.

Man Ray's photograph, which Aragon had brought to Rue du Château, is very reminiscent of what its model was like in 1928–29. Nancy almost always wore huge golden jewelry; she had a weakness for bracelets, which, squeezed around her forearms, looked like a piece of armor. The loveliest and strangest ones were enormous bracelets of ivory, from Africa or Asia. Her taste for them had been acquired from Aragon, who had given her most of them. Like many Englishwomen from a good social background, Nancy often drank too much. She would become nasty, aggressive, and brutal, slapping men with the back of her forearm, crushing their faces with the ivory or metal that squeezed her in from her wrists to her elbows. Sometimes she herself bore marks from those violent scenes, and she hid them under thick mauve veils attached to one of those small, absurd hats of the period. She also had a wanderlust and would cross the ocean at the drop of a hat, giving her friends bizarre addresses, sending surprise telegrams, often cryptic and written under the influence of alcohol, making dates in Bermuda or Naples the way other people would invite you for a weekend in Sologne.

At the time, I hardly knew Louis Aragon. I had rarely gone to the Café Cyrano, and Aragon, like Eluard, was almost always traveling. One evening, he just seemed to pop up on the terrace of the Left Bank café where I was sitting with a few young Surrealists. His sudden appearance was amazing, and quite fitted in with my conception of him. Aragon was swathed in a kind of black cape, which emphasized the hurried cloak-and-dagger aspect he often assumed. Instead of joining us, he greeted a few people rather patronizingly, exhibited a certain nervousness, and vanished in a swirl of mystery. More simply, he went to Nancy Cunard, I think, to spend some time with her on the Basque coast, which was very fashionable at the time.

Nancy had a house in Périgord and another in Chapelle-Réanville, near Vernon. She was mad about printing and had brought Aragon to share her passion. In Réanville, there was a press in an outbuilding; there was another in back of a store on Rue Guénégaud. Hours Press published chapbooks in limited editions, including Aragon's French translation of Lewis Carroll's *Hunting of the Snark*.

Nancy, who could be gentle, tender, loving, and attentive, was a difficult and devastating companion. More than anything, she loved men. Whenever she desired someone, he had to satisfy her wishes immediately; she would attack. It is hard to imagine the tortures that her unfaithfulness and her sudden cravings inflicted on her lovers. Aragon and Nancy had spent the late summer of 1928 in Italy. Their affair had already reached the phase of storminess, with bloody fighting and passionate reconciliations.

They moved to Venice, where they found a black American band, the Plantation Jazz, which was on a European tour with the Black-birds troupe. Nancy fell in love with the pianist, a likable, well-mannered, goodlooking black, who composed blues in the manner of Gershwin. For two or three weeks, Aragon went through agony. *Poem to Shout in the Ruins*, which appeared in 1929 in the collection *The Great Gaiety*, is a kind of epilogue to the affair and his sufferings.

It was time to break up and leave. And that was how Aragon came to Rue du Château in October, literally a broken man. The studio he had rented on Rue Campagne-Première still wasn't habitable. Above all, Aragon didn't want to be alone. He hadn't ended all relations with Nancy; her tenderness and snakelike power could go on fascinating her victims, preventing them from being totally free again. She made a point of seeing her ex-lovers. Actually, she accepted life in all its complexity and couldn't understand why she should force herself to stop loving Aragon just because she wanted to sleep with Henry Crowder.

Every week, or nearly, Aragon would spend a day or two in Chapelle-Réanville. And, of course, he would come back in pieces.

Emotional crises and absences were half-burned, glowing logs that kept lighting the hearth of despair where the residents of Rue du Château warmed themselves enthusiastically: Louis Aragon, Georges Sadoul, and the author of these lines. The sorrows of young Werther do not always lead to suicide; they can also temper one's sensitivity, intelligence, and self-awareness. The autumn was black, the winter promised to be bitter. The heat spread through all the rooms of the house as long as we left the doors open. That physical heat helped the despairing men cultivate their melancholy indoors, sometimes by taking a drop too much, usually just enough to liven up the conversation. Their mutual sorrows reassured them; a camaraderie of the wounded developed among them. Anything that could be regarded as an improvement in the life of one of the three men was instantly interpreted by the other two as a sign of renascence. Each one did his best to help the other two, either by bringing the most innocent news or by suggesting a stratagem to overcome fate.

Suzanne/Hélène was becoming more and more inflexible, alas, and Sadoul was getting on her nerves. She would go out with anyone so long as she didn't have to run into Sadoul. There was a good deal of honesty in this behavior; she was reluctant to encourage feelings that she preferred to ignore. Things went from bad to worse. Maurice Blech entered the scene. I don't know how far he got with her, but they were seen together several times, and she made no secret of the fact that she liked him. Since Blech knew that Sadoul was madly in love with her, Aragon and a few others, including me, thought very poorly of this friend who could not resist a pretty girl.

Aragon was a confirmed night person, as was the vogue in our *quartier*. The geographical center of our comings and goings was situated between Rue Delambre and Boulevard Raspail—to be precise, at the Coupole bar. The periphery, frequented more or less, ran along the Dôme bar, the Select, the Jungle (a very well-known nightclub that had taken over from the Jockey), Dominique, the Russian restaurant, the Vikings, and the Music Box. All I knew of Montparnasse was the terraces of the Dôme and the Rotonde, where I had gone in search of the shades of Lenin and Trotsky. I was rather embarrassed about entering the poisonous pleasure haunts of the capitalists. I felt in the wrong, and I tried to act as though I were outside it all, forced to do something I didn't want to do, a victim of transient obligations. But little by little, I got to like those places, and I discovered the charm of adventure and a thousand distractions.

The Coupole is still what it was in 1928—a sort of long, narrow nook, arranged at one of the ends of the huge room with which it is connected through a folding door. The main entrance is on the boulevard through a revolving door. The bar occupies almost the entire length of one of the long sides of the rectangle, Facing the bar, a banquette stands against the partition separating this area from the café-restaurant; between the bar and the partition, there are small tables and chairs. The bartender's name was Bob. People said he was a police agent; no doubt he contented himself with being a good informer. He was precise, efficient, slightly aloof, always on the alert, and very self-controlled, though he would have outbursts of cold anger when he threw people out of the bar.

The clientele was basically made up of regular customers, curiosity seekers, and tourists; the latter came mainly on weekends, when some of the regulars were in the country. The most notorious figures are mentioned in all the books on Montparnasse in the twenties. Journalists and politicians were quite rare. Gaston Bergery, a left-wing radical deputy, young and with distinguished manners, was sometimes there. Aragon had known him forever and would always ask him to step in when a Surrealist was hauled in to a police station: Bergery gladly interceded to get the offender out immediately. Aragon explained Bergery's political orientation by claiming that the radical deputy was the unacknowledged son of a Prussian general. He was almost the only member of Parliament to hang out with bohemians in Montparnasse. To compensate for this, the Coupole's restaurant on the other side of the bar was crowded with deputies, senators, and ministers every evening.

A few lovely girls came almost regularly to the bar. I kept watching two or three professionals, Norwegian or Swedish, who paid their hotel bills by going off around 2 A.M. with some well-to-do nighthawks. The prettiest one was a Eurasian who was only twenty. The most picturesque woman at the Coupole was an ugly well-built dancer who was temperamental, intelligent, lazy, and a drug addict. She had an extraordinary name: Caridad de Laberdesque.

In 1928, the Coupole was a flourishing and extensive enterprise: a pergola on the roof doubled the restaurant's capacity, one of the largest in Paris. There was dancing in the downstairs part, which opened at teatime for married women on the make. After dinner, three hundred people would dance until 4 A.M., and there were two orchestras, one for blues and one for tangos. The Coupole also had its proletariat, young intellectuals from all over the world, girls from the provinces, homeless and broke, who spent hours nursing the same cup of coffee.

These people also made up the bulk of the steady customers at the

Dôme, except on Sundays, when all the neighborhood tradesmen filled the terrace. In 1929, the Dôme opened up a rather immense bar, which soon had a clientele of its own, far more mixed than that of the Coupole. Once, in 1930, Harry, the bartender at the Dôme, helped me save Caridad. Following his directions, I found her downstairs, bursting with heroin. I brought her back to her hotel with the help of the Eurasian girl. And that was how I found out that the bar of the Dôme was one of the main drug centers in Montparnasse.

The Select had a rather poor reputation. Some of its patrons may have been well-behaved, simply enjoying the liquor and the excellent cuisine, but people claimed that it served mainly as a refuge for homosexuals and addicts. This was true, it seems, only after a certain time of night. Many of the Coupole's patrons sometimes crossed the boulevard to sit on the terrace of the Select. You could sometimes see Jacques Prévert over there. And there were a few painters who were steady customers. Oscar Dominguez was faithful to the Select until his death.

The Rotonde wasn't really in. But it was always full: with strangers passing through, who were unaware of the hierarchy of cafés, girls. students who were behind the times, a profusion of not particularly talented painters, people from the School of Fine Arts. Just the scene to drive out the snobs who had decided to reside at the Coupole.

Montparnasse was also filled with people who appeared more or less episodically, living in the midst of obscure groups, moving on the borders of the great tribes. Although they didn't hang out together, and didn't even know one another, most of them shared a taste for Oriental philosophy, a metaphysical anxiety, and a powerful interest in magic. Pierre de Massot, supposedly a historian, had split off from the Surrealists for personal reasons. Monny de Bouly had been a Surrealist, but Breton had driven him out. Georges Hugnet was part of *L'Avant-Garde*; friendly with Cocteau, Max Jacob, Pierre Roy, Virgil Thomson, and the musicians of the Arcueil school, he went out a great deal and showed no intention as yet of joining the Surrealist group. One might run into Arthur Adamov several times an evening between the Coupole and the Dôme. It was considered good form to insult the poor guy, who looked like a beaten dog.

Rolland de Renéville published *Rimbaud the Seer*. Although tendentious, his study is probably the most intelligent approach ever attempted to problems that do not need to be solved. In 1928, its nonconformity and honesty distinguished it from the various attempts to annex Rimbaud so strongly that it had to be well received by all unprejudiced minds. Aragon and Breton thought the world of it. But since it wasn't compatible with Marxism (the title, so true to Rimbaud, made my hair stand on end), I stood on the defensive. My hypocritical qualms multiplied. I forced Aragon to admit, at least to me, that René-ville had seen only one side of the poet.

In between two voyages to the Pacific, Savitry the painter had a show, and Aragon wrote the preface to his catalogue. Breton was more reserved about the quality of these paintings (two of which were reproduced in the special issue of *Variétés* on *Surrealism in 1929*); he compared them to the work of Georges Malkine, another protégé of Aragon's. Malkine's work had gone down in the estimate of the headquarters on Rue Fontaine, where he was regarded as a very likable amateur.

The Americans in Paris maneuvered their way over vaster grounds. Anyone who was to be anyone in the next twenty years was either in Paris or about to arrive. Cole Porter had bought a townhouse on Rue Monsieur. Gershwin was always a hit in the capital, but his longest visits were after 1928. His "Rhapsody in Blue" won the hearts of the younger generation and disappointed all the musicians who had expected something different from the composer of "Tiptoes" and "The Man I Love." Darius Milhaud, who loved Negro spirituals, deplored the harmonic language of "Rhapsody in Blue," which was very close to that of the *Fantasy* for piano and orchestra that Debussy wrote in 1890. Milhaud was sorry not to find the same melodic invention or even the rhythmic variety of musicals that had made George Gershwin so rich and famous. Edgard Varèse sometimes showed up at the bar of the Coupole: he was still French, and Parisian. I can recall a decent-looking man, athletic, and dressed in lovely tweed jackets. He already had a reputation for writing very new music. Since it wasn't part of the stream of modernism then in fashion, people granted him only a succès d'estime because of his personality and his persevering devotion to something unusual.

Georges Antheil also had a reputation as a vanguard musician. His *Ballet Mécanique* caused a scandal. It was the first attempt at writing a musical work by combining phonograph recordings with the crude noise of machines. Today such composition would be called electronic or concrete music. It had no antecedents: the sound effects imagined by Marinetti were merely an aesthetic distraction; the typewriters that Erik Satie made use of in *Parade* are a brief and fleeting episode in the path of traditional ballet. Some listeners—who evidently were unaware of Varèse's music—have claimed that the *Ballet Mécanique* was the only known example of music worthy to be called Surrealist. Less eccentric than the others, Virgil Thomson and Aaron Copland were studying harmony and counterpoint with Nadia Boulanger. Thomson, a friend of Crevel's, loved Montparnasse. I eventually saw a lot of him in 1945.

Gertrude Stein and Man Ray were ports of call for all the people who had crossed the North Atlantic to come and cruise in Parisian waters. Gertrude Stein was set up as sort of consul-general for modernism. But after Dada, she no longer understood any new languages. She hated Man Ray and was shocked by his sense of humor and his genius. Man Ray had an important position in Montparnasse because of his inexhaustible inventiveness, his friendliness, and the new use he made of the camera. He dazzled us all with his cars. And the girls he went out with were beautiful. For a long time Kiki was his official mistress. The headquarters for English-language writers, especially Americans, was on Rue de l'Odéon at the famous bookstore known as Shakespeare and Co., about which a great deal has been written. Aragon sometimes dropped in, presumably to keep in touch with Gide and Valéry, who were great friends of the place. Aragon thought a great deal of Sylvia Beach, the owner, and her friend Adrienne Monnier, who had brought out James Joyce's *Ulysses*. Another familiar of the bookshop, Eugène Jolas, would often come to the bar of the Coupole. He was living in Colombey-les-Deux-Eglises, in the Boisserie, which General de Gaulle was to make famous one day. Jolas was on very polite terms with Aragon. He put out *Transition*, the magazine that first published Kafka in French and Henri Michaux; Surrealists were working with him. I never met Hemingway (whom I saw for the first and only time after the liberation of Paris) or Fitzgerald or Faulkner, and I have only a very vague recollection of Ford Madox Ford. I didn't have the money to get involved in the literary world, and, besides, I didn't have the slightest wish to. The Americans also frequented the cafés of Saint-Germain-des-Prés, which were almost deserted in those days: Le Flore and Les Deux Magots. And they would often go over to the Right Bank. They had more money than the French. The British had an older, more solid, and higher social position in Paris than the Americans. They were mainly part of the gilded Bohème. Once, in 1930, at the Boeuf sur le Toit, Nancy Cunard introduced me to a shy blond man of medium height; his name was James Joyce.

On the other hand, Ezra Pound, bearded and always accompanied by a rather ugly but very excited little woman, was an assiduous habitué of Montparnasse. Aragon had put me on my guard against this admirer of Fascism, and so I was as unpleasant as possible to him, but I narrowly missed being kidnapped for a few hours by his small wife. The Montparnasse nightclub of 1925 was the Jockey, which Hilaire Hiler started. Buxom Kiki had drawn all of Paris there, and a good part of two continents, to show off her firm breasts, her brood-mare hindquarters, her dazzling complexion, and her unprecedented brio. She sang funny off-color songs. Sadoul knew them by heart and would sing them whenever he spent a furlough in Nancy, emphasizing the provincialism of the setting. The Jockey had failed around 1927. The mad, elegant clientele had gone across the street to the Jungle, which was run by a man in his late twenties who kept things lively. His wife, a beautiful brunette with a hint of a mustache, would dance with the best customers every evening. The Jungle was all the rage in 1928. People were packed into a gloomy, vaguely exotic setting. Cheek-to-cheek with their partners, people would dance to blues in an area the size of three sidetables. Some of the songs, sad and spellbinding (for instance, "Crazy Rhythms Crazy Blues"), were played over and over, creating a sensuous, sentimental, and depressing atmosphere. The most extreme tensions of love and desire were achieved by the tune "I Can't Give You Anything But Love." The crowd at the Jungle was younger and more "in" than that at the Coupole and other bars.

Piano bars were also "in." They had started on the Right Bank, where Harry's Bar, patronized in 1918 by Navarre, a war hero, and American aviators, and the Boeuf sur le Toit had perfected the formula. The pianist was generally a young American, more or less intoxicated, and often very talented. And people could dance.

In October 1928, I knew nothing about Montparnasse or the nightlife of Paris. Sadoul and our architect friends were already habitués of the Left Bank, but it was Aragon who finally showed us Paris by night. He loved bars and nightclubs. He had his favorite spots, often curious places, in all parts of town: small American bars, stylish, frequently unusual, generally discreet. For the young Surrealists and for those of our friends who never got to join the group but who were introduced to Aragon, he was the arbiter of etiquette. We thought that he knew everything; he happily gave references for clubs, brothels, trysting places. He was a triumph in Montmartre; I hardly ever went along with him, except to the Tabarin, where six or seven superb girls performed a dazzling French cancan. His favorite spot in Montmartre before 1928 was Zelly's.

Aragon's arrival at Brik Top, a cabaret for American Negroes in the Pigalle section, was something like a sacred rite. Brik, a big, stout, black songstress, had a soft spot for Aragon. I assume that the author of *Anicet* had spent many evenings there with Nancy Cunard. The moment he stepped in, the boss lady would welcome him with deferential friendliness and the band would start playing the new "Saint Louis Blues." At least that's what Aragon told us. But since I witnessed it once, it would be ungracious of me not to believe that the same thing happened every time he showed up. The last bar that I discovered through Aragon and which I went to only once thereafter, was the Bateau-Ivre, a fly-by-night drinking place one flight up on Place de l'Odéon.

André Breton hardly ever came to Montparnasse. He not only loathed the fashionable clubs in his own neighborhood, but despised the snobbish, café-society atmosphere of Montparnasse. And he cared no more for the "intellectual" and "artistic" climate of Carrefour Vavin. In either setting the role playing, the clever skill with which people presented themselves as painters or literati seemed to spoil the element of chance in advance and took away any sense of anticipation. The men or women he daily prepared to meet or get to know could not patronize the places reserved for the ambitions and self-display of a few dozen hangers-on or shrewd climbers. At the Coupole, there was every chance that Breton would find people he couldn't be bothered with. He considered them mediocre, had already insulted them or felt like insulting them, or had so little esteem for them than he didn't care to spend a couple of hours in their close company.

Sadoul's troubles and Aragon's presence had already begun to interfere with my fine resolutions. I wanted to help Sadoul find his happiness. Though he was older, I felt I knew more than he about tactics of love. I went along to Montparnasse with him, getting home very late and also sleeping very late, and kept putting off my plan to work in a factory. Finally, I screwed up my courage one day and went to the personnel office of Ernault a few minutes before 7 A.M. They sent me to the stockkeeper to handle machine parts in a dirty, freezing loft, under the quizzical eye of a man who knew all the terminology. I came home ten hours later, quite disgusted, and fully resolved not to try it again for some time.

The Party had assigned me to the 6th Section and to a neighborhood cell that met a block from my home. There I found a disorder such as I had never known. The section was one of those in which my criticisms of the previous spring had had the least effect. It was controlled by speechifying workers fully determined to make a career for themselves in political or union bureaucracy in order to avoid having to work in a factory. I knew them rather well, and we didn't get along. They were stupid and intolerant, and their vetoes and tongue lashings were draining all the ideological or corporative organizations that gravitated around the Communist Party—labor unions, tenants' groups, veterans, *Secours Rouge*, and so on. Their excuse was that they were eliminating the opportunists and the Social Democrats. They were outdoing the sectarianism that was taking hold of the entire Party. They organized meetings of the uncompromising members, regurgitating bufoonish secrets that could at best hold back the most honest, the least calculating, and the most lucid people from their daily work. They were not men of action. They devoted themselves to rhetoric and vituperation in a smaller and smaller circle. I was placed as an instructor in a cell of railroad workers, and all they talked about was the struggle against right-wing and left-wing deviationists. Ultimately, they expelled or disgusted nearly all the workers who had made the mistake of sympathizing with the militants who dreamed of a rapprochement between the two union centers, Jouhaux's and the Party's. After a few weeks of these aberrant exercises, which at times seemed to need some help from the police, I had no one left to instruct. I became less assiduous and, from a distance, merely helped prepare for the great demonstrations that recurred throughout 1929, with fewer and fewer participants.

Aragon threw quite a number of parties. They generally started a little before midnight in the large room on the ground floor. The small tea cart would offer a bottle of Noilly-Prat and very plain white table wine. The visitors included Pierre Unik, Jean Caupenne, occasionally some Belgian or other, and almost always Maxime Alexandre, who worshipped Aragon. The conversation would start with the news of the day: who had run into whom, who was going out with whom. The talk was filled with mannerisms, nearly all of them picked up from Louis Aragon. Thus women were hardly ever mentioned by name; we would say: "I ran into that woman." Everyone knew who was meant because we always talked about the same five or six young beauties who were on our minds or in our hearts. Aragon rapidly directed the conversation, telling tales, recalling his childhood and his youth, or improvising lengthy speeches to explain so-and-so's behavior, a motivation, a choice. His first novels contain all the yarns he spun at our place on Rue du Château. As fine as the written versions may be, they haven't made me forget the originals. Everything that wasn't episodes, experiences, or memories would deal with politics, philosophy, or morality, and resembled the *Treatise on Style*. I would participate in the discussions, trying to defend materialism and Marxist principles, Leninist and Stalinist interpretations, and I noted that Aragon never contradicted me on doctrine or on the general line of the Comintern. Gradually he accepted its cogency. I sensed that Aragon was daily taking the positions of the Party more firmly. I felt a great satisfaction, which in my eyes justified the abatement of my zeal in the Party organizations and the growing amount of time I was devoting to Surrealism.

But political or philosophical debates filled only a small fraction of the nights on Rue du Château. Memories of adolescence, the present state of hearts, poetry, and literature, a sort of collective introspection achieved through games, questions, and answers, took up most of our time together. And it was here that Aragon reached a high point, with his verbal talents and his quick, subtle mind. While speaking, he would pace up and down the entire length of the large downstairs room. He walked as far as the Caligari mirror covering the back wall, between the staircase and the door to my room. He would gaze at his reflection a long time and then come back. This little eccentricity was very amusing.

Conversation would sometimes give way to reading aloud. It was always Aragon who did the reading, while walking of course, and, again, he would look at his image in the mirror. He always read poems or prose pieces that he had just finished, or some book he had come upon. He read very well, particularly his own poems. They would acquire a dramatic touch and intensity that they don't ordinarily have when read silently. Aragon could read out loud all night long. I remember hearing *The Eleven Thousand Rods* and *Three Daughters of Their Mother* and, at one fell swoop, Apollinaire's and Pierre Louys's erotic novels, which we didn't know. Aragon read these texts the way he would have read Bossuet or Pascal. The most daring passages assumed a dignity that excluded any licentious or libidinous innuendo.

We sometimes tried to find out who we were or wanted to be by referring to historical figures. Aragon claimed that he aspired to be Benjamin Constant; he wanted to be both the politician and lover as well as the author of *Adolphe*. This wasn't such a bad notion, except that he was ultimately a more important writer than Benjamin Constant, and a more faithful lover. But his political role is really insignificant compared with that of the liberal who drafted the Hundred Days' Constitution.

12
ELSA

BRUISED AS THE THREE YOUNG MEN ON RUE DU Château may have been by their heartaches, they were unable to delight in their sorrows. It just wasn't like them, and the times weren't like that. Anyway, the three cases were not the same. As far as I was concerned, Katia was off on a sort of long voyage; the mails would ease our separation, and everything would turn out all right in the end—not immediately perhaps, but at least it wasn't a vain hope. Sadoul had to rely on chance, on the sheer force of his feelings: although he was melancholy, he never despaired. On the other hand, Aragon knew that it was finished. To return to Nancy, to admit that he still wanted her, would have been deliberately entering Hell. Sadoul and I felt enough commitment to prevent us, temporarily at least, from having other affairs, although we were not averse to them. But Aragon could consider himself totally free. Erasing caresses with other caresses, forgetting the impossible embrace in the arms of another, are highly effective remedies that have always been prescribed to unhappy lovers. Aragon's seductiveness seemed diabolical, and there was a touch of envy in our admiration. Sadoul claimed that when Aragon entered a room, all he had to do was flick a finger to get a woman to respond to him. And that was apparently just what happened to one or two passing fancies, until the day when, at the bar of the Coupole, Aragon met Lena Amsel.

She was a very young Viennese dancer who had been in a horror film, *The Woman in the Golden Mask*. Pretty enough, and very well built, with German breasts and thighs and an athletic elegance that suited her nicely, she commanded attention from the moment she arrived in Montmartre. Her high spirits, her joie de vivre, her openness, her ease, her desire to be liked, instantly won her a small court of cool handsome men. Always eager to meet foreign women, they longed to take her out—to go dancing with her, to escort her to the theater, to show her the gourmet restaurants around Paris—and did their best to get to first base. But Lena was rather prim (she had a lover in America), and most, perhaps all, of her dates had to content themselves with the prestige gained from spending an evening in the company of a lovely young lady. Lena wasn't after money. She genuinely wanted to have fun until she could go skiing or make another movie. She responded to Aragon as soon as she laid eyes on him, and she let him know her feelings. Before long they were sleeping together and had become quite infatuated. But Lena wasn't about to be kept on a leash; she was a flirt and a partygoer. It was obvious that the complications of jealousy and suffering were on the way when Elsa Triolet appeared on the scene.

In the midst of the Ilya Ehrenburg group, which occupied the same table, near the entrance, in the Coupole bar every evening, there was suddenly a small red-haired woman, with a full bust and a milklike complexion. She was neither beautiful nor ugly; her face was serious and far from relaxed. Her simple and aloof bearing contrasted with that of most of the habitués. And her voice was remarkable—a tiny voice with an intonation that could be imperious and disagreeable. Her zealous companions were always deferential, attentive to her every mood. She came and went, often accompanied by a prettier friend whose regular features were firmer and who was more carefully dressed, but far less interesting. A woman who would look men straight in the eye but didn't seem to pay them any particular attention, that was how Elsa Triolet appeared to me in the fall of 1928.

It was obvious that Aragon interested Elsa. She was acting like any girl who wants a man to notice her. When all else failed, she asked to be introduced. Her immediate, almost shameless, attack revealed the tenacity and patient will to conquer that she displayed all her life. Aragon was unnerved at first. With his taste for mystery and the Surrealist's obsessive fear of the police, he thought it was a trap. "She must be a spy," he said when he told us about their first meeting. But Elsa was stubborn; she tried for more and used any excuse to be near him. Whenever Sadoul or I entered the Coupole, Elsa (at the time, we called her Ella) would call to us gently and pleasantly. She never hid her feelings for Aragon, as she sat down and sympathized with our melancholy. But we were on our guard. We knew about Aragon's affair with Lena. He told us he was avoiding Elsa, that there was no question of his having anything to do with that unlikable woman who frightened him.

Elsa was approximately the same age as Aragon. Although still a young woman, she was far beyond my twenty years. To rouse my interest, she would have had to be ten years older or younger. At first I found her extremely pushy and indiscreet; she was almost impossible to shake off, and I didn't like the perfume she wore. Little by little, however, I began to find her charming and appealing. I was often alone in the Coupole for hours on end—sometimes without dinner, slowly sipping a mug of beer, waiting for Sadoul or Aragon to come so that I would have the heart to go home to bed—and she and I had long conversations. By repeating our talks to Aragon, I became part of her plans. The possible spy gradually gave way to a woman who was madly in love and had vowed to get her man.

Elsa came from a Jewish family of the Russian intelligentsia. They were understandably hostile to the Tsarist aristocracy because of the latent racism in the court's entourage, and they dreamed of a democracy along Western lines—an image that young bourgeois women tended to confuse with that of Parisian life and the pleasures of Monte Carlo. Elsa's older sister Lili, the kind of Russian woman whose charm, intelligence, and sense of life draw men, arouse passions, and defy all barriers, had surrounded herself with young poets and revolutionaries. (Her affair with Mayakovsky is well known.) She married Brik, a Menshevik who managed to adapt himself to every situation and served as a government minister for a long time. In 1917 Elsa was hardly an adult, but she soon lost her enthusiasm and came to hate the Revolution and the Bolsheviks. She believed that she wasn't meant for a life of misery and disorder, and all she wanted was to escape what she saw around her and avoid seeing what she sensed was coming.

André Triolet was a young bourgeois, from a family of rich land-owners. A man of pleasure, with an excellent education, he was determined to flee boredom no matter what form it took—all in all, a perfect product of the Belle Epoque. Intelligent, curious, and skeptical, he liked women and horses more than anything. In 1914 he was a young dragoon assigned to the English army as an interpreter, but he was lucid as well as courageous and soon became disgusted by the inconveniences and horrors of war. He felt absolute scorn for the skills of the Allied generals, and when the French government assembled a corps of officers to give the Russians fresh heart and keep them in the camp of the Entente, he volunteered. His interest in the Russian Revolution led him to join the mission that was to make some of its members famous because of their active sympathy for the Bolsheviks.

Triolet was far too shrewd not to realize that the new Russia was to be created by the Socialists. As part of Lili Brik's milieu, he felt —without sharing Captain Sadoul's ideas—a certain sympathy for the most determined revolutionaries, especially the Bolsheviks. They alone seemed capable of staving off anarchy: it was obviously necessary to make peace and give the land to the peasants.

But Triolet himself preferred to mind his own business. He fell in love with little Elsa Kagan, who was literally carried away by the elegant and forceful Frenchman. She followed him across Siberia during the pursuit of the Czechoslovakian contingents. Triolet liked to keep his adventures short, however, and managed to move on to Japan as quickly as possible. From there he traveled to San Francisco, which was where, I believe Elsa officially became Madame Triolet. After the demobilization, they traveled to Tahiti. But André Triolet, who was not a one-woman man, had grown tired of Elsa's small white body. And she, for her part, had reached her goal: far from Russia and its revolution, she had become French and had spent a honeymoon straight out of an English novel. It was time to return to Europe and live out the life in which her husband had been merely the first chapter. For the next few years this was not as easy as she had imagined.

I was fond of André Triolet, and he certainly liked me. His manner with women was enchanting. He had a strong sense of responsibility: each break-up involved obligations that he fulfilled with punctuality and discretion. "You can't spend more than three years with the same woman," he declared. But whenever he left a mistress, he would pay her some sort of alimony until she managed to get along on her own.

Thus Elsa received a monthly sum of three thousand francs from the husband with whom she did not live. Triolet would often invite her to visit, and she received him with his new and his old mistresses.

No one would have suspected that there had ever been anything but friendship between this man and this woman, if both of them, by mutual consent, hadn't told their story.

In 1928, André Triolet's mistress was a lovely brunette, named Nicole, not much older than I. He was preparing to break with her and counted on me to help him make it as painless as possible. While he was off playing around, Nicole was left in my hands. He gave me a bit of money to take her to dinner and escort her around Montparnasse. I was blind because I was in love with Katia, but I was also totally stupid. One day, Nicole brought everything to a head by proposing to me. "It will be a marriage of convenience," she said, "but it'll help me some into an inheritance." In order to speed things up, André Triolet took us to Saint-Efflam one day in 1929. There we joined Elsa, Aragon, and Sadoul, who were staying in a small hotel in the middle of Baie des Anges. I was still stupid, but light was dawning. Nevertheless, I didn't feel capable of anything more than a one-night stand.

André Triolet took over my education in the ways of Paris. He introduced me to ascot ties, took me to Washington Tremlett, the most elegant shirtmaker in Paris, and explained that only Englishmen could wear club ties; anyone else was merely an intruder or impostor if he wore colors he was not entitled to. "You can sleep with any women, with very few exceptions," he declared. "Do you know what cruising is? It's a sport I often practice. Around three o'clock, you stand in front of the first-class area in a Métro station on the Champs-Elysées: Etoile or George V. You wait a few minutes; that's the time of day they come out. As soon as you catch sight of something interesting, you get on the next train with her. And then you follow her. They always take you to the same places: Rue du Faubourg-Saint-Honoré, Rue Royale, or Rue de la Paix. They window-shop, stopping in front of a jeweler's, or a handbag shop, or a shoe store. Now you go up and ask if you can buy something for her. There's only a five-percent chance this will fail, and you get down to business within an hour—after the purchase of course. Not one woman in two has the heart to resist the chance to profit immediately from your good intentions."

My father's stove had made the place on Rue du Château very cozy. And Aragon had provided some financial help, even though the author of *Anicet* was very short of cash. His presence also attracted many visitors. I regularly vacuumed all the rooms, and waxed the linoleum in the studio to a dazzling shine, so the premises were ready for company. The decoration changed slightly. Following the direction of the original tenants, we brought in signs or placards stolen from shops in the neighborhood. Over the mirror, a superb advertising board announced, *Dry Vegetables Have Arrived.* We also displayed a bookmaker's sign.

But the great innovation was the objects stolen from churches. On Palm Sunday 1928, Blech, Baldensperger, Sadoul, Caupenne, and I visited our families in Lorraine. The car broke down in a small town in Champagne, immobilizing us for two hours. The whole group went to the church, which was still deserted. We started fooling around and finally carried off the fat book of the Gospels, reveling in this trick played on the priest a few moments before mass at which he was supposed to read the longest gospel of the year. The fruit of this larceny was carefully placed on the fur tabernacle with the human head. In November 1928, Jean Caupenne's father had to go to Gers, where he owned several farms. He was a very gentle and very middle-class man dominated by his son, who had resolved not to work. Caupenne saw this trip as a chance to drive his speedy Delage for 1500 kilometers, but the prospect of spending an entire week alone with his father and some farmers spoiled it. So he invited me along, and I liked the idea. I had exhausted all my financial means, and at least I would be properly fed for a couple of days. We were supposed to wait half a day in a huge county seat of Gers while Caupenne, Sr., visited his lawyer and his banker. But we were much too impatient for that. First of all, we lifted a splendid billboard that decorated the fairgrounds: *Nomads not allowed to park here.* It was just what we needed on Rue du Château. Next, according to a well-established Surrealist rite, we went to the church. It was deserted, so we conscientiously pissed into the holy-water basins, filled the collection box with pebbles, and filched all the ornaments on the altar, including the crucifix. Opening the tabernacle, we removed the ciborium, which was filled with consecrated wafers. That was a fine caper. At the general store, we bought the paper, cardboard, and string that we needed to make up a solid package, and we mailed the whole batch to Monsieur Louis Aragon, poet, 54 Rue du Château, Paris.

Our shipment met with success. When we came back, Aragon showed us how he used the stolen goods to decorate the toilets. (Two photographs were published in the special issue of *Variétés* on *Surrealism in 1929.*) The crucifix functioned as a handle for the flush chain, and that little closet became one of the prime attractions in the place. It had its finest effects when members of our families came to visit.

We hypocritically suggested the use of the sacrilegious rooms, encouraging people to satisfy a need they had neglected. When they came back out, the expressions on their faces were priceless. Surrealism was exactly what people wrote about it—scandal for scandal's sake. Often our guests were so terrified that they left at once. As for the sign warning nomads, Sadoul had hung it over the dining table, in the middle of the unbleached linen. Tint upon tint, that was the height of good taste.

Mayakovsky came to Paris. No other Russian poet could have aroused the interest of the Surrealists. Elsa Triolet was actually relying upon his presence to break through the hesitant courtesy that Aragon displayed toward her. Aragon wanted to meet Mayakovsky, and he decided to throw a huge party on Rue du Château in honor of this tall Slav with the frank, open face, who didn't speak a word of French. It was attended by all the Russians from the Coupole, a few Surrealists, and two or three pretty girls. Lovely Tatiana, whom Mayakovsky had been deeply in love with ever since his arrival in Paris, was also there. The phonograph played Duhamel's marvelous collection of blues, to which I had added the Armstrongs and Sophie Tuckers that I had begun to buy, plus a few current hits, such as "Ol' Man River" and "Hallelujah." I hadn't heard from Katia for several weeks and, in the throes of depression, wondered just what I was doing there. I didn't want to talk to anyone; so I went up to the loggia and opened one of the windows to look down at the others drinking and dancing. Suzanne II had just arrived; Sadoul was radiant with joy. Aragon's affair with Lena Amsel had completely transformed him. I felt desolate and unhappy. Since I didn't move from my window, Aragon, who saw everything, joined me up there; this kind of attentiveness is characteristic of him, and I was immensely grateful. Elsa caught sight of him and mounted the staircase: "You never showed me this," she said. "What do you do here?" Toward the back of the loggia, which was partitioned by a curtain, there was a large, low easy chair designed by Pierre Charreau. She took Aragon by the hand and dragged him behind the curtain. "What's this for, lovemaking?" I could see her hugging Aragon and kissing him on the mouth, and I realized what was coming. I was afraid to budge. I had to make sure that no one noticed anything and I was ready to use any excuse to prevent someone from coming into the loggia. Elsa had obtained what she wanted.

Neither party was disappointed. They left the loggia together and danced, but their way with each other had changed. In the eyes of the involuntary witness of that embrace, the small, plump, pleasant Russian woman, tenacious yet shy, had given way to a woman whose skin reflected caresses and love. She was defending herself as best she could, given her reserve and her obvious whims, against the weakness of her senses and her appetite for pleasure.

However, she still hadn't totally won. Aragon was only half conquered, and Elsa, even though she knew she had the trump cards, was not always adroit. She devised more and more chances for them to meet. Mayakovsky's presence in Paris supplied her with good excuses, but she knew she had to make Aragon absolutely lust for her body and yet she couldn't very well rape him every day in front of twenty-five people. Aragon put up a powerful defense. He admitted that he enjoyed sleeping with her, but he claimed that she bored him, that he didn't love her, that they had nothing in common.

Both Sadoul and I thought that Aragon had chosen Elsa. We regretted it slightly because Elsa often said disconcerting things to us. She didn't understand Surrealism and found Breton a crashing bore. Aragon finally declared that he had made up his mind to end things with Madame Triolet. He loved Lena Amsel, who had brought things to a head. "I don't want to see Elsa any more," Aragon said. "Please don't either of you ever tell her where I am. I'm not answering her letters any more, and I don't want to make any dates with her. Because of Mayakovsky, the Russians, and the intrigues that such a skillful and crafty woman can carry out, I don't want to quarrel with her. But I've made it clear to her that she can't expect anything of me."

Lena wanted to have a party on Rue du Château, to see the New Year in, if memory serves me. She invited Sadoul and me. Aragon hung up an enormous Christmas decoration with garlands and a profusion of birds made of feathers, paper, and sugar; birds were Lena's emblem. The great day was approaching. After a visit to the Cyrano, Aragon confidentially asked me to do him a favor. "Go to the Jungle tonight and sit down at a table. I've got a date with Lena there at eleven P.M. I may be a bit late. Keep her company and tell her that I'm really sorry about being late."

When I went to the Jungle before eleven, the place was almost empty. Little by little, the steadies, whom I knew quite well, were trickling in, and at eleven Elsa walked in. She confidently sat down across from me. The situation was becoming ticklish. Lena would show up at any moment and join me with just as much self-assurance.

Elsa was nervous and fearful. "André," she said, "where is Louis? I can't get hold of him. For ten days now he hasn't shown the least sign of life. He asked me not to come around. Is he sick? Is he in trouble? Is he coming tonight?" I replied evasively, not knowing what to do. "Answer me, André, I know that you know where he is. You're probably here because he's supposed to meet you. I beg you, tell me. He's supposed to come here, right? I'm very unhappy because I love him. You're in love yourself; you know what it means to be separated and to have to wait. I beg you, tell me where Louis is? And listen, do you know whether he's seeing a lot of that Lena Amsel?"

I decided to get it over with. After all, I knew—or thought I knew—what Aragon wanted. Elsa was probably pretending not to know anything. Or perhaps Aragon, who liked to maneuver, hadn't really leveled with her. "Elsa," I said, "do you really love Aragon?"

"I'm crazy about him."

"And do you think he loves you too."

"Of course he does. He's told me so."

"Are you sure? Don't you think you ought to figure out why he hasn't seen you for several days."

"What are you getting at?"

"You know I like you, Elsa. I don't want you to get on the wrong track. For Aragon, it's just a fling. Pull yourself together while you still can. You're barking up the wrong tree. Aragon doesn't love you. He finds you beautiful, intelligent, desirable, but he doesn't love you; he's never loved you. You've profited from his confusion; the break with Nancy Cunard destroyed him. He loves women, he loves to make love, but don't get excited. He seems to be interested in life again now that he's found a woman who may help him forget Nancy Cunard. Yes, Aragon does see a lot of Lena Amsel; he's really stuck on her, and I'm here to give her a message from him."

Elsa burst into tears. "No, no, you're wrong. That's impossible. None of this is true."

Lena and Aragon came in together. It was short and awful. "So it's true," said Elena to Aragon, "you had a date with her. Thirion has told me everything. He claims you love that woman, but I'm the one you love, I'm the one. I'm your mistress." Lena was dumfounded.

Aragon lost his temper: "That's insane," he said. And to me: "I didn't ask you to do anything." He took off. I stayed there with the two women, who were both nonplused, nervous, but flexing their claws, exchanging insignificant words. I myself didn't know what to do. I had assumed that as soon as Aragon saw Elsa, he would leave the Jungle with Lena or else stay there and act detached and sophisticated, as if it were natural for everyone to be here together. Elsa's presence could have given him a chance to make things clear with a minimum of explanations. Instead, Aragon had abandoned Lena as if caught in a mistake. "What's he doing?" said Elsa. "What a state he must be in. What if he kills himself? Go on, André." Elsa wanted to be alone with Lena. "He must be home by now. Make sure he doesn't do anything stupid."

Aragon had indeed gone home. Sitting before Nancy Cunard's photo, in the throes of a great agitation, he was drinking. All his strategy was overthrown; he had put himself in the position he hated most— having to choose on the spot. Usually he liked to let time take care of things. He greeted me with the most violent reproaches. "Who told you to interfere in my life? Who told you to speak about me and my alleged feelings? I asked you to wait for Lena, period! And you had to go and say things that were uncalled for to someone you hardly know."

I tried to make him listen to reason, without being too insistent. I believed that Aragon's confidences had authorized me to try and do him the favor of getting Elsa away, at least that night. I had thought I was doing the right thing. "But Elsa is really in love with you, and she doesn't want to let go." Aragon calmed down a bit. He got up, and began, as usual, to pace up and down, occasionally glancing at himself in the mirror. He launched into a huge tirade against women. "But what do you want?" I said. "Which of them do you want? I left them together. God only knows what they've been telling one another. Do you want me to call the Jungle and join Lena if she's still there, or should I say that you're coming?"

There was a knock at the door. It was Lena and Elsa. Sophisticated, at their ease, like two friends, they had walked over from the Jungle. Lena was now a little girl, submissive, caught in error, who admitted her naughtiness and promised not to do it again. Elsa was the winner, with the modesty of an older sister who's on to things a bit more than the younger one. "It was a misunderstanding," she told Aragon. "Lena now realizes I love you and that my feelings for you have nothing to do with what she's looking for and what she feels. She also knows you love me; she didn't know it before. A fling with you won't get her anywhere. She doesn't want to get involved; all she'll do is cause you more problems and anguish, which you don't need. She's leaving you to me, if you like. She's too honest and sensible not to respect you for what you are, and she's nice enough not to want to hurt me." Aragon had nothing to say. He knew better than anyone that silence will later be interpreted in terms of how things develop.

As I recall, Lena asked me to walk her to the nearest taxi station. Thus, Elsa Triolet entered Louis Aragon's life once and for all. She was never to leave it again.

Mayakovsky was a sort of giant with chestnut hair and craggy features. He had huge arms and enormous hands, made large gestures, and displayed the gentle manners of powerful men who can smash everything surrounding them if they're not careful. He moved with the deliberate slowness of people who need elbow room because of their size and who never feel the need to force others to give way or notice them. Listening to his sonorous, grave, accurate, resonant voice, one could easily picture the effect that this natural force of nature had produced when reciting his poems in the street during the worst days of the Russian Civil War. Nothing came of his meeting with the Surrealists except a confirmation of a favorable bias. He had two or three conversations with Breton. Despite the presence of an interpreter, the language barrier reduced their exchanges to banalities and generalities. Mayakovsky didn't speak French, he could barely get along in English, and if he knew German, that would have been useless with Breton.

The Russian poet was likable, but what could we say about works of which we only knew snatches in translation? How could we judge a mind whose communication depended upon an interpreter and which probably hesitated to give its all in such circumstances? Breton asked these questions of Aragon, who had Elsa as a witness and translator. At Niouta Simon's, I had a long and laborious conversation with Mayakovsky; I relied on my meager knowledge of English, and Niouta was willing to help us out. Mayakovsky claimed that the general line of the Party was as good a source of poetic inspiration as all the themes of Romanticism. The strides made by collective farming, the supplying of wheat towns, the importance of fine harvests for the building of socialism could become the substance of poems; the poet would decide on the means of expression. Did he really believe this? Was he so convinced of the excellence and even the aptness of militant poetry? Couldn't his need to write advertising verse for government products be interpreted as a sign of disdain for poetic language? Mayakovsky insisted that workers are alive to genuine poetry; they carry it inside themselves, unspoiled by academicism. History has proved him right —his poems have been acclaimed by huge crowds—but history has given academicism the last word in Soviet Russia. "What are you going to write when you're back in Russia?" I asked Mayakovsky.

"I'll go where the Party sends me. I'll receive my assignments from the Union of Proletarian Writers." This sentence, which ended our discussion, had the grandeur of Party discipline and the terrible beauty of a mission to be accomplished. I didn't yet know what the Union of Proletarian Writers really was—the mediocrity, vulgarity, and mindlessness behind that name. It wasn't until later that I fully realized the disenchantment, bitterness, and resignation implied in Mayakovsky's response.

Mayakovsky was visiting Paris for emotional reasons only. He was infatuated with a slender, elegant girl with regular features. She had been living in France for just a short time. Although his love was requited, things weren't going the way Mayakovsky hoped. He wanted to marry Tatiana and take her back to the Soviet Union. The young woman turned a deaf ear. She preferred clothes, luxury, and the West to the poverty she had fled and the uncertainties of socialist life. Mayakovsky spent a few days in Monte Carlo to try his luck, get his mind off his problems, and sacrifice to the old demons of Holy Russia. When he returned to Paris, Tatiana was still hesitant; she refused to go any further than Warsaw.

This emotional disappointment added further unhappiness to Stalinist oppression. Mayakovsky's position in Moscow became more and more uncomfortable every day. Isolated, in a society in which the men who had shone during the heroic era of the Revolution were suspected, disliked, and envied by the vindictive hacks of Socialist realism, who were setting themselves up as censors, claiming to teach literary form, taking over positions of command, and acclimatizing the police methods and tyrannical ways of the regime in the field of letters, Mayakovsky knew that his days of freedom were numbered. He was a living obstacle to the general cretinization being launched by the supreme authorities of all the Russias. For the time being, they could not only reproach him because he did not write canticles or monologues for the bosses, but they could also seriously challenge his activities during the Civil War. They brought up his personal relations with the heroes Stalin was beginning to expel and deport. As a further aggravation, Lenin didn't like Mayakovsky, and had said so on several occasions. He had criticized the poet's conduct as immoderate and costly, and his comments had been reported, collected, and published. What fine material for a trial! When Mayakovsky tried to leave Russia in 1930, he was refused a visa, and his closest friends deserted him. There is no proof that he was thinking of escape or that during the last few weeks of his life he ever considered treason. In 1930, no Bolshevik, no matter how threatened, ever thought of fleeing. Yet, isn't it significant that Elsa and Aragon waited until after the "thaw" before they published a volume of translations of Mayakovsky?

For several weeks after the liquidation of Lena, Aragon and Elsa lived on Rue du Château. Every day they were a bit more in love than on the previous day. Their presence gave life and cheer to a house in which the daily food and the heating remained constant problems. Sadoul ultimately detached himself from Suzanne II when he realized that the young coquette was making the rounds of all his friends before she granted him the slightest favor. Our young architects from Lorraine were starting to earn their livelihood, doing things which, for once, were of some use. Blech could go out with young women now, amuse them, take them around to nightclubs and bistros, whereas Sadoul had nothing to offer but passion, out-of-date cheap entertainments, and the privilege of witnessing at first hand the impecunious youth of artists who would someday be rich, famous, and honored. This was not a good recipe for seduction.

Blech's presence at Suzanne's side sobered Sadoul up. At the Coupole, he met Cora, a cynical German girl, lascivious and loyal, who had spent her last centimes on coffee and had no place to sleep. She moved in with us. She could have fallen deeply in love with Sadoul, but sensing that he wouldn't go along with it, she philosophically accepted her transient role. She had a marked penchant for sodomy; flaunting it, she set about making a list of all the slang or erudite French words designating that practice. She discovered De Sade and eagerly perused *Justine* and *Juliette*. I have never found another reader of the divine marquis as enthusiastic, avid, and industrious. Then she had a fight with Sadoul and started sleeping out, sharing the beds of some Swedish prostitutes who were steady customers at the Coupole, and whom I desired. She described them to me in detail, but she didn't advance my cause much. Although those opulent creatures condescended to say hello and goodbye to me, they were mainly concerned with their business.

Aragon brought in Frédéric Mégret, who wasn't even eighteen and didn't want to go home to his mother. He wrote delicate poems, did rather graceful drawings, and always manifested a childlike incoherence and timidity. He was in love with an actress at the Atelier. She was ten years older than he and, very amused by this schoolboy passion, drove him wild with her coquetry. Mégret slept fully dressed under the loggia, wrapped up in a torn and dirty Chinese bathrobe.

Once, after a fight with Sadoul, Cora came and lay down on the mattress next to Mégret's in the middle of the night. She couldn't resist the temptation to caress her neighbor. This took place right outside my door, which was always open. I was scandalized. According to our moral rules, Mégret and Cora had committed a misdemeanor. The next day, I criticized him violently and told him to go home to his mother. This episode shows how far the Surrealists were from group marriage in 1929! They were certainly amoral, but quite puritanical.

Elsa at first enjoyed herself on Rue du Château. She wanted to share her lover's life, to observe and get to know the rules of the Surrealist community, particularly the young men who seemed closest to Aragon. She also wanted to be sure of her ground. At night, she was always the first to turn in. With her plunging neckline, her lovely red hair falling about her shoulders, very sure of her effect, she would receive Sadoul and myself for a few minutes, abed like a *précieuse* of the grand century; we would gossip about trivia. She liked this court of young men, who were certainly respectful but whose eyes involuntarily dwelt on her neckline or on the freckles on her shoulders. She knew she couldn't hide much in that house; you could hear everything. Pretending to be shocked, she was amused at the admiration aroused by her sensuousness. Aragon cut her innocent bedtime ceremony as short as he could.

The modest comforts on Rue du Château could hardly satisfy a young woman once all its picturesque charms had been exhausted. There was no place to take a bath, and no hot water. Elsa felt very strongly about moving to Rue Campagne-Première, where Aragon had rented a large studio. His furniture, paintings, and books were already there, but it would take a woman to organize the place and make it livable.

In our pavilion, Elsa was still patient and prudent. Nevertheless, she knew what she was after. Once she was in her own home, everything changed. I have never seen a woman take a man so completely in hand. To establish herself in his life, she got rid of anything and anyone that bothered her. She reserved that man for herself alone, presented herself as his wife, and did away with the foundations on which he had constructed his entire existence.

It was as fascinating as a novel, and I would sometimes visit the studio as if I were reading the next installment. Very much the realist, Elsa first did a thorough cleaning in regard to women. Aragon was surrounded by former girl friends who had never wanted him for a husband but who were flattered and proud to have a place in what this brilliant man had written or was going to write. Only considerations of money, expediency, or status held them back from a mad passion; every now and then, they wanted a few more minutes of thrills. Then there was the redoubtable ghost of Nancy Cunard, her invitations and telephone calls. Elsa was an old hand at reproaches, threats, demands, and outbursts. She knew that Louis would always give in. It wasn't always easy at first, because Elsa, carried away by her impatience, would sometimes go too far. Shortly after they moved to Rue Campagne-Première, she got Aragon to break off completely with Nancy. Anyone wanting to remain friends with Elsa was forbidden to interpose between the former lovers, even for such inconsequential trivia as, say, publishing matters. Naturally, Aragon lied a bit, and Sadoul and I concealed the errands we got from Rue Guénégaud or Chapelle-Réanville. After two or three scenes, she got her way. In her presence, no one was permitted to utter the name of that Englishwoman. Her tyranny even went so far that she tried, unsuccessfully, to make us choose between her and Nancy; a trip to Chapelle-Réanville or accepting a dinner invitation was regarded as a gratuitous affront. I don't think Elsa was deluding herself: such demands were typical of the methods she used to assure her domination over the man she had annexed.

Then she got rid of the men. She found Aragon's friends indiscreet and something of a nuisance. She wasn't all that wrong. The door of their studio could no longer stand open like that of a bachelor flat. Aragon was a counselor and father-confessor to a good many young men, and even some who were not so young; they confided to him their troubles, money problems, failures, defeats, hopes. Aragon would listen patiently and gently, deal with mental or even linguistic confusion, and prescribe, sympathize, or comfort. Elsa brought some order into this constant parade. She reduced the frequency of visits. She did not cancel them totally, however, for after a short period of annoyance she came to understand the significance of this clientele both in Surrealist discussions and as a prop to Aragon's prestige.

The Revolution, Surrealism, the latent debate between materialism and spiritualism, war—none of these things really interested Elsa. "How can you be a Communist, Thirion?" she said to me in 1929. "Revolution is a dreadful thing. Perhaps you'd change your mind if you'd lived through a revolution, as I have. In 1917, I despised the Bolsheviks, and I'm not much fonder of them now." But what gradually made the difference and captured Elsa's attention was the fact that the Soviet Union had become a powerful state. It might be useful to have been born there and have connections there. She said she didn't understand Surrealism at all; she didn't like Breton, and he didn't trust her. She was particularly aware that within Surrealism, Aragon was not in first place, and that the constraints imposed by the unwritten laws of the group or Breton's whims were suffocating her lover's personality.

Elsa loved life. She had decided to take advantage of it and she knew the price. Ideologies and economic worries bored her equally. But she was realistic and courageous enough not to refuse a temporary political commitment or manual labor when necessary. If circumstances imposed such penalties on her, she knew that she wouldn't lose her way and that she'd quickly get out.

She always aimed high, for she felt that you only get what you aim for. Floundering obstinately in a dead end, breaking one's head against the wall, all the modes of behavior that she saw among some of us, struck her as the height of madness, annoying signs of mental instability or faulty character. She sensibly realized that human life lasts only for a few decades and that one-third of it is old age: everything you did during that brief journey had to focus on an intelligent distribution of the things you were capable of getting. First, you had to know what you wanted; then you had to want it very badly and go after it. Elsa loved capitalist comfort. She preferred success to money, as long as money wasn't lacking. In success, she was modest. She depended mainly on her own self-approval, and since she wasn't fanciful and tried never to lie to herself, she needed other people's opinions only to objectify her own stance. Once the goal was achieved, she didn't seek to elicit any new rounds of applause.

She gratified her ambition to the full. The only women that Aragon had known before her were the kind that just wanted to sleep with or go out with a man. Even if they were very much in love, they never cared about what that man might or should become. It was none of their business! Elsa desired the man she was about to take into her arms as much as any of her predecessors did, perhaps more, but she had no intention whatsoever of limiting his role to lovemaking or to a few social exercises. She didn't wish to leave the rest to chance and whim. She determined to build a life in which she would feel good with her man; she had made up her mind that he would bring her what she needed to be comfortable: love, ego gratifications, money, remedies for boredom. With this goal in mind, she took careful and objective stock of the treasure she had gained. She was certain she would make it grow, but in January 1929 she still wasn't sure how to go about it. She was in no hurry to decide, because she was counting on her practical sense not to let any valuable opportunity slip by. Nevertheless, things got off to a difficult start. In the scene at the Jungle, she had discovered Aragon's weakness: a certain lack of self-confidence could make that intelligent and alert man panicky. He showed an unexpected need to yield to a stronger authority each time his strategy and calculations went astray. As she got to know him better, she realized that it was possible to enslave Aragon because his emotions generally got the better of his reason. The success of their marriage thus depended on Elsa's lucidity and determination, and she could certainly lead her lover over to her views gradually. Aragon would furnish the weapons: he possessed a whole arsenal. He would have to use better ones and deploy them cannily!

As she approached fifty, Elsa became dazzling with good sense and tact. She replaced her vanishing beauty with the myth of eternal love and wanted the whole world to know that she was admired and loved. Thus was born the cult of Elsa's Eyes, which concealed the ravages of old age more effectively than any beauty parlor. No woman has ever obtained such an exaltation of her declining charms from her lover.

For quite some time, Elsa had been dreaming of becoming a French writer. I can recall a tearful scene after she had actually read some piece of hers to Aragon. The time for such exercises wasn't ripe. Elsa's greatest feat would have been to impose her novels on her husband. Not that her stuff was any worse than the writings of a few other successful women authors, such as Françoise Sagan. Thousands of people have read her things with a pleasure and gusto that they never granted to the charm and enchanting mystery of the tales of Lise Deharme, which were published at the same time. Indulgence comes with age, tastes change sometimes, though not so much that I cannot see Aragon's loving thralldom as fully responsible for his praises of his wife's writings.

So many men and women don't know how to fashion their lives that I am tempted to cite Elsa Triolet as an example. I wish that my granddaughter Marianne had as much skill, self-awareness, and sensitivity to others. To get what she was after, Elsa never took anything from anyone or hurt another person. On the contrary, she was generous. She allowed Aragon to fulfill his destiny, and if he failed in any way to become the major figure that we could discern on Rue du Château, that was his own fault, not Elsa's.

13
THE TRIUMPH OF PARANOIA

IN 1928, ONLY A VERY POWERFUL MIND WOULD
have been capable of refuting Marxism, Leninism, and the concept of
the Third International with decisive arguments. Marx's economic
determinism was as open to attack in 1928 as it is in 1975. Lenin's
theory of imperialism was as superficial in 1917 as it is now. Nevertheless, the least one can say is that these flaws weren't obvious then. *Das
Kapital* and the *History of Economic Doctrines* are major works, and
any criticism of them demands arguments stronger than those of the
conservative economists. For the last time, the Great Depression was
to prove Marx right, at least for the time being. There had been little
study of the German war economy during the First World War, of
American expansion, and of the premonitory symptoms of the building
of socialism in the Soviet Union. Certainly none of the works on
these essential factors of the modern world had reached the educated
public.

One can easily imagine my unshakable certainty in 1928. I was part of
the cohort destined to change the world according to laws as ineluctable

as those of gravity. We were emerging triumphant from a crisis of conscience, and all those who had questioned or expressed uneasiness were making honorable amends. I had shown my mettle as a militant: I knew how to organize a demonstration, direct a strike, set up a violent action. In art, I liked anything new, and nothing I liked seemed alien to the philosophical principles I had adopted. True, I realized there were hazy regions, the renowned superstructures, and that they were very widespread. But nothing prohibited my thinking that everything could be clarified and organized according to laws compatible with my principles. The fact that these laws were apparently still to be discovered simply made the undertaking all the more exalting. I might have the time to devote to this enterprise because the world was entering a new cycle of revolutions, and I would inevitably be one of its agents. The sacred law was loyalty to the working class, its historical development, and its party. By refusing any compromise with the adversary, by placing the superior interests of the proletariat above everything else, I would fulfill my life. This was, in fact, a new version of acquiring eternal salvation, but if anyone had pointed this out to me, I would have been absolutely furious.

The peremptory assertions defining the Third International, the intransigencies of class warfare, were not open to examination. Trotsky himself, during the last fifteen years of his life, devoted the essence of his prodigious intellectual faculties to problems of tactics that were often trivial and he was ill at ease with such rigidities. As for the members of the Communist parties, they asked no questions until 1933. Imperturbable, feeling that they had done their duty, the German Communists, under the watchful eyes of the Comintern, self-assuredly walked from the Third International right into the Third Reich.

Since the Surrealists apparently did not challenge any of the Communists' "immediate tasks" (to use the Party's jargon), I felt it would be a waste of time to sift through all the Surrealist writings in order to denounce every proposition contrary to the philosophical bases of dogma. Pierre Naville had been the editor of *The Surrealist Revolution* when the address to the Dalai Lama had been published and had advocated a rapprochement with René Guénon. After that, under the direct prompting of Breton, and despite *The Letter to the Seers*, the Surrealists had gone so far as to compose the tract *The Revolution First and Always*. They had also joined the Communist Party, which had involved a gradual acceptance of all the Party slogans and tactics. Could anyone ask anything further of them right away, especially af-

ter the incidents of the last few months? Lenin's most important contribution to the "ideological struggle" (another piece of Bolshevik
jargon, referring to the defense and demonstration of Marxism) was
Materialism and Empiriocriticism, the first French translation of which
came out in 1928. Although I was inclined to go along with Lenin, I
hadn't forgotten that he admitted that philosophy could be a "neutral
terrain, temporarily secluded" so that the more important "Bolshevik"
agreements on revolutionary action wouldn't be broken. Lenin was
never to regard philosophical divergences, no matter how serious, as
obstacles to the alliance of men interested in the Bolshevik party, in
which they even had important responsibilities.

The manifesto *The Revolution First and Always* mentions in its
preamble: "Our rejection of any legislated law is what makes us turn
our eyes toward Asia," This is accompanied by a note, of which the
most significant part reads: "Let us do justice to this image. The
Orient is everywhere. It represents the conflict between metaphysics
and its enemies, who are the enemies of freedom and contemplation."
Since this manifesto was published with the signatures of fifty people, it is difficult to attribute that astonishing sentence to any one of
them. Only Aragon might be able to identify the author. In any case,
it is highly reminiscent of René Guénon, the philosopher.

Guénon published the most significant part of his work between
1945 and 1960. At first sight, his influence on the people in this
book might seem insignificant. This may be true, in the literal and
personal sense of a writer's influence. But, whether conveyed by the
mysterious yet effective means used by sects or as a crystallization of
the antimodernist trends so widespread among the many Westerners
hostile to progress and to the notion of progress, the idea expressed by
Guénon represented a latent force after the First World War. Now,
looking back, I consider René Guénon one of the most important
authors for understanding the ideas and actions of men in the
twentieth century. His doctrine is the most accomplished and respectable manifestation of spiritualism since the great constructions of
the early nineteenth century. I am deliberately using the word "spiritualism" in a very general, popular sense, although I realize that
Guénon would have preferred "spirituality." I am thus, to a certain
extent, misconstruing, but, for convenience's sake, this term is more
clearly antithetical to the word "materialism" taken in the same way.
Guénon would not have been of his time if he hadn't succumbed to
the lure of paranoia, like the Marxists, and perhaps for the same rea-

sons. On the basis of a metaphysics, he proceeds, using the logic of twenty-five centuries of Western culture, to develop a well-ordered, satisfying overall system that will respond to everything (as long as a few embarrassing questions are eliminated at the outset). His adversaries tend to retain only his unlikely premises, contrasting the apparent inconsistency of the synthesis with the richness of the analysis, which demands the limelight. We have to ask ourselves to what extent a modern materialist dealing with Guénon as Marx and Engels dealt with Hegel might not set an equally respectable philosophy back on its feet.

Influenced by Leibnitz's ideas and discoveries, Guénon was a stranger to dialectics, whether Heraclitian or Hegelian. He didn't need them because in his system contradictions are all resolved in the knowledge gained through intellectual intuition when one moves beyond the level at which oppositions have their reality. Guénon does admit the reality of the external world, however, and the objective existence of matter. Berkeley is as foreign to him as the philosophers who believe only in the material. According to Guénon, unless the sciences are animated by metaphysics, their relative character will be even more sharply accentuated. Such is the case with the modern sciences, which sometimes study the same phenomena as that of the "traditional sciences." But the latter approach the phenomena differently, viewing them as the inevitable consequence of truths that are known intuitively through metaphysics. As examples of the "traditional sciences," Guénon cites astrology and alchemy, but he points out that fortune-telling is a vanishing deviation of astrology. Elsewhere, Guénon has explicitly condemned spiritism, theosophy, and reincarnation as fantasies of the mind.

Theoretically, the Sixth Congress of the Comintern had as its supreme goal the emancipation of mankind. Those who knew Bukharin, whose role at that congress may well have been the most important in his revolutionary life, unanimously saw in him a sense of the human, something one could not find in Stalin or Zinoviev and could not easily discover in Trotsky. The Congress's propositions are a concept of robots. *Materialism and Empiriocriticism* is an abstract polemic. On the other hand, all of Guénon's works, even the most extreme, even the condemnations of humanism and individualism, have a human resonance.

Late in 1928, a new poetry journal, *Le Grand Jeu*, appeared in the bookstores. It was edited and illustrated by René Daumal, Roger Gilbert-Lecomte, Arthur Harfaux, Maurice Henry, Joseph Sima, Roger

Vailland. The peculiar title revealed something about the character of the contents and the intellectual honesty of the main contributors; it was the same as the thick collection of poems by Benjamin Péret that the *Nouvelle Revue Française* had issued a few months earlier. At first sight, this new magazine presented itself as para-Surrealist. The influence of the elders was obvious and even annoying, though everything in it was several notches below them. Nonetheless, René Daumal and Gilbert-Lecomte were not lacking in talent or personality. The manifest content was a bit unsettling: it was a pale reflection, without the violence, of the first four numbers of *The Surrealist Revolution*. Stripped of any social reference, the anarchist bias even took on a rather mindless air; thus, the celebrated Landru, a common criminal, a vaudevillish and rather low bluebeard, was hailed. The new magazine also made an appeal to the East and to Africa in utterly dubious terms: "We are all yours, dear Negroes." The Orient they laid claim to was that of metaphysics, extrasensory perception, and drugs, according to those who knew the habits of Daumal, Gilbert-Decomte, and Vailland.

Aragon and Breton had already met most of the editors of *Le Grand Jeu*. They were not insensitive to Daumal's and Gilbert-Lecomte's literary qualities and to the Surrealist bent of their writings. These two men had sided with the Surrealists in certain public demonstrations. Yet this was not enough to win approval.

My own reactions were somewhat different. Over and above my reservations about its originality, *Le Grand Jeu* appeared to be taking up all the slag that Surrealism had discarded. I couldn't help worrying about a new wave of Oriental philosophies, anarchist attitudes, fakirish miracles, crystal balls, and hashish. There were passionate discussions on Rue du Château. Breton had just broken with Artaud and Vitrac, whose literary importance was certainly on a par with that of Daumal and Gilbert-Lecomte. The trials against Artaud and Vitrac furnished precedents for the condemnation of *Le Grand Jeu*.

I took part in these discussions all the more seriously because I had made up my mind to take a sort of militant stance among the Surrealists. My induction into the 18th Engineering Corps would take place by late April 1929. The growing disorganization of the Sixth Chapter, coupled with my interest in the life of the Surrealist group, had convinced me that I had a part to play and a duty to fulfill.

I hoped that Surrealism, as it presented itself, with all its richness and vitality, would join the service of the Comintern, which I identified with the development of the working class and, consequently, of the world. In contrast to other attempts since 1926, we had to avoid any temptation to reduce that immense innovation by forcing it into a mere political mold that was completely incapable of encompassing it. But any process of adaptation was doomed to failure if such encounters led the Surrealists back to the stammerings that had served them in lieu of political language before they had moved over to the Communist Party. It would be equally unendurable if new members were to increase the Surrealists' love of magic, or even subjective idealism. I therefore had to be steadfast and uncompromising in my defense of historical materialism, even traditional French materialism. Because I myself unequivocally recognized the objective reality of the outer world, the relations between production and exchange, and the nature of the means of production did not seem incompatible with the scientific study of dreams and psychic mechanisms, the existence of a human domain relatively independent of the socioeconomic context, a poetic and irrational approach of feelings and desires, I felt obliged to remain intransigent about any blindly dogmatic venture or superstitious beliefs. In short, I thought I could tolerate a few tendencies toward subjective idealism and philosophical passions for the marvelous.

At the end of 1928, the Surrealist world was aswirl with currents, attracted by outside lures, invitations, and vicissitudes, perturbed by André Breton's severity and his demanding personality. He was as severe in morals as in the criticism of ideas and works. It wasn't always easy to grasp his frames of reference and applications because he made a strict point of frequently redealing the cards and changing the rules in order to avoid any codification.

Soupault, Artaud, and Vitrac had already been condemned. All three of them belonged to that important faction that refused any political commitment. In mid-1928, I had participated in Breton's sabotage of a lecture Artaud was giving at the Sorbonne. The speaker had not yet become the lamentable, haggard, and rather disgusting wreck who was the joy of a number of epigoni during the last few years of his life. He was still a handsome man, at the peak of his acting career. I tended not to take actors seriously in regard to anything outside their métier. I seconded Breton's words, even though the gist of the lecture struck me as no more open to attack than most Surrealist writings. Artaud, very dignified, and overwhelmed by so much hatred and injustice, was on the verge of tears.

Breton was in the midst of divorce proceedings. He was separating from his first wife, Simone Khan, whose participation in Surrealist activities had been very vigorous. The divorce was not going smoothly, entangled in sordid problems of property rights. Some of us took Breton's side; others approved of Simone's conduct. The discussions that sprung up here and there followed hard upon the ones at Rue du Château in 1926–27. But they had moved beyond a rallying to the proletarian revolution and the Communist Party (on this point, the failure was patent) and had begun to question the very future of Surrealism and Surrealists. A thirty-year-old man's replies to such questions express his personal rules of behavior, his awareness of his own strategies and ambitions, and the demands he makes in life.

With the publication of *Nadja, The Treatise on Style,* and *The Capital of Sorrow,* Breton, Aragon, and Eluard had overshadowed the other Surrealists. Were these others willing to remain in the wake of the leaders? And just where were these leaders heading? Automatic writing and the cult of dreams defined the Surrealist aesthetic, or, more precisely, distinguished it from everything else. What would come from the acquiescence to Communist slogans? Where would the categorical refusal to cooperate with anyone belonging to established society take them? Eluard had no problem: he was not poor and could spend his life writing the fine poems that, by consensus, gradually assured him a top rank. But *The Treatise on Style* was nothing but a lovely display of fireworks. *Nadja,* to be sure, was a vast stride forward, like *Les Pas Perdus* or *The Surrealist Manifesto!* What were Aragon and Breton aiming at? Artaud had been ousted because he was a movie actor, Vitrac for writing plays, Soupault for publishing novels. Did the others intend to be satisfied with a long career as demonstrators and smashers?

When the head of a party or a group sees that he is no longer in a position to unify all his people wherever and however he wishes, when he senses murmurings among the rank and file, when he is no longer certain that an outside event, even when it abruptly proves him right, will actually quiet the qualms and criticism and discourage intrigues, then he simply has to work up a tempest in a teapot. Lacking new conquests to propose, he must designate a new enemy, fight against hesitation, set up bogus trials. At the same time, he has to gain new followers by favoring new, inexperienced people who are capable of enthusiasm and admiration. In them, he will find the absolute confidence that others refuse to offer. Among the novices, there are no mutual errors or failures as yet, and it is still too early for any recruit to set out on his own.

The December 1928 issue of *Le Grand Jeu* came at just the right time in the evolution of Surrealism. Brutal ruptures, solemnly performed major or minor excommunications, were typical of Breton. Aragon would rationalize afterward, but primarily he recruited, made contacts, and prepared new members. He wasn't always heeded, for Breton made the final decision, and Aragon's friends were not necessarily his. The most highly rated texts in *Le Grand Jeu* were by René Daumal and Roger Gilbert-Lecomte. The latter often came to the bar at the Coupole, and Aragon was interested in him.

Eighty-three students at the Ecole Normale Supérieure had signed a declaration against military preparedness. The civil and military authorities reacted promptly and, at their behest and with their help, the heads of the school, using pressure and threats, forced most of the signatories to withdraw their names. Nevertheless, there remained ten who refused to do so, and one of them was Paul Bénichou. Not only did they refuse, but they also drew up a new text. This longer, more violent, and more precise version attacked the army, the family, and the fatherland. This was sent to *Nouvelles Littéraires* in response to a vague survey on the younger generation, and since *Nouvelles Littéraires* didn't publish any of it, a few copies were distributed in the Latin Quarter. Some students in the various schools gave their approval—a very tiny number to be sure, but it was only 1929, and there was still a good deal of risk involved in demonstrating against the army and the family. Some of these students were contributors to *Le Grand Jeu*. After Roger Martin du Gard, editor of *Nouvelles Littéraires* had refused to publish the new text, Gilbert-Lecomte and Vaillant, both proud and embarrassed, showed the scandalous lampoon to Aragon, who instantly offered to publish it. It was thoroughly consistent with Surrealist practice. But in 1928, the university was less liberal than today. When he got wind of the new outburst, the director of the Ecole Normale forbade any publication, on the rather incredible grounds that the right of censorship was part of his administrative function. What's more, he announced that reprisals would be taken, and I think he actually raged a bit. The students gave in. That was all Aragon and Breton needed to decide to publish the text no matter what. But no one knew exactly what it said. In order to get hold of it, Aragon asked me to go to Bénichou, who was regarded as the most determined of the students. The discussion was laborious. The students had made up their minds not to let the Surrealists publish their text. They even wanted it to be totally forgotten. Bénichou himself seemed isolated. He rallied against their cowardice, but he had no wish to let Aragon and Breton use a declaration that had become so frightening.

Ultimately, Bénichou admitted that Gilbert-Lecomte had a copy, and that if he felt like giving it to me, I could make any use of it I wanted. I realized that the students were not ready to join in common action with Surrealists, any more than with the Communist Party. In short, they were like our friends from the Vosges, Blech and Baldensperger, who were certainly antimilitarist and ill-disposed toward most bourgeois values but who felt that the proletarian revolution did not concern them. Naturally when I went to Gilbert-Lecomte, he claimed he had returned the infamous text to Bénichou.

Breton felt like stirring up a rumpus. A scandal would show how various people would react to a subversive action. The publication of a text that the righteous and powerful considered infamous would fully expose the hypocrisy of the university heads. It would seriously compromise the cowards who had withdrawn their signatures and wished that all traces were gone; it would force the more steadfast students to put good fellowship beneath the defense of revolutionary principles, to overcome the scruples of friendship in the interests of an exacting cause.

The timing of this incident was just right for the clarification that Breton had been seeking. And Aragon too. In their progress toward the Communist Party, the Surrealists had formed a group of only five at the decisive point; now, suddenly, there were dozens of revolutionaries. It was with a view toward settling accounts that Aragon and Breton wrote their letter of February 12, 1929, and sent it out to eighty people. The text is a masterpiece of perfidy, demanding a choice between individual action and collective action (to be defined) and requesting the explicit names of those with whom one would agree to participate in any necessary joint activity. The accent was on the importance of individuals, and recipients were asked to judge whether they would refuse to take part in certain public *or private* acts. The addressees included all the old contributors to *The Surrealist Revolution* except for Delteil and Soupault, the group around Philosophies, the *Grand Jeu* people, Surrealists in Belgium and Yugoslavia, and such isolated figures as George Bataille and Pascal Pia.

I determined to devote all my energies to breach and rupture, preferring a small, hard, pure nucleus to any compromises or alliances that would lead to blazing conflicts. Such disagreements would go beyond my control and might unforeseeably throw people important to me far off the line I wanted to follow. The others would always be able to join this line on their own. I promptly replied to the letter of February 12. My response was published in full in the *Variétés* issue on *Surrealism in 1929*. It was essentially a list of banishment: Berl, Malraux, Barbusse, Naville, Francis Gérard, all the contributors to *Clarté* except for Fourrier, Artaud, Vitrac, the entire Philosophies group (Guterman, Morhange, Lefèvre, Politzer), and all of *Le Grand Jeu* constituted the long list of people with whom I would refuse to work. Along with everything else, I excluded from joint work anything concerning principles and anything that did not derive from the discipline of the Communist Party: the study of dialectical materialism, on the one hand, and revolutionary tactics, on the other. I suggested the immediate publication of several slogans from the catalogue of the Third International: statements against repression and war made up the fodder that I threw to collective activity.

My letter was well received on Rue Fontaine. I accompanied it with a campaign of explanations to the people whom I knew best. I frankly admitted to Aragon, whose indulgence toward Gilbert-Lecomte worried me, that the breach with *Le Grand Jeu* was, as far as I was concerned, a valuable first step in the pursuit of any Surrealist activity. I was as sullen as possible. I felt I had a strong position and that nothing should lead me to abandon it. I managed to convince Mégret, Unik, Caupenne, and Sadoul of the merits of my vetoes. They adopted them almost totally in their replies. I telephoned Fourrier to make him realize that the arrival of a few minor sorcerer's apprentices like Daumal among the Surrealists would reinforce the tendencies toward mysticism and definitively compromise the group's genuine adherence to historical materialism.

Would the people I was aiming at get wind of my intentions and the favor they were to encounter? Probably, for I didn't conceal them, and I was highly agitated. At any rate, André Delons, who suddenly appeared as a member of *Le Grand Jeu*, suggested in a letter to Breton on February 25 that as the first topic of common concern we ought to study a "protest against the more and more intolerable conditions being imposed upon Leon Trotsky." This was a peculiar proposal, since its author had never previously evinced any strong interest in politics. But the maneuver would inevitably divide the recipients of the February 12 letter along different lines than the ones I desired: the Party members, including myself, would most certainly be isolated, and their following reduced for the rest of the discussion—if indeed there would be any discussion left. Aragon, somewhat embarrassed, informed me about Delons' suggestion and admitted that it would be put on the agenda. "Fine," I answered, "but I won't take part in any examination of the conditions being imposed upon Leon Trotsky. This is an issue for the Party itself; it involves the internal life of the International. I've already expressed my opinions within the Party. Those people on the outside who want to question fully sovereign decisions in the Party and contest the absolute right of the Communists to get rid of their former leaders are committing an act of anti-Communism, and I'll have to treat them in that light." Aragon and Breton had fully understood the significance of Delon's maneuver. There was no way they could evade his suggestion, but they had made up their minds not to start any debate on such a ticklish subject. The Trotsky case was put on the agenda for the meeting of March 11, but it never even reached the floor.

Things were looking bad for *Le Grand Jeu*. Breton had just shifted his attention to the journalistic activities of Roger Vailland, who was editing *Paris-Midi*. Breton didn't much care for newspapermen, and Vailland's writings went beyond all bounds. We were in the midst of a full-scale police repression. Every week, vendors of *L'Humanité* and *L'Avant-Garde* and militants were being arrested and sentenced. The Parisian police, directed by the firm hand of Jean Chiappe, their chief, who made no secret of his right-wing leanings and his love of anything reactionary, distinguished themselves through their anti-Communist zeal. Chiappe knew how to win popularity, and he absolutely fascinated everyone by arranging little scandals and skillfully profiting from services rendered. In a rash of articles, Vailland outdid himself in paeans to the Paris police. But the height of bravura was a long article on a hymn composed by the head of the music section of the Police Department glorifying Jean Chiappe as the purifier of the capital. It was incredible! Vailland's comments were on a par with that choice bit of bootlicking. People who didn't know Breton can't imagine how furious he was when he came upon such pieces.

When the meeting was called to order in the back room of the rather sordid café on Rue du Château, several of the participants who had read Vailland's articles refused to shake his hand. The wind was blowing in the right direction: twenty of the people who had received the letter of February 12 had not been invited to the March meeting. Among them were Artaud, Vitrac, the entire Philosophies group, a good half of the old *Clarté* people. I advocated intransigence and vigilance, to the point of sabotage if necessary. Reading aloud Roger

Vailland's article on the hymn to Chiappe stirred up a fine row. The meeting went on to a trial of *Le Grand Jeu*. Ribemont Dessaignes was clumsy enough to challenge Aragon and Breton by comparing their former work at the *Nouvelle Revue Française* to Vailland's articles in *Paris-Midi*. He infuriated Breton. I felt that this might be very useful for properly orienting the debates, but they nevertheless went on and on. Daumal, Gilbert-Lecomte, and their friends were reluctant to condemn Vailland. I tried to help things along by making a scene: I jumped up and, after calling Vailland a cop, declared that I couldn't spend another minute in the same room as an apologist for Chiappe, and I stormed out.

For an hour, across the street in our house, I waited for the meeting to end. I was worried. Had I jumped the gun? I had counted on a general approval, a burst of indignation, and Roger Vailland's instant expulsion from the café. Instead, I had left alone. However, the trial continued, under Breton's guidance. The young men of *Le Grand Jeu*, who weren't used to political trials, were hoist by their own petard. Two or three friends, including Tanguy, came to join me. Aragon and Breton had heaped so many slurs on Vailland that he was totally demolished. They got him to agree to write a letter disclaiming and condemning his article in *Paris-Midi*. The text was to be published in *Le Grand Jeu*. All his accomplices declared their solidarity with his disavowal. As for the Surrealists, they could do what they liked with the text.

Naturally, once the defendants had left the tribunal, they took heart again and kept none of the promises that had been wrung from them. No one was surprised. The breach was consummated. I had won. Under the title *To be Continued, A Small Contribution to the File on Certain Intellectuals with Revolutionary Tendencies*, the results of the survey and an account of the meeting of March 11, 1929, were published in the special issue of *Variétés* I have already mentioned. The text was written by Aragon.

Today, my opinion of *Le Grand Jeu* has not changed. When Roger Vailland knocked at my office door in the Paris City Hall in 1946–47, I threw him out. This very mediocre littérateur joined the Communist Party after the liberation of France in order to run with the pack. After the war, it was no more glorious to serve Stalin and his reign of terror than to have supported Jean Chiappe, the Fascist-minded police chief, in 1929.

Gilbert-Lecomte's and Daumal's best writings aped Surrealism, with a lot of childishness thrown in, plus some mystical stuff based on a misuse of drugs. The things they wrote about the East and alleged experiments with extrasensory perception are juvenile attempts to turn the tables. Daumal never displayed the kind of honesty a witness and experimenter that Henry Michaux always evinced. The fact that he went to the charlatan Gurdjeff to learn the supreme truths is, in itself, enough to place him.

Since the Surrealists refused to contribute to any literary publication whatsoever, the editor of the Belgian magazine *Variétés*, which was widely distributed in France, suggested to Breton that he take over a special issue. Thus was born *Surrealism in 1929*, in which a good deal of space was devoted to Rue du Château. The cover reproduces the fur tabernacle decorating our large downstairs room. I myself contributed *Down with Work*, which was meant to offer the Marxist version of a frequently posed problem within a Surrealist publication. This piece is rather akin to Lafargue's pamphlet *The Right to Laziness* (*Le Droit à la Paresse*). Strange as it may seem, I hadn't yet read his text when I wrote mine. It was probably the only piece of his I was unfamiliar with. I had kept putting off reading it, no doubt because I thought its subject was useless. Sometime after the special issue of *Variétés* came out, I was curious enough to read *The Right to Laziness*, and I found that its conclusions were identical to mine. This was hardly extraordinary, because both of us had treated the same subject with the same method, but it did humble the pride I took in my dialectics. "I'll be accused of plagiarism," I thought, "if I haven't already been." I felt that my version was more amusing than Lafargue's, but generally not as effective.

Nothing better illustrates the crisis of Surrealism in 1929 than the laborious fantasy coauthored by Aragon and Breton under the title *The Treasure of the Jesuits* (*Le Trésor des Jésuites*). This was a series of sketches that were to be staged on December 1, 1928, by Musidora (Mme. Jeanne Roques) at the Apollo Theater on the occasion of a celebration, *Judex*, in memory of the actor René Cresté. Musidora had been the most noted French movie actress between 1914 and 1920. Her appearance in the serial *The Vampires* around 1916 was regarded by Aragon and Breton as a foreshadowing of Surrealism. Wearing black tights, she was beautiful and as sexy as one could wish in the rather thrilling role of a hotel thief. *The Vampires* and *Judex* were fairly dull productions by Louis Feuillade, a vulgar and untalented conformist, well-supplied with top actors and the good will of the public during the First World War.

In 1928, Musidora was fifty years old and several pounds overweight but dying to get back on stage in the famous black tights she had worn at twenty-five. Aragon and Breton were probably also seeking their mid-twenties. The sketches, which they wrote very rapidly, mixed minor reminiscences of the First World War (with a hallucinating recon-struction of the period style) with topical allusions to 1928. Monsieur de Peredes, the treasurer-general of the Catholic Missions, had been murdered in his office earlier that year; neither the motive nor the culprit was ever discovered. Peredes was the chief character in one of the sketches. In another, Aragon and Breton introduced two arti-cles of the Finance Law which were the object of a controversy between the left and the right. They facilitated free education in certain ways, and the "Republican" senate had separated them from the law. This was seen as a left-wing success.

All in all, *The Treasure of the Jesuits* was very poor. The perfor-mance of these sketches by Desnos or Soupault would certainly have prompted Breton to mobilize the group and create a scandal. His sud-den reluctance may be explained in terms of the emotional crises that the two men were struggling through during November 1928, but that is insufficient. The review, in my opinion, bears damning witness to the feebleness of Surrealism in late 1928 and to the fading creativity of its two most eminent representatives. Though they were barely past thirty, they had already written seminal works of twentieth-cen-tury literature.

14
ANDRE BRETON

IN 1929, ANDRÉ BRETON HAD THE NOBLE BEAR-
ing and dignity that he retained throughout the rest of his life. He
was tallish and robust, without even the slightest bit of fat, his erect
posture still allowed a certain litheness, and his gestures were infre-
quent but expressive. Carrying his head with a regal air, he always
dressed simply, with no concessions to any faddishness, whether of
Place Vendôme, the Latin Quarter, or Montmartre. He liked dark
shirts, preferably green; a discreetly eccentric tie sometimes lightened
a dark but studied outfit. I've known him to wear any number of red
ties. His hair was abundant and almost russet, slightly wavy, long, and
combed back, even when short hair was in fashion. At first glance,
one might have thought his mane a reminiscence of Symbolism, but
it actually represented an attribute of power, as in the days of the
Merovingians. His carriage had the nobility of his entire person. A
lightly gliding step reminded one of Versailles at the time of Louis
XIV, and there was something affected about his gait whenever he
approached people or things. His features were handsome and destined
to tempt sculptors; their regularity was deformed only by his character
and energy. His thick lips were wont to assume a sardonic cast, especially when he smoked a pipe. He would gaze calmly into his inter-

locutor's face with green-blue eyes, their expression both phlegmatic and pitiless. His eyes never laughed; like the rest of Breton's face, they were constantly attentive, sometimes mocking, always present, never distracted. Their activity could not fail to contradict the vulgar notions of what a Surrealist was like.

No matter where he was, no matter what the circumstances, Breton, through some sort of conditioned reflex or natural prudence, always kept aloof. His anger would never explode all at once, for it would thus have seemed unwarranted and would have lost its strength. It developed progressively, until a sort of outburst permitted him to reach Olympian heights; then he would roar. The hardening of his features augmented the violence of his words and the inexorableness of his pronouncements. If he suddenly felt an extremely intense emotion, he would muster an iron energy to control and conceal it; his voice would become only slightly graver and his eyes would dim with tears. He would never concede anything else, and he would very quickly pull himself together. Breton knew how to laugh, but his laughter was slow, contained, and limited to grave interjections. They not only responded to the humor of a situation or a comment but also expressed a nuance of sarcasm toward the people in question or the author of the text that had aroused the laughter.

He himself was never victimized by the reactions that his anger or his acquiescence provoked. His enthusiasm for other people and things, like his reprobation, had to be discharged instantly, for he liked to beatify and excommunicate; but his extreme attentiveness and his critical spirit would prompt him to changes of heart and re-examinations of works and people. He knew when it was advisable to rectify tentative opinions if the positions of the antagonists or new light shed upon a matter would allow for other views or justify greater hopes about individuals. He had no qualms about taking the first steps toward a reconciliation, which other people would have postponed indefinitely out of either prudence or selfishness.

He was a good friend; you could almost treat him like a buddy. Nevertheless, since he despised familiarity, informality, lack of constraint, he would naturally establish barriers between himself and others which were not to be crossed even in moments of relaxation. Although he knew how to keep his interlocutor in a state of relative dependence or discomfort, he was a good listener. When necessary, he would be very open about the esteem he felt, or appeared to feel, for the other party. He would, incidentally, play upon the intellectual well-being that his approval inspired in people. He could never be taken in, and he knew how to arouse confidences, confessions, and contradictions. He commanded a very wide range of intonations, with which he dosed his answers in order to specify or change their meaning as needed. Playing the judge or confessor, he would confuse his interlocutor, make him lose his foothold, or force him to confess or take a foolish stance.

He had the soul, the comportment, the resources, and the abilities of a leader of a school or party. I don't think it would be going too far to compare André Breton with the men of his generation who have exercised a personal influence that could hardly be due to their ideology or the available means of coercion: Hitler, Stalin, Trotsky, or Charles de Gaulle. Like some of them, he was absolutely selfless, had a taste for power, and fully believed he had a mission to accomplish. Like Hitler, he was subject to grandiose rages, and his polemical talent, vaguely mystical in tone, and his sense of leadership prompted him to march at the head of his followers if he thought it necessary. He had Stalin's need to put people on trial and to condemn and dishonor his adversaries; he had Trotsky's intolerance and polemical verve. As arrogant as Charles de Gaulle, he had the general's sense of humor and lofty style, his grandeur and his outbursts, and his concern with personal allegiance. He had no lack of political spirit. What distinguished him from dictators and heroes was his lack of ambition and his wide education, as well as the importance he attached to ideas, and to mankind and its creations. His aversion to the past and to social traditions made him more radical than Trotsky—the only man to whom he might be likened on that score, since the other three were various kinds of conservatives. Above all, Breton's preoccupations were more timeless than those of the politically powerful. Surrealism was not a collection of nonnegotiable demands or a program of reforms. It was a hazy whole, poorly delimited, that plunged deeper than Nazism, Communism, or nationalism into the human psyche because it did not limit its field of action to social or national life. I might define it as a religion without dogma or faith. The emancipating and revolutionary forces it called together would not be satisfied with a coup d'état or an insurrection, a new constitution or new economic structures. On these points, Breton was far ahead of his time. A member of the generation of pace setters, he had some of their appetites and used some of their methods. But the mass movements or intellectual developments that might be favorable to him could not come about in his lifetime. Nevertheless, the sort of spontaneous uprising that his passage through the Antilles generated in 1945 shows that the encounter of that man with a crowd could make the sparks fly and start fires.

André Breton's life and works will continue to be the subjects of theses for a long time, and someone is sure to write a book on Breton and women. Personal testimonies and correspondence will offer aberrant explanations like those that have been proposed for Baudelaire, Nerval, and others. Breton was on all occasions deferential toward women and never deviated from his delicate and slightly old-fashioned gallantry. His example made kissing a woman's hand a Surrealist rite. Breton didn't much care for libertinage. He encouraged his friends to follow the golden rule of elective love, which used to, and still does, attract so many young people to Surrealism. Like any number of men, he encountered love three or four times in his life, and each of his passions inspired texts or poems that are among the loveliest things written under such circumstances. Nonetheless, life set up harsh barriers against this quest for absolute love, and Breton sometimes found himself involved in self-contradiction. His difficult nature, and his indifference to luxury and security, along with the economic troubles he often experienced, made for more than one victory of sordid life over admirable love. He was greatly interested in the naturalistic descriptions of everyday life by lone men, the kind of descriptions at which Huysmans excelled. He relished their ferocious and despairing humor. When I asked him, after he returned to France in 1946, what the war, exile, and time had done to the woman who had inspired *L'Amour Fou*, he confessed that their marriage had not endured, that absurd details had destroyed everything. "She was incapable of turning off a faucet," he added. "Can you imagine how irritated a man can get in a hotel room or a tiny apartment, if the other person never turns off the faucets?" Although eroticism occupied a place of honor in Surrealist imagery, it was merely an intellectual category for Breton. He more or less explicitly rejected its presence in real life, accepting it only in the case of elective love, which was nearly tantamount to a negation. But he was not averse to a contradiction in that area; isn't a person's love life always a tissue of contradictions? Besides, he had his share of casual flings, though they did not militate against the value of his testimony to unique love. Like anyone growing old, he was fascinated by youth, a response that is probably nothing but one of the avatars of our dream of immortality. The last time I ran into him, as we exchanged a few pleasantries, a young woman came along on the other side of the street. Eighteen at most, in a rather jaunty black-and-red get-up, she was pretty and self-confident; her hair was streaming in the wind. Breton interrupted our conversation, stared as long as possible at the ephemeral apparition, and said: "Pretty little imp, isn't she?" The dictators and heroes with whom I've compared Breton had no distractions. Threatened and cloistered, they felt obliged to defend their virtue against any little imp who might ruin their projects. (Although I understand that Stalin had his imps visit him at home.)

André Breton exerted an immense intellectual and moral authority on a very great number of important men. His authority was deeper and more constraining than that of the master thinkers or leaders in the intellectual world. A letter that Georges Sadoul wrote to me on October 24, 1966, bears witness to that statement:

Dear André,
As you may realize, Breton's death was a terrible blow for me. We hadn't met for thirty years. But he had been a [spiritual] father to me, and I have wept for him the way you weep for a father.
You and I haven't seen each other for twenty years. But you have remained a brother for me. Couldn't we meet one of these days? I haven't had any news of you since I met your daughter Katia and her husband five or six years ago. But I came across you last year while rereading and filing your old letters, which are precious souvenirs and documents for me.

In November 1970, Marc Jacquet announced the death of General de Gaulle to Parliament in these terms: "Friends, the father is dead." This is rather confusing, but significant for the psychology of the generation of 1930. The odious pamphlet *A Corpse*, with which Bataille, Baron, Desnos, Vitrac, and a few others tried to reply to the *Second Manifesto of Surrealism*, was in the same vein. A perfect psychoanalytic document, it followed all the rules in expressing the classic revolt of the sons.

Breton often settled down in the cafés. The apéritif symbolized, for the Surrealists, a ritual of comradeship whose celebration took place only around Breton. In Paris, the settings were confined to a few specific areas: Place Blanche and its immediate surroundings, the great boulevards or, even better, the adjacent streets. I knew, among others, Café Cyrano, on Place Blanche, and Batifol, a strange café on Rue du Faubourg-Saint-Martin. Breton visited this café as if it were an office, with businesslike efficiency. The apéritif sessions became an almost permanent gathering for Surrealism. Assiduously attended, they were a ceremony of allegiance to Breton. The daily get-togethers of part of the group permitted the members to keep up with events, work out immediate attacks, devise ways to parry, and avoid any delays. The meetings were also a kind of test for newcomers; they sustained the leader's authority and allowed some participants to shine, others to elude oblivion and make up for their mediocre services by genuine faithfulness. The group went to the café around noon and again at 7 P.M. Breton liked to find his people there; he would amiably greet those who had not come every day and whom he would have liked to see more of. There was a hierarchy of apéritifs. All the anises, pernods, and so on, made up the aristocracy; their drinkers periodically regretted the long-standing prohibition of absinthe. Bitters were also held in high esteem, especially Mandarin curaçao, a black potion that effectively cleaned out your innards. Vermouths were tolerated with reservations and often elicited sarcastic comments from Breton or Péret. Aragon liked Noilly-Prat, and the appearance of this pale liquid before someone else always led to remarks. Day or night, it was identified with Aragon, which Breton, Eluard, and Péret did not quite approve of. They shrugged their shoulders and exclaimed: "That's Aragon for you." However, their minor qualms were never voiced in front of him. In Aragon's presence, no one would ever have gone that far; an imprudent person would have been faced with a lashing rejoinder in the inimitable tone of voice Aragon used to bring everyone laughingly over to his side.

Breton always addressed Aragon with a certain deference, even when their opinions diverged a bit. He acknowledged Aragon's preeminence over the others. They formed a sort of joint kingship, not only because of their great friendship, a brotherhood in arms and talent, but also because Breton needed it. Aragon had qualities that he lacked: a remarkable coolness (he never lost his temper), and greater perspicacity in handling thorny problems. When the outcome of a discussion became uncertain because the various interlocutors had strayed off in different, sometimes opposite, directions, when the give-and-take had thrown up obstacles on all roads, it was Aragon who worked out a balanced rallying point. Without resorting to a compromise, as some people claimed once the storm was over, he merely found a sensible solution to extricate the group from uncomfortable situations or hopeless entanglements. This made up for a certain weakness of character.

While sipping their drinks, the participants would comment at length on the daily news—the gossip about public officials, various sellouts by old friends, the ludicrousness of current events, the scandalous behavior of the police or the courts. Breton and Aragon would read aloud the most curious letters they had received. Strangers, some curiosity seekers, some invited by Breton, Eluard, or Aragon, would sit down at a table and be subjected to an entrance exam. Breton was the final judge of admission. He would lace his welcome with an ironic politeness, and his tone of voice was filled with many nuances. The condemnations were quite deafening, but the nuances quickly gave the newcomers guidelines as to how often they should come, or even whether their presence was desired at all. There were nearly always one or two more or less transient neophytes, dumb-struck with fear and admiration.

Important issues were debated at Breton's home after dinner. Invitations were tendered during the apéritif hours or via petit bleu. The Surrealists, particularly Breton, were especially fond of these messages transmitted by pneumatic tubes. The intimates of the moment set up the agenda during dinner. Breton would often dine in a restaurant; he liked cheap or reasonable places as long as the food was of a good quality, the wine pleasant, and the clientele didn't make too impudent a show of bourgeois mores and manners. Breton didn't care to eat alone. Aragon or Eluard would sometimes come along, and he would ask two or three young Surrealists to join him. It was always Dutch treat, but if someone was obviously low on cash the invitation would also cover the bill. More often, the poorer individuals would spot whoever had money and touch him for something during the meal. If the restaurant turned out to be expensive, Breton would use all sorts of excuses to prevent anyone from feeling left out for financial reasons. He didn't always succeed. Except in 1931–32, and probably in 1935, there was a rather wide gap in the Surrealist group, and, like anywhere else, money contributed to this. In his choice of cafés, Breton bore in mind the financial situation of anyone who might come along, not just his own. For example, there was a decent and modest place on Rue Lepic where the menu was not beyond my means. Sometimes, I came to the Cyrano on foot from Rue du Château and did not always have the wherewithal for even a glass of beer. Now and then, Breton would invite a few of us over for dinner but would ask us to bring our own food. We would buy some cold cuts, potato salad, and a bottle of wine—always on Rue Lepic.

On Rue Fontaine, when there was no debate on a topical subject, we would play cards, preferably tarot, or any of the numerous Surrealist games of chance: "exquisite corpse," "questions and answers" (you wrote down answers without knowing the questions), "portraits" (something like American "twenty questions"), and so on. Coincidences or irrational responses gave rise to astonished or admiring comments and developments during which some of the players showed a conformity that was peculiar, to say the least: they tried to get Breton to like them, even going so far as to ape his phrases or judgments. The most extraordinary and most typical Surrealist game was "exquisite corpse," literary or pictorial. Somewhere there are collections of amazing figures, with heads by Miró, bodies by Max Ernst, and legs by Tanguy; others are the products of less dazzling but no less successful collaborations of the imagination or talent of Max Morise, Georges Sadoul, Valentine Hugo, Georges Hugnet. The most fearful collective pastime was "inquiry," a public debate in a sort of general assembly of Surrealists and sympathizers. The most famous inquiries dealt with sex, but other subjects were also treated. Breton used these inquiries as a test for unwitting neophytes and people he was thinking of dropping.

Like "Truth or Consequences," the inquiries precipitated deadly quarrels, brutally separating or bringing together people who hadn't realized how far that perilous game could go. Sometimes, we listened to records. Breton said he wasn't interested in music, but he did like songs. There were also readings, which were very instructive because Breton used them to introduce unfamiliar texts to people whose curiosity might otherwise have never led them in that direction. The choice depended on Breton's moods, his discoveries, his concerns as a man and a writer. In 1928, the works of Huysmans were held in high honor, followed by other Naturalist books, such as *The Evenings of Médan* and *Earth* by Zola. Some of these readings reflected the obstacles, traps, and petty betrayals in Breton's private life. The interest in Naturalism coincided with the aspirations of populist writings and discussions about proletarian literature. Among the other phantoms who materalized for a few hours were Forneret and Sade, whose unpublished works were uncovered by Maurice Heine. In 1930 and 1931, there were public readings of texts by Dali. And some authors read works of their own: Breton read *The Second Manifesto*, Aragon read a few poems from *The Great Gaiety* and a novel, since destroyed, to which I shall return. Breton read solemnly and with virile grandiloquence. His voice would swell to emphasize fortuitous expressions or grotesque forms or situations; his intonation was somewhat like that of the actors in the Comédie Française, but simpler, truer, more modern, less affected. His readings always had a great effect; I have never again experienced so exalting a diction, except in Malraux's great speeches, in which his voice would often surpass the ideas, expressing a richer and more mysterious meaning.

Paul Eluard finally came back from his travels and trips for his health, which had often taken him away from Paris in 1927 and 1928. He enjoyed particular prestige in the group, because of his growing renown, his talent, and his parents' affluence. His real name sounded like that of a character in Balzac: Eugène Grindel. Nearly all the Surrealists were, in their heart of hearts, grateful to Monsieur Grindel, Sr., for the social standing he had given his son. Eluard's money and generosity meant a great deal in all the Surrealist undertakings.

Photographs of Eluard are astonishingly good, much better than those of Breton or Aragon, largely because of his innate hieratic qualities and his facial immobility. Eluard was a man of few words, but whatever he said he said well; he rejected everything that might ruffle his life. He was tall, slender, blond, with a poet's noble and faraway gaze and an asymmetrical but handsome face. His manners were distinguished and serious, and slightly condescending. At thirty, his hands trembled like those of an old man; his voice also trembled when he read, but he managed to draw very poignant effects from this. When he recited his own poems, his voice at first was blank, almost noncommittal, unintoned. Slackenings and heightenings of the timbre made the poem sound like a declaration or a warning, and the final words resounded for some time on the same level after the poet had fallen silent. Well dressed, in good health, he looked like *someone*.

Shortly before the First World War, Eluard had discovered a young Russian woman, Gala, whom he had married in 1917. A nude photograph of Gala never left his billfold, and he readily showed it to others: it revealed a marvelous body that Eluard was very proud to have in his bed. Even more than Elsa Triolet, Gala knew what she wanted: pleasures of the heart and senses, money, and the companionship of genius. She had no interest in political or philosophical discussions, and she judged people according to their effectiveness in the real world, eliminating the mediocre. She knew how to inspire passions and exalt the creative force of men as diverse as Eluard, Max Ernst, and Salvador Dali. In 1929, Gala was unemployed and without any commitments. Paul, rather libertine, was still very attached to her, but from afar. Max Ernst had just seduced Marie-Berthe Aurenche, a young and very conformist beauty, the kind of girl that every man wants to possess for his personal ravishment, at least for a while. Gala, never impatient, was waiting for destiny.

A captive of women, a captive of love, a captive of his dazzling gifts, of the sympathy and respect he inspired in all others, Eluard, in 1929, was less troubled than his friends by ideologies and revolution. He shared their opinions—he had gone along with the move toward the Communist Party in 1927—but his writings did not commit him as much as the others. His works were neither scandalous nor blasphemous; they were lovely but prophesied nothing. Max Ernst's collages and paintings, on the other hand, shocked many because of their obvious content, their implications, their challenges, and their graphic force. Eluard won't disturb the most conformist reader as long as he likes poetry and doesn't set too much store in classical form.

Eluard was also an exceptionally discerning collector and an alert buyer. His fortune allowed him to purchase any number of paintings and objects; he always acquired masterpieces. His relations with painters, writers, dealers, and musicians were very close, and he even refused to be on bad terms with people whom Breton had condemned and the group execrated. The Surrealists liked Picasso's paintings and respected Picasso as a man; Eluard was an intimate friend of the greatest painter in our century. He moved through contradictions with ease. His financial independence permitted this balancing act, and the only other person to do likewise was René Crevel, for the same reasons. During discussions in the group, Eluard would successively advocate contrary opinions, never retracting anything, moving from the most sordid opportunism to verbal extremes that were all the more violent in that they signified absolutely nothing to the man who used them so suddenly.

From 1928 to 1935, Eluard restrained all political activities as best he could and continuously defended a Surrealism maintained in the traditional terms of artistic creation. He was drawn to libertinism, brothels, group sex, more as a spectator and dilettante than as an active participant. Like all the Surrealists, he put elective love above everything, but any passion he felt for a woman never prevented his having flings on the side. Breton even reproached him for these characteristics, and went so far as to establish a parallel between Eluard's self-indulgence and the disagreements between the two men. Actually, Breton's judgment isn't convincing. Although it may sometimes have been difficult to tell whether Eluard's love was as great as he claimed— he may have had no marked preference or simply been afraid of being alone—I feel that by giving in to temptations, explaining that affairs weren't detrimental to an exclusive feeling, Eluard was being more honest than Breton, who refused to even admit that he was tempted. Nonetheless, the behavior of the two men toward women was quite dissimilar. Eluard had a sensuality that was totally lacking in Breton.

In 1929, Eluard was interested in a young woman from Berlin. Pretty as a picture, she looked like Gala, and since her name was Frau Apfel, he called her La Pomme. The Berlin express had left her in Paris, fickle and voracious, together with Rudolf von Ripper, a talented draftsman and engraver. That adventurer, grappling head on with life, was alien to our group. He was more or less truly accused of homosexuality and a penchant for drugs. Ripper and La Pomme had a social life in which the Surrealists did not participate—except for Crevel, a few painters, and episodically, Aragon. La Pomme liked Eluard, but she had a lot more fun with Ripper, who accompanied her to London, Berlin, Saint-Moritz, or Vienna indefatigably.

One rainy day in autumn Eluard met a tall twenty-year-old girl in the street. Dressed in a harum-scarum sort of way, homeless, penniless, starving, she was ready to turn a trick with someone just to have a warm place to sleep. Eluard was deeply moved. His tact and kindness multiplied the effect of his natural charm tenfold. Nusch, fresh from Mulhouse and about to go under in Paris, instantly fell madly in love with Paul. The poet was not insensitive to the physical appeal of his new conquest, but an immense pity also warmed his heart. He fulfilled himself as a man in the adoration that this young, insignificant Alsatian felt for him. But Nusch had to fight resolutely and stubbornly to keep the little place he had granted her and to conquer "her Paul," as she used to say in her Mulhouse accent. For a long while, La Pomme maintained the prestige of her easy ways and her life style. With the perturbations of the Depression, however, Nusch carried the day by means of love and tenderness. She espoused him totally: the man, his libertinage, Surrealism, his friendships and his quarrels, poetry, and, lastly, the Communist Party.

In June 1926, Kra published a new edition of *The Surrealist Manifesto* and *The Soluble Fish* together with *The Letter to the Seers*. The latter, written in 1925, had come out in the fifth issue of *The Surrealist Revolution*, which constitutes a sort of rift. The same issue contained *The Revolution First and Always* and a long and important discussion by Breton of Trotsky's book on Lenin. The simultaneous publication of such different texts must be seen as a definite desire to strike a sort of balance between the contradictory commitments of Surrealism. In 1925, and even more in 1926 and 1927, I had been bothered by *The Letter to the Seers*. True, this apologia for clairvoyance was essentially poetic and symbolic, but how could the rationalist founders be made to accept such an extension of metaphor? The new edition contained a preface of great interest in terms of understanding Breton's ideas, his development, and his contradictions (if the reader will bear with me until the end of this book, he will see I do not attach a priori any derogatory meaning to the word "contradiction" for an intellectual development. After explaining that he valued life and that this was a rather recent discovery, Breton wrote: "I realized that life was a *given*, that a force independent of the force of expressing and spiritually making oneself understood controlled a living man's reactions of an inestimable interest whose secret would be carried off with him. This secret was not revealed to me, and, for my part, recognition of it in no way invalidates my declared inaptitude for religious meditation." This introduction of metaphysics into Surrealism went almost unobserved. A bit further on, Breton defended his desire to judge his earliest friends who have taken fright and withdrawn. A few months later, he wrote *The Second Manifesto of Surrealism*, in which he attacks those early friends.

The Second Manifesto was an indispensable document. The meeting on Rue du Château and particularly the special issue of *Variétés* marked a virtual breach. Daumal and Gilbert-Lecomte, somewhat traumatized by their trial, had separated from Vailland, but too late. The publication in *Variétés* of *A Small Contribution to the File on Certain Intellectuals with Revolutionary Tendencies* and the favorable reactions to some of the answers to the survey (including mine) threw doubts not only on Vailland but on all the people involved in *Le Grand Jeu*. Aragon felt things had gone far enough. He and Breton tried to let Daumal and Gilbert-Lecomte know that the discussion could be resumed. Whereas Breton was preparing to break off with Desnos and circumstances were hinting that Queneau, Prévert, Max Morise, Tual, and Leiris were similarly doomed, even without having been personally challenged, it seemed time to start recruiting again. A reconciliation with Tzara was decreed. Tzara was alone; the reasons for the breach, when examined, seemed flimsy. On Rue du Château, Aragon gave public readings of Tzara's poetry; Breton did the same on Rue Fontaine to prepare us. Everyone already knew that Tzara was a great poet; they would even had turned to Reverdy if he hadn't espoused an intransigent Catholicism. Tzara had never taken a philosophical or political stance inconsistent with Marxism-Leninism. His good will was total.

Daumal and Gilbert-Lecomte hesitated. They wanted us to revoke the condemnations that Sadoul, Unik, and I had uttered against them. Aragon knew I wouldn't retreat. I could probably accept the idea that a Surrealist publication might include both an article of mine and texts by Daumal or Gilbert-Lecomte, but I would never modify my judgment against *Le Grand Jeu*. The affair led to nothing, even though the findings of the inquiries against *The Devil* (by Daumal) and *The True Phantoms* (by Jean Audard) were prominently published in No. 12 of *The Surrealist Revolution*. Despite the ten laudatory lines on Daumal in *The Second Manifesto*, the reckoning was wrong. Daumal, Gilbert-Lecomte, and Renéville added their little pieces of filth to the package of excrement that the authors of the libelous *A Corpse* were flinging in Breton's face.

In any event, there was no other choice, for Daumal and Gilbert-Lecomte were heading more and more toward theosophy, artificial utopias, a belief in supernatural realms and divination. All of these were antithetical not only to dialectical materialism but also to a metaphysics devoid of godhead, tradition, and drugs.

If we can form an exact notion of Breton's philosophical thought at the time of *The Second Manifesto of Surrealism*, it is far more difficult to do so in regard to the others (except Naville). All the Surrealists were atheists, and they all believed in the objective reality of the sensory world. They refused to admit that dreams and reality could not be reconciled. In this sense, they were expressing an absolute scientific truth, but most of the doctors and psychologists of 1929 who ignored or rejected Freud were still inclined to regard dreaming as merely a pathological phenomenon rather than one of the basic mechanisms of man's spiritual life. The claims of the Surrealists went a lot further than a reintegration of dreams in the ego; they sought a mode of existence in which waking activities and life in dreams were not obligatorily opposed or separated by social habits or constraints.

Peter Ibbetson, a fine film that was being shown around 1936, is an almost ideal expression of Surrealist life in which waking and dreaming are complementary; the only difference is that because the hero is locked up in a prison cell, he escapes many of the obligations and worries of everyday existence. Another example, also from the cinema, can be seen in *Nosferatu*. The hero rides a coach through mountain forests; at the turning of a road, the extraordinary road sign "Here begins the land of phantoms" doesn't alter the appearance of the firs or the mountain in any way, yet there is something over and above the waking reality: the Vampire. It is difficult to list all the traps lurking for explorers: the temptation of drugs, a belief in the material reality of phantasms, communication with the beyond, dialogues with Martians, and so on. Surrealism managed to sidestep these traps, although it barely grazed past them, putting them on a level with cheating at cards. The call to a total liberty that led to automatic writing, for example, excluded neither lucidity nor the use of reason.

Most of the Surrealists—at least in their texts—did not get beyond the demand for liberty in writing. Only Breton and Aragon forged further ahead. In *A Wave of Dreams*, Aragon speaks about a hypothesis formed in the group during the time of sleep: "The existence of a mental matter which the similarity of hallucinations and sensations forced us to envisage as different from thought, and the thought of which could be . . . only a particular case." This highly materialist hypothesis precedes an affirmation of absolute nominalism in the same pamphlet: "There is no thought outside of words." This idea had little appeal to Breton; he would never have written such a sentence. To say the same thing, he would have used the term *esprit* (mind). It is not uninteresting to stress this difference of language between the two men who were both preoccupied with the same issues.

None of the Surrealists were interested in scientific discoveries. André Breton didn't care for the practical side of research. The actual production or exchange of things seemed ludicrous to all the Surrealists and was likely to create unbearable constraints. Surrealism "tends to ruin definitively all other psychic mechanisms and replaces them with itself in solving the main problems of life." Of course, society in 1929 did not permit anything of the sort. Unless we had admitted that Surrealism was merely a utopia or simply another point of view, we had to want that society destroyed and replaced with a society of freedom. This train of thought resulted in *The Revolution First and Always*. The exercise of total freedom, the emancipation of the mind, apparently had to come after the destruction of the capitalist regime.

From that point, everything became more contingent, for these men who were passionately interested in dreams and the unconscious and were exceptionally gifted for artistic creation began to move in a direction where action was more important than any other behavior.

Breton's respect for Hegel, his openness to him despite everything, had facilitated his rallying to dialectical materialism. Nevertheless, Breton persisted in hoping that through transformations and negations, one could ultimately reach a favored intellectual zone, a sort of sublimation of the mind akin to absolute knowledge. As for historical determinism, it did not contradict a Surrealist idea of the time because it had to lead to the emancipation of man. One could regard that emancipation as total, for it was consistent with Marxist principle that once the human condition had changed and the wage system vanished, the mind in its turn would be freed of any debilities that can be conveniently ascribed to the capitalist system. All things considered, however, this reassuring determinism had several gaps. If men living in the capitalist regime could imagine the moral and mental behavior of individuals after the abolition of wage earning, imagine it in a state that was about to disappear, wasn't this a formal contradiction of the theory of superstructures created by the structure? If a few people were already capable of elevating themselves above and beyond the present, couldn't others, and still more people, imitate them? How would the destruction of the system benefit the mind? The contradiction was apparently resolved by admitting that the prophets could rely on prophesy because they belonged to a privileged milieu that simulated certain conditions of life in a classless society. The Surrealists managed to score a point by quoting Lautréamont: "Poetry has to be made by everyone and not just one person." Russian and Chinese society turned out to be rather disappointing in that respect.

Marx and Engels had had the same experiences. Since not all workers are conscious of belonging to a social class with a messianic destiny, it is at the very least peculiar that historical determinism needs a combination of propaganda and explanations in order to work, and that the ways and means have been pointed out by people from the bourgeois class. But let's put that difficulty aside! Let's grant that workers with a class-consciousness, bourgeois men with a sense of history (Marx) or embracing the proletarian cause despite their own position in the production process (Engels) and their followers have thought out revolution for others. Those men who have a better view of things, who are alone capable of conceiving their essence and isolating their movement, are the Communists. Destined to grasp the conditions and the mechanism of the emancipation of the mind because, through their daily action, they convey the means of that emancipation, they are distinguished from the Surrealists only by habits of language and by the skills they have acquired as agents of the proletarian revolution. Ergo . . .

I'll leave it up to historians to work out the comparisons. It may be necessary to go back to the period between 1820 and 1848 to find antecedents for the politicizing of the Surrealists. Lamartine, George Sand, Victor Hugo, Baudelaire, became supporters of the Republic and vague Socialists. Chenavard wanted to do popular art. Delacroix painted the victorious insurrection, and later on Courbet had the Vendôme Column toppled. They all fought for greater liberty or for the exercise of freedoms already gained. But in 1930, for the first time in history since the Reformation, poets, painters, filmmakers, wanted to hitch their hopes, their lives if need be, their creative activity, to the daily life of a political party. They all bet on a coming social transformation through violence, regarding it as a necessary stage for the trial against society, thought, and reason. Joining the cause of proletarian revolution was not just a manner of speaking or a pose on the part of the Surrealists. They expended an enormous amount of effort to participate in that revolution, which, to their chagrin, was not being prepared anywhere. The most eminent Surrealists had always shown a highly characteristic willingness to take part in direct action and a manifest taste for violence.

Thus, the cleavage signalled by *The Second Manifesto* is thereby significant. Tzara, one of the chief smashers of the Dada movement, got back into line. There appeared a pleiade of men whose talents were to be affirmed in this sortie (I'm thinking particularly of Prévert and Queneau), though all of them, apart from Desnos, were uninterested in action and hostile to any political commitment. Here, too, historians will establish parallels: the birth and development of Dada in Switzerland, Germany, and France coincided with the renewal of proletarian internationalism and the flowering of Communist uprisings, in which a number of Dadaists participated. (Marinetti's rallying to Italian Fascism was of the same order.) A short-lived Association of Revolutionary Writers appeared in Germany. Dada wore itself out in a series of demonstrations, none of which claimed to represent a new aesthetic, at least until the performance of *Coeur à Gaz* (Gas Heart), but which did tend to shake things up.

To a certain extent, the mass effect was achieved because the words "Dada" and "Dadaist" passed into various languages and spread through the press, even in provincial gazettes. In 1923, Breton tried to coordinate individual activities by organizing the strongest partisans of the modern temper. Neither he nor Aragon were seeking a purely literary or artistic adventure. As of 1924, Surrealism made a reputation for itself through physical violence and commando raids. Thus, there is nothing astonishing about *The Second Manifesto*. When the Comintern declared that a new era of revolutions had begun, Breton replied "present" and gathered around himself all those who had resolved to make the same commitment.

Another line of cleavage cut through the first: French society was becoming more and more hostile to the Surrealists because of their anti-imperialist positions. In the world of arts and letters, the Establishment, mostly mediocre and now forgotten people representing stillborn aesthetics, defended their annuities energetically and methodically. The more their self-importance, stupidity, and bumptiousness weakened the nation and paralyzed the economy, the more the representatives of the ruling classes, especially the intellectuals, became sectarian, selfish, and petty, the more a disgusting chauvinism spread. The opposition to academicism and official art was embodied in a well-to-do and well-bred left that was as terrified by Surrealism as it had been by Cubism and all the challenges of the last twenty years. The most eminent representatives of that left were Gide, Valéry, Alain, and Giraudoux, and the most widely read publication of liberalism was *La Nouvelle Revue Française*. These notables had no lack of talent, especially Valéry. But they were weak and flabby and delighted in a molly-coddled mandarinism, an anachronistic intellectualism, refusing to surround themselves with even a few of the marvelous paintings or sculptures that their contemporaries were lavishing on the world. In 1934, during *Counterattack*, Breton went to Gide to get a signature from him—but in vain. The aesthetic mediocrity of Gide's apartment, as well as the feebleness of what he had to say, astonished Breton. He told me about his visit a few days afterward, describing Gide's prudent conversation, the conventional furniture curiously devoid of anything fine or singular. Such things were well within Gide's means, and he wouldn't have felt out of place in such an aesthetic domain. Yet objects and furnishings were humdrum; there were no Seurats or Renoirs on the walls, no Bonnards or even Signacs, but instead Laprade, Aman-Jean (or Lebasque), and so on.

By 1929, all the dissidents from Surrealism had money or were about to come to terms with money. That comment should not be understood as a value judgment, or even a criticism. The stubbornness of those who remained with Breton was dazzling but senseless. Perhaps they didn't want to leave because they couldn't afford to. Leiris, Masson, Prévert, Baron, Bataille, to mention just a few, never sold out. Nevertheless, economic circumstances were better for them outside than inside.

As I have already said, personal issues played a very large part in the ruptures. In October 1929, when Breton was terminating *The Second Manifesto* and starting, with Aragon, to prepare *The Surrealist Revolution*, No. 12, he didn't calculate the scope of the breaches that were to follow. The quarrels gravitated in part around Breton's divorce, but excuses were found for resurrecting past disagreements.

It was thought at the time that Surrealism would be impoverished by the expulsion of Desnos, Masson, and Artaud. However, Desnos and Artaud had already given their best. Masson's work hasn't developed to such a degree that one can say that the things he painted from 1930 to 1938 could have added anything to the Surrealist shows in which he did not take part. In 1929, nothing was known of Prévert's work, and next to nothing of Queneau's; the two of them had to get out in order to be able to produce. Breton knew the group was losing talented men. He committed himself very strongly to political action and Bolshevization. As a counterpoise, he rolled out the red carpet for Tzara and made overtures to Daumal. But the crisis was already past. That autumn, in 1929, Surrealism welcomed René Magritte, René Char, Luis Buñuel, and Salvador Dali. Gold by the cartload! The event was a major one. All the political risks were conjured up.

The Second Manifesto came out in favor of the position I advocated by condemning Pierre Naville, and it also slandered the men involved in *La Revue Marxiste* (which I didn't mind either). Still, it wasn't a pure and simple rallying to the dogma of the Third International. Prudently, Breton mentioned Trotsky to justify his move toward the Comintern. For issue No. 12 of *The Surrealist Revolution*, I wrote a sort of Marxist fantasy called *Notes on Money*. It was an apologia for poverty, and its sole retrospective interest is a fleeting qualm about Marxist theory, the value of which I was to ponder ten years later.

The publication of *The Second Manifesto* in issue No. 12 aroused, as we all know, extreme reactions and mudslinging from nearly all the Surrealists challenged. I have already described the singular character of those disciples. I have good reason to believe that Bataille played a large part in the strange pamphlet *A Corpse*, and I have a feeling that his own personality and his constant malaise in Breton's presence set the general tone of the insults. It was an exorcism following a rite, and in the filthy terms that only Bataille could think up. Breton was upset. For a while he thought that everyone would desert him. Men who hadn't signed the pamphlet declared their solidarity with it. In those days, I never went to the Cyrano. My state of health forced me to stay in my room for several weeks. Aragon would often drop by to keep me posted about the current defections and find out what Sadoul and I thought about the explosive situation. It even came to a quarrel between Breton and Aragon, which made us fear the worst. But they made up again.

Aragon asked me and Sadoul to come along on a walk one night. This was, I think, the first time I had gone out. Aragon was very nervous. He spoke even more and even better than usual. He took us over to the Pont des Arts, and we walked from one end to the other several times. It was past midnight. "My friendship for Breton," he said, "and my agreement with what he thinks and what he wants must be regarded as a natural phenomenon, as a force permitting the two of us to be what we are. Our rapport is very old; it's part of our destiny. Both Breton and I know that there is always a risk of misunderstandings between people and things that we may fail to comprehend. We realized long ago that we might encounter some of the wrecks that occur so abundantly in life. We agreed upon a signal of recognition, a sort of password to put everything in shape again and to irresistibly remind us of our absolute and fundamental understanding."

These lyrical words, spoken by a man who was being even more romantic than usual, in the tragic darkness of a winter night, among the galleries of Catherine de Médicis, were as solemn and fateful as the revelation of a state secret. What part did delirium play, what part truth, and what part worry in that confidence? I asked myself these questions without finding any answer, but I admired the quality of the monologue and the choice of setting.

Aragon then launched into an amazingly intelligent and well-styled definition of Breton. I'm afraid it has been betrayed and weakened by my memory:

"Breton isn't merely the writer you admire," Aragon told us. "Everything in him goes beyond his own words, beyond the things he writes, the things he does: he's also a crucible in which a central fire is burning. That could very well be his essential function in our time. And he fulfills this function with an almost magical and exceptional gift. He alone can fuse together the various materials that all of us bring him.

He can work dazzling transmutations. Avoid dwelling on his moods or contradictions so that you can be surprised by the admirable development that even his weaknesses and character faults can reveal to us."

Although *A Corpse* disgusted both of us, Sadoul and I still did not totally break off with the signatories and their friends. We were less friendly toward but would still speak to Desnos, Prévert, or Tual whenever we ran into them. This crisis had taught me two things: first, that one could be induced to leave the Surrealist group in order to escape suffocation, and secondly, that invention and decision belonged almost wholly to Breton. Aragon fixed things up, explained, corrected, but the creative force was Breton's mind.

Breton slightly altered *The Second Manifesto,* and it was published by Kra in June 1930. He asked Eluard and me to write a statement "for the favor of publication in your columns," and to make it so meaningful that it would express an agreement on principles that each member of the group would sign. I have kept the initial version. It is written in Eluard's hand and constitutes a first draft of the collaboration. After copying the twenty-five lines or so that I had suggested, he sketched out a concluding paragraph. The difference between what was finally published and the draft concerns that conclusion; the first two sentences were interchanged and the end was more forceful than in the first version. That little exercise was carved out with a good deal of honesty and skill.

The long central portion of the *Manifesto* is a call to Marxist dogma and an act of faith, written both to the Surrealists who were to sign their names and to the readers, so that no one would be left uninformed. The opening is almost entirely a very important statement by Breton, defining what was to be the properly Surrealist activity and elucidating the author's philosophy.

"The limit at which contradictions are no longer perceived," a phrase from *The Second Manifesto* which, along with others, drew Georges Bataille's attention, greatly pleased me for its poetic value and the deliberate imprecision of the idea of perception. I appreciated its modesty and ambitiousness. The aim was not to obtain some sort of golden age of classless society in which most contradictions would supposedly be solved or surmounted. It was enough to disregard those contradictions. The day I stopped believing in the infallibility of the dialectical method, I replaced Breton's utterance with "the point at which contradictions are no longer troublesome, which amounts to the same thing for the person in question." Since Breton was not habitually an advocate of any sort of renunciation, we can see this marvelous wish as a wisdom to be acquired or as the announcement of new and interesting mental gymnastics. Today, I must admit that that little sentence is very close to the most topical and reasonable of Guénon's ideas: the notion that man, through his own effort, must keep somewhat aloof from other people, feelings, mechanics, habits, perhaps even destiny.

Bataille, in *Documents*, reported on the publication of *The Second Manifesto*. Despite his disparaging bias, he admitted that the tone was very Hegelian. He also quoted the little sentence, without drawing any particular conclusions. One can't help being struck by the similarity between *The Second Manifesto* and *The Phenomenology of the Mind*. The Surrealist approach, which includes dialectics, seeks to recover the intrinsic force of the mind. To do so, it provokes a new approach to the object, but material life, other people, society, hide the object, reveal it, or offer only bogus and deformed images of it. So Surrealist thought rises up against society, arouses a revolutionary action that modifies the conditions of social life from top to bottom, emancipates desires, establishes a classless and stateless society. Surrealist thought, freed of all material constraint, purified and enriched by the dialectical exercises which it has undergone, flowers in a supreme knowledge in which the notions of reality and unreality, reason and unreason, and the like, lose their meaning. *The Phenomenology of the Mind* describes a similar, albeit more complicated road from the perception of the object to the concept, then to despair, revolt, heroism, good citizenship, and religion. For Breton, the end is neither the absolute idea nor sovereign thought, but a kind of ultimate state which, at least in 1930, could signify that there is no final stage but an indefinite and privileged zone of accomplishment and rest after the journey. Breton believes it can be reached only by passing through the proletarian revolution. Later on, he suggested shortcuts, magic in the final analysis, not so much to obtain absolute knowledge as to "recover the intrinsic force of the Mind." But, as in Hegel, the end of the process is contained in the beginning, and the entire interest of such gymnastics resides in these vicissitudes. Since there is neither dogma nor rule, the road to knowledge seems to be some sort of happening. After the Revolution, man, by multiplying Surrealist gymnastics, will manage to no longer distinguish between "a flame and a stone." This degree of uncertainty in knowledge is one of the great discoveries of Surrealism, but Breton gradually forgot it when he was in bondage to determinism, against which he always defended himself quite badly.

In 1930, the exploration of the unconscious ascribed a good deal to chance. The manifest content of dreams could be almost anything. The symbol was identified afterward, and the various schools argued about the level at which the cascade of associations stops and about the nature of motives and residua. In any case, the inevitable inter- actions between the analyst and the object of analysis introduce a principle of uncertainty that Freud evades by claiming to subject all transformations to simple laws. Automatic writing also opened the way to chance. On the other hand, Breton's and the Surrealists' worship of coincidences rehabilitated destiny, whose concatenations Breton sud- denly toned down in 1930 when he took up Hegel's dazzling notion of objective chance.

The weakest part of *The Second Manifesto*, which was anathema to Marxist hard-liners, was the note on Choisnard and the horoscopes of Aragon, Eluard, and Breton. These came as a surprise to anyone who read it. Guénon, whom I voluntarily consulted in order to com- pare the desire for "total recuperation of our physical force by no other means than a dizzying descent into our own selves" with an exaltating of intelligence, contemplation, and "completely speculative" cognition, tended to condemn that gross superstition, which, he writes, has de- graded the traditional science of astrology to the level of charlatanism. It is certainly amusing to cast inborn characteristics according to some sort of formula. The distribution of human personalities into twelve astral signs is one of the best possible topics of conversation with the opposite sex. The least we can say is that astrological soothsaying is a lofty fantasy, even if the positions and conjunctions of stars have been calculated within a tenth of a second by a graduate of the Ecole Polytechnique. The explanation of the laser effect and the elemental forces in the makeup of a bundle of light seemed more delirious to Claude Bernard than the "remarkable conjunction" of Uranus and Saturn, which, according to Breton, "characterized the sky at Aragon's, Eluard's, and my birth." But nothing now enables us to say that the exact sciences have made any strides in regard to horoscopes and astrologers. We cannot see astrological claims as anything more than incantation, and the results that stargazers wave about are no more than an applied reckoning of probabilities.

The Stalinists and Trotskyites made a point of harping on the note about the conjunction of Uranus and Saturn and did a good deal of shouting. They didn't bother to count how many of their militants believed in newspaper horoscopes, and they never asked themselves how many of the people attacking the Winter Palace in November 1917 would have been left out if they had had to be examined for superstition. The horoscope note certainly deserved more than a summary condemnation. It marked a reintroduction into Breton's thought of a belief in determinism. Outside the Communist world, no one took notice of that curious innovation.

The little note on the conjunction of Saturn and Uranus had no immediate consequences, aside from the coat-of-arms on the cover of *Surrealism in the Service of the Revolution*. On the other hand, before we even knew Dali, the call to a "dizzying descent into our own selves" greeted his bewildering arrival in Surrealism. The principle of indetermination was to be triumphant for over ten years.

On October 1, 1929, Studio 28, a film theater, presented the first showing in Paris of *An Andalusian Dog*, Luis Buñuel's film of a scenario by him and Dali. Until then, Surrealism had produced only one movie, *The Sea Star*, devised and filmed by Man Ray. This was the first time that a professional moviemaker, who was to become one of the greatest of his time, devoted his knowledge and technique to a Surrealist inspiration.

Buñuel was nearly thirty. Despite long sojourns in France, he had never had any contact with Breton and his friends. Dali, a Catalonian, was several years his junior. Both of them came from a well-to-do background, especially Buñuel. That was fine with us because Surrealism was in no position to absorb any more paupers. The two had a very good Catholic upbringing, which Buñuel has never shaken off. In 1929, the maker of *An Andalusian Dog* had an athletic build and round, prominent eyes. He was a man of few words, very active, as good as gold and as sound as bread.

Dali, despite his studies at the Ecole des Beaux-Arts, seemed (wrongly) to have just freed himself from his mother's apron strings. He wore a fine mustache, like the film actor Adolphe Menjou. Slender, shy, phlegmatic, well-mannered, he had an inexhaustible gift of gab, which his natural humor and his Spanish accent sprinkled with comical effects. But he knew when to hold his peace, and he would hold it for a long time, curled up, attentive and serious, in an easy chair. Enormously intelligent, he was obviously capable of wrecking any mental construct whatsoever simply because he was so marvelously funny; he could make everyone but himself howl with laughter. Eluard had spent the summer in Cadaqués and he had brought Dali back in Gala's baggage, along with Goemans and Magritte. Dali himself brought a dozen paintings which Goemans exhibited on November 20, 1929, in the short-lived Surrealist Gallery he had started at 49 Rue de Seine.

In Paris, Dali was completely lost. He couldn't even cross the street. His only means of transportation was a taxi. He fell down several times a day. He always paid with large bills, often forgetting to pick up his change.

He was crazy about Gala, who was available. She instantly took possession of the handsome Spaniard. Nevertheless, she waited awhile to think things over before casting herself head over heels into that immense adventure whose outcome no one could predict. Dali, when he met Gala, was practically, if not technically, a virgin. He absolutely needed an expert and loving woman who would remain undaunted by his penchant for masturbation and would know how to capitalize on a genius and an imagination that could easily be frittered away. Gala's tenderness rapidly made Dali self-confident to a fault. With his natural bent for eccentricity, Dali, in 1929, still managed to keep a tight hand on his demon with the help of his Spanish rigidity. But he discarded these annoying trappings and gave free rein to his exhibitionism. Jesting and talent alone do not assure total impunity for such behavior, of course, but Gala knew how to censor, whenever necessary, the most shocking excesses.

Dali's passion for Gala was exclusive and sweeping, which fitted in with the Surrealist tone in 1930. Once, Gala had to undergo a serious but basically safe operation, which nevertheless shook up a man very much in love with her. So Dali painted several pictures which are among the finest and most poignant testimonies of love that a man has ever given a woman. I'm thinking particularly of *Gradiva* and *The Old Age of William Tell.* I wish that every young woman who ever sees these paintings could be aware of their background so that she could demand, if need be, an adoration and concern equal to Dali's for Gala.

Eluard and Breton were wonder-struck by the paintings that Dali showed them. They instantly bought some, which were reproduced in issue No. 12 of *The Surrealist Revolution.* Their format was small. Dali's virtuosity worried Breton. His hesitation is apparent in the catalogue for the Goemans show. When Breton showed me some of the paintings that were going to be in the exhibit, he particularly stressed their character as miniatures. I agreed with him on that point, and we wondered whether larger formats wouldn't make Dali's paintings look like photographic blow-ups. The year 1931 proved us wrong.

Dali's contributions to Surrealism were of major significance for the life of the group and its ideological development. Those who have denied this have either lied or misunderstood the situation. Nor is it true that Dali stopped being a great painter in the 1950's, even though his alleged conversion to Catholicism was rather disconcerting. Like any other artist, Dali has not enjoyed a constant inspiration. Some of his commercial works are mediocre. They are not all bad and never indifferent. Despite everything, there is always an exemplary draftsmanship, a surprising inventiveness, a feeling of drama, and a sense of humor.

Imagery is very important to Surrealism. After Dada, the most exalting discoveries were made by Max Ernst: an unlimited inspiration in his collages, a new vision of plants and animals. Masson, Miró, and Tanguy did admirable paintings, like nothing ever seen before, and Man Ray invented ceaselessly. But the language of these four great artists was not as rich and workable a mine as Max Ernst's. The collages for which Max Ernst cut up old magazines, the body of Man Ray's photographs, are anthropomorphous, but the human body, the face, and both life and death were alien to Surrealist painting. Chirico aside, the few exceptions, all of them in Max Ernst, merely confirm the rule. Dali renewed Surrealist inspiration by reintroducing men, women, nudes, and animals into paintings. Magritte did likewise, with frozen and timeless figures. He was followed by all the northern Surrealists. Dali returned to the smooth and modeled technique of the sixteenth century. Since 1945, lovers of material effects and abstraction have actually been waging a skillful campaign against Surrealism, labeling it literary and even academic. The enormous boredom in so many abstract or Tachiste compositions, the poverty of expression, significantly contrasting with the ranting and gibberish of painters at a loss to explain their own works, have hardly helped the theoreticians of abstraction.

Dali supplied Surrealism with an infernal machine that continued to explode, and the various showers of rubble covered the prospects of the Third International, historical materialism, and the science of horoscopes. In late 1930, he proposed that "an activity with a moral aspect could be prompted by the violently paranoid desire to systematize confusion." That was the well-known paranoid-critical method. Any discussion was by definition impossible because to discuss paranoia one had to enter, for reasons of self-defense, the imagined system and acknowledge the "patient's" obsession. Dali's utterances have a very high literary quality; they are compelling in the singularity of their similes and in the hallucinatory beauties they evoke. The psychoanalysts had their work cut out for them with Dali, who meticulously cultivated the complexes he was aware of, admitted everything, and put his interlocutor in a grotesquely awkward position. Starting off with an obsessive idea, he would prepare to carry out varied, delirious, and exemplary constructions for anything on any occasion. These exercises were far from safe for a fanatic Communist. I greatly admired Dali. I was captivated by his brilliant inventiveness and his gumption. His position in Surrealism was so important, he gave it so much new energy, that there was no queston of a separation. He wasn't a Marxist, thank goodness! He poked fun at Bukharin and Plekhanov, and reduced Lenin to a subject of ornamentation! I could sense the emerging distrust: Dali was about to shock all the petty-bourgeois minds in the Party with his painting, irritate the theoreticians with his references to psychoanalysis, and scandalize the militants with his lack of interest in social problems. They should have been relieved that he didn't maliciously apply the paranoid-critical method to their problems. He accomplished that a bit later by introducing Hitler into his demonology. At the time, Breton and the others lost their tempers. Now that Nazism has been conquered and Hitler has come to dust, we can admit that Dali's feat was amusing and less catastrophic than the tasks most intellectuals and politicians in France and England were setting themselves.

In 1930 and 1931, I did my best to conciliate. I didn't feel it made any sense to harp on doctrinal deviations, statements of troublesome principles, absurdities that were apt to make the Tribunal of the Holy utter as many qualifiers ending in "ism" as the epithets that Dali used without rhyme or reason and so effectively. Everything boiled down to the one question that had been asked so often. Was or wasn't Dali's activity revolutionary? I didn't hesitate to answer in the affirmative.

The autumn of 1929 also brought us René Char. He arrived from his native Vaucluse, where, for a long time, he had been playing rugby, which fitted him to a T. Char also had a personal fortune that assured his independence. He became the most intimate friend of Eluard, whom he greatly admired. From the very start, there was a definite kinship of inspiration between them, an identical tendency toward an immobile and transparent poetry. Nevertheless, objects are treated much more roughly by René Char than by the author of *Immediate Life*. Little by little, violence and even brutality distinguished Char's work from Eluard's and placed it in the hard, cruel line of cutting and thrusting traced by the sparkling, flashing dagger of Agrippa d'Aubigné.

Their lively interest in women also brought Eluard and Char together. A handsome man, the author of *The Hammer without a Master* had little difficulty with the opposite sex. For a while, he lived at Eluard's place on Rue Becquerel. The chambermaid was a pretty brunette, very young, nice-looking, discreet, and well-dressed. There was nothing unusual about the way she worked. "Nevertheless," René Char told me, "when she helped me on with my overcoat I found her graciousness a bit clinging. She was really a very pretty girl. One day, I couldn't help it, I took her in my arms. She went along with it readily and turned out to be quite an expert. I told Paul the whole story, and the next day he had breakfast served in bed and straightaway made a pass at his lovely servant. She told us she had been waiting for a long time; she had come to think that there was something wrong with us and had been just about to give up. She would have made her feelings obvious if she hadn't been so unnerved by our serious ways and our courtesy. She had been at her wits' end about making things come to a head." Her job at Eluard's home was just a cover-up. Nearly every evening, she would go over to Boulevard de la Madeleine, where her true job was. She didn't stay on Rue Becquerel for long. The two men kept her too busy. It made very little sense.

I lived in the Buttes-Chaumont area because of René Char. One stifling summer evening in 1931 or 1932, Katia and I went to dinner at a studio on Rue Manin, the home of a very appetizing Belgian girl who was the official mistress of Fernand Léger. She had gone to bed with Char. Night came on, deliciously cool, balmy with all the fragrances from the park. In 1932, life on Rue du Château was as unpleasant for Sadoul as for me because we had had a parting of ways over the Aragon affair. Katia found an apartment on Rue Manin, unfortunately without a view of the park. I left it the following year for a place with windows opening wide over Paris, from Vincennes to Place de l'Etoile, about a block from Buttes-Chaumont. It was there that I recently reread *Artine*, the slender volume of poems published by René Char in 1930, so characteristic of his early style. I perused it no doubt to thank *Artine* for having taken me to the top of Belleville.

"Despite animals and cyclones Artine maintained an inexhaustible freshness. When strolling, she was absolute transparency."

Wasn't she coming straight from La Fontaine-de-Vaucluse?

15
THE INQUIRY INTO LOVE

WITH PREVERT AND TANGUY, LIFE ON RUE DU
Château had been homey, alcoholic, and irreverent. It had also been
sheltered from the great debates on the politicizing of Surrealism. With
Sadoul and me, the little house became a serious place. It was bohemian
and a bit licentious but for the most part severe and ideological. One
can imagine what might have become of a small pavilion as well situated as ours if it had belonged to young men with less moral rigor
and sincerity and with more money. But objects and dwellings follow
their destiny no matter what: on various occasions, the pavilion nearly
drowned in merrymaking and sensual delights. Nonetheless, such occasions were as brief as they were bright. Reading, thinking, talking,
preparing subversive projects were the things I spent most of my time
on from 1928 to 1933.

The tenants were poor. I myself was very poor in 1929 and during
the better part of 1930 and 1931. Sadoul worked at Gallimard until
a court sentenced him for having written an insulting postcard to the

commandant of a class at the Saint-Cyr military academy. He received a bit of money from his family and did some relatively well-paid work for publishers. In 1929, my relations with my father had grown worse. I was actually quite unhappy about it. All I received now was two hundred francs a month: my laundry was still being done in Nancy, and that was all. Twenty days a month, I would live off my friends. Back home, Sadoul had learned thrift and how to cook; he made sure we had fairly steady meals, with herring filet soaked in oil and chopped horsemeat as the pièces de résistance. Sadoul had his own life, his appointments and meetings with our architect friends, his walks through Paris with Unik, Breton, and Aragon. He often went to the movies, spent more time than I did at the Cyrano, and afterward would dine with any of the apéritif crowd who felt like relaxing a bit. My own life was partly devoted to politics: I would go to the Union House at 111 Rue du Château (which is now an experimental theater), to the Party headquarters at 120 Rue Lafayette, or to other meeting places. Usually I walked, preserving my precious reserve of a few francs which I might need to buy a drink in a café.

My father had a quarrel with his brother over some sordid money matters. I had no particular grounds for siding with my father, and yet I stopped visiting my aunt and uncle on Rue César Franck, where I had always been able to count on an excellent dinner once a week. My overwhelming moral sectarianism led me to that decision. I would stop all contact with anyone who wasn't revolutionary.

I didn't like my cousin René Thirion's crowd. They were social butterflies, mostly homosexuals, à la roaring twenties, and quite antithetical to my needs. The only people I still kept up with were Darius Milhaud and Signac. Milhaud, so marvelously kind, pretended to show interest in my political doings; from time to time, he would invite me to lunch on Boulevard de Clichy. He introduced me to Desormières, and to Robert Caby (then the music critic of *L'Humanité*), because these young men were more or less close to the Party. Milhaud, to my mind, was the greatest French musician alive; I learned a lot from him, and I was proud of being able to visit him while he was exercising a musical talent that I considered one of the best in my time. I once asked him to play parts of *The Creation of the World*—a piece I was dying to know—because I couldn't afford to attend a concert and didn't have the nerve to ask him for tickets. Milhaud is a mediocre pianist, but this private performance, with his explanation of the planned instrumentation, was worth more to me than the best orchestra. I asked him about the musicians I cared for most: Bartók, Sczymanovski, Rieti, Schoenberg. The recital of *Pierrot Lunaire* had intrigued me. I had been disappointed by Webern's short pieces, which I had had performed in Nancy. But I wanted to hear them again: the Pro Arte quartet allowed me to attend two or three working rehearsals, and at one of them, they were kind enough to give me a private performance of Webern's famous pieces. Milhaud enjoyed my curiosity. In 1927, he had introduced me to Negro spirituals. In 1929, he had me listen to Chinese music, fragments of an opera that takes twenty-four hours to perform. It made a very keen impression on me. The Chinese struck me as going much further than Schoenberg in regard to freedom of expression. Milhaud explained that this music obeyed very strict laws.

I would have liked to bring all my friends together. But Breton felt only a polite consideration for Milhaud; he didn't like music, and, besides, Milhaud was friendly with Cocteau and Claudel, which was enough to make him suspect. Milhaud's tastes in painting amazed me. Of course he liked Braque and Picasso, but he set great store by mediocre painters and a high-fashion modernism like Jean Hugo's and Pruna's. Actually, this was a sign of the absolute loyalty that Milhaud always showed his friends. My intransigence, coupled with provincialism, must have amused and sometimes irritated him. "What if you took me to the Café Cyrano one evening?" he said. "What would happen?" That was certainly the most embarrassing question he could ask. I could picture Breton's annoyed and severe expression, the icy wind that would pass over the tables, the critical remarks: "What's he up to? Why did he do it? If he wants to be on good terms with a musician, fine, but he ought to realize that we're not interested in anything that Monsieur Darius Milhaud may write. Besides he's one of Claudel's most loyal collaborators, that pig." And so on.

I explained to Milhaud that I still considered myself a guest at the Cyrano and that I would first have to ask the hosts if they would be agreeable to a visit from him. I added that I keenly hoped that good relations would be established between Milhaud and Surrealism. What a narrow escape!

I would see Paul Signac when my father came to Paris. My father had known his second wife, Jeanne Selmersheim-Desgranges, ever since her first marriage to Pierre Selmersheim. Jeanne Selmersheim's daughters all had nicknames. Poucette, the youngest child from her first marriage, would often visit them. She was about my age, and I found her very exciting. Pich, Jeanne's daughter by Signac, was still a kid. Intelligent, headstrong, curious about my relations with the art world, which was so different from her own milieu, she asked me a lot of questions about various people. Knowing that I had met Honegger three or four times, she made me describe him in detail.

The Cachins were her parents' most intimate friends. Marcel Cachin, the most widely known Communist in the Chamber of Deputies, was one of the most honorable of the old Social-Democrats, but I viewed him as merely a sentimental Communist rather out of touch with Leninism. He was a man of few words. Sitting in an armchair and looking very important, with his big, broad mustache, he was stately, in a very pre-First World War way. His unfailing loyalty to the Party didn't make a cat's paw of him. In 1930 (or 1931), in Moscow, he had attended one of the early witch trials of the Stalin regime. As I recall, it was the trial of the Industrial Party, when a dozen engineers and managers, and a few foreign specialists, were prosecuted for sabotage, destruction of material, industrial espionage, and so on. Naturally, the defendants, who had until recently been directors of the most important enterprises in Soviet industry, had admitted everything. Marcel Cachin had been astonished to hear one of the defendants declare that he had met Poincaré and Briand on the terrace of the Café de la Paix to plan some sort of sabotage in Soviet factories. As an old Parisian and a deputy, Cachin knew that Poincaré and Briand didn't get along. The last thing in the world they would have done was to conspire together against anything. They disagreed about Soviet Russia, and it was inconceivable that a Russian engineer could meet with a former President of the Republic and a former President of the Council and sit with them at a table in the Café de la Paix like vulgar shopkeepers. Paul Signac had Communist leanings, but he was clearheaded. He reported these matters to me when the conversation turned to the strange occurrences of everyday life in the Soviet Union and I tried to explain that the famine, the terrible and unprecedented housing shortage, the abandoned children, and the like were caused by imperialist plotting.

I didn't find Marcel Cachin or his wife very interesting. She was a tall American straight out of Sunday school. On the other hand, the three children were utterly likable. Especially Marie-Louise: I loved her slow and melodious voice and her passionate melancholy, which was typical of Brittany. The presence of Poucette and Marie-Louise, two such dissimilar and interesting girls, transformed those rather dreary evenings for me. I would gladly have dated either of them. But back in Saint-Germain-des-Prés, I quickly pulled myself together. What could I do, since I had absolutely nothing to offer? I didn't even have the power to love, because Katia was mistress of my heart. So I contented myself with gazing at them a good deal and paying them a few compliments.

I ate very badly. Often, a bowl of tea and two slices of bread and butter were my food for a whole day. At most, I never had more than one meal daily. What little money was left went for Métro fares. At the Cyrano, I generally ordered the cheapest drink, a bock beer, which I couldn't always pay for; I would usually manage to excuse myself when the ceremony was over so I wouldn't have to admit I simply couldn't afford to go to a restaurant. It wasn't always easy to steal off so quickly; Aragon, Eluard, and Crevel, who sensed what was up, would sometimes take me out; I was abashed, mortified, and content.

Poverty didn't solve the problem of girls. I still got awfully horny every so often. I used a technique of immediate and brutal conquest to avoid any subsequent date, which I was almost certain to break for lack of money. I tried to talk the girl into coming over to Rue du Château. From Montparnasse, it was only a fifteen-minute walk. The streets were badly lit and just right for hardy enterprises. A taxi would have cost three and a half francs, and everyone knows that a taxi helps things along. But girls like to be courted a bit; if I couldn't get her to make up her mind right away, everything was lost—unless the girl in question said she would meet me at Rue du Château the next time. The thing I had to avoid at any cost was agreeing to go to a restaurant, a movie, or a dance! All in all, my conquests were few and far between. Fate would have had to deliver them to my door.

There *were* miracles. The most charming was Florence. She was pretty, covered with freckles, and barely twenty. Along with twelve others, she had come to a scratch dinner, in the throes of the most violent despair. A few weeks earlier, she had met Max Ernst in Mégève. It had been as beautiful and as refreshing as snowfields in the sun. She had fallen madly in love with him. But he was soon singing a different tune. In Paris, Max Ernst had met Marie-Berthe, a demanding and jealous woman. I consoled Florence as best I could. I didn't believe I would ever succeed with her. I didn't dare continue. Florence, I believe, thought otherwise. She hinted as much, astonished at my discretion, before returning to her conjugal home somewhere near Saint-Raphaël. In late 1929 she wrote that she wanted to come to

Paris, implying that she would be glad to live on Rue du Château. I had not expected anything of this sort. It was flattering; even better, I liked her a lot. The prospect of living with Florence for a while bathed my return to Paris in a soft light. I wrote to tell her when I'd be back in Paris. Some projects with Hainchelin kept me in Nancy during the first few days of October. Florence's dates corresponded to mine. No sooner had I unpacked my suitcase in the pavilion than someone knocked at the door. It was Lasserre the sculptor. He had been looking for me in Montparnasse since the day before, and had only just learned my address from the first Surrealist he managed to reach by phone. "You know Florence," he said. "She went to Barbizon yesterday with Derain and Lena Amsel. Lena had taken Florence in her Bugatti. Derain also owns a Bugatti. After breakfast, Lena wanted to get rid of Derain on the road back by claiming her car was faster than his. This is sugar-beet season, you know. Lena's car skidded on some wet leaves, turned over into a field, and caught fire. The two women were burned alive. All you could see from the road was their legs. I was with Derain. It was horrible. I knew that Florence was supposed to meet you today or tomorrow. You're the only one who knows her name and her family's address." It was as though I were fated never to see Florence again.

Another encounter had more severe consequences, as we shall see. Returning from Nancy, where I had gone to show my father some of Tanguy's paintings (he bought one), I found Sadoul in an unusual euphoria. The Jockey had just reopened, and there he had met Monique, a model who was out for a good time. He gave me a long description of her face and profile; she was a tall girl, slender as models usually are, with delicate features and a pensive, almost doleful expression. The first night had been conclusive, but Monique had disappeared. He had to find her no matter what. So that same evening we went to the Jockey. Monique was nowhere to be seen, but we located one of her friends, a platinum blonde with large, hazel eyes, a very white, finely grained skin, pure and regular features. All in all, she was a lovely, well-built girl, and she was naked under her cheap dress. Her name was Jackie; she was eighteen. She finished the night in my bed. Her breasts and behind were enough to damn the son of God. But she also had money problems. We parted, after making a date for which she never showed up. Nor did she send us Monique, despite her promises.

Jackie returned a few weeks later, in a cab, high on ether. She immediately lay down on one of the leather cushions near the fur tabernacle. She reeked and she felt ill.

Youki Foujita, who was visiting us, was more familiar than Sadoul or I with those young drug addicts. Jackie slept off her ether for hours on end. She left exactly as she had come.

I dressed very badly and looked like a miserable minor clerk. When I went without a tie, nothing distinguished me from my worker friends, except for my well-kept hands.

When I first arrived in Paris, I had ordered an elegant suit from Zeff. I took care of it as well as I could, but it was irritatingly worn at one elbow. Mending it would have helped, if dry cleaning and mending had been within my means. Most of the time I wore a black suit, made over from a tuxedo I had worn at sixteen for my cousin's wedding. During the winter I added an old checkered beige sweater and a black double-breasted overcoat that kept getting shabbier and shabbier. My socks had been mended to death, my shirts were threadbare at the collars and wrists, my ties were shapeless and colorless, aside from one red masterpiece I had bought at a market in Raon-l'Etape, which showed a naked woman amid playing cards. I hardly ever go bareheaded in winter, so I donned a worker's cap that I was very proud of. In summer, I wore a light-gray suit with wide trousers, which had been my pride in 1925. The cloth was solid; it was the jacket that split first. In 1929, Aragon gave me a gray-blue sweater, in which I managed to look almost elegant for three straight months. In winter I slept in military shirts of heavy linen, which I had inherited from my father. I had no pajamas. Nevertheless, I owned some good footwear, sneakers with rubber soles. Sadoul had the same; we liked them because we could walk noiselessly.

I spent two hours a day cleaning and waxing our place. I could have been a good valet. Dust and dirt have always been anathema to me. I was more or less defying my lack of money. The house became as inviting as those shiny northern European homes. In this respect, I was the contrary of Sadoul, who could survive amid dirty dishes, overflowing garbage cans, dust, and cobwebs. These housewifely exercises included a sound linoleum polishing. I would do it almost every day, like push-ups. This regimen, together with my walks across Paris and my uncertain and irregular food, was hardly suited to an adolescent with no money. Well-meaning souls dwelt on the tuberculosis that ran in our family, predicting disaster. In 1929, it was snowing in Lorraine during Easter week. Sadoul and I decided to spend a few days hiking in the mountains. Without skis or snowshoes, we reached the fresh snow of Champ de Feu. It was a magnificently heady experience. I felt in excellent form. A few dozen yards from the peak, Sadoul had out-distanced me slightly; I suddenly felt worn out. It was like drudgery. My legs were bundles of rags. I halted. I couldn't move another step. I found a road where the snow had piled up and I stretched out to regain my strength. When Sadoul could not see me, he doubled back. I told him I was feeling a sudden, intense, and uncanny fatigue; we would have to curtail our outing. I stayed there lying in the snow for nearly an hour. We had brought along some plum brandy, and one gulp brought me back to my feet. I was able to climb the last stretch to the summit by following a marked road. A farm offered us shelter in a barn. I knew how to sleep in a grange and protect myself against the cold. In the morning, I felt rested, but not capable of doing the day's march that we had planned. We cut our excursion short. Again, the hike through the snow drained me.

In Paris, I discovered abscesses, with practically no fever. Dr. Simon, a friend of Elsa Triolet's, didn't like the turn the infection was taking. For the first time, Elsa Triolet played the part of Providence, which she was to repeat during the next two years. I had no way of taking care of myself, and my father returned to pay some minimal attention to my health. I needed an operation. Through Elsa's agency, the Simons took over the costs and put me in a clinic at the very moment when I was supposed to join the 18th Engineering Corps in Mayence. An army doctor came to check my unavailability.

My convalescence was long and tedious: I had to avoid all fatigue, and I didn't eat much better than before. André Triolet's girl friend Nicole came by often, and her visits helped me to bear my isolation. Nicole was unhappy; she knew that André was being unfaithful, and he was gradually getting her to accept the idea of splitting up. I spent the rest of that summer in Baccarrat, either at my sister's or at my cousins'. My father didn't mind offering me inexpensive hospitality.

I stayed on in Nancy to work with Hainchelin on a magazine for Marxist studies, which we had been toying with since the fall of 1928. Some extracts from a letter that Hainchelin wrote to me in early 1929 describe this undertaking and its goal:

Yesterday morning, another letter from Riazanov. He's sending me *The Marxist Annals*, the philosophical works of Plekhanov, the works of Deborin, and several periodicals (*The Academy Bulletin*, etc.).

Furthermore, and this is important, he's asked me to collaborate on some scholarly Marxist publications, at least for a critique of the French social and historical works. He's also asked me to send him a copy of everything I write, and he's promised to help me and supply me with any scholarly material I may need.

This augurs well for the review we're thinking of starting. As soon as you can sketch out some plans, send them to me so that I can let our Russian friends know.

From the very start, we have to totally drop literature, which is of secondary interest, and we have to be resolutely Marxist. I intend to remain firmly on the terrain of the Marx-Engels Institute and the red professors. Under no pretext can we get involved in Luxemburgism or the Bukharinades that occasionally blossom in Russia.

Launching the *Devenir Social* (*Social Development*)—the title that I had chosen and that Hainchelin had accepted—surpassed both my strength and my means. In October 1929, with no great conviction, we decided to draw up synopses of the first two issues. The financing, which was to come from Russia and Germany, had been rather hypothetical. At any rate, the project that we had formed in October 1928 was supposed to "come out" at the latest by the end of spring 1929. The delay was due partly to my own inexperience and my poverty and partly to Hainchelin's Machiavellian scheming, which often prevented him from carrying anything out. In October 1929, our plans were almost fully ruined by the appearance of *La Revue Marxiste*. Breton's attacks on Morhange, Politzer, and Lefebvre made a favorable impression on Hainchelin and helped make him more attentive to the results of my crusade among the Surrealists.

Hainchelin gave me deplorable news about the state of the Party in the Eastern Region. The regional secretaries had been stealing one another's wives, and these bedroom intrigues had degenerated into political conflicts. The police had sent informers into the very ranks of the Party. The effectiveness of the United Unions was diminishing; most of the cells were no longer meeting. My successor in the Nancy chapter, totally absorbed in "antimilitarist" work, had absolutely no political sense at all and took refuge in a passivity induced by the leftist rhetoric then in vogue and the desertion of militants. Hainchelin foresaw that the fine network of regimental cells covering Lorraine, Alsace, and the Rhineland would soon crumble under the blows of the police. The old Party members I went to see confirmed Hainchelin's description of havoc.

I was glad they had missed me, of course. The organization was reeling; obscure but active militants had spent three or four days in prison, which was all it took to break up their cells or their union sections. They had often lost their jobs, and their old friends in the factories were scared. Hainchelin was pessimistic about the future of the entire French Section of the Communist International. The only remedy, to his mind, was a more direct intervention by the Comintern.

Shortly after my return to Paris, there was a minor incident that took on a greater significance for me a few years later. During my second year of special mathematics, the philosophy teacher had introduced me, as his best pupil, to Jean Wahl. Wahl knew I had given up any notion of a scientific career in order to throw myself body and soul into Communism. He came to see me on Rue du Château and asked me why and how I had become a Marxist.

At the time, I was chock-full of the famous *Materialism and Empirio-criticism*. I ended a conversation which Jean Wahl had probably expected to be more serious and more profound by asking him to read that Summa of all revolutionary philosophy. I lent the philosopher Volume XIII of Lenin's complete works, which had recently appeared. Three or four months later, Jean Wahl dropped by to return the book. "That's simply not philosophy," he said. And he immediately left. I instantly classified that opinion with those that Marx ridicules in *The Holy Family*. What did we need philosophers for in 1930 to *interpret* the world, since now was the time to *change* it? In seeking a new interpretation, Wahl was unaware of the need for transformation; he failed to understand that Lenin owed it to himself to wreck the hopes of anyone who still wanted to chatter about the nature of the world!

I felt no hint of doubt, but the philosopher's comment was astonishing. I could not forget his brief dismissal of such an immense book, and even though I marshaled my defenses against Wahl's criticism, it gradually started its destructive course through me.

The Surrealist event of October 1929 was *The Inquiry into Love*. It reflected the incitements of passion among these young men (none of whom were much over thirty) and the interrogations by Breton, who was both at the zenith of happiness and in the depths of disquiet. Rarely had the future appeared so uncertain, no matter what rational arguments he used to try and repel a vague fear, the icy fog of which slyly enshrouded his heart even during his moments of happiness with Suzanne. Her presence overwhelmed him; she restored his faith in life and in the constructive power of love. Yet he feared the demons he had already seen revolving around his mistress. He had exorcised them several times, but he realized that they could take shape once more. To my mind, the danger was perfectly symbolized by Melmoth, the pampered dog with the long gray fur, with whom Suzanne liked to play perverse games.

The *Inquiry* questionnaire composed by Breton is admirable. It wrests the idea of love away from the etiquette of bourgeois marriage, the chains of Christian wedlock, the optimism of fortunetelling. What sort of hopes do you set on love? Are you ready to sacrifice your freedom and your convictions to love? Can love conquer all? That is a rather poor synopsis, just barely enough to orient the reader.

The original text of the questionnaire, on page 65 of *The Surrealist Revolution*, No. 12, is followed by the most characteristic replies. Inside the issue, the photographs of sixteen Surrealists with eyes closed enframe a reproduction of Magritte's painting *i dont see the [female nude] hidden in the forest.* Issue No. 12, in its exergue, has the life-sized imprints of female lips: those of Suzanne, Elsa, Gala, La Pomme, Jeanette Tanguy, Marie-Berthe Ernst, and Goemans' wife (or mistress).

Like all good questionnaires, *The Inquiry into Love*, as insidious as its terms may be, calls forth by its very wording some of the answers that its author awaited. Suzanne lived up to the task demanded of her. Her responses brought Breton to a towering point of exaltation; he countersigned the text to make it a sort of declaration of love *urbi et orbi.* A canny analyst might discern some qualms and reticence in Suzanne's words.

During the time I was working out my answer to *The Inquiry on Love* (a sort of act of total faith in love), violently focusing my undivided attention on Katia, I often wandered about Montparnasse with Sadoul. We were driven by the intoxicating demon of the flesh. I ran across Jackie, the girl from the Jockey, sitting at the Coupole or the Rotonde, with a girl friend who was less attractive but pleasant to look at, plump and full of promise; her name was Lucette. The girls welcomed us with open arms: they had no place to sleep.

Sadoul hadn't forgotten Monique. Jackie and Lucette might be able to get them together again. We brought the two girls over to the pavilion. They immediately displayed the gaiety and enthusiasm of children, telling us everything. At the moment they were working the Stock Exchange district; they had left a hotel because the owner was starting to show too much interest in their activities. They had to be at the Stock Exchange by around one. At five, it was all over. They were free, they could see friends, go dancing, sit around in cafés, take in a movie.

Lucette and Jackie offered to move in with us, do the cooking, keep the place clean, make love, and continue their Stock Exchange operations so as to pay all our expenses. It was funny, and sad enough to make us cry. We answered that we couldn't go along with them because of moral scruples. We were not about to describe these, but they constituted imperative rules for us. We proposed an arrangement: they would live with us but would not be either man's private property. They promised that they would get Monique to come, and she would belong exclusively to Sadoul, at least for the moment. The girls would make the beds, wash the dishes, and clean the house; at one o'clock they would be free to go about their serious duties. Everything they earned would be theirs. But they had to be back by 1 A.M. They would prepare a soup and wait for us in their most suggestive negligees. We would then all eat together and entertain our friends. Next, they would share our beds according to whatever arrangements we agreed upon. For a start, Lucette would go with Sadoul and Jackie with me.

The girls punctiliously carried out the terms of the contract. When they heard us cursing about money, counting our sous to see whether we would be going to the Cyrano on foot or by Métro, they were always amazed that we flatly refused their kind offers to help us out.

Word got around that they were living with us. We never had so many nighttime visitors. By 2 A.M., we would have finished Lucette's fragrant and delicious garlic soup and be chatting like pashas, while the girls, dressed only in the suggestive underwear of prostitutes, filled our glasses with the white wine we had obtained with great difficulty at the nearby tavern.

Sadoul's nights were well occupied and satisfying. Mine were paradoxical. Jackie was no doubt the loveliest and shapeliest of the girls, but she obstinately refused to have sex, always for trivial reasons. She wanted to go to sleep, though she affected a very great emotional attachment to me personally. Moreover, she was dirty; I had to show my temper to get her to wash even slightly, and, to begin with, I had to clean her up myself.

One evening, I confronted Jackie with a choice between total surrender or exile in the downstairs room. Jackie wept: "I feel like it too, but I can't. It's for your sake that I don't want to have sex." I could not understand, and since Jackie considered exile a demotion, she gave me everything I wanted. And she did it with lots of tenderness.

After two or three sessions with Jackie, I found out the reasons for her prudence. She was ill, and I realized she had been nice enough to pass her gonorrhea on to me. Busser, the son of the director of the Opera, was then practicing at Saint-Joseph's Hospital; he confirmed the diagnosis.

I asked Jackie to go to a clinic and to stay in the downstairs room. Three days later, Sadoul had the same troubles. Lucette was more sensible than Jackie. She said it was her own fault because she had agreed to take on a customer without a condom, which she usually never permitted. Lucette and Jackie moved out. We bought milk, permanganate, and douches (the only known treatment at the time) and every morning and evening underwent the necessary ablutions.

At the Cyrano, everybody laughed at our troubles. Nearly all of them had had similar misfortunes. Everything went well until I awoke one morning with a painful testicle the size of an orange. Busser ordered me to stay in bed and fixed up a small board on which the cumbersome gland was to rest day and night, smeared over with a blackish pomade. He sent an orderly over two or three times a week to fix my coffee and vacuum my rug. But once again the fairy godmother turned out to be Elsa Triolet. Sadoul came home only at night, and eventually he went to Nancy for a few days. I would have starved to death if Elsa hadn't made a point of coming by every evening, often after the theater. She would bring butter, fruitcake, sometimes a slice of ham. Brewing some tea, she would sit on the edge of my bed, sharing a charming little snack and telling me all the gossip, all the tales from the Café Cyrano; she was an oral gazette of Montparnasse. She also sent other people over to visit me, and she would mail my letters.

At the time, I wasn't on speaking terms with my father; I had good grounds to be angry at him because he was leaving me sick and penniless. For his part, he had reason to think I was leading an easy life. I wrote him a very nasty letter. My sister intervened. She understood what was happening and what sort of situation I was in. And she sent me a bit of money.

My forced rest was good for reading but put an end once and for all to the *Devenir Social*. I outlined a few chapters of *La Vie de Château* (*Castle Life*), which became *Le Grand Ordinaire* twelve years later. I already had a conception of the book as I was to write it in 1941–42, but I wasn't quite sure where I was heading with it. I took the pages which I had managed to put in the shape I was after and read them to Aragon: he encouraged me to keep on writing, but this wasn't enough to help me over two or three hurdles which I felt loomed in front of me. The first obstacle was the question I had been asking myself since 1925 and had apparently resolved between 1926 and 1929: Should I write, or should I prepare the proletarian revolution? The second obstacle followed from the first: If I wrote, what should I write? Did I have anything to say that hadn't been said already and far better than I could say it? Comparing myself with Breton or Aragon, I felt so inferior! I lacked education, imagination, the gift of poetry. The only thing I knew better than my two elders was the Communist doctrine and Leninism. What could I conclude but that I should not continue writing, that my vocation lay elsewhere? After a few brilliant starts, I would stop before a mass of banalities, at the foot of walls in which I could find no door, though I suspected I would discover marvels on the other side.

The things I had written I found flat and impersonal. Whenever I left the political or moral framework which I had chosen several years earlier and inside which I felt safe, I could find only vague, shapeless thoughts. I refused to recognize them as anything but vapor. I concluded from these self-examinations that I knew nothing and that I had to learn to see. Aragon's alertness, his knack of saying the right thing, his sure-sightedness, filled me with envy. It was obvious that unless I were illuminated with inspiration, I would have to postpone my literary ambitions.

In the early days of our friendship, Aragon had got me to read Jouffroy's celebrated article, *How Dogmas End.* This was a sly but polite attack by Aragon, who was still undecided, against my Communist orthodoxy. Aragon claimed he wasn't aiming at Marxism or the Comintern; Jouffroy's text, of course, concerns the Catholic religion and the Royalist Party. But, *mutatis mutandis,* couldn't it be applied to the discussions ravaging Bolshevism between 1923 and 1929, and even to Leninism?

Jouffroy's tone, the quality of his style, his rigorous description of phenomena, with hardly any interpretation, did not produce the desired effect, although they did exert a different sort of fascination. First of all, I found in the article a model of exposition and construction which I hoped to follow. I particularly noticed the fidelity of such objective description: dogma evolves through the ripening of its content, through the successive conceptions of it by men and the use they make of it, by rubbing against the world and its wear and tear. It ages through a natural process until it loses its character as dogma. Jouffroy describes a behavior process which a sophisticated man can recognize in various individuals and states during the last few centuries, especially during the forty years preceding the writing of the article. The argument does not gainsay any "materialist" explanation of the phenomena in question, though it doesn't resort to one. It struck me as remarkable that the mechanism of aging could be so independent of the nature of dogma and apply to other cases with little chance of error. The famous ultimate causes of Marxism would, I thought, supply the key to the elaboration of dogmas and show the elemental forces undermining them. I was not certain, however, that they could account for the mechanism of evolution apparently determined by the existence of the separate external world, a dogma in itself, and of men who believe, doubt, undergo, and establish.

I planned to use Jouffroy's approach to explain the origins of opportunistic or leftist deviations and the development and issue of socialist heresies. I was going to call my article *The Birth of Error,* and I spent two years outlining it, especially in Belgrade during 1930. I never got very far, but ultimately I realized that I too was working on a dogma. The victory was Jouffroy's, at a point very close to that which Aragon had wanted to lead me to.

I was feeling much better. The end of my troubles was in sight, but I still had to stay in bed for a few more days. One December night I heard the latch scraping under the pressure of an unfamiliar hand. Someone hesitated in the large room, switched on the lights, took off a coat, and with a very unsteady gait came up the stairs. A woman of about thirty, visibly intoxicated, dressed in a black fur, with ten bracelets on each arm, stepped into my room. "Hello," she said as she entered. "I'm Nancy Cunard. You've never seen me but we've often spoken on the telephone. You're André Thirion." She sat down on the bed. I stammered a few words of excuse for not getting up (luckily I no longer had my board). "I know," said Nancy. "I know you've been sick. I'm worn out. I'm going to stay here." She undressed straightaway, and wearing nothing but a black silk slip, she crept into bed next to me. "Good night," she repeated. "You can put out the light and go to sleep if you're tired."

Sleep was hard to come by. I couldn't do very much. I had no right to do anything, and, besides, I didn't know as yet whether I was cured. So my relationship with Nancy was established on a basis of loving friendship—which was much better anyway.

She didn't particularly want to become my mistress, but the thought of being naked in the arms of a young guy who wasn't supposed to have sex must have been rather exciting. When she had fully sobered up, we talked for a long time about different people, herself, me, Katia.

"Why don't you go after her?"

"I've been thinking about it a good deal," I replied, "but the time isn't ripe."

I saw a lot more of Nancy. Her kindness was marvelous. She was attentive, discreet, and as tender as one might wish. She was always ready for serious discussion, which she pursued with a poetic bias but with a lot of good will. She claimed she wanted to learn. She had polite society's habit of never contradicting the other person and of changing the subject when the conversation began to get boring or her interlocutor was getting entangled in pedantry. She acted as though she needed my company and asked me to come look for her in the nightclubs, where I would often find her quite drunk. Each of us would then go to our separate homes; I always felt as though I had saved her from ending the night badly. She asked me again and again to tell her what I'd been doing, and what I intended to do about getting Katia.

Our intimacy was peculiar. Nancy invited me to spend a few days in Chapelle-Réanville. Play-acting, I found myself in the hostess's bed. We were rather content with one another, yet we never really made love. And we never tried it again. This reinforced our friendship. We wrote lengthy letters to one another, often expressing a mutual longing and tenderness. In other circumstances, our loving affection would have changed into a somewhat exalted affair. But both of us knew how to keep things within proper limits and to husband our own feelings.

We often talked about my emotional confusion. I hadn't heard from Katia. I could no longer pretend that she would ever return of her own accord; either she herself was hesitating or something was preventing her. I would have to go and either bring her back to Paris or else officially acknowledge my defeat in Sofia. This idea loomed larger and larger in my mind. I threw myself into the history and geography of the Balkans and looked for addresses and correspondents. Nancy helped in my search; everything she brought me was hysterical or absurd, but never useless because it enabled me to think out loud and correct myself.

With my threadbare clothes, I must have cut a wretched figure in the places Nancy invited me to. She gave me a black cape tailored from the cloth with which Venetian gondoliers cover baggage. This romantic accessory made up for everything else.

16
THE STORY OF AN ABDUCTION

MY SISTER WAS CARRIED OFF BY DOUBLE PLEU-
risy in January 1930. Her death totally upset my father's life. Nothing
could replace the movement, the gaiety, and the optimism that Françoise had taken with her to the grave. The tragedy reunited father and
son. What I was planning to do suddenly acquired an emotional importance far greater than the disturbing picturesqueness of my current
activities. For my part, I felt that I had reached most of my goals: I
belonged to the Surrealist group, I was a militant Communist appreciated by others, I would probably help carry out the revolution I was
awaiting. But the things that had been happening to me since late
1928 resulted more from a combination of circumstances than from
my own determination. I realized that my emotional disequilibrium
and my celibacy were seriously detrimental to any deliberate and continuous action. I had to get Katia, bring her back to France, and marry
her. I told my father about the difficulties of this undertaking, which
I felt I could nevertheless carry out if I had enough money to go to

Bulgaria and spend the necessary time in whatever situation I found there. I believed that, by selling the objects my father had given me in October and by accepting any necessary help from my friends, I could leave very soon. It was agreed that once we were back in France, my faither would help Katia and me along until I found a way of taking care of our needs.

Nancy Cunard had been calling me almost every day since Françoise's death. She wanted to come and see me the very night I returned to Paris. I met her at the Grand Ecart. She was slightly high, but fully attentive and affectionate. "You've got to leave for Bulgaria as soon as possible," she said. "Make your plans. We'll review everything together, because I'm more experienced in traveling than you are. Don't worry about money. I'll give you anything you still need. If things go badly in Bulgaria, I'll come and get you; I know all the British ambassadors."

We discussed the essentials during a long luncheon. I hadn't heard from Katia for several weeks. Where was she? Maybe it was better to give her as little information as possible about the exact date of my arrival in Sofia so as not to risk alerting her husband. All the same, I couldn't leave her totally in the dark.

Entering Bulgaria was no problem in those days, and finding Katia wouldn't be difficult. If her papers were in order, if her husband didn't oppose her leaving, if she herself consented, the operation would be carried out easily. But we had to plan for the worst: How could we get a young woman out of Bulgaria illegally? By sea? Would we find a skipper in Varna or Burgas who would agree to a clandestine departure? By land? The borders to the west and the south were very mountainous; we would need expert guides. The passes were being closely watched by the old enemies of Bulgaria because of Macedonian agitation. To the north, the Danube separated Bulgaria from Rumania for nearly the entire length of the country. Over half a mile wide, the river can be crossed on a good boat despite the rapid current, and we could do it at a point where we would not risk gunfire from a border guard.

"I'll give you some letters of recommendation to English companies," said Nancy. "There are sailors in every port ready to deal in any sort of traffic. It's just a question of money. I gather from your description that you mustn't give yourself away too soon. That means that you must have a plausible reason for your trip: journalism, for instance, or some commercial mission. It would be better if the mission had an official character. If they arrest you because of the people you hang out with, then you can say goodbye to Katia. The Bulgarians are probably simple and proud. As a Frenchman, a citizen of a victorious nation, you must fulfill their image of the wealth and fearlessness of the French. When you're there, hang out only with the upper classes and make sure you have one or two certain and accessible references in Paris. That way you'll be safe from any maneuvers that the petty bourgeois in your friend's circle might try. The people you cultivate in Bulgaria will have to be brilliant enough to make an impression on her family and disarm them." Nancy repeated my thoughts, arranged them in her own way, and made me understand their weaknesses.

I sold my paintings at rather low prices, especially Angran's pastel *The Apple Pickers* (now in the Metropolitan Museum in New York).

First off, I got a new wardrobe. Zeff made me a superb navy-blue suit of English fabric, for ambassadorial luncheons. I bought shoes, socks, ties, shirts, gloves, and an overcoat. Any of my clothes that I felt could still be worn, I had fixed up. Nancy gave me a valise that was covered with international stickers.

Gabriel Cudenet, editor-in-chief of the left-wing daily *L'Ere Nouvelle*, was fond of me. I knew him from the Coupole bar. Telling him a bit of the story, I asked him how I could pretend to the Bulgarians that I was a French newspaper correspondent. "No trouble," he replied. Pulling out one of his calling cards, he scribbled a certification and a recommendation. "It doesn't look like much," he added, "but these few lines will be enough. I won't spoil it, don't worry. I'll leave the necessary instructions at the paper and I'll inform the proper office on Quai d'Orsay. *L'Ere Nouvelle* is quite popular in those countries. If you send me a good article, all the better! But don't feel obliged to do one, especially because the interesting things you'll see might not be right for publishing."

My situation in Paris appeared to be improving. It was understood that upon my return I would become the director of the Goemans Gallery. International Surrealism was coming to my aid. My work on *Variétés* and my very friendly relations with Aragon had brought me together with Belgian Surrealists. Goemans and Mesens hardly ever went out of town. Of all the Belgians, Valentin seemed to be the most gifted in literature. Aragon liked the tone of the novel that *Variétés* was running. Nougé was considered the most solid member of the whole bunch. Breton had full confidence in him. Magritte had added his painting, his childlike simplicity, and his desolate sense of humor to the group.

We were going through a time of plotting, rigor, and violence. The dissidents, those who had signed *A Corpse* and those who had joined them, were meeting at the Deux Magots, which they had turned into an anti-Cyrano, with the same rites. They overwhelmed Breton with insulting phone calls and poison-pen letters, challenging him to fights and wanting at all costs to welcome the new Surrealists with their fists. Both sides were ready to settle the quarrel, but with no great enthusiasm. However, Breton didn't want a pitched battle in which we would all have lost face. He decided to finish off with the Maldoror cabaret.

On January 1, 1930, a new nightclub opened at 60 Boulevard Edgar-Quinet, not far from Rue du Départ. It was Maldoror. The sign announced dancing, bar, dinner, and late supper. It had been decorated by Mayo, a young Montparnasse painter who had roamed about in the outskirts of Surrealism. Breton didn't find out about it immediately. It was Aragon who first got wind of it. On February 14, the Cyrano was in a towering rage. I was the last to arrive. At that time, there weren't very many faithful, and they were waiting for me. Breton did not hide his indignation. Aragon clued me in on what was being done. They had decided to go and kick up a row. I said that the operation ought to be organized in some way. We first had to reconnoiter the terrain and establish some plan of attack. Sadoul and I were dispatched to Boulevard Edgar-Quinet, and we left instantly. Once there, we had no trouble working things out. The personnel were putting the last touches to the preparations for a party; the club had been hired for the night by a Princess Paléologue, who was giving a private late supper. We brought the information back to Breton, and then alerted all the Surrealists that we would strike that night at eleven.

We pushed aside the doorman when he asked for our invitations. Char went in first, met the bouncer head on, lifted him up, and threw him against the screen in front of the entrance. The screen came crashing down, some windows were broken, and the four of us—Char, Breton, Noll, and myself—stood there facing the supper guests. The others—Aragon, Elsa, Eluard, Sadoul, Tanguy, and his wife—had stayed outside. Supper had already been served at the little tables; the guests were seated, their glasses were filled with champagne. The women were all in evening gowns. "We are the guests of Count

Lautréamont!" shouted Breton with enough rage and solemnity to give our undertaking suitable gravity. While Char was violently arguing with a large athletic fellow, a denizen of the Coupole bar, Breton and I violently tore the tablecloths away, flinging down the plates, glasses, bottles, and champagne buckets, kicking over the tables and chairs. Confronted with such determination, the Princess's guests took fright and fled screaming toward the orchestra in the back. The women jumped up on barstools; most of the men accompanying them showed no more courage than the yelping beauties. Standing on a chair, George Hugnet shouted, "It's the Surrealists." Realizing that there were only four of us and that our strongest man was involved in an unusual struggle, a few young men advanced toward us and formed a sort of barricade around the owner.

Char was struggling toward the bar. To help him, I hurled a few bottles at the bartender and went after Char's attacker. Breton called me over, and he, Noll, and I faced the barricade. The damage was already serious, and we were not sure about what to do next. We exchanged insults with two or three people surrounding the owner. The young women in back become less fearful. They called us names and tried to hit us with crêpes or bottles of Perrier, but they always missed.

The police had been summoned. They were at the entrance but were careful not to come in. Sadoul was methodically pulling the glass fragments out of the door; he realized that in a few seconds we would be thrown through that exit and decided, quite properly, that getting shredded en route wouldn't do us much good. I was facing a man who was smaller than I was but strapping and very excited. He became more and more provoking as time sped by, and we manifested a certain indecisiveness. I knew I could get the upper hand as long as I attacked him brutally. But that would be a bad move, and the free-for-all would turn into a massacre. I chose a middle course, wiser but obviously weak. I grabbed his tie and collar. We were fist-fighting and grappling. My friends were retreating toward the door. I followed as best I could, trying to extricate myself, and I rolled around on the floor with my strapping opponent. I tried to limit the damage, to avoid the broken glass. I felt our mission was accomplished. But I was getting the worst of it. One guy was holding me down, another was banging my head with a Perrier bottle. He wasn't hitting me very hard, and I've got a solid head anyway. All the same, this couldn't go on for long. Caridad de Laberdesque leaped upon my attacker. "Stop it!" she shouted. "Stop it! It's Thirion." She intervened and managed to calm down the bottle-wielder. I scrambled to my feet, a bit bloody but safe.

The police were finally entering. Char had a knife wound in his thigh; he accused the bartender of having stabbed him while he was trying to shake off his first adversary. Aragon and Eluard immediately pointed out what a dirty trick this was, which brought the cops over on our side. I think that Char brought charges.

All in all, the caper was a success. We didn't count the torn or stained dresses or the messed-up jackets. We had sacked more than half the supper arrangements. According to Sadoul and Tanguy, the sight was impressive and the cops had hesitated to enter the scene of such destruction. The next day at the Dôme, I had a picturesque mug, somewhat bruised. I was quite the hero. *Paris-Midi* had run a front-page story with a headline. The women were looking at me. One of them said she had been disappointed in me, expecting a lot more aggression. She was right. My heart hadn't really been in it. The prospect of leaving for Bulgaria very soon had made me take care of myself.

On March 13, 1930, I boarded the Continental for Belgrade. It was made up of sleeping cars and first- and second-class coaches. I had a second-class ticket.

Aside from Belgium, the densest national nucleus of Surrealists was in Belgrade. The Spanish did not form a separate group; they were an integral part of the Paris set. Aragon and Breton knew only Marco Ristitch, the leader of the Yugoslavs. They had met him in Paris. Issue No. 5 of *The Surrealist Revolution* had included a poem of his. I had written to Ristitch to tell him I was coming, and the exact reasons why. It was agreed that I would stop in Belgrade for a few days to put the final touches to my plans.

The royal court of Belgrade and the army were Francophiles. Nearly all the Serbian intellectuals had been to French universities. Some of them had even received their secondary education in France or Switzerland. They had returned home with liberal ideas. Even those in the government or in high army and administrative posts were somewhat open to the rights of man. The rest were hostile to despotism and King Alexander's police regime. French liberties were consoling points of reference for them.

I shall never forget the welcome I received in Belgrade. Since I am ignorant of the Serbian language, I cannot judge Marco Ristitch's work objectively. What I know of it, thanks to the author's French translations, prompts my admiration. To my mind, the intelligence, the forceful thought, the quality of expression, place these works among the best of their time. Ristitch was regarded as a past master by everyone I met around him.

Marco Ristitch lived in a large apartment with his charming and gentle wife, Cheva, and a tiny daughter. All the Serbian Surrealists had a good knowledge of French. Ristitch, like Kotcha Popović, spoke it without any accent and wrote it better than most of my compatriots. With one or two exceptions, the Yugoslav Surrealists were all natives of old Serbia and their families were part of the ruling castes. The Popovićs were a feudal family. On the eve of the Second World War, Kotcha's brothers and sisters were either diplomats or wives of diplomats in important positions. In 1930, Kotcha was studying at the Sorbonne. I didn't meet him in Belgrade but got to know him in Paris a few months later. His friends considered him an exceptionally gifted person. He was one of Tito's main collaborators. As chief of staff of the Yugoslav army and foreign minister of his country, he fulfilled all his promise.

In 1930, Alexander Vućo had a major place in the group. The Vućo brothers dealt in raw leather and American cars. Alexander was said to be very rich. His dinners were sumptuous. The dining room was enormous and noble, with high-backed chairs in seventeenth-century Austrian style. Behind the guests stood a profusion of white-gloved butlers. Vućo was just over thirty; on the verge of turning plump, he had soft features, blond hair, and an easy and cheerful character. He wrote poems in the style of Eluard. His wife, Lula, was one of the loveliest and most poetic creatures I have ever met.

Ducan Matić, a large, thin man, never laughed. He and Ristitch were the intellectual leaders of the group. He too spoke excellent French. He is supposedly the greatest Yugoslav poet of the twentieth century. He had met Eluard in Paris around 1926. He was prudent and scrupulous, and his way of thinking was deeply marked by his French studies. In 1932, he allowed himself to be tempted by the trickery and the grimacing which Aragon has always confused with the political spirit, but he never became a true Stalinist. In 1930 he was a teacher.

A letter from Breton to Ristitch had preceded me to Belgrade. I described my plans. The romanticism of my escapade filled my friends and their wives with enthusiasm. Ristitch immediately perceived the weaknesses in my project. I would have to have a more serious accreditation for my alleged journalistic mission. I wrote a mild article for a French-language periodical in Belgrade, devoting part of it to a laudatory description of the Kalimegdan Promenade, which was built on the city's old fortification. At the express request of Cheva's father, Minister of Transport Koumanoudi received me and presented me with a first-class travel permit for all the Yugoslav railroads. This precious document added weight to Cudenet's calling card, which was actually a bit light for my mission. Ristitch recommended me to an old school chum who was then attached to the Yugoslav legation in Sofia and a correspondent for *Politika*, the most important daily newspaper in Belgrade, read and commented upon throughout the peninsula.

The Serbs, the Greeks, and the Bulgarians were fighting over Macedonia. No area of the Balkans was the scene of so many intrigues. The Macedonian Interior Revolutionary Organization, founded in the late nineteenth century to fight against the Turks in the old tradition of outlaws and honorable bandits, remained popular and powerful. In Bulgaria, it reigned supreme. The royal court of Sofia, aided and abetted by the secret agents of the various powers, supported the right-wing tendency of the M.I.R.O. In return, the M.I.R.O. helped the King wipe out the revolutionary parties. Italy furnished the necessary money and advice to torment the Serbs, Greeks, and Bulgarians and poison the relations between Sofia, Athens, and Belgrade. France and England demanded the dissolution of the M.I.R.O. But this led only to subterfuge, and Bulgaria became the favorite area for terrorism. The historical leader was Todor Alexandrov, a man of considerable prestige and uncontested disinterest. Assassinated in rather mysterious circumstances, he had been replaced by General Protoguerov, a right-winger but hard to manipulate. A cruel and ambitious young wolf named Ivantcho Mikhailo had loomed up opportunely. Under the pretext of loyalty to the teachings of the historical leader, he inaugurated a campaign of assassinations. It was estimated that during 1929 there were more than two hundred assassinations in Bulgaria, a good third of them in Sofia.

In 1930 Mikhailov was boss in Rhodope. A full-length portrait of Todor Alexandrov, all abristle with cartridge pouches, was enthroned in public places, but it was almost impossible to find any pictures of King Boris. The functionaries had to knuckle under or else leave the country. The M.I.R.O. levied taxes. Every so often, it would arrange a border incident with the Serbs or the Greeks, to remind the world that the Macedonians were not disarming and that Bulgaria was submitting to the Treaty of Neuilly. When the victims complained to the Bulgarian authorities, they would lift their arms to the sky. "How do you expect us to police our frontiers with the army of twenty thousand men that the Treaty allows us!"

I focused most of my attention on these border incidents. As a revolutionary, I felt I had a great deal to learn. And since I would soon have to prepare to solve a problem of border crossing, I intended to take a close look at the scene of the action.

The day before I was to leave Belgrade for Sofia, the Yugoslav press announced in huge headlines that the Macedonians had committed acts of violence in Pirot, a village near the Bulgarian border. A bomb had been thrown into a café, injuring several people; the police were hunting for the culprits. Again I boarded the Continental. I had a first-class compartment all to myself, and the conductor, once he had seen my travel permit, was at my beck and call. In Yugoslavia, the average speed of the express was about fourteen miles an hour; often it went no faster than a man on foot. The trip was rather tedious. In a corridor, I met a very comely young Frenchwoman who was traveling to Athens to join a troupe of actors. She was as bored as I was. We started flirting, which seemed appropriate to the character of the French newsman I was playing. In Niš, the train was to split in half. There would be a two-hour wait. The Athens cars of the Continental were to be hooked up to those of the Simplon, which form a mixed express bound for the Greek capital. I had the conductor lock up my compartment and took the actress to a buffet in the station.

It was a hot, lovely day. I wore no hat or overcoat. We were chatting away gaily. I was rehearsing my role by describing an imaginary life. She was talking about her loneliness, her problems, and her career, when all at once she exclaimed: "Look, your train's leaving." Sure enough, a huge express was slowly starting toward Bulgaria, a few dozen yards away. I dashed toward it, easily covering a hundred yards in twelve seconds. I made the train, which was rolling very slowly. It was the Simplon, not the Continental. The latter would be coming in about three hours! I could get it in Pirot. My travel permit would take care of everything. I paid extra for the sleeping car and then got the idea that proved to be the most useful one for my mission.

In Pirot, I introduced myself to the stationmaster. My travel permit was the best I.D. card. "I've left my luggage in the Continental so as to have a few hours available in Pirot. I would like to make inquiries about the assassination. Could I meet the chief of police or the military governor?"

The stationmaster was terribly excited! A French journalist, with a recommendation from the Minister of Transport; in this tiny village it was practically an affair of state. A quarter of an hour later, the colonel in command of the town called personally for me in a car. I got in next to him. On either running board stood a militiaman with a drawn sword. The colonel was a rather young, handsome man, elegant in the large gray-green cape that the Serbian army had inherited from the Austro-Hungarians. His French was good. He immediately took me to the scene of the crime. It was a vast Balkan café on the main square: wide, lofty windows, a cement floor, and wooden chairs. The windows were undamaged, the furniture was also apparently intact. At the point where the missile was said to have hit, the ground was scratched. I looked in vain for traces of splinters, a broken chair. "Do you have any idea what kind of device was used?" I asked the colonel.

"A grenade like those used in the Italian army," I was told.

"I hope there weren't many people in the café," I said. "It would have been sheer butchery. Could we see the victims?"

The colonel was uncomfortable. I helped him out. "I suppose they're back with their families. It's more humane. You're always better taken care of at home than in a hospital." The colonel was visibly relieved by my explanation. I looked him straight in the eyes. "When I got the wire about the attack, I was talking with a member of our legation who knows your country very well. He praised the perfect organization of your services; he wondered how a terrorist could manage to elude the vigilance of your security system."

"The French are very smart," replied the colonel. "I ought to bring you back to the depot; we can have a talk there."

The station was quite far from the center of town. We drove back and settled down in front of a cordial slivovitz at the police station. We were becoming good friends.

"The Italians' grenades are more or less the same as ours," I told the colonel. "If I had thrown one of them into your café, I would have brought down all the glass and absolutely riddled the furniture. The Pirot glaziers repair things quicker than the ones in Paris."

The colonel laughed heartily. "So you don't believe in my *attentat*?" he said.

"I didn't say that," I replied hypocritically. "Miracles do happen over here, and, besides, the investigators may have been mistaken about the device. It could have been a crude bomb, made with a tin can, black powder, and a fuse."

The colonel now started talking to me about the feelings of the people in the villages and the way he saw his role as a military man and patriot. "What people think and say to one another isn't very important. It's none of my business. I've got propagandists, of course, but the purpose of my mission is to get results, not to convince people of anything. The Bulgarians claim that the Macedonians belong to them and that we are occupying a foreign territory here. Keeping the propagandists and terrorists away is not my concern. Others are in charge of that. But it's up to me to safeguard the order and cohesion of the people. Every now and then, I have to frighten them and find a good excuse for seizing individuals that my spies have identified. At the next market day, when all the peasants from the surrounding countryside will be in Pirot, I'm going to close down all the roads leading out of town with the soldiers from the regiment that I command. My men will push everyone into the square that you have just seen. My speaker will harangue the crowd; witnesses who will have seen everything will condemn assassinations, and I will have them vote by acclamation for an address of loyalty to King and Country. I'll also have photographs. After that, they can all go home. There was a bomb after all, enough to make some noise and justify a few accusations. It wasn't necessary to go any further."

My train was entering the station. The colonel was glad to see that I hadn't been lying. My first-class compartment was locked up, my luggage and belongings were inside, and the conductor was more obsequious than ever. "I'll come along as far as the border," said the colonel. "I'm so happy to be chatting with a Frenchman." All I had to do was listen in silence. The colonel praised the provocation as a choice police method. Wasn't it the best way to unmask the people who were preparing something? "In order to find out who they are," he added, "we have to help them a bit: we uncover them and at the same time we have excuses for dealing severely with them." He told me he had first served in Hungary, against Béla Kun. Ever since then, he claimed, Communists and terrorists had no secrets from him. I was highly amused.

We were nearing the border. "We've got two secret agents on this train," he said. "I'll point them out. One of them is a friend of the correspondent for the newspaper *Politika*. He has a thorough knowledge of the entire Bulgarian organization along our border. Take a good look at him. He'll notice we're together, and if you need his help in Sofia he'll be able to give you some good tips." The colonel left me at the border stop in complete friendship.

As I crossed the Bulgarian border, I pulled myself together, overcoming as quickly as possible the kind of anxiety you get before an exam. The first test took place at the press service of the Ministry of Foreign Affairs in Sofia. I had been received by an official in his early thirties, the assistant director or perhaps director of the service, Ivan Stamenov. He complimented me on the brilliant article he had read, a few days earlier, he said, in *L'Ere Nouvelle*. I was unabashed: "Either you're confusing something with what I published in the French-language Yugoslav press, or you're crediting me with something I didn't write. I've never sent them anything, but perhaps they've used my name in commenting upon an agency dispatch." Stamenov realized that his play was crude and that I had responded well. He immediately wrote a letter asking the Bulgarian railroads to give me the privileges I had had in Yugoslavia. He decided to introduce me at the Union Club, a meeting place for diplomats, where I would find a pleasant dining room and meet all the leading people of Bulgaria. I had passed my entrance exam with honors, for two days later Stamenov found me at the Union Club on the best of terms with the *Temps* correspondent Georges Hateau, to whom Cudenet had been kind enough to recommend me.

The Pirot affair had deeply affected the Allied legations. The French had strongly advocated a good deal of effort toward relative tolerance, which would replace the hostility of previous relations between the Serbs and the Bulgarians. They congratulated themselves because the Bulgarians had slowly returned to government methods close to the rules of Western democracies and had renounced terrorism as a means of arousing the Macedonians in Greece and Serbia to a national consciousness. These political commitments were the counterpart of the financial aid granted to Bulgaria under the aegis of the League of Nations so that it might try to solve its agricultural problem in some other way than through collectivism.

Georges Hateau felt that the Bulgarians had the right to take part in Macedonian affairs. But he didn't think that justice had any need for bombs. He praised the moderation of Bulgarian leaders during the past few years, as opposed to the pride and authoritarianism of the royal court of Belgrade and the airy vanity of the Rumanians. If the M.I.R.O. aroused the Serbs again, all efforts at conciliation would be in vain. So Hateau was relieved by the brief account of what I had seen and heard. After a few days of conversation, I felt enough trust in Hateau to pass on to him most of the Serbian colonel's secrets. I knew he would use them carefully, without getting me into trouble but with just enough indiscretion to help me with the Bulgarians whom I would have to trust.

Together with Stamenov, I made up a schedule of visits to Bulgarian political figures. I wanted to meet everybody. Bulgaria seemed to be moving toward an honest parliamentary government. The chief political force was the Peasants' Party, whose strength was both the confidence placed in it by most peasants and its old and solid organization on the local level. Totally free elections had given it preeminence within the Sobraniye! In 1923, it had a majority in Parliament. Its leader was a tall, dynamic, and able man, demagogic and subtle, one of the breed of individuals who often appeared on the political scene of agricultural nations during the past century. His name was Alexander Stambuliski. One can liken him to Nasser and Fidel Castro. The Communist Party was very insignificant, even though it was numerically larger and more firmly implanted in Bulgaria than in the other Balkan countries. The Bulgarian proletariat was tiny, and the Communist Party mainly represented the traditional Russian influence through the intellectuals and a few military men.

Stambuliski's government anticipated the socialism and nationalism now in vogue in Damascus, Algiers, and Havana and had a very marked peasant character. Stambuliski didn't like the cities, in which he saw nothing but waste and evil. His ideal was to establish a harmonious peasant society without abolishing private land ownership. The whole economy, including banks and industry, was to be in the service of the peasants, which might involve some nationalizing. The Communists had been puzzled by Stambuliski's actions, an indication of the hesitancies of the Comintern hard-liners. A captive of his background and prejudices, overconfident of his prestige, Stambuliski lacked political realism as much as Nasser or Castro. But he never had the chance to receive the corrective and unconditional help of one of the great world powers. His peasant hatred of squandering and his devotion to the family virtues of the village led him to propose ludicrous laws and to curtail liberties. There was a tax on women's hats (peasant women wear kerchiefs), for example, and a fine for anyone found in a park during working hours. Lovers were a special target: young people were supposed be at school or out in the fields; they could embrace later on. These foolish and vexing measures, which formed a long catalogue, obscured his judicious decisions against usury or in favor of cooperatives and poor peasants. They added to the bitterness engendered by the peasant leader's manners: he would always affect a scornful condescension toward young King Boris, whom he treated like an urchin, literally placing him at the end of the table. He was rude to the leaders of the army, making mortal enemies of these men who were absorbed in their ranks and their titles. He probably regarded them as useless expenditures to which he was temporarily obliged to consent.

Stambuliski might have got outside financial support if he hadn't been determined to establish a Grand Southern Slavia. This intellectual chimera has always aroused the militant hostility of other powers, little and big. In Stambuliski's time, it could only frighten the royal court of Belgrade and Athens and their English and French protectors. After 1945, Stalin opposed it with equal force.

A military plot, hatched in the palace, put an end to Stambuliski's quasi-dictatorial regime. He was assassinated, and his followers were up in arms. The Sobranye was dissolved, and the white terror was imposed throughout the land. Naturally the Comintern accused the agrarians of all the errors and stated that things would be handled right under the leadership of the proletariat and the Party. This marvelous recipe resulted in a host of massacres, as it did everywhere else. With their astonishing political sense, the Communists hadn't defended Stambuliski.

Consul Gerhardy was a gourmet. He claimed to have the best table in the Balkans. He was probably right. In any event, his cellar was incomparable. He would always inquire about the local background of his guests and make it a point of honor to serve them an excellent wine from that province. He had a reserve of local anecdotes stressing some specific wines which he served as a contribution to folklore. After performing his act, which amazed and enraptured his guests, he would take them down to his cellars, which contained more than ten thousand bottles.

Consuls are always spies. I was careful not to offend him. He forced me to tour all the Bulgarian secular schools and religious boarding schools, sparing me nothing. I saw girls' schools as immaculate as a nun's coif, and capuchin institutions as dirty as pigsties.

At Varna, a second-rate port town, I found a French consul-general, and nothing could better illustrate the absurd conservatism of the

Third Republic's administration. The post had been created during the Crimean War and had remained significant throughout the first Balkan Wars. But after 1878, nothing justified anything more than a consular agent in Varna. The state had maintained this position for imbeciles whom it felt obliged to promote and who could not otherwise be placed. In 1930, the consul-general was a well-known, ridiculous-looking fool, the laughingstock of the area. He was living with his cook, making every effort to prevent his legal wife from coming from Paris. He was successful, presumably because he had married a woman stupider than himself. He described imaginary horrors and dangers, assuring her that cholera was raging again as in 1854, the days of Marshal Saint-Arnaud, that European women would be abducted in broad daylight by suppliers for Turkish harems, and so on. His wife knew something was up and became stubborn. She made inquiries and found out that Varna had been cleared of cholera. When she announced her arrival for the summer of 1929, the consul-general, dumb-struck, wired her that packs of starving wolves were ravaging the streets of the town. The text of the telegram made the rounds of Varna and Sofia and became the hit of the embassies, but the lady canceled her trip.

The cretin of Varna put me in touch with transport agents and shippers. But the best contact was with Louis-Louis Dreyfus's representative in Burgas. At the time, I suspected neither the importance nor effectiveness of that great enterprise. Its Burgas agent was a smart young Jew who had his wits about him. His freighters also took passengers.

But my chief interest was in the borders. The Bulgarians were very eager to prove they had no part in the M.I.R.O.'s terrorism and that the reason they couldn't do any better along the border with Serbia and Greece was their lack of military means. "You have to meet the inspector-general of our border troops," said Stamenov. "He's in command of one-fourth of our army, an excellent officer whom your attaché appreciates. He'll personally show you how poor our installations are and how ample the outworks of the Serbians are. They've fortified the entire mountain opposite us."

So I decided to go along the border. It was off limits, but I soon had all the authorizations necessary. I made no secret of my trip. Quite the contrary. Georges Hateau, who had never obtained such a favor, made it clear he would like to come along. That was exactly what I had been hoping for. Hateau, the colonel-inspector, and I started off on a cool April morning in an old Fiat convertible. Our driver was a civilian (in reality, he belonged to the police force). For four or five hours, we drove along incredible lanes and forded rivers, amid a countryside in which nothing had stirred for centuries. We were stopped near a gorge, below a slope; on the other side, a field dropped steeply down to a stream. "That's where Stambuliski was killed," said the colonel. "He was in this very car with this very chauffeur. The car was stopped by people who probably belonged to the M.I.R.O. Stambuliski tried to escape toward the river. They got him in the meadow."

The border passed along lofty peaks, some of which were as high as six thousand feet. The Serbs outnumbered the Bulgarians everywhere. We stopped at the last village of the kingdom, at the foot of a hill leading into Yugoslavia. It was the headquarters of the general staff of the company commanding the two-hundred square-mile sector. The company's armament consisted of a German light machine gun, the soldiers' rifles, and a few hand grenades. The equipment of the border guards was meager and picturesque. The soldiers had no shoes, only peasant sandals, curved at the end and held together by thick laces, like the puttees worn by the French but far more Merovingian. The peasants were dressed in the same way. I had to review the munitions. We climbed up to the border post, a small peasant hut located about a thousand feet higher, beside the road up at the peak. The mountain landscape was impressive. The colonel explained that this road had once been one of the main exchange routes in the area. Now it had been closed by the Serbs. A hundred yards from the post, the road was barricaded, a thick network of barbed wire stretched on either side as far as the eye could see. "There's the border," said the colonel. "The barbed-wire network is in Serbian territory. You can see their little forts." Sure enough, on each peak there was a watchtower, and some of them were very big. Three hundred yards in front of us, on the other side of the barbed wire, stood a kind of big blockhouse.

I wanted to have a closer look at the border. At the foot of the blockhouse, I could make out a large group: officers, soldiers, civilians. I walked toward the barricade. No one had followed me; I was all alone. A few Serbian soldiers ran over to the barriers and started pushing them aside. I entered Serbian territory, among soldiers standing at attention. The troop of civilians and soldiers were coming toward me with broad smiles. At their head, there were several superior officers. Photographers started taking pictures. The most important officer was wearing a greatcoat; the others had the elegant capes of the Austro-Hungarians. They halted three feet away from me and saluted: "General X," said the officer in the greatcoat (perhaps Zivanovitch). "I command the —th division. This is the sector brigadier and"—indicating a civilian—"the governor of the province. Monsieur Thirion, we are happy to welcome you to Yugoslav soil. It's lunchtime. Naturally you will be our guest."

I thanked him profusely and added that I wasn't alone. "Of course, your friends are also invited. Isn't Monsieur Hateau French like yourself? As for the colonel, I shall be delighted to finally have him at my table instead of peering at him through barbed wire."

My companions couldn't believe their eyes and ears. The general led us to the little fort, where the table was already set. Except for the provincial governor and the two journalists, the only other guests were officers of at least the rank of colonel. We were served by captains. It was irresistible. We had to toast peace, international understanding, the two Kings, and the President of the French Republic. When the convivialities were over, the general took me aside and said: "We'll show you our installations and positions. But only you and Monsieur Hateau. We have nothing to hide from the French. The Bulgarian colonel will stay here with my staff officers."

We walked over to a gray tower atop the nearest peak. A bit lower down, we could discern the large network of barbed wire. We passed along a few firing positions. The general explained the disposition of his territory. "We've constructed a line of posts along the border. They're linked by the buried positions that you've already seen. In back, we have another line of barbed wire and operations bases for the infantry. A bit further on, we've put up a series of artillery installations. At strategic points, we're finishing more important things. Furthermore, we're very well informed about what's happening on the other side. You can see, *messieurs*," he added with a satisfied laugh, "that we know how to maintain what our common heroism has given us!"

My return to Sofia was a triumph. The Bulgarian colonel was as flabbergasted as Georges Hateau. Stamenov invited me to dinner. He did not conceal his admiration, especially since the entire press corps had been talking about our visit and had shown photographs of Serbian and Bulgarian officers side by side with the two French journalists. "Our dear inspector-general still hasn't recovered," said Stamenov.

"Just imagine, last week, Serbian soldiers shot at him because he was getting too close to the barbed wire. But," he added, "did you let the Serbs know you were coming?"

"Not at all," I replied. "I only spoke about it at the Union Club. Evidently your neighbors have a good intelligence network here. The waiters at the Union Club, for example. It's quite classic."

We talked about secret agents. "They're never who you think they are," I told Stamenov. "For instance, at first sight, you might be taken for a secret agent from Russia." (I said this deliberately, for Stamenov's talk was often very pro-Russian).

"Why on earth?"

"I find there's something very Caucasian about you. You look like Mikoyan—you know, Stalin's friend, the one the Soviets have put in charge of their foreign commerce."

"That's true," said Stamenov. "Other people have told me the same thing. But I'll have to pay you in kind. When you came to my office, I was on my guard. I had just received a telegram from an anti-Communist agency we subscribe to; it's in the Balkans. They announced the imminent arrival of an agitator with your name. I'll show you the wire tomorrow."

"Ah well," I answered, "we've both missed a career as secret agents. Unless we've succeeded, because you have the rank of minister and I have been welcomed to Serbia by the entire major staff of a division."

I still had to make sure about the M.I.R.O. I told Stamenov that I wanted to know more about that renowned organization than its legend and the tales of its exploits. "I can't be of any use to you" was the answer. "Go to Macedonia, and ask direct questions. You'll probably make contacts. Use them without frightening people. Speak to your military attaché. It's a problem he's interested in."

I followed his advice. I went to Kyustendil and Macedonian villages, where the photograph of Todor Alexandrov was flaunted everywhere. I found people who were affable but knew nothing. At the Union Club, I ordered champagne for the Italians I met. Some sort of journalist presented himself at my hotel; his name was Radev. He brought me a volume of propaganda, written in French, on the Macedonian question. "This won't teach me a thing," I said. "The French are confused about the rivalries within the M.I.R.O. What's it all about? What do the antagonists stand for?"

That was a good opening. I was given an appointment in one of the cafés that served the tasty appetizers that Stamenov called "Bulgarian atrocities." I got into a limousine with lowered curtains and was driven through badly kept streets to what seemed like a suburban house. I spent an hour waiting on a couch covered with worn velvet, in the company of appealing "atrocities" served on a small round table with a horrible but touching embroidered doily. Then, in the same car, Radev took me to a caravanserai full of peasants, and from there to a sort of bedroom with whitewashed walls, an iron bed, two chairs, and an old sewing machine. Two young men with angular, chiseled, sun-tanned faces and dressed in wrinkled shirts and shapeless suits, were waiting for me. One of them spoke fairly good French. "Even though Ivantcho Mikhailov doesn't like journalists, he probably would have made an exception for you. But he's traveling now. We are men without a country. Here, even the Bulgarians arrest our people and don't make life very easy for us. The Serbs are certainly worse, but you can believe that the conditions of our struggle are uncomfortable."

The rest of the conversation was uninteresting. The M.I.R.O. was not attempting any assassination. If they sometimes killed a traitor, it was because the people had condemned him. What should a people do if it is not allowed the right to constitute an independent state and therefore has no tribunals, lawyers, ambassadors, schools, press, or army aside from the clandestine institutions forged by its patriotism? We never got beyond generalities. I praised Mikhailov, who seemed to have the confidence of the Macedonian people, as far as an outsider could tell. We parted on cordial terms. A third man escorted me on foot through streets that were unfamiliar but probably were not far from the center of Sofia. I finally found a barouche back to my hotel.

It was time to get on to more serious matters. After six weeks of inquiries, visits, and interviews, my position was secure enough for me to take the final plunge. My last official visit had been to the metropolitan Stefan, a high church dignitary with a lubricious and dishonest look about him. I gave him some money for his good works, stressing the emotions I had felt during the night and day I had spent in the picturesque monastery of Mount Rila. I wanted him to remember my good will in case he would have to intervene for an annulment or divorce.

Where was Katia? The poetess Dora Gabé had obtained this crucial information for me. Dora Gabé was, I understand, a talented writer; she had aroused great passions. Still beautiful, fortyish, with very dark hair, she was not unappreciative of admiration by a young French

journalist well thought of in diplomatic circles. I courted her lightly.
I confided that a young friend of mine, the poet Pierre Unik, had had
an adventure in Paris with a Bulgarian student and hadn't heard from
her for over a year. He had given me a message for the young woman,
but I had qualms about delivering it, for if she had married one of
her countrymen, as I assumed she had, my mission would have been
in very bad taste. Dora Gabé was sentimental and basically favorable
to love intrigues. I gave her Katia's name and her parents' address. Dora
Gabé could obtain the precious information through a friend who had
connections in Orekhovo.

The inquiry was handled with much discretion and care. I learned
that Katia was no longer living with her family there; she was now
in Vidin with her husband. Prepared as I was for the bad news, one
of my working hypotheses, I was nevertheless very upset. I decided to
go to Orekhovo myself and wrote to Katia's mother, giving her the
date and time of my arrival.

Orekhovo is a large village on the Danube, at the edge of a fertile
plain formed by thick strata of sediment. The countryside and the
village are several dozen yards above the river. In 1930, Orekhovo
looked like the straggling hamlets that can still be seen in Asia Minor.
Anything built after the wars of independence showed various Western
influences, but no differently or more strongly than in Smyrna. These
influences, blending with the old Greek and Turkish traditions, lend
great harmony to the entire Balkans.

Katia's parents kept a sort of inn, a one-story house. It had a large
public room with tables, chests, chairs, benches, and a sort of grocery-
store counter with a *fin-de-siècle* bar. In the chests, there were mats
that could be unrolled so that the peasants who had to spend the night
in town could sleep on the floor fully dressed. Next to the public room,
there were whitewashed rooms for the family. The furniture was very
scant. The inn was kept by the father, Tomo, an enormous Bulgarian
with very gentle and slightly tired blue eyes. He was helped by his
second-oldest son, his oldest daughter, Mara, a shy, gentle girl who
did not have her sister's beauty, and two bustling servants who were
straight out of a folk play and slept behind the counter. Katia's mother
was a slight woman, typically Slavic, with fine features; their natural
distinction contrasted with the coarseness of the people in the hamlet.
Katia's youngest brother was training to be an army officer. His military
career was interrupted in 1945 by Stalin. The eldest brother was a

doctor in Orekhovo; he had married a rather attractive woman who spoke a bit of French.

They welcomed me with great kindness and prudent curiosity. The family knew the whole story. They hadn't expected me to come and thought the matter had been settled by Katia's going back to her husband. Yet they quickly acknowledged that her return seemed merely like a final experiment. They found me to be more Parisian and more French than they had imagined, and this exoticism was greatly in my favor. I declared that I wanted to marry Katia. I told as big a story as possible about the life awaiting us in Paris. The well-meaning and shaken family finally gave me Katia's address in Vidin. I said I wanted to see her, and unless she refused to follow me, we would leave Bulgaria together. I asked my future parents-in-law to give me all their help and returned to Sofia.

I had no doubts about Katia's answer. I knew it was exhaustion that had carried her off to Vidin. She also had an Oriental or Slavic passivity, which I wasn't aware of at the time. I had to go to Vidin. There I might be handicapped by language problems. In Sofia, where French was understood or spoken by every educated person, I had never had any trouble communicating. But Vidin might be different, especially if I needed people from the lower classes.

I went to the correspondent of *Politika*, the young Yugoslav from the embassy, Ristitch's friend, an antenna for the secret agents of the colonel of Pirot. We had spent a few evenings together. He was a very likable person. Like all the diplomats in Sofia, he knew all about my escapades. He was ready to accompany me anywhere in my next undertaking.

"I need your help," I told him. "I'm taking you along to Vidin. But I won't tell you the purpose of my trip until we get there. You'll be essential because of your good knowledge of Bulgarian." What more does it take to attract a guy of twenty-five to an adventure? T. was very excited. (He was still excited in Lisbon in 1951 when he was representing his country at some kind of celebration. He told the entire story to Pierre de Gaulle, president of the Municipal Council of Paris, who was amused but not exactly overjoyed, because we were both in love with the same woman, and Pierre de Gaulle did not particularly appreciate any reminder of how much ardor I was capable of exerting to get the woman who had entranced me.)

T. and I left for Vidin. This city, the most important one in Danubian Bulgaria, played a major part in the history of European

Turkey. An important communication point, it had a first-rate administrative and military role until 1878. It still possesses fine fortifications.

We went to see the sights—the mosques and fortifications—to keep up our act. In between two bastions, I told my companion the aim of my trip. He wasn't disappointed. "Here's what I want you to do," I said. "Go to the Popov home, and try to see Katia alone. Use any excuse. Say you met her in Nancy in 1927. Her husband doesn't know French. Just avoid using my first or last name. She either has to know where to find me or else arrange a meeting with me!" T. accomplished his mission with all the efficiency and discretion I wanted. The Popovs were out of town. They would be returning tomorrow on the evening boat. We took rooms at the best hotel and decided to act as though we had come to Vidin as tourists, for entertainment. A troupe of Hungarian actors were there on tour, doing an operetta in a kind of casino. I got a front-row seat. One of the Hungarian sopranos, good enough to eat and as lively as fire, kept staring insistently at me. In full accordance with my role, I made a date with her after the show, while T. went out with another girl. However, I had other things on my mind. Once again, I realized the weakness of the senses, the danger of certain games, how easy it is to become sidetracked. I really wanted that singer. Like many Hungarian women, she had an electrifying and provocative power that made her irresistible. Nevertheless, I had enough strength not to go all the way and got out of the situation by making a date for the next day, knowing I wouldn't show up.

The next day wore on and on, broken by our having drinks with the singer and other members of the company. The boat was late. One can imagine how feverish I became when I caught sight of Katia at the gangplank. I think she turned pale when she saw me, but she retained her native calm. During that moment which I had been looking forward to for so long, and which cast off all the vaguely romantic quality of evocations and dreams, the very intensity of my emotion struck me with an almost paralyzing astonishment and calm. On the other hand, all my sensations were heightened tenfold. I saw, I heard as I had never before seen or heard. I registered every one of Katia's gestures, every expression on her face, every movement of her husband, everything that happened around the two of them. I feigned indifference, however, murmuring a few words to T., who, as I had asked him to do, replied in Serbian. Time seemed suspended, but I knew that every second counted and that I had to act as quickly as possible

without making a single mistake. I wanted to give Katia the name of
our hotel. In the hubbub of disembarking, it was relatively easy. A
blinking of her eyes showed she had understood.

Katia was at the hotel the next morning. Her visit could have been
fatally imprudent. But sometimes there is a God for lovers. We agreed
that she would return as soon as possible to Orekhovo, using any
pretext. After warning her parents and getting her passport, which
fortunately was still valid, she would immediately get to Sofia. She
would go directly to Dora Gabé, who would have my instructions.
"We'll have to leave the country right away. It's the most difficult
part," I said, "but I think I've found a way to do it as long as you
follow my plan blindly, no matter how bizarre it may seem. If your
parents give you a little money and you have the time, go see a lawyer
about starting annulment or divorce proceedings."

T. and I returned to Sofia that same day. He had gathered some
information about her husband. He was considered important and
sophisticated in Vidin, but he evidently didn't belong to the political
clan in power.

I told Dora Gabé everything, and she was wildly amused. The whole
thing was crazier and more romantic than anything she had ever written. I gave her permission to write a short story about it, but she
immediately wanted to start it in a way that I considered vulgar. Of
course, she knew nothing about the Surrealist and Communist parts
of the adventure and believed I was really a journalist. I had just
enough time to make the final arrangements and assure the denoue-
ment. Katia still had the passport she had obtained before her marriage. I had no trouble getting her a French visa from Gerhardy; I
didn't have to offer any explanation whatsoever. But to leave Bulgaria
legally, she needed a visa from the police. If her husband didn't go
after her immediately, the matter would be relatively easy. Otherwise,
we would have to resort to absolute illegality. Above all, Katia's retreat
might be revealed, which would prevent me from communicating with
her directly in Sofia.

I discussed all these problems with T. I had ruled out going to
Serbia through the mountains; the barbed wire seemed impregnable
and my relations with the M.I.R.O. too distant. T. told me that
Yugoslav agents used the railroad and the Danube. I stuck to a dual
plan. Katia would go to Plovdiv, where she had friends, and then on
to Burgas, and sail off on a freighter. Or, if things went wrong, she
would return to Vidin; I would go to Rumania and rent a motorboat;

T. would also go to Vidin and take Katia by ship to meet me in my boat on the appointed day.

I waited for a week, studying all the details of the two possibilities for secret departure. The Vidin plan was the easier, because it could be carried out in broad daylight. Katia finally showed up with five suitcases and a naïve unawareness; she was bringing her trousseau.

"We have to let Stamenov in on it," said Dora Gabé. Her feminine intuition was excellent. Stamenov was fairly surprised, but he was forced to save face. Once Katia was in Sofia, Stamenov realized my determination and my love of risk. He was into it so deep that he couldn't possibly abandon me.

"Let's first try to do it legally," he said, when I spoke to him about the M.I.R.O. and escaping to the mountains in order to unsettle him a bit. "The most convenient way of going to Paris is to board the Simplon at the station in Sofia. I'll take care of the exit visa, but it can't be done overnight. Her husband is more powerful than you think. We'll have him on our backs within three days. If he gets angry, he mustn't be able to find his wife under any circumstances. Katia will stay with Constanza Kirova. She must not leave and you must not see her until further orders."

Madame Kirova was a charming young woman, a member of the Sofia opera. She was said to be kindly disposed toward the King. It was certainly an inviolable asylum, and one which a provincial lawyer would never think of.

Sure enough, Popov came to Sofia and kicked up a fuss. Too much of one. He couldn't prove a thing. Katia had vanished. No one had ever seen us together. The police were reluctant to accuse a foreigner when there was no crime. Stamenov calmed everyone down. He made Popov realize that I could not be touched, even if his gratuitous charges could be proved; the Bulgarian government would not care to risk a diplomatic incident with France for an affair of the heart in which a Bulgarian citizen cut such a miserable figure. He advised him just to write off a marriage that had been doomed from the very first day. Popov returned to Vidin, crestfallen.

Katia, with her papers in order, boarded the Simplon with her five valises. I imprudently joined her. I should have realized that Stamenov's plan stipulated Katia's crossing the border all alone. I was held back on the pretext that my passport lacked a seal. I returned to Sofia, where I stayed for another forty-eight hours. It was the national holiday. In the diplomatic tribune, a few feet from the King, I watched the parade of the garrison of Sofia. The next day, with my passport in order, I caught my old Continental. Twelve hours later, I was in Belgrade, at Ristitch's home, where Katia was waiting for me.

A lot had changed in Belgrade during two months. The depression that had begun in the United States had already reached Yugoslavia. The Vućos were ruined; they had sold everything and had moved to a poky little apartment. Atsa might have saved quite a bit of money if he had been less scrupulous. He hadn't known how to choose between the banks and his own fortune.

Under Ristitch's direction, the Surrealist group was preparing to publish an important pamphlet, more or less a single issue of a magazine. The title chosen was *Nemoguée, the Impossible*. Aragon, Breton, Char, Eluard, and Péret had sent texts. For my part, I promised them *The Birth of Error*, but I could not turn out more than three pages of acceptable material. I threw up my hands, for time was pressing, the printer was growing impatient, and I had to return to France. Ristitch was kind enough to translate some of the manuscripts for me. Together we chose the illustrations. At first blush, the ideological and literary content was better than the drawings and photos that had been proposed. Ristitch and I did the layout. All in all, the works reproduced were better than we thought. Thanks to Tito and his Surrealist companions, Yugoslav painting has escaped Bolshevik and Stalinist stupidity. This is one indication of the relative liberalism of that regime. I personally did the whole cover of *Nemoguée*, black and pink on glossy paper, for a few special copies. I was very pleased. Breton was less enthusiastic. "I figured you did the cover," he said. "It's very Baudelairian." It revealed my penchant for the useless complications I had devoted myself to during my Balkan voyage.

My literary contribution to *Nemoguée* was limited to one poem, which was really by Desnos. I had reversed word by word a text from *Corps et Biens*, a recently published collection, so as to show my friends that if forward was the same as backward, they were wrong to take such disoriented pieces seriously. Ristitch and his friends were suffering from the condemnations in *The Second Manifesto*. The violence of *A Corpse*, the rifts and polemics during the last few months, disturbed them greatly. They were all very great admirers of Desnos, whom they revered over Eluard. I had to take them in hand. I commented on the meeting at Rue du Château, the *Grand Jeu* affair, the Naville case, the Artaud case, the Desnos case, the Bataille case. I explained that the period of hesitations and literary flirting was past.

Surrealism could no longer stay aloof from Communism. No matter what you thought of Trotsky, his fate was one of those things that had to be forgotten.

We discussed the relations to be established between the Yugoslav Surrealists and the Yugoslav section of the Comintern. The Party had been forbidden. I advised my friends to keep in direct contact with the underground, but it didn't seem necessary for everyone to be a member. It would be good if those who were more interested in political life, and accepted the personal sacrifices demanded by revolutionary militantism, joined the organization and kept the others abreast of the problems posed by the conquest of the masses and the secret struggle. "If you depict Communist ideology with enough purity, then you'll be more useful outside than inside the Party, as long as it remains illegal. But despite any conflict, of which there will be plenty, between relatively protected intellectuals and the strugglers who'll be thrown in prison once they're found out, never swerve from the fundamental principles and always recognize the Party's leadership role. Don't get involved in secondary and violent quarrels; they always destroy any kind of sect. Stay local to the general line of the Comintern." I approved of going to the sources, of using the Hegel centenary in 1931 to encourage intellectuals to study dialectics. "They may put you on trial if you attack the King or demand revision of the 1919 treaties. Repression will be more difficult if you define historical materialism and defend liberty of speech. We are entering a period of revolutions. We have to be prepared. Anyone who isn't with the Party will miss the boat."

Thus, I fulfilled my role as a propagandist. It would be vain and foolish to credit me with anything but a temporary and episodic influence in the intellectual evolution of the young men who were ultimately to serve so brilliantly in Tito's ranks. Objective conditions led them to success and glory, but in 1930 I may have been a modest aspect of those objective conditions. I returned to Paris knowing I would find only trouble. I was bringing Katia to love but perhaps also to misery. With a touch of melancholy I thought about that spring spent in relative luxury, which I would abandon the moment I opened the door on Rue du Château. I also realized that I had demonstrated certain talents that would now lie fallow. It was not that they weren't suited to the areas in which they might be exercised, but because I didn't have the key to those areas, which I had encountered by chance or illicitly.

17
SURREALISM IN THE SERVICE OF THE REVOLUTION

AFTER RETURNING TO PARIS, I WENT TO THE SEC-
retariat of the Party's Paris region, at 120 Rue La Fayette. The same
building contained the bookstore of *L'Humanité*, the Central Committee, the political bureau, and the technical sections (agitprop, organization, and so on). The man in charge of the Paris region was
Pierre Célor, one of the members from the Communist Youth, to
whom the Comintern had entrusted the Party in autumn 1928. These
young men had put their own people everywhere they could. They had
been practicing a verbal leftism that the leagues and sects of 1971
recently restored to honor. They blissfully emptied the Party and the
united trade unions of their members. In June 1930 they were still
powerful, but when they let Maurice Thorez become number-one man,
they signed their death warrant. Thorez was determined to stop the
loss of members, but his objective was also to establish his personal
power. He too was starting to recruit a clientele. He wanted to halt

the waltz of the secretaries-general of the Party by consolidating his own position and assuring its permanence.

Pierre Célor had many titles, both in the Party and in Moscow. He belonged to the Politburo and to the Comintern. He was intelligent, likable, and indefatigable despite his poor health—a man of committees, cadre meetings, cabinets, the very opposite of a democratic leader or a demagogue. He was later accused of being an informer. This seems to be standard procedure when the Communist Party is determined to malign those who no longer toe the line. No proof for the accusation of Célor was ever advanced. The counterevidence sought by less than scrupulous historians merely points to an unconscious complicity with Stalinist methods. Célor did remain firm in refusing to knuckle under and go to Moscow to negotiate a nauseating compromise like the one accepted by another member of the group, Raymond Guyot. An agent provocateur would have taken the trip to Moscow, equipped with all the relevant documents, and would have obtained the change of opinion so urgent to his career. Célor was ousted. He joined the French Popular Party, a Fascist group founded by Jacques Doriot, and ultimately went so far as to fight on the Nazi side. Célor remained a member during the war and supposedly died after 1945, an anti-Communist and a good Christian.

When I told "Pierrot" Célor about my Bulgarian caper, he was amused, astonished, and interested. "Your true path," he said, "lies with partisan warfare." The Communist organizations were in a pitiful state. The Comintern was beginning to react carefully against leftist sectarianism, but it was itself a prisoner of the leftist and sectarian conceptions of the Third International. I reproached the Party for its political passivity masked by a verbal intransigence swarming with hasty judgments and stupid assertions. I felt I could be a better interpreter of the ideology of the Third International. I still didn't realize that the views I was criticizing originated in Stalin's profound indifference toward anything that wasn't Russian. The Comintern? A veneer! The Communist parties? A device to create fear. True politics took place on the level of states and ambassadors.

Stalin assumed his power through police tactics. But he had assumed a task beyond his scope (no matter what people may have claimed) and was erecting monstrous obstacles in his own path. To grapple with the gigantic difficulties he couldn't handle temporarily, he resorted to a Reign of Terror on a level unparalleled in history, at least on such a scale. He used the Communist parties in 1930 to maintain a shining red beacon for the national proletariats until the Five-Year Plan would, he thought, give the U.S.S.R. irresistible strength. A prisoner of his own insane directives and the boasting of an apparatus that was more and more intent on maintaining its privileges, he lived in an unreal world. Since his pride would tolerate no competition, he vituperated against the social traitors and Trotsky. He expressed consideration only for the bourgeois leaders whom he was intent on reassuring.

These contradictions were implicit in the resolutions passed by the Congress of 1928, but at the time I wasn't aware of them. The Depression was expected to radicalize the masses, and the Communists would thus automatically profit; we would have to know how to wait and remain uncompromising. The chief, perhaps the only, danger was a capitalist crusade against the U.S.S.R. By developing a love of peace, a refusal to wage war, we would be objectively helping the radicalized proletariat, and this brilliant tactic would bring the Revolution on a silver platter. The bugaboos brandished in Russia and elsewhere, with their accompanying terrorism, were mainly feeding the cult of fear.

In June 1930, the radicalization of the masses was revealed to the Communist Party by the flight of its members. There were only about three thousand people left in the cells of the Paris region. Thorez wanted to stop the loss of blood. He didn't feel total confidence in his prefects, the regional secretaries. He wanted to get at the bottom of things himself. "You've got to see Thorez," said Célor. "He wants to meet the militants. He'll give you an assignment himself."

I saw Thorez within three days. He received me on one of the upper floors at 120 Rue La Fayette. His office was modest and narrow, no bigger or better equipped than that of a supply officer. The administrative apparatus of the Party seemed to be sharply reduced. Thorez didn't hide the fact that he was facing a very serious situation with limited means at his disposal. People have often described his cordiality and humanity, his intelligent and sympathetic face, the impression of balance and thoughtful wisdom given by that massive man. Thorez had a physiognomy like Danton. He had the oratorical force of the great democratic leaders. He had become one of the best journalists in the Party; I sometimes heard Breton lauding his editorials in 1930 and 1931. The faults of the "son of the people"—vanity, servility toward Stalin, the political dishonesty learned in Moscow, the dread of risk—were revealed only gradually during his career.

Maurice Thorez was probably a superior bureaucrat. He could have been an effective collaborator. General de Gaulle made him a minister. But Thorez's scope was no greater than a clerk's. He was the very opposite of a revolutionary. His temperament was more conservative than that of his rival, Doriot. He belonged to the race of high priests so numerous in western Europe since the late nineteenth century. Indeed, their proliferation under all sorts of labels makes one doubt whether the working class, within the narrow context of Marxism, can produce anything but administrators.

"We shouldn't underestimate our crisis of strength," said Thorez. "Too many good comrades have scorned the masses and mistaken the militants for future corporals. Leftist rhetoric has permitted them to conceal an opportunistic appreciation of events and to justify passivity. They've been treating reformist or partyless workers as if each of them were a petty Social-Democratic leader. They've neglected to explain patiently the line of the International; they've failed to seek contact with the socialist or reformist workers. We've staked more than we should have on our young. The Party needs men like you, familiar with the trade-union struggles, the life of Parisian workers, the implacable strength of the bosses' repression.

"Barmotte and you had good ideas in the Fifth Chapter. You were active and you fought against opportunism. But you were in too much of a hurry; the workers got left behind. You've got to get the local cell in Plaisance back on its feet and sink your teeth into the companies. There are supposedly a lot of union members there who are afraid of the Party. You've got to convince them. Go see the old members, the ones who were never at odds with the general line, who were looking for explanations that we couldn't give them. Talk to them. Bring them back into the Party. Don't hesitate to come and see me if you run into any trouble."

Plaisance belonged to the Sixth Chapter, which was ruled by J.-Pierre Timbaud, whom I didn't like. When he discovered that I had been put in office by the secretary-general himself, Timbaud became very hostile. He saw me as a probable rival. A big talker, sectarian and stupid, he had almost no following among the metallurgists and owed his position only to his gift of gab, his natural baseness, and the rapid advancement of the cadres in his union. He was mainly bent on making a career by pleading his quality as a onetime worker, in order to avoid ever returning to the factory. Arrested by Daladier, he was part of the lot of hostages handed over to the Germans by Vichy. He died bravely. He had been a Stalinist all the way, passing through the approval of the Stalin-Hitler pact and organizing sabotage in the armaments factories during 1939. A street in Paris is named after him, whereas the names of the true heroes of the Resistance are gradually fading from memory.

The meetings were held at the Trade Union House at 111 Rue·du Château. Lénard, the concierge, was a former secretary of the Federation of Metallurgy. He had been dismissed and had lost his job with the union. He was rather stupid, but no more incompetent than Timbaud, lazier and more honest, with enough sense to see that his successors, with their big mouths, had lost a good part of their manpower. He knew me and put me on my guard: "First you've got to straighten out the two or three guys who joined the Party in 1929 because of its sectarianism. You may be able to do something with them; they're not bad, just lazy. But watch out for X. He wanted to be secretary of the cell. He'll inform against you to the Chapter. Don't expect anything of Timbaud. He always messes things up wherever he goes. The only guys here who are ready to work are in the International Committee, but they're old-timers." Everything he predicted came true. In 1932, X. became secretary of the cell. He was a mystic who would have been more at home with the Trotskyites, if they had been capable of recruiting workers, than among the Stalinists. He refused to accept the Popular Front. In disgust and out of revolutionary idealism, he joined the International Brigades and was killed in Spain.

One of the habitués of Rue du Château was Le Goff, a giant from Brittany, nicknamed Red because of the color of his mop of hair. He was a boilermaker in a small firm. In summer he wore a simple black T shirt on his Herculean chest, and in winter he added an old jacket. He chewed tobacco, and during demonstrations he would use the jets of brown saliva as a defensive weapon. He was very fond of red wine and often got drunk. He lived in a rather large room in a hotel on Rue du Texel with a thin ageless wife and two children. Le Goff earned a decent living and was never work-shy. For him, the working class, the trade union, and the Revolution were sacred! But he wouldn't have anything to do with the Communists. "They're liars," he would say, "and they politicize too much!"

In every May 1 demonstration, Le Goff was at the front. He was afraid in brawls, although he could knock out a cop. He was extremely powerful and indifferent to blows. He never went out of his way to start a fight. His adversaries were very cautious and respectful, and he would always come out of an affair with honor. I have seen him keep a dozen policeman in awe before the Trade Union House. He was playing with a beam he had taken from a construction site. "If you try to enter," he shouted, "I'll smash you to a pulp, and if you don't let us out, I'll do the same."

We became very good friends: "Thiriun," he would say in his Breton accent, "you're on the wrong track. They're gonna have your hide because you wanna dent them, and all they like is talk. You don't ask nothin' from no one and you're in front. They don't like that because they wanna be in charge. No matter what you do, it'll be wrong!"

After the inspection commissions in 1931, he was very comforting. "Just stay here. They're gonna kick you outta the Party, but they'll keep you right where you are, 'cause they know we won't go along with them; we'll always be on your side." He invited Katia and me to lunch in his hotel room. Just before dawn he had been to Les Halles and had brought back more than twenty crabs. They were lined up on the floor, cooked to a turn. We bent down to pick them up and ate them with an extraordinary succulent sauce which we poured into the shells. The sauce had been prepared by Le Goff himself.

In 1930 the traditional celebration of *L'Humanité* took place at Bezons, in the miserable park around a mansion pompously referred to as a castle, which belonged to the Communist municipality. The government had turned down everything. Not even five thousand people were present. I counted several times. There couldn't have been more than fifteen hundred. I spent part of the afternoon stretched out on a lawn, next to Thorez, concerned about the way things were developing, gauging the scope of the ravages caused by sectarianism and repression. But neither of us questioned tactics! The Party had been badly managed, that was all: it hadn't involved itself in the daily struggles of the workers; it hadn't profited from the famous radicalization of the masses. Thorez was not given to despair. His tranquil and winning presence reassured the militants. I mentioned the Surrealists and Aragon. "Oh, yes," he said, "the guy who wrote a treatise on style. I read it. It's really pretty good. But do you honestly think those people are close to the Party? Aren't they mainly bourgeois intellectuals?"

The year 1930 was to be one of the most important for Surrealism. Eluard and Breton published *The Immaculate Conception*, and Dali *The Visible Woman*. *L'Age d'Or* was premièred, Aragon and Sadoul went to Russia, and two issues of *Surrealism in the Service of the*

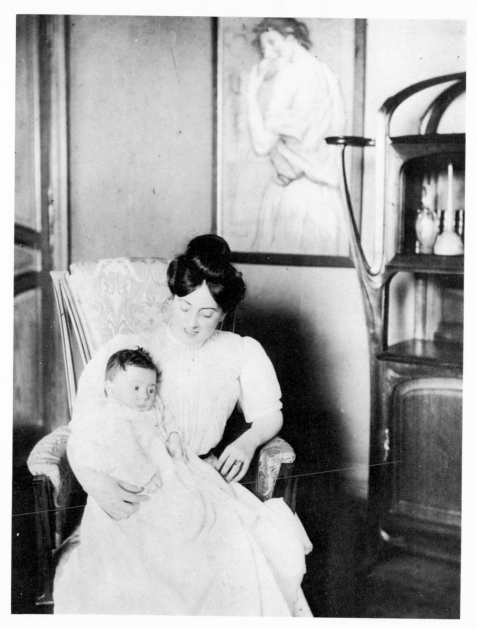

Above: The author in July 1907, probably on the day of his baptism, sitting on his mother's lap. The photograph was taken in the "pink parlor" of the Baccarat house, which was burnt down on August 25, 1914. Furniture by Tony Selmersheim. In back, a pastel by Victor Prouvé. (Photo, Collection André Thirion)

Right: Louis Thirion, father of the author, in 1919 on the banks of the Meurthe in Baccarat. (Photo, Collection André Thirion)

Françoise, younger sister of the author, at the age of seventeen. (Photo, Collection André Thirion)

Above: Jean Ferry, 1932. He had not yet joined the Surrealists. (Photo, Denise Bellon)

Right: In the High Vosges, in 1926, during a hike of over 300 kilometers. Standing, André Thirion; seated, Georges Sadoul. (Photo, Collection André Thirion)

Breakfast at rue du Château, February 1929. At the foot of the stairs in the main room; from left to right, André Thirion, Cora, Georges Sadoul; standing behind Sadoul, Frédéric Mégret. (Photo, Man Ray)

Right: The toilet in the pavillion on rue du Château, decorated by Louis Aragon (1928). (Photo, Man Ray)

Below: Yves Tanguy, 1929 (Photo, Man Ray)

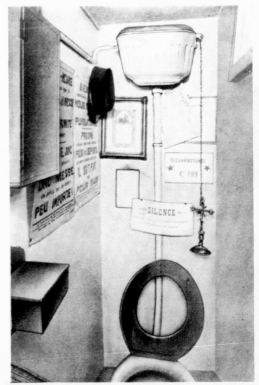

Above: Louis Aragon, c. 1935. (Photo, Keystone)

Left: Jacques Prévert, 1942. (Photo, Denise Bellon, *Images et Textes*)

Elsa Triolet, rue Campagne Première, 1931. At left, a drawing by Miró; at right, a North American totem pole. Elsa is mounting one of the necklaces that she was making for the high fashion world of Paris. The studio belonged to Louis Aragon (above). (Photo, Collection André Thirion)

An exquisite corpse, a collective drawing done c. 1933 at Valentine Hugo's by Tristan Tzara, Yves Tanguy, Paul Eluard, and Valentine Hugo. A sheet of paper was folded in four; each participant drew part of the figure without seeing what the others had done. (Plate, Ed R. Laffont)

Below: Suzanne-Hélène and André Thirion (bearing the traces of a recent brawl). (Photo, Collection André Thirion)

Bottom: The painter Georges Malkine, 1927. (Photo, Man Ray)

Paul Eluard (*left*) and André Breton, 1934. In those days, their intellectual rapport was absolute. (Photo, Atelier René-Jacques)

A montage published in issue 12 of the *Révolution Surrealiste* (December 1929) to illustrate the inquiry into love. Surrounding a Magritte painting, most of the Surrealists of 1929. From left to right, line by line, starting on the top: Maxime Alexandre, Louis Aragon, André Breton, Luis Buñuel, Jean Caupenne, Salvador Dali, Paul Éluard, Max Ernst, Marcel Fourrier, Camille Goëmans, René Magritte, Paul Nougé, Georges Sadoul, Yves Tanguy, André Thirion, Albert Valentin. The handwriting says, "I do not see the [woman] hidden in the forest."

Above: Raymond Queneau, 1928.
He had not yet written his novels.
(Photo, Man Ray)

Right: Maurice Thorez, secretary
general of the French Communist
Party, 1935. (Photo, Roger-Viollet)

From left to right, Vera Popović, Kotcha Popović, Nusch, Paul Eluard,
photographed by André Thirion in July 1939. Kotcha Popović was a chief of
staff in the Yugoslavian army and Minister of Foreign Affairs. He was one of
the Yugoslavian Communists to have been recently designated to act as
deputy for Tito in case of an emergency. (Photo, Collection André Thirion)

Above: Georges and Germaine Hugnet during the preparations for the Surrealist Exhibition of 1938. (Photo, Denise Bellon, *Images et Textes*)

Right: André Breton and Leon Trotsky in Mexico, 1938. (Photo, Archives of Editions Seghers)

Above: The Eleventh Company of the Sixth Foreign near Palmyre in September 1940. Photo taken by André Thirion. (Photo, Collection André Thirion)

Below: Georges Bernier and Max Ernst, 1958. Max Ernst and May Ray had become household words. Georges Bernier had often put his gallery and his review *L'Oeil* in the service of Surrealism. He was responsible for enabling André Breton to stage his last major event, *L'Ecart Absolu*, dedicated to the memory of Charles Fourier. Younger painters and writers exhibited an unblemished revolutionary ardor, the effects of which will be felt despite the disappointing forms that the mirage known as *revolution* will take.

Photograph taken in the *Le Paradis* cabaret on Boulevard de Clichy, 1929. Originally meant for *Variétés*, the photograph was never used. From left to right, seated, Elsa Triolet, Louis Aragon, Camille Goëmans and his wife; standing, Jean Arp, Jean Caupenne, Georges Sadoul, André Breton, Pierre Unik, Yves Tanguy, Suzanne Musard; behind the latter, René Crevel; seated on the chair, Cora; with his back to the camera, Thirion, his hand on Cora's chest; holding up the Key of Saint Peter, Frédéric Mégret. All the people in costume are employees of the cabaret. (Photo, Collection André Thirion)

Above: May Ray in Hollywood, 1948.

Right: Post card sent by Georges Sadoul to André Thirion in 1930, the day he mailed the famous Saint-Cyr card.

The text of the Saint-Cyr card that ultimately sent Georges Sadoul to jail:
"Dirty swine, you're hiding your game, you've just been made 61st in your
class at the Saint-Cyr Military School. I know how greatly you admire armies,
you fistulous and grimy officer you. If you do not hand in your immediate
resignation to the Commander General of the Saint-Cyr School, then you're
nothing but a pile of refuse and a garbage can full of shit. Furthermore, you can
go eat shit, with your fancy white gloves, you dirty Saint-Cyrien. DOWN WITH
YOUR SHAKO PLUME. We'll manage to kick you out and hang you high
clip your Marshall Joffre's tail, the master of your young years, fuck off you dismal
Cyr, you dirty little creep. Signed The Unknown Soldier. THE UNKNOWN
BELGIAN SOLDIER." (Photo, Collection André Thirion)

Right: Marie-Laure de Noailles, 1932. (Photo, May Ray)

Below: René Crevel, 1929.

Katia in Dubrovnik, Yugoslavia in 1930, after the "abduction."

Several Surrealists in Tzara's home during the writing of the pamphlet, *Mobilizing against War is not Peace*. From left to right, above, Paul Eluard, Jean Arp, Yves Tanguy, René Crevel; below, Tristan Tzara, André Breton, Salvador Dali, Max Ernst, Man Ray. (Photo, Atelier Rene-Jacques)

Several Bulgarian and Yugoslavian officers, in April 1930, at the Belgian border post at Guetchevo. At left, wearing caps, André Thirion, Georges Hatteau (the Sofia correspondent for *Le Temps*); in the middle, the Yugoslavian commander general of the sector and the Bulgarian colonel and inspector of the border troops. A week before this photo was taken the Bulgarian colonel had been shot at by Yugoslavian border guards at this very spot. (Photo, Collection André Thirion)

Left: Benjamin Péret and his son, Geyser, in Paris, 1932. Photograph taken by André Thirion (Photo, Collection André Thirion)

Below: A croquet game in Belgrade, 1930. Cheva Ristić, about to tight-croquet the poet Atsa Vućo. Standing, Marco Ristić, who was the Yugoslavian ambassador to Paris from 1945 to 1950. (Photo, Collection André Thirion)

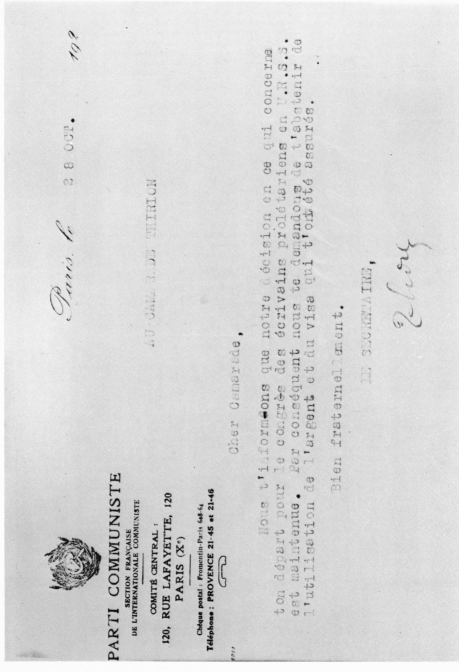

The letter of October 28, 1930 from Maurice Thorez to André Thirion, informing him that the Party secretariat did not authorize his participation in the Congress of Proletarian Writers in Kharkov.

Revolution appeared. The birth of this magazine was the main event of spring. I don't know whether the title was hit upon before or after the exchange of telegraphic correspondence filling up the first page. The coincidence, in any case, is remarkable.

The Depression was reaching one country after another. France still felt no direct effects, but England and Germany were gradually being hit. The Comintern specialists recognized the well-defined features of cyclical crises. According to their terminology, this one was frightening because it came on top of a general crisis of capitalism which they said would get worse and worse. The implication was that the political prospects outlined two years earlier were correct. We could now expect the workers' struggles that would engender revolutions.

The Moscow soothsayers came to a completely different conclusion. The crisis would increase the danger of war, and the U.S.S.R. would be in greater jeopardy than ever before; the masses would have to be mobilized to defend it. Stalin, who was deporting millions of peasants to Siberia and organizing famine, was particularly bent on arousing fear and making possible opponents feel guilty. The other Communists took that bugaboo seriously!

In late spring 1930, André Breton received the following telegram:

International Bureau of Revolutionary Literature asks response to following question. What will be your position if imperialism declares war on Soviets?

This is the answer that Aragon and Breton drew up. It was wired to the bureau in question:

Comrades if imperialism declares war on Soviets, our position will be consistent with directives of Third International position members of French Communist Party.

If you judge a better use of our faculties in such a case we are at your disposal for mission demanding our use as intellectuals. Submitting suggestions to you would really be presuming on our role and circumstances.

In conflict situation nonarmed we think it useless to wait to put in the service of revolution the means that are particularly ours.

This commitment was just the right move. At the time, there was nothing like it in the left or far-left wing of intellectuals and artists anywhere. It was to define the Surrealist position up to the very moment when Hitler's threat to all civilization would make Stalin's blackmail against the anti-Soviet crusade odious, ridiculous, and provincial.

In Paris, the Surrealist reply embarrassed the intellectuals who were starting to paddle around the review *Monde,* edited by Henri Barbusse. They were pacifists but not revolutionaries. They didn't like Surrealism, which made their artistic ideals look retrogressive and defended a very strict morality. Their consciences were generally rather elastic, and they placed their bourgeois comfort over anything else.

To the extent that Breton's telegram became known, it was welcomed by the Russian Communists, who staunchly believed that the powers were preparing a war against the U.S.S.R. The truth, however, was quite different! The armed forces of the "imperialists" were at their lowest. All strategies were defensive. Armaments were old-fashioned!

Suzanne had left Breton once and for all. Lise Deharme believes that Suzanne had always loved Emmanuel Berl, and that her affair with Breton was a misunderstanding or a dare, a rash act provoked by Berl's bad manners toward her. The young woman went to Lise Deharme's place in Saint-Brice for a while, which cast a shadow over Breton's very affectionate relations with Lise. For some time now his feelings for her had been keener than admiration and deeper than friendship. Lise was a very attractive sorceress, with the voluptuous and seductive eyes of the Queen of Sheba. She was singularly fond of objects, forms, and colors that had any connection with magic; she surrounded herself with oddly behaving animals and wore jewels that most women would have regarded as baleful. Breton was certainly in love with her. Circumstances prevented any realization of this love, but for the rest of his life Breton remained under the spell of his first meeting with Lise Deharme. Thus he was especially responsive to what he might interpret as a complicity in treason. But Lise had invited Suzanne only because she found her amusing. It seems that Suzanne was accompanied by Berl, and their presence in Lise's home might seem to be a masterpiece of perversion.

Suzanne, in my opinion, had loved Breton. She had been flattered but outdone by her lover's position. Versatile, flirtatious, and frivolous, she was always open to flings, but Breton's exclusiveness permitted her only temptation. Breton was too lucid, too intellectual, and too passionate for a woman like her. The break-up caused him a good deal of suffering, but his admirable strength of character helped him remain calm, and he tried not to lose interest in ideas and people. He confided only in Eluard and Aragon, forcing himself to stay as serene as an analyst; he was as unwilling to compromise in that private domain as in any other. All of us were totally scornful of Emmanuel Berl and his writings. Nevertheless, Crevel, Aragon, and I would certainly have attacked him less often if he hadn't been responsible for our friend's suffering. Our solicitude for Breton was all the greater because he was the only member of the group with an unhappy love life. Gala and Dali were having their honeymoon. Eluard had no problems. Nor did Aragon as far as his heart was concerned; he had regained his equilibrium, and his only troubles were his financial security and certainty about his literary career. Sadoul was in complete disarray, which made him more like Breton, but his emotional void was merely one of the causes of his state, and probably the least important of them.

The ridiculous story of the insulting postcard he had drunkenly sent to the Saint-Cyr major was reaching a bad end. Katia and I had found the pavilion extremely dirty and disorderly. The unwashed dishes, the decay everywhere, the distressing traces of temporary tenants all reflected the bad state of the master of the house. Sadoul's life was more irregular than usual: he often got drunk, and he had an episodic affair with an acrobat, who left after giving him syphilis. Sadoul went to the provinces, where he spent several months, interrupted by brief visits to Paris; he wanted both to escape possible arrest and to take care of his shaky health. He was in great need of rest. His doctor had discovered that he had a lung disease that required immediate attention. Sadoul stayed away from Paris all that summer. In the fall, after being sentenced to three months in prison because of the postcard, he left France in a catastrophic mood, physically undermined, to join Aragon in Moscow.

France's right-wing government was bumptious and boastful. Reactionaries of every sort were in the saddle. The terms "bourgeois power" and "bourgeois dictatorship" made sense. The moralizers were making the law, censorship was king. In the mother country, repression was revealed in stiff prison sentences; the laws against anarchist plots were applied to simple matters of opinion. No one was burning cars, raising barricades, sabotaging the railroads, or blocking the highways. Such activities would probably have led to deaths. Molotov cocktails were still unknown. A conspiracy of silence was organized around the Surrealists. The major papers avoided mentioning them, and publishers turned down their books. José Corti, an independent publisher, decided to buck the trend and take the risk. It was he who brought out everything, or nearly everything, in 1930 and 1931. The prefecture of police refused to give Paul Eluard a passport, and police investigations of various individuals became more and more frequent.

Almost the entire younger generation was prudently conformist. The trade-unionists were driven out of the factories, the strike leaders dismissed. Voicing one's demands was a misdemeanor. In the colonies, the least attempt at emancipation, even within the legal framework of the empire, was drowned in blood. Petty colonial officials were laying down a meddlesome, vexing, and often racist law, and yet the masses generally remained attached to the tricolor, Bastille Day, and the vague ideal of Republican glory and liberty. Despite everything, the Republic had brought peace, relative prosperity, and a little education to the territories it had conquered. Nothing was absolutely rotten, especially in the old colonies, where the fairly strict administrative rules of the French, a certain freedom of speech, the opening of schools and lycées, and the practice of elections brought forth gifted individuals, set up a local intellectual life, and enriched the French universities, the theater, and the army. In regard to the "colonial question," Surrealism violently opposed the official ideology, the prejudices of almost all the French. This clash was not simply the consequence of political options or the result of our alignment with Communist ideology; it also had its roots in our refusal to consider Christian civilization as absolute progress and in the Surrealists' interest in the customs and traditions of savages. The Surrealists professed that the myths of the native peoples were better than those of Christianity, and that the artistic creations of the African Negroes, the Papuans, the Aztecs, the American Indians, and the Eskimos were no less meaningful and beautiful than the most celebrated works of Western civilization. Aragon and Breton sometimes liked to indulge in simplifications and programs. Now and then they would draw up lists of what and what not to read, which tended to wreck most reputations and disqualify anthologies. The world map published in the *Variétés* issue on *Surrealism in 1929* is both an affirmation of several political preferences and an indication of the areas that produced the art that was particularly admired. Half the globe is reduced in favor of New Guinea and Easter Island. The Surrealists' attitude toward the thought and art of the "colonial" peoples and the oppression victimizing them determined a line of rupture with the right and with most left-wing and far-left intellectuals. This attitude aroused militant hostility, but in itself it was a more coherent and obvious force than our Marxism.

It resisted the test of time and permitted the extraordinary worldwide expansion of Surrealism.

Breton, despite Suzanne's departure, had regained all his creative energy with no loss of lucidity (partly perhaps under the lash of the unexpected help of Salvador Dali's paintings, writings, and statements). Eluard effortlessly maintained himself on the heights he had reached. But Aragon was passing through the most serious crisis of his career as a writer. In 1929 he published *The Great Gaiety*, and in 1930 a thirty-page brochure, *Painting in Defiance*, as a preface for the collage exhibit at the Goemans Gallery. Some of the poems in *The Great Gaiety* were written in 1927 and 1928. This was a small output for the most gifted Surrealist, the only one other than Crevel who was capable of finishing ten pages by noon with a minimum of revision—especially if you compare those two rather slender volumes with his production between 1923 and 1928 and with the reams of paper he used up after 1934. *Painting in Defiance* was the last Surrealist text that Aragon wrote. It contains a sentence that everyone has noticed. In regard to the origin and development of collages, Aragon cites the photomontages of the Russian constructivists: "It is not up to me to neglect a phenomenon," he writes, ". . . that marks one of the swings of painting in our time and that is primarily an indication of the necessity of signifying." In introducing political collages between 1921 and 1924 into the Surrealist museum, with some hesitation, Aragon did not shock any of his friends. But what did he mean by "the necessity of signifying?" Is Klee less meaningful than George Grosz? As an admirer of Klee, Aragon, could have replied that this was a false issue in 1930. Couldn't Duchamp have suggested to him—in case he forgot—that it takes so little artifice to remove or change the meaning in a collage, that painting must distrust any "necessity" so contingent and transient? What was one to admire in Lissitski's or Rodtchenko's collages? their meaningfulness or their political bias? Reproducing Rodtchenko's collage, Aragon was forced to admit that its meaning is extremely obscure. I knew Aragon well enough to assume that the juxtaposition of Man Ray's *Eau de Voilette* and Lissitski's collage showing a tiny Lenin on an imaginary tribune marked the limits he assigned to the necessity of meaningfulness in the illustrations of his brochure. In 1930, all the Surrealists were willing to let their own means of expression be used, if necessary, for Communist propaganda, but their concept of service to the Revolution went far beyond a few practical tasks.

For Breton, for Dali, or for me, it couldn't be a matter of forcing artistic or literary creation, moral or philosophical inquiry, into the molds of slogans. The same apparently held true for Aragon. But, without his realizing it, the importance of the manifest content, the necessity of an almost vulgar meaning, expressed in the most questionable literary tradition, imposed itself upon him more and more as a rule of creativity.

Not everyone admired Aragon's poetry. Eluard and Tzara deemed it minor, Breton thought it peripheral. In *The Great Gaiety*, Aragon writes:

> People insistently ask me
> Why I occasionally go by
> The line. . . .

This was a question that most of his friends were asking. His early poems sometimes derive from Apollinaire, whose breeziness he pushed into paroxysm in 1927 and 1929. Eluard, Desnos, and Tzara couldn't keep their bearings in it, but Aragon's verdict was based partly on his wariness of the excesses in the great genre. The last two poems in *The Great Gaiety* remove those barriers. The necessity of significance obtains, and the poet is no longer very demanding in regard to the means. The authenticity of feeling, expressed in *The Ruins*, about the poet's affair with Nancy Cunard, saves a text that nearly plunges into banality at several points. When all the political disputes of the twentieth century have become as vain and distant as the theological quarrels of the religious wars, it will be obvious that the imprecations hurled in *The Ruins* anticipated the eight pages of *Hurray the Ural* or *Red Front* as well as all the logorrhea of *Elsa's Eyes*, *Broceliande*, and other works. The Congress of Kharkov merely accelerated a process that had already begun. Nevertheless, if the cretinizing doctrines laid down by Stalinist illiteracy had not crushed all of that vulnerable poet's motives for rebellion and all his critical impulses, there is no certainty that he would have abandoned himself to the verbose academicism which he dubbed poetry.

In 1929, I asked myself about Aragon, and I know that other people also asked, "What on earth could he write after *The Treatise on Style?*" I was waiting for an answer that would astound me. Aragon may have replied with one or more of his novels. But in 1930 the writer was on the wrong track. Aragon began a kind of bastard book, a mixture of a pamphlet, an imaginative work, and an edifying composition. He introduced inept and vile characters who embodied all the bourgeois vices, at least the ones we saw at the time. The main figure was a police chief whose ridiculous and extravagant name Aragon borrowed from a judge who was then professionally involved in all the scandals: Faux Pas-Bidet. The text had the panache and brilliance of *The Treatise on Style,* but it left the reader as puzzled as a perusal of Léon Bloy. Was it necessary to set off on this road, along which certain poems of Péret's seem to exhaust everything that could be found and said in thirty lines and that led directly to skits for red headquarters? Aragon gave a reading of his sketch at Rue Fontaine. The audience was Breton, Sadoul, myself, and perhaps Giacometti. Breton's response was icy. When Aragon finished reading, Breton simply said, embarrassed but firm, "If you publish that, people will once again say that you're a genius. This won't be news to anyone. But I don't think that piece adds anything at all to your last books, or that it can achieve the effect you're looking for, that both of us are looking for." Aragon was not insistent. We never heard another word about that sketch.

The Third Faust also hung fire. It was to be an opera with a libretto by Aragon and Breton and music by Georges Antheil. The title might ultimately have tempted Breton, but he could never forget the miserable *Treasure of the Jesuits.* The thought of collaborating once again with Aragon didn't excite him, and he was even less enthusiastic about becoming a librettist. All that remains of the project are some preliminary fragments sketched by Aragon, which leave little room for regret. On the other hand, Breton and Eluard coauthored the remarkable *Immaculate Conception.* Returning from a vacation in Vaucluse with Eluard and Char, he brought back the poems of *Slowing Down Work,* a joint effort of the three men. These two works, Max Ernst's *The Dream of a Little Girl Who Wanted to Enter the Carmelite Order,* and especially Dali's *The Visible Woman,* all of which appeared in 1930, provided the Revolution with a choice of frightening explosives powerful enough to act spontaneously, regenerated, like endlessly recharged and re-energized mines. For quite some time these books have created very wide danger zones, to the great peril of the conformists and conservatives who ventured in upon them. Their effect will outlast all the harangues of congresses, the shouts of demonstrators, the lyrics of the International or the Marseillaise; they will endure long after the condemnations of all the Republican, Fascist, or Communist tribunals have been forgotten or purged. Nothing justified my presence in that team better than the judgment by Charles Hainchelin, who was nevertheless so unwilling to veer from Marx or Lenin. After receiving *The Visible Woman,* he wrote to me: "I've lost Dali's address. Please apologize to him for my not having acknowledged the receipt of his book. Tell him I've found remarkable things in it, *truly revolutionary"* (underlined by Hainchelin).

L'Age d'Or was screened at Studio 28, in October, a few days after Aragon left for Moscow. Today it's hard to describe the effect in 1930 of a film so scandalous in comparison to the productions of the time, which were tightly supervised by various forms of censorship, of which the prior control by producers was not the least. I sat next to Breton during the screening. He was seeing the film for the second time. During the first part, you hear a fragment of Beethoven's Fifth, the opening bars of the andante. Breton, who wasn't interested in music, leaned over to me: "Who wrote that? It's very beautiful." After the screening, the Viscount and Viscountess de Noailles, who had backed the film, gave a reception in their townhouse on Place des Etats-Unis. Everyone was invited. At the time I didn't know Charles or Marie-Laure de Noailles. But I was not unaware of their patronage of and interest in Surrealism. I knew they were responsible for *L'Age d'Or.* My intolerance at the time was so total that the role played by rich or titled people in making a revolutionary work greatly troubled me. I saw it as a stain. However, thinking it over a bit, I had to admit that without the Noailles there would have been no *L'Age d'Or.* Eluard and Breton dragged me over to Place des Etats-Unis. At first I didn't want to go. My curiosity got the better of me. Mounting the grand stairway, which was flanked by butlers in French get-up, my anger burst out. I went over to the buffet to start a row, smashing glasses, hurling bottles at the mirrors and the stewards, knocking over anything that could be knocked over, spouting insults. Charles de Noailles remained impassive. Marie-Laure was a young, slender brunette with a winning décolleté. She was elegant enough not to notice anything. Neither of them was unforgiving about my incongruous and gratuitous violence. My behavior was even more foolish because I could reproach the Noailles with their fortune alone, not with their use of it. The following year, Crevel patiently explained to me who Charles de Noailles was and the genius inhabiting Marie-Laure. I sensed that the world was less simple than the schemes in which I wanted to enclose it. (In fact, Charles and Marie-Laure de Noailles were ousted from the Jockey Club for the crime of supporting *L'Age d'Or.*)

The screening of the film had been planned as a Surrealist demonstration. In the lobby and the corridors there were paintings by Dali, Max Ernst, Man Ray, Miró, and Tanguy, books, and very successful photographs that Man Ray had taken of each member of the group. We drew up a program catalogue containing a preamble and five fragments. I am the author of the last of those statements, *Social Aspect, Subversive Elements*. It's the one that has been most frequently quoted and reprinted. The rest were written by Breton, Crevel, Eluard, and Aragon, in that order.

On December 3, members of the Patriots' League and the Anti-Semitic League sacked the moviehouse, smeared up the screen, lacerated the paintings, ripped the books and photos to shreds, and threw stink bombs, interrupting the screening. They anticipated the actions of the Nazis in Germany in 1933. The evening of the next screening, I was at Studio 28 with a few workers from the fourteenth arrondissement. We were armed with bludgeons. When any young men tried to enter, we first frisked them summarily to make sure they weren't carrying any instruments of sabotage or aggression. Two or three suspects were kicked out without further ado. The film was banned on December 11 and seized on the twelfth.

The Provost de Launay, then the municipal councilor of Paris, in an open letter to the chief of police, denounced the review *Surrealism in Service of the Revolution* as anti-French. From 1947 to 1953, I was in the Municipal Council along with Provost de Launay. We were registered in the same Gaullist political group. The Provost was now an old man in his dotage, indulgent toward anyone, including Communists. He had done some sort of favor for the general in 1935 or 1940, demonstrating perspicacity as well as courage, and he was proud of it. A very handsome man, he had been quite successful with women. He remembered the *L'Age d'Or* affair very well. "Today," he said, "I would gladly go and see it and ask you to explain anything I didn't understand. Dali is about to become famous, you and I vote against the Communists, and if an anti-Jewish league were to form again, I would instantly write to the chief of police demanding its dissolution. In 1930, a lot of things passed me by. But perhaps you didn't see so clearly either. I didn't realize that one shouldn't toy with freedom. Naturally, I'm still attached to a lot of my prejudices; I despise bad manners. But, believe me, the only thing that counts is time, and it's time that play the dirtiest tricks on us. I would give anything to be like him," he added, pointing at one of our Communist colleagues, a tall man about thirty, "even in his place! I wish you the ability to grow old gracefully!"

My position in the Party was strong. I had revived the Plaisance cell and all the auxiliary organizations of the fourteenth arrondissement: The International Red Aid, The Friends of the U.S.S.R., the Committees of Defense of Humanity. I had set up a Marxist study group attended by store employees and Communist Youth members. I had organized a dance at the Trade Union House to fill up our treasury. I had breathed life back into some company newspapers.

At one of our work conferences I ran into Darnar. Imprisoned in Nancy with Thorez, he had left the Saint-Charles Prison as secretary of the Central Agitprop Commission. He asked me to organize an exhibition in Bellevilloise. The Political Bureau wanted to celebrate the tenth anniversary of the Party. I had carte blanche. The Party was putting its archives and a credit of two thousand francs at my disposal. However, sixteen hundred francs of that sum had already been used to pay Cabrol, a cartoonist, for portraits of the four main leaders: Thorez, Doriot, Cachin, and Monmousseau. With the documents of the Congress of Tours, the most exciting piece was the congratulatory telegram sent by Doriot to Abd-el-Krim during the War of the Riff. I had mistakenly worked up a project too difficult to carry out, given the means available to me: four hundred francs, a worker from Bellevilloise, Yves Tanguy, and myself. Tzara gave me a thousand francs. The great auditorium of Bellevilloise was dreary. I wanted to paper it white and make a false ceiling with rolls of paper on a framework of metal wire. With Tanguy's help, I slaved away on that structure, while Clovis Trouille did the decorations we had agreed upon. We had asked Trouille and Dali to design them. Trouille painted a life-sized *trompe-l'oeil* guillotine, dripping with the blood of the condemned of Yen-Bay. Dali had done two projects, which Trouille, Tanguy, and I had to carry out. The bigger one was a depiction of an enormous stake, its flames consuming ciboriums, government bonds, weapons, decorations, and other paraphernalia symbolizing capitalism. The other project was to present the famous telegram to Abd-el-Krim. Arrows and bloodstains were to lead the visitor to it.

Aragon's financial situation was unenviable. He was starting his life with Elsa, who absolutely refused to live in mediocrity. But assuring Elsa's comfort in 1930 was not all that easy. The new household could no longer accept the pension that André Triolet was elegant enough to continue to offer. Aragon was bent on terminating that morally embarrassing dependence as soon as possible. Happily, Elsa was of a practical mind and by no means lazy. She hit upon the idea of creating high-fashion necklaces. She designed imaginative jewelry that was easy to make with pearls, plaits, rings, and the like. Her very lovely things instantly met with great success. Worth, Molyneux, Chanel, Piguet, Schiaparelli introduced them in their collections. On Rue Campagne-Première, Elsa set up a little studio with Katia and herself as the workers; she also recruited one of Triolet's friends. Once the necklaces had been shown in collections, Aragon went to show them to foreign buyers in the retail houses on Rue Paradise. He got himself a traveling salesman's kit. I accompanied him several times, for he asked me to take over during his trip to Russia. Aragon's commercial shrewdness was stupefying, almost embarrassing, for he had acquired the manners of a real drummer. I was quite shocked to see the author of *Anicet* forced to stoop so low in order to survive, and I was annoyed that he could play such a servile role.

Business prospered, but Elsa never hid the fact that she had no commercial calling. They began talking about a trip to Russia. At first, they discussed it as a simple tourist venture, which is all it really was. Elsa wanted to see her sister again and buy herself a beautiful fur coat. Aragon was curious. But as the time drew near, political aspects began to emerge. The Surrealist defense of the U.S.S.R. was favorably commented upon. It was inconceivable that such a well-known author as Aragon would not be received by the Russian poets and novelists and that his conversations with them would be merely trivial, or that the authorities would not acknowledge his presence. Finally, we learned that a Congress of Revolutionary Writers was to be held in Kharkov during Aragon's sojourn in the U.S.S.R. The plot thickened. Eventually, Sadoul decided to go along. More and more nervous at the possibility of imminent arrest, he requested a visa at the Soviet consulate.

It all moved along swiftly. The departure was feverish. I felt that our two friends in Russia, presumably after conversations of definite political importance for the development of everything of concern to me, had to hold all the trumps. Aragon and Sadoul had joined the Party in 1927. They had never been expelled. I knew they approved the general line. Aragon had been defending it within the limits of his activity for over a year. I suggested that they register in the Plaisance cell. I had a formal mandate to get back the comrades who had left the organization but were not in political disagreement with it. Aragon and Sadoul accepted. I sent a note to the Party secretary, informing him about the voyage and giving my opinion of its significance and its political advantages. I suggested that a contact be established in Moscow between Aragon and one of the Frenchmen in the International delegation. As a precaution, I asked Hainchelin to inform his friends in Russia, which he did. But I was committing a monumental tactical error: I wanted to increase Aragon's and Sadoul's authority, but I merely rendered them more vulnerable.

The political line that Aragon and Sadoul might possibly have to defend in Russia was the one I had drafted in 1929 in a document reprinted in *Variétés*. This fairly leftist line began by asserting the existence of a nucleus of intellectuals very close to the Party, devoid of any bourgeois attachment, firmly settled on the positions of orthodox Communism and the possibility of activities based on precise objectives set by the Party's guidelines. That nucleus would temporarily enroll any person ready to take part in such activities as long as his character would not weaken the rapprochement by confusing its goal.

The Second Manifesto had endorsed the line that would form the substance of Nos. 1 and 2 of *Surrealism in the Service of the Revolution*. Consistent with the spirit of the Third International ideology, leftwing and far-left intellectuals who were not Surrealists were the object of savage attacks. One of our essential aims was to dispell the fog of confusion surrounding the weekly review *Monde*, to identify it as one of the most dangerous adversaries of the working class, and to discredit its editor Barbusse, to whom we denied the right to present himself as a revolutionary intellectual. Our ideas were subject to the rules of historical materialism and Leninism, but everyone acknowledged that the Surrealists still had a long way to go in interpreting and using the Holy Scriptures correctly. Nevertheless, Surrealism was to cover wide areas in which Marxist orientation was unknown, if indeed it would ever be defined there. It was agreed unambiguously that the development of Surrealist investigation in those areas would not be trammeled by political action, since the resulting achievements could be reckoned as objectively revolutionary.

In October 1930, I set greater store by purely Surrealist activities than I had in January 1929. On that head, I was as firm as Breton. My admiration for Max Ernst's paintings, and for those of Tanguy and Dali, my respect for Dali as a person, in the texts of *The Immaculate Conception*, were the factors in that evolution, which was quite feeble in scope. The Dali case was a test. Any necessary concessions would have to be made in that domain. Aragon apparently concurred. Nevertheless, there were slight indications that he didn't feel as committed as Breton, Eluard, Crevel, or I to defending the delirium that might develop in Cadaqués.

I married Katia in Malakoff on September 30, 1930. It was a rainy day. The then Communist mayor Piginnier, a fine, bearded Social-Democrat, who a few years later was to join the ranks of some rightist dissidence, officiated. Our witnesses were Aragon and Breton. My father and Tanguy were also present at the brief ceremony, which verged on parody. By mutual agreement, Piginnier wore against his flesh the tricolored sash that, according to regulations, he was supposed to girdle himself with. Breton made a funny remark about the allegory painted on the ceiling of the wedding chamber. Tanguy seriously offered to improve the composition by adding a few symbols, such as a small sickle and a small hammer. But Piginnier did not take his offer seriously, so the town of Malakoff really lost something. The wedding dinner took place on Rue du Château. Eluard joined the newlyweds and the witnesses. My father, at my request, had personally prepared an enormous *quiche Lorraine*. He had started learning how to cook three years earlier, and was particularly adept at that regional specialty.

We had acquired a first-class recruit. In the middle of 1930, a skinny fellow of medium height, with hair like a Sicilian shepherd, joined the Surrealists. He said he was a sculptor, and his name was Alberto Giacometti. Shy and fidgety, he was careful not to support any opinions condemned by the chieftains. He even went so far as to utter nothing out of line with their judgments, so he might contradict himself three times in the same evening according to the way the discussion was evolving. We were not very familiar with his work. He would sometimes bring tiny sculptures; he didn't really compel recognition until three months later with a few symbolic objects. He gradually found his bearings in his art and soon hoisted himself to the front rank. For a long time, he was torn between Breton and Aragon.

With the autumn, a group of young vagabonds heaved into view. The most active was a man of vague nationality who said his name was Bauer, a sort of red-haired hippy. He may have been an illuminato, provocateur, or humbug; we were never to discover which. The others included Rolf Ubac, Michelet, and Malet. There was at least one girl in the group—an unfrocked nun in her twenties, very attractive—plus a few more or less episodic and vague students.

Michelet wasn't even eighteen. His father was a police chief in Clermont-Ferrand. He had run away from home and was living in

Paris. Malet flaunted anarchist ideas. He was more mature than the others and hadn't yet started writing detective stories. Ubac still wasn't sure about becoming a painter. He spoke hestitantly and modestly. He had the gaze of a mystic and a candid soul. It was very hard to judge people that young. At first sight, Breton felt that Michelet was the most solid. Of all of them, only Ubac had something to say.

I was seeing Breton every day. Our opinions on everything had never been so close. I received an express letter asking me over to Rue Fontaine without delay. Aragon had been in Moscow for some time now and was starting to send us optimistic letters. He had written that Sadoul and he had been invited as observers to the Congress of Kharkov.

I found Breton in a state of agitation. He had had several conversations with Bauer, who rather intrigued him. Breton's curiosity was fired by Bauer's claiming to be a Party member (which he was, in fact), by his hints that he belonged to the secret apparatus, and by his flaunting a major and deferential interest in psychoanalysis. He argued that the essence of Freud's work can easily be integrated into Marxism and insisted that this was the point of view of a good many comrades abroad. Such statements were so new, though they mirrored hopes that were so old, that Breton was all set to give them much attention, so long as the man expressing them wasn't a fraud or a spy. Everything spoke against Bauer—his physical appearance, his manners, his clothing, a certain linguistic confusion he made excellent use of when at a loss, claiming he couldn't find the right French expression (although he spoke the language very well). Nevertheless, he knew Freud and the psychoanalysts. Breton asked me to clarify the whole thing about secrecy. It was hard. Not everything was made up. Bauer seemed to be carrying out minor tasks in a vague espionage network attached to the International Workers' Aid or to the movement of working correspondents (the rabcors, after the Russian abbreviation).

Emphatically, and in a tempting way, Bauer straight off proposed assembling all the revolutionary artists in a large association. He claimed that only the Surrealists were capable of carrying out such a task and that he would do his best to get them the necessary support.

It was a splendid opportunity. Breton was all the more tempted by the idea because Bauer gave him a preamble text which he claimed had been endorsed by "foreign comrades." Its arguments were new because of its comprehension of Freud and the skillful bridge between Freudianism and Marx. We decided to use this text as the basis of a kind of inaugural manifesto. I feel it bears reprinting. The first three paragraphs are pretty much Breton's polished form of Bauer's draft. On the other hand, the *nota bene* was entirely by Breton and me, taking into account the syndicalist aspect of Bauer's proposals.

Preamble:

The desire for self-affirmation as an individual is innate in any living creature, and this creature therefore tends essentially to survive beyond itself. This desire seeks fulfillment generally and primarily in the organic cell that appears to retain in itself the quality of the individual: the child.

Under certain conditions and, as is admitted nowadays, if a human being presents, in relation to the normal, a certain organic * insufficiency involving feelings of inferiority, a *sublimation* occurs within him, permitting him to externalize himself in other areas. The work he creates serves primarily as compensation. And the remarkable acquisitions of the mind resulting from the psychic enrichment that is thereby realized give this work an undeniable social usefulness.

The values man creates by grappling with the universe through sound, line, color (if, on the one hand, they are fundamentally important for explaining the creative process and if, on the other hand, they are indispensable to the existence of any society), depend absolutely on the social structure of his environment. The artist must always be considered a biological and sociological product; the material basis of his existence rests on the economic conditions of the society he lives in.

N.B.: The nature of human needs is indifferent; it scarcely matters whether they come from the stomach or the imagination (Marx). By "artist," it is clear that we very rigorously mean only the intellectual producer who seeks to satisfy man's *spiritual and intellectual* appetite. We need not say that we distinguish him from the unscrupulous trafficker who usurps his place in bourgeois society by making himself to any degree whatsoever the apostle or the mere accomplice of that society.

The artist, who by definition cannot submit today to the ideology of the ruling class, is barely tolerated by that class, and his means of survival in the capitalist regime are the most precarious. He does not control the markets, which are almost exclusively in the hands of the great bourgeoisie. It would do the painter no good to enter into competition with the art dealers, who are united in trusts and cartels. But in this transitional period, the proletariat cannot be reckoned as a buyer. Unless he organizes, the artist has no chance whatsoever of improving his economic situation, a situation as bad as, if not worse than, the proletariat's. His

* The concept of artistic creation as the result of organic insufficiency struck us as somewhat suspicious: a police provocation or a Germano-Russian obsession?

only means of safeguarding the independence of his work is to struggle side by side with the exploited workers against capitalist society.

His guide in this struggle can only be the organization of the conscious proletariat: the Communist Party. For the artist, it is crucial that he create his own trade union so as to make sure that the destiny of the revolutionary proletariat is linked to his own.

This text, which may have been deliberately provocative, still maintains an interest today that the laborious Marxist "analyses" of artistic creation do not approach. The most consummate of these pedantic stupidities that Marxists have vied with one another to lavish on us since Plekhanov and Bukharin were the products of the Stalinist era, The Soviet "ideologists" viewed the impressionists, Picasso, Matisse, etc., as evidence of the disintegration of the bourgeoisie, at the same time that the Nazis were denouncing the degenerate art of Paul Klee. The Trotskyites were no less foolish. The use of biology to discover the sources of artistic creation was, of course, bound to irritate "consistent" materialists of the Party, who were prepared to outdo the most questionable issues in Friedrich Engels. When I presented the "preamble" to the Party leadership, the intellectuals, including Hainchelin, grimaced. Bauer's "foreign comrades" were probably out of town!

It was decided that the group would be called Association of Revolutionary Artists and Writers. Breton and I spent two days drawing up the statutes. The leading idea was to create a sort of syndicalism of letters, arts, and sciences aligned with the trade-unionism of workers. The choice of the program was simple: all we had to do was adopt the program of the Red Syndical International (or Profintern), to which the Communist or sympathetic trade unions belonged, in France the C.G.T.U. We could thus rid ourselves of liberals, lukewarm followers, and conciliators. The door would be closed to the intellectuals on the weekly *Monde,* who refused to repudiate national defense in the capitalist regime and bourgeois democracy. We included a protective clause stipulating that no one could be admitted to the A.R.A.W. if it were proved that he was working for any counterrevolutionary newspaper or publication. In short, the defined criteria of membership established a permanent reign of intellectual terror.

We regarded as revolutionary "any moral or philosophical idea compatible with Marxist morality or philosophy." We regarded as "revolutionary propaganda any propaganda useful to the Red Syndical International or the Communist International and recognized as such by these organizations." These statutes contained one crucial point that was deliberately inserted. It clearly shows how far our loyalty to dialectical materialism extended in 1930. I have every reason to assume that I was its author. Any man of science was eligible for membership in the A.R.A.W. if he could "furnish proof that his scientific activity is revolutionary in nature and in conclusion." Considering the definitions cited above, this astonishing sentence anticipated both Lysenko and Hitlerian science.

I informed the agitprop section of the Party of these statutes, indicating that their publication could, if necessary, involve a slightly different preamble. Five years later, the Revolutionary Writers and Artists was to turn against Eluard and Breton with weapons from the arsenal we set up in 1930. Our definition of revolutionary ideology and propaganda in 1930 may have been contingent and debatable. But our successors in 1935, who deserved none of the adjectives they decked themselves out with and counted for nothing in literature and revolution, were to illustrate their claims by silencing Breton, one of the major writers of the twentieth century, universally acknowledge as having embodied more than anyone else the spirit of revolution. This pattern always arises whenever people venture into theology and churches.

All the Surrealists present, including the newly arrived sympathizers, were called together to a sort of general assembly, during which the preamble and the statutes were ratified. Breton sent these texts off to Aragon, explaining how they had come about. Max Ernst designed the seal of the A.R.A.W. We instantly did a stereotype. This, like so many documents from that era, is probably in the possession of Georges Hugnet.

18
THE CONGRESS OF KHARKOV, OR THE HAND OF MOSCOW

THE FIRST LETTERS THAT BRETON AND I RE-
ceived from the Moscow travelers were enthusiastic. We were assured
that Aragon had established the necessary contacts and that misunderstandings were being cleared up. Aragon seemed to be an excellent ambassador: Breton agreed that the author of *The Peasant of Paris* could
make decisions there that would commit us all. The negotiator's
finesse, after ten years of close collaboration, of jointly resolved conflicts, of doors broken down and new worlds discovered together, gave
Breton the highest guarantees of the quality of the action undertaken.
Or at least so he thought. We felt our friend was carrying out a
campaign of methodical explanation. The following letter, written to
me by Aragon on October 10, 1930, at the start of his sojourn, indicates the subjects he was discussing with his hosts. They were not
always austere political problems.

Dear chum, send me all the things you have handy as soon as possible
by return mail:

1. The bulletin of the *Société d'Editions* (*To Know Marxism*)
2. The review
3. A clipping of my article on *Le Monde* in the S.R.
4. Clippings from *Le Monde* of any articles you think might interest me (Einstein, Habaru on Mayakovsky, you know the kind, I'll rely on you). A good many. And several copies at that.
5. Find the articles on Mayakovsky and M. Mir's translations in *L'Humanité*.

Register your letters. Georges is probably arriving tomorrow. You can see the kind of things that are occupying me now. If you come across any newspaper articles that might interest me, cut them out and send them over before I have to ask you. . . . If you happen to find these books in what I use as a library, please send me *Maisons de Société* and *Le Marseille Curieux*. You know them. A registered package, okay?

Above all, write me. Don't tell me any jokes. My mind has been slowing down terribly; I won't understand a thing. I have enough trouble expressing myself. I hope you know me well enough not to be annoyed. Affectionately,

Aragon.

On October 22, Aragon wrote to Breton that Sadoul and he would be taking part in the Congress of Kharkov not as mere observers but as official French delegates to the plenum of the International of Revolutionary Literature. Ultimately, Aragon himself denied this. In *Surrealism and Revolutionary Development*, published in December 1931 in issue No. 3 of *Surrealism in the Service of the Revolution*, he claimed that he and Sadoul merely had an advisory capacity in Kharkov. All in all, however, the lessening of their role between October 25 and November 10 may have been the consequence of events I shall describe later.

No sooner had he informed us of this success than Aragon relayed an astonishing piece of news. He felt that my presence in Kharkov was indispensable. His opinion was shared by the organizers, for I received an invitation to the Congress. On October 25, Aragon sent me the following telegram:

Visa money sent. Get passport immediately. Indispensable presence desirable November 3 Moscow—if impossible directly before November 10 Kharkov—telegraph Brik. Bring documentation.

Sure enough, a notification of the transfer of sixteen hundred francs, I believe, from the International Bureau of Revolutionary Literature arrived the next day on Rue du Château. The sum was available to me at the Bank of Northern Europe.

This invitation could be interpreted in various ways. Despite the telegram of October 26—"Immediate results, Unhoped-for feature, Confidence"—not everything may have been arranged, and Aragon may have needed reinforcement and a Communist backer. I reported the matter to the Party secretariat and asked for instructions. Their reception was measured. Initially, there was doubt whether my presence in Kharkov would be opportune. I wrote to the Secretary-General of the Party, enclosing the invitation telegram. On October 29, I received the following reply from Maurice Thorez:

Paris, October 28
To Comrade Thirion
    Dear Comrade,
We have to inform you that our decision concerning your departure for the Congress of Proletarian Writers in the U.S.S.R. is upheld. In consequence, we ask you to refrain from using the money and the visa that have been made available to you.
Fraternally yours,

THOREZ,
Secretary.

Discipline had never been my forte. I decided to go anyway, and I requested a visa at the Consulate-General of the U.S.S.R. Nobody knew anything about it. All precautions had been taken so that Aragon would not receive the help he was awaiting.

There were two questions to ask. Where did the order against my departure come from? And what were the reasons for it?

Only forty-eight hours had elapsed between my application at the Secretariat and Thorez's reply. It was thus a purely bureaucratic decision made in Paris. The secretariat was stunned when Moscow confronted it with a fait accompli by an organization "next to" the Party. It felt that it was up to Paris to designate the French representative to Kharkov. By insisting on obtaining the Party's concurrence, I had probably provoked a fundamental debate. The membership of the Surrealists in the International Bureau was episodic. On the other hand, Barbusse was untouchable. This thesis was defended by those who set great store by the moral influence the author of *Le Feu* exerted on the old-timers. The more the French Communist Party saw its following shrink within the working class, the more importance it attached to the intellectuals who maintained a tie between the Party and the petty bourgeoisie. Hypnotized by the theory of a growing danger of war, most of the members of the Political Bureau refused to break at any cost with their great pacifist comrade. In Nancy, I had expressed qualms about Barbusse. Heaven only knows what intrigues I might have started in Moscow with the members of the French delegation to the Comintern! Prudence as well as bureaucratic ethics demanded that I stay in Paris. The matter went back to Moscow—but rather slowly, it seems.

Two main topics were discussed in Kharkov: the establishment of a sort of inventory of revolutionary writing and the development of proletarian literature. Aragon's contribution on the first topic was rather important, and he probably felt he had won several points. The inventory of revolutionary writing in France is presented in two resolutions: a so-called general one and another concerning the weekly *Monde*. The sole merit of the general resolution was that it classified the Surrealists at the far left and admitted that their evolution would lead the best of them to proletarian ideology. A rather lengthy paragraph defined Surrealism as "a reaction of the younger generations of the petty-bourgeois elite to the contradictions of capitalism in the third phase of its development." The conclusion condemned "the errors that found expression in *The Second Surrealist Manifesto*."

The "resolution" on *Monde* owes a great deal more to Sadoul and Aragon than the preceding one. Aragon has written that it is a résumé of "his report aside from a few terms." It severely condemns the contents of that publication and he attributes responsibility for them to its editor, Henri Barbusse. But the judgment against him, hard as it may have been, was merely an exercise of style. Barbusse himself, though absent, had been elected to the Presidium of the Congress, and the overwhelming enumeration of the faults he had covered up did not bring him down from his pedestal. After this resolution had been passed, Aragon and Sadoul sincerely thought they had won, for none of us would have dared to hope a month earlier that Moscow could so easily convict *Monde* of promoting "ideologies hostile to the proletariat." Our two friends weren't politically experienced enough to gauge the influence of Barbusse's defenders in the Comintern and Soviet leadership. Barbusse and Romain Rolland were a source of pacifist propaganda, which the "politicals" valued more highly than the ideological contest of *Monde* and the anger of the Surrealists.

There was a great deal of concern in Kharkov about proletarian literature, a subject often discussed during the thirties. Among Marxist and sympathetic intellectuals, it aroused a prodigiously foolish competition. Even today's leftists have forgotten the delirious texts that treated proletarian art with high seriousness, using sheaves of quotations from the Church Fathers.

The debate was regularly reopened by mediocre writers who were trying to force their dreary naturalism on the wide market of the world proletariat. The Russians obtained that effortlessly within their frontiers thanks to their police and their reign of terror. Outside Russia—to the great benefit of culture—the masses, scarcely interested in difficult reading, showed a preference for detective novels and revelations about movie stars, queens, and torch singers.

Aragon participated in the Congress discussions of that white elephant—without the least sense of humor (which he seemed to have lost forever upon crossing the Berezina) and with his characteristic tendency to elaborate. He announced that the cautious letters sent by working correspondents, the rabcors, to Communist newspapers were the source of proletarian writing. His remark was very sensible, for those efforts did fulfill all the criteria of that genre. Aragon was not completely guileless. He knew it was good form in the Party to encourage the rabcors. And as a professional writer, he knew it wouldn't get very far.

The rabcors were one of the pseudo-democratic deceptions invented by the Communist bureaucracy. Theoretically, these "readers' letters" should have revealed the opinions of the "rank and file" directly rather than through the filter of professional journalists. In reality, a network of informers had been created. Their totally unspontaneous writings not only were censored by the authorities, as was the entire press, but also showed a distinct tendency to discredit or insult those whom the authorities wanted to attack. This rather efficient system is still in use. It seems to have wreaked havoc in People's Republic of China. In France, the rabcors became an espionage network which collapsed after a trial that aroused worldwide interest.

The Comintern representative to the Congress of Kharkov was a fat Marxist lady, Comrade Gopner. She acted like a schoolmarm in her guardianship of dogma. No one has ever found out what particular talent had given Comrade Gopner the right to head the flock of revolutionary writers. Perhaps she had come to Kharkov to expiate some mysterious deviation. In any case, she supposedly took her role seriously and was respected. She really attacked Aragon; she wasn't the least bit taken in by the sleight-of-hand that confined proletarian writing to the domain of complaints and denunciations. "To state," she replied, "that the 'rabcors are the only source of proletarian literature' is tantamount to formulating a far-left assertion that is nonetheless right-wing and 'opportunistic.' "

Statements like this should have alerted Aragon. But he was still a novice in the techniques of congresses. His optimism was unshakable. He sent Breton a wire on November 17, "Here complete success," while they were finally getting around to serious matters. Comrade Gopner and, I was told, the Comintern secretariat wanted some information on these two French intellectuals and Party members who were so fiercely committed and so nasty about Barbusse. The information relayed from France was accompained by vehement protests against the presence of Surrealists in Kharkov. Opinions in Moscow were split. The Russians responded to Aragon's charm and talent, and even more to the brio with which he conducted his commando operation. After all, in September no one had even been thinking about him. In a few days, that wicked Frenchman had got himself invited to the Congress of Kharkov, had actually given a report, obtained more and more recommendations, won supporters, and submitted conclusions. Spurred on by his criticisms, the Congress had condemned *Monde* and attacked its editor. In the tableau of French literature, brushed with colors supplied by Aragon, Surrealism was on the top level of revolutionary writing. The Congress had compromised itself with Aragon and Sadoul, an incontestable achievement! Furthermore, there was nothing much that the two men could be reproached with: they behaved well, their orthodoxy was meritorious, they had made a number of right-thinking declarations. When they had been taken sight-seeing with the Congress delegates, their comments were exemplary.

But for the French Communists, there were dangers inherent in the situation. So Aragon and his friend Sadoul wanted to play teacher to Moussinac, Barbusse, Jean Richard Block, Politzer, Fréville, and their followers? The Congress had decided to create an association of revolutionary artists and writers in France. Hadn't it already been created by Breton and Thirion, who had probably been instructed in time by their friends? The Party intellectuals would thus be forced to affiliate themselves with this new phenomenon Surrealism! And so on.

In extremis, the Russians and French reached agreement on an emergency procedure. The French were determined to give the two travelers the worst possible welcome if they didn't get protection and assurances against further harm. A few hours before their departure, Aragon and Sadoul were visited by emissaries who presented them with an ultimatum: the Kharkov decisions would have no force if the two Frenchmen didn't sign the long confession that was handed to them. Aragon and Sadoul admitted to guilt on the following counts:

—Their literary activity had not been supervised by the Party.

—They had not been consistently militant in the rank-and-file organizations of the Party.

—Aragon had attacked Barbusse and Robert Caby outside the organs of the Party.

—Sadoul had adopted a joking tone in the letter of insults to the valedictorian at the School of Saint-Cyr.

—They had allowed criticism of the Party press to appear in the Surrealist reviews.

Furthermore, Aragon and Sadoul declared their rejection of any idealist thought (especially Freudianism). They committed themselves to struggling constantly against counterrevolutionary Trotskyism, broke with André Breton's *Second Manifesto*, and agreed to submit all their literary activity to Party supervision.

As we know, Aragon and Sadoul signed this rather defamatory confession (the entire text was reprinted in the brochure *Paillasse*, published in 1932) which invalidated anything they had achieved at the Congress. Their signatures were obtained in part because of the hallucinatory effect of the intellectual, moral, and political conditions of Russia in 1930. Breton felt that if Aragon had traveled alone he would never had signed a thing. In his *Conversations* with Parinaud, Breton implicitly put the responsibility for the decision on Sadoul; Elsa Triolet's role was suspect but not crucial. But Elsa's wishes actually had no political weight until 1932. Everything seems to indicate that Sadoul gave Breton a detailed account of that adventure during the summer of 1931, which the two men spent in Castellane. Before he returned to Paris, Aragon was not sure that he had done the right thing. He sent Sadoul on ahead, apparently to say: "You were the one who insisted we sign. Shift for yourself and do the explaining." Breton thought that Sadoul's sole motive for signing was his three months' prison sentence. He imagined he would be put under the protection of the Communist Party. This explanation is probable, since it takes into account a psychological step identical to that behind Sadoul's collaboration with Aragon in 1932, when the future film historian had become a journalist on *L'Humanité*.

As one might suspect, Sadoul, after twenty minutes of shouting and yelling on Rue Fontaine, disavowed the annoying confession. Breton was dumbstruck by Aragon's unexpected betrayal. He was impatient to straighten things out, because for ten years nothing had ever come between them. I felt hit below the belt. The confession had ruined all my efforts. I realized its full significance. Once every writer for a Surrealist publication was required to condemn Freudianism beforehand and to ask for the Party's imprimatur if he himself were a member, there could be no more possibility of joint actions. Even worse, this complete break would benefit only the most sectarian and most conservative intellectuals in the Communist world. Breton and I meticulously sifted through the text of our friends' "self-criticism." It seemed both embarrassed and embarrassing. What possible interest could there be in disciplining Sadoul for the minor and fairly ridiculous incident of Saint-Cyr? What sense was there in forcing literary activities to be supervised by the Party? Such precensorship had never before been required, except for texts involving the Party. One couldn't be certain that it existed at *L'Humanité* outside of editorials and foreign politics. And just who would be qualified to apply such censorship to Aragon's poems? Was there any need to ask our friends to reproach themselves for not having been assiduous militants and to repudiate Trotskyism, aside from the desire to indicate that their political convictions and their will to revolutionary action were open to question? Even more Machiavellian were the affirmation that *"The Second Manifesto* of André Breton opposes dialectics (to some extent)" and the repudiation of Freudianism as idealist. The imprecise language, which would have annoyed even a grade-school teacher, permitted a condemnation of all Surrealist activity, halted any literary creation beyond 1880, and confined writers to a leadership-approved naturalism. That could very well have been the whole point of the thing!

This confession, which had been extorted at the very last moment, betrayed a distrust and hostility inconsistent with Aragon's enthusiastic statements and Sadoul's summary of the Kharkov debates. Could our friends have been so deceived that they had mistaken a cordial welcome for an approval of their ideas? Were they lying? Had they been victims of an abrupt reversal? If this last hypothesis was true, then their signing was even more inexcusable; they had uselessly yielded without a struggle to demands that were all the more dishonorable in that they had previously given all possible evidence of conformity and had thus been grossly manipulated. In point of fact, however, they had been mistaken about their welcome and had been lying about the results. When we finally got hold of the text of the Kharkov resolution on Surrealism, we found a sentence about "the errors" of *The Second Manifesto*, which our friends had approved along with the entire contents of the resolution ten days before their confession on December 1.*

I suggested that we regard that imposed "self-criticism" as a compromise between the demands of the French Communist Party and the desire of the Russians to do something with the Surrealists. Breton saw the whole affair as the beginning of a betrayal. In any event, his efforts had been wrecked. What about the position I had been taking for two years? And yet I persisted in it. "By continuing along the same route," I said, "we'll win out: we'll bring a lot more than Aragon and Sadoul, who are throwing up their arms and surrendering. The International and the French Party will understand."

In any case, we had to wait for Aragon's return to clear things up. But Aragon did not bring any clarity. He protested his good intentions, claimed that the declaration of December 1 gave all the Surrealists the possibility of an agreement with the Party, cited circumstances beyond

---

* Extract from the Resolution of the Second Conference of Revolutionary Writers (*Littérature de la Révolution Mondiale*, special issue, 1931):

"Surrealism. This movement is a reaction of the younger generations of the petty-bourgeois elite to the contradictions of capitalism in the third phase of its development. From the very start, the Surrealists have not been capable of proceeding to a deep Marxist analysis of the cultural reaction they are rebelling against. They are seeking a way out through literature by forming a specific method of creation. The first attempts at struggling with the aid of that method against bourgeois intellectualism still confined them to idealistic conceptions, but they enabled a few members of the group to pass to Communist ideology, which is still manifested with insufficient precision in the political activities of the Surrealists. The acuteness of the class struggle has been perceptible even within this group in the elimination from its ranks of elements with bourgeois tendencies. The true face of 'the inner opposition,' a reactionary face, was revealed after the dislocation of the group and the declared adhesion of the opposition to the bourgeois camp, whereas the central nucleus, which had maintained the Surrealist title, continued to evolve, not without groping and jolting, toward Communism. The development leaves room for hope that the better part of the current Surrealist group, while continuing to evolve toward dialectical materialism, will ultimately adopt the proletarian ideology once and for all, after revising its theory on the 'disintegration of the bourgeoisie, a consequence of the development of its inner contradiction,' as well as all the errors that found expression in *The Second Surrealist Manifesto*."

his control, announced that we would change our minds once we saw the Kharkov resolutions, did his best to put the debate within the area of sentiment, trust, and friendship, and was as evasive as possible. The discussions were confused and distressing. I again saw the uncertain, shifty Aragon I had first come upon in the Jungle, when Elsa Triolet had barged in on his date with Lena Amsel.

The Sixth Chapter, on the basis of information from the regional secretariat, was barring Aragon's and Sadoul's reintegration into the Party. Rumors had been circulating since early November. I had requested—without finding a second—that they be submitted to a commission of inquiry. They came just in time to buttress the discriminatory thesis that I got the Surrealists to agree to: the declaration of December 1 was the product of an intrigue of the French Communist Party. If our friends hadn't signed it, those behind that evil move, probably some of the *Monde* intellectuals, would have gone to a lot of trouble for nothing. If Aragon and Sadoul disavowed their signatures of December 1, I said, the risk would be slight. Who should be charged with applying the Kharkov resolutions in France except the very same people who had been delegated to that task by the Congress before the fateful first of December? The major problem in our friends' "confession" lay in the implications of the condemnation of Freudianism and Trotskyism. By signing an explicit manifesto, including a specific recognition of the association we had founded as the indispensable meeting place of revolutionary intellectuals, Aragon and Sadoul could erase the effects of their panic.

It took several days of effort and discussion to bring Aragon around to that point of view. He prepared a text, and I examined every word of it. This was the *Manifesto to Revolutionary Intellectuals*, signed by the two travelers and publicized (rather poorly) by them and by us in December 1930. The text was reprinted as an appendix in the brochure *Paillasse*.

The crisis was theoretically overcome. Sadoul, in a bad state, left Paris to spend a few months in Switzerland. Aragon resumed his place in the Areopagus, but everything was cracked and inharmonious.

The Association of Revolutionary Artists and Writers remained as we had left it when the statutes had been approved at a sort of general meeting. The Party leaders, whose consent and support were the primary condition of sucess, were lying low. Aragon wouldn't lift a finger to help. He abstained from any outside activity and went back to hawking necklaces. From time to time, he explained his immobility by saying he couldn't undertake anything until he got hold of documents, debates, and resolutions of the Congress, which were to be published in French by the periodical *Littérature de la Révolution Mondiale*. Neither Breton nor I had the enthusiasm we had shared in November. For my part, I was wracked by terrible doubts, which I mentioned to Breton without revealing how great they were. Once the association was set up, what were we going to put into it? Were we really resolved to organize and direct a trade union of painters and writers, to which a whole mob of would-be's and has-been's would most certainly flock? What unbearable compromises were we heading toward? Two names stuck in my mind when I thought about possible members: Francis Ponge and Clovis Trouille. Ponge's texts have nothing to do with Marxism or the ideology of the red unions. On the other hand, Clovis Trouille would be accepted right off. We had only just met that artist, who had shown Breton his realistic paintings of fairs. They were violently and unequivocally anticlerical and antimilitaristic, with a touch of sex.

Trouille painted only on Sundays. The rest of the week he made mannequins for Siégel, earning a good living. "I can make a new man out of you," he said to me one day. "If you have to hide out or escape the police, come and see me. I'll change your features so that no one will recognize you." (I would evidently have looked like a shopwindow dummy, which would certainly have produced an entirely different effect in the Métro.) While working on the exhibit for the Party's tenth anniversary, he described the picture he was painting. It was a vast composition: a naked priest bathing amid naked women and staring lecherously at them. "But how can you tell he's a priest?" I asked. "By his tonsure," he replied. He reflected silently for a moment. "Maybe it's not enough. I'll let him keep his bands."

This charming painter certainly belonged in the A.R.A.W., and he would be admitted on the basis of any one of his paintings. But what about Jean Arp or Yves Tanguy? If we admitted these two as a favor, who would guarantee that other leaders might not hit upon the idea of asking Arp to do a head of Lenin or a worker kicking a capitalist in the ass? Our association would be wide open to any foolishness whose manifest content reflected the statute definitions. It would soon become unbearable, and Breton would be the first to reject such doctrinaire thinking.

So why bother? What would the proletariat and the Revolution stand to gain from red publicity and proletarian kitsch as monstrously

stupid as any other? Wouldn't it be better, as Breton had written in
The Second Manifesto, to be "closed to the public"?

I had to submit to the campaign of the Communist bureaucracy,
which was probably intent on condemning my analysis of Aragon's
misadventures in Moscow. *L'Humanité* ran a series of anonymous
features casting doubt upon the Surrealists. One of its goals was to
persuade the Party leaders to call off the tenth-anniversary exhibit.
This goal was achieved. I was asked to return the documents that
had been entrusted to me and to stop work. The inspection commission
of the Sixth Chapter ordered me to appear before them on January 8,
1931. As witnesses, there were some vague intellectuals who didn't belong to the Party. At the start of the meeting, a stout and suspicious-
looking man named Wisner submitted an eight-page typewritten document filled with garbled quotations, slander taken from the bourgeois
press, to demonstrate that Surrealism was harmful to the working
class and that the Surrealists would have to be expelled. This outburst
of stupidities and insults was directed mainly at Aragon, Breton, and
Sadoul. I got Wisner to admit he was speaking on his own behalf and
that his little literary masterpiece did not involve any Party agency. If
the discussion went on in that tone, we would be left open to the
worst. I reported that incredible scene to Breton, and we discussed it
at length in his home. I think that Aragon, Eluard, and Crevel were
present. To cut short any further spilling of bile, I decided to resign
immediately from the Party. In my letter of resignation, I related the
essential points of the incidents involved. I had the letter printed in
order to assure it sufficient publicity within the organization.

Everything calmed down, as if by magic. I continued my militant
work, although I stayed away from my cell meetings. I found out that
the workers hadn't understood anything about the whole rumpus. They
had refused to vote me out, and the matter had gone no further.

The next turn of events was extremely peculiar. In November and
December 1930, my first reaction had been to keep Maurice Thorez
abreast of the Kharkov debates and the incidents accompanying Sadoul's and Aragon's return to France. My requests for an appointment
were ignored. Breton hadn't lost all hope of getting Suzanne back, and
she enjoyed torturing her ex-lover and blackmailing her husband Emmanuel Berl. Breton told Suzanne about our Soviet dealings, expressing his astonishment that I had obtained no support from the Party
secretariat. He found it odd that Thorez, with whom I was on good
terms, had taken the trouble of asking me not to go to Kharkov with-

out explaining why, though I was entrusted with a job as important as the tenth-anniversary exhibit. "Berl and Barbusse are the ones against you," said Suzanne, "and Thirion isn't strong enough. We entertain Maurice Thorez fairly often, and you can imagine that in our house he doesn't hear anything favorable about the Surrealists." *

I had to settle a few details concerning the liquidation of the abortive exhibit. It was soon after my resignation from the Party. I gave Darnar a copy of my letter, telling him what a defeat this meant. For five years now the Party had been the center of my hopes and my life. I had sacrificed almost everything to it, and I had nothing left. I wanted to let Darnar know the position of each Surrealist. Hoping that Aragon and Breton would as quickly as possible obtain some revolutionary employment, I insisted that the hairsplitting discussions had lasted long enough and had been carried on by the rearguard struggles of the *Monde* people. Since they had been condemned in Kharkov, why should they be granted a lost importance? Darnar was reticent. He took refuge behind the fact that the Party was unaware of all the things that had happened at the Congress of Kharkov.

"I don't believe it," I told him. "I'm afraid that all of us, and you too, are dupes of people who are better situated and more cunning." I told Darnar what Suzanne Berl had been saying. "I wanted to speak to Maurice about it personally," I added, "because she's surely told other people what she's told Breton. But I haven't been able to get through the door of the Party secretariat. Could you report our conversation to Thorez, and tell him who's doing the talking? I'll be at his disposal if he wants to know anything else about the indiscretions of the Berl circle."

This conversation took place in January 1931.

On May 5 I was summoned to the Party's central inspection committee; the summons was signed by Comrade Dupont, one of the last survivers of the Paris Commune. Dupont was an alert little old man of noble bearing, with a long white beard that had turned yellow around the mouth. He received me in the company of his assistant, Gourdeaux, a slightly younger but nevertheless very representative syndicalist of the old C.G.T. Both of them were disciplined Communists, fervent but honest.

I was being indicted on three counts:

1. I had accepted Sadoul's and Aragon's membership in the Party.

---

* This was either an invention by a woman who wanted to muddle things up or a misunderstanding by Breton of some ill-considered words.

2. I had written without authorization for the review *Surrealism in the Service of the Revolution.*

3. I had accused the secretary-general of the Party of frequenting a bourgeois salon.

Dupont and Gourdeaux did not conceal the fact that this last charge was the most serious. The C.C.C.P. had been seized by Maurice Thorez himself. "The Party," said Gourdeaux, "has suffered long enough from unstable and controversial leadership. We now have a unanimously respected secretary-general. The Party cannot tolerate personal gossip and incidents."

In Charles Hainchelin's demonology, a leading role was played by Alfred Kurella. This is how he appeared in a letter that Hainchelin had written to me in May 1928:

"An excellent comrade, delegate of the Communist International, Kurella, whom I've spoken to you about, has seen the faults we are suffering from. You simply have to use the article he had in the *Communist International* in 1926, which you are familiar with. Kurella resumed his attacks afterward in *Le Bolchevique*, the organ of the Soviet Communist Party . . . All you have to do is allude to Kurella if you want to get certain people to shut up."

One spring morning in 1931, there was a knock at the door of our pavilion. A slender man of medium height, in his late thirties, dressed simply, was standing at our threshold. "André Thirion," he said, "I'm Alfred Kurella."

It was really incredible! "I got your address from the Party," he said. "We have friends in common. When I come to Paris, I don't like to rely on the special agencies for a place to stay. I think you could help me a lot more."

Katia and I were alone on Rue du Château. I gave Kurella the downstairs room, showed him where the key was kept, and asked him to join us for lunch.

Kurella was as discreet a guest as could be. For some time now, he had been one of the traveling salesmen for the Revolution; known as Cominternians, these extraordinary men, efficient, intelligent, and modest, were occasionally called upon to play essential political roles. Staying in the shadows, with no hope of any advantage other than the pride of having corrected an error, they restored a jeopardized situation or planned major actions. Most of the Cominternians died during their lives as missionaries, either at the hands of the governments against which they were acting or because they had incurred the displeasure of the Kremlin and were caught in one of Stalin's purges. Some were assassinated, while on an ill-defined mission, by a professional killer or even the young female comrade who had been sent to distract them.

Kurella was a German national. During the First World War, he had been buried alive by French shells that were demolishing his battery. Another round of shells freed him from his tomb, but he had an intermittent stutter for the rest of his life. He spoke French well, with no accent. Punctual, patient, and hard-working, he loved modern literature, poetry, and painting. He was very close to Bertolt Brecht. He become a minister under Ulbricht, in charge of something cultural. His sectarian and intolerant writings, which the French press reprinted with a sense of embarrassment and pity, aroused Western attention in 1969.

I told him my whole story—what I knew about the Congress of Kharkov, my conflict with the inspection commission, and so on. He was greatly amused, seemed to attach no importance to it all, and took greater interest in my article against Berl and my activity as a militant. What interested him most was my opinion of the Party's line, my criticism of the Party's daily activities, and the way I went about applying the line, requiring the committees to live according to stipulations and animating the intersyndical committee, of which I had become secretary.

The belated publication of an account of the Kharkov debates and resolutions exposed the embarrassment of the manipulators. The participants at Kharkov were mere underlings; they had no part in the elaboration of general policies. It was decided to distribute in France the copies of *Littérature de la Révolution Mondiale* on the Congress of Kharkov while the Comintern specialists were planning another operation, The International Congress Against War, to crown the Third International. Barbusse would be given a leading role, since he and Romain Rolland were to sign the call to the congress. The Kharkov resolution had become inopportune because it denied the editor of *Le Monde* the right to call himself a revolutionary writer. The wording was slightly modified so as not to antagonize the author of *Le Feu*. Here and there, he was turned into an upstanding revolutionary writer in the resolution that had had nothing but criticism of the "ideological" contents of his review.

One of the objectives of the International Congress Against War was to create cracks in the liberal and Social-Democratic world. A few of the more lucid communists were beginning to have qualms about the "Social-Fascist" tactic, which claimed that the Socialists had moved from the position of objective allies of Fascism to that of the main enemies of the proletariat. They thought they could overcome the difficulty by obtaining the support of liberal writers for militant pacifism. If they succeeded, they would try to mobilize the masses around these great names and break the isolation of the Communist parties. They might also find new sympathy in the middle classes for the U.S.S.R.

Such an enterprise was not without its threats to orthodoxy. So the Comintern was resolved to keep several irons in the fire. There was no question of applying the Kharkov resolutions, driving a wedge between the French Communist Party and *Monde* (which was probably living on Russian money), of giving Aragon even the slightest responsibility in an association of revolutionary writers, or, most of all, of permitting the association founded by Breton and Thirion to exist anywhere but on paper. The Surrealists were to be clamped down, but they were also to be kept on ice. This, among other things, was Alfred Kurella's mission. He knew the French Communist Party very well. He had repeatedly fought against its "opportunistic" deviations (that is, any sliding toward the ideas of prewar Socialists and bourgeois democrats). What could be more natural than his contact with a militant who had invoked the Party's authority during the discussions of 1928 and was said to be the political counselor of the Surrealists?

As for the association of revolutionary writers, it would be created a bit later, with a core of non-Surrealist Party members who had no allegiance to the Barbusse group. Meanwhile, the practical results of Kharkov were paradoxical. Strengthened by their impunity, the *Monde* people counterattacked. Their target was Surrealism. Instead of engaging in debates on dialectical materialism, which would have been embarrassing for them—first of all, because they knew nothing about it and, secondly, because they felt beaten in advance within the area of philosophy and Marxist exegesis—they waged their battle in the name of proletarian art and literature. They returned to the academic quarrels of yore, the Romantics vs. the Classics, the Parnassians vs. the Symbolists, and so on. The terrain was excellent because the public could follow and comprehend the argument. Furthermore, they were assured of solid support from Russian littérateurs. The forms of art being imposed in Russia were the most reactionary and old-fashioned ones ever known. Barbusse and *Monde* defended the same aesthetic. The positions taken by the Surrealists against imperialism or in defense of the U.S.S.R. had absolutely no importance. What mattered was the refusal to accept automatic writing, Picasso's paintings, Max Ernst's paintings, psychoanalysis, Sade, Tristan Tzara, and so on.

In Kharkov, Aragon had secured ratification of Breton's excommunications of Artaud, Vitrac, Bataille, Desnos, and others. The resolution turned even that incident into an episode of class struggle by labeling the dissidents "bourgeois!" But the preposterous result of such burlesque dialectics was a general outcry against Surrealism and Breton. The latter was quite aware that he was the target. Anyone else would have been flattered or might have negotiated and given in. Breton's behavior during the next four years is the greatest example of intellectual honesty, modesty, and revolutionary faith that a writer has ever furnished. Within the arts the flow of new talents was gradually assuring the triumph of the aesthetic that he had always defended and in part created. All he needed to do was to retreat slightly and wait until the commentators had exhausted their energy. His adversaries, given the success of Surrealism, would ultimately have solicited rather than censored him. Breton, however, was so scrupulous that he questioned everything he had previously thought about traditional materialism and seriously considered the accusation that he had written things incompatible with dialectic materialism. In order to put an end to the confusion following the Congress of Kharkov, he asked for a definition, by consensus if possible, of future Surrealist activity. He was worried about the "secondhand value" of Surrealism's creations in 1931. He thus triggered a general discussion that continued throughout the spring.

Nothing could differ more from Breton's dynamic and sincere approach to the problems posed by the general hostility of the outside world that Aragon's passivity and reticence. The declaration *To Revolutionary Intellectuals* we had dragged out of him could terminate the state of distrust only if the attitude and words of its principal signatory were not likely to stir up everything all over again any minute. I ferried between the two men in order to explain and correct errors, to obtain a gesture of good will here, a bit more patience there. I felt Elsa's growing hostility toward Breton, who would sometimes fly off the handle at some incredible remark of Aragon's, a sign of the total transformation of his personality. Aragon, who had lost the arrogance and breeziness that had often mesmerized anyone who encountered him before 1930, was growing more and more intolerant of Dali's natural absurdities, which could scarcely be exported to the Soviet Union. Dali's constant references to Freud and psychoanalysis tormented Aragon's conscience; he acted like a true believer who had been forced to read a book that was on the Index. He was preparing the publication of his book of poems, and the title itself is most revealing: *Persecuted Persecutor.*

The revolutionary incidents in Spain and the opening of the Colonial Fair reestablished apparent cohesion in the group by providing material for action. Three leaflets were run off and handed out; they were widely read, especially by the young. Profiting from the relative liberty granted by the recent Republican government, the Spanish anarchists had begun a short-lived uprising, in the course of which some hundred churches and convents were burned down. We were all shaken by this spontaneous insurrection. Once again, I noted that the Communist Party was not involved. Aragon and Breton asked me to write something as the basis for a sort of proclamation. Imprisoned by dogmas and rites, I turned out a bit of good Marxist homework. The task of the Communists was to substitute mass terrorism for individual feats of arms. Popular violence, exercised against the clergy and its property, would bring about the true separation of church and state and start a process that would move from the expropriation of monks to that of bankers. I advocated an international antireligious program to help the Spanish, advising them to strike harder at that comparatively weak spot in the carapace of oppression that was stifling the people.

The final text took the fullest possible account of my plan. It retained the essential terms, but added a tone of anger that was not in my learned statements. The writer was, I think, Aragon. On the other hand, the two leaflets on the Colonial Fair were proposed by Eluard and Breton, and the latter was their main author.

To settle once and for all the uneasiness caused by Aragon's evasive ways, Breton decided to submit all the Surrealist activities to critical examination. Each member of the group was to advance his opinion. I have already indicated that these discussions went on throughout the spring of 1931. They were resumed in October, before the publication of Nos. 3 and 4 of *Surrealism in the Service of the Revolution.* The minutes of these debates, kept mostly by me, still exist. In 1950, nearly all these documents were in the hands of Tristan Tzara.

The most important meetings took place in Tzara's small townhouse. Tzara had married a graceful and talented Nordic woman, Greta Knutson, who had some property. Tzara's daily life was free of economic cares. His pleasant home was maintained in Swedish style. We met in a large room elegantly furnished in the most advanced style of the era, surrounded by some of the objects and paintings in the lovely collection that the owner was assembling.

The founder of Dada had come over to dialectical materialism, a shift that would have appeared improbable in 1927. His *Essay on the Situation of Poetry*, in issue No. 4 of *Surrealism in the Service of the Revolution*, is to some extent the fruit of our discussions in 1930 and 1931. It already reveals Aragon's influence, which was to steer the poet into Communist waters after 1945. In 1931, however, Tzara was far more interested in primitive societies, stimulated by the many excellent works on that subject during the thirties. Unfortunately, *The Origins of the Family, Private Property, and the State* by Friedrich Engels, the first French translation of which had just appeared, was so heavy with dialectical force that it made the objective study of those problems very difficult for Communists and sympathizers.

Tzara, short and slightly fat, looked like a comfortable bourgeois, more inclined to sedentary work than to any kind of aggressive activity. He wrote. In 1931, Fourcade published his *Approximate Man*, a monument of French poetry that will probably become an object of worship for students in 1990, when the syllabi will have abandoned Alfred de Vigny's works to the dust of tombs.

The participants in the discussions of 1931 were Alexandre, Aragon, Breton, Char, Eluard, Buñuel, Dali, Giacometti, Crevel, Tzara, Malet, Unik, Ponge, Tanguy, Sadoul, and I. I think that Max Ernst, Michelet, and Pastoureau were sometimes also there as supernumeraries, and, in addition, Mesens and Ristitch during their stays in Paris. Two groups took shape during these debates: the Communists around Aragon and me, and the poets around Eluard. In voting, a majority, of which Breton was the pivot and in which I always took part, prevented us from sliding toward excessively partisan politics or toward attitudes that were exclusively aesthetic. Giacometti and Unik often sided with Aragon, with whom I sometimes disagreed. Crevel, Tanguy, and Buñuel were never at odds with Breton. Aragon did not act as leader; I was generally the custodian of dogma. A manifest enmity separated Aragon and Eluard. I tried, to the extent of my means, to reduce their disagreements to terms compatible with a common action, without giving up hope that Eluard's ideas would also evolve.

The growing difficulties of financing Surrealist activities were always on the agenda. The Depression was starting to ruin, dry up, and compromise everything. The hostility of the social environment was becoming so powerful that anyone who didn't experience it cannot possibly imagine it. Serious emotional disorders arose in some of us. André Breton, with an extraordinary precision and a hallucinating evocative power, had described what he went through during the first few months of spring 1931. The images which form the warp and woof of the central part of *Les Vases Communicants* depict a psychic state halfway between dreaming and waking, in which the individual is not fully conscious of what he sees, does, or wants. As for me, I had gone through a terrible experience, and only those who have had similar ones will understand what it can cost a human being. Katia had given birth to a son in late winter. Not having the means to bring him up, we were ready to give him out for adoption. We would have rid ourselves of the intruder sooner if there hadn't been an absolute medical counterindication to abortion during the early months. Good Dr. Simon and Niouta decided to adopt the child. It was Elsa who arranged it all. Thanks to their kindness, Snejan was born in a clinic on Rue de l'Assomption.

"You're building your life," said Breton, when I announced the birth to him, "and I'm destroying mine." The sight of the baby, which I found so beautiful, changed everything. There was no longer any question of abandoning him to the Simons. This was rather tragic for Niouta, because she wanted him so badly. She elegantly suggested a transitional solution. Snejan would be declared as my son, the Simons would take care of him for a year, and then we would perhaps discuss the issue of adoption. But, day by day, Katia and I became fonder and fonder of the child. He died at the age of one month, a victim of those epidemics, sadly familiar in those days, that sometimes rage in nurseries. Our grief was immense. I now think that my awareness of fatherhood, albeit so natural, grew even more forceful because several of my undertakings failed and I was extremely tormented in regard to my creative powers in the areas closest to my heart.

The discussions were endless. Nothing came of them except that once again Eluard and Tzara would financially back any Surrealist publications. Breton suggested designating a commission for submitting concrete proposals that could be carried out immediately, taking into account everything that had been said. This task fell to Dali and me. Our work sessions took place on Rue du Château and Parc Montsouris. While Gala and Katia talked about clothes, Dali and I tried to find some central points that would allow each Surrealist to exercise his talent in a joint project anchored in a mutually accepted discipline. One of my concerns was to avoid letting our interest in psychoanalysis, in the relations between the conscious and the unconscious, slip toward the philosophical statements that our adversaries labeled "idealist" and that would give substance to accusations of "Freudianism." This wasn't particularly easy because Freud and Jung exerted a powerful attraction on Tzara, Dali, and a small fringe of sympathizers and occasional writers for the reviews. Dali had no fundamental objection to the insertion of his ideology, willy-nilly, into dialectical materialism, whose standards are given by the relations between production and exchange and the nature of productive forces. Consistently paranoid, he was open to any concession—provided it pertained to subjects he considered trivial—in order to obtain general recognition for his current mania. That mania was worthy of his genius, for, apart from the fascination of any Surrealist work because of the unwonted arrangement of forms and material, it fitted in with the most intimate problem of a number of our friends. Dali suggested manufacturing symbolic objects meant, writes Breton in *Les Vases Communicants*, "to procure by indirect means a particular sexual emotion."

Although I felt that such objects might soon represent an interesting and temporary crystallization of Surrealist activity, a new episode worthy of earlier ones, I was as favorably disposed toward the value and significance of the political proposals I was about to submit to the group, with Dali's approval. For lack of anything better, I had chosen the antireligious struggle, under the influence of the events in Spain and because of the natural developments that such a statement might involve in the study and illustration of dialectical materialism. I was convinced there would be a rapprochement between the Surrealists and the secular circles, particularly people in education. Besides, Aragon had proposed it. A number of Max Ernst's works and many parts of *L'Age d'Or* run in that direction. The writings of the Marquis De Sade were strongly present in everyone's mind. Like Sade, the Surrealists, if they thought about religion at all, associated the propaganda of atheism with the criticism of the family, the challenge to traditional morality, and investigations on eroticism. I was hoping the Surrealists would agree to bring some of their philosophical or literary efforts to a critique of Christian dogma. Without limiting themselves to a denunciation of everyday morality, they could draw on the writings of eighteenth-century French materialists and make Feuerbach topical again. This viewpoint was sharply criticized by Sadoul, who wanted to place our activity in a more concrete realm, to show less ambition, and to stick closer to the programs of existing organizations, such as the Proletarian Free Thinkers. Sadoul and I had more and more disagreements about details and tactics. I was beginning to question certain statements by Friedrich Engels (in purely formal terms), which is something neophytes detest. I felt that in his critique of Eugene Dühring, Engels isn't always sincere, even when he appears to be right. But I had stronger reservations about *The Origins of the Family, Private Property, and the State,* which some of us read in 1931. For Sadoul, it was gospel. I was beginning to find its dialectics a bit simple. First of all, the fact that a large part of the argumentation was based on Morgan's theories, which, as I learned the very same year that I discovered Engels' book, had been surpassed and challenged by more recent works, obliged me to stop reading with a believer's eyes. My scientific education kept me aloof from any blind faith, whereas I sensed a sectarian intransigence developing in Sadoul, which did not augur well. I wasn't convinced. Engels seemed to disregard the constants that force one to think that man in capitalist society may not be as far from the caveman as we are led to believe by historians in thrall to the principle of economic necessity as the ultimate constraint: for example, cannibalism cannot be explained by hunger alone. I was not yet familiar with the letters Engels wrote in the decline of his life: this great mind, without retracting what he calls the materialist conception of history, admits that a large number of determinants (not solely the economic factor) can intervene in the relations that cause the development of human societies to appear as more than pure effect of chance. For my part, I had qualms about the refusal to ascribe any value to the two great motivating forces that Freud isolated to explain human behavior: the sexual instinct and the death drive. Since I couldn't integrate them in *The Origins of the Family* without quashing Engels' reasoning, I was extremely unhappy. I half reassured myself by subjecting the manifestation of instincts to economic laws, but, for all my good will, I had to admit that the problem remained untouched.

I had never assumed that the writings of Marx and Engels shed light on everything, but I saw them as fundamental. The thought that they might be vulnerable had never before crossed my mind. I needed to find my bearings in the "superstructures," and it was with the lamp of Marxism that I ventured into them. Now not only was the light poor, but I saw other sources of illumination. In 1931, I still kept hoping it was only an optical illusion—until the day I found myself thinking about the folly of interpretation while rereading *Anti-Dühring.*

Yet it wasn't until Hitler slowly set fire to the world that I managed
to grope my way to this rather simple truth.

The conclusions of the small commission were approved by the
Surrealists in late spring 1931. *Les Vases Communicants* was written
as evidence that Breton had "rid himself of any idealist attachment"
and to urge his readers to do likewise, if necessary. The first part,
devoted to a psychoanalytical and materialist interpretation of several
dreams, aims to destroy any theory that presents dreams as anything
but a new elaboration by the dreamer of impulses from the outside
world. There is a curious polemic against Freud, as though the author
were bent on emphasizing his aloofness. The second and most engaging part is a series of variations on solitude and love, which occasionally achieves the tone of *Nadja*. The philosophical texture derives
from Engels' *The Origins of the Family*. For Breton, human love has
to be "reconstructed like everything else" by making a clean sweep of
capitalist society. The third part is more subtle. It develops the notion
that the "need to radically transform the world" cannot be set against
the "need to interpret the world." In more down-to-earth terms, the
revolutionary intellectual is not just a propaganda agent. This is simply
a reaffirmation of one of the fundamental theses of Surrealism, to
which I totally adhered. "The harmony of opposite tensions," Breton
wrote, quoting Heraclitus.

The last few pages of *Les Vases Communicants* may have been
rewritten in 1932, after Aragon renounced Surrealism. But it seems to
me that the measured and prudent critique of Soviet culture and its
methods figured in Breton's readings even before the February incidents.
In any case, one must admit that the first two parts of *Les Vases
Communicants* made short work of the accusations of Freudianism.
They completed the author's evolution toward dialectical materialism.
Just as the Kharkov resolution demanded, they revised all the so-called
errors of *The Second Manifesto*. One might infer that the author had
moved over "once and for all to the proletarian ideology," to use the
jargon of revolutionary writers. This expression made no Marxist or
Leninist sense. But for the impoverished figures crowding around the entrances to offices and associations, it expressed the essence of the
debate. We had had a foretaste of their miserable aesthetic in the
schools, the city halls, and the post offices of the Third Republic and
in the oppressive poetry and literature of the secular inspector-generals
and the clerical academicians prior to 1914.

Kurella seemed mainly occupied with shaping up the Anti-Imperialist League. He was deeply struck by the almost total lack of reaction on the part of the French Communist Party to the demonstrations and eloquence accompanying the Colonial Fair. "The Surrealists are practically the only ones who have demonstrated an intelligent hostility against that enterprise, and shown their disgust through specific action. Why don't you do something bigger under the aegis of the Anti-Imperialist League? What do you say to a counter-fair? As world head of the League, I'll let you have the Soviet Pavilion and some money. I'll put you in charge of the whole thing. You can represent the League, and you and your friends can handle it yourselves."

The Soviet pavilion was the lovely wooden structure that the Vesnin brothers, who were constructivist architects, had set up at the Exhibition of Decorative Arts in 1925. It had been one of the main attractions and the most modern building at the Exhibition. Transported to a lot belonging to the Association of Trade Unions of the Seine, on Avenue Mathurin-Moreau, it was still in good shape; it wasn't being used for anything. Sometimes it housed a syndical or political conference, but the militants preferred the leprous halls of a sort of barracks nearby. All these structures have been torn down and replaced by the new building of the Communist Party, designed by Niemeyer.

Kurella's suggestion was just the thing to restore my prestige as a militant, which had been damaged by the events of the past few months. Down deep, Aragon and Sadoul would not forgive me for the way I had received their December 1 "confessions" and were taking advantage of my difficulties with the Party. I divided my program into three sections. I put Aragon in charge of presenting cultural problems, Sadoul in charge of proselytizing, and kept the "ideological" part, Leninist theory on imperialism, for myself. "The Truth about the Colonies" opened its doors on September 20. I had the ground floor, the least attractive area in the building. Michelet and a few friends helped me put up posters and slogans. The main room on the second floor, designed by Tanguy and furnished by Eluard and Aragon with fetishistic and primitive objects and a few of the most foolish devotional ornaments from Rue Saint-Sulpice, looked very becoming.

The exhibit drew a lot of visitors, although it did not benefit from any strong publicity. The members of the Party's Political Bureau stayed away, except for one syndicalist who came by for other reasons. I had installed loudspeakers to broadcast political commentaries from time to time and to urge passersby climbing to Buttes-Chaumont to stop in at "The Truth about the Colonies." Aragon and Elsa brought records of any Polynesian or Asian music they could find at special shops. Elsa had added a few hit songs, including a nice rumba (or some other Caribbean rhythm that had just become the rage). I worked hard on the exhibit, organizing the guard. To make sure that all my people were present, I spent long hours on Avenue Mathurin-Moreau. I was often the first to arrive and the last to leave. I can still hear that rumba, and I can visualize a late and very lovely afternoon in September, perhaps a Sunday.

Aragon, Eluard, and Elsa had been showing a young couple, who had nothing proletarian about them, through the exhibit. They were leaving. Elsa had put the rumba on the phonograph herself. I was suddenly aware of my loneliness, my failures, and the mediocrities toward which the stream of life was bearing me. Aragon and Sadoul were no longer the beaten dogs they had been in December. They had regained their self-confidence and their status. Sadoul was dying to get into *L'Humanité*. I couldn't help noticing the touch of condescension that my two friends had introduced into our relationships. Aragon— and Eluard, too, incidentally—had just shown it again while visiting the exhibit of which he was the star. But didn't he owe this stardom to me? I was scarcely more than a porter. The rumba was beating its obsessive rhythm and tantalizing melody. The friend who had come to help me had a date. The guard asked me when I wanted to close for the night. He offered to do it for me. I sensed that he too was in a hurry to finish work. The last visitor left.

A moment later, I found myself out on the sidewalk. The sun was setting, and it was pleasant. The guard had put the rumba back on. I decided to save the carfare and walk home to Rue du Château. The rumba evoked pleasant evenings in the restaurants with friends and the "in" nightclubs. "It's all over for you," I said to myself. "Listen carefully to that rumba. You'll never hear anything like it again, first of all because you'll never again know the hit songs, and, if you do happen to find out what they are, you'll think twice about spending money on a record. You're going to change the way you're living. Next month, you'll be a white-collar worker. You'll be like all the people you've been concerned with during the last five years, but you'll have had your leisure. Now you have to start all over again and show your mettle. Consider everything you've done so far as wiped away, except in your own experience. Don't complain. You've got what you wanted, but not the way you wanted it. You wanted Aragon to have a career in the Party; you wanted him to become a top Communist writer.

That's not accomplished yet, but it's sure to be soon. You've seen him succeed at your expense. You wanted Breton to abandon subjective idealism. You've won. Tomorrow Breton will be a recognized force in materialist dialectics. He'll become the reference point for lots of others that he's been for you.

"You're on the outside now because you wanted to help them across barriers. But wouldn't they have made it without you? What use were you really? What right have you to teach others when you don't really know what you believe in yourself? Your only strength may be your recognition in the problems of revolution certain forms and obstacles that your friends don't see. But your humble position and your disturbed sense of doubt won't allow you to tell anyone else about these things. They'll see everything you say as negligible. Be modest. Rejoin the ranks. Go back to school. Clamp down on your ego. Later on, much later, your turn may come."

Walking past shopwindows, I thought of the symbolic object that I had dreamed up but not constructed, for lack of funds. Considering how modest the expense was, I am less certain today that that had been the real hindrance. Here is the design: A ball, hanging from a sort of pendulum by an elastic band, is kept balanced on an inclined plane (a small plank). With a slight impetus, the ball can drop down the inclined plane and partly lodge in a cavity of the same shape, padded with cotton wicks. With the inclined plane placed in a horizontal position, the ball, acting like a pendulum, can be impelled to move back and forth, slightly muffled by balls of cotton pasted to the board. None of this should be shown working, but the object has to be capable of being started at any given moment.

The symbolism was simple: I felt the movement of the ball as a gentle caress on my testicles. I thought I understood why I had imagined that object and why I hadn't put it together. My sexual relations with Katia were becoming grating. Desire was slackening off, and I occasionally wanted other women, carnal pleasures I wasn't getting at home. I could still master this problem easily, but clouds were gathering. Since I was still deeply in love with Katia, I drove them away.

Almost all the objects made by the others revealed sexual dissatisfaction or fantasy. Did Elsa and Aragon give in to that temporary craze? I don't think so, or else I can't remember. I suspect that Aragon's "Victorian" reactions got the better of him. Today, one can imagine an exhibit of erotic objects by Surrealists taking place in a factory or working-class district. But in 1931 "left-wing" modesty and hypocrisy were too strong for Aragon to risk defying them. Furthermore, Elsa and Aragon were lucky enough to have solved, at least temporarily, the problem of sexual satisfaction for themselves.

The most moving object (apparently still in existence) was by Valentine Hugo, who had just entered Breton's life. This adorable, intelligent, inexhaustibly sweet woman was passionately in love with him. He, however, felt merely the emotional and slightly irritated tenderness of a man who is still thinking of someone else and knows that this new woman has lost in advance. Valentine may have been a bit too old for him. On a roulette cloth, a black-gloved female hand clutches the wrist of a white-gloved hand. The woman's forefinger has gone through the white glove and is caressing the skin of the palm. The white-gloved hand is holding in its thumb and index finger a die showing a trey. Valentine was to create several discreet declarations of love during the next few years by making the most of her lovely, unacademic draftsmanship, which had an uncommon sense of enchantment.

The group meetings resumed in the fall, as I have said. Breton read *Les Vases Communicants* to his closest friends and asked that an assembly debate the problem of the public. For whom were the Surrealists writing? Who were their readers? Was everyone satisfied with his audience? Shouldn't they try to change to new readers? I am not sure that Breton genuinely wanted to answer his own questions. His action was more of a provocation than an inquiry. He wanted to shake up his people, drive them out of their comfortable shells, get at something new, break through the reserves he felt in certain individuals. I have in my possession the minutes of the meeting of October 6, 1931, in which Eluard and Tzara, on the one hand, and Aragon and Breton, on the other, violently opposed the advisability of putting out *Surrealism in the Service of the Revolution* and disagreed about the audience it should be aimed at. The debate concerned issue No. 3 of the magazine; we had learned that 350 copies of the first two numbers had been sold, which was 700 fewer than issue No. 12 of *The Surrealist Revolution*.

BRETON: At the moment, we know what's going to be in issue No. 3. This won't bring any different readers. If I pose the question of audience, it's because I feel that the answer will bring about a change in the contents of the magazines.

(The priority of examining the question: "For what audience

are we writing?" is passed, with Eluard and Tzara voting against it.)

ELUARD: I'm not looking for any public. Keep them out.

TZARA: The audience is to be judged in terms of quality not quantity.

ELUARD (to BRETON): Are you capable of changing a text so that some particular person can read it?

BRETON: Yes, I think I'd be capable of that, since I don't want to provide any food for thought to the aristocracy and bourgeoisie. I aim to write for the masses.

ELUARD: I wonder whether Breton and the others feel that what we know of Breton's book [*Les Vases Communicants*] is the sort of thing to reach to masses.

BRETON: My role is to show how, in my development, I can be led to a purely Communist determination.

BRETON: Even though we may have to abandon Surrealism, we've got to refashion our audience at any price.

The meeting adjourned in an uproar. A motion formulated by Aragon was passed:
"Considering that a result of the entire debate is that agreement between the persons present is absolutely impossible if no philosophical postulate for further debate has been accepted, permitting us to orient future discussion, the undersigned accept as a basis of discussion, postponed until [date missing] . . . dialectical materialism in its uttermost consequences." These words are followed by the signatures of Breton, Sadoul, Aragon, Buñuel, Thirion, Eluard, Tzara, Giacometti, Malet.
I reprint these notes to show how far Breton was willing to go in working with the Communist Party. In October 1931, Breton and Aragon seemed to have become close again. Each had taken a step toward the other. A few days after the meeting, we decided to put out issue No. 3. I suggested that Aragon do a thorough article with an account of the Congress of Kharkov and the decisions made that summer in regard to the directions we had agreed upon for Surrealist

activities. I attached great importance to the publication of such a text, knowing it should dispel Breton's lingering fears and rally the final opponents. Thus *Surrealism and Revolutionary Development* was written, to everyone's satisfaction.

On November 13, 1931, I received the following note from the Party secretariat:

THIRION CASE

The investigation of the case of Comrade Thirion has revealed:

1. That Comrade Thirion writes for a review that is not subject to inspection by the Communist Party and does not spare it its hostilities.

2. That he has been suspended from his chapter for six months for having improperly given Party cards to two of his friends.

3. That, in protest against this sanction, he has resigned from his cell.

4. That he has falsely accused the secretary of the Communist Party of frequenting a bourgeois salon, a collusion that Thirion himself should have recognized as nonexistent.

5. That, under the pretext of exercising his right to criticize, Thirion has formulated completely unfounded complaints against the people in charge of the Political Bureau.

The Inspection Commission of the Communist Party

Expels Comrade Thirion from the Communist Party

1. For his repeated undisciplined acts.

2. For having formulated against the people in charge of the Communist Party false accusation liable to harm the Communist Party.

The I.C.C.P. July 9, 1931

Ratified by the Political Bureau

The secretariat

Paris, November 2, 1931

Dupont and Gourdeaux had been paternal and courteous throughout the "cross-examinations." I thought the matter had been settled. It was this note that informed me that my cell had taken action against me. No one had ever told me, though I had met members of that cell several times a week. My investigations revealed that the cell itself knew nothing about it. They had discovered it, as I had, from the note of November 2. My "suspension," which had been invented by Timbaud, was needed to obstruct Sadoul and Aragon administratively.

Nos. 3 and 4 of *Surrealism in the Service of the Revolution* came out simultaneously in December 1931.

The only cheerful event of that year was the incident concerning Michelet's father, the police commissioner in Clermont-Ferrand. Michelet didn't want to come home. Furthermore, in a letter to his father, he had made some rather unkind observations on that man's profession. Monsieur Michelet, Sr., tired of begging, admonishing, and scolding, decided to act on his own. He came up to Paris. He knew that his son was staying on Rue du Château. One morning, he had the house surrounded by policemen and, after hesitating quite a while (because at the precinct station they had drawn a horrible picture of his son's hideaway), he knocked at the door. He was wearing his frock coat, which he donned for important professional occasions, and one end of his sash was sticking out of his pocket. He was a small, dark man, rather agitated, and typecast in his role as the noble father.

During our conversation, Michelet was in Sadoul's room, I think. (Helping the eighteen-year-old escape paternal solicitude was no easy matter. His father had him arrested twice.) In the most hypocritical tone of voice, I expressed my sympathy with the father's misfortunes. I pointed out to him that our pavilion had nothing that could tempt an eighteen-year-old boy or make him stay, that if he didn't want to leave Paris, it would be wiser to seek the reason in a girl friend, who could probably be found easily enough around Boulevard Saint-Michel. I was amazed that a magistrate accustomed to investigations and the weaknesses of life hadn't considered that obvious hypothesis! The poor man was embarrassed! After discreetly remarking that it had been kind of me to receive him, that his rather brutal manners (he had knocked very loudly on the door and, I think, uttered the word "police") would have entitled me to leave him outside and bring charges. "After all, you have no warrant. What you're doing is completely personal, and that's how I wish to take it." I promised to let him know as soon as I had any news of his son and said that I would certainly make the young fugitive realize how grief-stricken his worried father was!

When Sadoul returned to Rue du Château a few hours later, we had a good laugh. But we had to take the matter seriously. After deliberating, Sadoul took Michelet to Nancy Cunard's place in Chapelle-Réanville, and Nancy gobbled down that fresh body in no time.

19
DULITA

ON DECEMBER 1, 1931, AT 8 A.M., I BECAME A
bookkeeper at France Mutualiste, an autonomous pension organization
on Rue de la Douane. The war veterans were the most powerful lobby
in the Republic. They would demonstrate in the streets at the drop
of a hat, and they were the terror of all the politicians. Their leaders'
ambitions was fairly mediocre, and the authorities did their best to
keep them that way. They confined themselves to demanding all kinds
of subsidies and favors. Besides the payments to invalids, widows, and
orphans, and discounts in most public services, the veterans' groups
had managed to get the parsimonious government of the Third Republic to grant them a small free pension and subsidies that would increase
the interest on the savings accounts of the most farsighted among
them. The right-wing veterans were affiliated with the National Union
(U.N.C.). The leftists, or more precisely those who didn't want to
compromise with the right, had founded the Federal Union. A mixture
of diverse tendencies, it lacked the cohesiveness of the National
Union. The Communists kept to themselves, within the Republican
Association of War Veterans headed by Henri Barbusse. The offices
of the associations were sometimes held by men who had seen little

combat, though that didn't prevent them from shouting louder than the others. Those who had genuinely risked death twenty times over were offended. They set up the Cross-of-Fire groups, which at first recruited only among men who had been decorated at the front. The solidarity of danger and glory was one the germs of Fascist ideologies throughout Europe. It encouraged nostalgia for the authoritarian and hierarchical Communism of the trenches of the First World War and the cult of platoon leaders. The Crosses-of-Fire appealed to the left as well as the right. If they had been led by a man of the people instead of an aristocratic career officer like Colonel de la Rocque, the chances for French Fascism would have been much stronger.

Each of the national groups had founded an autonomous mutual benefit society to provide government-subsidized pensions for the members. But such societies were already in existence. The product of the timid social laws of the late nineteenth century, a welter of tiny groups, touchingly humanitarian, had appeared, often in the shadow of fraternal organizations. The leaders were well thought of at the Ministry of Labor. They annexed the Federal Union. Within three years, the mediocre resources of the old fraternal group were increased a hundredfold. The Autonomous Fund took in more than a billion Poincaré francs. It launched one of the most important housing programs of the era, building nearly ten thousand apartments in five years.

The staff comprised about five hundred people, almost all of them employed at the pension service where I began working. Three-quarters of them were women. All of them sat behind large tables of pale oak on two stories of an old store. The manager occupied a gloomy glassed-in office. The discipline was strict. The offices were vast, drafty, but well heated; the whole place was more like a factory than an administrative department. The manager, a young man of peasant stock, who looked like a junior officer, ordered his people about like a company of foot soldiers. The working conditions were fairly nineteenth-century. The toilets were rudimentary. There was no lunchroom or canteen. Silence was compulsory. Smoking was forbidden.

Half the employees lived outside the city limits, which reflected the pattern of the population of greater Paris. One of the girls in the first group I supervised in 1932 lived in Pontoise, another in Ermont, and a third in Nogent-sur-Marne—three out of a total of six. Fernande, the girl from Pontoise, had to commute three hours a day. She ate lunch at her aunt's, near Boulevard Voltaire. Yvonne, the girl from

Ermont, had no family in Paris, and she too spent three hours a day on public transportation. Simone could make it from Nogent-sur-Marne in an hour, provided she didn't miss her train. Today such commuting has been perceptibly reduced only by private cars. The railroads, despite electric power, have made little progress, and the subways and buses have remained what they were in 1920.

The regularity of my schedule and my office work interfered with my Surrealist activity. There was no longer any question of my joining the midday apéritif. I had to devote my days solely to the office, except for Saturday afternoons and Sundays. During the evenings political or union meetings competed with Rue Fontaine. I had to be up and about by 7 A.M. I couldn't read or write except on Sundays. Outside of Malet, who sold newspapers, I was the only one among my friends who led a worker's life.

Nos. 1 and 2 of *Surrealism in the Service of the Revolution* had sold badly, but the agitation of 1930 and 1931 had caused greater excitement than the scandals of 1925. They seemed more terrifying to the conservatives in both the bourgeoisie and the Communist Party.

If the hullabaloo in Kharkov, our leaflets, and the anticolonial exhibit were bearing fruit, not all of it tasted alike. I had been kicked out of the Party. In November, the French police prohibited and seized the issue of *Littérature de la Révolution Mondiale* containing Aragon's poem *Red Front*. On January 5, *L'Humanité* announced the founding of an Association of Revolutionary Writers and Artists. Its creators hadn't gone to any great trouble to find a name; except for the inversion, it was the same one that Breton and I had chosen the previous year. None of the Surrealists had been informed, consulted, or invited, of course, not even Aragon, despite all his blessings from Kharkov. Finally, on January 16, 1932, Aragon was charged by Judge Benon with inciting soldiers to disobedience and provocation to murder for the sake of anarchist propaganda. He could draw five years in prison. The ground for the indictment was the publication of *Red Front*.

I have deliberately put all these events in one summary. The coincidences and correlations are disturbing, to say the least. Since from 1930 to 1940 the Political Bureau of the French Communist Party included at least one permanent policeman, since the editorial board of *L'Humanité* and the Communist or sympathizing intellectual circles were crawling with informers, the political manipulation of the Communists by the Ministry of the Interior had approached near perfection in 1932. It was, incidentally, no different later.

Red Front, a poem made famous in 1931 by the public prosecutor, is now forgotten. So much the better for its author. One cannot deny a certain lyricism in the first part of this long bravura piece (which runs to nearly four hundred lines). There are still traces here of the early Aragon's insolence. The poem is a description, in the style of George Grosz and Mayakovsky, of middle-class Paris. It's not very different from the things the young leftists of Neuilly were saying in the 1970's.

The end of the poem is as banal and weak as the worst articles in *L'Humanité*, despite the sound effects reminiscent of certain Dada poems of 1920. The middle part, which claims to have a political content, is totally inept. Aragon outdid the delirious thoughts and linguistic excesses of the Third International and what I called the Social-Fascist line, whose absurdity I criticized as strongly as I could. There is a revolution; the proletarians gather, seize the Madeleine, the Bois de Boulogne, and the Elysée palace, kill a few cops, and carry out a huge massacre of Socialist members of Parliament. Here are the most significant lines:

> Kill the cops
> Comrades
> Kill the cops
> . . . the Social-Fascist doctors
> . . . will fall at the hands of the rioters who'll put them up against the wall
> Fire at Léon Blum
> Fire at Boncour, Frossard, Déat *
> Fire at the erudite bears of Social Democracy
> Fire fire I hear death
> passing pouncing upon Garchery.† Fire, I say.

At the start of the peroration, Aragon inserted a text explaining in all seriousness how the unfortunate engineers Ramzin and Larishev (the first victims of the negligence and disorder of full-scale collectivization, who were shot after an Ubuesque trial), recruited forcibly by the Soviet district attorney for an industrial party, had organized the

---

* Socialist deputies. Frossard was one of the founders of the Communist Party.
† For a long time, a municipal councilor and Communist deputy. He had already left the Party to form a group of independent Communists.

imperialist intervention against the U.S.S.R. "The leading role," wrote the poet, "belongs to France, the country that has been directing the preparation." It's unfortunate for certain texts that we know what actually happened afterwards.

According to Surrealist tradition, whenever any of us was in serious trouble, the entire group would go all out for him. When the legal action against Sadoul had become known, for example, each Surrealist had written a postcard to the general in command of the school of Saint-Cyr, informing him of the writer's intention of publicly spanking the valedictorian. Breton, as usual, took charge of the response in this case. He stirred up the art and literary world and brought the discussion to a level far beyond *Red Front*. Politically, the affair was ticklish. Neither Breton nor I had any intention of answering for the notion of Social Fascism, much less taking responsibility for calls to murder Léon Blum, Paul Boncour, and others. Although the *Aragon Affair* tract, written by Breton and a couple of his friends, remained within Third International ideology, it used reasonable language to explain the precise political situation of the Surrealists. It justified Aragon's imprudences by referring to the laws of an "exalted diction" that poetic speech obeys. This distinction was astonishing, but such a misunderstanding of poetic language was not all that surprising in a country where people express unconditional admiration for the *Fables* of La Fontaine. True, the subject matter of *Red Front* wasn't well suited to support such an issue. One could easily refuse to accept *Red Front* as a "model of aware thought," but that couldn't be blamed on Aragon, who had merely intended to give it the "expressive" value that he had been obsessively seeking for several months. The interpretation of a poem is not exhausted by a reading of its literal sense, the Surrealists wrote in *The Aragon Affair*. Isn't this just as obvious in a passage like this from *Elsa's Eyes*?

> I crossed the Bridges of Cé
> That's where it all began
> a song of times gone by
> Speaks of a wounded knight
>
> . . . .
> Of the meadow where just now
> an eternal bride has been dancing
>
> . . . .
> The Loire carries off my thoughts
> With the overturned wagons. . . .

What gives this bit of fluff true character, beyond its uninteresting literal sense, is its silliness. In the same way, *Red Front* in 1930 was a fine evocation of Stalin's criminal madness. These prophetic lines bear excellent witness to the author's rhetorical ignorance:

> The burst of shooting gives the countryside
> An unfamiliar merriment
> Engineers, doctors are being executed.

Appended to the tract was a petition against the trial. Everyone went off to get signatures; Aragon, Eluard, and Crevel had the most luck. I called on Paul Signac, for the last time. He didn't like Aragon or Surrealist painting. "Fire at Léon Blum" had aroused his long-standing horror of violence and killing. The whole affair struck him as rather frivolous.

"People have to take responsibilities," he said. "Aragon doesn't. Every day, people selling *L'Avant-Garde* are being arrested and convicted. Is anyone making as big an uproar about them as about Aragon? I'm not going to sign. But tell Aragon that if he wants to avoid the police, if he wants to escape arrest, my house is open to him, here or in Britanny. If necessary, I'll take him across the Channel myself on my own boat."

The protest was signed by one of the members of the Communist Party's Political Bureau, a quaint academic named Bouthonnier. For various reasons, some of the other names ought to be mentioned: Benoist-Méchin, Le Corbusier, Braque, Matisse, Picasso, Fernand Léger, Jean Luchaire, Bertolt Brecht, Thomas Mann, Federico García Lorca. On the other hand, Georges Bataille's signature was not included.

Once it was under way, the Aragon affair embarrassed everyone. The government didn't want to be saddled with a spectacular trial, a defendant renowned as a fearful debater, and an interminable parade of well-known character witnesses who would have made a laughing-stock of French Justice. Nor did the Communist Party want any litigation. If the Surrealist Aragon were in a martyr's position, the hacks splashing about in revolutionary literature would be reduced to insignificance. On January 9, 1932, *L'Humanité* let the cat out of the bag: "We vigorously denounce any use of this affair by the Surrealist group for publicity. . . . The bourgeoisie, in its repression of the revolutionary proletariat, occasionally strikes out at people who happen to latch on to the working-class movement. That is the significance of the Aragon Affair."

Things were getting confused. We had to bring them to a head, both for the sake of the people who had been following the Surrealists, refusing "any effort at interpreting a poetic text for judiciary ends," and for the edification of those who had preferred to hold back. We also had to situate *Red Front* within modern poetry and to show the kind of art and writing that would be endorsed by the official Communist intellectuals in the association whose founding they had just announced. Breton had regained his total mastery. He could see what the crux of the debate was. During the last week of February 1932, he wrote the brochure *Misery of Poetry*.

First of all, the brochure reprints a curious conversation between Gide and Crevel as well as Romain Rolland's letter. Gide and Romain Rolland refused to sign the Surrealist protest, which showed how foreign to them the idea of a particular poetic language was. Gide, the old hypocrite, pretended to believe that the Surrealists were asking that literature be granted impunity. Although Rolland was quite sympathetic to the Surrealists, he sincerely likened the invectives in *Red Front* to the cries for killing Jaurès, which Maurras had written in July 1914 and which, as we know, were horribly realized. Anyone with half an eye could see that Aragon had never intended to kill Léon Blum or have him killed, but the ambiguity of the work, which Breton felicitously called a "circumstantial poem," had deluded more than the police.

As soon as the Minister of the Interior, partly because of a governmental crisis, withdrew his complaint and the Minister of Justice decided not to prosecute, this curious incident lost all power to become a literary quarrel with unforeseeable police and political consequences. Breton liked *Red Front* no more than most of Aragon's poems—even less. He was primarily aware that the text was "poetically regressive." André Breton was more sensitive than any other writer of his time to modernism; no one paid less tribute to the classical "legacy." But his exceptional sense of evolving forms and genres, of creativity, hampered his objectivity about works in which he sensed or thought he saw a "danger." It was as if he had put on blinders. He tied himself to rules that, unfortunately, reduced his vast field of vision and inhibited his genius.

Lise Deharme has told me several times about visiting the Louvre with Breton to show him two small paintings that had been recently discovered, still lifes by Baugin, which were both rigorous and unreal. Breton, who more than anyone else could appreciate the quality of painting, had to admit that these pictures were very lovely. It was like pulling teeth to get him to say so, however, no doubt because their beauty had congealed or appeared to have congealed around 1660. They disturbed certain ideas he had developed on the seventeenth century in France, an era he didn't care for. Furthermore, he couldn't fit these still lifes into his projections of the future.

In reading *Red Front*, he felt as though he were facing a kind of denial, even more serious than that of the false alexandrines that Desnos had been writing in 1929. The curiosity aroused by legal prosecution of the poem aggravated the basic misunderstandings. That was why Breton wanted to devote a major part of his brochure to a sort of historical critique of the text. He relied on Hegel, an approach that other important writers have used when disturbed by external circumstances. Hegel defined the dangers threatening art as the servile imitation of nature in its accidental forms and humor. The possible resolution of these two tendencies lies in "objective humor." Breton writes: "In art, we are, whether we like it or not, in total objective humor. To what degree is this situation consistent with what the revolutionary requirement demands of us?"

This question called for a negative reply. The Surrealists registered it for a long time without believing it. Perhaps if there had been a genuine "revolutionary requirement," the answer would have been positive, but given the revolutionary requirement as we saw it at the time and given those who claimed to represent it, no hesitation was possible. The answer had to be negative. Our hope in 1932 was to obtain a positive response from the men apparently in charge of the Revolution by going over the heads of the creeps entrusted with the "cultural sector." It was in this spirit that Breton, after affirming once again his complete adherence to the policies of the French Communist Party, insisted on denouncing the stupidities and petty treachery habitually indulged in by the two *L'Humanité* journalists who signed themselves Moussinac and Fréville. At the same time, he polished off that bad joke "proletarian literature," of which the February 20 issue of *L'Humanité* had run a particularly distressing "sample."

Although the preparation of Nos. 3 and 4 of *Surrealism in the Service of the Revolution* had seemed to put an end to the latent tension in Breton's relations with Aragon since Kharkov, problems cropped up again. Aragon used the word "dialectic" irrelevantly and ubiquitously.

He also added the adjective "idealist" to just about anything, as though he hoped, through his manner of speech, to give evidence to mysterious eavesdroppers. Sadoul had taken over the antireligious activities on a very low level, in the style of "opium of the people," "flunkeys of capitalism," and so on. It was as remote from Péret's grandiose insults as from Feuerbach's disturbing explanations. Elsa Triolet began to go along with him. She had been deeply hurt by the reception of the Kharkov travelers. She loved Aragon and was unhappy at his maltreatment. As a Russian, she had a much better understanding than her companions of the evolution of Soviet minds and institutions. Her subtlety and intuition helped her guess what rites were to be observed and what manners were to be assumed. She had never liked Surrealism, nourished as she was on Turgenev and Tchaikovsky. She was amazed that Paris was attaching so much importance to the *Exquisite Corpse*, automatic writing, and formal problems, which she knew nothing about because she still had everything to discover (which she did do later on). Breton, she felt, was very unfair, demanding, partial, and domineering. Although Char, Eluard, Crevel, Sadoul, and I had gradually awakened to Elsa's charm, to her skin and her freckles, for Breton she had always been the very opposite of a woman. "Breton will destroy Louis," she said to me any number of times. Just what were the scruples, the childishness of the Surrealists leading to? Misery. Couldn't they see that Surrealism was getting nowhere, that it was outside of everything, that it merely served to amuse a few snobs who, in return, were quite resolved to let the Surrealists wither away?

The big nuisance was Dali. Anyone could see he wasn't a Marxist and didn't give a damn. There was no way of getting him into proletarian art. Since Aragon had lost all sense of humor, he found nothing funny about Dali's whims. The flaunting of his manias, the cruel sincerity with which Dali described his own intimate life, his priceless experimental contributions during the thirties, shocked Aragon. Although Aragon had written three erotic books, including *Irene*, first published as *Irene's Cunt*, he always exhibited a restraint and modesty in regard to his own personal life that might someday tempt the psychoanalysts. He frequented brothels, but he had inherited the outer reserve and the frock-coat-and-butter-colored-gloves attitude of the high officials of the Third Republic. Finally, Dali's big mistake was his references to Freud. He was a living illustration of psychoanalysis. But, ever since Kharkov, Aragon had viewed the Viennese scientist as a counterrevolutionary. A large part of my persuasive efforts during 1931 had been spent on pointing out to Aragon that Dali was necessary to Surrealism, that we had to put up with his deviations and merely make sure that they weren't overly obtrusive. But by late 1931, Aragon was becoming more and more intolerant of Dali's presence and activities. He may have been voicing the Victorian reactions of the Russian circles that Elsa led him to.

Sadoul and Aragon had resumed contact with the Party organization, with their cells, and with the people on *L'Humanité*. But things weren't going smoothly. The attacks started in again toward the end of 1931. Our friends had to admit that their reintegration in 1930 had been against the rules; they had to recommit themselves to Party supervision of their literary activity and to abjure their real or imaginary errors of the past. In the feature that ran in *L'Humanité* on February 9, Aragon was designated as a person who happened to have "latched on" to the working-class movement.

Aragon suffered as much from the distrustful reception of the Communists as from the slow ruin of his long-standing friendship and collaboration with Breton. If he had listened to Elsa, he would have broken with the Surrealists twenty times over. He resisted because of a sort of sentimental cowardice. Yet day by day he realized more and more that he could no longer breathe in the Surrealist atmosphere. Surrealism itself—its inspiration, its rules, its interdictions, its cults—could no longer be endured. Aragon was first and foremost a littérateur. For two years now, it had been obvious that he could no longer write within the Surrealist camp, that what he had to say could not mature or even be put forward unless he separated from Breton. But, as usual in such cases, others had to choose for him and force him to make the break.

Breton read *The Misery of Poetry* to him as soon as it was completed in manuscript. To tell the truth, Aragon probably didn't know the definitive version of the polemic against Moussina and Fréville. Breton was more and more exasperated by the insincerity and stupidity of *L'Humanité* in regard to everything concerning Surrealism. And then came the Dulita incident.

Issue No. 4 of *Surrealism in the Service of the Revolution* ended with six pages by Dali, entitled *Reverie*. This was a very precise description, full of Dali's intellectual candor and honesty of 1931. Its images and reflections were drawn from that intermediary state so dear to the Romantics, reverie. To my knowledge, it was one of the first authentic testaments of daydreaming in which nothing erotic was censored. The comparable texts by the German or French Romantics always eliminated or neglected thoughts and images of that nature. Dali's text is beautiful, poignant, complex; the descriptions are very exact, and most constantly evoke masturbatory practices. The very touching heroine of that reverie is a little girl of eleven, Dulita.

L'Humanité was all agog. Dali's text was judged to be pornographic. An investigating commission was set up. Aragon, Sadoul, Unik, Alexandre, were summoned, and reproaches were showered on them. Wasn't Dulita a challenge to the class struggle? They were called upon to set things aright, to publish a condemnation.

Breton blew up when Aragon told him about that incredible and burlesque investigation session. He felt he had to mention it in *The Misery of Poetry*, and devoted a brief note to it, including the following:

"Poetry . . . is called upon to no longer draw upon those areas in our person where these collisions [of human life] are by far the richest. I mean the social domain. . . . I hope that one day the Surrealists will be credited with having refused to comply with an interdiction on that order, of a spirit so remarkably petty bourgeois."

Whereas the Moussinacs, the Frévilles, and the Parains have gone to indistinct dust—they are saved from oblivion only because of the Surrealist polemics—everyone knows that the day of honor has come. The Communist Party cannot even forbid its members to enter porno shops. But shortly after *The Misery of Poetry* was published, *L'Humanité* ran the following note:

"Our comrade Aragon informs us that he is absolutely a stranger to a recently published brochure entitled *The Misery of Poetry: The Aragon Affair before Public Opinion* and signed by André Breton. He insists on clearly pointing out that he totally disapproves of the contents of that brochure and the fuss it can raise around his name. Any Communist must condemn the attacks contained in that brochure as incompatible with the class struggle and therefore as objectively counterrevolutionary."

This rift had no political character. There was no disagreement on principles in 1932. It was an incompatibility, a far more serious matter than the Marxists were capable of explaining, or even comprehending. Their criteria were losing their value, and their logic was slipping. Even in terms of discipline, the incident was a minor one. What did Moussinac and Fréville represent in the Party hierarchy? Absolutely nothing. As troublesome as Breton's criticisms may have been, they related merely to details and hardly merited a press communiqué about counterrevolution and class struggle.

Actually, it was useless for the Surrealists to go on making declarations of political adherence and protests of loyalty to the Party and its doctrine, or even to follow the Party line. The Surrealists had lost in advance simply because they represented another realm of art, literature, and morals. Their adversaries didn't want to carry the issue into these areas because it was there that they felt weakest. But they stuck even more firmly to their conceptions of writing and painting than to Marxist theory on value or Lenin's theses on imperialism. The conflict that had developed between Aragon and Breton concerned Surrealism, not dialectical materialism or the building of socialism in the U.S.S.R. As unsatisfying as Marxist methods and references may be for understanding that quarrel, it is amusing to apply them, at least to a few aspects. Thus, it is peculiar that the French Communists had given aesthetics priority over any other criteria for determining their behavior toward the Surrealists. Lenin never confused the quest for a political agreement with the statement of divergent opinions on subjects not directly concerned with revolutionary action. By using the language of Marxist criticism, I could write that Barbusse, Moussinac, and their consorts, who ruled the roost at *L'Humanité* in 1932, and had taken offense at Dali's *Reverie*, were a good example of the petty-bourgeois prudishness of nineteenth-century society, which was born within the monogamous nuclear family, which was a slave to private property, and so on. On the other hand, the destruction of sexual taboos, generally begun during the thirties by the Surrealists, accelerated with the development of productive forces—the massive arrival of women in the production apparatus, causing a weakening of bourgeois constraints, and so on—and coincided with the almost worldwide triumph of the Surrealist aesthetic. Of course, I can't accept such artificial "explanations," which strain to link objective effects with imaginary causes.

This abyss of stupidity that Aragon had seen opening at his feet when the astonishing censors had asked him to reproach Breton for the "pornographic" character of *Surrealism in the Service of the Revolution* had troubled him no more than the sight of a proletarian misery in Russia far beyond anything in France. Masses with retrogressive minds as the hope of the world, and underfed workers building socialism! Only an intellectual can be content with that kind of

dialectics, which ridicules all experience and sanctions the most audacious frauds. Total submission to the Party brought Aragon (like so
many other weak minds) a cozy spiritual comfort. Aragon had always
preferred having others choose for him, but the most important thing
for him was that, by renouncing all exercise of the intelligence and
critical spirit, by replacing cynicism with love of good feelings, he was
acquiring the freedom of the littérateur that Surrealism refused to any
of its practitioners. From now on, he could let himself go, giving free
rein in his writing to the marvelous facility he had received as an exceptional gift of nature, which the demands of Surrealism had bridled
and bullied. Loyalty to the Communist Party was to take the place of
thinking and conscience; in return, it offered him an audience, the
entire public, any public.

This was the shipwreck of one of the most celebrated dandies of
the Western world. He remained at the prow of the "superb and un-
masted ship" that was rushing full speed at mirages. The hold of this
ship was filled with fermenting discoveries meant for the end of the
century. The studious Dali had been beating his naked belly with his
penis while he watched a nubile and blushing Dulita leaf through an
album of pornographic drawings. The author of *Irene's Cunt* was
suddenly shocked by this spectacle. He was thinking compassionately
about those unhappy jobless proletarians who may have been also mas-
turbating in front of little girls but didn't have the money to buy them
any pornographic albums. He was embarrassed and dove into the rolling sea that was rocking the boat. He really felt he would reach the
destination before the others. But the current was flowing the other
way. He hadn't realized this. He was rescued rather far away by girl
friends of his grandmother. First they stripped him naked, for they
were perverse, old as they may have been. They dressed him like a
little boy and sent him to the New Jesuits to learn good manners. He
became an even better pupil when he stated that anything he had
learned before his shipwreck was of no use to him. He forgot that he
had been an eccentric and rather devoted to all the practices of the
cult. He liked to write. They furnished him with no end of pens, ink,
and paper. He was assigned the task of inditing compliments, anthems,
and odes for parish feasts. He achieved moderate success by rhyming
verses for the albums of young girls. They got him to travel. Since
he liked dialectics, they taught him that white was black, that slavery
was true liberty, that poverty brought more goods and pleasures to
people than opulence, that the love of humanity was never better ex-

pressed than by countless imprisonments and capital punishment, and so on. Nevertheless, toward the end of his life, he began to have doubts and wondered whether, ultimately, he wouldn't have done better by marrying Dulita, and so on.

Maxime Alexandre, Pierre Unik, and Georges Sadoul followed Aragon. For all three of them, the determining factors were simpler. They went over to the Communists because they needed employment. Sadoul's decision surprised the people who knew him best. I thought he was emotionally attached to Surrealism and to Breton. It had never occurred to me that a political opinion could alter the course of his life because he acted only on intuition. At this juncture, he behaved like an employee who did not want to lose his livelihood. What did Surrealism offer him besides intellectual pleasures? He refused to work in an office or a store but was devoted to journalism. The Communist press gave him a chance to use his talents, along with a small monthly salary and moral approval, by which he set great store. Breton's frame of mind during the summer in Castellane had led him to believe that Breton's conversion to Communism was accomplished. He did not understand that Breton would never stop questioning anything that happened to him, that his rallying to historical materialism and to the ideology of the Third International could never involve any concession on his part to honor, any abandonment of his lucidity and curiosity, any renunciation of what he felt ought to be his personal service to revolutionary activity.

The communiqué of March 10, 1932, and what followed, led to my break with Aragon and Sadoul. During the next forty years, I saw Aragon only twice. In 1946 or 1947, I ran into him in the Catalan, at Georges Hugnet's table; I usually sat there whenever I came to the restaurant, which was almost every day, and I saw no reason to change my habits just because Elsa and her husband were at the same table. Besides, the thought amused me. He and I maintained a polished and courteous reserve toward one another. I complimented him on *The Bells of Basel* and *The Voyagers of the Imperial*, and he appreciated what I said.

I saw him again in 1967 at Georges Sadoul's funeral. He had changed very little. In his funeral speech, he took pleasure in revealing his Surrealist past. His speech was not without regrets. More than thirty-five years had elapsed since the rift of 1932. No revolution had occurred, Soviet socialism was just as unsatisfying, and oppression, massacres, and the enslavement of whole nations had downgraded

Communism. The man who may be the greatest novelist of the twentieth century could not pretend that his own life, and that of his comrades, other than a ruin, more and more decrepit and shapeless year by year. The ferment of its destruction was nothing other than loyalty to the Party. A few yards away from this mediocre ceremony, the great boulevards, totally untroubled by the inconsistent words of the orators of duty or expediency, were filled with the tumultuous torrent in which Surrealism and capitalism triumphed together. The funeral march before the premises of *L'Humanité* added a ludicrous touch.

I moved from Rue du Château in the fall of 1932. Living with Sadoul was no longer possible, and I was sick of the place. I didn't see Sadoul again until 1945. *Volontés*, the weekly periodical of *Ceux de la Résistance*, for which I wrote the editorial, had published a favorable article on André Malraux. Sadoul sent me a very short note reminding me of what I had written in 1929 about the author of *The Conquerors*. I replied, asking him to dine with me in La Villette, of which I was representative in City Hall. The man who sat down at my table was the kind of narrow-minded, bumptious, mendacious Communist that I encountered every day. We exchanged some memories of the Resistance and sent our books to one another. I received the first volume of *History of the Cinema*, and sent him my *Grand Ordinaire*. I don't think his letter was inspired merely by the recollection of an old friendship. Sadoul was undoubtedly carrying out an order. These love feasts coincided with the last attempt of the Communist Party to get me back, which I'll come to a bit later. When Sadoul learned a few months later that I was moving toward the R.P.F., whose list I was compiling in the nineteenth and twentieth arrondissements during the municipal elections of 1947, he assumed that his mission was over. I had become an irremediable adversary. For my part, I had no desire to see any more of him.

In an earlier chapter, I reprinted Sadoul's brief note to me after Breton's death. His article in *Les Lettres Françaises* on the author of *Nadja* had greatly pleased me. It was as if nothing had happened between the two men. The article drew my attention for more than one reason. Its very entertaining description of a nocturnal Surrealist caper in the reservoir of La Villette comes from a letter that Sadoul had sent me in Nancy the day after the adventure. Between 1946 and 1948, I was in effect no longer living on Avenue Simon-Bolivar. Katia, with whom I was on bad terms, had become a Communist out of love. She was preparing to return to Sofia to marry the embassy attaché she had met in Paris. She had become a radio announcer, and her broadcasts aimed at the Bulgarians largely expressed the viewpoint of the Communist Party. Those old friends of ours who were the intellectual feathers in the Party's cap—Eluard, Sadoul, and the Yugoslav ambassador Marco Rististch—received her with open arms. Fifteen years of Stalinism had taught Sadoul that archives, too, can be used against one, and he asked Katia to give him back anything she could find in my papers of his correspondence to me between 1925 and 1932. Katia was weak and inelegant enough to do what he asked. Communist morals are such that a theft of that nature becomes a pious deed when perpetrated against a "class enemy." Since I had been elected in a proletarian district by majority vote against the Communists, I could only be an enemy of the working class.

By 1967, however, a lot of water had passed under a lot of bridges. The Communist rivers had carried off piles of corpses—the victims of Stalin, Stalin himself, the workers of Budapest and Berlin, the Chinese killed along borders, and so on. I was no longer a class enemy because I was a brother. I asked Sadoul to lunch. Calmer, almost objective, liberal, sentimental, disillusioned, he strongly resembled the young man he had been in 1930. He spoke only about our friends of the past. I repeatedly had the impression that the Communist Party was wiped away. It was true that Breton's death had upset him. He was unshakably convinced that if Breton had lived a few more months, we would have witnessed a total and spectacular reconciliation with Aragon. These gratuitous words betrayed regrets and remorse; they also implied that Aragon was about to accomplish a prodigious about-face, that he was rattling the chains of his intellectual dungeon.

The man sitting before me was the Sadoul of our youth. I recognized the precise and amusing stories that showed the exceptional knack of observation which had made his conversation and his letters so interesting. He told me about the end of Nancy Cunard. Alerted by a hotelkeeper in the Latin Quarter, he had been brought to an old woman, ravaged and haggard, a dead-drunk *clocharde*, at the foot of a stairway she couldn't climb. In a flash, he recognized a familiar gesture, a look, an intonation that instantly vanished but made it clear that this wreck had been Lady Nancy. He had to help her up every single step; she kept falling, so Sadoul decided to sit down and slowly lift her up one step at a time. A deliriously incoherent conversation began; all she talked about was death and the past. In a sort of disordered litany, Nancy mixed up people who had disappeared with those she hadn't seen for a long time. At the end of that crazy climb, incessantly broken by halts and pleas, Nancy finally staggered into her room. Michelet, who had come to lend a hand, put her to bed. A few hours later, a fire broke out in her room, kindled deliberately or through drunken inadvertence among piles of old newspapers. The old ruin was taken to the hospital. Then perished the fascinating lady with a hundred bracelets, who had once horrified and abashed old England by flaunting a black lover in London.*

Sadoul and I decided to see each other again. He was fitting out a country house he had bought near Rambouillet. He planned to write a book of memoirs about our youth and asked me to return the letters he had written to me. He said they would help him put some order in mine, which were never dated. I replied evasively. I said I had only a dozen letters from him that had escaped the ravages of 1947. Most of them were from 1930 and 1931. Why did he want them? Was he after a formal authorization that would free him of all remorse? Was he afraid to leave the slightest trace of his earlier hesitations?

I called him before going on vacation. I can still hear the grave, slow, diligent voice that answered. Sadoul explained that he was still suffering from drastic treatment for a serious indisposition he had had in Moscow a few weeks earlier. "I was about to cross Red Square," he

---

* Michelet has given me some details about Nancy Cunard's agony which Sadoul had forgotten or felt he shouldn't tell me. Sick, in straitened circumstances, and in a terrible state of physical weakness (she weighed seventy-seven pounds), Nancy somehow got off a train that had brought her from Nice to Paris. She wandered all over Paris, where not a single door opened to her. Her incoherent odyssey ended in Lilas, at Michelet's home, just as the taxi driver was getting nervous. Nancy was penniless. Once she had been carried in, she asked for rum, and then for Aragon, Beckett, Sadoul, and Thirion. Sadoul happened to be the only one of the four men whose address Michelet knew and who was in Paris at the time. Sadoul was not the sort to back out of a situation like this. Nancy demanded that they drive her to a hotel on Rue Cujas, where she said she was supposed to meet Neruda. I have described the hallucinatory scene of the staircase and the start of the fire.

Sadoul informed Aragon about these horrors. Elsa opposed the idea of sending help to Nancy, and she grew as violent as in 1929. Despite this disheartening reception, Michelet practically broke down Aragon's door. He wanted to make Aragon realize that the two men who had been so important in Miss Cunard's life, and who had received so much from her, had to take care of her during the last few days she had left. If Elsa hadn't become so furious, Aragon probably wouldn't have hesitated, but he was still not free to act. He tried to convince Michelet that "a person has to know how to die properly." Once again, he would have done better to hold his tongue. That very moment, a taxi was delivering Nancy, unconscious, to the hospital, where she died the same night.

said, "which, as you know, is much smaller than Place de la Concorde, when my legs simply refused to move. I stayed there, like a post, unable to command my lower limbs. I'm much better today. I'll get in touch with you in a couple of days. I'd like you to come over for lunch and meet my wife, Ruta. You once met her a while back." Alas, I understood everything! It was the young acrobat's syphilis that was striking Sadoul's nerve centers. He had started cleaning it up in 1930, but with his devil-may-care attitude about his health, he hadn't felt it necessary to continue treatment until it was clinically certain that he was absolutely cured.

A few days later I was at his home. It was gentle Ruta who opened the door. She remembered having met me during our days of anti-religious activities. Georges was waiting in the vast, lofty, book-filled main room of his apartment. Behind a cluttered desk, he stood up with a great deal of effort, and I saw before me a stiff, massive statue with Sadoul's voice and features and even his ink-stained hands. The eyes were peculiarly fixed, but the arms were moving. Georges brought up his letters again. He asked Ruta to show me mine, classified and bound. I absently leafed through them, barely recognizing the handwriting. The conversation was trivial and mainly about the host's health; in the same words he had used on the telephone, he told me about his sinister adventure on Red Square.

Ruta announced lunch. "We've got to go up to the kitchen," she said. "It's up those stairs." The stairs were rather steep. Ruta asked me to sit down at the top, from which I could view most of the staircase. I heard dull noises from the large room, as though someone was shoving large things around, knocking furniture over. And suddenly, at the bottom step, I saw the fixed features of Sadoul, who was climbing on his knees, using his hands to pull his semiparalyzed massive body from one step to the next. It took him several minutes to climb the twenty-five steps separating the library from the kitchen. It was horrendous. Arriving at the top, he paused to catch his breath. Ruta helped him to get up and then sit down.

I left that house terrified and sad. Afterward, I described those horrors to Nicole, with whom I was going to be vacationing. Nicole, who was still under twenty-five, was a movie buff. As a denizen of all the film clubs, she knew who Georges Sadoul was. When we returned to Paris, I delayed calling him up. I feared a depressing conversation with a man who was gradually turning into a wooden statue. When I learned of his death, I decided to go to the memorial service, which was to take place in the hall of *L'Humanité*. I have already mentioned the ceremony. Numerous speeches were given before his coffin; the representatives of one or another group felt obliged to utter distressing orations. I pictured the Sadoul of 1928 at my side, tapping his thighs and joking with a typical gesture of his at each of the pearls that were destined for his corpse. Aragon was very much the priest. If "Party" had been replaced with "God," we would have had an excellent traditional sermon.

Nicole wanted to come along. I felt a certain pride. She was probably the youngest woman there; her presence brought me even further away from my past. During the orations, I tried to sum up the thirty-five years that had passed since the Dulita incident. Aragon and Sadoul had been Communists to no purpose. The Revolution had not taken place. Their Party had sabotaged any possible chances the Revolution might have had. Both of them had adulated Stalin, a murderer, and one of the men responsible for the Second World War. If the French workers in 1967 had a better and less "alienated" life than in 1932, they owed it not to the Communists but to technical progress, capitalist know-how, to reforms often made despite the Party's opposition. Had Aragon and Sadoul at least made a success of their lives?

Aragon's lengthy speech tended to make the answer to that question negative. It struck me as a statement of great disenchantment. I spoke about it with Nicole several times during the next few days, to confront the ideas I was gradually forming with an impartial judgment; but because she knew only the outcomes and was unfamiliar with the events leading up to them, she could merely confirm my hesitant impression. Aragon had hinted that loyalty to the Communist Party had sometimes been *trying* for the two pilgrims to Kharkov. What a euphemism for thirty-five years of bearing false witness! Party loyalty had led Aragon from Social Fascism to the Popular Front; from the alliance of the democracies to the Stalin-Hitler pact; from hymns to Stalin to canticles for Joan of Arc; from celebrating the massacres of peasants, engineers, doctors, and revolutionaries to feigned indignation at the imprisonment of the least Soviet spy; from cheering the crushing of the Hungarian rebels to ovations for peace congresses. In an area of which he was totally ignorant, he had agreed, in the name of dogma, to defend Lysenko against the science of his time. In an area where he was expert, he had silently allowed Matisse, Picasso, and Cézanne to be taken off the walls and relegated to the attic as culturally unworthy. Yet he never stopped lauding the stupidity that the

Communist leaders were inflicting upon the Russian people. Aragon had become the theoretician of Socialist Realism, borrowed from Stalin, in order to excuse the excruciating stuff engendered under the aegis of Comrade Gopner and her successors, while the G.P.U. was murdering the Czech Surrealists whom he had known and quoted. Here he was, expressing doubts in front of the coffin of a man whom he had dragged into that mire. And he was letting his audience think that he had lied on command and that it hadn't been so easy!

(While he was speaking, Dulita stood on the sidewalk of Boulevard Poissonnière, her arms crossed, and looked Aragon straight in the face as she chewed her gum. Since she bore him no grudge for his low trick of 1932, she made a sign of acknowledgment and fixed a date for the following year, certain he wouldn't stand her up.)

Sadoul had received moral comfort from Communism as well as certain material advantages that had permitted him to be independent of work throughout his life. He had been constrained in his thought but free in his occupations. He couldn't stay put. No one had tied him down to an office. After all, thanks to the Communist organizations, he had led the life of travel and study that he wanted. His monumental history of the cinema, supposedly begun at the advice of Moussinac, will, despite its biases and overstated appreciations, assure him some sort of survival. But was that his destiny? In 1926, I pictured him writing novels or chronicles in which very realistic observation of behavior and situations, a consistent interpretation of what he saw, an imagination stressing the ludicrous and absurd, a candid amorality, and a calm sense of humor would bring a completely new tone to descriptive literature. Had I been mistaken? Was I describing books I would have wanted to produce myself but which Sadoul had never even thought of? Nevertheless, I am sure he could have written a most extraordinary *Voyage to China* if he had undertaken such a trip without previously denying himself the right to see everything.

Aragon and Sadoul were the prisoners of their era, the victims of the aggressive "nowness" that, at noon, unsettles and transports journalists intent on bringing out the evening edition. They invent headlines, believing that they're summing up what's happened; anyway, the paper will sell, which is already an end in itself. At midnight, the paper has become garbage. The fever has dropped, and new dispatches have belied the old ones. The journalist forgets everything and prepares to start all over again, for he lives by the minute, myopically, at what he thinks is the pulse beat of the world. The next morning, he passes into another trance, becomes enthusiastic, jubilant, again thinks he understands everything. Doesn't he have firsthand documents on his desk? His excitement won't abate until the moment the newspaper is "wrapped up" and sent to the printer. "Realism" permits him to be blind to reality.

A few weeks after Sadoul died, his lovely, erudite book appeared: *Jacques Callot: The Mirror of His Time.* This title, in which I see a final thought of the author's, strengthened my conviction that Sadoul and Aragon had been victims of appearances, deceived by reflections, fooled by gross superficialities. In 1932, Aragon viewed the problems of literary creation in the hypnotic terms of "realism." He chose the freedom of a writer over Breton's demands and scruples. Did he have to obtain it at the cost of enslaving his conscience? The same reason sent Sadoul to the historian's delight, the worship of detail. Since he refused to seek truth in life, since even in his documentary task he was unable to stop being partial, he was ready to cross the Atlantic just to check the date of a screening or the format of opening credits. Realism permitted him to be blind to reality.

Dulita was on time for her appointment. She waited for Aragon as he left a session of the Party's central committee. A few of her girl friends had come along, Maoists, Trotskyites, left-wing Gaullists, and anarchists. They were all rapturously leafing through luxurious albums of pornography. The little slut, still nubile, saw that she had won when Aragon reddened and grew nervous when he spotted the tiny bare breasts under the transparent Indian blouse. She took the author of *The Bells of Basel* by the hand and led him to his publisher, where he signed the agreement to reprint *Irene's Cunt.* Now his self-image was secure. It was Dulita who removed *Cunt* from the title. "We've all got one," she said. "You're not teaching anyone anything. Besides, now the public prosecutor, that big grouch, won't have your book seized." As she left her old admirer, she hinted that next time she'd be nicer—as long as he made an immediate public declaration denouncing the new misfortunes of Czechoslovakia.

Aragon, wanting to see Dulita again, did make the declaration, albeit halfheartedly. Like the priest of a worn-out religion, who assiduously celebrates rites he doesn't believe in, Aragon embarked on a difficult old age. He was tempted by apostasy and convinced that, all by himself, he would have a hard time making up his mind.

20
THE SECOND
DEATH OF LENIN

ARAGON DRAGGED ONLY ALEXANDRE, UNIK, AND
Sadoul along in his surrender. There were certainly a few hesitant souls,
including Giacometti, who were more concerned about friendship than
principles. Eluard and Breton were out of town. I was down with a bad
case of flu on Rue du Château. Char and Crevel came to see me in a
catastrophic mood. "We've got to answer," they said, "and explain
everything. Breton gave us carte blanche, but he says we can't do anything you don't agree to." My two friends handed me a rough draft
that I found dangerous and unconvincing. Our final version should be
addressed primarily to the members of the Communist Party; it would
have to be prepared with that aim in view.

I was in bed with a high fever. Crevel and I worked out a detailed
plan of the pamphlet, and I let him do the final draft, adding two or
three sentences that I considered essential. "We mustn't force anyone's
hand," I said. "Above all, we mustn't fall into the trap that's been laid
for us. Aragon's communiqué is a piece of shit, and it concerns only

him. It doesn't alter our desire for revolutionary action, or our political convictions; it can't modify the position we've all adopted concerning the Party." In *The Misery of Poetry*, Breton describes the political line of the Party as "the line that I approve and that would be the only right one for me." We even rallied, quoting Breton again, "to the modalities of the recent application, in France, of the Kharkov theses." We couldn't write anything that might disturb such a clearly defined position, from which we expected to gain something more than Aragon's enrollment in a Party cell. I suggested that we try to demonstrate that the sole bone of contention was the Communists' failure to appreciate Aragon's instability, his foul language, his retractions. Crevel shared my viewpoint. I worked out an outline of the pamphlet. Through some rather audacious legerdemain, I insinuated that we regarded the declaration of December 1, 1930, the fateful extorted confession, as a mere safeguard, a desperate shift to corner a man who was hard to pin down, an erratic specialist in ambiguity.

Thus was born the brochure *Paillasse* (the title suggested by Char). The most important thing about the brochure is the inclusion of the main documents of the case (the communiqué of March 10, 1932; the declaration of December 1, 1930, published as a corrigendum under the title *To Revolutionary Intellectuals*). The editing was very poor. There are misprints galore. Char, Crevel, Dali, Eluard, Max Ernst, Péret, Tanguy, Thirion, and Tzara were the signatories. Péret was still in Brazil.

Eluard found our text weak and inadequate. That was probably what Breton thought also. Eluard composed the tract *Certificat*, severely settling some old accounts with Aragon. On a Surrealist and human level, *Certificat* is a better piece than *Paillasse*. But I feel that our brochure attained the goals I had in mind. It pointed out the erroneous premises of our Party adversaries and Aragon, and it exposed the episodic, personal, and tendentious nature of the communiqué of March 10, 1932.

For almost two years, Aragon and Sadoul scarcely profited from their repudiation. Sadoul got the better of the deal; he obtained small journalistic jobs to pay his bills, completing his apprenticeship in servility. It wasn't until the collapse of the Third International, long after Hitler's takeover, that Maurice Thorez, preoccupied with his coming political switch and probably at the urging of shrewd counselors, discovered that Aragon had received no employment.

As for the members of the Surrealist group, their daily lives had become more difficult as the Depression wore on. Eluard moved into

Breton's place on Rue Fontaine. This modest studio contrasted with the comfort of the middle-class apartment on Rue Becquerel. Eluard was in financial difficulties. He joined the International Red Aid, and throughout the winter of 1932–33 he took part in collections, humbly hoping to be a rank-and-file militant. In a sense, this was a concrete protest against Aragon's dilettantism and careerism, which he had denounced in *Certificat*.

The tone and substance of the March 10 communiqué had annoyed everybody. Friends and foes of Surrealism agreed that the procedure was shameful. The younger generation ignored it. Throughout 1932, there was a steady flow of new recruits: first Roger Caillois and Jules Monnerot, then Georges Bernier accompanied by lovely Yolande Oliviero, Maurice Henry and Arthur Harfaux (deserters from *Le Grand Jeu*), Gilbert Lély, Georges Hugnet and Marcelle Ferry, Zdenko Reich, Alquié, Denise Bellon, Guy Rosey, and the West Indians brought by Monnerot: Moro, Léro, and Yoyotte. Unik returned to the fold. Evidently Aragon was not a drawing card.

Though the bridges had been burned, there were emissaries. Since I remained on Rue du Château until the end of 1932, I was forced to run into Georges Sadoul frequently. Our relationship grew colder and more distant. He behaved like a new convert. I think he saw Breton a few times, in 1933 and 1934, until Stalin's atrocities made Breton feel that anyone who could approve of them must be infamous.

Crevel, until his death, tried to bring about a reconciliation, but his goodwill never altered his admiration for Breton and his disapproval of Aragon's conduct. Beyond personal issues, Crevel wanted to realize all the hopes we had set in 1932 on a definitive and total union of Surrealism and the Communist Party. The author of *My Body and I* was one of the most likable people imaginable because of his modesty and kindness, and his elegant behavior. Handsome, chubby, and by no means effeminate, even though he was said to have affairs with men, well dressed, and a model of correctness and good breeding, he was always even-tempered, never became angry, listened to others, and excelled at putting things back in order or clearing up misunderstandings. In 1925, he had turned to Marx and Lenin, who were totally alien to him, and during his last few years they supplied the essence of his inspiration.

The great problem in Crevel's life was his frail health. Bouts of tuberculosis had attacked him in his adolescence, and he had overcome them only by means of a pneumothorax and long periods in a sanatorium. The disease had made his inner life blossom, given him a kind of detachment from things, fostered a courageous pessimism. Endowed with an absolute moral rigor, he put his honor as a free man above everything else. He readily connected this moral integrity with a physical integrity and had decided long ago not to tolerate any lasting impairment of either. Life did not strike him as something to be lived halfheartedly. Aside from Tzara, he was probably the richest of us all, the only one who was really part of "society," where he maintained himself, never copping out or selling out. The success of his first few books and his great affability made him popular everywhere. He won neither glory nor profit.

It was hard to imagine that the health of such a tall, well-built man was frail. He was vain about hiding his fatigue, and when he couldn't keep it up, he would go to Switzerland for a rest. He was very close to Eluard, Dali, and Aragon. In all quarrels, he always unhesitatingly sided with Breton. In 1932, we assumed he was cured. He could often be seen with a young German woman, Mopse, whom he appeared be in love with. Mopse was intelligent, addicted to drugs, and attractively ugly with an overlarge nose, lovely eyes, and the mouth of a Lesbian. She swung both ways.

The young men drawn to Surrealism were ideologues or poets, sometimes both. Caillois and Monnerot belonged to the first category. Caillois was a solid man of above-average height, with a face that was almost immobile. He was severe and questioning, with a reserved demeanor. His obvious shyness was the product of both his diligence and the slight stutter that sometimes troubled his speech. In regard to his recent election to the Académie Française, well-meaning critics have gone so far as to write that the young student at the Ecole Normale had *fortunately* merely passed through Surrealism. But the better part of Caillois's work belongs to Surrealism, whether they like it or not. It often treats futile things with monumental seriousness. Besides his broad philosophical background, Caillois, like Ponge two years earlier, had a curious view of nature. Within a very narrow area, his rather fixed gaze became piercing, first scrutinizing insects and objects, then minerals. This interest in details connects him with the author of *The Story of the Eye*. None of this was in any way disturbed by the concept of class struggle.

Monnerot, the boy-husband of a ravishing West Indian, was a completely different type, lively, cheerful, a good friend, dynamic, sensitive to everything, lucid, and endowed with scrupulous intellectual honesty. He anticipated the changes in Surrealism after the forties, when the revolutionary ideologies in which we were all ensnared began to dry out and fall apart. Through a kind of reversal, Monnerot, the prophet of a sanctification of the poetry and even of the magic that Breton was soon to put at the heart of Surrealism, was seized, as of 1940, by the new aspects of politics and dogma.

The best way to illustrate the contributions of these two men in 1933 is to quote short passages from their articles in No. 5 of *Surrealism in the Service of the Revolution*. These are presented, not as brilliant observations, but as examples of keen awareness. There is a clear continuity of intellectual investigation between what these young men inherited and what was to be painted, written, and conceived during the next half-century. At the same time, Aragon, in *The Anti-Religious Struggle*, published tearful poems for his bosses, and Sadoul turned out Boy Scout yarns.

"It is obvious," writes Caillois, "that the utilitarian role of an object never completely justifies its form; in other words, the object is always more than the instrument." Monnerot, in an article entitled *Civilized Mentality*, concludes: "In using the findings of an era that has denied sorcery, we have to dialectically reinvent sorcery. . . . Morality devours psychology, poetry devours verse, acts devour individuals, man devours the ego, the world devours objects. The lucid roads convey their continuous diamond."

These two young men came to Surrealism in the midst of the Depression, when the revolutionary pole, designated as such by the Surrealists, was thought to be the Communist Party. In principle, they accepted the idea of the proletarian revolution, but they didn't feel that this perspective exhausted the issue. Besides, the Communist Party's credibility in regard to revolution was open to question. I didn't realize it at the time, but popular common sense was not deceived.

True, *The Bells of Basel* and *The Voyagers of the Imperial* have a different dimension than the works of Caillois or Monnerot. But Aragon, for all his narrative talent, for all his penetrating insight into the psychology of young men and women, contributes merely an enormous emotional fog, in which the beauty of the episodes, although it occasionally dispels the vapors, simultaneously reveals a perjury and fraud more odious than, and as reactionary as Balzac's royalism. Caillois and Monnerot, however, remained watchful and never tried to hoodwink their customers. Small as their field of vision and framework of experience may sometimes have been next to Aragon's vastness of scope, their writings, through a kind of reversal of dialectics, contain a human quality that *The Communist Man* totally lacks. They latch on to the future, whereas everything of Aragon's belongs to the past.

Thus any members accepted by Breton after the publication of *Misery of Poetry* and the Dulita affair were also opting for intellectual honesty. In addition, they marked a vague defiance of the Communists' revolutionary sincerity. None of these nuances will be perceptible in thirty years, however. As in politics, nothing succeeds like success, and being better is not good enough. Literature sloughs off morality the way an insect sheds a useless cocoon. The generations judge it by its own codes, nearly every article of which is favorable to Louis Aragon.

Spring 1932 brought Benjamin Péret back to Paris. He had been living in Brazil with his wife, Elsie Houston, for four years. They had just had a son, whom they named Geyser. Several of us welcomed the Pérets joyously. Péret hadn't changed a bit; he was as easygoing and disarming as ever. She was a bit more opulent than in 1932, with a slightly bigger nose, but still a beautiful woman. Aragon's repudiations came as no surprise to Péret. He had always regarded the author of *The Peasant of Paris* as a weather vane, and has never missed an opportunity to "let him have it." The group's Stalinism troubled him a bit more, but Péret had never bothered himself with proselytizing. He was a Trotskyite, as he repeatedly declared, but he signed along with everyone else so as not to annoy Breton, though he had the usual reservations. He was more intractable than intransigent anyway. He was not always affected by his friends' maneuvers. He declared that he was opposed to something, that everyone knew he was opposed, and that he would go along with us. His Trotskyism wasn't very well thought out. What he had was mainly a moral stance of hostility against any compromise, an absolute nonconformity that might have seemed a bit too facile if Péret hadn't repeatedly been willing to face all the consequences.

After two or three months of relative tranquillity, all sorts of hardships, which were the facts of his life, began to beset him. He met them with a candor and a kind of fatalism. He had the courage to content himself with little and totally lacked ambition, even though he was as sensitive as anyone else. He became a proofreader again. Elsie got a job in a cabaret. Péret went to call for her every evening after her performance. To save money, and probably to avoid bothering her, he would often wait for Elsie at the cloakroom or outside. What had to happen finally happened. One morning, Elsie refused to come along with him and left with someone else. Péret became even poorer. Badly dressed, slovenly, he lived a hand-to-mouth existence, begging a dinner here, fifty francs there. This poverty never altered his rough good humor; it even reinforced his general refusal to obey and ultimately led him to join the Trotskyite Revolutionary Party in Catalonia. After a few months in the barracks of Barcelona and on the Aragon front, he came back to his poverty in Paris. Frankly, he hadn't been of much use in Spain. He wasn't cut out to be a soldier, and he found the whole thing badly organized. But no one had asked him to join, and even if his trip had an emotional basis, one must agree that it was a rather peculiar flight. Thus one of the greatest French poets, whom anthologies, of course, still ignore subsisted, with difficulty, until the war.

The legislative elections of 1932 brought me so close to the Party again that the only effect of my expulsion was that I was freed from high-level meetings (and what's more, my cell often summoned me to discuss local work). The fourteenth arrondissement was divided into two electoral districts. In the less proletarian of the two, the Party candidate was a rather pathetic artisan, Poulet. He had been a young Socialist before 1914, and we mistakenly thought he could draw the small tradespeople to us. In the other district, the candidate was Léon Mauvais, a member of the Central Committee, perhaps already secretary of the Party organization. I liked Mauvais, and I think he liked me. We had known each other for several years. He was an old employee of the gas works, lusty, robust, cool, but by no means stupid. He owed everything to the Party, which made him a member of Parliament, a widely heeded union leader, and a robot. Mauvais never had any problems of conscience, but he was sometimes more lucid than others. By 1932, he had already acquired the mental ability of never being surprised at anything. Everything was explained in terms of class struggle, with the bourgeoisie represented as an active and rascally old lady, whimsical but always aware of her pocketbook and her station. The strategy of class warfare was an inexhaustible mine for the kind of teleological explanation adored by the Party leaders. Lady Bourgeoisie became a slut, artful and crotchety, flirtatious, capricious, amusing herself by pushing some people ahead, keeping others on ice, offering and withdrawing her trust in order to hoodwink the proletariat and play with it the way a cat toys with a mouse. Fortunately, the valiant Communist Party was there, austere, vigilant, incorruptible, denouncing and vilifying all the artifices of the old lady in terms of rigorous if paranoid analyses.

Poulet was a very bad speaker. Besides, he hadn't quite absorbed the strategy of class warfare. It fell upon me to direct the election campaign in his district and to explain the Party line. To do so, I had to endure two public meetings a day and sometimes an additional rebuttal session.

The Party had launched its election battle with confidence and a certain braggadocio. Objectively, the situation was favorable: unemployment, lowered salaries, depression, all, in terms of good Marxist analysis, led to an aggravation of class struggle, the proletariat's realization of its true interests, and the success of the Communists. We had a resounding failure! The Communists lost 30 percent of their 1928 votes. The unemployed and the little people impoverished by the Depression hadn't believed that their lot could be improved by an all-or-nothing policy, the "all" being improbable and the "nothing" fairly assured.

Kurella came as soon as he heard the news. I fulminated. "No united front is possible if we start off with insults, especially if our insults are uncalled for. Besides, all these insane clamors are the best excuse for doing nothing no matter what happens. 'They're all traitors, sell-outs, or pigs. I alone am pure and sincere. Look at me, admire me, but whatever you do, don't touch me. I don't want to get dirty.' That's the language of the average Communist today."

The rash talk and highly touted leftism of the French had never been to Kurella's liking. The Party's passivity in practically all political circumstances worried him even more. Meanwhile, Barbusse and Romain Rolland called for the union of all those against war "regardless of political affiliations." This appeal was also aimed at all the labor organizations, "no matter what they were."

Barbusse and Romain Rolland's appeal, printed in *L'Humanité* on May 27, 1932, promptly aroused the anger of the Surrealists, who had already been enraged by several rather scandalous passages in that newspaper. At the evening apéritif hour, I found Breton in the throes of great decisions, backed up by Eluard and Crevel. "We have to go to Amsterdam," said Breton. We're joining the Congress, and you'll defend the viewpoint that we'll define in a pamphlet." With no prior discussion, we all had the same opinion of Barbusse and Romain Rolland's appeal. I insisted that our pamphlet emphasize the obvious fact that the horrors of capitalist peace were sometimes equivalent to the horrors of imperialist war, and that we underscore Lenin's old tenet: We struggle against war by bending our efforts to transform imperialist war into civil war.

The text was largely written by Crevel. I had given him issue No. 11

of *The International Communist*, from which he drew a large number of quotations. The pamphlet was finished by the time the signatories met. I think that the happy phrase "If you want peace, prepare for civil war" was by Eluard. After carrying out all the membership formalities for the Congress, I was unable to get time off from my job to go to Amsterdam, and I didn't have the money for the trip.

Kurella greatly appreciated our pamphlet *Mobilization Against War Is Not Peace*. Its publication was used in Amsterdam by the manipulators of the Congress, who depicted our position as a sectarian aberration that nevertheless had to be taken into consideration. The names of André Breton and Paul Eluard were included in the list of celebrities under whose auspices the Congress took place.

The Congress itself came as a surprise to everyone. The stunning ascent of Hitler and the troubles of capitalism, which seemed incapable of managing its own affairs, were fostering a latent anxiety in leftist circles. Socialists and radicals were very displeased by the vetoes of the parties, and several Communists were fed up with the imprecations. But illusions were tenacious!

Kurella had put me in touch with another Cominternian, Hans Glaubauf, who was spending long periods of time in France. I had told him about the entire Aragon affair. I wanted to improve the relations between the Party and the Surrealists and, particularly, bring about their admission into the Association of Revolutionary Writers and Artists, which was then being formed. Despite Kurella and Glaubauf, my efforts were largely wasted. Under the pressure of pacifists, Marxist intellectuals, and proletarian writers who abhorred Surrealism, the Party secretariat was planning to sick a few of its dogs on Breton. The long letter that Glaubauf wrote to me on September 17, 1932, partly devoted to a polite criticism of *The Misery of Poetry*, made me fear the worst. This letter speaks volumes on the blindness of the Communist leaders three months before Hitler's takeover. "You're wrong to quote Lenin the way you do," wrote Glaubauf. "Today, the watchword 'peace' is playing a seminal role. Thousands of people are still following the Social-Democrats and the bourgeois pacifists because they see the Communists as champions of war. We've heard too many tirades like 'Let the war come; it will bring the Revolution that much sooner.'"

This evidence of an absurd pacifism, to which the policy of the Comintern and the Communist parties was to be reduced for several years, upset me all the more because I was still reeling from a lengthy conversation I had had with Kurella about Germany during the final days of August 1932, before I left on vacation.

Despite the increase of Hitlerian voices, the disorder in Germany, as seen from France, seemed to imply a revolutionary outcome. There were battles every day in the streets of German cities. The workers were reacting to the Nazi provocations. On July 17 the Communists of Hamburg had attacked a police-protected Nazi parade; there were nineteen deaths and hundreds of wounded. In the July 31 elections, the Social-Democrats had lost 10 seats, and the Communists had gained 12, bringing their total up to 89. (True, the Nazis had 230.) I had kept the faith in the German Communist Party that Barmotte had inculcated in me. I told Kurella how impressed I was by the electoral gains of the German Communists.

Kurella became very grave. "Since you're asking, I'll tell you the truth. I know you well enough to be aware that you think as I do about the present tactics of the Comintern. Everything's down the drain. Hitler's won; he'll be in power before six months are up. And the German Communist Party won't do anything serious to oppose him. The workers *are* fighting against the Nazis, of course, but they're fighting either because they can't stand the brown shirts or because the Nazis are provoking them. You've got to realize that they're fighting against the wishes of the Party.

"There won't be any United Front. There won't be any serious resistance. If there is any token fighting for the sake of honor, it will be a small Paris Commune. Do you see why, despite everything, I'm interested in the Amsterdam movement?"

Kurella's pessimism, the inexorable rigor of his analysis, terrified me. "But then, was Trotsky right," I asked, "when he accused the German Communist Party of sabotaging the United Front?"

"What Trotsky thinks and writes doesn't change anything because he influences only about fifteen intellectuals. And even if he should happen to win over another fifteen, there would be an immediate schism. But we have to credit him with having made a revolution and knowing what you use to achieve power. Trotsky's opinion has less influence on the German proletariat than the Pope's."

I had some small assignments from the Anti-Imperialist League. Once or twice, I met German Communists who were passing through. I questioned them eagerly about Germany. The sinister forecasts were confirmed: the Party was letting the workers fight all alone. It rejected any alliance and persisted in the chimera of a rank-and-file United Front. The Comintern was supporting that suicide. In the elections of November 6, the Nazis lost 34 deputies and the Communists gained 11; the Communist and Socialist strategists were already shouting victory. Yet it was evident that the power was practically in Hitler's hands. On January 29, 1933, old Hindenburg offered him Germany on a silver platter.

The Communists didn't fire a single shot. They didn't raise a single barricade or start a single strike. The 300,000 Party members stayed home and waited to be arrested. Half the members of that model Party joined the Nazis within a year. The Social Democrats let themselves be hauled off to prison after a few fake protests.

This tragedy was accompanied by comedy in France and other countries. The Comintern explained with a straight face that never had Germany been so close to revolution. The Communist newspapers unanimously accused the Socialists of treason. Naturally, the Communist Party, which had acted no differently from the Social Democrats, had not committed treason! If one thought of the way such a capitulation would have been met during Lenin's lifetime, one could not help concluding that even Leninism was gone. The Third International, which the Communists were to go on invoking throughout 1933, was obviously paranoid nonsense.

Little by little, the truth came out. Stalin's personal responsibility for the criminal tactic imposed on all Communist parties was crushing. It was he who had demanded that the German Communist Party stop the street battles with the Nazis, who had insisted until the very end that the German Communist Party regard German Social Democracy as the chief enemy. What good was the Comintern, which hadn't even been able to save face?

In·February 1933, Communist refugees gave talks to small groups of militants. I still wanted to hope: these men seemed to come from another world, and they all had fear in their eyes. "They're in for fifteen years, maybe a generation," they said, "and during all that time there'll be no more opposition in Germany."

I experienced a kind of inner trauma, a far more serious and more profound wound than when I had been ousted from the Party. I had to bow to the evidence. Helpless and shocked, as after the worst treason, I did not relax any of my militant activity. In fact, I worked twice as hard. I learned I had received an important promotion in the C.G.T.U. The Association of Seine Trade Unions, headed by Henri

Raynaud, decided to create five organizations to coordinate union activities in Paris and the northern, eastern, southern, and western suburbs. I was entrusted with the Paris sector. That was the highest rank I was ever given in the Communist world. I lost it shortly after February 6, 1934, when a new (and final) sectarian offensive was launched against the partisans of an agreement with the Socialists, "so that we can be among ourselves," as some big-mouth or other in the Building Federation said to me!

21
DREAMS AND
STRENGTH

ARAGON WAS FORGOTTEN SIX MONTHS AFTER HIS
disappearance. The newcomers didn't know who he was. They were
beguiled more by the Surrealist games, the (for them) completely new
atmosphere of collective creativity, the rigorous principles, the anathemas which called forth pride among those who figured in the elect,
than by the procedural aspects of establishing relations between the
Communist Party and Surrealism. With a childlike joy, they went
about discovering a vast and hidden world; they unquestioningly accepted all the edicts that came out of Rue Fontaine. The Café Cyrano
had become a harum-scarum hive, adding new recruits every month. Its
effervescence masked the financial straits of Surrealism, and these troubles rather seriously interfered with the activities of the group until
the Exhibition of 1938. The last two issues of a publication covering
all facets of Surrealist thought, Nos. 5 and 6 of *Surrealism in the
Service of the Revolution*, came off the presses in May 1933. Events
were about to furnish a massive series of instigations, but Surrealism

would be almost totally without any means of expression except in the area of the plastic arts. *Minotaure* was essentially an art magazine. This impotence was the result of the poverty of the group as well as the conservatism, stinginess, and blindness of the French political parties and French society. Stalin's crimes brought about a total rift between the Communist Party and the Surrealists. Breton's move toward Trotskyism left him outside French political life without placing him in a revolutionary line. Within Trotskyism, the Surrealists again found the hostility and strict submission from which they had suffered among the Stalinists.

None of the political or economic powers in French society were prepared to give Surrealism even a tiny spot in the inventory of those who were threatened by Hitler and whom they claimed to be defending after 1935. The cultural ideal during the final years of the Third Republic was made up of reminiscences of 1920 and memories of 1910: Giraudoux and Dufy, Valéry, Gide, and Claudel, plus Romain Rolland and Péguy. Except for Claudel and Péguy, these men were representative of France's parliamentary democracy and liberal regime. But they were a far cry from "Surrealist" freedom, which was frightening everyone. Thus Surrealism had to content itself with handouts.

As for the Surrealists themselves, their contradictions were not, on the whole, likely to be resolved (which is not their least contribution in this universe of scholastic or dialectical optimism) and these prevented them from imposing any of the ideas that might have allowed them to take over. But the time probably wasn't ripe, for the world was evolving in such a way that it misunderstood the Surrealists even while it gradually opened the entire future to them. In 1932, nationalism was forcing its constraints on the world for a good forty years. Breton and Péret, to cite only two writers, couldn't escape their nation. Language was one factor. Furthermore, the very essence of their personalities, in spite of themselves, made them part of a demanding tradition. Breton, incidentally, gauged it rather exactly while he was in the United States during the war. But the notion of one's country, which could present itself to Breton and Péret only in the caricatured and sometimes obscene terms that it had assumed during the First World War and in victory, was part of the Surrealist hell in 1933. In the same way, Breton, like many other French intellectuals, could not understand in 1935 or 1936 why the concept of National Defense was suddenly becoming a capital element in the defense of freedom.

Perhaps it wasn't unfortunate that this prodigious brew, which began in 1933 and was to become the basic thrust of the world for the next forty years, left Breton and most of the Surrealists behind. Surrealism was not a political party. The events of 1927 to 1934 showed that it had nothing to gain from attempts to integrate itself in a contingent and limited political program. Soon it would have no more "politicians" among its activists. Luckily, it gave itself plenty of elbow room and managed to go beyond the present, even if it didn't always understand it. It is clear now that it was to Breton's credit that he never came to terms with nationalism. I write this with great certainty because I myself did come to terms with nationalism; it was necessary, and it was a matter of honor as well. But Breton, although he took a stand and admitted the inevitable, never abandoned the internationalism that was one of the major characteristics of Surrealism between 1933 and 1940. Whereas other French writers who had fled to the United States during the war acted no differently from political refugees, Breton helped create a melting pot with a high temperature. New materials of all sorts, brought by men of all races and nationalities, were thrown into it. To be sure, Surrealism was not going to halt and defeat Hitler. Others accomplished that with the appropriate means. But, after the death of Stalin, we still had to find the flame that might permit us to illuminate the end of the century.

In October 1932, there was a sudden relaxation in the Association of Revolutionary Writers, which reflected a new attitude on the part of the Communist Party. Fréville informed Breton that his membership in the Association had been accepted and gave him a list of the Surrealists admitted. Crevel brought the information that I needed to get my bearings. Aragon had taken another trip to Moscow. He may have been behind the "unblocking," for he had fought hard against the anti-Surrealism of his new comrades. Aragon had an important position in the Association, and he told Crevel he would be glad to work with Breton, despite everything, in this new framework. But he absolutely refused any joint work with me. The Association had no clear attitude on that point, but it deliberately ignored me. Somebody had to pay the piper. I had enough human and political experience to know that I had nothing to hope for from this situation, whether it was moving in the direction I had wanted or the opposite. I was still under a disciplinary sanction by the Communists. They couldn't very well punish and congratulate me for the same things within a few months. Following the principle that the Party is always right, the presence of Breton on the Association's board of directors and that of Aragon and Sadoul in the cells were perfectly acceptable now that the Party had decided that these things had been a mistake eighteen months earlier, when they had been done on personal initiative. That's how bureaucracy works, no matter where it may be, regardless of the domain in which it exercises its talents. I was nothing to the Association, totally useless because Fréville was the Communist on duty. The Party was interested in me not as a revolutionary intellectual but as a militant political and union leader. That was the category in which it had assigned me a function. For the Surrealists, I had lost the keys to a house the doors of which opened by themselves.

Eluard and Breton were preparing Nos. 5 and 6 of *Surrealism in the Service of the Revolution*. I hoped to offer them some literary contribution. Once again I announced an article, *The Bohemian World*. I had taken notes. But each time I gathered them, I was sterilized by Marxism. The result was so meager that, after I had revised the first three pages ten times over, I gave the whole thing up.

Nor did I make any progress with the political or polemical articles I drafted several times. On reflection, the topics I had chosen seemed futile, and my treatment of them no better than that of a journalist on *L'Humanité*. The essence remained, the main points, but my analysis diverged further and further from that of the French Communist Party and even the Comintern. I was striking out on a dangerous terrain. What good would it do to add a feeble voice to the rather discordant and unheard chorus of opposition? I fell back on scholarly study. I had asked Hainchelin to collaborate on the magazine, and he had sent me Lenin's notes made while rereading Hegel's *Science of Logic* at the outbreak of the First World War. The manuscript reached me at the same time as the announcement of Hitler's rise to power. With all due allowance for the differences between Lenin and the commonplace militant that I was, the shocks were comparable. Hainchelin informed me that he didn't feel up to an interpretive article, and that I should do what I thought best with the text he had sent me.

Nothing was more exalting or fearful than presenting Lenin's posthumous work on Hegel in the magazine. We had to be modest but truthful and leave its providential character to objective chance. The thirty-odd lines that started off issue No. 6, though they could have been improved by greater formal rigor in the writing, still seem worth the effort. My friends didn't comprehend their full significance until two or three years later.

This minor project took up all my free time during the first third of 1933. It determined my reading and thinking for several years. I shall try to define what I comprehended at the time and what germinated slowly. First of all, note 144 (*Elements of Dialectics*) enumerates an almost exhaustive description of the mechanism of logical thought. Today, I would have two crucial reservations, but these do not impair the validity of Lenin's analysis; one of them is in a way implicit. I would first emphasize the subjective character of the examiner, the shadow he himself casts on his examination, which he will never be able to discard fully, the modifications he brings to the object by examining it. The second criticism is an offshoot of my first observation: Is the object studied the one the examiner thinks he is studying? It seems that the relation of the object that one thinks one sees to that which one does see will appear in the second phase of the examination. Finally, since I now think that the unity of opposites is an exception, perhaps even an optical illusion, and that the notion of "opposite" is in itself difficult to establish (particularly because of note 10), I can reach only an approximate understanding of notes 5, 9, and 14. Each of these steps along Lenin's road will not lead to a closed or a secure enclosure. In most cases, the door will not shut, the enclosure will remain open. But remarkable residues will be revealed and new perspectives will be provided, as pointed out in note 10.

144   (ELEMENTS OF DIALECTICS)

1. The objectivity of the examination (no examples, or digressions, but the object itself);
2. The totality of the varied relationships of that object with other objects;
3. The evolution of that object (or phenomenon), its particular movement, its particular life;
4. The internal tendencies (and the faces) contradicting one another in that object;
5. The object (phenomenon, etc.) as a sum total and unity of opposites;
6. The struggle, or the development of these contradictions, the contradictory character of efforts, etc.

145   (145 IS ACTUALLY THE SECOND PART OF 144)

7. The union of analysis and synthesis, the decomposition of the isolated parts and the total, the addition of these parts. (Dialectics

can be briefly defined as the doctrine of the unity of contraries. Thus the essence of dialectics is understood, but that requires explanation, development);

8. The relations of any object (phenomenon) are not only varied, but general, universal. Every object (phenomenon, process, etc.) is linked to everything else;
9. Not only the unity of contraries, but the passages of every determination, every quality, every feature, every property into every other (in an opposite direction?);
10. The infinite process of the appearance of new faces, new relationships, etc.;
11. The infinite process of deepening the knowledge of the object, of phenomenon, processes, etc., by man, from the phenomenon to the essence and from the least profound essence to the most profound;
12. From coexistence to causality and from a form of connection, from a reciprocal dependency to a more profound and more general one;
13. The repetition of certain features, certain properties, etc., from the lower stage to the upper;
14. The apparent return to the former (negation of the negation);
15. The struggle of the content with form and vice versa; the rejection of form with the transformation of content;
16. The passage from the quantity to the quality and vice versa (15 and 16 are examples of 9).

In 1933, I was only half aware of these responses. I particularly valued notes 17 and 135 because of their absolute condemnation of the Bolshevism of 1932.

17. A magnificent formula "not only the abstract universal, but a universal such as contains in itself the richness of the particular, the individual, the isolated, all the richness of the particular and the individual"! Very good!
135. Practice is higher than (theoretical) knowledge for it has the dignity of not only the universal but immediate reality as well.

Finally, notes 82 and 107 opened two sluices through which my faith in Marxism and dialectics was gradually to flow. Note 82 reads as follows: "Necessity does not vanish upon becoming liberty." This is a refutation of dialectics. It is also an expression of great disenchantment. Note 107 concerns the dialectics of nature: Lenin subscribes to the Hegelian division of natural laws into *mechanical* and *chemical*. This division, taken up by Engels, no longer made sense in 1889. What was there to be said about it in 1914, or, a fortiori, in 1933? I already knew that modern science never valued Hegel, and even less Friedrich Engels. In 1933, I held scientists responsible for a failure that I believed was due to "bourgeois" education. Whatever good will a Marxist might show toward Hegel, Engels, and Lenin, he had to blench in 1933 when he read that Lenin set store by the Hegelian division of natural laws into mechanical and chemical. After all, Bohr's atomic model had been described in 1913!

Note 107 contains more than this extraordinary indication of datedness; Lenin also writes: "The laws of the outer world, of nature . . . are the foundations of human activity toward a goal. In his practical activity, man has before him the objective world on which he depends and which governs his activity." What does this mean? Does the objective world choose man's goals, like Allah? Does it impose them on man, like predestination? Does man choose what is necessary to him on the à la carte menu offered by the objective world? Or does he take just anything? How can one apply the term "materialist dialectics" to this fragment, in which one also finds the following sentence: "Human consciousness, science (notion) reflect the essence, the substance of nature, but this consciousness is simultaneously an outer thing in relation to nature (it does not coincide with nature immediately. Simply)."

That "simply" struck me as so outrageous that I asked for confirmation of the translation. Lenin was actually introducing into dialectical materialism a short period during which man's consciousness would be outside of nature, would detach itself from the objective world, which it would reintegrate after some sort of automatic adjustment. Nature, propelled by something or other, moves toward conscience, or it may be that conscience, directed toward a goal, reintegrates nature after a brief solitary stroll. I recalled Jean Wahl's serious qualms about the philosophical inconsistency of *Materialism and Empiriocriticism*. Thus began the slow demolition that I was to complete around 1945.

The French, including the Surrealists, attached merely transitory importance to Hitler's victory and to the passive surrender of the German labor parties with revolutionary pretentions or reformist goals. The diplomats, who regarded themselves as shrewd, attempted moves that were both clever and crazy. The most useless was the attempt at a rapprochement with Mussolini. A portion of the property owners as well as the men of "law" (from the rural policemen and, if need be, the schoolmasters to the big bosses) were not unappreciative of the fact that an entire people had been brought to heel, that strikes and street fighting had been brought to an end, and that Parliament had been housebroken. The left didn't care for Hitler; it disapproved of his edicts but it didn't really understand them. The Communists were still not facing reality, predicting imaginary difficulties for the new regime, though they managed to chalk up a point when Goering foolishly accused Dimitrov of having started the Reichstag fire. Dimitrov's courage before his judges and his political intelligence slightly redeemed (for foreigners) the cowardly collapse of the German Communist Party.

In February 1933, the problem of the Treaty of Versailles could be considered a thing of the past. Hitler was doubtless a product of that treaty, but now the issue was his ambitions, not a revision of the clauses. Digests of *Mein Kampf* appeared in France during the first few months of 1933. In a booklet of some 150 pages entitled *Selections from Mein Kampf*, one can read the following:

> The goal of re-establishing the borders of 1914 is a political insanity both in its scope and in its consequences. . . . Not to mention that the Reich's borders in 1914 were anything but logical. In reality, they did not group all people of German nationality nor were they strategically national; there can be no question for anyone that the borders of 1914 cannot be restored without bloodshed. Only childish and naïve men can delude themselves into thinking that a revision of the Treaty of Versailles can be brought about through humility and supplications.

Until the *Anschluss*, very few Frenchmen attached any importance to *Mein Kampf*, from which I could have drawn ten even more explicit quotations. French political circles were accustomed to election promises that were rarely kept; the voters were only half deceived, albeit willingly. The French were so used to playing this game that it never occurred to them that someone might be playing a different one. Even the horrible beginnings of anti-Semitism didn't revolt the French. On the contrary, they roused a whole group of riffraff.

The French political spirit between the two wars was characterized not only by the traditional chauvinist boastfulness (the most painful examples involved aerial prowess and athletic competitions) but also by pettifoggery accompanied by a declared and dogged pacifism. In the early sixteenth century, the French were conquerors and adventurers. During the 1930's they were mainly intent on preserving their domestic tranquillity. Pacifism had different names within the two great currents of opinion among the French. The right used the word "security" and manifested it through its attachment to uniforms, to the great leaders of 1914–18, to the flag, to garrisons, to the cult of Verdun. All in all, a historical panorama. Later it took pride in the Maginot Line. Until 1933, it did a great deal of shouting against a disarmed Germany. In reality, the right was scared. It also promoted fear by describing imaginary dangers (gas warfare, for instance) but was uninterested in strengthening French military power, primarily to avoid any tax increases. Besides, strengthening (but not modernization) would have been absurd before 1933. Once Hitler became Chancellor of the Reich, the conservatives didn't shout as loudly and showed they were willing to grant political concessions to maintain the social regime. A conflict with Hitler or Mussolini looked dangerously like a leftist fight against order. In 1933, France had a large but old-fashioned army. Military appropriations were never fully spent. The prototypes of new weapons were administrative alibis. On the other hand, the vaingloriousness of the old generals still fed the illusion.

And the left labored under this illusion. Whereas in the first half of the nineteenth century the French army was part of the left's political panoply, since 1870 the army had been considered a right-wing institution. The Republicans were deeply enamored of peace, which was understandable after the great massacres of the First World War. As victors, the French had escaped German imperialism, which, if it had won, would have lowered its adversary's standard of living by reducing France to an agricultural nation. Those who had fallen in combat had probably sensed the importance of what was at stake. The survivors and the new generation had no idea of it, and they felt that anything gained by the people from those great killings was meager. The Communists had theoretically adopted Lenin's views on war. They distinguished between imperialist war, civil war, and revolutionary war. They had tried to give a concrete substance to their struggle against colonial warfare; the rest was kept in the abstract realm. The far-left intellectuals, including the Surrealists, were the prisoners of these abstractions as the Second World War became more and more probable. In 1928, despite Leninist principles, the Communists had slid into pacifism because of the myth of "defending the U.S.S.R." and the extraordinary repercussion of Soviet statements in favor of general disarmament. Once Hitler was in power, they gained a good conscience by vituperating against the Treaty of Versailles. No one understood that the political cards had been dealt in such a way that any change in the clauses of that treaty would strengthen the Nazis, whether the democracies made concessions or Hitler used crude methods to nullify the agreement. The sole approach unfavorable to the Nazis was a defeat of their brutality.

Accepting the absurd idea that the danger of war depends on the amount of armaments a nation possesses rather than on antagonisms and ambitions, the majority of the left wing refused to study military problems. The Communists, who prided themselves on their loyalty to Marxism, occasionally quoted Clausewitz, whom Engels and Lenin had held in great esteem. But after repeating the famous aphorism "War is merely a continuation of politics by other means," they revealed themselves as incapable of analyzing the "politics" of a conflict between Hitlerian Germany and the France of the Third Republic and the meaning of that conflict for both nations.

Just like the Trotskyites, they resorted to the concept of imperialist conflict, which was merely an additional proof of their childishness. This inability of professional revolutionaries to grasp the development of an idea—"the appearance of new aspects, new relationships," as Lenin would have written—disturbed me almost as much as the passivity of the German Communists in January 1933. Such inadequacy, which was disastrous in 1940, still hinders the left's objective analysis of various conflicts.

Just what did Hitler and the Nazis represent? The dictatorship of big business, as the Sixth Congress of the Comintern had said? No one explained why "big business," composed of a few dozen industrialists and bankers (assuming they could have agreed on politics), should have needed a minor Austrian painter, how they got him to write *Mein Kampf,* and by what miracle they had obtained 13,245,000 votes for him in July 1932 and 17,217,000 votes after he had been in office six weeks. Hugenberg's funds didn't explain everything. The Marxist tradition was more powerful in this large country than anywhere else. Had the Socialists and Communists silently accepted Hitler's nomination as Chancellor because they did have faith in big business after all? Old unionists swore allegiance to Hitler on the eve of May 1, 1933 (only to be arrested the next day). Did they feel they were bowing to big business? In the plebiscite of November 12, 1933, 95 percent of the German voters approved German rearmament, thereby ruining once and for all the scattered and sporadic opposition organized by the Communists a few months too late. Was a whole people thus approving the wishes of big business? All the experts have maintained that the counting of the votes was honest. "Even in Dachau, 2,154 inmates out of 2,242 voted for the government that had imprisoned them." (William Shirer, *The Rise and Fall of the Third Reich.*)

The German tragedy proved to me that the Comintern and the Communist parties had no right to claim that they were organizing and guiding the class struggle. It was easy to find fault with tactical errors committed in 1923 and 1925 in Europe and China. In all wars, there are defeated generals. But after piling up the stupidest tactical plans, the Communists decided it was useless to fight. Thus they went from incapacity to treason.

Still a Communist, I immediately referred to Lenin: "parliamentary idiocy," "bureaucratic degeneracy of the Party," "spirit of capitulation," and other phrases he had used in 1914 to condemn the Second International came to my mind. But I could discern something more serious, something that challenged the entire doctrine. To follow the example of Lenin, who had opened Hegel's *Science of Logic* in Berne to see where Marxism was, I tried to resume an analysis of Fascism in the light of dogma. This sent me back to the nonsense of the Sixth Congress and Engels' and Lenin's uncertainties about the state.

Summing up Engels, Lenin writes: "The state is the product and the manifestation of the irreconcilable antagonism between the classes." (*The State and Revolution*, Chap. 1, p. 1.) This literally means that the state is a tournament field! A bit further on, Lenin, employing a quotation from Engels (*The Origin of the Family, Private Property, and the State*), offers the following correction:

"The representative modern state is capitalism's instrument for exploiting salaried work. There are, however, exceptional periods in which the struggling classes attain a balance of strength so that public power momentarily acquires a certain independence from them and becomes a sort of arbitrator between them." (Quote from Engels in Part I, Chap. 1, p. 3.)

I noted in passing, and with Lenin's help, that these exceptional periods occurred in the seventeenth, eighteenth, and nineteenth centuries in France, and during the reign of Bismarck in Germany! Thus, in Germany, Hitler was the instrument for exploiting the oppressed class that, after eighty years of Marxism, and through a masochistic reflex unanticipated by dogma, had given its executioner 95 percent of its votes. I closed *The State and Revolution* (which I nevertheless consider one of Lenin's seminal works) as though I had closed the Old Testament after reading Genesis!

A new political force was in power. It couldn't possibly have caught us unawares, since it was the force that had made the nineteenth century. It had ridden roughshod over the class struggle, in the very midst of capitalism's depression, whereas, according to dogma, everything was tending to open the proletariat's eyes to the "meaning of history." This force, nationalism, was to lead German workers to six years of fighting with insane heroism for a myth that had nothing to do with the proletarian revolution.

I can now state my thoughts of 1933 with a clarity that they hardly manifested at that time. I was trying to retain as much as possible of the Marxist theories that the events I witnessed were condemning. I militated like a madman, in quest of new proof or to invalidate the evidence I had already gathered. I took advantage of my position in the Regional Alliance of United Unions to set up committees open to members of Socialist sections, reformist unions, and even the Republican League of Human Rights.

At the other end of the world, Japanese militarism was bursting across borders. Japan was under the yoke not so much of Fascism as of a sort of vestigial feudalism coupled with a ferocious capitalism, at the same time modern and reactionary, imported from the West. Japanese ambitions were impregnated with racism. They seemed aimed at the whole of Asia, but this continent, except for China, was controlled by the "whites," and no one knew which "whites" the Japanese would first pounce on. The most consistent information emphasized the army's virulent anti-Sovietism. The military felt that a new conflict with Russia was inevitable. They desired it, were making preparations for it, and were convinced they would be as lucky on the battlefield as in 1905. The politicians thought otherwise. They saw Russia as a minor adversary. When, later on, the Japanese leaders arrogantly attacked the United States, that decision probably saved Stalin from annihilation.

In any case, Japanese ambitions were as disturbing as *Mein Kampf,* and the U.S.S.R. was very attentive to them. China was the first country to bear the brunt of an aggressive Tokyo, whose troops had occupied Manchuria in 1931. In China, nothing was simple. The development of the revolutionary war proved both Stalin and Trotsky wrong: Chinese Communism could only have a peasant foundation (according to dogma, a petty-bourgeois and uncertain basis) or none at all. The Anti-Imperialist League had drawn up vast plans for Asia. Their objective was not to arouse the proletarian revolution, nor even to emancipate the colonial peoples. The main goal was to create difficulties for the Japanese in order to aid and abet the Soviet Union in case of conflict. All things considered, this strategy was realistic enough from a Soviet viewpoint. It was also the strategy of the Americans. It succeeded in breaking up Japan's war effort. And, ultimately, it also led Mao Tse-tung to victory.

The League wanted to muster all the democratic and nationalist forces in Asia against Japanese aggression. It tried to do this through a cluster of groups, personalities, and tendencies. But Kurella regarded those as political odds and ends. The people to convince were the entire Kuomintang and its generalissimo, Chiang Kai-shek. It was also necessary to pressure the Communists to make peace with their adversaries, and even agree with them on common actions against the Japanese. The League thus did its best to replace civil war with preparations for a national war and to subordinate class struggle to nationalism.

During the summer of 1933, these prospects were still hypothetical. Chiang Kai-shek was totally involved in preparing a new campaign against the Communist armies. He wanted it to be decisive. A further complication was the fact that he had entrusted a military mission from Nazi Germany with the task of reorganizing his general staff. The Anti-Imperialist League wanted to hold a congress in Shanghai. Kurella asked me to polish up some notes for a French edition of the League's publications and to write a few propaganda features.

Kurella and I were aware of, and terrified by, the dimensions of the conflicts that Japanese ambitions could trigger. A general strike in Canton or Shanghai was not the sort of thing to stop the Japanese divisions. Mobilizing the people against the invader is an academic notion when that people cannot be armed or led and are in no position to fight steel with steel. No guerrilla has even been able to achieve victory unaided. Pitched battle was the only possibility. The thought of changing imperialist war into civil war made no sense, at least during the initial phase of fighting.

Organizing a rebellion in China or provoking strikes or peasant uprisings would have meant helping the invaders. This would also be true if the 200,000 men of the Communist armies were to take on the Chinese nationalists, who were busy repulsing the Japanese. The

Manchurian attack had, incidentally shown the birth of a true national feeling in China. The Chinese had battled fiercely in the North, and the Nineteenth Chinese Army had been tenacious and heroic. One could also refuse to act, leaving Chiang Kai-shek to pour out his strength against Mao Tse-tung and abandon the latter to his mountains. That would spell sure defeat in case of an all-out Japanese offensive. An agreement between the Communists and the Kuomintang on a common war effort against the Japanese was the only reasonable objective. Was this consistent with the means available to the League? Not at all. We both agreed that all we could expect of any congress in Shanghai, and of our propaganda operations, was a clear statement of the problems to be solved, which would also draw the attention of the responsible leaders to the urgency of a solution. I was asked to cooperate. I felt that what we had to do was prepare for war, make the means available, and forge a politics that would permit the victims of aggression to form a joint force superior to the enemy's. I don't know what became of these texts. Some of them were printed and distributed. I am not certain that the Shanghai congress actually took place. The important thing for me was that I had been able to discern the probable course of events and to avoid any ready-made ideas.

It was impossible to limit these projections to the Chinese. In case the conflict were to spread, could Singapore be defended without the English, Batavia without the Dutch, Saigon without the French? Asia was simply dependent on Europe, which held Saigon, Singapore, and Batavia.

We agreed that we still hadn't reached the point where revolutionary tactics would require that we demand a fleet of cruisers for Saigon and the reinforcement of the English and Dutch fleets in the Strait of Malacca. We ourselves were content to think out loud. But we were also moving toward a politics of states rather than social classes for Europe. The political privileges and financial interests of the ruling classes in England and France were threatened by Hitler's ambitions just as the working class saw its organizations and liberties challenged by the spread of Fascism. German nationalism could become a mortal danger to the French nation. By comparison, the Hitler regime offered proof that bourgeois democracy was worth defending. Nor was it fair to say that the Third Republic, for instance, or the United Kingdom represented only the will of their bourgeois classes. We were faced with at least two examples of states whose leading social groups were capable of convincing all the classes that they had a common destiny in conquest: Japan certainly and Germany probably. Not only had their nationalism wiped out the basic freedoms of press, assembly, and association; they were also replacing the hope of proletarian emancipation with the notion of collective brigandage through war.

In order to preserve peace in Europe, would we have to rely on a proletarian takeover in France and England? In 1933, there was no serious prospect of revolution in either of these countries. The war or the enslavement of half the world would not be conjured away by the feeble action of the French Communist Party, the heroism of Mao Tse-tung's 200,000 soldiers, or possible general strikes in England, Holland, and Czechoslovakia. To fight Hitler, the proletariat would need the French army.

The working class would have to work for the salvation of the democratic countries threaetned by Fascist ambitions. The preservation of fundamental liberties justified the use of force. It appeared that the time had come for audacious alliances and great risks. The proletariat, to avoid bearing the brunt of a new war, would have to establish its representatives within the threatened governments if the need arose. The salvation of the working class depended on preserving bourgeois democracy, not on weakening it.

This is a schematic summary of the rather long discussions whose conclusions were more subtle. It expresses my thoughts more than Kurella's, whose opinions were a bit less distinct and whose reasoning was more faithful to dogma. These differences were primarily a matter of presentation. Thus I was convinced and Kurella fairly certain that French domestic politics had assumed an international scope. France was the foremost country in which to strengthen democracy (Trotsky said that France would be the next victim of Fascist leprosy). The proletariat's representatives ought to set about acquiring an influence on the state as quickly as they could. Things would be hopeless if the Communists and Socialists were unable to reach some understanding, if they remained hostile to coalition governments that were capable of combatting Fascism. Such ideas were new: the Socialists, in national councils, had periodically resisted such temptations. Communist writings tirelessly gave the masses a choice between an improbable revolutionary "all" and the "nothing" of an academic opposition.

We were thus revising the doctrinal taboos that had been established through sixty years of Marxist exegeses by the "pure." Kurella affirmed that several dignitaries of the Comintern were very close to these ideas; the most realistic members of the Russian Communist Party were not averse to them. Doriot had defended very similar ideas, and they had listened to him attentively. But a change in Comintern policies would have to be based on a worldwide strategy in which the U.S.S.R. was the pivot, no matter what.

Kurella encouraged me to continue setting up committees without worrying about the French Communist Party's sectarianism. He was a bit anxious about my burgeoning reservations about such sacred texts as *Anti-Dühring*, for I was claiming that Friedrich Engels had not always been sincere. I had hidden from my friend the gravity and extent of my criticism of the Comintern's actions. Nevertheless, I did say that the prestige of that venerable institution had, to my mind, been greatly shaken by what had happened in Germany. Kurella agreed, but he had faith in quick remedies.

As I diligently tried to put in order what remained of my old convictions, the new truths that I could see, and my vague misgivings, I included my position in Surrealism in my efforts. The goals I had been striving for in that area since 1928 had been reached, largely to my detriment. I still had a sentimental attachment to the movement and showed its morality and tastes, but I couldn't quite see what part I might play in Surrealist activities. The rapprochement with the Communist Party had apparently been achieved. A number of Surrealists were Party members or were militating with a conviction and ardor that they hadn't shown back in 1927. Breton, Eluard, Char, and Crevel, along with several others, were in the Association of Revolutionary Writers and Artists, and Breton was one of its leaders. His lecture on February 23, 1933, in the auditorium of the Grand Orient de France, on proletarian literature (see No. 6 of *Surrealism in the Service of the Revolution*) had marked a great evolution on his part toward militantism. The author of the *Manifestoes* advocated preparing "a Marxist manual of general literature" to fill the gaps in primary secular education. I began to feel that I was no longer "in." A future reconciliation with Aragon was not out of the question.

I have mentioned that I was the only Surrealist not admitted to the Association. There was no question of my begging for admission. After all, the situation was no worse this way. What would I have done in the Association? I was a writer who didn't write. Was I to join the ranks of the men preparing a "manual of dialectical materialism" at the very time when my confidence in dialectics was riddled with doubts? On the other hand, I saw all the Surrealists perfectly at ease in the blind and sectarian politics of the Party, whereas I myself was trying to invalidate them, to struggle against them, denying the Comintern's right to be the leader of the world proletariat. I regarded those policies as criminal and wanted them replaced by new logical constructions, which were only just being hinted at, though I knew that as soon as they took the shape they were heading toward, they would leave all my friends nonplused. The Surrealists had reached the goal at the very moment that I realized that goal was a decoy.

My political role in Surrealism was over. At this point, I could only hinder the evolution of my friends. Others had taken over for me. Crevel was as good as I, and perhaps showed greater ease in writing the texts I had more or less specialized in. The proof was in *Notes Toward a Psychodialectics* (*Surrealism in the Service of the Revolution*, No. 6), the first French attempt at a Marxist critique of certain Freudian ideas. For the moment, my purely literary participation in Surrealist publications was inconceivable. I certainly felt capable of it, but my crisis of conscience was inhibiting all my creative power.

Furthermore, family reasons kept me from frequenting the café as much as I used to. I felt slightly out of place among all the newcomers. As for Breton's studio on Rue Fontaine, I no longer went to the meetings there. I decided to abscond. My decision wasn't irrevocable. I myself didn't know where it would lead, but I had made up my mind. I stopped going to the Café Cyrano.

Besides the militant activity that still kept me extremely busy, I had good reasons for staying home. Since mid-January, Katia and I had been living in a barely furnished apartment in Rue Manin, on the fifth floor facing the court. Françoise was born in April. I wanted to have a child by Katia, preferably a girl, whom I would name after my sister. With Katia, love was gradually changing into tenderness. Day by day I came to realize more and more that I wasn't cut out for marriage and that my domestic responsibilities ran counter to my self-realization. I was an anxious father, solicitous and scrupulous, hoping to give his daughter a childhood that he himself had never had. The hours of children's games, the walks, the lullabies, the stories I invented, were probably the essence of happiness that had come my way. They compensated for a great many frustrated creations and secondary occupations. I also devoted to my daughter the time I once spent on Surrealism. Watching a ravishing baby awaken to life, I had an easier time accomplishing the change that totally brought me away from Stalinism and then from the Marxist faith.

The Stavisky affair was a minor swindle, but it was discovered after many similar dishonesties and right in the midst of a recession. The President of the Council was Camille Chautemps, an honest man, a radical and a Mason, who excelled in the art of putting off all important decisions and governing in a liberal spirit with no thought for the morrow. Two of his ministers, as well as several members of his family, were directly accused, although such operations were no doubt fairly common in what a polemicist might call a republic of comradeships. A few members of Parliament were seriously compromised; they were all in the same boat. Chautemps resigned. He was replaced by Daladier, an academic who was said to be the head of the foremost vanguard in the radical party. He had a reputation for energy and Republicanism, and his integrity was absolute.

The parliamentary majority was to the left. Since the establishment of the Republic, the French right had been more aggressive than the left. Always beaten in elections by a center more or less liberal according to circumstances (but always conservative), the right was accustomed to taking the debate out into the streets. Ever since 1925, the right had been producing organizations more oriented toward civil war than the peaceful securing of votes; they were good recruiters, and they had a paramilitary air. They were known as the "Leagues." The oldest and smallest, although most effective in battles, was L'Action Française.

The ideologist of the right was Charles Maurras, a decided paranoiac who explained each morning in *L'Action Française* that there was a gap between the "legal country and the real country" and that electoral opinions could not possibly represent the will of France. In his eyes, France had only one option, royalism, and its sole manifestation was in the defeat of the French armies in 1940. At least half of the metropolitan press paraphrased Maurras's shabby and antiparliamentary nationalism. The financial scandals of politicians were given exaggerated importance, and any pretext was good enough to ridicule or attack the left. The Communist Party and its newspaper weren't any better.

Since 1920, French political life had followed a sort of regular alternation. Relative prosperity would bring a rightist government to power, directly representing the interests of industry and finance. Their financial experts were unimaginative administrators, who knew only the techniques learned in school. Their shortsighted administration, coupled with the authoritarian pettiness of the politicians, created enough discontent to bring about a left-wing success through a slight swing of votes in the next elections. The distinguished academics who came to power did not offer any better economists (when they weren't the same). They translated the strivings of their voters into a less conservative foreign policy, a touch of anticlericalism, and a rather pleasant domestic liberalism. Incapable of overcoming the economic and monetary troubles inherited from their predecessors, they even tended to aggravate them (thus, ultimately seesawing the right back into power). Once the left was in the driver's seat, the right would start yelling at the top of its lungs, multiplying its press campaigns, demonstrations, and maneuvers, which terrified their timid adversaries and set up the next elections. The whole situation had become worse and worse, however, because of the Fascist influence on the right and the growing sentiment among all the French that most administrations were weak and powerless. The political parties were losing themselves in Byzantine quarrels, vetoes, and ambitions that enflamed two thousand initiates in Paris, less than two thousand in the provinces, but bore no relationship to any of the nation's problems.

All that was needed was a lengthy and serious depression to transform political quarrels into street bands. The Communist Party had shown that it was totally incapable of understanding the distress of the unemployed, the difficulties facing small tradespeople, and the impoverishment of the peasants. It had used all its strength calling for the defense of the U.S.S.R. and blaming the left, especially the Socialists, for economic problems, which, as anyone could see, the Socialists were in no way responsible for. Thus, in 1934, the conservatives, and not the Communists, were the prime force in French politics. The Veterans' Association was indignant because its members had been hit by the Depression and because the regime's immobility disgusted them. Was that why they had risked their lives and gone through the worst torments, for these routine bureaucrats, these transient and insubstantial governments, these ministers who were partners in swindling? Luckily for the regime, the youngest of the veterans were thirty-five years old; that age can still produce some violence, but no commando tactics or unconsidered daring.

For various reasons, the demonstrations of the veterans multiplied during the winter of 1933–34. They were generally organized by the National Union (U.N.C.), the huge rightist group. Since they were supposed to be working for all veterans, the left-wing group, the Federal Union, felt obliged to follow suit. After Chautemps resigned and Daladier succeeded him, the National Socialist Council once again refused to assume its responsibilities, invoking the principles passed by the party around 1905 in regard to bourgeois governments. The Communists had no parliamentary strength (only ten members!). They heaped scorn upon Daladier. Everything was set for a parliamentary victory of the right, which was determined to use the extra-parliamentary means that the Communists had forgotten. The Prefect of Police, Jean Chiappe, was sentimentally devoted to the right. All the Leagues were dreaming of a mass demonstration that would put that "Chamber of paralytics" out of existence.

When the great demonstration that the Leagues were planning was announced, Thorez alerted all the chapters to make sure the Paris Communists would form small groups in the midst of the Fascists. They were supposed to yell "Down with the thieves" but give the protest a "proletarian" character. The idea that 5,000 Communists could set up cells among 60,000 Leaguers and deliberately yield to the tactics of their worst enemies was straight out of a dream. *L'Humanité* on February 6 asked the Communist veterans to be at the crossroads of the Champs-Elysées and strengthen the ranks of the U.N.C. reactionaries! Shortly after 8 P.M., I was on Rue de Rivoli, where I found a section of the Veterans' Association (half a dozen people) who hadn't managed to join the group at the crossroads because of the charge on Place de la Concorde. A few Communists from the 19th and 20th precincts, slightly lost, had also come here. I was horror-stricken. I remembered the Berlin transit strike in 1932, which the Nazis had started and the Communists had joined! I tried to reason with the militants I knew. "You're crazy! You must think there aren't enough Fascists in the streets. What do you intend to do? Don't you understand that you're under their orders, that they'll force you to help them? And when you've made them stronger, can you explain to me what good it will do? Who's anti-Fascist today, you or the Republican Guard?"

Their answers were sheepish. They insisted that the Party had assigned them. Their curiosity and the vertigo of a riot got the better of them. A young woman who belonged to the United Union of Clerks sided with me. We talked until the Jeunesses Patriotes started marching toward Place de la Concorde. "You're a bunch of fucking idiots," I shouted. "Don't count on me!" I took off. The young woman followed me. She said she also belonged to the Party, but now she was at her wits' end. She was a pleasant girl, who had been wavering between streetwalking and selling in a department store. She compromised by combining the two. She confided her troubled conscience to me at the end of the evening after we'd made love in a cheap hotel.

The story of the February 6 riots is well known. Over and over again, the police and the Republican Guard had to use their weapons to keep from being overwhelmed. Score at midnight: fifteen dead and hundreds injured.

I tend to think that the Italian and German governments had a hand in these disturbances. I would be the last to be astonished if, during my lifetime, someone furnished me with proof that the Leagues and Political Bureau of the French Communist Party had less liberty than they thought when they reached their ominous decisions.

After fascism had been banned by humanity in 1945, everyone who might have told about February 6 agreed to keep mum about it. Either they didn't want to aggravate the situations of people already discredited by their behavior during the war or they preferred not to cast aspersions on former leaders or old comrades, to whom they would rather issue warrants of patriotism for the honor of a common past. The basically confused character of most of the known or assumed actors in that drama has probably puzzled more than one historian. Since these mediocre activities ultimately ended in one of the greatest national catastrophes, no one has found it necessary to boast about having participated in them.

L'Humanité, on February 7 and 8, broke all records for stupidity. For the first time in Europe since Hitler's attempted putsch in Munich, the police had fired on a right-wing demonstration and had killed Fascists! The Communist Party's daily lashed out against "the government of snipers." The right announced stronger demonstrations. The Leaguers would be armed. But their bark was worse than their bite. The size and quality of their arms could never have compared with the arsenal of the police and the riot squad. Furthermore, the majority of policemen were not favorable to the right. When they had "cleaned up" the Champs-Elysées with unusually murderous rage, they hadn't appreciated the violence of the young bourgeois men in L'Action Française. The police had even gone through gunfire. A new rightist demonstration would never attract the same crowd as on February 6. The halfhearted and the idlers had no desire to face bullets.

Although it had obtained the massive approval of the Chamber, the Daladier administration nevertheless handed in its resignation, as though it had been guilty. Next, the Third Republic offered still another example of its knavery and shrewdness by putting in office one of the governments of trickery and perjury that it was so adept at coming up with. During the interregnum, the Leagues thought they could regain the upper hand. The police once more became tolerant, and the Leaguers seemed to be the masters of the street. The newspaper kiosks on the boulevards were the main victims on the evenings of Fascist rejoicing.

The Socialists reacted promptly; on the eve of February 7, the left-wing Socialists went over to *L'Humanité* to propose joint action. Wisely, Léon Jouhaux, secretary of the C.G.T., suggested a general strike for February 12, along with mass demonstrations everywhere. February 6 had been Parisian. The provinces were agitated and replied in the negative. Hundreds of protest letters against the Party's conduct were pouring in to *L'Humanité* and the Party seat. Members and sympathizers came to protect the union offices. The decrepit premises on Avenue Mathurin-Moreau were put in a state of defense, under constant guard, day and night.

In the provinces as well as Paris, demonstrations were bringing Socialists and Communists together. But the Party leaders persisted in their refusal to understand. When Doriot suggested contacts with the Socialist leaders, Thorez objected that this would be contrary to the decisions of the Central Committee! Realizing that it was cutting itself off from the masses, the secretariat of the Communist Party called upon the workers to demonstrate on February 9. The demonstration was forbidden. So the Party hurled the workers against the police, who had killed over fifteen Fascists three days earlier!

On February 9, Paris was covered with an exceptionally dense fog. The militants were out in the streets because of reason and discipline. They could not understand why the anti-Fascist struggle consisted in attacking the police. The police fired at sight without asking questions. Fortunately, they didn't see very much. All the Surrealists were out in the streets. Tanguy was at Gare de l'Est, where he was struck by a bludgeon. There were several dead, all Communists.

The whole business disgusted me. The Party was going from stupidity to crime. It was stupid and criminal to send its militants to Place de la Concorde on the sixth; it was no less stupid and criminal to mobilize them against the police on the ninth in order to make people forget the insane orders of the sixth. Nearly all the workers and militants that I ran into during the next few days agreed with me. But they were eager for a show of force and wanted everyone threatened

by Fascism to reach some agreement on action. The preparations for
the strike and the demonstration of the twelfth were exalting. Spontaneous contacts were established between the cells, the sections, the
unions, the committees. Ambassadors were exchanged. The Communist
cadres were snowed under.

On February 12, the strike was general. Very few subways, buses, and
streetcars ran. Factories, warehouses, offices, and stores of any significance had to shut down for lack of personnel. In the provinces, the
strike was no less powerful. The enthusiasm and the feelings of the
crowd were intense, like the mood after the liberation of Paris. The
demonstration had mobilized more people than the Leagues had
managed to get on February 6. The working class was affirming its
strength against the right with some success.

On February 8, Crevel and Marcel Jean came over to Rue Manin,
sent by Breton. They brought me the plan of a pamphlet which Breton
had initiated on February 6. The text was published on the tenth, under the title A *Call to Struggle*; it was signed by a good many writers
and artists who weren't Surrealists, such as Elie Faure, Jean Guéhenno,
Félicien Challaye, André Malraux, Henri Jeanson, André Lhote, Maxi-
milien Luce, Henri Poulaille, and Paul Signac. The labor organizations
were summoned to reach an immediate agreement on unified action.
I naturally went along with it, but I couldn't attend the meeting scheduled, I believe, for February 10, because of organizing work I had
taken on elsewhere. I told my friends that I didn't think that manifestoes by intellectuals could change much in the conduct of the parties.
Only the workers could exert enough pressure (especially on the Communist Party) to make the leaders stop quarreling and start acting.
Direct action by a united working class—strikes, demonstrations, street
battles—was definitely a cardinal element in the anti-Fascist struggle,
but it would also be valuable to obtain the support of the government
and the state apparatus. We couldn't overcome Fascism without the
help of the police and the *garde mobile*. The evening of February 6
had reminded those who had forgotten of the decisive value of armed
force when violence in the streets escalated beyond a certain point. We
had to have that force on our side.

My reservations concerned both the significance of manifestoes by
intellectuals and the effectiveness of a united front made up only of
labor parties. I was eager to sign the document, which I felt was good,
and I was amazed not to find my name on it. They probably held a
grudge against me because of my involuntary absence from the meeting

and the skepticism with which I had received my friends. I had certainly made a mistake. *A Call to Struggle* was useful. It preceded the birth of the Committee of Vigilance of Anti-Fascist Intellectuals, which retained some influence, at least during the long period in which the Socialist and Communist parties rid themselves of their quarrels before signing a political pact.

I tried to create local vigilance committees. I couldn't do it all alone. The leaders of the Communist Party were still far from realizing that an understanding on all levels with the Socialists was a matter of life and death for democracy and the labor movement. The Party was torn by the more and more acute conflict, now public, that had broken out between Thorez and Doriot. Thorez was more interested in power than in the success or failure of Fascism in France, and since he had a conservative nature, he was loath to veer from the policies defined by the Congresses. But he opposed Doriot's propositions, not because he considered them false or harmful (their contents actually were closer to his temperament than sectarianism), but because they came from a man whom he wanted to overthrow. Thorez had the Party apparatus on his side, which is a major trump in such a case. All Doriot had was the workers. The Comintern had not yet chosen between the two men, but Doriot was less and less interested in the Comintern, which he regarded almost bankrupt. As the days went by, the absurd and esoteric character of the policies that Thorez was defending became more and more obvious. Doriot was gloating. He became arrogant about his correctness and the approval he received from the workers. His colossal prestige in Saint-Denis, the absolute trust placed in him by almost all the proletarians in the most industrial suburb of greater Paris, blinded him. He held more and more public meetings. The workers came in throngs to acclaim him. Thorez didn't risk venturing outside the meetings of the Party cadres. Doriot had gathered around him all those who had had difficulties with the changing moods of Moscow. The sequence of events shows how unprincipled most of the Communists were, particularly those who had basked in Moscow's favor.

Once the February tempest was over, the Party apparatus pulled itself together under Thorez, who didn't want to admit that Doriot was right, and returned to a sectarian line. The Party's daily newspaper continued to lie, to attack the anti-Fascists, to advocate stupid tactics, and to oppose any agreement with the Socialists or the C.G.T. Thorez knew where he was heading: he was forcing Doriot's partisans to reveal themselves, so that he could fight them better. Thorez was also blinded by pride. As a good bureaucrat he could not be unaware of the fact that by early 1934 the Comintern had already abandoned sectarianism and that after the success of Hitler's plebiscite in November, Russian diplomacy was even more clearly seeking a counter force to Hitler among the Western nations. George Dimitrov was more or less in charge of the Comintern. Alfred Kurella had become one of his closest co-workers.

Thorez wanted to drive Doriot to breaches of discipline, to get him to make statements about Moscow that would ruin any confidence the Russians might still have in him. He was fully successful.

Doriot first got caught in a legalistie trap. He was reluctant to start a national campaign against Thorez, preferring to hole up in his Saint-Denis fief, where he was legally unassailable. Anywhere else, he would have been doing "factional work," according to Communist terminology. (Later on, however, he did hold two or three public meetings in the provinces.) Everything indicates that reliable information conveyed at the beginning of spring convinced Doriot that he was out of favor with the Comintern and that Moscow much preferred Thorez's stupid discipline to Doriot's intelligent indiscretion. The last time I saw Kurella, in June 1934, he didn't hide the fact that the Comintern was considering Doriot as an individual and his faults rather than his politics and his influence on the masses. "We're quite familiar with Doriot," said Kurella. "We have a file on him; we know he's doomed." Little is known about that dossier: vague tales of hush money, like those uncovered in nearly every suburban municipality, dissolute habits that were ill defined. In any event, there was nothing new about it. But with a psychological confidence paralleled only by the Company of Jesus, the Comintern and the Russians opted for Thorez, who gave every guarantee of being a good servant. The political line being debated by the two men was unimportant. It was the Comintern who would define the policies to follow: Thorez would make the necessary corrections, as we all knew, and become an excellent defender of the Popular Front. Doriot was sent off, not because of his shortcomings, but because he had rebelled.

I never liked Doriot personally, and I did find Thorez sympathetic. Nevertheless, I feel that Doriot would have given the Popular Front and the actions of the Communists a dimension that Thorez was unable to achieve. True, with Doriot the French Communist Party might have held aloof from Moscow, particularly in 1940. But if Doriot, who fought courageously against the German army in 1940, had been head of the Communist Party, he would have become the chief figure of the Resistance (barring difficulties), or at least the far-reaching popular politician that General de Gaulle lacked in London on June 18.

Kurella came to Paris at the end of June. I think he was supposed to attend the conference at which the French Communist Party, not without friction, decided upon an unconditional understanding with the Socialists. I was happy to see him again, for I esteemed him greatly and admired his political courage. But I was afraid of disappointing him. We made an appointment to meet at the apartment of another Cominternian on Rue Manin. There I found two or three young and likable men, and a Rumanian woman who may have been Anna Pauker. Everybody knew my name. They gave me a warm welcome; one of them said he was happy to meet me. "We've often spoken about you," he added. The great show of friendship somewhat astonished me. Kurella suggested we take a walk along Buttes-Chaumont. He had an appointment. We would go look for a taxi.

"Our victory is total," he said joyfully. "You know I've been working with George [Dimitrov] for six months. He's completely in favor of ideas we've so often agitated for together, and now they're the official line of the International. We had to bang our fists on the table for the French Communist Party, but Thorez understood, and the necessary decisions will be taken. By the way, your cell has reinstated you in the Party. We'll be able to do some fine work together."

"Who's going to head the Party? Doriot?"

"Why Doriot? We're about to expel him."

"I apologize, Alfred, for the disappointment I'm about to cause you. Nevertheless, I thank you from the bottom of my heart, for if I still wanted to rejoin the Party, I'd have *you* to thank for it. It's as important for me as you imagine, because I regard it as reparation for a foolish injustice and as a sign of esteem on the part of several true Communists. But I can't accept. I no longer believe in the Comintern.

"You know I've never particularly liked Doriot, and I care even less for the people around him; they're practically all contemptible opportunists. But I don't think I can ride roughshod over truth and honor in the name of the Revolution. This time Doriot was right; he fought with a great deal of courage so that an objective truth could win out. The others, inept, lying cowards, insulted and slandered him.

"If you make Doriot a leader of the Party, then, despite my rather serious qualms, I'll become a member again. And I won't spare any efforts. But you're kicking Doriot out and yet adopting his politics.

I'm quite willing to admit that he's a bastard, and that you may have to get rid of him someday. I thought as much in 1928. But not under such conditions. It's too much like the practices of the Catholic Church, and it immediately wrecks any idea of a better world.

"Goodbye! We may never meet again, except in the democratic and revolutionary labor party that I would so much like to see and that would be honored to have leaders like yourself. There I could serve without being ashamed of myself."

22
FAMILY MYTHS AND PHANTOMS

IN 1934, THE ACTUARIAL DEFICIT OF FRANCE
Mutualiste—that is, the difference between the amount that the company should have had to be certain it could meet its commitments and the assets it actually held—ran to one billion francs. The commanders of the Veterans' Association of the Federal Union, who represented nine-tenths of the paid-up capital, took over the administrative positions in order to reorganize the management of the business. The new general manager, Maurice de Barral, was in his fifties, tall, distinguished, slender, and nervous. He suffered from a tenacious acne that tormented his hands. He was authoritarian, intelligent, and brusque. Otherwise, he had pleasant manners. His political opinions were very leftist. He had an inborn sense of negotiation and compromise; at times he seemed as able as Aragon. He had strong political connections in all circles.

Barral was stuck with an assistant manager who was the very opposite of him. A disabled veteran who dressed like a burgher of

1914, he came from a modest background and was conservative. A workhorse, harsh and guileless, he regarded the funds of the war veterans as something sacred. We didn't always see eye to eye with one another, and he made me pay dearly for the strike of 1936. We eventually became good friends because he appreciated my enthusiasm at work, my talent for modern administrative methods, and my conduct during the war. I was promoted to the position of assistant head of my department, and I became one of the most respected technical co-workers of the director-general.

The studies I had to undertake in order to set up projects for straightening out the pension fund taught me a great deal about French society. Working on the budgets of the war veterans, I came to appreciate what government subsidies meant to millions of citizens and the panicky attachment of the pensioners to the value of money. Every lowering of the franc, every devaluation, was more directly felt by these people than the stagnation of the economy. Monetary changes sent them seesawing between the right and the left, a response so characteristic of French elections from 1920 to 1936. I had already come to realize that the working class forms an entity only in *The Communist Manifesto*. Marx himself had to distinguish subgroups within it every time he delved into history: first he designated the *"Lumpenproletariat,"* then "the working aristocracy." Their economic functions are so different, and political stances so often oppose these groups to what remains of the "proletariat," that one is tempted to ask what good the Marxist definition of social class is anyway. My daily practice as a militant obliged me to differentiate, within the proletariat itself, between the journeymen of the artisans, the workers in small businesses (with less than ten employees), the personnel in medium-sized and large factories who showed all the characteristics of the proletariat, and the technicians. I could also distinguish other subclasses: the workers from the country, the owners of a house or field, those who were government pensioners, and the huge body of functionaries. The post office, telegraph, and telephone workers were assured of a pension, but depended on administrations that had not yet been nationalized. Gas men, electricity men, the public-transport workers were set off from the ordinary proletariat because they worked under contract. And what about the ever-growing service sector, whose members, at least theoretically, are not involved in the process of production? Without their services, the manufactured object cannot fully realize its exchange value in order to become a use value.

Chapter 52 of *Das Kapital*, entitled "The Classes," which should have been one of the most important if not *the* most important in the work, runs to only five paragraphs. The manuscript breaks off. One of the most dramatic episodes in Marxist history is the sterile interrogation of a dead man by a man living on borrowed time. In 1936, in Amsterdam, Bukharin was assigned to obtain the original notebooks of the second part of *Das Kapital*. He eagerly read the almost indecipherable notes of the "Interrupted Manuscript," on social classes, written by a man in bad health, cognizant perhaps that he had reached the major difficulty of his undertaking. Bukharin himself, fifteen years earlier, had devoted the last chapter of *The Theory of Historical Materialism* to social classes, extrapolating Marxist particulars in the spirit of traditional Socialism. Since publishing that work, Bukharin had learned to his cost that the revolution he had participated in was not building a classless society. In 1921, he had written, "The society of the future will witness a grandiose overproduction of organizers, and there will be no more stability in the ruling groups," but what he witnessed in the U.S.S.R. flatly contradicted that utopia. Hitler had broken the social classes of Europe's most industrial nation with the help of nationalism and racism, proving once again the strength of the "relative solidarity" that Lenin had denounced in 1914.

Bukharin also knew that if he ever went back to Russia, Stalin would have him killed in the name of class struggle. Here he was in Amsterdam, face to face with the myth. The myth was no better or worse than the ancient or modern deities that people think are hidden in the depths of sanctuaries. Their silence, in reply to even the most anguished interrogations, is the most terrible of the torments inflicted on the faithful. Bukharin held the sacred books in his hands. He got nothing because there was nothing to get.

I know the end of Marx's manuscript only in Engels' edited version. Supposedly he scrupulously respected the thrust of the notes left by Marx. Here is that version in translation:

We first have to answer the following question: Who is it that forms a class? And the answer quite naturally comes from the answer to another question:

What actually constitutes the salaried workers, the landowners, the capitalists, as the creators of the three great social classes?

At first sight, the identity of income and the sources of income.

But from this point of view, doctors and functionaries, for instance, would likewise constitute two classes, for they belong to two different social groups in which the income of the members comes from the same source. The same reasoning would apply to the infinite number of interests and jobs that the division of social work creates among workers, capitalists, and landowners (vine growers, farmers, owners of forests, of mines, of fishing grounds, etc.). THE END.

The question thus remains open, and we must note that Marx seems far less comfortable with these lines, written around 1870, than he had been when he adopted the grandiose simplifications of *The Communist Manifesto* in 1847.

In 1921, Bukharin tried to complete the interrupted manuscript, for better or worse, by analyzing, with filial piety, the axioms and categories of Marxism. His confused analysis merely reflects the vagueness and confusion of the basic assumptions. The proletariat, which Bukharin admits is heterogeneous, encompasses most of the productive individuals whose wages represent only a fraction of the value of what they produce. However, it doesn't necessarily follow that this class constitutes a political entity whose interest lies in suppressing capitalism. For the professions, groups, and so on that constitute it play different roles in production, suffer different degrees of exploitation, and want different things. Certain technical groups do participate in decision making. If you cut away the technicians in order to affirm that their interest, like that of engineers and all bosses, can accord easily with that of the holders of capital, if you link those groups with the technocrats and the distributers of merchandise because the latter groups have some control over the means of production and exchange, you will obtain a good idea of societies known since 1934. In any event, it will be a more precise image than the Marxist caricatures of Russia, Germany, the United States, and France. The existence of the Soviet bureaucracy as a social class is all the more obvious in that its members draw their income from the same source. In the United States, technicians, administrators, accountants, distributors, executives, and the like hold an important part of capital. The appearance of a new social class is the phenomenon of the twentieth century. Neither Marx nor Engels foresaw it.

Every day I spent some two hours commuting, and I used the time to draw a balance between the elements of "historical materialism" I was keeping and those I was rejecting. At the end of the week, I would sum up the outcome of these discussions with myself in a school notebook. I began a new and somewhat advanced outline of historical materialism in January 1944, thinking of publishing my thoughts. The manuscript was lost with several documents that I had hastily removed from my home for safekeeping. At the time, I felt that the class struggle was one historical driving force *among many*, that the distinction of three "great social classes" represented merely a rough approximation of the structure of modern societies, that the corporative interests of what Marx calls the proletariat nearly always triumph over what Bukharin, in line with Marx, depicts as "class interest." Once the pressure of history forced me to relegate these great monsters (proletariat, bourgeoisie) to the status of abstract categories and replace them with more homogeneous groups (professions, for example) truly capable of displaying a collective consciousness in certain cases, I finally gave manifestations of class-consciousness the right to exist, even if they didn't bear directly on satisfying economic needs, and I reintegrated the famous superstructures into daily life. They do not figure as a setting or as appearance: they express the complexity, the variety of individuals, their hopes and their follies. They also became causes. Thus, the German proletariat—or, rather, the social strata conveniently designated under that heading—had not behaved as a political class in 1933, even though they had been more nourished than anyone else on Marxism and controlled powerfully organized unions and parties. If we abandoned that vague entity and tried to comprehend the true communities of interest, we would reach a much better understanding.

All the Marxists devoted themselves to the parlor game of trying to determine whether a train engineer, a merchant sailor, an engineer, a foreman, a bookkeeper, and a salesclerk produce surplus value or, in other words, are doing productive work. I was no different. The game is all the more amusing in that Marx doesn't waste words on any labor outside the factory. In 1860 technology, research, transportation, and civil services had not assumed any of the economic and social importance they have today. As far as I was concerned, the answer was direct. By calculating pensions and tables, by determining the interest rate on a bond, by dealing with the mortality rate and evaluating its risks, I wasn't being productive. Mine was a function of distribution. I was adding my wages to the general expenses of the system; that is to say, I was living on the product of unpaid work, ultimately sponging off the people who had produced the wealth and the capitalists whom I was cheating of a part of their profit. The same held true for functionaries, soldiers, and shopgirls.

I had thus reached a conclusion diametrically opposed to the Bolshevik view that Bukharin formulated at the end of his chapter on classes. I refused to consider the proletariat, so vaguely defined, as a political class. An enormous mass of wage earners (all those who were in office agencies, for instance) were set aside as nonproducers of surplus value and therefore undeserving of full entrance into the revolutionary force. But this mass, which includes people earning very low wages, was steadily growing year by year in the industrial nations. Stinginess of the capitalists in regard to office personnel may have characterized the first half of the nineteenth century, but by 1935 it had given way to an endlessly growing concern for everything bearing on sales.

A Socialist revolutionary party should not, I felt, be homogeneous. It ought to represent all the social strata oppressed by the system, those who are robbed of part of the product of their labor and those whose salaries are too low in relation to the value of other people's production. If the interests of these groups are sometimes contradictory, solidarity can be based on their common suffering because of the way those interests are dealt with by the capitalists. Two of the revolutions that history has experienced, that in France in 1789 and that in Russia in 1917, were achieved by alliances between parties and social categories. We can assume that the degeneration of the Russian Revolution resulted from a desire for homogeneity, which led to the dictatorship of one party over all social groups. The revolutionary party will be heterogeneous, I thought, so that a true inner democracy can preserve the power and capacity for action that are killed by sectarianism and blind obedience to dogma.

France Mutualiste moved from Rue de la Douane to the old Hôtel Mirabaud on Avenue de Villiers. This was a large building in the style of Henri II, dating from the era when La Plaine Monceau was the elegant part of Paris. From the window of my office, in a former bedroom two flights up, I could see Aux Délices, the quaint and charming pastry shop that was one of the best caterers in Paris, and the always empty Henner Museum. The ground floor and the upper story of the Hôtel Mirabaud harbor a profusion of woodwork, coffered ceilings painted in the style of the castles on the Loire, and Spanish leather. The stairway, with its sculptured wooden banister, is very beautiful. The Mirabauds, one of the high Protestant dynasties that financed the industrialization and colonial expansion of the Third

Republic between 1870 and 1914, had kept a rather spacious pavilion on the other side of the main entrance.

From 1935 to 1940, I was the technical adviser to several mutual-aid societies affiliated with France Mutualiste. One of them was called The French Chefs. Its object was to obtain pensions for the old chefs of wealthy families and big hotels. The treasurer was a fine-looking old man, as straight as a ramrod, who put out an amazing bulletin, partly devoted to the recipes of grand French cuisine. They were simplified, he once explained, to make them accessible to modest budgets, but the preparation of each dish required at least half a day's work and would have cost a whole day's wages for any typist who might have wanted to take the risk. When the King and Queen of England paid an official visit to Paris in 1938, I showed the President's menus to my chef and asked his opinion of them. He was very severe. "That's no cuisine for a king. The great traditions are dying out. I've worked at all the courts in Europe," he went on. "Before 1914, of course, when there were still a dozen kings around. My greatest joys were in Germany. The princes wanted only French cooking, and yet the Germans have excellent recipes for game and treat pork very well.

"I like coming here because this is the place I started in. I was only thirteen. I've seen sauces being stirred for twelve hours. That was the kids' work; we would take turns. It's all part of a past that's quite dead. The great French cuisine is gone! It's been replaced with approximations. They may taste almost the same, but the dishes are heavy and indigestible. If you correctly follow the true recipes, they're much much better for the stomach. The great principle of the French cuisine, monsieur, is reduction. By reducing a sauce as long as necessary, with the proper attention, you burn out or decompose all the harmful or indigestible elements. All that remains is the aroma.

"But living conditions aren't the same any more. When the Mirabauds had this house, there were twenty people at lunch every day, and a few dinners for thirty people every week. Where are the Mirabauds today? It's the automobile that killed French cooking. In the old days, the guests at a castle would stay for at least three days. They would arrive at the nearest railroad station, several miles away, and be called for in a barouche. And once they were there, what could they do? You can't go hunting all year round! The main resource was the table. Nowadays the guests show up in a car ten minutes before lunch, and three hours later they're off again to Deauville or to other friends twenty miles away. People are in a hurry. The grand cuisine was not meant for people in a hurry."

I still regret that I didn't ask the fellow about anything else he had seen at the courts of German princes. My other clients weren't as picturesque or as interesting.

By the end of 1935, the general impoverishment of the country struck harshly at the artists, intellectuals, and bohemians. It was good to be a functionary or a civil servant. I had to hire dozens of clerks to handle all the paperwork. Georges Hugnet came to see me about a job. He was followed by Leo Malet and Pastoureau. In their group, they ran into Degottex, whose father had been in my department for several years. Degottex was young and slender, dreamy-eyed; he didn't seem very comfortable in an office despite his good intentions. Whenever he spoke, he acted as though he were looking at something else and was not very interested in the topic he had broached. It was probably by calculating the pensions of the war veterans and being in touch with the three Surrealists that he thrashed out his vocation as a painter. A young Nordic, very tall, a perfect Aryan by Nazi standards, fresh out of high school, also came looking for work. We needed an accountant who knew what an integral was. So we hired him and were very satisfied. His name was Van Hejenoort, and he had been one of Leon Trotsky's secretaries. He had entered into the service of the great man as one enters into a religion. Modest, gentle, but uncompromising and stubborn, intelligent and hard-working, he lived on very little. He was spellbound by a revelation that saved him from impurity, qualms, doubts, and filled him with ineffable joy. He brought along two or three Trotskyite militants, including Craipeau and a dreadful shrew of twenty, who was attracted by the many opportunities such a group offered for gossip and slanderous denunciations. She sowed discord, quarreling about everything and nothing. Hopelessly in love with Van Hejenoort, she belonged to the race of gossipy concierges.

During the time they spend in the office, men and women reveal their oddities, their manias, and even their vices. Secretaries are given to exaggerating the merits of their bosses, but anyone who doesn't work very closely with an executive has no way of appreciating his professional value or his services to the company. On the other hand, the lower personnel or the intermediate workers judge their superiors in terms of certain repeated gestures, words, and manners. These may define an office creature, but they do not reveal much of that creature's essence or strength (or even weakness). The generally malicious talk of colleagues and underlings sometimes makes a reputation. Those who are cunning enough to conceal their insufficiencies or faults so that they give no excuse for harmless spite have an easier time with their careers than others, since informers abound on every level. But, ultimately, it's the opinion of the superior that counts most. The wisest thing is to avoid taking any risks, to act as little as possible, to ask for a bigger and bigger staff, and to "reorganize." Reorganization provides a helpful pretext for flow charts and promises. It justifies delays or mistakes and takes place entirely within a closed system that tends to become an end in itself, especially in public administrations. One should also be very respectful of manuals. By knowing them thoroughly, one can put a stop to any sort of action, with irreproachable motives. Finally, the foremost quality of a department head is writing good reports and furnishing his superiors with frequent memos, not so much to keep them informed as to give them the impression that everything is going well, that they are abreast of everything, and, perhaps, to cover oneself. Bureaucracy thus develops terrible faults: self-importance, servility, laziness, and administrative falsehood. In a private office, the possibility of firing an employee or transferring him to a disagreeable position limits the damage somewhat. Within the civil service, the permanence of officials, old school ties, and union fellowship have created a kind of feudalism that gradually leads to the same results as its illustrious predecessor.

I used some of these gimmicks myself, although throughout my life I had always tried to give top priority to the goal, sacrificing my personal interest. I soon realized to what extent the purely administrative aspect of an office, what I call the comfort of the executives, is more important than the work itself. But my experience in supervising people has convinced me that a large part of humanity is totally useless. How often, trying to determine the aptitudes of somebody or other for some sort of work—an operation in which I strove to take into account as far as possible the person's social background, character, and ignorance—have I begun to wonder whether Marx's peremptory judgment on the alienation of workers was not simply romantic optimism? It may have been an intellectual chimera or a nostalgia of the 1820's for German artisanry, something like a philosophical translation of the perils awaiting Hans Sachs the shoemaker were he to become an industrial worker. I admit that the beginnings of capitalism, like production-line work, offered and still offer some fine examples of alienation, but can we really be sure that the *form* of work is the cause? Isn't it rather *work per se?* Two-legged creatures are born by chance into a family they haven't chosen, with their physical and intellectual capacities limited by fate. They are more or less the prisoners of habits, complexes, and taboos forced upon them by external conditions. Their only vocation is to live for a few decades, constantly waylaid by nature and their fellow men. They work, because if they don't do anything, society won't satisfy any of their little needs, first and foremost the need to survive. They feel little solidarity with that social machine over which they have so little control. They played no part in constructing it, and its complexity is too much for them. But they don't feel like changing it because they don't give a damn and because the replacement models don't seem to hold water. These people are mediocre. They are neither intellectuals, artists, nor Jacks-of-all-trades. They are neither dexterous nor intelligent. They lack courage. Most of them go to work of their own accord, under the sway of necessity. They recognize that necessity, and the only freedom that this awareness gives them is the desire to change bosses or jobs. But things never get better. Do they at least have their share of what the lovers of illusions call human qualities? Sometimes, but not always. A lot of them are mean, envious, mendacious, dishonest. But who can blame them? The only way to prevent it would have been to kill them at birth.

Manufacturing employs some of them, even though they generally prefer offices, where they can find jobs that are easy to keep. Because of their indolence, they produce little. Ultimately, they live largely off the work of others. Society receives from them only what they can give it. The same would hold true for a Communist society. Aside from the tiny fraction of capitalist profit that could be distributed among them (I mean that part of the profit that isn't spent on new investments), their condition could be ameliorated only by increasing the number of objects produced, which would mainly come from the work of others. Stakhanovism emphasizes, for the benefit of an elite, the differences in wages between good workers and indolent and incapable ones. Isn't that further proof of the heterogeneity of the proletariat? Even though, in *Down with Work*, I granted a larger place to unwilling workers than Lafargue did in *The Right to Laziness*, I had reached the same optimistic conclusion as Karl Marx's son-in-law: work could be eliminated through automation. At France Mutualiste, I had just installed some calculators to replace the tedious work of adding and sorting with surer and more rapid automatic operations. Nevertheless, one-third of my personnel were incapable of learning and carrying out the sorting operations. I had managed to train only one operator, and the mechanics that were sent to me from time to time had technical qualifications that none of my employees would have been capable of acquiring. Faced with apparently insurmountable contradictions between society and the individual, the producer and the incapable worker, I was inclined not to renew my blind faith in Hegelian dialectics. Could it be that many opposites are irreducible, that they do not permit synthesis, or that the syntheses proposed were merely acts of faith?

In 1938, I needed operators for my calculators. A woman who came to my office one day in July was both young and lovely; her complexion reminded me of the nymphs in the Fontainebleau School. Her face was right out of a Greek statue: a straight nose, well proportioned and prolonging the forehead, large eyes forming an isosceles triangle with the mouth. I asked her to give it a try, certain beforehand that this young beauty would fail. She came back. The man in charge called me up to say she was excellent. I complimented her and asked her when she wanted to start.

"First I'd like to go on vacation," she said, unembarrassed. "And I'd want to start as soon as I get back, if that's all right with you." I liked her very unadministrative reply. Monique was hired; she was an excellent recruit. Despite her cheap clothes, she was quite chic. Her mother was a factory worker. She lived in Charonne. A few months later, I saw a young middle-class man waiting for her in a small sports car after work. "It had to come sooner or later," I joked. "She's too beautiful for us. We'll soon be losing her."

We didn't lose her. It was a rather virtuous flirtation that flattered her ego. When I came back from Syria in late 1940, some of my employees took me out for a welcome-back drink. To my great surprise, Monique was still there. "She's in love with you," said a young woman whose political opinions were close to mine. "That's why we invited her. She's sort of shy, and she'll never tell you herself, but people in her department kid her a lot about it." I took it to heart, but a few months passed before I was tempted enough to clear the whole thing up. My colleagues hadn't been lying. So I followed up on it. Our affair lasted for four occasionally stormy years. I owe my life to her beauty, which I'll explain later on. It was partly on her account that I wrote *Le Grand Ordinaire*.

Breton's "Stalinism" progressively wore down. The February 6 riot shook his faith in the French Communists. During 1934, and until he was ousted in 1935, he became more and more heretical within the organizations more or less under the thumb of the Association for Revolutionary Writers and Artists, in which he sat, albeit not enough to prevent the Czech Communist Party from rolling out the red carpet for him in Prague during the spring of 1935. Little by little, Breton came around to Leon Trotsky's theses.

Reference to Leon Trotsky was the spontaneous reaction of anyone who was worried about how to stop the expansion of Fascism and tried to understand the easy surrender of the German working class. As of 1931, Trotsky had explained what was the "lesser evil" for the working class. It was pointless to talk about revolution and taking power if the proletariat were robbed of its organizations, particularly its party. In 1932, he foresaw the victory of Fascism "if the United Front fails to materialize." He regarded this United Front as an entente between the Socialist and Communist parties, but was vague about the necessary form and motitivations.

Trotsky had created a scandal when he wrote that, to oppose the Nazis, the Communists would have to ally themselves with the devil, the devil's grandmother, and even Greszinsksi, the Socialist police commissioner of Berlin. This outburst was prophetic. The important thing in 1933 and 1934 was that Trotsky saw in time that a United Front of Communists and Socialists was *the* political necessity.

The principal articles written by Trotsky in 1932 on Germany were published in the pamphlet entitled *And Now*. When I recently reread it, I was struck even more than in 1934 by the old-fashioned quality of these articles. They are often too long. There are constant references to the history of Bolshevism, with parallels between the actors of the 1933 drama and the Russian political figures of 1914–17. These comparisons made sense for the author, and for the historian, but they do not correspond to any reality most militants or readers knew in 1933. Here and there, however, an admirable formula compensates for everything, even though it may not always be in perfect agreement with what precedes or follows it. Thus I came across a sentence that I had noted in 1934 because it fitted in exactly with what I was thinking. It inspired my political activity until the Liberation.

"For its struggle, the proletariat needs the unity of its ranks. This unity is as important for the economic conflicts within the domain of a business as for the national struggles such as the defense against Fascism."

Trotsky's political writings are measured and decent in contrast with Stalin's, but all they could lead to was quarreling. The excited tone, the partial judgments, the violent personal attacks—all qualities that tended to isolate the great man in the haughty solitude of an accursed prophet—make for grand pages of polemics but render the argument inadequate to the enormous events that were sweeping past us. The most courageous and most intelligent Marxist still on his feet when Hitler seized Germany did not know how to be the guide and leader that the nations needed in 1939.

I thought no differently in 1934. Trotsky seemed a point of reference, a vivifying source of ideas, but not a master thinker. People are quick to cite his prophesies; they forget the erroneous judgments, the brisk but soon belied analyses that should never have been regarded as anything but tirades or hypotheses. Unfortunately, they were ranked— until they lost all probability—among the revealed truths, the foundations of true Bolshevism, the guideposts of the "only revolutionary road." Leon Trotsky never realized that he might not have achieved a proletarian revolution so much as a coup d'état followed by an atrocious civil war that gave birth to a new social class.

I'd like to present two quotations from Trotsky. Although I subsequently tried to incorporate these fragments in a whole, I was frightened of criticizing bluntly and in detail the judgments of some of the most important people in our era on events, ideas, and men. The first quotation is from 1932. I didn't know about it at the time, but it clearly illuminates the author's self-delusions. The quotation is from an article published in *Forum* on April 15, 1932:

"Would Hitler's coming to power mean peace? No. If Hitler comes to power, he will merely reinforce French predominance. . . . War not against Poland and France, but war against the Soviet Union."

These words are as preposterous as what Stalin told the unfortunate engineers whom he accused of sabotage. And yet: Everything that Hitler was to do was written in *Mein Kampf*.

The second quotation is from the article *Where Is France Heading?* published in October 1934. Its analysis, like the advice given to Germans in 1934, wiped out any slight impulse I might ever have had to get any closer to the Trotskyites.

"Capitalism has raised the means of production to such a level that they are paralyzed by the poverty of the broader masses, who are themselves ruined by that very capitalism. For this reason, the entire system has entered a period of decadence, decomposition, decay. Capitalism not only cannot give the workers any new social reforms or even merely small alms; it is forced actually to annul the older reforms. The whole of Europe has passed into an era of economic and political counterreforms."

In 1934, two fundamentally Marxist tenets—the definition of the worker's wage as the price of reconstituting the work force and the principle of the growing impoverishment of the proletariat—struck me as erroneous. Although the standard of living of the French working class in 1934 was quite low and retrogressive, it already involved a considerable consumption. One merely had to glance at the precise descriptions in Zola's novels and compare them with the daily life of Parisian workers or northern miners in 1934 to see that no impoverishment had taken place. Certain Marxists, to save dogma, explained these anomalies by citing the surplus profits of imperialism, thanks to which a few crumbs dropped down to the urban proletariat. True, the quantity of unpaid work done by the colonial peoples for mine owners and other reapers of natural resources was appalling; but the sequence of events has shown that that was not the factor preventing impoverishment. The principle itself was false; that was all. Trotsky's categorical statement could not be taken seriously. It was based on the errors Marx had committed in his discussion of labor's earnings, it applied a simplistic and subjective judgment to the capitalist crisis, and it was swarming with terrible contradictions.

Between 1939 and 1941, Hitler successively invaded Poland, France, and Soviet Russia, in accordance with what he had announced fifteen years earlier. Between 1935 and 1940, social legislation throughout Europe made immense progress, and the workers' standard of living rose everywhere except in Spain and Russia. A few months after the publication of Trotsky's article, France instituted social security. Next came the reforms of the Popular Front, collective contracts, labor delegates, paid vacations, the forty-hour week. The Scandinavian countries and England followed suit; the advantages obtained by the working class in Germany (and even Italy) partly explain how Hitler could so easily lead the German people to massacre.

Nevertheless, in 1934, under Leon Trotsky's moral guidance, I became a member of the S.F.I.O. Socialist Party, which all the Trotskyites had joined. I was not, however, among the ranks of those turbulent and presumptuous recruits.

23
THE POPULAR
FRONT

IN CONTRAST TO THE COMMUNIST PARTY, THE
Socialist Party favored free discussion and criticism. Its members had
the right to challenge its politics at any time. They were at liberty to
gather in like-minded groups and were allowed to have their own press,
which was not restricted to Party members. Their publications were
openly sold or distributed to anybody. These rules of internal democracy, this tolerance, the preparations for congresses through large-scale
discussions, had been traditional in international Socialism, including
Bolshevism, before the First World War. The bickering that agitated
the Second International led to rifts, reconciliations, and schisms. The
Bolsheviks kept some internal democracy until 1921, when the Russian
Communist Party became totalitarian and autocratic. Trotsky himself
had added a good many stones to that jail.

Three groups divided the Socialist Party at the time the Popular
Front was created: a rather heterogeneous majority around the uncontested leader Léon Blum and the secretary-general Paul Faure; a

Marxist left around Jean Zyromski; and a far left, no less heterogeneous than the majority, led by Marceau Pivert. This last group united pacifists, anarchists, Trotskyites, and others, recruited from an impatient younger generation whose revolutionary will was quite firm although it was manifested with much confusion and many contradictions. Actually, the political makeup of the Socialist Party was more complex than this scheme might indicate. The Party was mainly provincial, although its leftist groups and its leader were typically Parisian. It drew its chief strength from the confidence of workers in northern France. In all industrial centers of the provinces, except Gard, the Socialists had a following that the Communists lacked.

Even though several of its leaders, and not the least important ones, were neither deputies nor senators, the activities of the Socialist Party were essentially parliamentary. That was one of the grievances of the Comintern against Social Democracy, but the history of the last decade had established that the Communists were acting no differently. Hitler's success showed up the weaknesses in the dogmatism of the Communists, who considered elections superfluous. Elections brought Hitler to power through a process somewhat comparable to the changes of the majority in the Soviets. And, just as the Bolsheviks had done before him, Hitler, once he was in power, immediately smashed the democratic mechanism he had used. Western nations were accustomed to expressing their opinions by way of free elections, in which the Socialists rightly saw the ultimate guarantee of democracy. This explained the absence of any response to the watchword "The Soviets everywhere," which the people felt was more like anarchy than popular power. The United Front of 1934 and the Popular Front of 1935 were virtually an admission that Leninism had been promoting a utopia since 1918. The Communists fell into line with the Social-Democratic tradition: to govern, one must gain the assent of a popular majority clearly expressed in free elections designating representatives with legislative power. There was no sign of a revolutionary situation in France.

On the Communist side, political analysis was not carried out by the Political Bureau (and even less by the Central Committee); it was in the hands of "instructors," whose intellectual capacity was far superior to that of the national leaders. Inspired more or less directly by Stalin and his collaborators, they benefited from information received from Soviet services.

Leftists and Trotskyites disapproved of the transformation of the United Front into a Popular Front and of the agreement with the

Radical-Socialist Party, especially as it was represented by Daladier. Instead, they suggested a return to class warfare, forgetting that, despite his weaknesses, Daladier was the only European politician ruthlessly opposed to Fascism. Furthermore, in electoral terms (and there were no others), the success of the left was impossible without the radicals. Although the polls of May 1936 gave a majority to the left, they registered only a slight shift of votes. The left could talk about a success but not a triumph. The United Front received only about 35 percent of the votes. It would have had even less if the voters had been asked to endorse a position whose electoral victory didn't seem credible. Even more than in 1928, the voters had given the Communist Party a firm demonstration that they weren't ready for the worst.

The Socialist section of the nineteenth arrondissement met in the vast basement of a café on Place du Combat (now Place du Colonel-Fabien). It had more than two hundred members. On good days, more than one hundred would attend a meeting. A rough four-part division, representing the four electoral districts, took shape before the elections. Their strength was swelled by the supporters of the candidates or the elected.

There were few workers, a great many functionaries and clerks, a few tradesmen, and a small nucleus of schoolteachers and lawyers. Coming from the Communist Party, I found myself in a different world, one strongly dedicated to political debates and oratorical effects but quite removed from action and completely isolated from factory life. The language was also very different. The Church Fathers cited in discussions were Marx and Jaurès, more rarely Engels. Lenin and Stalin had more or less the status that Luther and Calvin have among Catholics. Trotsky was seen in a better light because of his misfortunes. Léon Blum had an intellectual prestige that Thorez acquired in his party only toward the end of his life.

The Doumergue administration, which intended to appease the right and make it forget the casualties of February 6, would have preferred to amend the Constitution in order to do away with six-month governments. The Cross-of-Fire groups tried to help the former President of the Republic through "mass pressure." Their vast provincial rallies alarmed the supporters of the Republic. The systematic hostility of the left, which had the majority in the Chamber of Deputies, easily overcame the reformist projects, which they labeled authoritarian, because the huge proletarian demonstrations that took place almost everywhere, in response to the automobile rallies of the Cross-of-Fire groups, re-affirmed the zeal of the left-wing deputies.

The most notable administration of that period was Pierre Laval's, which obtained its power by passing so-called decree laws, on whose validity the Parliament would not pass judgment until later. The grand plan of the Laval operation was to reduce the French standard of living by 10 percent. This would balance the national budget, protect the franc, and revitalize the economy. Thus pensions, salaries, rents, and, if possible, prices, were to be cut by 10 percent.

Laval couldn't have done anything better to assure the success of the Popular Front. Management took advantage of the situation to lower salaries. The working class's standard of living reached its lowest point since 1918. Since the deflation never managed to enliven the French economy, the 1936 elections were heralded as a victory of the left.

The first ballot took place on April 26, 1936. The Popular Front was present everywhere. By April 27, its success was beyond all doubt. There would be a Léon Blum administration in a few weeks. Millions of Frenchmen felt as though they were emerging from a tunnel. The workers were more responsive than anyone else to this new vision. Until then, they had been fighting against management and the state. Tomorrow the state might be favorable to labor's demands, something unheard of since the beginnings of the Republic. Thus it was not astonishing that the workers who were more daring, more impatient, or felt more threatened than others triggered off strikes as early as April 27. After May 3 came the avalanche. To show their strength, the workers occupied the factories, a tactic that had already been used abroad.

Strikes broke out in factories where there were no union sections. The federations and the unions were overrun. All the available militants were detailed to control the strikes and start discussions with management. Appeals were made to the politicians in charge, to all those who had some practice in trade-unionism. Wildcat strikes had to be supervised, and coherent lists of demands drawn up. Such activities increased steadily. The workers were happy to be able to strike legally, with no fear of dismissals or "scabs." Occupation of a factory was both a guarantee and an act of revenge. "We're in our own place," they could be heard saying. But most of the strikers handled that weapon awkwardly. Lists of demands were hard to work out without the help of professional unionists.

I was known to both Socialists and Communists. I had been on all the United Front committees and was one of the founders of the Popular Front. Militants and sympathizers came to see me every day, for want of anything better, because some factory or other had gone on strike. I helped workers set up their strike committees and organize the occupation of factories. I tried to put them in touch with the proper trade union. I also had to harangue the mass meetings to keep up morale.

I came to work late and left early. In the general euphoria, I decided to get all the factories in the district to go out on strike. I intervened in the most direct manner by marching into the establishments, authoritatively calling the workers away from their posts. and persuading them to vote for the strike. This threw administrators, directors, and bosses into a dither. Sometimes they helped me convene their personnel. I must admit that I was pretty rough.

The occupation of France Mutualiste came just in time to allow me to devote myself all the more to the factories that had been neglected. Comrades asked me to take over the conflict at the rag factories.

The Dufour plant treated the discarded rags that were gathered by the garbage pickers. It not only supplied the papermakers but also manufactured buffing wheels with old pieces of bed linen.

More than three hundred people were employed to sift the rags, clean them, and, if necessary, fashion the buffing wheels. Most of them were women. The working conditions were abominable, like something out of a report on Shanghai or a Zola novel. The personnel sorted filthy rags in decrepit, badly ventilated, and unheated buildings that were even poorly lit. Since it had never occurred to the management or to the work inspectors to install exhaust fans, the workers, recruited from the poorest section of the populace, were terrifyingly dirty. The salaries ran as low as fifty centimes an hour. In two or three suburban locations, smaller enterprises also dealt in rags, and they were even more horrible to see. In Montreuil, I came upon some forty haggard creatures, dirtier than the rags. Looking like they had emerged from a cellar, they squinted their bloodshot, filth-lined eyes as though the sunlight were painful.

I drew up a provisional collective agreement raising all wages by 50 percent. I doubled the lowest salaries by fixing a minimum wage rate. Dufour was the only employer who drafted a defense. My response was arrogant. His colleagues were panic-stricken. After several days, the agreements were signed.

Work resumed slowly. Quite a number of workers had participated in the strikes. The ample raises in wages, unprecedented since the first factory began in France, were mouth-watering. If the bosses had yielded, and so quickly at that, wasn't it logical to assume that these concessions were insignificant compared with their fortunes? Weren't their profits theoretically immense? Couldn't the workers obtain more? As the discussions dragged on and on in some of the factories, political circles became disquieted. We could see armed *gardes mobiles* at strategic points. Maurice Thorez wrote the oft-cited article *We Have to Know How to End a Strike* for *L'Humanité*. This piece is a primer of trade-unionism. The labor movement had appealed to so many partly because it expressed a new legal concept. The workers had sensed that the government would support them or at least not bother them. As soon as the most leftist political group announced that recess was over, it would have been absurd to continue. One would run the risk of finding oneself without further support, whereas the advantages already gained were enormous. Nevertheless, new strikes broke out in June and July because employers and workers still hadn't learned to bargain without losing their tempers and because discipline has never been a strong point among the French.

These strikes gave the Communist Party the chance to implant their organizations in the factories, to the detriment of the Socialists and the reformists. Thus it profited from ten years of Bolshevization. At the behest of the Comintern, it had recruited hundreds of militants from the working class. Their function was to build up unions rather than to make the Revolution.

In September 1936, the refusal to intervene in Spanish affairs, advocated by Léon Blum, dealt a severe blow to the prestige of the Socialists in a number of industrial centers. Since the strikes were always victorious because the government was so meek and because the arbitration procedure almost systematically favored labor, every group could urge its claims on its own terms. Nevertheless, in the long run, this system worked against any kind of rash agitation. It would have changed the union leaders into hairsplitting lawyers and assured the triumph of reformism if the Second World War hadn't interrupted.

Despite the abominable trials in Moscow, in which Stalin equaled Hitler in refined savagery and falsehood, the influence of the Communist Party in France spread through both the intellectual circles and the Parisian proletariat. This was the era of Aragon's rise, when he became editor-in-chief of the daily *Ce Soir* (circulation: 300,000). *Commune* became one of the most widely read literary reviews, and the author of *The Peasant of Paris* was no longer an avant-garde writer but a front-rank literary personality. The leftist intellectuals and bourgeois who read *Ce Soir*, received Aragon with open arms, or joined the Communist Party were moving more toward Russia than toward the ideas of Marx and Lenin.

The Soviet intervention in Spain, which had been crowned with success in 1937, reassured all those who were beginning to fear Hitler and had less than full confidence in French military might, which had been reduced to a minimum by an unprecedented defeatist campaign inspired by the right. Russia had become the symbol of armed force for the intelligentsia and part of the left (and even for some conservative circles, since the traditional distinctions were disappearing in 1936). They were relying on the Soviets' strength and anti-Fascist determination to dissuade Hitler from going any further with his disquieting plans. For once, the policy of the Communist Party was sound and didn't stray into wishful thinking. It was entirely dictated by the secret leaders bestowed upon the Party by the Comintern. Thus it was a Russian product. But it was a good thing. Since the interest of the U.S.S.R. and of France coincided almost everywhere in the world, the Communist Party was sometimes more precise than the Quai d'Orsay about what the country needed.

On the other hand, this Russification had a ravaging effect within the Communist Party. All those who still had friends there were terror-stricken by the progress of its "Prussianization" and blind authoritarianism. The Stalinist methods of spying and informing had been introduced into the organization, where something like a control board used unheard-of inquisitorial procedures to destroy the personalities of the militants. This agency closely examined the relations between members and with the outside world to make sure that no aspect of their private lives wasn't known to and accepted by the Party. For this activity, which was more monstrous than any police investigation, the agency used not only reports and informers but also a technique that had been perfected in Russia, the questionnaire. Each member was required periodically to fill out printed forms indicating what he knew about his relatives and friends and mentioning the names of all the policemen, military men, magistrates, capitalists, and so on in his family, within his circle, or even in his neighborhood. The Party had to nip in the bud any stray impulse toward independence. Each individual was to be trained so that he would never undertake anything without first asking himself if it would be approved by the Party. If there was any doubt, he was to abstain or inform upon himself, and he was expected to be always ready to feel guilty. These extravagant precautions were primarily intended to obtain a worshipful and absolute submission to Thorez and Stalin and a respect for the hierarchy (though they failed to protect the Party against police infiltration and Hitlerian counter-espionage). Their corollary was the systematic use of slander against political adversaries or anyone regarded as an enemy. Defamatory procedures which until then had been the prerogative of the far right and the admirers of Fascism were perfected by the Communists.

The Communists accused the Socialists of sacrificing everything to formal legality. "They can't be revolutionaries because they respect the law." Within the framework of the anti-Fascist alliance, the members of the Communist Party and the young revolutionaries, including myself, readily quoted an axiom on civil war and terrorism: "There can be no liberty for the enemies of liberty." But the historic importance of the Socialists, and even the radicals, the reason they were at the center of the popular coalition, depended almost entirely on the belief that the enemies of liberty could enjoy liberty even while they intentionally threatened it. In Russia, the Communists had suppressed liberty, denied it to their adversaries, and refused to grant it even to themselves. Fascism, in its turn, had taken over this total suppression, and it was precisely this that the Popular Front was fighting against. The Socialist scruples, which I had ridiculed in 1928, had, thanks to Hitler (and Stalin), gained the exemplary force that triggered the revolutions of the nineteenth century.

The Trotskyites, and to a lesser degree the Communists, saw the United Front as a tactical phase that would lead to something else. But in the United Front, and even more in the Popular Front, the political goal, following Clausewitz's formulation, yielded to the nature of the means and became something different. The Communists were still inimical to the governmental institutions of bourgeois democracy which, in 1922, they had wanted to use only in order to destroy them, but they were forced to side with the defenders of these institutions in 1936. In France the struggles taking place outside Parliament reached a climax with the election of deputies according to constitutional laws and with Parliament's passage of laws improving the situation of the working class, in formal contradiction to the Comintern's prophesy.

All the Socialists were attached to universal suffrage, a representative government, and republican institutions, to which they attributed democratic virtues that were sometimes lacking. They meant to respect popular will, not to interpret or violate it. The Communists misunderstood such scruples because the main feature of the Soviet constitution was that it was not applied and the major characteristic of Soviet elections was that they were not free. Human rights were sacred to the Socialists, whereas the Bolsheviks, as of 1917, considered them optional, and Stalin, in 1936, trampled them underfoot as deliberately as Hitler.

Despite, or perhaps because of, these divergences, the evolution of the United Front toward Proletarian Unity was much discussed. The Stalinists pretended to favor unity. They expected it to destroy the Socialist Party, its leaders, and its political influence, through the methods that had been used in Poland (and in "Democratic" Germany after 1945). I, for my part, saw unity as a synthesis of the two parties: internal democracy and freedom of speech would serve as fuel to burn off the slag of Bolshevism and Social Democracy, which covered the gold of the Revolution.

There is a myth of the abortive revolution in June 1936. "Everything is possible," wrote Marceau Pivert, leader of the Gauche Révolutionnaire, in *Le Populaire* of May 27, 1936. But although this article caused a great to-do, it is merely a confused and ranting tirade. Its sole concrete element is a ridiculous tale of blunderbusses sold to Poland.

Was the Revolution already under way? At the high point of the strikes, there were more than a million participants. Yet none of the public services was affected. Trotsky advocated setting up workers' councils, a good example of parody. The French had just elected a Chamber of Deputies, to which they gave their trust. This confidence had not been disappointed in June 1936—quite the contrary! Liberalism such as had never been seen before allowed the workers to exercise their right to strike and to occupy the factories with impunity. The Blum administration was forcing management to engage in a nation-wide discussion on wages and reach a favorable settlement of labor's demands. It was also announcing considerable reforms. Why, then, should the workers elect councils? Because an old Russian revolutionary was asking them to do so? Even though the remedy had often been worse than the evil, the Russian workers had needed councils in 1917 to try to solve, among other things, administrative problems that the ruined and disintegrating Tsarist state was incapable of handling. But the French workers in June 1936 had no desire to govern or administer. When it came to politics, they had had their say at the June 3 elections, and since that day everything had been going in their direction. They were actually quite satisfied with the government. Having raised the problem of wages and working conditions, they were settling it to their own advantage, with the moral support of the political powers and the effective help of the unions. They didn't want to start a revolution; they only wanted to enjoy the benefits they had obtained. Nowhere did the striking workers move from labor concerns to political issues. The strikes dragged on mainly in the areas where the federations and management attempted to avoid applying the agreements and to make the workers back down.

In June 1936, the Communist Party's main objective was to strengthen its efforts at organizing and taking over union leadership. The Socialists, for the most part, were helping the administration extricate itself from the chaos by the extended strikes. Almost all of the "leftists" were in the Socialist Party. They had little contact with the working class, and their exhortations had little appeal to the proletariat. They did not constitute a homogeneous political entity and didn't know themselves where they were heading—aside from a far-off revolutionary Eldorado ritually evoked at the close of every speech.

To gain the confidence of the workers, they first had to show interest in their immediate demands and see to it that they were met. Credit with the baker and the grocer has a deadline, and wives were always impatient for payday. These are imperatives that most revolutionary intellectuals are unaware of or misunderstand. The leftists regretted that collective agreements put an end to strikes and factory occupations, as though the proletariat were an experimental resource rather than a mass of men and women dominated primarily by material needs, the fundamental cause of their real or alleged revolutionary destiny. The Trotskyites, faithful to all the errors of Marxism, learnedly announced that the gains were illusory. This argument never got beyond the hermetic world of their study groups; no worker whose wages had gone up by at least 20 percent, who for the first time in his life was preparing to go on two weeks of paid vacation, and whose work week now ended on Friday evening was at all disposed to pay attention to such nonsense.

Most of the leftists were unrepentant pacifists. To deal with Hitler, they advocated disarmament. In June 1936, they wore out their listeners with their tales of munitions dealers, all of which had a false ring. They began to play the deadly game of giving way before Nazi strength.

Nothing the leftists had to offer could help the workers move from wage demands to political demands. At best, one could hope for positions that would not cause a revolution so much as they would preserve the advantages obtained and bring the French proletariat a place in government leadership. Between 1920 and 1960, the changes necessary for France were not posed in terms of government by one class, whichever class that might be, but in terms of government of class balance. This phenomenon, which was nothing new in history, particularly French history, was never recognized by revolutionary intellectuals because it is far less heroic than the notion of the Grand Revolution.

In June 1936, other reforms were possible—notably those carried through by General de Gaulle in 1945, which proceeded from the ideology and experience of the Popular Front. The liberal government of 1936 was helpless in the face of the leakage of capital and the drop in industrial production. Nationalization in certain areas (credit, for instance), or at least increased power of government intervention (which Léon Blum so painfully lacked) and a lessening of the Senate's political influence, could probably have been obtained under the impact of strikes. These changes would have been more useful than nationalizing the deficits of the railroads or the aeronautics industry. The Popular Front missed the boat here, just as it lost out on its foreign politics.

I ran into Crevel on Rue Saint-Lazare on June 16 or 17, 1935. He spoke of his worries about the Association of Revolutionary Writers and Artists and the Congress for the Defense of Culture. Breton had slapped Ilya Ehrenburg; this well-deserved reproof delighted me, for I had always hated the man. Crevel had done a good deal of work organizing the Congress. He was afraid that Breton would be left out and insisted that the idea of a reconciliation between Aragon and Breton, which he had supported so strongly, was utopian. His judgment of Aragon was severe. Since I had kept aloof from all cultural activities for two years now, Crevel wanted to have my opinion on the problem. I think he was looking for subtle judgment on the respective positions of those involved and a disavowal of Breton's "oppositional" stances. He knew that I was deeply committed to the politics of the Popular Front. He was somewhat surprised to hear me say that culture was as much jeopardized by Stalin as by Hitler. Although a political understanding with the Communists was, to my mind, indispensable to the anti-Fascist struggle, there should be no excursion into cultural areas. The only outcome would be the worst sort of confusion. "When you joined the Association for Revolutionary Writers and Artists, I first thought that Breton had won. Although I found it harder and harder to see what that association had to offer, I felt it would be good if all of you had the experience. Ever since Hitler's takeover, I've known that Breton would be leaving those stagnant waters before long. The Communist Party is no more revolutionary than the Socialist Party. At least the structure of the Socialist Party permits the development of ideological currents that won't be wiped out at once by official conformism and that may offer protection against new capitulations. Some of the political activities of the Communist Party may deserve support or assistance, but anything the Communists undertake in the cultural area will be reactionary simply because of their subordination to Moscow." On June 19, the newspapers informed me of Crevel's suicide. His testament was his pointless struggle against Aragon, Nizan, Fréville, and several other members of this Congress, which, although it was supposedly hostile to book burning, to arresting apostate writers, and to banishing poets and painters, would not give the author of the manifestoes of Surrealism the right to speak!

Breton himself did not think he was beaten. In October 1935, a pamphlet ran the *Counterattack* resolution sealing the temporary pact between the two French writers with the richest minds in the twentieth century, Bataille and Breton. The progressive and inexorable entrance of nationalism into world politics was sure to disturb all those who refused to be slaves. Although no one had foreseen that development around 1930, it was now anticipated by those who were more alive than their contemporaries to the evolution of the inner forces of the world. They were conscious of the fact that any prospect of revolution would not therefore be eclipsed and appreciated the role that this new monster might play in preserving freedom.

My response to the *Counterattack* declaration was a mixture of satisfaction and irritation. I consider it one of the most significant documents of the period because it attempts a precise and new definition of revolution and makes an awkward attempt to liberate it from any nationalistic commitment. Recognizing the socializing of the means of production as a basis of social law, the authors of the declaration identify revolution not only with that socializing but also with the constitution of a new social superstructure. The point of departure will be less "a reduction of the middle-class standard of living to that of the workers" than an end to "economic impotence." The revolutionary means are the foundation and action of a party ("a vast composition of forces, disciplined and fanatic, and an uncompromising dictatorship of the armed people"). Finally, the declaration refused to allow the "revolution be enclosed within the framework of a dominating and colonialist country."

I was astonished by a text signed by my friends that so perfectly expressed the faults of revolutionary intellectuals. The disciplined and fanatical party is the idealization of the Nazi S.A., and the dictatorship of an armed people is reminiscent of the Convention. The socializing of the means of production is an unexamined concession to Marxism, which is nevertheless challenged by placing "the study of social superstructures . . . at the basis of all revolutionary action." The fundamental hostility to the ideas of nation and country, together with the demand for universal revolution, stunningly belies the will to eliminate "anyone incapable of passing on to realistic considerations." How right I was not to get involved in positions that led nowhere! But the paragraph concerning the refashioning of superstructures, the formal position against a Communism of poverty, as well as the call for a world revolution (despite its unattainability), are worthy of the double seal of Bataille and Breton. My reaction to this unwonted rapprochement was one of intense curiosity. I predicted that it wouldn't last.

Counterattack completely dissuaded me from returning to the Surrealists, an idea I had had on Place du Panthéon on February 17, 1936, during the demonstration against the unprovoked assault on Léon Blum. I ran into Breton almost directly across the street from the Hôtel des Grandes Hommes, whose façade is the first setting in *Nadja*. We joked a bit about the coincidence, wondering whether the crowd was wiping away any traces of the people who had previously walked up and down in front of the hotel or whether a clairvoyant would be able to superimpose a female silhouette on that gray mass. He had qualms about Bataille. He spoke about *Counterattack*: they were planning a series, and he felt that my help would be useful. I took advantage of his offer to tell him how greatly my concept of the role of nations in the anti-Fascist struggle differed from the ideas expressed in his resolution. Pointing at the throng around us, I said: "Here is your struggle. The threat is across the way. The revolutionary forces are those surrounding us. Their points of application are Paris and France. We would be unarmed anywhere else. As for Germany, all the evidence indicates that internationalism there is dead." I couldn't meet Breton without wondering whether we could resume the collaboration that had meant so much to me. I felt that this extraordinary man was out of place, that it was the duty of his friends to alleviate his modesty and awkwardness. He was simply part of the crowd. He deserved to be recognized, not only because on that knoll said to be dedicated to exceptional men one of these fabled figures, in the flesh, was marching in the procession, but also because he more than any other participant, embodied everything that Fascism wanted to annihilate and that the official anti-Fascists didn't have the nerve to defend. But I still hesitated. A few weeks later, the appearance of the pamphlet *Under the Fire of French Cannon*, which refused to "qualify" the bourgeois democratic nations against Hitler, demonstrated to me that *my* road was not Breton's.

The expansionism of the great Fascist and reactionary countries (Germany, Italy, and Japan) was the driving force of the world. I recognized their leaders' ambitions. They wanted to replace the power of the imperialists with domination through nationalist power. The new factor in the imminent conflict was entirely grounded in a racist and authoritarian notion of conquest. Extending the methods of the Wild West, certain races were to be exterminated like the Indian tribes, and any survivors would be penned up in moral dependence and economic inferiority.

If warfare favored the totalitarians, the French ruling classes had as much to lose as the classes they ruled. Democracy, liberty, national independence, every cultural principle was being challenged at every level. Certain members of the propertied classes might try to sell off this enormous historical, intellectual, and moral capital in order to save what they considered most important: the social structure. But that would be a pointless sacrifice. Hitler's and Mussolini's victories would reduce these fine gentlemen to the state of petty provincial nobodies, ruined and without honor. Their workers wouldn't even be laboring for them any more, but for the Germans. Such degradation would soon prove unbearable for everyone, except the handful of collaborators such defeats unfailingly produce. Despite the foolishness that the French bourgeoisie often calls realism, I felt that this unattractive view of the Nazi victory would soon be shared by a good many others. It would change people's heads. Wage earners, who had become a second-degree proletariat, would lose their parties, their unions, their cultural associations, perhaps even their native language. They would have to choose between unemployment and ill-paid labor in the Germanized territories.

The rise of French Fascism had been definitively halted by the reaction of the united left and the electoral victory of the Popular Front. In France, Fascism was not a national phenomenon: in 1936, it looked like reactionary defeatism and sabotage. At best, it could rule as a prison guard over the provinces conquered by Hitler. The French Fascists had lost the opportunity of creating a mass party. The force of events had crystallized them into hard-core cells of sellouts, fanatics, and restless souls who saw terrorism and defeat as the only way out. Their excesses would give their adversaries the best chances to declare themselves true patriots; they would confront the traditional nationalists with dilemmas that would force them to accept the initiatives of the left. Hitler's aggression would produce cracks in the political bloc of the propertied class.

The transformation of the Cross-of-Fire groups into a powerful party that was more and more amenable to democratic rules confirmed this analysis. The French Social Party became the political organization of the moderates, more interested in the elections of 1940 than in extralegal means of interfering with French politics. It adopted the social reforms of the Popular Front, and its influence grew because it simply shirked the administrations on economic matters and because people naïvely believed that the rightists could reach an honest understanding with Hitler.

With two million members, its potential electoral force in 1938 disturbed a good many radicals. Despite the relative skill with which the French Social Party played with an imaginary Communist danger, however, its membership was not animated by any spiritual life; it was incapable of any specific reaction to the Hitlerian danger that was remodeling French political life from the ground up. The F.S.P. was pro-Munich in 1938. Resigned and uncomprehending, it accepted the war. After the armistice, it dissociated itself only through a fundamentally contradictory attempt to oppose patriotism to the political organizations that, often despite themselves, represented the nucleus of resistance to Hitler. With France conquered and the left crushed by Hitler and Pétain, all that remained for the F.S.P. was the old war veterans' spirit, which was quickly exhausted around Marshal Pétain during the destructive colonizing of France.

I have dwelt on this evolution of the F.S.P. because it seems the best possible illustration of my conviction that the propertied classes and their political organizations had not been able to cope with circumstances since 1936. In the war, which I considered inevitable, the primary concern of wage earners would be the defeat of Hitler. The crushing of the most reactionary forces in the world through a coalition that would have to include the U.S.S.R. could only reinforce democracy and freedom and accelerate the emancipation of its subjects. The proletarian revolution might be the outcome of the participation by revolutionaries in the national defense of France and England. It could survive defeatism only in Germany.

The intellectuals who refused to acquiesce in the most vulgar pacifism (for instance, the Surrealists) held on to the old slogan: "No national defense in a capitalist regime." A revolutionary illusion might have been understandable in 1936, but by 1938 the tide was obviously turning. One had to make the best of it and recognize the stakes rather than divert political battles toward irrelevant issues. Further strikes would merely play into Hitler's hands; he had outlawed them in Germany. The forty-hour week would only help the Nazis. The hardening of social conflicts in France could only weaken the main military foe of Fascism: an uncompromising management would tend to make the workers think that they had nothing to defend and that their worst enemy was their bosses, or the excess demands of labor could challenge the very existence of business, spurring the bosses to wish that a foreign army would save them from bankruptcy or ruin. Since neither the play of forces nor the state of opinion permitted the working class to impose itself as the exclusive ruler of the nation, it was imperative to reach a political balance. The representatives of the social classes most devoted to liberty and democracy would have to have enough power to preserve, during the preparations for war, the economic and administrative advantages they had already gained. In fact, a closer alliance between labor and political leaders implied, as a corollary, wider participation by the working class not only in the decisions but also in the growth of productive forces and the power of the nation.

In other words, we should have laid the foundations of a new nationalism, which would simply have expressed a de facto solidarity. Pacifists and people with old formulas were afraid that French nationalism would furnish the German nationalists and Hitler with more excuses. They talked like lawyers preparing a defense brief! Only Hitler's defeat in 1938 or 1939 could have challenged his emotional rapport with the German people. The end of the Second World War revealed the weaknesses of Lenin's theses on revolution through defeat. Once their nations were crushed, neither the German nor the Japanese proletariat made the slightest attempt to transform the imperialist war into a civil war. And in June 1940, the French proletariat wasn't particularly tempted to do so.

The future confirmed the basic features of this political analysis, illustrating it with dramatic images of defeat and liberation. The Spanish Civil War offered arguments galore. The anarchists and Trotskyites thought they were involved in a revolution, but they were actually starting a war. While they were bogging down in quarrels and vetoes, the Communists turned into examples of discipline and efficiency. The qualities they displayed in forming an army and in fighting might have led them to supremacy if Stalin (from behind the scenes, in the worst traditions of Bolshevism) hadn't brought things to an end. But the Communists lacked men of real ability; their professions of faith in a unified Republican Front and the priority of the war didn't prevent them from cultivating sectarianism or hounding their rivals. If they hadn't spent most of their energy in attacking the Trotskyites or the anarchists, they might have noticed that those who were shouting loudest in their ranks were agents of Franco. This initial confrontation between Fascism and the Western democracies was a dress rehearsal in which all the big arias were sung. The inability of the spectators to comprehend it made me feel that history may never have been anything but a struggle of the blind and the deaf.

One aspect of the war eluded almost all the observers. There was great heroism in both camps: the anarchists in Barcelona, the cadets in Toledo, the women and children in Madrid, had equaled the great traditions of Saragossa and the Golden Age. Nevertheless, month by month, the people were moving slowly and steadily toward Franco. The unmethodical nature of Republican action and the cowardice of France and England weighed on Spanish consciences. Even more significant, perhaps, was the lack of faith in the beneficial effects of a revolution that would make the state the proprietor. The Spanish Republicans fought fiercely for liberty, not for collectivism. But the mass of the Spanish people, including the Republicans, gradually became convinced that the revolution would not solve anything, that the war would continue after Franco's defeat, and that nothing would be gained from supplanting the landowning system with an administrative order. And, at the same time, lassitude and discouragement overcame the best people.

From the very first, I had pondered this conflict in terms of a struggle between nations. My political friends were shocked by the tranquillity with which I advocated an intervention in Spain by the French army—accompanied, if necessary, by a declaration concerning Catalan integrity. Those who were most aware of the danger continued to advocate the supplying of weapons, but they did not ask themselves whether the Republicans, deprived of officers and specialists, would have time to use the arms that were sent. They still believed in the virtues of class struggle: the Italians and Germans, or so they thought, would play a deadly game by overcommitting themselves in Spain. But the Germans and Italians intervened as nations, with all their weight, not just as munitions dealers. The German navy settled in the Mediterranean to protect the unloading of its armaments and specialists. German and Italian submarines sank the Republican cargo boats. Three complete Italian divisions were placed under Franco's command. The sons of workers and peasants did not come to Spain for one of those colonial conquests that had hitherto been accepted by all the armies in the world (they often flattered the racism of the simple soldiers); they came in order to fight against other workers and peasants. These sons of workers and peasants had accepted their mission. They were sent out against (among others), the Garibaldi Brigade, which was mainly composed of Italian anti-Fascists. Mussolini's divisions were beaten because their adversaries were more skillful and better commanded. But this defeat did not suddenly arouse the vanquished men to "class-consciousness." And, two years later, the disciplined soldiers of Fascist Italy captured Barcelona.

No one was more remote than the "revolutionary left" from the ideas I have just expressed. Marceau Pivert's prestige was very probably founded on his perfect concordance with a whole petty-bourgeois generation. The exact contemporaries of the Surrealists of 1925–30, they were viscerally allergic to the army, to veterans, to monuments for the dead, and to the excesses of marauding armies. These young men had been slightly tempted by Marxism, but the brutality, cynicism, and warlike aspect of Bolshevism had kept them away from the Communist Party. Holding aloof from big industry, they did work that required thinking. These people liked systems, and their morals were austere. A good many of them were Masons, and although this affiliation with an ancient and respectable power may have furthered their careers and strengthened their convictions, it detached them a bit more from the real world. They saw progress as destined and indispensable, threatened only by obscurantism and saber rattling, and believed that the failures or setbacks of the Socialist idea were merely the consequence of the abandonment of principles by those who had let themselves be bought or who had compromised out of weakness.

Marceau Pivert taught in a school for elementary-school teachers. With his little mustache, his beret, his modest clothes, his activeness, his camaraderie, his vague but inflamed eloquence, this skinny man inspired confidence in all those who sought a certain stylish conformity more than truth and efficiency. René Modiano, who represented absolute pacifism, came out in favor of unconditional surrender. He claimed that only peace is revolutionary; if the Nazis won, then the proletariat would continue the underground struggle until victory. It was as simple as that! Daniel Guérin was somewhat less categorical. Guérin is probably the most perfectly consistent utopian I have ever met. All his life he has subscribed to the myth of the proletarian revolution and, what's more, to the myth of the betrayed revolution. He did everything he could to prevent that revolution from having even the slightest chance to come true. He lived in the marvelous and simple world in which wicked capitalism is sometimes pounced upon by the good and generous proletariat, who would ultimately triumph and bring about the happiness it holds in reserve if only the Stalinist traitor in office didn't force it to relent.

Danile Guérin has a Saint-Simonian heritage. Around 1948, he took me to the top of Rue de Ménilmontant to visit the abandoned but still solid house in which Father Enfantin had founded the sect. The building had been transformed into an apartment house. In the tangle of studios and shanties one could make out the long avenue of lime trees that the Father and his disciples had strode along while they preached respect for the passions and a reform of marriage. I tried in vain to interest the City of Paris in preserving that landmark. At the municipal council I obtained a short-lived success based on curiosity. But those illiterate agencies who have such a knack for making Paris ugly found, after the usual red tape, a thousand reasons for replacing the old ruin with horrible middle-income housing.

Daniel Guérin deserved the restoration of that house. It should have been dedicated to sweeping pacifism, and generations of dreamers could have used it to rail against war and advocate group marriage, provided that they always dressed with as much imagination and symbolism as the Saint-Simonians. A subsidy from the City of Paris could have assured rent, water, and electricity to these successors of the Supreme Fathers.

The war in Spain broke up the Popular Front and dulled the charm that Léon Blum had exerted on the workers since the attempt on his life. Because of commercial agreements, the renewal of matériel for the Spanish army was largely confined to France. On July 25, in a subtly and perfidiously anti-Semitic article in *Le Figaro*, François Mauriac called upon Léon Blum to stop the shipments of weapons to the Republicans. The English government began to worry. Blum invented nonintervention and kept up that fiction despite the activities of Italian and German submarines in the Mediterranean, the massive landing of German aviators and tank companies, and the presence of several regular Italian divisions in the battle. The attitude of the French government remained ambivalent until Blum finally realized in which direction the balance of power was moving. He responded to the *Anschluss* by planning to send troops to Catalonia in order to prevent Barcelona and perhaps Valencia from falling to Axis weapons. But when the general staff was consulted, it raised administrative objections. The government capitulated to the agency heads who were supposed to obey and carry out orders. The Senate subverted Blum. The Communists did nothing to defend the Socialist leader.

There couldn't have been a stupider policy. In the inevitable struggle against Hitler, France's political assets would have to be symbolized by an association between her military victory and the setback of oppression. The French Republic could not desert the Spanish Republic without losing face, in spite of the strategic facts of the problem. But it was necessary to act quickly and effectively.

Through a dialectical mutation of effects and causes, the prolongation of the civil war served France's interest. It relieved General Franco of any colonial ambitions in Africa. The reactionary general turned out to be a great statesman. If the Spanish people are no freer today than the Russians, Franco at least has brought them meat, more oil, more refrigerators, more clothing, more washing machines, more new apartments and automobiles than Stalin and Brezhnev have given the Soviets. Spain has gone through an evolution that the Marxists didn't foresee in 1937.

I had run into Marcel Fourrier again in the Socialist Party. We realized we had the same ideas. Fourrier had moved away from Trotskyism for much the same reasons that had led me to abandon Stalinism. We had the same opinion of Fascism, Blum, the Socialist Party, Marceau Pivert, and nonintervention. We saw proletarian unity as safeguarding the idea of revolution. Zyromski's extreme leftist attitudes toward Spain, the United Front, and the Hitlerian danger were more to our taste than the insubstantial words and the hazy pacifism of Marceau Pivert.

One of us put the other in touch with André Ferrat, whom the Communist Party had just ousted for "leftism." My memory is a bit shaky on that point, but I tend to think that Fourrier deserves the credit for the disputes within the Communist Party. Ferrat, who was slightly older than I, had been a leader of the Communist Students, then of the Communist Youth. In 1929 he was supposedly the theoretician of the Barbé-Célor group, and he held very high offices in the Party and in the secretariat of the Comintern. From the sectarian and conformist viewpoint of the 1930's, he had written a *History of the Communist Party*. André Ferrat is for me the living evidence of the destructiveness of bureaucratic structures. With his education, his hard work, his intelligence and courage, he deserved to be one of the political leaders of the workers' parties throughout his life. The only things that went against him were his intellectual and moral honesty, his great lack of ambition, and his fundamental disinterestedness. These uncommon qualities should have been enough to make him win out over anyone else. But, to the contrary, they explain why Maurice Thorez had him thrown out, and why Guy Mollet granted him only a back seat.

Of medium height, but massive, Ferrat, wearing glasses and smoking a pipe, looked like a Bolshevik of the grand generation. He was married to a gentle and intelligent woman and lived right next door to me on Avenue Simon-Bolivar. His breaking with the Party had concerned the agreement with the radicals on the Popular Front. But this was a poor excuse. In reality, Ferrat no longer believed in the Comintern, whose functioning he was quite familiar with, and he regarded Stalin as a bandit. In 1936, he shared Trotsky's ideas on the bureaucratic degeneration of the U.S.S.R. "If Stalin were assassinated," he told me in 1937, "he would be replaced by some Postyshev or other, who would follow the same policies, perhaps with a few less massacres." It was Postyshev who was killed first, on Stalin's orders.

Ferrat had started a Marxist-Leninist magazine called *Que Faire* (*What Is to Be Done*), after Lenin's little book, which had been published in 1902. In 1937 I became an active member of the *Que Faire* group and wrote several articles for the review. Convinced by events, Ferrat soon adopted the viewpoint I have just outlined. He joined the Socialist Party, and we set out together to give the La Bataille Socialiste group a more coherent ideology. We planned to unite the Socialists and Communists in a single, democratic party and to prepare for a revolutionary war to be led by members of the united working class.

During 1938 and 1939, we made huge strides in that direction. We managed to achieve a solid agreement with Jean Zyromski and several of the most serious representatives of La Bataille Socialiste, which we then extended to the members of Parliament favorable to the notion of labor unity. The events that came rushing upon us proved that we were right and cracked the Socialist Party asunder. Soon after Munich, which we stormed against, Paul Faure and Severac, the secretaries of the S.F.I.O., separated from Léon Blum and tried to isolate him in the name of pacifism and the most disgusting kind of defeatism. Severac became openly anti-Semitic. La Bataille Socialiste, in which we were solidly established, hoped to join Léon Blum's friends at the next congress, where he would take over leadership of the S.F.I.O. and, if necessary, expel the cowards and rightists.

War was not within our range in 1939. We were convinced that an alliance between the Russians, the English, and the French would be concluded by the end of summer and that the great military confrontation would take place in 1940. I was fairly certain that by 1940 I would be one of the leaders of the Socialist Federation of the Seine, with Jean Zyromski or a left-wing "Blumist" as secretary-general of the party. Thus we had taken no precautions to ensure and maintain relations with like-minded friends in case of an armed conflict, even though we regarded it as almost inevitable and we intended to play a political role in it.

France Mutualiste, like all large French concerns, was preparing for war. Intending to transfer its offices, it had bought the picturesque castle of Bonaban and its lovely park near Saint-Malo for a song! A small study conference took place in July 1939 in the office of the president of the Administration Council, and I was asked to participate. At the end of the conference, the president invited the directors and two or three functionaries, including me, to stay for lunch. The conversation never got away from international politics and the military possibilities of the conflict. Maurice de Barral was a reserve commander. He was fairly optimistic. Paul Boë, the president, was less sanguine. Someone mentioned the Russian army. "Who says they'll be with us?" said Boë. "I was very shaken by some harsh words of a friend of mine who teaches history at the Sorbonne. He's a knowledgeable historian, and he assured me that every time Prussia and Russia quarreled over the activities of the Poles, they always found a means of understanding: the division of Poland." I can still hear Barral's laughter. Of course, I simply forgot these words. Whatever qualms I had about Stalin, I didn't believe him capable of such out-and-out highway robbery.

Doctrines about the use and general organization of the army were the subject of several study sessions at Ferrat's place. I hadn't yet read the books of Colonel de Gaulle, thought I think Ferrat was familiar with them. A professional army met with unanimous opposition. Like all Socialists, we saw it merely as a corps of mercenaries at the disposition of the bourgeois state for all its tasks. We were (or at least I was) skeptical about the Gaullist concept of blitzkrieg.

The stodgy doctrine of the French general staff, largely inspired by Pétain, seduced all the leftists traumatized by their memories of the bayonet charges and uselessly bloody attacks of 1917. The prudence of that doctrine looked like wisdom, its geometrical form looked like rigor, and, to be fair, it showed a reassuring concern for human life. All these errors of judgment show the mental laziness and conformity of the French political class. Any citizen at all concerned with government problems ought to be in a position to form an opinion on the doctrine of his military leaders, just as he does on the construction of speedways or national education. The lack of interest in or response to Colonel de Gaulle's ideas corresponded to the backwardness of the French in regard to their time. Ferrat's skepticism, mine, and Marcel Fourrier's were merely the survival of a pedantic Marxism that automatically identified any military thinking with a "class" ideology. Such facile reasoning always tends to further the most backward sort of conservatism.

André Ferrat was particularly interested in the organizational structure of the French army and its connection with social categories. After long reflection, he felt that Jaurès's theses were as valid as ever. He called my attention to the social makeup of the military caste, which was recruited almost exclusively from the bourgeoisie and the landowners. Ever since a distinction had been made between the active and the reserve corps, the military caste constituted the most solid group possible, with its own rules for promotion and assignment. It denied nonprofessionals and rank-and-file soldiers any advancement and eluded any governmental supervision through a childish blackmail that invoked secrecy and patriotism. André Ferrat expected nothing good from this self-indulgent and self-assertive bureaucracy. He read a few recent military analyses and was terrified by their intellectual mediocrity. It seemed consistent with the disappointments one expected from the system. Nonconformist superior officers, who had lost all ambition, had drawn portraits for him of future army commanders. They were even drearier than Radical-Socialist ministers. Ferrat feared the worst.

Munich dealt the coup de grâce to the Spanish Republic. Negrín wanted to separate from the international brigades in order to have an easier time negotiating peace. The heroes were welcomed at the French border by *gardes mobiles* who interned the foreigners at Gurs and Vernet in rather miserable conditions. Lula Vućo, more beautiful than ever, suddenly showed up at my home. She told me that Kotcha Popović was at Gurs. We had to get him out!

Kotcha was Lula's great love, though it was a hopeless passion. She was married, and Kotcha had a very beautiful girl friend, Véra. But Lula heeded only her passion and promised Véra she would get Kotcha out of the camp.

I took Lula to Jules Moch, who received us very kindly. I explained to this important man that Kotcha had been my friend for ten years. I was ready to have him come to my place and keep him there as long as necessary. Moch did not hesitate. "Madame," he told Lula, "you can take the next train to Gurs. The orders will be given."

Two days laters, Kotcha was in my apartment, where he spent the entire winter. He was a bit skinnier, and not very enthusiastic about the French Republic's welcome for the international brigades. He told several stories about French soldiers who openly disobeyed absurd orders to bully the prisoners. There had been no backlash from the officers. "So there's still something to defend after all," said Kotcha.

A reserve artillery lieutenant in the Yugoslav army, Kotcha Popović had joined the illegal Communist Party in his country during 1933. In 1936, sectarianism or stupidity had forced him into a kind of opposition. His manners were unpleasant. He was asked to join the international brigades, and he spent a whole year sweeping the courtyard of a politicized barracks at Albacete. André Marty was in charge. The army lacked officers, specialists, and, particularly, artillerymen. During a huge commotion at Albacete, Marty had a stroke of genius. "I suppose none of you is an officer?" he asked the sweepers.

"I am," replied Kotcha. "I'm an artillery lieutenant in the Yugoslav army." They could have found that out merely by looking at the very thorough forms that every international had to fill out!

A few days later, Kotcha was commanding batteries on the Aragon front. He had to protect the army's retreat. "I did everything I could," he told me. "I got results, but I never had the luck to have shells that were exactly the same caliber as the cannon I put them in."

Kotcha was still suffering from a wound in his leg. He was furious. "It's not a glorious wound," he declared. "I was thrown into a ditch with one of my guns. The axle gave way, and big pieces of wood tore open my calf. The wound was dirty and got infected. It took a long time to close."

My political analysis didn't surprise him. It was rather close to the Communist position. But my emphasis on the ability of the Socialist left to put the workers' party back on its feet struck him as bizarre. He believed that the Communist parties were enough for anything!

French hospitality was distrustful. Kotcha periodically had to report to the police station to renew his residence permit. This operation was supervised by a police inspector who was a member of the Socialist section of the nineteenth arrondissement. He warned us whenever the moods or the instructions of the Palais de Justice were unfavorable to the internationals.

Kotcha sent for his beautiful girl friend, and the two of them settled down on Rue Botzaris. In July 1938, he told me he thought he might soon be returning to Yugoslavia. He wanted to meet Eluard before he left Paris. Together we went to Rueil, where Eluard and Nusch had rented a house. Eluard had just recently broken with Breton. He was already thinking of joining the Communist Party.

My relative optimism about the development of French politics, the progress of La Bataille Socialiste within the S.F.I.O., and the influence that Marcel Fourrier, André Ferrat, and I exerted on that group was partly based on the deterioration of class relations in the country and the lowering of all prestige. Wage earners were disappointed in the unions and the Popular Front. The price rises had wiped out a good part of salary increases. The people themselves were divided about a policy of resistance to Hitler. The general strike of 1938, organized under pressure from the Communists to protest both Munich and the abolition of the forty-hour week, was a failure. It made no sense in either political or labor terms. The C.G.T. had lost millions of members. The Socialist Party was in shreds, and Léon Blum's authority was shaky. The ruling classes didn't know what they wanted, apart from respect for the bosses, whose authority had never been enough to make a business go. The Popular Front had been unable to finance both its social reforms and the rearmament of France, or to make the country aware of the Nazi danger. The class known as the bourgeoisie, waning for several years, was equally incapable of facing the responsibilities of a ruling class, that is, to assure both production and national defense. It was divided itself and defeatist to boot.

The only political organization that temporarily resisted the rising turmoil was the French Social Party, which gradually buried itself in the past. Only the Communist Party still seemed to be a coherent force conscious of inner and outer dangers. The Stalin-Hitler pact blew it apart. Overnight, the Communists had to decide between breaking with the U.S.S.R. and retracting everything they had been defending for four years. Would they have the courage to snap their links of allegiance to Stalin and drag the French working class along into the first episode of the struggle to the death against Fascism? A few of them, including Nizan and Darnar, did not perjure themselves; a good many others, full of shame, cowered and kept quiet; a few fanatics opted for treason. Daladier and Albert Sarraut did Muscovite discipline the immense favor of dissolving the Party and arresting militants at random. Maurice Thorez took the middle way out: he deserted and fled to Russia.

Stalin's dirty trick, for which Russia had to pay dearly in 1941, opened the Second World War with the fourth partition of Poland. It wrecked any prospects of proletarian unity for half a century and ensured unexpected political success to the French right wing. It was disunited and incapable, but all the pacifists stuck to it like maddened butterflies. A series of weak and modiocre administrations led the nation to defeat, enslavement, and shame.

24
HIT AND MISS

FOR TWENTY YEARS, GEORGES HUGNET WAS MY best friend. Some people were amazed that two such different individuals could meet so often without coming to mortal blows. The explanation is simple. We both were careful not to intrude on any private domains that were none of our business or that would have given rise to rivalry and disagreement. Hugnet's life was devoted to commercial activities which did not attract me at all, because of my incompetence, my lack of natural aptitude, and the bad state of my resources. Hugnet, for his part, showed only a polite interest in my devotion to politics. He never tried to criticize, approve, comment on, or even comprehend my attitudes toward events or the positions I wanted to occupy on the chessboard of political parties. Fortunately, we never became interested in the same women, at least not at a time when the interest of one of us could have been annoying or tormenting for the other. Each of us needed a buddy, with everything that that word implies about trivial talks, irrational tastes, confidences, minor complicities, favors, and the like. We had many friends in common and shared an artistic and literary background.

Men who have accepted all the risks of emotional lives and who have exposed themselves to all the elements by refusing the security of such social guarantees as marriage or professions are often eager to unburden themselves. They like to talk and be given reassurance. For fifteen years, Georges Hugnet lent a willing ear to my emotional problems. It made up for a good deal. From 1930 to 1938, I said nothing to anyone, keeping it all to myself. After 1953, I reverted to silence. Little by little, I drew away from Hugnet, who, for his part, had nothing left to confide in me.

My oldest memories of George Hugnet go back to the years 1929–30. Anyone who knew him after the war can't imagine what that little bullet-headed twenty-five-year-old from Saint-Male was like. Agile as a monkey and lively as an eel, he could never stay put. The Surrealist-inspired film he had made before joining the Café Cyrano shows him running along cornices sixty feet above the ground, whereas at forty-five he couldn't even cross the street alone and panicked as soon as he reached the first landing of a house. His character developed in the same way. A good comrade, attentive, and generous, he gradually turned into a monstrous egocentric. His all-embracing interests changed into a morbid acquisitiveness. Reacting against his family, he had at first shown an astonishing lack of business talent, but later he became a businessman straight out of Balzac. Dozens of people of quality enjoyed talking to him because of his caustic mind, his wit and sense of humor, his precise observations, his lively repartee, and his wide literary background. But he became unfair and nasty. He was always a collector, but when he started amassing things like a miser, this eccentricity irritated even those who know how discerningly he gathered his treasures. From 1933 to 1938 he was a strictly orthodox Surrealist. His *Small Poetic Anthology of Surrealism* is sometimes annoyingly right-thinking. In 1933, he broke with Breton, for what reasons I don't know. His subsequent hatred for the author of *Les Pas Perdus* became monumental, somewhat akin to the reactions that had produced the pamphlet *A Corpse* ten years earlier.

Georges Hugnet is now living in comparative isolation, surrounded by astonishing objects and paintings. Most of the people who knew him well, who needed his dynamic qualities, his intelligence, his worldly wisdom, have stopped seeing him. When the difficulties of his personality are forgotten, we may be able to understand who and what he was. He had the pride of being a poet, but in regard to his own works he showed a shyness and modesty that poets laureate and professionals have often lacked. But Hugnet's works are far above the oppressive things honored by the critics, the government, or the universities because of the political or religious opinions of their authors or their assiduous presence at dinners in town.

Most of the poets of Hugnet's generation were fascinated by a return to the rules of poetic art: rhyme, meter, even classic forms. It was in defiance of the flirtatiousness of a young woman who, like so many others, preferred industry to Bohemia that Hugnet hurled himself into such fearful gymnastics. He didn't come out of it unscathed, although he was certainly better off than his contemporaries. His melancholy *Chèvrefeuille*, which came out in 1943, did not make me forget another booklet of poems, *Non Vouloir*, published in April 1941 and also illustrated with Picasso engravings. It contains all the bitterness and secret rage that was ours in those days.

> Asleep and betrayed
> They scarcely refused to see
> The night fell heavier
> On the error of this world
> Without hope without desire
>
> You have to hold out your hand
> Which was done in the past
> And to know to know this time
> If it's to beg for alms
> To love or to kill

I had never stopped seeing Péret regularly. He came for dinner nearly every week. Tanguy would also drop by. He was an avid reader and borrowed serious books from me. He always returned them promptly. In 1935, he was very poor, and his work wasn't selling. I had him do a map of Greater Paris that, for three years, decorated the back of the receipts of France Mutualiste. He got a few hundred francs for it. The last time he moved, on the sly, was in 1936 or 1937. He told me that if he lost the little furniture and china he owned, I would have to forget about the books he had never brought back. By way of compensation, realizing that I was the only one of his friends who had never asked him for anything, he brought me a delightful drawing with a nice dedication to Katia.

I couldn't confine myself to politics or hang out only with middle-brow militants. That was why, as of 1937, I often went to Georges Hugnet's home on Rue de Buci and occasionally popped up at the Surrealist cafés, which had shifted slightly. There were also meetings at the Deux Magots or near Saint-Lazare, in an atmosphere where one could finally feel success.

The preparations for the International Exhibition of Surrealism in 1938 gave anyone who had suffered the "hard times" of 1930 a sense of revenge, a sort of moral justification. I felt a touch of regret because I wasn't in on it, even though there was no way I could participate since I had nothing to exhibit. But I was there in spirit.

All these new ideas astonished me. One mild evening in the autumn of 1937, I was was on the terrace of the Deux Magots with some of the organizers. They were worried about how to greet the public and direct its attention to the objects on exhibit. Dali, in his habitually detached tone of voice, suggested that at least one room should be transformed into a wheat field with very narrow footpaths for the visitors. The wheat would be very thick and high enough to prevent anyone from seeing anything but the heads of the tallest visitors. The smaller ones would have to stand on tiptoe, or be carried by the taller ones, in order to see. The proposal was not accepted.

Shortly after he returned from Mexico, Breton insisted on speaking to me about creating the Fédération Internationale pour un Art Révolutionnaire Indépendant (International Federation for an Independent Revolutionary Art). I agreed to join, but I didn't want to become any more involved. After the opening salvo, Breton said he wasn't made for the organizational responsibilities that such an enterprise required. He did know that I could handle them, however. He would have liked me to agree to help him, but he had the impression that I wasn't willing. "I've sworn an oath never to get involved again with revolutionary intellectuals," I replied. He burst out laughing. "And I don't believe in the future of the F.I.A.R.I.," I added. "I only agreed to it for your sake. An independent revolutionary art doesn't need any guarantee other than yours. All in all, Surrealism can do without allies."

This wasn't altogether true. The joint signatures of Breton and Diego Rivera at the bottom of the manifesto *For an Independent Revolutionary Art*, dated July 25, 1938, demanding "full license in art," gave this little declaration of principles a worldwide reputation that would never have been gained by one of Breton's texts or Rivera's proclamations alone. The conjunction of these two men with such different aesthetics had a special exemplary value, but I couldn't help thinking that such stunning declarations were of little immediate use. Despite the Trotsky-ite paragraph in which Breton and Diego Rivera rejected democracy as a thing of the past and called for a social revolution to pave the way to a new culture, nothing was less certain than that social revolution to guarantee the license they demanded.

Trotsky himself was not reassuring. I questioned Breton about this legendary figure. The simplicity, education, intelligence, and gentleness of the old revolutionary was attested to by this most demanding witness —as were, incidentally, his love of hunting and his marksmanship. How had he received Surrealism? Leon Trotsky believed that the Revolution and Communism would transform society and man. That was the order of the day. Everything else, including independent revolutionary art, was subordinate to it. Breton felt that liberty was being challenged by Hitler and Stalin, who had suppressed it even in artistic creation. Breton appealed to Lenin's last companion. But Trotsky was ready to grant rights and hopes to anyone who would endorse the chimerical slogan of social revolution, with which he proposed to conquer Hitlerism. Breton could hardly resist this new attack of that celebrated childhood disease, Communism, for the inoculator was none other than the man who had overthrown Kerensky in November 1917. I told Breton that he alone needed license, and that there was less and less proof that a Bolshevist social revolution would admit license. My support of the F.I.A.R.I. covered everything Breton had introduced in the prefatory declaration but did not pertain to the rest.

This severe judgment, which events confirmed, does not apply to the historic importance of André Breton's visit to Leon Trotsky. Since their areas of specialization were quite different, these two men, drawn to one another through a mutual liking, marched cautiously side by side through the rather narrow territories they shared, though they were not always at their ease. Leon Trotsky was sometimes disturbed by the violent fragrance of the spiritualistic roses that Breton couldn't resist gathering from his secret garden. But the strange new world that Trotsky sensed did not leave him indifferent, even though it was stained with heresy.

We know that the four pages of the F.I.A.R.I. manifesto were written by Leon Trotsky and André Breton. Together they rejected the maxim "neither Fascism nor Communism," which, for more than thirty years, had served to define the regimes in which the independence, indeed the very existence, of artistic creation, revolutionary or not, was assured.

But the chief interest of this text lies less in the demand for "full license in art," however fundamental that may be, than in Trotsky's approbation of it. This was the superb climax of Breton's struggles. In 1938, the demand for absolute liberty received the guarantee of the most indomitable revolutionary of all time. This ruined more than half a century of Marxist attempts to enslave the intelligentsia. Alas, the contribution of this great man was not on a level with his guarantee: Leon Trotsky's vigorous hand opened only over the ashes of fires lit from 1905 to 1925, which had consumed the last utopia of Socialism. A Marxist—and what a Marxist!—had turned to Surrealism. But nothing gives anyone the right to assume that the revolutionary of 1905 and 1917, if he had lived, would have failed to draw any inferences from the disappearance of the proletarian revolution.

My main reason for visiting Hugnet was to meet girls. I liked Jo, the sculptor sister of the poet Alice Paalen. The restaurant we haunted was Le Petit Saint-Bernoît. The decor, with its imitation-leather banquette, embossed ceiling, and mocha-colored false-wood paneling, has not changed. I used to kick up a rumpus there all the time; I baited the guests and propositioned the women quite openly. We would sometimes have a nightcap in a painter's studio. Oscar Dominguez had been in Paris only a short time, and we used to drink a lot at his place. The jokes were brutal; Victor Brauner once lost an eye there. In Seligmann's studio, the rite was more curious. As soon as his girl friend had company, she would take her clothes off. She was beautiful. I've seen four men carrying her stiff and naked on their shoulders. They marched around the room several times, singing, and finally stood her on a big table in order to render Bacchic homage. I don't know whether these astonishing scenes, encouraged by Seligmann, were limited to such rather lovely pagan rites, or whether there was a more orgiastic aftermath.

A few months before the war, I found out, from Georges Hugnet, about the rift between Breton and Eluard. That was the last thing in the world I would ever have expected. Hugnet sided with Eluard, and the dissident Surrealist publication *L'Usage de la Parole* (*The Use of the Word*) saw the light of day.

For several years I had taken only two-week vacations in order to increase my income. In 1939, I decided to take the full month I was allowed. Katia and Françoise were in Bulgaria, where I was to join them. First I intended to spend a short time in Germany, especially Munich, and I would come back via Vienna. I set out in mid-August.

In Munich I had a lot of trouble finding a place to stay. A reception office got me a furnished room. I was astonished at the sense of gaiety I felt in Germany. The people were better dressed than in France and seemed happy. I made a point of walking back and forth in front of the medieval-style building which contained the ashes of the victims of the 1923 putsch, simply so I could refuse to give the obligatory Hitler salute. I wasn't taking any great risk, since I was openly holding the French Blue Guide in my hands. The sentinels glared at me ferociously but never broke their statue-like immobility.

In Bavaria I stopped several times to see the lakes. Wherever I deposited my baggage, whether in a checkroom or a hotel, my suitcases were thoroughly searched. The train to Belgrade was full of tourists, but there were also young men who seemed to be going to work. Two of them asked me lots of questions. What did I think of the Czechs, the Poles, the Russians, the Belgians, and so on? Were the French afraid of war?

I took a Hungarian boat heading down the Danube toward Orekhovo. The skipper talked to me about the Treaty of Trianon, for which he held me personally responsible! The boat was carrying a heavy load of German tourists, including a large and beautiful girl dressed in the tricolor. "This is the French flag," she said, and I never understood whether her choice was an indication of sympathy or a matter of personal aesthetic taste.

In Bulgaria, I learned about the Stalin-Hitler pact. I couldn't believe it. But I had to bow to facts. It meant war and in the worst way. I decided to go back to France immediately. By the time I got to Sofia, war had been declared. I spent a day with Sazy, a commercial attaché at the French legation, whom I had first met in 1930. We accompanied a legation official to the train that was to take him to France; he was being mobilized because he was an officer. Every day more and more Germans were arriving to swell the diplomatic ranks in Sofia.

French bureaucratic idiocy was as hearty as ever. I went to see Stamenov, and we spent two long hours locating the positions of the various sides in the conflict and discussing the prospects for Bulgaria and France. Stamenov was principal adviser to the King. "We're a very small country, poor, badly armed, and we have no choice but to remain neutral. Depending on the way the conflict develops, we'll tend to go along with the stronger power so as not to have to pay for any operation in which our neighbors will be able to participate. You know that my personal sympathies are with France, but we have to admit that everything we use in our factories, everything we find in our stores, comes from Germany, which buys everything from us except essence of roses. Please believe me when I say that I deplore your country's failure in the Balkans. Now everyone will be looking toward Russia. You've probably noticed the sudden inflow of commercial travelers and technicians from Germany. It's been a genuine invasion for several weeks now. My information from Rumania and Yugoslavia indicates that the same thing is happening over there. Hitler is using modern methods of war. Just think of the impact of all these propagandists who are businessmen and buyers to boot. The English and French still think it's 1918!"

I saw Stamenov for the last time at the royal palace. He turned around to wish me good luck. I had been deeply moved by the sight of his Caucasian face, his little Mikoyan mustache, his affability, and his lucid mind. When he had spoken about France, I had comprehended the collapse of our national prestige because of internal quarrels, political hesitations, and old-fashioned traditions of diplomacy, industry, and commerce.

Sazy was no optimist either. "In any case," he said, "we have nothing to prepare with. Look at the difference in methods. The Germans are setting up their fifth column. Here we're mobilizing diplomats! Most of the Frenchmen living here have received their marching orders, whereas the government ought to bring in three times as many. You, for instance, have connections here. You know Bulgaria fairly well. What are you going to accomplish in your regiment? Are you irreplaceable?"

I hopped the train for Belgrade, where I intended to spend a few days with Ristitch. I arrived in the midst of total chaos. The Stalin-Hitler pact was worrying everyone. Wasn't this an imperialist war? The favors I had done for Kotcha Popović had preserved my prestige with the Serbian friends I had made in 1930. Since I didn't approve of the Stalin-Hitler pact, Ristitch convened a sort of general assembly to hear me out.

"This war is not an imperialist war," I said in substance. "The great confrontation with Fascism is now beginning; the democracies must be defended, and the revolutionary content of this struggle will be affirmed during the course of the war by the defeat of Hitler. Stalin's agreement with Hitler is a monumental error. It will someday be amended. If we win, Russia will lose her role as an example forever, unless Stalin joins us in time. Stalin may be playing a peasant's waiting game. By turning the storm against others, he thinks he's going to win on all counts. But in war the victor nearly always grows stronger. At this point the only effect of the pact is to help Hitler spread Fascism through Europe.

Should the emancipation of the proletariat be based on the sacrifice of Poland? After Poland, it will be your turn next. For the time being, the only guarantee of your independence and the few liberties you have left is the military force of England and France. I am going home. I intend to join the French army, because today that bourgeois army is the army of liberty."

Not everyone was convinced. Ristitch was happy to hear me. "Nevertheless," he said, "on the one side, there's Goebbels, and on the other, propaganda is assigned to Giraudoux. It's not the same thing."

I spent two nights in the lovely circular house of the editor-in-chief of *Politika*. That young journalist was fully aware of Stalin's sellout.

I found out that Kotcha had come home and wanted to see me in Zagreb. He was waiting on the station platform. He brought up the "imperialist war" immediately, but without conviction. I think he was in uniform. "Goodbye, Kotcha," I said, returning to my railroad coach. "Today it's up to me to relieve you. This is a new stage of the struggle of the brigades in Spain." But I never did relieve Kotcha Popović. I wasn't up to it. The young officer I was leaving was to become one of the heroes of the war of liberation. In 1944, he commanded one of Tito's divisions.

I traveled through a deserted Venice, where I was served by waiters who were thankful that Mussolini hadn't entered the war. My train took two days to go from the Italian border to Paris: we had to let the north-bound convoys of heavy artillery pass. The trip was so full of adventures that I didn't sleep for seventy-two hours, which was relatively easy for me then. As soon as I arrived in Paris, I hurried over to the nearest recruiting station and signed up for the duration of the war. I was immediately declared fit for armed service. I had asked to join the artillery or the tank corps, but the unimaginative military bureaucracy, using its up-to-date files, sent me to the 18th Engineering Corps.

Thus, one day in September, I landed in the village of Houdemont, near Nancy, where my regiment's training battalion was billeted. The battalion was a motley crew of young volunteers and draftees from professions that might have something to do with communications. The junior officers were decent, and most of them wanted to do something. The soldiers were lazy and had confused ideas about the war. No one liked Hitler, but if by negotiating the government could have managed to stop the whole thing and send everyone home, they would all have applauded, without worrying about the Poles, democracy, or revolution. The officers themselves were mediocre; their main concern was their uniforms. At night, they went to Nancy for entertainment; the commanding officer was lax in his administration. We didn't learn much. Besides, there was very little equipment.

Winter set in rather quickly, and it was very cold. The public fountain on the square was covered with ice. I would wash there every morning before roll call. These ablutions were an object of general curiosity. When the thermometer had dropped well below freezing for several days, the battalion was brought to barracks in Nancy. We didn't know very much, but the commanding officer had probably decided that we were trained.

Nancy was a very merry town, full of soldiers and joyously undisciplined. There was a speakeasy in the Hôtel de l'Europe. I went there in civilian dress after changing clothes in my father's home. There I ran into a lot of reserve officers I had known in school. A record player was playing "J'attendrai" ("I'll Wait"), and two or three beautiful dance hostesses seemed overly curious about military details.

Only some aerial reconnoitering reminded us that we were at war. The newspapers were full of the exploits of French fighter forces, which seemed to be putting up a fairly good defense. The Russian assault on Finland had crowned the embarrassment of all the leftists. Russia seemed to have slipped to the other side and to be behaving even more badly than the most militant imperialists. The Finland war didn't help her much. The triumphant shouts of the conservatives, who were overjoyed to catch Stalin in the act of robbery, were odious. Daladier wanted to send matériel and soldiers to aid the Finns. Whom were we fighting: Hitler or the Russians?

I learned that the training battalion would be dissolved. Part of the force would go to Versailles to make up the transport company of a North African division that was then being formed. There was talk of Finland for a second lot. The rest would go to the Levant. I obtained information about what was going on over there. They were gathering the equivalent of an army corps, with tanks and cannon, to reinforce the Turkish contingents. But, although France continued to furnish the Turks with large quantities of arms, especially antitank guns— which would have been more useful in Sedan—the expeditionary corps to the Levant, which had been formed with the stinginess and flightiness typical of French general staffs, was merely a modest force. It was commanded by the most remarkable show-off in the French army, General Weygand.

When the Panzers pulverized the Polish army, I was obliged to revise my somewhat hasty judgment of Colonel de Gaulle's ideas. By chance, one of our fatigue parties witnessed a drill involving some sixty tanks. It was very cold, but those machines looked ferocious. "It was probably very optimistic of me," I thought, "to believe that a heavy-artillery barrage could wipe out all those tanks. Any tanks that got through would storm the batteries and destroy them. Only other tanks can stop them; otherwise they'll ravage everything. They'll take Nancy or Trèves while the French army is still fighting on the Maginot or the Siegfried Line."

In March, I got brand-new khaki and more modern weapons. My detachment, reinforced with soldiers from the 8th Engineering Corps, was sent to Marseilles, then to Beirut. In Bizerte, our transport took on a superb squadron of spahis (Algerian native troopers), which Weygand needed for display.

The Beirut barracks faced the ocean and the mountains. The streets around it were lined with leafless or nearly leafless trees covered with mauve flowers. The nights were luminous and fragrant. The moon, brighter than in Lorraine, left a sparkling trail on the sea and shed a milky light upon the white houses that were dotted with a thousand twinkling fires. Biblical landscapes began toward the south. The town seemed to contain every possibility for corrupting an army.

Again I found myself in a training unit. The barracks housed another company from Lorraine, a radio corps. They knew their stuff and had the right equipment. We had drills on the seashore, and I finally became useful. Except for a collection of brightly colored chemisettes, with which I remedied the supply corps' parsimony in regard to linen, I was an attractive soldier, disciplined and hard working.

On May 7, as I was mounting the stairs from Bab Edriss to the Grand Seraglio to see the sights, I heard someone calling. It was Mégret. The war had caught him in Egypt as editor-in-chief of *La Dépêche d'Alexandrie*. Before that, he had spent a long time in New Caledonia with Suzanne I, Breton's passion in the thirties. He had been mobilized to Weygand's general staff and lived in a pretty house with a slender and delicate wife. She asked me to come to dinner on May 11, the day after the great offensive. The conversation was rather disorderly. Also present were Chambard, who had been consul in Hankow, and his very attractive wife, who told funny stories about Abyssinia, Japan, and China.

The best story concerned the dinner to which General Chang-Hsueh-liang had invited the whole consular corps after his troops had occupied Hankow. The general, young and rather handsome, had a disconcerting reputation for savagery. Suzanne Chambard was sitting opposite him. He couldn't take his eyes off her. He launched into more and more daring compliments, making passionate declarations and very direct propositions. Some of the guests tried to change the subject, but he grew more and more animated. Silence fell around the table. The object of his attentions tried to keep her countenance. She was slightly nervous, but she was the only one having fun. She was waiting. She could hardly say no to him: she had to think about the safety of her husband and the other diplomats. "As long as he's not a sadist," she thought to herself. She decided to act as though she were going along with him.

The general never stopped talking, and all he talked about was the object of his sudden passion. Happily, he drank as much as he spoke. Suzanne Chambard managed to make him drink a little more. Chang had already asked his servants to prepare a room worthy of this dreamlike creature; everyone was waiting for the climax. The general was very drunk. He got to his feet, and all eyes turned to Madame Chambard. The general collapsed in one fell swoop. He was carried to his quarters.

The next day, our heroine was no more reassured than the previous evening. They cast about for some way of organizing an escape. But then a captain brought a cartful of flowers and a very respectful letter from the Chinese general, offering the consul's wife all his apologies.

No one could believe that the 9th and 2nd armies had collapsed on the Meuse. The fighting at Dunkirk aroused stupor; there was anti-British talk. I was in the midst of a drill on the rocks facing the sea when a van came speeding up and ground to a halt near me. "Get back to the barracks right away; you're going to see action." At the barracks, I found the commander, Captain Fleury, and two or three other officers. All of them were grave and nervous. "Thirion, you're leaving for Palmyra immediately. You're being transferred to the 11th Company of the 6th Foreign Legion. You've got to make it tonight if possible. They've installed a transmitter on the car so you can work with the tanks and the airplanes." This was the only piece of equipment in the French army I wasn't familiar with. All the same, I got a short explanation and realized that essential parts had been omitted. We found them in a store. We had no maps, and we didn't know how to get to Palmyra, which was over a hundred miles of desert away. I got hold of a compass, and off we went as though the entire German army had marched across the Euphrates the previous night.

I didn't realize that I had just been transferred to a company whose troops were supposed to work with armored vehicles. For some mysterious but urgent reason, the general staff had set up a motorized mobile force, consisting of a company of legionnaires, to defend the precious pipeline of the Iraq Petroleum Company. They had added three modern planes and a radio car, mine. But none of these things ever functioned at the same time. Fortunately, we never met the enemy.

Most of the legionnaires in the 11th Company were Germans or Spaniards. Nearly all the junior officers were German. We were billeted in the Weygand post, a sort of fortified barracks which could house a five-hundred-man garrison. It was off toward the west of Palmyra and also functioned as the food depot and ammunition dump for the region. It was completely surrounded by a network of barbed wire. On the terraces of the barrack rooms, pigeon holes hung with sackcloth sheltered machine guns and a small 65-mm. cannon.

A few hundred yards from the Legion post, aviators occupied another, more luxuriously equipped, blockhouse. To the south, the quarters of the Sudanese camel corps sheltered the 1st Light Company of the desert, a detachment of automatic machine guns, and a few hundred Sudanese. Their hair was long, sometimes reaching down to their knees, and they braided it and coiled it up under their headbands. They had signed up for five years in the French army. After their hitch, they would return home with their equipment. Their officers, wearing red dolmans, looked like characters in a novel. A small hospital and a military field brothel with five or six prostitutes completed the military equipment of Palmyra.

During the days of Queen Zenobia, the city had counted at least twenty thousand inhabitants. The ruins were a mile away from the military posts. Toward Damascus, they stretched to the foot of some medium-sized hills; further north, toward the trail to Homs, higher and steeper hills framed a real mountain pass. It was in the valley leading into it that tombs had once been built. Some of the towers in this necropolis were filled with niches where the corpses were placed. Others were probably muck heaps. The passage to Palmyra via the valley of tombs produces a powerful effect of grandeur and desolation.

The largest monument in Palmyra is the Temple of Bel, at the eastern edge of town. It is as large as the largest buildings in Baalbek. After the Arab invasions had totally destroyed Palmyra, the remnants of the population took refuge in the Temple of Bel, which, because it was easy to defend, became a citadel. The French evacuated the temple to get rid of the rubble and built a dreadful suburban village with wide, dusty avenues running alongside the palm grove.

The western skyline goes along a mountain chain that reaches as high as 2,500 feet. In the gravel and the rocks one can see herds of gazelles during the day and hear hyenas at night, shrieking like women. The sunsets are very long and magnificent. Toward the north, a kind of peak towers eight or nine hundred feet over Palmyra. At the top, there is an almost intact Arab castle from the fifteenth century, Qalaat Ibn Maan, which was used as a garrison by Turkish soldiers during the First World War. The walk up this peak was one of my favorite promenades. In 1930, the Queen Zenobia Hotel was constructed between the Arab castle and the old city. Its owner was killed in the gardens just before 1940 by his wife, a French adventuress and a friend of Mussolini's; she claimed she had spent several years of her life in a harem.

Palmyra was a strategic position from which the army could protect the French branch of the pipeline that brings crude oil from Mosul to Tripoli. The pipeline passes slightly south of Palmyra. The Sudanese camelmen supervised the movement of the nomads and their flocks which came up every year from the confines of Arabia Felix to the borders of Turkey, after the sun had burned out what they called their pasture lands. A police force was necessary to protect the nomads from the rebels, to prevent smuggling, to insure respect for law and customs, and to obtain information on the groups that were always ready for plotting and adventure. Sometimes, at night, two of these superb soldiers would come trotting home to Palmyra in their slovenly way, flanking some unfortunate Bedouin leading his donkey along by the halter. The Sudanese looked like two gendarmes from the French countryside bringing a chicken thief back to town—except that they were as dazzling as a man must be in a desert where almost all the divinities in the world have manifested their anger or dictated their laws.

I had arrived in Palmyra on June 1, 1940. Tragedy was unrolling so rapidly in France that it was beyond our understanding. My sources of information were the radio at the Weygand post and my own apparatus, which I set up every morning on the other side of the barbed wire. After four or five days of hope, the disaster became obvious.

The changes in French politics were no less disquieting than our military fortunes. Weygand's nomination as commander-in-chief was, for me, replacing a one-eyed horse with a blind horse. I was biased against Weygand because of his Fascist sympathies. Ferrat and I had studied his actions during the First World War and in Poland. There was no reason to consider him a valuable general. All the information I had gathered in Beirut depicted him as vain and arrogant, devoid of intellectual curiosity and attached to all forms of conservatism. The takeover by Marshal Pétain, an avowed defeatist, boded no good.

We found out about the fall of Paris on the very day it happened. Most of the German legionnaires looked overjoyed. I wept with rage. Spanish legionnaires came and shook my hand as though I had lost someone near and dear. I was friendly with several German junior officers, who were correct to a fault. One of them made a point of telling me that a military defeat had never diminished a great people.

I think I heard the call of June 18 on the same day, for I was constantly listening to the British stations. On the other hand, I have a vivid memory of the call of June 19, which was firmer and more precise and was aimed particularly at North Africa. It included the following sentence: "Any Frenchman still bearing arms has the duty to continue resistance." The request for an armistice struck me as all the more scandalous because I was part of an intact army beyond the reach of the Germans.

For about a week after the armistice, I really believed that the Empire (as we used to say at that time) would refuse to go along with it and would continue fighting. There was talk of disbanding the Legion, which aroused a good deal of worry in Palmyra, but that was a minor detail. Just as my friends and I had foreseen, Hitler's victory led to a throttling of the Republic and the establishment of a regime that instantly wanted to ally itself with the ideology of the victors. My mind was made up from the very first defeats. The world had entered into a war that would totally consume it; the war would be long and hard and would end only when the Fascists were crushed. The installation in Vichy of a government of docile slaves made the duty of a revolutionary even clearer: he had to fight against Hitler and his French allies.

Since the colonial governors had joined the camp of shame, what path could I take? I listened to General de Gaulle's appeals on the radio. But who was De Gaulle? Who was in his entourage? True, someone had to represent France and her honor on the outside. But wasn't the main struggle for a Frenchman *inside* France? Where could I best be of service? At first sight, my background and everything I knew about revolutionary fighting called me to the anti-Fascist struggle in France. I was sure that the war would resume someday. With an Allied landing, we would have to organize partisan groups and prepare a national uprising. But how could I get back to the mainland?

It was too early for any decision. Other opportunities might arise in the Levant. In any case, I had to regard myself now as part of a world subject to the rules of secrecy.

Mers-el-Kebir came like a bolt from the blue. British aggression against the fleet at first implied that Pétain's government had secretly linked itself with Germany. As of July 9, the idea of a French-English conflict, which would have seemed a monstrous idea in late June, was welcomed in some places without protest. Seals were put on the telephone stations connecting the French with the English posts. The fever subsided quickly. But for three weeks there was uproar. Discussions and rebellion were taking over the army!

On July 14, flags flew at half-mast when we assembled for a parade in front of the post. The commander of the 3rd Battalion, a big earthy drunk, reminded us of the Legion watchword and the legionnaire's oath. Before he left for Damascus, he was assailed with questions about the future of this elite corps. He was as reassuring as he could be, but he himself was worried. That evening, the junior officers of my company invited me to a drinking bout in the Queen Zenobia Hotel, which had been deserted for months but whose cellar was still well-supplied with whiskey. First we took a nocturnal dip in the milky water of the swimming pool. The young wife of the security chief of Homs joined us. She was having an affair with one of the aviators in the garrison.

The Germans were very attentive to me. The most likable one, Gerhard Pasche, was a section leader who was regarded as a future officer. A former midshipman in Kiel, he had come to the Legion after a scandal with a girl. Although I had concealed my opinions and plans, he had an intuitive sense of what I intended to do—and so, it seems, did the lieutenant of my company. When I was trying to bring some order to the post library, Pasche reached into a stack of books and pulled out Ernst von Salomon's lovely story *Die Geächteten* (*The Pariahs*). "Here's a book for you," he said. "It's the story of our Freikorps, especially the Hamburg battalion." That book was very comforting. Only those who admit their defeat will lose. Through this viewpoint from the other side, I rediscovered the agitation in Germany between 1919 and 1922, which Barmotte had described. Once more the force of the national sentiment—or, even worse, of nationalism—was stronger than any other. But in the situation that France and the French found themselves in during 1940, no book could provide greater hope than Ernst von Salomon's.

An ovenlike heat suddenly rose from the stones of Palmyra. On July

16, at midnight, three French Sudanese and two legionnaires took off for Palestine with several machine guns. As an added precaution, they had sabotaged the other vehicles. Damascus gave the alert, and my radio car was mobilized to follow the airplanes that were hunting the fugitives. I was listening together with the sergeant-major. I prudently told him of my scruples if a message led to an organized pursuit. I disguised what I said as an expression of humanity. The sergeant-major told me he was not ready to promote a fight between Frenchmen. Besides, he knew one of the camelmen. "Nevertheless," he said, "we have to see the problem as it is. If they haven't got lost by now, they must be on the other side. We won't be alerted unless they've gone astray here or got into trouble. In that case, it would be better to go look for them." I realized that the alert had been deliberately sent too late.

Delaunay, one of the sergeants of the 18th Engineering Corps whom I had known in Houdemont, had managed to be transferred to Palmyra. He was intelligent and extremely honest; if he had been lucky enough to be born into a wealthier family and gone on to higher studies, he could have attained very high positions. He was exactly the type of person whose future, I felt, would be changed by the Revolution. The destruction of a state based on bureaucracy and diplomas would make way for careers based on merit. Delaunay had left-wing opinions. Although he was not interested in politics, he couldn't help seeing through the regime that Pétain wanted to set up and the Nazification that could be expected from it. He shared my reaction to the bureaucratic stupidity of the French army. I was overjoyed by his coming, for I needed his common sense to work out all the ideas I was developing.

Delaunay drew a funny and saddening picture of a rebellion filtered through red tape. President Puaux and especially Commander-in-Chief Mittelhauser had at first rejected the armistice. Telegrams from Noguès led them to believe it would be possible to create a council of pro-consuls to continue the war. But first there would have to be civil war! Orders were given to keep an eye on the "partisans of capitulation" in each unit. Haphazard proscription lists were drawn up in the company offices, and a camp was opened for undesirables. Then, less than a week later, Mittelhauser and Puaux finally sided with Pétain. They took over the proscription lists. But now there had been Gaullist plots. The army had to be purged. Once again, the company offices provided names. The same men often figured on both lists. What counted was not Fascist sympathies, pacifism, Anglophilia, or support of the Resistance, but the opinion of the sergeant-majors.

More men escaped: six junior officers from the air base. One of them had informed Delaunay and me about their plans. The arrival of the Italian armistice commissions in the Levant caused confusion. The demands of these inspectors shocked the military men. The Italians intended to strip the troops of part of their weapons and store all the ammunition reserves in depots that were easy to guard. One of the junior officers in the 9th Company called me into the company office. "I'm a soldier," he said, "and nothing but a soldier. I served in the Dutch Legion, then in the French Legion. I've been demoted twice. But each time I got my rank back. I'm forty-three years old. Are they going to throw me out like an unsavory outcast because I'm a legionnaire and a German, and because I don't want to serve Herr Hitler? Where am I supposed to go? To Chiang Kai-shek?"

Mégret came to Palmyra with Captain Fleury. I asked him about the June fighting. "Apparently there aren't a hundred thousand casualties, but close to two million prisoners. First the officers, then the men knuckled under!" He said nothing about the command, the strategic positions, or the way the battle had been conducted. Although Mégret was quite capable of objectivity, he always tended to side with whoever happened to be stronger at the moment. He spoke with humor and scorn about the Gaullist conspiracies that had been agitating Beirut since the armistice.

Fleury escaped from the hospitality of the officers of Palmyra to talk about service with Delaunay and me. We immediately got to war and politics. Fleury didn't see things the way Mégret did. Each of them remained cautious, but it was easy to discern the drift of his thoughts. Who was De Gaulle? Who was with him in London? First of all, De Gaulle was the only French general who had achieved any successes during the six weeks of war. We tended to exaggerate their significance. He was also the only soldier who thought in terms of modern warfare. Mégret envisaged the defeat of England, but Fleury and I recalled that a maritime power had never been beaten by a continental power. I pointed out that I knew one of the men in the London Committee, Professor Réne Cassin, who had been president of the Federal War Veterans' Union. "He's a leftist," I added, "and in those terms he's certainly a moral safeguard."

"For all its faults," said Fleury, "the Levant army, as it is today, represents a force. But the Italians will insist that it be dispersed. We'll all we demobilized. No one here will want to take the slightest risk."

I didn't have much to do. I was interested in archaeology. I also learned some marvelous recipes. I spent my evenings on the public square. Around 10 P.M., a cold wind arose. You had to bundle up, and you blessed the arrival of the bitter tea. Afterward, all you could do was listen to tales of the Arabian Nights.

A woman in Palmyra had been robbed. The police had arrested a suspect. Despite the usual beating, he hadn't confessed. The police had to try something else. They resorted to a dervish, who had a marvelous crystal ball. Seated before the ball after she had read a certain number of verses in the Koran, the woman had seen the stolen object, then the larcenous hand, and finally the place where the object was hidden.

A Mecca pilgrim asked a barber to shave his head. The razor didn't cut. The angry barber tried to slash the pilgrim's arm, but his skin wasn't even grazed. After studying his customer closely, the barber asked him to put his ring on the table. Then he was able to shave his head. He had recognized the stone that makes the wearer invulnerable to side arms.

Nevertheless, everything was going downhill in Palmyra, even the fine discipline of the Legion. We were hatching out plots to get to Palestine, but we wanted to leave with weapons and baggage. It was more difficult in October because the distributor caps were taken out of the motors every evening and put under careful guard.

We heard that we were to be relieved by the 1st Company of the 1st Battalion. The legionnaires would return to Damascus, and I would be repatriated and demobilized. The arrival of the 1st Company was impressive. They all looked like buccaneers. Apparently they thought the same of us. The night they arrived, Pasche, Delaunay, and I treated Ledinneg, the regimental sergeant-major, to whiskey at the Queen Zenobia Hotel. He was a small thin, lively, and very Prussian soldier, the kind of sensitive man who feels sorry for the people he is punishing but who punishes them anyway, perhaps even a bit more harshly to guard against his unsettling pity. He told us about the recent mutiny in the 1st Battalion. His unit, which included many Spaniards from the Republican army and a few volunteers from the international brigades, was the regiment's marching battalion. It had gone on all the alerts. At the time of the armistice, it was in the Cedars opening a road for tourism. The armistice infuriated the legionnaires and their officers. They conferred and decided to join the British and continue the fight. The troops fell in and marched back down to their quarters in the valley. It was a grand adventure, rebellion, but they preferred to be realists and wait for their pay. Their pay was distributed. Still no departure; they requisitioned a few trucks. Ledinneg asked the captain to explain.

"We don't want to leave the families of the officers and the non-commissioned officers behind. Ledinneg, do you have any family in Lebanon?"

"No, sir. But we've already waited for our pay. If we now wait for families, we've got to think of the legionnaires too; some of them have very solid ties here."

"Let's have the addresses. Ledinneg, what are they saying in the company?"

"Sir, I'm German. There are German legionnaires here. The armistice is signed. The battalion wants to go and fight the Germans. We've all sworn the Legion oath. We'll go wherever you go, even if we have to turn rebels, but don't ask the Germans to squeal. We have to act quickly."

They finally loaded the families and were about to leave. An alert. It was General Mittelhauser. He had the battalion pass in review. He exalted obedience to the Marshal. He ordered an end to the preparations for departure. The trucks were unloaded, and the battalion set out to finish the tourist road.

In Beirut, I ran into Jacques Baron and Mégret. Baron was also to be repatriated. He had me transferred to the Theater of the Armies, which permitted a pleasant return voyage on the *Athos II*. Marseilles was filled with thousands of refugees. It was impossible to find a place to stay. The prostitutes used couches and elevators to practice their trade. I bumped into Jeanine Picabia. She reported incredible things about the demoralization of the German army at the mere contact with Paris! The wildest rumors were circulating. Fleury, Baron, and I managed to have a decent dinner at Bassot. We were about to go our separate ways. This was a moment of truth. Jacques Baron was ready to come to terms with the Marshal. Fleury and I had chosen a different road. "We're not quite sure who De Gaulle is," was what we said in substance, "but we feel that he is the government of France."

I added that I was returning to Paris. "I'm joining the underground. The final outcome will be accomplished by our insurrection."

I was not a hero of the Resistance. On a rather low level, I did some patient and mostly useless organizational work. But I never sold out.

25
ORDEAL BY ORDEAL

ON OCTOBER 28, 1940, I WAS BACK IN PARIS, demobilized. Katia and Françoise were still in Paramé. After a cold bath (this was to be a daily rule for more than five years), I began to look up my old political friends. I started with Ferrat, who lived fifty yards away from me. "They haven't come home," said the concierge, "and it's better if they don't. Tell them to stay where they are. The Germans came right after the armistice—soldiers and civilians. They ransacked the whole place and carried off boxes full of papers. You can go up if you want to see the mess."

I went to see Fourrier the same day. He didn't know that Ferrat's place had been searched. But he wasn't worried. Ferrat, he reported, had fought courageously against the Nazis and had been seriously wounded behind his machine gun. He was still being treated in Lyons. Was the house search a Communist maneuver? Were the Party representatives, who were trying to get the Party legalized and to be able to put out *L'Humanité* again, also trying to get rid of the enemies of the Stalin-Hitler pact? We were inclined to believe that it was a purely German operation, possibly prepared with the help of information from Doriot's French Popular Party—that is, from people who had been in the service of the Gestapo before 1939.

Marcel Fourrier drew a rather gloomy picture of the Socialist and Communist circles. The Stalin-Hitler pact had ripped the "Socialist Battle" to shreds. The Communist Party was hardly any better off. "It can't be possible," I told Fourrier, "that all the Party militants approved a pact with such terrible consequences for the French proletariat. Party discipline won't stand up under a prolonged flirtation between Hitler and Stalin." Fourrier accepted this view. There had been many activities that contradicted the official party line, which favored a compromise with the Germans.

The bourgeois parties were acting pretty much as we expected. The new element was the collapse of the labor parties, which none of us had foreseen. We were more attached than ever to proletarian unity. The way to it seemed open because—or so we thought—Social Democracy and Stalinism had mortally compromised themselves. We could appear as the champions of national independence and liberation, the gathering point of a revolutionary party expressing the historical interests of the wage earners. Now that the Republic of 1875 had been suppressed by the French state, Socialism could succeed the Vichy regime; it would be forged in victory. We had nothing to use for making the slightest start on such an ambitious program. But that was the road we were going to take.

In November 1940, the French population, whether leftist or rightist, was passive. Only in scattered groups could any desire for action be felt. The Germans hadn't landed in England, so hope was returning. But since liberation wouldn't come overnight, no one wanted to take any chances, and they credited Vichy with a certain ability to negotiate. The only "resistance" activity that had any popular character was assisting escaped prisoners. The escapes, relatively easy and numerous in June and July, and even in August, had become more perilous and difficult by autumn because the organization of the camps and the occupation techniques had been perfected. The assistance to escaped prisoners may have been amateurish, but many organizations that had formerly been associated with the parties took part in the network.

The main change was the appearance of a new faith. Little by little, on this occasion, as during all the times when French interests were directly opposed to German interests, the left and the right made common cause. One of the resources available to a lone man in a strange situation was the village priest. In addition to his usual interests in the catechism, encyclicals, and various obligations, the churchman was an enthusiastic worker for charity. The endangered Saint-Cyrian also realized that the public-school teacher could not, on principle, support Hitler, so he knocked at the door of the school.

Month by month, the spread of misery engendered a kind of community of paupers in the towns, where material goods did not mean very much. Everyone, whether he had voted for the Popular Front or had cast a more conservative ballot, was hungry and cold and survived only through barter and the black market. The people longed for their lost liberties, suffered from the insane bureaucracy of the Nazis and the Vichyites, came to abhor the occupiers, and realized that state management of the economy was bedlam.

Then there was General de Gaulle. In late 1940, everyone was wondering about this man, who had been unknown six months earlier and whose prestige was growing faster than his military strength. The product of a right-thinking, reactionary family, whose formidable rise was based on work, classical education, loyalty to the Christian tradition, honor, and a love of history and the great heroes, De Gaulle was a proud Bergsonian and a nonconformist soldier. In 1933, he had flouted the idea that France could be protected from invasion by fortified works "manned by novices." The natural authority and a slightly cynical lucidity of the man inspired respect.

In late 1940, some Frenchmen saw General de Gaulle as a seer and a hero; others regarded him as a careerist in other people's service, either Pétain's or Churchill's. But almost no one trusted him. If presidential elections had offered a choice between Pétain and De Gaulle, the Marshal would have won hands down: many veterans would have voted for the only great leader of the First World War who had been interested in the soldiers. That egotist, eager for servility and honors, looked good. The Marshal asked the French to stand still and let themselves be fleeced; that platform would have been more seductive than an appeal to vanquish someone stronger than oneself. The conservatives would generally have voted for Pétain because of the old man's reactionary nature. Most of the left would have preferred him to De Gaulle because of his pacifism, because he came from a modest background, and because he pronounced the word *patrie* with a radical-socialist sonority. De Gaulle would at best have gotten the votes of the consistent nationalists and the lucid revolutionaries. But there weren't many of them around then, and those that there were voted more for a position than for the man taking it.

What bothered the left about De Gaulle was his tinge of Maurras. In his writings published before 1939, one sensed a great scorn for representative assemblies and a marked preference for a monarchic form of government. De Gaulle had a critical attitude toward the great ancestors; the Convention did not inspire his respect. People couldn't forgive the General for advocating a professional army. The left felt that this notion masked dark designs on the people, although history teaches that no professional army has ever been immune to a revolutionary contagion. Slogans were stronger than reason. I heard arguments that went on all evening whenever I visited the militants I had known. But the immediate results were rather disappointing.

I had been in Paris for less than three weeks when, as I arrived at France Mutualiste one morning, I caught sight of Fougerolles, who had formerly been in charge of Foreign Labor for the Eastern region, standing in front of the entry gate. I knew that he had been a police agent since 1928, so I simply walked over to Bonnet, my immediate superior, who was waiting at the door.

"Hello, Martin," Fougerolles called out with the coolness of a policeman. I was very uneasy. Martin had been my pseudonym when I headed the Nancy chapter. I didn't answer.

Fougerolles planted himself in front of me. "Well, Martin, don't you recognize me?"

I shook my head. "You must be mistaken. My name isn't Martin." I asked him up to the office I shared with Bonnet. I let him stand.

"Come on, Martin, don't you remember? Nancy, the Rue Saint-Nicolas?"

"You must be mistaking me for someone else," I said. "Of course I know Nancy, but I left it a long time ago. The name of that street doesn't remind me of anything except the patron saint of Lorraine and my childhood toys. We have work to do, so please leave. I can't be of any help to you." Bonnet was elegant enough not to ask any questions.

Fougerolles roamed around Avenue de Villiers once or twice more. Then he vanished. But I had to be careful. What was it all about? It was probably connected with the Ferrat raid, though the approach was peculiar. I told Fourrier about the incident and warned him that I would stop seeing him or calling him up until further notice.

Barral had spent several weeks in Vichy after the armistice. He had returned horrified. He had been opposed to Munich. We trusted one another. In one or two sentences, each of us found out what the other thought of the defeat. Barral had no intention of making a revolution, but he wanted Hitler crushed and the Republic and its liberties restored. He also felt that we should rally to De Gaulle. René Cassin's presence in London was, in his eyes, a powerful guarantee that a free France would observe Republican principles.

Barral was quite satisfied with the state of mind of the veterans in the Federal Union. The associations of the free zone had been forced to join the Legion, but they retained their own characteristics. A few openly Masonic leaders had been forced out of their positions. Vichy would someday pay for these persecutions. Only the unconditional pacifists were leaning toward the wrong side. The spirit of capitulation had not yet penetrated France Mutualiste. There was no portrait of Marshal Pétain anywhere.

At this point, any work Barral and I planned couldn't go beyond a condemnation of Vichyism. In December 1940, as the Riom trial against Daladier, Blum, and other leaders of the Popular Front approached, both of us, without making common cause with these men who bore some responsibility for our misfortunes, felt that the Republicans had no interest in authorizing the greater culprits to use a proceeding against such people as a trial against democracy, Parliament, freedom, and armed resistance to Hitlerism. We could not know whether we were in any position to accomplish anything useful. Our means could just about cover the costs of two or three hundred copies of a leaflet. But this would be an extremely limited operation. What good was it next to the commentaries of the B.B.C., even if they were jammed? We were almost ready to throw in the towel when Barral told me about a simple chalk graffiti he had seen in the Villiers subway station, *Vive la République*. It had been eradicated within twenty-four hours but it had exerted a comforting and defiant power. Now we had a new angle. Our leaflets would not be instruments of propaganda, but expressions of nonalignment. By their example, they would arouse further manifestations of defiance.

We set up three rather short texts. The first explained that in 1940 France had enough tanks to move against the Germans with some chance of success. Almost all these tanks had been built in the days of the Popular Front, but, despite De Gaulle's warnings, the general staff hadn't bothered to use them in a modern way. The second leaflet asked why the some two hundred airplanes that had bombarded Gibraltar on September 26, 1940, in reprisal for the Dakar affair hadn't been employed on the Meuse in May. A third asked who was responsible for our military insufficiencies: the generals who had insisted in 1939 that France had never been stronger, the M.P.'s who had voted for the military appropriations requested by the generals, or the workers who had agreed to work overtime to fulfill armament orders? This last leaflet was the subject of rather lively controversy between the two writers and never got past the stencil stage.

I thought it might be possible to publish and distribute a book attacking the principles of Vichy and Hitler, provided that it made full use of the approximations and licenses of poetic language. The watchword *Work, Family, Country* was a good source of inspiration. I took up the fragments and drafts I had written in 1929 and 1930, and I read the main chapters of *Le Grand Ordinaire* to Hugnet in 1942.

I soon became convinced that most of the members of the old parties had no desire, at least at that time, to take up any political activity. We had to recruit new people. Nevertheless, I made a point of following the development of the former Socialists, unionists, and Communists I visited. I devoted myself to the easy work of writing graffiti on walls. Unfortunately, the means of execution were very poor; most of the time, I had to make do with chalk, since spray paint was still restricted to automobile manufacturers. I indoctrinated a few people.

Sometime during the spring of 1941, I was engaged in my activity in the tenth arrondissement. It was past midnight, and the streets were absolutely deserted. There was a risk that I would be caught in the act. Two policemen stopped me. Since I was hanging around after curfew and had no permission to be out, I was at fault. One of the cops suspected I might be the author of some insulting partisan phrase on the walls of the factory. I put on airs, trying to embarrass and frighten him. Why go to any trouble if the German occupation wouldn't last forever? I ended the night at the police station. An official report was drawn up, and legal proceedings were set in motion. I asked Marcel Fourrier to defend me. The affair dragged on, but, despite the special notation some pig made on the record itself, the case was not handed over to the Germans. When I appeared at the Civil Court on January 25, 1943, Fourrier managed to play down the incident. I was merely sentenced to a fine, which I never paid.

The spirit of resistance was coming out in the open. The Musée de l'Homme affair was the first manifestation of our recovered honor. The occupation authorities put up yellow posters with black stripes in the subways and on the walls of Paris announcing the death sentence for and execution of Commander d'Estienne d'Orves. This voluntary publicity for acts of resistance was fantastic. It expressed the Germans' drive to terrorize in response to the bad conscience they got from partisan actions. But nothing was more contrary to their interests. The posters aroused hatred for the Germans and pity and admiration for the victims; they incited the French to resistance. They multiplied enormously the effects of any seditious activity.

When I came to work one day in the spring of 1943, I learned that Barral had been arrested by the Gestapo that very morning. He was still assistant secretary-general of the National Confederation of War Veterans. His boss, Rivollet, was a government minister and said to be on good terms with the occupation authorities, so the leaders of all the veterans' organizations dashed over to ask him to get Barral released. A delegation left for Vichy to lay the matter before Pétain. Rives, the assistant director, summoned me to his office the day after the arrest. "Here's the information we got from Rivollet. France Mutualiste is said to contain a resistance cell with Thirion at its head and Barral as an active member. The Gestapo wanted to set an example. Rivollet doesn't know how valid this accusation is. He himself stands behind Maurice de Barral, who is being transferred to Compiègne today. First we have to see to it that Barral doesn't get sent to Germany; then we have to get him released. We'll do all we can for him. Rivollet asks you not to change anything in your habits or behavior. The Gestapo's charges seem to be mere generalities." I followed his advice assiduously. Maurice de Barral, thirteen pounds lighter, was set free after several weeks of detention.

The Vichy regime probably accumulated every defect that a state can. Essentially an absolute monarchy, it was subject to the laws of chance. The monarch was not a madman, a drug addict, or a simpleton, but an unstable old man no longer in full possession of his faculties. This decrepit king was actually a vassal; he instructed his army to shoot at the English, the Free French, and the Americans, supposedly to protect the integrity of overseas possessions, yet there wasn't even the faintest gesture of defense when the Germans invaded the Kingdom of Vichy. As in any court, intrigue reigned supreme. The administration controlled goods and people. The things most necessary to life could be obtained only by grace of the Prince or by trickery. The Prince's grace was confused with that of hundreds of petty potentates.

The regime was also one of hypocrisy and derision. In 1942 work for Germany became obligatory. This pharaoh-like requisition of civilian manpower had already been recommended in *Mein Kampf* as one of the foundations of the Great Reich. Family legislation to produce children who could not be fed was the monstrous product of a narrow-minded nationalism and of the worst Christian superstitions. Its main accomplishment was the death penalty for abortion.

"Justice" took up where the Inquisition had left off. In further loyalty to monarchic traditions, *Le Journal Officiel* of June 24, 1943, promulgated the law instituting within each Court of Appeals a special section to judge any infractions that might encourage terrorism, Communism, anarchy, or social or national subversion or provoke or incite a state of rebellion against the legally established social order, whether the crimes were against individuals or property. Arrested individuals would, according to this law, be prosecuted immediately, with no previous hearing, by this new court, whose judgments could not be appealed in any way and were to be carried out immediately. The sentences included imprisonment, forced labor, and death. They varied according to the activity being prosecuted, and functionaries of the state always incurred the maximum penalty.

Economic regulation was the most interesting part of Vichy's laws. Each morning I began work by reading *Le Journal Officiel*, in which a theory of an economic system was being worked out. I could then test the effects of that system. This was especially thrilling for a Socialist because I knew that within the agencies producing all these articles there were many people from the far left. To begin with, a very simple truth, though one to which the revolutionary propagandists had never paid any heed, imposed itself upon the French: you can distribute only what has been produced. A second truth was equally obvious: the market economy was shown to be more effective than any bureaucratic system for distributing products. The doctrinaire experts who railed against "wallet rationing" to justify their determinism refused to see that a rationing system involving inspectors, offices, and cards would ultimately be grinding up thin air. They should have realized that the very principle of rationing multiplies tenfold the force of individual initiative. In fact, they were starting the infernal process in which the Russian Revolution had exhausted itself. So that nothing might escape the supposedly equal distribution, they had to turn the farmers into functionaries and keep a close watch over them. As a result, agricultural production decreased, and negligence, dishonesty, and disorder came to stay. In towns and cities, the endless lines of housewives at shop doors became an institution.

The organization committees who beguiled General de Gaulle in London—he saw them as a starting point for a unified organization of the nation—were merely a replica of Russian planning agencies. It didn't matter whether the professionals on the committees that distributed raw materials, arbitrarily set quotas and prices, and divided the products among the consumers were capitalists or managers of state-owned factories. But the Vichy system did have one advantage over the Soviet organization: it left a margin of initiative to the producers. Vichy offered a good image of the "construction of Socialism": the workers had no right to strike, rationing was universal, as was poverty, and a vigilant police bore down brutally on any infraction of the community law. An endlessly growing, endlessly heavier bureaucracy did a very poor job of distribution. Favoritism and the black market prospered. The individual was not obliged, as in Berlin or Moscow, to report for periodic cultural drills—although every program of the petty tyrants in Vichy tended toward that goal—but, as in Russia, people had to bow to strict rules just to be fed and clothed. To meet these elementary needs, one had to lengthen one's workday by the time needed to convert one's salary into poor-quality merchandise. Eating one more loaf of bread than the ration was considered a crime against society.

Daniel Mayer, who had made up his mind to devote all his energies to defending Léon Blum, leaned toward joining Free France. It was no longer possible to regard De Gaulle as an agent of Great Britain. Fighting Hitler meant fighting Pétain, and the regime established in Vichy reflected their deep aspirations. Everyone felt that a conflict intended to restore liberties and democracy was inevitable. Hence General de Gaulle was pushed toward politics, the Republicans, and the idea of a social revolution.

Russia's entry into the war did away with the qualms of the revolutionary forces and those workers for whom Stalin still symbolized emancipation. Not the least paradox of this war was the fact that one of the most oppressive regimes in the world was in a position to stimulate the struggle of the masses for liberty. National independence was the first of the liberties to be recovered. That objective explains better than any other ideological consideration the attraction of Russia. The Marxists of western Europe, accustomed to enjoying these benefits, had forgotten that national sentiment had raised redoubtable forces whose goals were different from those they attributed to the class struggle. De Gaulle knew this better than anyone; but he also saw that in France class-consciousness could either strengthen or weaken patriotism, depending on whether one focused on the people or the ruling classes. He still hesitated to come out in favor of the Republic. He realized that while almost all the *résistants* were ready to die in order to overthrow Pétain's reactionary monarchy, barely one of them would have lifted a finger to enthrone the forty-first king of France. The intellectual and moral effort required to overcome his qualms was virtually an abjuration. His torments were sensed in France and interfered with the spread of Gaullism. De Gaulle wore a kepi, which the people did not regard as a sign of political intelligence or the spirit of democracy.

I imagine that this solitary man had to settle a number of conflicts between the tradition that had shaped him and the person he had become. He was aware that to found a new tradition he would have to use elements he had been taught to despise. The General's destiny was to become the president of a sort of Committee of Public Safety. He reestablished in his majesty the Declaration of Human Rights and on these premises rebuilt a state of which he would be king. Three —Robespierre, Bonaparte, and Louis-Philippe—haunted him for thirty years. He had to exorcise all three of them. Like Robespierre and Bonaparte, he loved power and the state, but not the disorder or order established by others. Like them, he preferred a storm to everything else. This austere moralist, whom certain Frenchmen would one day regard as a kind of regicide, shared Robespierre's need to find a simple hermitage that nothing would trouble, where he could isolate himself in retirement or sulk after an outburst. Like any member of the National Convention, he favored a constitution and laws, but not of ramshackle construction. Like Bonaparte, he cherished grand plans and blew up over quarrels. He fought any temptation to be a dictator. He feared that he would end up like Louis-Philippe, though he made sure to lean upon the notables. His final battle, which he lost, was waged to correct the image that the rebels of May 1968 wanted to make of his old age.

Nothing better illustrates that great man's contradictions than one phrase he uttered during his famous passage down the Champs-Elysées on August 25, 1944. "Here is . . . the Louvre, where the continuity of the kings succeeded in building France." This may be a discreet tribute to juvenile enthusiasms. But what a blunder! The Louvre is an example of discontinuity of spirit and continuity of expense. Charles V's castle was razed, the Renaissance was continued through a classic colonnade, and construction was abandoned in favor of Versailles. The final result: a pastiche!

In 1942, the domestic Resistance was large and well-organized enough to operate a secret press. Its declarations were well distributed within the kingdom of Vichy, but rarer and less widely read within the occupied zone. A statement by General de Gaulle, published in June 1942, specified the war aims of a fighting France. I remarked on the use of the slogan "Liberty, Equality, Fraternity," and the new idea expressed in the formula "As long as they [the people] subscribe to victory, they will gather for the revolution." But there were complaints in my circles that the word "republic" did not figure in the declaration. It was because De Gaulle represented democracy and Socialism that he gained the support of the left wing all around the world. He won popular support in France. The progressives joined him because they felt he would go fairly far along the road of reforms, the moderates because they understood that he would not wreck society. The Saint-Cyrian regretted that he had to prepare to bury the part of Vichy's legislation that was inspired by the Action Française economists, by the admirers of Italian Fascism, and the priests. But the rebel was about to foment a national insurrection, use Lenin's and Trotsky's methods to destroy a state, and complete the work of the Popular Front.

After *Le Grand Ordinaire* came out during spring 1943, I suddenly felt dead tired. The doctor prescribed rest. I chose the Department of Orne, where I had already sent several young men who didn't want to go to Germany. I settled in Mortagne, an area far away from the war. There were no Germans around, and there was white bread in the bakeries and an absolute scorn for the food agencies, with their inspections and rationing stamps. Since the farms needed manpower, they were glad to get young people from towns who, in turn, were happy to be sheltered and fed. Several other Parisians had come to the hotel for a rest. The most curious guest was a thin, rather tall man, no longer young. He was a grandson of Alexandre Dumas, and his name was Alexandre Lippmann. A former Olympic champion in saber or sword, an untalented watercolorist, a first-rate bridge player, he had an inexhaustible store of anecdotes about the brothels of the 1920's.

The undulating countryside was very beautiful, with hedge-lined fields intersected by small woods and horizons filled with great forests. I was obsessed with the idea of the *maquis,* the French underground. It was forming everywhere in France, and some of its people were in Orne. New ones came to me every month. I didn't ask anything in exchange, but I didn't hide the fact that I might need them very soon.

After two months of relaxation, I was in a better state. My doctor said I could do some bike riding. I tried to make contact with some people in the underground. I got to know Mulot, railroad worker from the Mortagne station, who belonged to the Railroad Resistance. Able and resolute, he was more than eager to participate in activities more violent than petty direction giving. I talked with him about men I had sent into the area. Mulot showed me two maps of a good portion of the department. One suggested destruction on the railroads, the other indicated how demolition and ambushes on the roads would slow down tank movements. Mulot's plan was very thorough. He knew where the explosives should be placed and had calculated the amounts necessary. But he had no manpower. Together we checked out certain parts of his project. Because of the number of objects to be destroyed, we studied alternatives.

Orne, which had been unoccupied, suddenly filled up with **Wehrmacht** units that had been brought back from Russia. They were reinforced with young recruits to whom the veterans were teaching their trade. I decided to join my Parisians and form a few small groups, with Mulot adding some Normans, to carry out some minor propaganda assignments. I went to Paris and, using a false name, sent a box of underground newspapers to Mortagne.

Our men turned out to be quite capable. I worked out a few orientation and reconnoitering exercises within a radius of fifty kilometers. By the time autumn interrupted those maneuvers, we had a good dozen scouts. After I returned to Paris in October 1943, I went to Orne three times a month, using food as a pretext. In Paris I joined the little group that put out the newspaper *Libertés.* Most of them were former editors of *Que Faire.* The kingpin was a typographer who had once belonged to the Communist Party. His name was Rimbert, and he was as simple and as courageous as he was intelligent. We had liaisons with *Franc-Tireur,* where Ferrat was working, and handled the distribution of that paper in Paris. Rimbert was a typesetter in the shop that printed the German weekly of Paris. There, under the very noses of the Nazis, he composed and printed *Libertés*. In early 1944, he was very nearly caught in the act by the Gestapo, who recognized the paper stock used for the Hitlerian news. He had to escape through a window at the very moment that the Germans were entering.

We resumed the discussions of 1939. We decided to work out a plan for the political unification of the workers' parties. First we would publish a manifesto explaining our intentions, then follow it up with a program. Rimbert set greater store by this than anyone else. "The Communist Party," he said, "has abandoned all propaganda for the traditional objectives of the proletarian revolution. It's limiting itself to a kind of sacred union for the liberation of the country. We are faced with a new, slightly more radical version of what the Popular Front wanted, or what it could easily have accomplished." Rimbert had always been the "leftist" in our group. An uncompromising Marxist and Leninist, he wanted to go all the way with the general line that we had defined in 1940. I didn't belive that we could reach the point of a revolution like Russia's. "We're moving," I argued, "toward coalition governments. Is there any need to harp on reforms that can't be realized because of both the political and the economic situation of the country?"

The discussion grew very lively when it touched on the colonies. Rimbert, loyal to the Comintern of the great era, demanded immediate recognition of their independence. "What does their independence mean in 1944?" I objected. "It's because of these colonies that the Republic has been able to enter the war."

I wrote out a draft for the manifesto. The first part was an indictment of Vichy. The second was the minimum program of a labor government. The third was an outline of the political emancipation of the colonial people within the context of France as a whole. Rimbert kept the first two-thirds of my text but replaced my views on the colonies with a proclamation of their independence. This document never reached the First Army, where it would undoubtedly have had a disastrous effect.

Léo Hamon, newly arrived from the southern zone, joined the *Libertés* group. He had done a lot of work in the resistance movements of the so-called free zone since their establishment. Small and dressed like a worker, with his nails chewed and his pockets crammed with papers and magazines, he was so active that he seemed to be everywhere at once. Serious and a good organizer, he had excellent contacts with everyone who was to play a leading role in the first few months after the liberation of Paris.

Libertés was absorbed by Ceux de la Résistance (Those in the Resistance), one of the main movements in the northern zone, which was striving for a position in Greater Paris. Its president, Lecomte-Boinet (Mathieu) was a gentle man, heroic and timorous at once. I know that he has written his war memoirs. This splendid observer, with a strong sense of humor, a conservative who strayed into the Revolution, has probably written an excellent book. Ceux de la Résistance had done an enormous amount of useful work along the coasts in Normandy, in Seine-et-Marne, in Marne, in Lorraine, in Burgundy, and even in Luxemburg. Active underground groups, large and fairly well-armed, had begun to interfere with the communication routes of the Germans in 1943. The losses were always heavy, but the results were especially spectacular at the time of the landing in Normandy and throughout the battle. The tracks of the eastern railway network were cut again and again. Attacks on the trains delayed the delivery of supplies and reinforcements, providing the Allies with assistance equivalent to two extra divisions on the battlefield.

The Parisian chapter of Ceux de la Résistance first assembled around Bourdeau de Fontenay. We brought together all the scattered groups that had been kept more or less alive for the last three years. When Bourdeau de Fontenay was named Regional Commissar of the Republic in Rouen on January 10, 1944, he was replaced by Léo Hamon, who within a few months managed to expand the organization so that it became one of the chief Resistance forces in the Paris area at the Liberation. Many Socialists joined the organization. The most picturesque left-winger was Pierre Stibbe. Ugly as a scarecrow, tall and thin, with the fiery gaze and sonorous voice of an anathematizing prophet, Stibbe, a courtroom lawyer, always wore an enormously checkered tweed jacket. It was so extraordinarily loud that it was easy to recognize. He never took any precautions. In the subway, he would talk loudly about anything, as though no one were listening. After you left him, he would stick his head through the window before the train got under way again and shout out a last goodbye from twenty yards away, mentioning the precise time and place of your next meeting. Although he was afraid, he withstood every difficulty and never caused any arrests. Throughout his life, he remained a nervous leftist, tortured by the fear of staining his pure soul.

Once during the spring of 1944, after a friendly and harmless get-together, we were about to part when Stibbe, as usual, clearly and specifically mentioned the work I was doing. I was with Monique, to whom I had said nothing about my activities. I couldn't hide anything after that. "You know everything," I told her. "It would be better if you joined us. I need a liaison like you." Monique accepted immediately; she was very adroit. Since she didn't look the least bit militant, she was very useful. Taciturn and discreet, she knew how to discourage questions by opening her eyes wide in astonishment, so that the other person was forced to think of something else. Each of the principal agents of Ceux de la Résistance had a young woman as a liaison agent. The person in charge of them was a left-wing intellectual, devoted, punctual, and a bit bohemian; her name was Jeanne Mathieu. The girls met almost every day in different squares or parks. They knew each other only by first names. Amid pointless gossip, they would exchange the instructions and information that their bosses needed. They wrote down as little as possible, memorizing everything they heard. Then they would return to their men, as they might have gone to their boyfriends, which was often the case.

In August 1944, this regional organization covered Paris, the Seine, and the adjacent departments. The military leader of Ceux de la Résistance was Vaillant (Jean de Voguë), who had been in the resistance from the very start; he came from *Combat*, and his entire family had hurled themselves into the battle. A slender man of about forty-five, with hard features, he looked very distinguished and cold. He had been a naval officer and is still an unrivaled navigator. But he resigned from the navy when he was a lieutenant commander and devoted himself to the sugar industry. Endowed with a highly curious mind and terribly introverted, he could be selfish and nasty. But he was the best friend in the world. He had a sailor's love of adventure and the mute dialogues between man and space; an aristocrat's horror of a certain vulgarity and need for hierarchy, good manners, cliquishness, and haughtiness; and an industrialist's sense of efficiency and cost. During the Resistance, he had been seduced by the selflessness and courage of the Communists. He would join anyone who flattered him a bit, and he could overlook anything as long as his contacts knew how to utilize the panic that sometimes overcomes a lone man. General de Gaulle hated him and refused to use him.

In January 1944 the National Resistance Council created a Military Action Committee; its counselor was General Revers. France was divided into regions designated by the letters of the alphabet. Each region was headed by a colonel. The designation of these regional commanders was a bit haphazard; it depended mainly on the action of the Gestapo. A military chief usually survived for three months at most, before he was arrested by the enemy, shot, or sent to a concentration camp. The replacements were never chosen as carefully as the initial nominees. Certain disappearances were inadequately explained, and the frequency of Communist "replacements" was totally out of proportion to the activities and manpower of the Party as of 1944.

The Domestic French Forces were granted legal status only on June 3, 1944. The underground organizations and combat groups were generally arms of the resistance movements. There were also the Secret Army and the Snipers and Partisans (F.T.P.), a Communist group. The unification of all these forces, for both operational and logistical reasons, became essential as soon as they were able to liberate, even if only temporarily, certain parts of the national territory. It became urgent when the Allies were fighting in France. But this unification wasn't easy. Several units maintained their autonomy until after the Liberation.

Early in March 1944, I gave Vaillant an account of the state of the organizations in Orne. I was still sending young men there who didn't want to go to Germany. Almost all of them were of modest background and come from insignificant neighborhoods. Whereas in the summer of 1943 my recruits had shown no particular enthusiasm when they declared themselves ready to take part in resistance acts (though they did in fact participate), those who joined in 1944 were resolved to fight. I had obtained precise information about the weapons received and stocked in Orne. There was talk of seventeen tons.

"We've got to get those weapons out of the depots," Vaillant said. "Arm some combat groups and form an underground. Some of our comrades are afraid to arm the Resistance. They're waiting for orders, which may very well come too late. I'll help you. You can expect the Allied landing to take place between May 1 and June 15; there will be a beachhead in Normandy. The strategic location of Orne is excellent." I had a force ready within a week. But as soon as those young men were formed into regiments, they would have to be fed. We worked out the budget problem with Vaillant, and the money was left with old Socialist Party comrades in Paris, people I trusted. For treasurer, I chose Mortagne's bailiff, who traveled around a good deal and who could receive both visitors and sums of money in the course of his work.

I got hold of dressings, sulfa drugs, and enough material for a good field pharmacy. I also assigned a young instructor named Denis, who knew how to use a Sten automatic and German hand grenades. I sent him to Mulot, and a few days later I was at the Mortagne depot to see how things were going. The young men were enthusiastic and were armed immediately. The weapons were hidden in a barely discernible hole in the ground. This operation claimed the lives of two overly curious Germans. Mulot informed me that an Australian aviator, the sole survivor of a bomber crew, had been provisionally assigned to the *maquis* as an instructor. Young Denis didn't quite fit the bill; they were keeping him in reserve in Mortagne, where his girl friend had joined him. I didn't like that at all.

I went to see my men. My work in Paris was absorbing me more and more, and I was getting worried about the command of the operation. The simplest solution would have been to find some local person. But Mulot couldn't get any of the many ex-officers in the area, who were presumably anti-German, to resume active service.

That May was very sunny in Mortagne. An armored S.S. division (Hitlerjugend) was billeted in the area. There were black uniforms everywhere. The roads were furrowed by armored vehicles, and here and there drill detachments were doing real shooting, which turned out to be very fortunate. Mulot took me to the underground barracks. After several miles along the roads which the Hitlerjugend couriers were cruising, we crossed a field and left our bicycles in a small wood. On the other side of the wood, slightly lower, stood a rather large isolated house. A dozen yards away, on the enclosing wall, there were field defenses, with gun slits. An armed sentinel was posted at the door. In the meadow, a half-dozen armed young men were drilling like cadets, under the command of a sandy-haired man who ordered them around in English. The S.S. vehicles were driving down a road less than five hundred yards from the house.

I gave our men a good bawling out. I ordered them to go indoors, camouflage the battlements, station sentinels in the bushes, and make up their packs. "You," I said to the Australian, "the only risk you're running is an officers' POW camp. But if the others are caught, they'll be shot. Evacuate the barracks in three distinct groups. Six miles from here you'll reach a base that some of you know."

Mulot had been responsible for that absurd performance. But he finally understood. That very evening, the bailiff of Mortagne reported that he had received a visit from the mayor of a tiny hamlet less than half a mile from the farm we had visited. "A group of *résistants* are practicing their shooting every morning within my parish," the mayor had complained. "I don't want my houses burned down and my villagers shot. If they're still there in twenty-four hours, I'll denounce them to the German commandant!" At the very least, the organization I had set up wasn't very secret!

We urgently needed a firm command. The episode with the Australian had had one benefit: all the men knew how to use machine guns. We couldn't let these young men remain idle. I told Mulot to blow up some electric-power lines. The objectives were to be within one or two hours' march from the quarters. The men were to move at night in groups of three, and they were not to stay in the same hiding place more than five days. Finally, without even waiting for the requested officer, we spread the men around the countryside in groups of six. We could then call them together whenever we had to.

I had designated Noël, a tall blond man, serious and resolute, to head the group. Around May 20, I was astonished to find Noël in my office at France Mutualiste. He was worried about the lack of action, which weighed heavily on the group, and he complained a lot about Denis. "You can kill some Germans," I said. "But the very first time you do it, they'll take blind revenge on the peasants. Up till now, Normandy has been a paradise, far from the war. Won't the population turn against you after the first massacres? But I must admit that such inactivity is bad for the cohesion and valor of the group. Why don't you stage a small ambush, but far away from your zone? I'll let you be the judge.

"As for Denis, I can see that his presence in Mortagne is a nuisance now. Take him into some operation and kill him. But don't leave any evidence of his identity on his corpse. His girlfriend will raise a row. If she carries it too far, go to bed with her. In any case," I added, "the Allied landing isn't too far off. The officer I asked for has already been announced. [He never came.] As soon as you start an operation, don't let anything stop you. Personally, I favor your breaking up into little groups. If things become too hot for you, get back to Paris."

On June 3, Denis was in Paris, complaining about everything. He claimed that the alarm messages had already been intercepted. According to conventions, this meant that the operation we had been waiting for so long would take place within five days. I still didn't have an officer to lead the groups. My work in Paris was completed, so if the landing took place in mid-June, I could spend a month in Normandy. I had become a permanent member of Ceux de la Résistance, receiving a monthly salary. I made an appointment to meet Denis in a café on June 6 at 7 A.M. We would bike out to Mortagne together. Although my military knowledge was very weak, I had decided, because there was no one any better, to take over the command of the *maquis* groups. I told Monqiue that I was only going to get things started. "I'll be back before two weeks are up. But I want to bring back some weapons. I'll return with four or five well-trained men, automatic pistols, and explosive gelatin for Paris. I'd like to find some abandoned house to use as a relay station."

On June 5, Monique and I found the house I was looking for. I think it was in Chevreuse. On the way back, in Massy-Palaiseau, next to the still undamaged railroad station, we were caught in an air raid. "We'll never get out of this alive," I thought, and I started running. Monique, as I had always told her, threw herself down immediately. Some ten yards away, I found myself on my belly, with a terrible pain in my kidneys. It felt as though I had been sliced in two. I was sure I was about to die! I looked up at the sky and thought, "Too bad." But since death didn't come, I felt my kidneys with my right hand. There was no blood. I could move my legs. I noticed that my left hand was in a strange position in front of my nose. My left arm was broken. I picked up my hand. It hurt very badly, but it still hung together. I stood up. Then a second squadron started hurling bombs, and I threw myself down, my left hand dangling about. The pain was very sharp. I got up again. The squadrons kept coming. "Too bad," I thought. "It hurts too much. I'm not lying down any more."

In the first period of whistling, you felt directly involved. During the last few seconds, you felt a sort of iron curtain unrolling over you and sliding toward the point of explosion. The bombs were now dropping a bit further away. I managed to get to a small house whose walls were trembling. Two German soldiers who were greener than their uniforms had taken refuge there. They were supposed to be the targets! I went to the nearest hospital. They bandaged me up and gave me an injection.

Monique and I got back to Paris on a vegetable truck. I went to a Resistance doctor. "Major fracture of the left arm. Tomorrow morning you're going to the hospital."

"But they're waiting for me in Mortagne!"

The next morning I was in surgery. After twenty-four hours of observation, they opened up twelve inches of my left arm, and stuck me in an enormous plaster cast that I had to keep on for three weeks. The landing had taken place. I was deeply moved by the thought of the *maquisards* in action. I saw them covered with glory.

They put me in a room with a man the militia had wanted to arrest. He had got a burst of machine-gun fire in the stomach. His room was guarded day and night. The young hero died after forty-eight hours. This incident, more than the landing itself, made me realize that the nurses were for De Gaulle and that the surgeon was in very good spirits.

Around June 20, I was visited by a liaison agent I had met in Mulot's office. I knew that people were suspicious of him and that the Railroad Resistance had transferred him. My suspicions were instantly confirmed.

"I'm isolated, and I want to get back into the Resistance. I can't go back to the West because of certain things that happened there."

"You're knocking at the wrong door," I said. "You can see what condition I'm in. How did you manage to find me anyway?"

"Through France Mutualiste. I dropped by your office."

I pretended to be indignant. "What? You still don't understand what *their* liberation means? No one asked them to destroy the city of Caen, or Lisieux, or to smash up my arm and nearly kill me!" And so on. I was extremely vehement and violent. But the traitor listening to me, slightly taken aback, was annoyed only about the reward he had been promised.

"But you sent crates and an instructor to Mortagne."

"Crates? Yeah, medicines. They can be useful. An instructor for what? For tasting cheese probably! I won't deny that for a while I really believed their bullshit. But now I can see what came of it! So don't count on me any more."

"But I can't go on alone. I need money or leaflets or newspapers."

"Money!" I said. "All I ever had was my salary. And now, thanks to those creeps, I'll have to pay a hospital bill. Leaflets? If I found one, I'd burn it." I didn't know how to get rid of that pushy guy. I gave him the address of a girl in my office, a sort of a nun, who supported the Marshal and could think of nothing but God. He left.

I took my nurse aside. "I'm leaving tomorrow. That guy you just saw probably works for the Gestapo. Let me see the surgeon as soon as possible." The young intern realized I had the best reasons in the world for wanting to get out of the hospital.

Something had happened in Mortagne, but for the moment it was better not to try and find out what. With my plaster cast, I was pretty obvious. I decided not to do anything else. I tried to find a place to stay, but nobody would take me in. One of my cousins, who spoke against the Germans all the time, wouldn't even offer me a single night's hospitality. I went home to Avenue Simon-Bolivar. I preferred to spend the night out and went to my office every now and then. I acted the convalescent. As soon as I could move my arm, I resumed my activities. I was closely watched. A stocky man, honest-looking and calm, with a small black mustache, sometimes sat in front of my place for hours on end. If he came to the the small bar where I met Monique, I would kiss her even more tenderly when he was at the next table. I used every known stratagem to shake him off whenever I thought it necessary.

One July morning, I met a police sergeant on the Métro. I knew he had Socialist sympathies. "There's a Gestapo agent on board," he told me. It was my shadow with the mustache. "He comes to the precinct house a lot." I knew enough now. The joke had gone on too long. I jumped off the moving train and didn't go back home until after August 19.

It wasn't so easy to find places to stay. Furnished with a false I.D. card, I took refuge in hotels. I was checked twice. Everything was in order. Thanks to my nurse, I finally found a safe haven with a Security Commissioner on Rue Saint-Gilles.

After the Liberation, Denis came to Paris. Mortagne's organization had been destroyed. The men had been captured. All of them, including Mulot, had been shot on June 30 near Alençon.

As soon as I could, I sent Denis to Mortagne. Then I asked the police to question him thoroughly. I started an inquiry. They sent me an informer who had tried to blackmail the family of one of the executed men. But I didn't get very far.

The whole story finally came out a few months later. One evening in December 1944, an Algerian, Ahmed ben Mohammed, had come to the office of Ceux de la Résistance on Avenue des Champs-Elysées. A junior officer in the infantry, he had been captured in Sedan but had managed to escape. Around May 25, he had joined our group. Captured and sentenced to death like the others, he had been taken to the place of execution. He had witnessed the death of his comrades.

When his turn came, he was told that his sentence was commuted because he was North African and a career soldier; he would be deported to Germany. Luckily for him, his convoy was attacked by planes. He escaped once again.

He wanted to find me and tell me the whole story. The one who had sold them out was a Frenchman who had been mobilized for forced labor but had escaped. After the Germans had arrested him as a black-marketeer, he was sentenced and shipped back to Germany. But he managed to get away. When he was rearrested, he was offered a choice: deportation to a German concentration camp or working for the Germans. When my friends began forming the group, he got wind of it. He had finally hit upon a way of not going back to Germany. He presented himself as a volunteer. He didn't know very much; only that there were sessions of gun practice in Mortagne. That, unfortunately, was enough to kill fifteen men! Apparently young Denis had not been a provocateur. Nobody had been interested in getting me back to Mortagne, where I could be arrested, between June 1 and 5. Shadowing me in Paris was probably supposed to be more profitable.

I have often thought about that unhappy affair, which shows so many errors in thinking and execution. The Breton underground revealed how effective partisan operations could be provided that there were enough arms and, especially, qualified leaders. In Orne, the *maquisards* had operated in a highly concentrated military zone. Even though the terrain lends itself to guerrilla warfare, the underground groups would almost certainly be destroyed in short order unless they were extremely mobile. But that presupposed training, leadership, and logistics, all of which we totally lacked. There were two contradictory possibilities: on the one hand, immediate action would arouse retaliations but would also get the fighters hardened to war; on the other hand, action against an enemy already demoralized by defeat would have been very profitable in the month of August but waiting until August would have created a phony-war atmosphere. While the Germans were withdrawing, the armed Resistance of Orne added to their confusion by stepping up guerrilla actions better suited to their means and to the general situation than I had foreseen in the month of May. The Germans were apparently amazed at the size of the armaments that our unfortunate comrades had at their disposal.

The preparations for a Parisian insurrection had both a political and a military character. For the political action, we set up something like soviets, which were supposed to seize power. These Committees of

Liberation had not been elected, and their version of the Resistance gave the lion's share to the Communists. The secret Liberation Committee was theoretically the supreme authority, sharing power with the prefect in administrative matters. But during the agitation and preparation for the uprising, it was the sole master, exercising power in the name of the Provisional Government of the Republic. Most of the members of the National Resistance Council were in Paris, which made for interference with the actions of the Paris Committee, especially since personal ambitions were coming into play.

The Seine Department was divided into four sectors under separate commands. There were 10,000 men in the Domestic French Forces on August 19. They had four machine guns, twenty Lewis guns, eighty automatic pistols, about a hundred rifles, and six hundred revolvers. Thus only one out of every six soldiers was armed. The Patriotic Militias constituted by the Liberation Committees added up to less than 1,500 men, most of them in the factories. By the end of the uprising, they included as many as 30,000 men and women. By August 27, their weapons, almost nonexistent on August 19, included hundreds of arms of all sorts taken from the Germans. The Paris police were the backbone of the insurrection. They numbered some 12,000 men, each armed with an automatic weapon, and they had a good stock of ammunition. Aabout two hundred Republican Guards assisted the garrisons, especially in City Hall, or assured the occupation of the ministries or public services.

The coordination of all these elements was very lax. Most of the time, each fought on his own and in his own sector. The northern half of Ceux de la Résistance of Paris fell into my hands. But this was merely a name on an organization chart.

I tried to draw up a general plan for the insurrection. Control of the canals and the railroads would create a sort of partitioning meant to prevent the Germans from maneuvering. In imitation of the Germans, I wanted to use survey points in the sewers as firing positions by surrounding the entrances with sacks of earth. I figured out how many guns I needed. The number was impressive. My requests for weapons, like those of the other *résistants* in Paris, were never followed up. Perhaps they never even reached their destinations!

After August 10, everything moved very fast. The fear of a Paris uprising took hold of a good part of the "bourgeoisie," who, nourished on the history of France, hoped, as they had in 1871 and 1940, to salvage, above everything else, a reactionary social order that was far less profitable to them than they thought. The Resistance people attached to structures and hierarchies, whether Socialists or conservatives, were just as infected. They refused to make an intelligent analysis of the ratios of forces and the political objectives. The old Communist bugbear was evoked. "You know the Party so well," Léo Hamon said to me at one of the last meetings of the secret committee of Ceux de la Résistance, "and you're in contact with its militants. What do you think of the following hypothesis? The Germans will have been driven out, the leaders of the Resistance will be in the City Hall, and the square will be black with people. Marrane will appear at the window and proclaim the Commune."

I burst out laughing. "That reminds me of the way the National Convention invoked the ancient Romans. You have no idea how weak the Communist organizations are numerically and how limited their influence is. But you're doing everything to increase their power by giving them positions. You're being taken in by the sustained pressure of the Communists. You're letting yourselves be victimized by their wiles and their sense of organization. You've already given them a majority in the secret committees. This doesn't correspond to the political opinions of the population.

"I'm really terrified by the flimsiness of the Communist organizations in the precincts I know best. There can't be more than five thousand Party members throughout Greater Paris. Whether they stay put or increase depends on you, on us, on the Provisional Government. If the throng gathers on City Hall Square in a few days, it will be ninety percent non-Communist. Don't fabricate a danger that doesn't exist today, but could come true tomorrow, if they steal a march on us. For the Parisians, the Resistance is General de Gaulle. The General will be acclaimed. The Communists gain importance only when others resign and you agree to put in office the political leaders of a possible Stalinist insurrection."

We had more and more contacts with the Resistance workers in the Paris police. It was a police officer who taught me how to steal bicycles. We were drinking on a café terrace in front of the Stock Exchange. "Nothing could be easier," he said. "There's one right in front of you. Take it. It has no lock, and its owner just went into the house next door. Hurry up!" I didn't have the nerve. We walked toward the Comic Opera. A cyclist went into a bank after leaning his bike against the entrance bars. "Go ahead," said my friend. "The guard is looking the other way." It was very easy. A bit later, I needed a good many bikes, and I mounted a few operations near black-market restaurants. The chains didn't resist good wire cutters. Poetic justice: a superb bicycle, the first one I had stolen, which I held on to like a fetish, was stolen from me in January 1945 while I was dining at the Catalan.

The head of the Liberation Committee of the nineteenth arrondissement was a history teacher, Pioro. A bit solemn, he was a bon vivant, interested in modern art, fond of sex, and indefatigably attached to the Communist Party. Marcel Bour, the delegate of the Civil and Military Organization, was, along with Pioro, one of the most likable persons on the Committee. A former student of the Central School, he owned a small cable shop on Rue des Annelets, just above Belleville. He employed some forty workers. He and his wife managed the place, which was one of the dozens of small industries scattered throughout that neighborhood of ill-proportioned lofts and small houses. Rue des Annelets was our secret Communist cell. You could get out of it easily, and an unexpected visit from the Gestapo would never have surprised us. But Bour, Pioro, and I had nothing against living well, and we often met for lunch at the Pavillon du Lac, one of the three restaurants inside Buttes-Chaumont, in the shade of age-old trees. Opposite us, a suspension bridge led to sheer rock surmounted by a replica of the Sibylline temple of Tivoli. The restaurant owner, old Latour, didn't like the Germans or rationing. Throughout 1944, he was able to serve us decent meals with excellent wines that had been bought before 1939.

In August 1944, I was in charge of some fifty men in the nineteenth arrondissement—more people, probably, than in any Communist cell. There were former Communists among them, and they rejoined the Party in late 1944, when it looked as though the Resistance movements had no political future. Vast lofts and warehouses contained gas masks, hundreds of steel helmets, fatigues, uniforms, and plenty of tools (shovels, pickaxes, picks, etc.). The workers constructed a lot of three-dimensional swastikas from thick iron wire. One of their sharp points always stuck up, no matter how the thing hit the ground. They were very effective against tires.

I inherited a mounted orderly with an enormous black motorcycle. He was a fairly well-known tap dancer and had all the German papers he needed to run his machine. I wondered whether his marvelous bike hadn't come straight from the militia. His brother joined us on August 19.

On August 12, the railroad workers went out on strike. On August

14, the Parisian Liberation Committee decided on an all-out strike. The order was given on August 16. All services except those involving water and hospitals stopped work. On August 15, the police, threatened with disarmament by the Germans, also struck. The Republican Guard declared iself neutral, except for two hundred men who rallied to a fighting France. There was always negotiating and discussing to do. The battle was led by a multitude of local commands, some of which were improvised. On August 17, around 6 P.M., I was riding across Paris on the back seat of the superb motorcycle (on which I considered myself invulnerable), trying to get to the terrace of the Deux Magots, where Monique was waiting for me with reports from several colleagues. My bags were full of armbands with the stamp of the F.F.I. (Domestic French Forces) and some two dozen swastikas for puncturing tires. Along Boulevard Saint-Germain, beneath the trees that lined the sidewalk, there was a long line of Wehrmacht trucks. I threw a few loads of swastikas under the vehicles and asked my driver to step on the gas. That was my only brilliant feat of arms. I went to pick up a shipment of posters announcing the insurrection. They were up on the walls of Paris that very same night.

On August 18, early in the morning, the last meeting of the secret regional committee took place in the seventeenth arrondissement. Hamon notified us of the insurrection order for the next day. The City Hall and the municipal offices were to be occupied by noon on August 19. Within our respective sectors, each of us was to supervise the seizure of essential factories and power stations and organize the defense of these strongholds. There were hardly any weapons; during the night small commando actions against isolated Germans by the workers and the *résistants* occupying the factories put some rifles in our hands.

The city was quieter than any countryside. It was a stony silence, interrupted only by the noise of shooting. The firing was sporadic but ubiquitous. Early on August 19, I took my motorcycle and toured the "bases" of the tenth, nineteenth, and twentieth. The streets were deserted, and traffic was easy, except around Place de la République. At about 11 A.M., with our bands on our arms and wearing, I think, sashes that Madame Bour had made, Pioro, I, and three buddies entered the office of the mayor of the nineteenth arrondissement. I had my revolver in my hand; two policemen were covering us from a distance. "In the name of the government of the French Republic, we hereby take possession of this office. Monsieur, you are removed from office. Please go home." I don't know whether that solemn sentence was addressed to the Vichy-appointed official by Pioro, who tended to be a bit timid on grand occasions, or by me. Pioro took command of the entire staff. No sooner were we installed than the slightly abashed clerk notified us that a young couple was waiting. Their marriage had been scheduled for August 19. The national uprising didn't apply to weddings. We all went into the Marriage Chambers. Pioro read the sacramental formula. He was deeply moved. This romantic episode was just the right thing for a man who thrived on historical anecdotes.

Everything had gone very well. But the Germans were beginning to plague the Prefecture of Police. Some of the policemen of the nineteenth arrondissement left for the Cité, the center of town, as reinforcements or to repel counterattacks. We held a short meeting with Charles Bour, the commander of the F.F.I., and his chief companions. They had installed themselves on Rue Tandou. Their morale was confused. As soldiers, they were there to fight, but their weapons consisted of two or three rifles and a half-dozen revolvers.

Two black cars with front-wheel drives brought us a group of *résistants* that refused to obey anyone except, at a pinch, the Communist Party. There were seven or eight of them, all students, including a rather pretty girl; they had two automatic pistols, rifles, and revolvers. Feeling very superior because of their weapons, proud of being Communists (the future of the world) and even prouder of being very young, they disdained sedentary resistance and immediately set up a military operation. But the only serious force was the precinct policemen. They were all armed with pistols, but they had no rifles, hand grenades, or automatic pistols. On August 19, the three brigades were complete. But we had to get as many men as possible to the Cité, which the Germans were attacking. So all we had left were a few policemen in civilian clothes. We did have means of transportation, however: the police vans and the police chief's car. The municipal building had a well-equipped first-aid station. It was in the hands of fine men, Vichyites who were hostile to the Resistance, especially to the far left, but who didn't spare their efforts or their devotion.

Our immediate adversaries were the convoys of Germans retreating northeastward along Rue de Flandre and Avenue Jean-Jaurès. The police had begun to attack them, but only sporadically. Toward the south, on the edge of the precinct, Gare du Nord and the warehouses on Quai de Valmy housed small German garrisons, approximately the size of two companies, equipped with a few French tanks from 1940.

Villette station, five hundred yards away, was occupied by about a hundred Germans. A small train bristling with guns shuttled between Pantin and the nineteenth arrondissement.

Communications were easy. The telephones worked better than they do today. Things got worse in the afternoon. Besides rather serious attacks against the Prefecture of Police and the barricades of the Latin Quarter, the Germans laid siege to the municipal halls of the twentieth arrondissement and Neuilly. The Resistance had to evacuate them. The enemy fire was fairly slack, but their strength was such that our comrades were well advised not to put it to a test. On the other hand, the Germans were repulsed from the Prefecture of Police and the Latin Quarter.

At dawn on August 20, left-wing Franc-Tireur-Partisans (F.T.P.) killed one of the sentinels at Villette station. In reprisal, machine-gun bullets came whistling toward Place Armand Carrel, but far too high. I had settled in the Hôtel du Parc, a former nest of the Feld-Gendarmes, so that we could join the return fire, if we had weapons. The Feld-Gendarmes returned and fired their rifles into the elevator cage. A wild flight. We were very scared. We ran across the roofs into an adjacent house. Our panic was pitiful. The Feld-Gendarmes left again. I was not very proud of myself.

In the municipal building, the atmosphere was gloomy. We brought the French flag. "The essential thing," I said, "is that we go on occupying places and attacking Germans wherever we can." Considering our equipment, my words elicited ironic exclamations. With a rumble of motors, two tanks and a few armored vehicles filed past the building. I compassionately felt my revolver in my pocket; it was probably the only weapon protecting the dozen people in the mayor's office. Two policemen came in. We agreed on what to do in case of attack. Those with weapons would try to contain the assault by defending the main staircase. We would build a small barricade with furniture and filing cabinets in the hall at the bottom of the stairs, soak the whole thing in gasoline, set fire to it, and try to escape through the sewers. The tanks rolled slowly around Place Armand Carrel and then rumbled away.

A call from City Hall informed me that a truce had been concluded. The insurrection was going very badly. Our garrison of policemen withdrew following appeals from the Cité. Bour, Pioro, and I got over to Rue des Annelets. I called Monique in City Hall. She gave me very precise data on the truce. Things still weren't very clear.

Fighting was continuing on the Left Bank, but the cease-fire had been sounded at City Hall. Monique added that at City Hall and the Prefecture of Police, they were starting to worry about the lack of ammunition. "I envy you," I said. "Here we don't have any weapons."

Much has been written about the truce announced by the loudspeakers on the municipal police cars. It was negotiated by Parodi. The Prefect of Police and his entourage went along with it despite the hostility of some of the policemen. The Germans agreed to cease their attacks on the public buildings occupied by the Resistance; in return, the *résistants* were to stop their skirmishes against the Germans. The military forces of the Resistance could stay in their positions, but they were not to construct any new barricades. Two withdrawal routes were conceded to the German army. The truce was effective until August 23.

To cut a long story short, the Parisian Liberation Committee was deeply hostile to the agreements that had been reached. Some of the men advocating the truce feared a popular victory more than any reprisals. This opinion eventually won over several of the *résistants*. All those who were afraid of a Communist success failed to realize that, by refusing to direct the insurrection, they were actually giving the Communist Party, at little cost, the very advantage they were trying to deprive it of. But there were also other, nobler motives, both military and humane. By emphasizing reprisals, the supporters of the truce were yielding to the apparent logic of those sentiments that so often prevent people from comprehending the real forces at play. The Germans couldn't do very much for the time being; they had to preserve the streets and bridges of Paris for the passage of the retreating troops.

The truce didn't last even twenty-four hours. No one respected it. It may have given the outlying precincts a breathing spell and allowed the units in the center of town to receive ammunition. The sudden revolt on August 22 involved not just a few hundred more or less novice fighters, but the entire city.

On August 21, Pioro, Bour, and I went to have lunch at the Pavillon du Lac. We were still uncertain about what we were going to do and we felt like the teeth on a tiny wheel in an insignificant machine. As we were sitting down in the restaurant—we were alone, since all the gates of the park had been closed—a German detachment parked its vehicles against the bars of the main entrance. Their guns were pointed at the municipal office. There were two tanks and three or four armored vehicles, all full of soldiers. They were less than two hundred yards from our table. We agreed we weren't risking anything: the poor fool commanding the detachment was supposed to observe the municipal building and, if necessary, use his guns to finish off our personal exploits. But he was not expected to have lunch at the restaurant. And the only people left in the office were the watchman and the clerks. The policemen were occupying the other side of the building, and none of them would have dreamed of attacking such a force. One of us wondered whether we should invite the detachment leader to join us, on condition of a general surrender. The idea was funny, because the situation was so very uncertain. We ended our lunch in a very selfish mood. After an hour's waiting, the tanks and vehicles went away. The Germans' stomachs were, we trusted, still empty.

A catastrophic event took place that afternoon. The F.T.P., which had had a few successes and captured some Germans, had captured a Vichy militiaman. They brought him as far as the strip of ground between the police station and the Hôtel des Postes and killed him. This was too much for the divisional commissioner, an unrelenting Vichyite, who wanted to make some arrests. The policemen were grumbling that this kind of civil war was a luxury. "You're in charge of the police," Pioro said to me. "Take over the station." The policemen had recommended this plan. I sent the commissioner home, informing him that I would ask for his dismissal, and installed myself in his office. The staff received me favorably and carried out my orders with great discipline. I began by taking the young F.T.P. lieutenant to task: "Such incidents mustn't happen again. All prisoners must be brought here, where they will be properly treated; we will keep good watch. Any people who have something to account for will be tried before regular tribunals. In exceptional cases, only the Liberation Committee is authorized to constitute itself as a court-martial." During the next few hours, I was obliged to demote the militia "colonel" and get rid of him. Thus I was in direct command of the largest military force in the precinct. I took advantage of my situation as interim "divisional commissioner" to work out the necessary coordination with the other forces.

The order to build barricades was brought to me during the evening of August 21. I had gone home to change clothes. I returned to the police station, and we worked out a plan of the barricades. They had to be built no matter what. I borrowed the necessary tools in the middle of Rue de Meaux. The barricades were to be up by daylight.

The truce was forgotten. We had a great many more weapons. A few German prisoners were held in the basement of the municipal building. The Germans on Quai de Valmy were upset when they saw the construction that had taken place during the night. A squad of infantry, covered by a tank, attacked. There were people in the street. The German bullets killed one man and wounded several others. Some Germans were hit, and they shot back under the protection of their tank.

This small incident and a few successes during the day lifted the morale of the combatants very high. My motorcyclist and his brother brought back two prisoners, a young officer and a soldier who had been imprudent enough to ask the way to Bourget. We decided to hand out bottles of gasoline. With no materials for Molotov cocktails, we had to resort to bottles of pure gasoline ignited by a wick.

On August 22, 23, and 24, we tried to interrupt or interfere with the trucks that were taking the retreating German detachments to Pantin or Bourget. From Avenue Laumière to the Villette slaughterhouses, policemen lay in wait in the gun pits they had fitted out. When they shot at the trucks, the passengers fired back as best they could, causing more casualties among civilians who had ventured outside than among the combatants. We did the same thing on Rue de Flandre. Twice we hit the drivers of the vehicles, so we had more prisoners on our hands, as well as more arms and ammunition. We seized a tank but no one knew how to run it, and the explanations we got from our prisoners weren't very clear. To add to the fun, we had planted a few antitank mines on Rue de Flandre and Quai de Seine. They were brand-new and had been taken from a small factory that manufactured them. The mines were empty, but the sight of them made the trucks slow down abruptly and head in another direction. Our men took advantage of this moment of uncertainty.

The Germans on Quai de Valmy and at Gare du Nord collected some two hundred French civilians and put a few of them in each truckload of soldiers to act as shields. This infuriated us. But, for the moment, we were not equipped to attack the German garrisons, which had machine guns and tanks. I assembled all our prisoners on the strip of land between the two buildings. We had about fifteen Germans. I told the officer and three young soldiers to step forward. I then had them tied to each of the fenders of an F.T.P. car and a Citroën. Next I sent for a noncommissioned officer. This prisoner was in his forties and wore a Red Cross armband. There was an interpreter in every police station. I asked him to translate everything I was going to say to the prisoner. To make an even stronger impression, I began to shout as I had seen the Bavarian major do thirty years earlier when he had assembled the troops billeted in my uncle's lemonade factory. I didn't realize that this unrestrained loudness is peculiar to southern Germans. The Prussians are calmer.

After telling the medical sergeant what I thought of his leaders' methods, I showed him his compatriots tied up on the front fenders. "I command you to go to the coward who gave the order to take hostages and use them as shields. You will deliver a letter ordering him to stop these degrading practices immediately. He is surrounded by the Americans; he cannot escape us. And he will answer with his life for his behavior, which is contrary to human rights. But I'll teach him a lesson right now, without waiting for the Americans. We're going to attack his barracks. We're going to mount machine guns on those cars and drive straight at him. I assume that the coward will fire on our vehicles and the four men you see will be shot into sieves. I've got hostages too. Just a few feet away from here, there are fifty wounded Germans in the Rothschild Hospital. I'll set the rooms on fire and broil your wounded men alive. The flames and smoke will be visible from your retreat."

The German was as white as a sheet. I signed the letter in front of him. He had taken barely ten steps from the police station when I called out to him. He turned around and stood at attention. "As for you," I shouted, "you know I've kept your identification papers. Don't forget that you're a prisoner of war. If you're not back within twenty-four hours, I'll hunt you down in the prisoners' camps and I'll hang you up on that tree." The sergeant did return the next morning.

The interpreter had translated faithfully. Within half an hour, the telephone rang and a German voice asked to speak to the commander of the nineteenth arrondissement. It was incredible! The man who had received my letter wanted to negotiate. We quickly came to an agreement. He would release the hostages, and my inspection groups could come as observers. He asked me to untie my prisoners from the cars. The conversation went on. I said, "If you want your men to escape our bullets, the simplest thing would be for you to surrender."

He replied, "I can't make that decision on my own."

A bit later, the telephone rang again. Our interpreter began a long talk with one of the German officer's men, then with the junior officer in charge of negotiations. The latter claimed that the garrison was willing to stop fighting but had very little confidence in the concern of the "terrorists" for their prisoners. There were several more phone conversations on the same subject.

I counted up the forces I had left. I had already spread two-thirds of the garrison all over the precinct, to man the barricades or wait in ambush. There were five or six rifles and some twenty automatic pistols, but we were running out of ammunition. I received another phone call. It was the German officer. "How much time will you give us to surrender? I'll surrender only to a regular troop officer."

I turned to Marcel Bour. "What should I say?"

"A quarter of an hour." (Another mistake. We should have been more patient.)

This was an incredible conversation. A quarter of an hour later, we could not even simulate an assault without revealing our weakness. I went to reconnoiter the area and to work out some plan of action for the moment when I could reassemble less miserable forces. I tried to get hold of an officer's uniform that would more or less fit me. I envisioned the following scenario: My troops, well provided with bottles of gasoline, would take up positions on the elevated Métro line. They would cover a group moving along on the other bank of the canal to attack our enemies from the rear. After a fusillade for the sake of show, I would send one of our prisoners to the Germans with a new request for surrender. A dozen uniformed policemen and the pseudo-officer, perhaps myself, would be ready in the ceremonial dress demanded for the ritual of capitulation. Zero hour: Dawn.

This operation never took place. My adversary tried to get his men out through the subway. He gave up the idea because of our reaction. His skillful use of the telephone led us to converge all our forces on Place de la République for a premature attack. I could not oppose these maneuvers, even though I suspected a trick. In the middle of the night some infantrymen made it through the poorly guarded Métro line. Before dawn, the two tanks moved into Avenue Jean-Jaurès at a point where there were only a few inadequately armed policemen. One of the tanks managed to smash through the barricade that we had hastily set up on a railroad bridge. The second got stuck in it. The policemen gathered around immediately and broke two bottles of gasoline on its armor. But they didn't catch fire. The tank finally managed to extricate itself from the barricade and left the sector as fast as possible.

The Villette station, at the foot of Buttes-Chaumont, some three hundred yards north of the municipal building, had been attacked, or at least harassed, several times, with no apparent result. Only a few Germans were occupying it, and they found their situation uncomfortable despite the train that shuttled between Villette and Pantin. It just wasn't very pleasant to be German and to be forced to remain in a station. During the morning of August 23, the train started back toward Pantin, taking most of the members of that small garrison. Another train loaded with various kinds of equipment stayed in Villette. Then that convoy took away the last twenty-five Germans, mostly railroad workers.

The Buttes-Chaumont tunnel opens at the intersection of Rue Manin and Rue de Crimée. After a subterranean passage of 1,200 yards, the tracks are out in the open, in a cut along Rue Emile Chevreau for about 200 yards. In 1944, this quarter, the twentieth arrondissement, was one of the most picturesque in Paris and one of the most leprous. It had hardly changed since the times of Eugène Sue. After this passage, the tracks enter a second tunnel that opens near the municipal building of the twentieth arrondissement after going along Père-Lachaise. It runs over some viaducts and joins the Vincennes Railroad and Bercy station.

Dillot, the Ceux de la Résistance officer in the twentieth, called me during the morning of August 23. A German train emerging from the tunnel had been attacked by the F.F.I. there; there had been one casualty on each side. The Germans, impressed by the attack, had reentered the tunnel. They were retreating toward Villette. "We'll keep up our pressure here," added Dillot. "If the train comes out of the tunnel, it won't escape us. Get it at the opening or else block it." I immediately sent ten policemen over to Rue Manin and ordered them to fire a couple of revolver shots into the tunnel in order to make some noise.

"Block the Buttes-Chaumont exit of the tunnel," I said to Charles Bour, "and make sure there's a defense of the Buttes across from Pantin. I know you've got troubles with your troops; they're still not ready for a disorganized and improvised insurrection. But tell them it's time to act. We can handle this operation. You can take command of the area. I'll coordinate with the twentieth."

Throughout the day we exchanged information with the twentieth, preparing a decisive attack and checking the strength of our arrangements. I decided to throw containers of burning gasoline down the air holes of the tunnel. Marcel Bour ·was in favor of benzol and set about getting hold of some.

That evening, the Germans surrendered to the twentieth arrondissement. We got a share of the booty and were especially glad to have a few more weapons. I never did find out what that train was carrying. One of my men brought me a swastika flag. At the same time we seized hold of Villette station and found large stocks of gasoline.

On August 24, the Germans were beaten. At 10 P.M., the bells of Paris rang out full blast. It was extraordinary. I called together the policemen and other forces, which were two companies strong. Dressed in sackcloth captured from the Villette train or taken from the depot on Rue de Meaux, and wearing helmets from Rue de Meaux, the formation did look like a military unit. I ordered a review on Place Armand Carrel and a huge Marseillaise soared forth from hundreds of chests.

On August 25, we were surprised by the arrival of the Americans, whom we hadn't been expecting. Three soldiers in a jeep explained that they belonged to a Civil Service that had been set up to help govern France after the Germans had left. Pioro, Bour, and I couldn't believe our ears. It was hard for us to imagine that our Allies could be so psychologically blind. Furthermore, the three men were likable. One of them, Ramon Guthrie, was a teacher of French at Dartmouth College.

We received these three strange visitors as courteously as possible, putting them up in the Hôtel du Parc until we could find an attractive apartment opposite Buttes-Chaumont. I showed them the cells in the police station, which held the first collaborators to be arrested. We asked them to dinner but explained that we represented the government of the Republic in our modest sector, that we were qualified and mandated for civil administration. What we had just done to Vichy and the Germans showed what the French thought of any foreign meddling in their domestic affairs. Having said this, we did our utmost to facilitate the action of the American units against the common enemy. I admired our visitors' weapons. Before he left for Bourget, Guthrie (I think) lent me his rifles, cartridges, and a few of the excellent grenades that the American army inherited from the French army of 1918.

August 25 and 26 were devoted to setting up communications in all directions and reconnoitering toward the northeast. If we met up with the Germans, we were to dash into the houses in order to fire our weapons and throw our famous bottles of gasoline. "It's a terrifying weapon!" I said. "You'll see." My driver passed me a bottle. I lit the wick and hurled it a few yards away on the sidewalk. The bottle broke. Nothing happened. This wasn't the effect I was after. Two bottles later, I still hadn't achieved any better result. It was useless. A cyclist signaled that he had seen tanks toward Crancy. I thought it wise to retreat via Aubervilliers and return to the nineteenth arrondissement, a notion that met with general approval.

The last episode of the battle, for us, was the German bombardment during the night of August 26. I believed that the Nazi planes, flying rather low, were trying to hit bases identified during the fighting of the preceding days. Tanks advanced as close as three hundred yards behind the barricades on Pont de Flandre.

I immediately assumed a counterattack was afoot. We had several fires in the precinct. I sent some policemen to reoccupy the northern barricades, and I tried to put the municipal building and Place Armand Carrel in a state of defense. The rest of the night was calm. The next day, the Germans were driven away.

Several major Gestapo archives, especially those that have been discovered in Strasbourg, reveal that during the final months of the occupation, the Germans were willing to neglect a number of the networks and organizations they had identified. They made only whatever arrests were necessary whenever activities became too troublesome. This attitude was based on the principle that what you know well is more reassuring than what you don't know.

By September 1, 1944, new authorities had taken over in Paris. The prefects tried to reshape the state by installing a great many new clerks who had been in the Resistance. Plenty of political careers began with such administrative positions. There was a swarm of Liberation Committees, within which the Communists acquired a dominant position. The Communist Party seized all the important posts. A merrily picturesque military disorder governed Paris for several months.

All the printing establishments and press services were in the hands of the Resistance. The Communists did not innovate: they began to issue *Ce Soir* and *L'Humanité* again, adding *Libération*, which a team of their men had taken over. The most original creation was the newspaper *Combat*, with Camus as one of the leading editors. Ceux de la Résistance founded a political weekly, *Volontés*. Michel Collinet became editor-in-chief, and Pierre Stibbe was the publisher. I wrote almost all its editorials and I was virtually in charge politically until its brief career came to an end.

In the next chapter, I shall mention the behavior of the Surrealists during the German occupation. After the tragic death of Desnos, it is best to pass over his cooperation with the "pacifist" rag *Aujourd'hui*, published in Paris by Henri Jeanson in 1940 and 1941, with the authorization of the Germans. This kind of exploit confirms Breton's severe judgment against the snares of journalism. Maurice Henry agreed to publish, throughout the war, cartoons in the Nazi daily *L'Oeuvre*, put out by Marcel Déat. Although these drawings were often funny and politically neutral, they were self-serving and boosted Hitlerism to a most regrettable degree.

26
THE PRICE OF LIBERTY

GENERAL DE GAULLE HAD UNLEASHED THE TEMpest: he had nurtured it and directed its ravages by giving the domestic Resistance its means of action, by identifying the authority of the Resistance fighters with that of the Republic and the Fatherland, and by deciding to encourage the Liberation Committees. As a result, he found himself grappling with a dual monarchy: one problem grew out of the Vichy economic system, and the other was caused by the committees. Like the entire left wing of the Resistance, he was ready to make the best of the former, but he was quite allergic to the latter.

Among the many hypotheses of Marxism, that concerning the appearance of great men is one of the most unusual, even gratuitous. Through the process of historical determinism, the places to be taken are always taken; if De Gaulle had been killed in June 1940, the resistance against the invader would nevertheless have found its leaders. Such is the Marxist view. But, while it may be true that situations tempt men, history abounds in roles that were not taken or that were poorly carried out. In more or less identical circumstances, no one stepped forward in Norway, Holland, Belgium, Czechoslovakia, Rumania, or Greece, except on a purely functional level. There was Tito in Yugoslavia and De Gaulle in France. And even a very subtle analysis of the social structures and power relations in Yugoslavia and in France would not have provided a forecast of Tito's triumph, much less his heresy, or of the phenomenon of De Gaulle.

External information about the Resistance and the underground groups, anything you read in the papers, pictured a Marxist 1793 for France. The revolutionaries were winning everywhere. France only seemed to be a revolutionary power. The moderates complained about extortions in the central and southern departments, but these were a somewhat hasty and blind purging and some minor robberies of banks and properties. Otherwise, the Liberation Committees tried to maintain an administration that would have collapsed without their impetus. The country was centralized, but no order was coming from the top. There were so many movements and armed forces that no party could impose its dictatorship, although the Communist Party circulated everywhere, full of boastfulness and pretentiousness. Nowhere did the politics of the Liberation Committees move beyond daily or immediate problems. The regional police commissioners and police chiefs did not represent an authority superior to that of the committees; they rested on the same legal structure.

The power of the Liberation Committees weakened as soon as the traditional hierarchy of the state recovered its ability to regulate and control, which it had lost in the general disorganization of discipline and communication. The revival of the centralized and effective state apparatus came out by itself, thanks to the innate perseverance of that organism, the support of the great corps, and the internal dynamism of the trade unions, whose members were more than anyone else attached to restoring the edifice. The municipal elections of April 1945 relegated the Liberation Committees to history once and for all.

The leaders of the African army were faithful to the memory of Pétain. But they were not unconditionally Gaullist; far from it. Their relations with the great units of Free France were distant and distrustful. Arguments about rank were prominent from September 1944 to March 1945, and members of the First French Army bitterly commented on Gaullist promotions. In fact, the traditional De Gaulle was horrified by this tumultuous growth of military medals, so reminiscent of the Paris Commune and so contrary to the principles by which he had been formed. But the revolutionary De Gaulle—that is, the intellectual and ambitious man—realized that one sometimes has to jostle tradition. He didn't like anyone else to do it, however.

De Gaulle first approached insurgent Paris as the traditional officer. Quite deliberately, the General went first to the Ministry of War, which was empty, then to the Paris Police Department, and finally to City Hall. These precautions were futile. The population was unaware of them; if someone had explained the legal subtleties involved, it wouldn't have understood. As I had told Léo Hamon, the people were determined to acclaim General de Gaulle, which they did on August 25 on City Hall Square and on August 26 on the Champs-Elysées. But the direct, human contact with the leaders of the uprising and the Resistance went badly. The General was icy at City Hall, and he was no happier during the stiff and painful audience he granted on August 27 to the Parisian general staffs of the insurrection. This man, who later was so often charming and deceptive, and whose sense of humor became famous, acted, according to those who were there, more like a combination regimental colonel and headmaster. This was especially disappointing because everyone had been expecting some kind of emotional encouragement. An injection of that sort would have enabled them to hold aloof from the sordid games that were imminent.

The Resistance circles, perceptibly larger in September than in April, were in the throes of a great intellectual agitation. People were writing and talking about "Revolution." As De Gaulle remarked in his memoirs, "That watchword dominated speeches. But no one was very precise about what it meant exactly, about what effective changes were to be achieved by will or by force. Mainly, no one specified what authority, endowed with what powers, would have to bring them about." This concisely sums up the debates of politicians at the end of their luncheons or unrationed dinners in Paris during the winter of 1944–45.

The General, who wanted to hoist France "by will or by force" to the legal status of the great victors, needed an "impartial and powerful" state. He personally preferred Socialism of a sort that would preserve the essential structures of the old society, particularly the bourgeois system of social castes and intellectual hierarchies. The chief of state would arbitrate the distribution of tasks and assure promotions. To govern, he would rely on a sort of balance of power and conditions. He was particularly distrustful of politicians and prepared to implement considerable changes in the leadership of the

Republic. But he saw these modifications in purely administrative terms: the hierarchies and offices would be preserved, and, if necessary, others would be added to make the methods uniform. But the positions were to be filled with new men who had been steeled by the war or the resistance. They would be adverse both to the system of the Third Republic and to totalitarianism.

De Gaulle permitted the parties to reorganize. This was part of his program for restoring liberties, though he regretted that some of his best colleagues succumbed to the seductions of parliamentary government. He would have preferred to urge them toward administrative functions and positions, to keep them solely in the service of the public interest. This soldier couldn't quite get his bearings among the parties, but foresaw their development with frightening lucidity. "The factional character of these parties, which strikes them with infirmity, is matched by their own decadence; the latter feature is still hidden behind rhetoric. But the doctrinal passion that was once their source, the attractiveness, the grandeur of the parties, could not endure in this era of a materialism indifferent to ideals." This sentence seems to be aimed particularly at the Socialist Party. It was written after 1953, however, and may not represent what De Gaulle was thinking in 1944. The General had appreciated Léon Blum's homage. He was beguiled time and again by the grand loftiness of thought he found in the political speeches and the words of the Socialist leader.

Blum, when he came back from captivity, had apparently been converted to the system of presidential power, to the notion of a strong and relatively free executive. De Gaulle, annoyed by the words and maneuvers of the Communist Party, urged the *résistants* to join the Socialist Party. "It has leaders," he thought. "It already has part of the administration. It will absorb all the bourgeois individuals who want revolution; it will not turn away the civil servants who will be anxious to forge Socialism in order to strengthen the state without destroying French society." In 1945, De Gaulle, who was far from willing to assemble his own partisans, who didn't realize that he was in a position to coalesce almost the entire Resistance around himself, provided he suggested some ideology slightly less mysterious than the one that could be discerned in his speeches, almost handed his power over to Léon Blum. He thought that Blum was more capable than he of restraining the growth of parties he was powerlessly witnessing, despite his gigantic political capital.

As early as 1944, the Communist Party falsified the entire political game. Its goal was not honest alliances but hostages; it wanted to impose a program that would lead not so much to revolution (which seemed chimerical for the moment because of the Allied presence in Europe and the agreements concluded with Stalin) as to strategic positions after the war. Remembering what had happened in Eastern Europe between 1919 and 1921, one might think that, after Hitler was crushed, a cadaverous and ravaged continent could be the scene of proletarian upheavals, or at least of putsches by armed and resolute Communist minorities. But the Party had learned nothing and forgotten nothing. The Stalinist principle of Communist infallibility was stronger than ever. The Stalin-Hitler pact was seen as a brilliant maneuver on the part of the Russians, who had been hoaxed by England and France. No mention was made of the division of Poland, the internment of Polish soldiers, the massacre of their officers, and the invasion of the Baltic countries.

This wasn't far from 1940. In June of that year, the leaders of the Communist Party had supported the armistice and were prepared to get on with the Nazis. But they had told the very opposite to the young men in the *maquis*. The fortunes of war, which had saved Stalin, were modestly ignored. On the other hand, a bright spotlight was projected on anything that might portray Stalin as a superb statesman or, for instance, as a prudent, economical, if rather inflexible father. Even the courage of the Russian people was described as a virtue of the system, although it mainly revealed the force of nationalism to which the Soviet leaders had capitulated. The colossal defeats of the Red Army between 1941 and 1942, the aberrant strategic arrangements so characteristic of decadent regimes, the warm welcome millions of Soviet citizens accorded to the Germans a quarter of a century after the October Revolution, the presence of quite a number of former Red Army soldiers in the Wehrmacht—all these things were denied.

Marxism is based on the knowledge and interpretation of history. To make the interpretation of history favorable to dogma, and especially to Stalin's megalomania, world Communism had launched upon the most systematic and brazen revisionism that the world has experienced since the triumph of Christianity. For fifteen years, the French Communist Party devoted itself shamelessly to falsification. Since Stalin's death, the French have habitually laughed at all that. Anyone who knew the truth about the Moscow trials and the Comintern might have imagined that the Stalin-Hitler pact and the bloodbath that ensued would restore to the French Communists the honesty that is indispensable to revolution. But proof of the contrary had been administered since 1942. And this proof became dazzling as soon as France recovered her liberty. One of General de Gaulle's cardinal errors was his hurried parrying on this point. The recent Hitlerian examples of administrative measures ought to have shown him the limits of that approach, and during political negotiations he failed to realize that his partners would only concede those things that were already in his hands. When he recalled and granted amnesty to Maurice Thorez, for example, the Communist Party could be reconstituted as it was in 1939. But this renaissance would also apply to other parties. Thus all hopes of national unity, including proletarian unity, were coming to naught.

General de Gaulle thought he could reintegrate the entire French working class in the nation by calling Communists into the government. The idea was superb, provided that the Party could break its ties of allegiance to Moscow. The operation was worth trying, and only the leader of Free France could have succeeded, for throughout 1944 he had the necessary means of pressure and corruption. The process of self-criticism so dear to the Communists might have enabled them to obtain a text condemning the Party's attitude after the Stalin-Hitler pact. This would have been consistent with political morality; the other parties had condemned Vichyism and purged themselves. But the Communists had secretly separated themselves from the second-grade robots who had been on the wrong side in 1940. This purge had actually begun during the occupation.

The Resistance had brought the Communist Party more intellectuals and bourgeoisie than workers. For thirty years, the younger generation continued to discover Marx and Lenin, hurling themselves, trembling, into a paranoid cure. The young cannot be cured by the force of reason or the refutation of dogma through information. Such purely intellectual approaches rarely dim faith. The Communist Party itself, its sectarian immobility, and the foreign policy of the U.S.S.R. managed to enlighten the intelligentsia. But I'm too optimistic. The pure and the fanatic maintained their blind faith in dogma despite everything, like those Dutch pastors who won't allow the natural sciences to be taught in their schools because they imply that the world wasn't created in six days.

General de Gaulle, fully occupied with getting France into the forefront, wasn't particularly concerned with Communist messianism. Perhaps he even felt that a collective social system—one founded on the absolute primacy of the state, the negation of all private interest, one which reduced popular representation to the confirmation of expert decision by recognized specialists to insure the nation's happiness and the country's grandeur, one in which undivided power was exercised by pure and virtuous men—would be more to his taste than any other system, if it could be established without the disorder of a revolution. On the other hand, De Gaulle could not tolerate the existence of private armies or a police force that was not part of the state. He issued a decree integrating the Domestic French Forces in the French army. He enjoined the Patriotic Militias to disband and hand in their weapons. He had to negotiate this with Maurice Thorez.

In the twentieth arrondissement, the senior members of Charles Bour's F.F.I. demobilized. The others followed their captain to Lorraine with other Parisian forces. Joined together with the F.F.I. from Champagne and Lorraine, they constituted, until November 1944, the only French infantry fighting outside the First Army. In December, Grandval showed me his battalions in Nancy. Though they were rather badly equipped, Bradley asked whether he could use this force in the event that the Battle of the Bulge lasted longer than expected.

In late September, our Patriotic Militias amounted to a battalion. They were more or less billeted in municipal buildings and were fed through the good offices of the municipality. Around September 15, I told Pioro, the Communist mayor, that I felt it was time to transfer this battalion to the F.F.I. He refused, arguing that he needed a force strong enough to protect the people against the fifth column. It was true that not everything had been cleaned up.

Members of the Communist Party, including the newcomers, increased the size of the militias. The Party began to choose the leadership with its usual seriousness. The Socialist commander resigned and was replaced by a former officer of the merchant marine whom I had known as a Party member before the war. His nomination, prepared by the Party, was accepted by the Liberation Committee, which had no other candidate. Nevertheless, the majority of the militiamen escaped Communist influence. They were mostly jobless men attracted by the small profits the Resistance offered. It was more like a race-track audience than an industrial proletariat.

The purge was a test. Many businesses were vulnerable. Bosses were arrested, and plants were sequestered. These were good methods of expropriation. I used them on the managers of a large printing press and the owner of a factory that had worked exclusively for the Wehrmacht. I turned over the management of those two establishments to business committees elected by the workers. In the first case, they were assisted by the company's technicians, and in the second by the boss's daughter. These activities had no support from the Communists, who were more anxious to get an owner's stock than to prosecute him, except in spectacular cases.

In terms of "class" relations, the purge presented complex problems of morality and justice. The printing-press case was simple enough. The proprietor, who should have had every reason in the world to be an anti-Nazi, was actually an admirer of Hitler. In 1944, the business was running a secret printing shop for the Gestapo. One of its jobs was to typeset and run off the yellow posters listing the victims of German firing squads. When I entered the factory on August 21, 1944, there was an enormous poster on the press announcing to the Parisian people all the dreadful punishments that would be visited upon them if they dared to attack the German army. I demanded a galley proof of that fine piece of literature.

The most elementary patriotism should have forced the managers of that business, which was in no dire need, to refuse to have anything to do with the Germans. But what about the workers? It was in their nature to work in order to subsist. But were they obligated to offer their technical knowledge to the Gestapo without wondering whether they should betray that trust for the benefit of the Resistance? The thought passed through the mind of only one now, the head of the workshop. The industrialist who headed a small sheet-metal concern was not forced to manufacture mines for the Germans. Nor were his workers. They might have compensated with patriotic responses, but they never did.

The concept of national interest was richer and more demanding than the concept of class interest. In the case of the printing press, despite the owner's wiles and sordid schemes, Hitler's victory would have taken everything away from him. His workers should have looked for their wages in Germany. Justifications based on an alleged class interest (I negotiate with the Nazis to retain the ownership, if not of the factory, at least of my trade name; why not go and work in Germany, what's the difference between a German capitalist and a French capitalist?) or pride were no different from the Vichyite arguments. National interest was not the untimely abstraction that the Vichy soldiers evoked while they stood at attention. Nor was it that untimely abstraction that the parlor Trotskyites called imperialism. It was a cultural complex within which the bosses probably developed rather short-range ambitions concerning their own enrichment—their profits were not seen as the price of posters listing the names of the fifty hostages shot the day before—and their workers could plan strikes that would not lead them to the firing squad.

The docile workers paid little heed to the management rights offered them after the Liberation. They gained some knowledge about the significance of the celebrated surplus value and the role of the owner and the manager in the workings of a business. But this moral responsibility brought them no satisfaction. They felt that their chief concern was to defend their wages and working conditions, not to run the business.

The armed and victorious *résistants* had the power. More precisely, the power was crumbled among the hundred or more committees that still possessed, in September 1944, some of the violent means they had used to take the lead. No one knew where to begin, however, except that it was necessary to solve local problems and then move on to the national level. The Communist Party was better organized than the others, with all its numerous associations, and therefore had excellent chances in all the meetings of groups and committees—provided that there were no elections, for they would have put the Party back in its numerical place. There was a vague, sometimes explicit, need to set up, alongside the government, a popular expression of the domestic Resistance, which would serve as a means of checks and balances, or at least give advice. But De Gaulle decided to create by decree a consulting assembly within which the various groups would be honestly represented, and nothing prevailed against the system he devised.

This was not just a paper government. De Gaulle took charge of the agencies and their personnel. The masses put their trust in him. They were not urging revolution. They wanted to be governed, but they were in a hurry to free the nation from the trammels and controls the joint administration of Vichy and the Germans had forced upon it. De Gaulle helped bring the masquerades and quaint doings in which the Resistance had bedecked itself to a painless end.

The "patriots" had mixed feelings. A small faction of *résistants*, both to the left and to the right, regarded General de Gaulle as a clumsy and arrogant soldier, incapable of understanding political complexities because of his atavistic deference to hierarchies and unconcerned with domestic problems. His mind was thought to be clouded with vanity and problems of precedence, in which he tended to confuse the nation with his own person. The Communists sought to strengthen the National Front, which they controlled under the cloak of hostages, the most eminent being François Mauriac. They proposed mergers. I suggested to Vaillant that we keep Ceux de la Résistance out of the conflict and propose a federation of all the movements. This refusal to choose was well received by the provinces. But the position that I had recommended was precarious, because the Communist Party, despite its tricolored disguise, was returning to Stalinist methods and principles. Thus even the most ardent partisans of Resistance unity— nay, proletarian unity—were forced to take a basic position. What were we to think of the Communists, their doctrine, their aims, and their methods?

The Germans had provided a good deal of information on conditions in Russia. The revolutionaries who had followed the "Socialism" being built there had nothing to learn about the terror methods, the "cult of personality," the dictatorship of the bureaucracy over the Party and the dictatorship of the Party over the people. The force behind that monstrous deformation of principles was the formation of a class of technocrats and bureaucrats. But no one had suspected the magnitude of Soviet negligence or the backward, downright elementary character of the daily life of Russian citizens. Poverty was everywhere, and, in comparison to Germany, the lack of conveniences had surprised even those who were most hostile to the regime. The reaction of the German troops to the Russians was edifying. Here and there, former Communists who were now soldiers in the Wehrmacht had shown humanity to Soviet citizens and prevented barbaric orders from being carried out.

As serious as these reports may have been, they became peripheral and episodic when I compared them with my hesitations about the very basis of Marxism. Dissatisfaction with Marx's notion of class and, more particularly, with his definition of the proletariat led me to reread *The Process of the Production of Capital* carefully. When I was twenty, that brilliant text, full of stories about the lot of British textile workers during the second quarter of the nineteenth century, was thoroughly convincing because of its dogmatic simplicity, which youth always seeks. Now everything proceeded from my rereading of *The Critique of the Gotha Program*, the only Marxist text that shed some light on the future Socialist society. The producer, writes Marx, "receives from society a ticket stating that he has done so much work and, with this ticket, he withdraws from the social stocks a quantity of consumer goods corresponding to the value of his work." The price of merchandise, according to Marx, is always close to its theoretical value: constant capital + salary + surplus value. One might add the costs of production, but this last factor is always underestimated by Marx. Since the additional expenses are supported by nonproductive work, it must be incorporated into the traditional scheme. What good is nonproductive labor? It pays for the expenses of the sale that transforms the profit contained in the merchandise into money; it supports the innumerable services that abound in a modern society; and, last but not least, it enriches the capitalist or the state. This enumeration makes it clear that the societies of today are differently organized than England of 1860, where the market was elementary and there were far fewer services. In Marxism, however, wages and surplus value are no longer economic categories, but symbols. The view that wages represent the cost of maintaining the work force and that surplus value essentially comprises the boss's profit, already inadequate in 1860, has dwindled to a mere theme of public meetings a hundred years later. The wages of a French, German, or American worker cover, beyond what is necessary for his physical restoration, payments on his car, television set, household appliances, even his apartment, and his weekend and vacation expenses. Surplus value pays for an ever-increasing number of services, and management's profit forms a smaller and smaller fraction.

This already destroys the fine dialectical construction in which the proletariat is balanced against capitalism. Each state has defined so many distinct "spheres of production" that a hundred different figures are used simultaneously to measure the work socially necessary for producing an object. From the perspective of specialization and qualification, we can now observe hundreds of irreducible values for the work force. Marx caught a glimpse of this development, since he discusses it briefly in *The Critique of the Gotha Program,* but in the latter part of the twentieth century it has reached such proportions that it definitively demolishes the highly touted class solidarity on which the concepts of the proletarian revolution and the proletarian dictatorship are based. In the twentieth century, the proletariat in the Marxist sense of the word has diminished in the advanced countries. The salaried mass, ever on the increase, is divided among the proletariat, which nevertheless enjoys economic advantages beyond the mere maintenance of the work force; a growing number (large in proportion to that proletariat) of workers, technicians, engineers, and scientists directly involved in capitalist expansion; and a multitude of service workers who produce little surplus value. The last transport, distribute, sell (and consume) the objects produced by the first two categories.

Nevertheless, it is true that the whole society—and perhaps what we care most about in society—is partly financed by the value of non-productive work. The hypocrisy of the so-called Socialist societies that arose in the first half of the twentieth century (Russian, Yugoslav, Cuban, Chinese, and so on) is that they disguised this truth in vain and mendacious professions of faith. Moreover, their efforts to elude the laws of market economy have merely created gigantic and inefficient bureaucracies, at the expense of the proletariat whose destiny they claim to embody. Hence, in late 1945, it seemed obvious to me that, for the sake of the workers, the work force would have to be and remain a commodity. Defended by the traditional means of a market economy—coalitions (trade unions), regulations (social legislation), violence (strikes)—wages have managed to escape the iron law to which Marxism subjugated them. In the totalitarian countries, Fascist or Socialist, the first act of any government has been to suppress the right to strike, and the trade union has been reduced to gathering dues and finding jobs for its members. Today these patent truths, which American, Swedish, and British workers have known for a long time, still haven't quite sunk in among all the French intellectuals who claim to be revolutionaries.

I abandoned the idea of the "dictatorship of the proletariat," not only because of my horror at "dictatorship" but also because there was no proletariat capable of practicing it, or even willing to. I replaced "proletariat," a convenient but relatively ambiguous term, with the plural "working classes"—or even better, "wage earners"—and I noted that in these categories, a kind of class was gradually coming to power. It would relieve the traditional bourgeoisie. This class included administrators, technicians, and leaders of all sorts—from foremen to executives, from heads of sales to refrigerator salesmen, from organizers to department heads, from trade-union secretaries to postmasters. All these people already had some segment of power more durable than that of the Liberation Committee I was in, and they were far more apt to coalesce and suffocate the state than all my colleagues in the Resistance. I was frightened of this future ruling class, which would have the use of other people's money and statistics as well as the distribution of material goods, knowledge, and administrative procedures.

To exorcise this peril, I held fast to the idea of a proletarian and democratic party, which I balanced with the concept of a bourgeois and capitalist party freed from any influence by the trusts. The state's authority would be strengthened if it gained economic control of these trusts, especially in credit and energy. The state itself would be organized in such a way that the elected bodies could insure its control. The government would serve as an umpire between the social classes. General de Gaulle seemed more capable than anyone else of embodying that conjunction of contrary forces, which had already been expressed in the resistance to Fascism.

I guided my political activities in that direction throughout 1945. The editorials I published in the weekly *Volontés* of Ceux de la Résistance bear witness to my development. Those I wrote in fall of 1945, stating that General de Gaulle's government was putting through a program of reforms very close to the revolutionary plan Lenin worked out in July 1917, establish the foundation of a Socialism that would end the quarrel against nascent capitalism that Marx opened in 1848. These extremely modest suggestions do not represent a ridiculous termination to one of the richest lives of thought in modern times. In fact, thought leads to nothing; it is too elusive to come true. It exists and suggests, but it may even be alien to the edifice constructed by the formulas and logical obligations that are its vehicles. Thus these propositions should be seen as the residue of some of the most stimulating concepts of one of the grand utopias of the nineteenth century: the proletarian revolution and the classless society. The trial begun, in the name of "scientific" Socialism, against so-called capitalist economy was very probably a good cause, and it was supported by prodigious talents. But the file was slim and the argumentation too subjective. It is time to get on to other things.

The Patriotic Militias did not disband. I had imagined a statute that would depoliticize them by giving them a civic function. They would be commanded by the police, recruitment would be subject to strict rules, and their task would be to guard the roads and communications, the electric-power stations, and the important depots. But De Gaulle got Maurice Thorez to write an article in *L'Humanité* advocating that they be disbanded. The Party was ordered to make sure that the law was applied. I had been named inspector-general of the Patriotic Militias, a bombastic title that I shared with Jean-François Chabrun and that never corresponded to any real power. Thorez achieved the effective and immediate disbanding of the militias. Were all the weapons given back? That is another story.

For some months, I had been accusing the government of being soft. This intervention by a feudal grandee annoyed me deeply. I said so in a very long article appearing in *Volontés* on February 2, 1945, entitled *Who Governs?* My article caught Pleven's interest. He asked me to dinner on Rue de Rivoli. The fare was meager and the apartment unheated. I had to disappoint the Minister of Finance. "General de Gaulle," I said, "owed it to himself to unify the Resistance and become its leader by forcing the political parties to spend a time in purgatory. I think I can say that all the movements, and probably many of their Communist members, would have accepted both unification and the General's leadership. Now it's probably too late. Working-class unity would have been a good joke on the re-Stalinization of the Communist Party; it would have got the entire working class away from Moscow. But I'm afraid we can only take it as a utopia. Restoring the parties will rob it of any chances. The war effort and the reconstruction will have been spurred on by a popular enthusiasm, not by officialdom." In February 1945, the fate of the Fourth Republic had already been decided.

The affair of the F.F.I. commissions was more amusing and highly instructive. After the last gunshot, stripes proliferated. The manpower of the Domestic French Forces doubled and tripled during September and October. Improvised lieutenants, captains, and commanders cropped up, in many cases merely because someone had to command the troops. I myself tried to put some order into three or four large battalions stationed in forts or barracks in the Paris area by naming some thirty officers. The solution seemed simple enough. The men and their officers would have to be instructed without preconceived ideas. Officers' schools (there were some in existence) would be able to provide rapid evaluations of the worth of the F.F.I. ranks and the demotions that were necessary, provided that we followed those rules that were not of the traditional army. But the war offices and the hundreds of active or reserve officers who reemerged after the Liberation, were unwilling to surrender any of their rights. The General leaned toward tradition, and things bogged down in red tape and quibbling. This benefited only the Communists, who were happy to foment discontent and protest against such administrative decisions. There was enormous confusion within the military. A new leadership was constituted for the First Army, and Vaillant assigned Rosenfeld to it. I must devote a few lines to this picturesque man, whom I brought back from Orne in late September 1944.

When I went looking for scattered groups more or less attached to the Ceux de la Résistance which had been very active during the last few weeks of the battle of Normandy, I encountered Colonel de Pelet in Courtomer. A retired officer of the Lunéville hussars, he had been recalled to service in 1939 and driven to Vichy in July 1940. He was part of the social class to which Marshal Pétain was ready to offer all positions. Unfortunately, the colonel's opinions in regard to both the armistice and the coming legislation were quite nonconformist. They got rid of him by making him a State Commissioner for the Gypsies. This was an extremely fortunate choice. Pelet virtually fell in love with that proud and threatened people. He rightly felt that the Gypsies had a human value far superior to that of most of his fellow citizens. He became the protector of a small kingdom, at Sainte-Marie-de-la-Mer, until his generosity and patriotism aroused displeasure. He was sent to Orne and he went underground.

The first time I saw Pelet, he was with a red-faced man who sported a uniform that, at first sight, seemed to be that of a cuirassier colonel, but, on closer look, turned out to be from the Army Service Corps. This was Colonel Rosenfeld. Indefatigable, a big eater and drinker, he never contradicted anyone and was extraordinarily dexterous in dealing with army rites and traditions. He never neglected any nuance of any token of respect. He was unbeatable in regard to regulations. Always early to rise and late to bed, as precise as a stationmaster, he was *the* soldier. No one knew exactly where he came from or who he was. He lived with a rather attractive woman, whom he introduced as his wife, though gossips quickly identified her as having come straight from a brothel. For several months, he somehow settled all the problems involved in integrating the F.F.I. into the First French Army. He died the evening before a holiday, after a Rabelaisian dinner. Someone later told me that he was merely a sergeant-major and had been about to retire when fortune smiled at him in the guise of Ceux de la Résistance.

In 1944, the French were more interested in stripes than in strengthening the French armies. The officers' corps ruthlessly defended itself, and the newly commissioned men were uncompromising.

To fully appreciate their position, we had to consider their pay, which no one overlooked. But there was clear evidence of the value the French place on noble titles and legal authority. Once the war was over and the Resistance was well entrenched in official commissions, hundreds of officers were legitimized, to everyone's satisfaction. These men had their stripes, but the army paid little heed.

The defeat of the Nazis had ended in a sort of apocalypse. Severe blows had been dealt to Russia. The victory of democracy was encumbered by a thousand ties but full of promise. These events seemed to increase the difficulties that had been weighing so heavily on the determination of revolutionary intellectuals before 1940. I wanted to profit from my front-rank position on a weekly that sold twenty thousand copies in France, so I drew up a list of intellectuals who might participate in some kind of manifesto. I said a few words about it to René Char during one of his first trips to Paris.

Char's behavior had been exemplary. He had fought well, as an officer in the underground. He told me about his parachuting behind the lines of the Wehrmacht. "Just imagine, the parachutes were calculated for guys weighing a hundred and seventy-five pounds with normal equipment. I weighed two hundred pounds and, with my guns and hand grenades, I was sixty-five pounds too heavy. I was falling fast. I could already see myself plummeting onto stones with my explosives. Well, it was all right. I landed on soft ground. But, believe me, while I was coming down I wasn't calm at all!"

I had run into Péret in Paris on October 29, 1940. He was the same as ever; he didn't understand a thing. The arrival of the Germans, I think, had led to his release from the prison where the imbeciles of the phony-war administrations had incarcerated him. He was nevertheless sensible enough to go to the "free" zone and then head for Mexico. He was safe. Now he could be against everything with impunity. His prudent retreat and his writings about the poets of the Resistance are hardly exalting.

Eluard had stayed in Paris, where he was never disturbed. Aside from *Liberté*, toward which I may be overindulgent, the poems he wrote between 1940 and 1945 are not his best. But his presence in Paris was somehow reassuring and exalting. His life and personality were an intrinsic challenge to Nazism, to the gains Vichy sought from military defeat.

In 1944, I had asked Prévert to write a poem on Hitler, which I would then publish and distribute. "Describe him without using his name," I told Prévert. "No one will be fooled, but the effect will be powerful." It was a huge risk to take. Prévert didn't want to run it.

Desnos was against Hitler: he demonstrated it, and died for it. Picasso was theoretically a national of a neutral country. But his anti-Nazi opinions were well known. He received a few German visitors in his studio on Rue des Grands-Augustins. He told me about two young officers, shy and fearful, who may have felt they were doing something wrong, behaving badly.

As absurd as it may sound, until the end of 1943 the occupied zone, and especially Paris, enjoyed a climate of relative intellectual liberalism, in contrast to the so-called free zone. Certain German authorities or collaborating French agencies permitted nonconformist thought to express itself. Carné and Prévert could film *Les Visiteurs du Soir*. Dominguez exhibited his works. Sartre staged *The Flies*. And so on. These instances of liberalism may have been due to the influence of men like Luchaire or Drieu La Rochelle or to the presence of officers like Ernst Jünger in the *Kommandatur*. In any case, books that Vichy might have prohibited were published. These included Pierre Naville's *Holbach*, Queneau's novels, Georges Hugnet's *Non Vouloir*, and Noël Arnaud's chapbooks of poetry, *La Main à Plume*, one of which was Paul Eluard's *Poésie et Vérité 1942* (which contains the poem *Liberté*). This list isn't complete.

Despite the jammings, André Breton's voice, which was easily recognizable in the broadcasts from America, resounded like an encouraging call. I have already indicated that Georges Hugnet was the principal collector of the secret publications of the Resistance poets. The first Catalan was a café on Rue des Grands-Augustins, on the odd-numbered side of the street. It was founded by a dealer of Les Halles who looked like François I. This loyal and curious man, popular with artists, was accompanied by a young, ardent, sly woman. He was discovered by Picasso. Every Wednesday, Georges Hugnet gathered around himself Eluard, Dominguez, Picasso, Desnos, Leiris, Baudin, Auric, Charles Ratton, Jean Bouret, an old friend of Apollinaire's known as Baron Mollet, and a few others. Patrick Waldberg made a theatrical entrance in an American uniform shortly after the liberation of Paris.

I thought of asking that fine group to collaborate on a manifesto that would express an intellectual and artistic solidarity. Char pointed out that I couldn't do without Aragon's cooperation. And he would either drown the statement in a catalogue of Elsa's attributes or make sure the whole thing collapsed. But I didn't even have to ask Aragon. All the Communists, recent or ancient, were unwilling to join together with orthodox Surrealists.

The second Catalan opened across the street, occupying a ground floor and a second story in 1945 or 1946. The owner was the same, and Hugnet was again the chief animator. At his table were all the poets that were then being talked about. Pierre Emmanuel, Lescure, Guillevic, Jean Follain, and Camus, Nicolas de Stael, Leibovitz, Yves Allégret, Balthus, Félix Labisse, Coutaud, Francis Grüber, Max-Pol Fouchet, Germaine Tailleferre, in addition to the faithful from the first Catalan. Off to the side, Claude Mauriac, reserved and silent, dined at the Catalan several evenings a week with a ravishing girl friend. Lise Deharme, Nora Auric, Marie-Laure de Noailles, and Pierre Boulez also attended Hugnet's "Wednesdays." François Mauriac and Cocteau put in occasional appearances. People drew a lot on the paper napkins. There was a piano on the ground floor. It was tended by Pierre Barbizet, but this innovation wasn't much of a draw. I could be seen at the two Catalans almost every night.

Seized with the frenzy of freedom and food, happy as children escaping restrictions, Hugnet and I took off every weekend in the old Peugeot which had been used in the Liberation. I had bought it from the widow of a collaborator (who had been executed in Marseilles) and arduously rebuilt it and got it into shape. The two of us took enchanting trips all around Paris. We were happiest when Georges Bernier joined us. He had an unbeatable sense of humor and was as fond as Hugnet and I of wines, alcohol, and fine cooking.

The conversation at the Catalan and during our weekend outings was often brilliant. Although most of the intellectuals had converted to Communism—blind adherents occupied almost all the positions in radio, theater, movies, and literary and art columns, which made for odious, miserable, and disgusting conformism—the Party never laid down the law at the Catalan. Eluard sometimes showed an annoying zeal and intolerance, however. A rather funny political episode happened in November 1947. I was lunching alone when Eluard came in with his grandiosely solemn expression. He sat down next to me. "I've just broken off with Picasso," he said in the gravest tone of voice.

"Broken off?" I replied. "You mean you had a fight?"

"No, broken off, once and for all. I'll never see him again. Our friendship is dead. I won't put up with what he said or with the tone

of voice in which he said it. I wanted him to join the Communist Party and he refused."

I burst out laughing, of course. A few weeks later, Eluard (or Casanova) renewed his attempt and won his case.

I was elected to the Municipal Council of Paris in April 1945 on the ticket of the non-Communist Union of Resistance Movements. I had been one of those who first recommended this organization, though Léo Hamon and a few others brought it into being without my participation. These were the first political elections after the Liberation, and they changed four-fifths of the councilmen. All the Communists were removed from office in the provisional assembly.

Marthe Richard tackled the brothels during the first few Council sessions. Bourgeois hypocrisy and clerical prudishness were unleashed. In order to protect the Christian family, which was already beginning to crack, prostitution—a kind of divine boon that had survived all regimes and religions—was pounced upon. This was merely the opening phase of a cunning project to moralize Paris. It was carried out with considerable hostility by people whose private lives were not always consistent with their loudly proclaimed principles. Only the younger generation was able to hamper these idiotic efforts.

The swashbuckle opponents of the brothels had all sorts of tales of collaboration. But the management of these houses, as of so many businesses, had been shared by patriots and enemy agents alike. I tried to bring up the condition imposed by society upon women from a modest background and unwed mothers. For them prostitution is the only resource. My aim was to thaw out the Communist group and avoid a law that would only benefit the consciences of a few churchwardens and ladies of good works. But the minds of these robots were already made up. Their consent to such moralistic preoccupations was one of the terms of the new apportionment of France. I abstained from voting.

A few days before the brothels were closed, Jean de Vogüé, who smiled at my almost complete lack of experience and appreciated my hostility toward Marthe Richard's proposal, decided that I needed further information. This was neither a debauched excursion nor an intimate tête-à-tête, but merely a simple act of sightseeing. We went to the famous One Two Two on Rue de Provences, which was as renowned as the Chabanais. The proprietors had been alerted. We were welcomed by a ravishing woman who wore hardly anything but had the good manners and decency of a Mother Superior. I was shown everything; the pirate's parlor, the torture chamber, the selection hall, all the rooms. My attention was gripped, not by the picturesqueness of the whole place, nor by the women, but by its isolation from the outside world. The calm, the comfort, the silence, the extraordinary pleasantness of that "ambiance," were intended to tear a man away from all his worries, all his problems, no matter what they were. I talked freely with Vogüé. I understood how a man like Toulouse-Lautrec and so many others could have spent most of their time here. "You're beginning to see," said Vogüé. "These houses don't provide just custom-made sex, although that may be extremely important. They are extraordinary places of relaxation. I'm not surprised that petty-bourgeois men who are afraid of their time are desperately eager to destroy these venerable institutions. True, this is a very luxurious and very expensive house, to which only the very privileged have access. Presumably, a worker might also need the intellectual, moral, and physical relaxation that his boss sometimes comes here for. Instead of outlawing brothels, the state might be better off if it had a lot more."

The gentle young woman who was pouring champagne for us talked at length about her own happiness. "I'm not cut out to be faithful, and I've never been vain or arrogant enough to order men around or shake up their lives. I must admit that I'm a submissive girl, and I really enjoy being submissive. It's all relative, anyway. The man who goes to bed with me here is just like a child as soon as he's in my arms. He needs a girl friend who means nothing to him, whose only function is to restore his self-confidence. That's one of the nice things about our work."

I thought of a story about Drieu La Rochelle that Aragon had told me in 1929. The two of them had gone to a brothel, as they often did. From time to time, Drieu, a man of contradictions and complexes, worried about his virility, which bothered him a great deal. Aragon heard someone calling him from a nearby room. It was Drieu, carrying a naked woman whose thighs were wrapped around his hips; the woman was solidly nailed by the virility upon which she writhed, sighing. "Louis, Louis," Drieu was crying in true anguish. "Louis, Louis, I'm impotent!"

During the municipal election campaign of 1945, Ceux de la Résistance gave me the quarter-hour of radio time allotted to the national organizations that were running candidates. My broadcast was scheduled just before the one by Thorez. I had not met the Secretary-General of the Communist Party for fifteen years. He heard my broadcast and congratulated me warmly as I left the studio. "I have some qualms about speaking after you," he said, "because I'll be saying the same things." I had strongly advocated a united stand. That conversation was the penultimate episode in my relations with the Party.

The final episode was a luncheon in Villette. I was invited by Mayoux, the Party's representative to the Liberation Committee of the nineteenth arrondissement, soon after I had been elected to the Municipal Council. I think Pioro was also there. After the usual small talk, Mayoux got down to business. "What we have to tell you is very important. All in all, we have nothing to reproach you with. You're undisciplined, but that's in your nature. No one's going to do you over. In fact, there is no political disagreement between us. Come back to the Party. You can retain your seat in the Municipal Council, of course, and we'll guarantee your nomination as a deputy at the elections for the Constituent Assembly."

This was totally unexpected. My reply was evasive. "You don't know everything. Perhaps I'm basically in disagreement with the Communist Party. Furthermore, how do you know for sure that I want to be a member of the Constituent Assembly?" Naturally, the matter got no further.

The behavior of the Communist group at City Hall did not encourage me to take a road that I already refused to follow. Impervious to any argument, concerned above all with the demagogy which it saw as the interest of the Party, this monolithic group was exclusively preoccupied with wrecking any initiatives that were not its own and with supporting any motions that could rouse agitation and propaganda. It did work with others on the outlawing of brothels, because this was a sensitive voter issue and had occasioned political bargaining.

In the center of Place Armand Carrel, a small miserable bronze to the memory of Jean Macé, the founder of the League of Instruction, had been put up in 1939. Vichy, always glad to take cheap revenge on secular authority, had handed the bronze over to the German war industry. I suggested that it be replaced with a piece by Giacometti. Pioro liked the idea. Alberto came to the office one day with a marvelous filigree figure. The Communist Party didn't want it. I asked the Council for seven million francs to buy works by Bonnard, Matisse, Roualt, and Picasso, so that the Paris City Hall could have some trace of the great French painters of our time. I proposed that we hire one of these artists to decorate one of the few rooms whose walls and ceilings hadn't been completely covered up by official painters of the

1890's. My proposal was rejected on the basis of a report by Gourdeaux, the trade-unionist who had expelled me from the Party in 1931. None of my colleagues were interested. One old reactionary concerned with the fine arts, Contenot, confused Henri Matisse with a nineteenth-century stained-glass artisan, Auguste Matisse, who had once been summoned to decorate municipal buildings. The men in the prefect's office knew who Matisse and Picasso were, but they had sworn never to allow the scandalous products of these painters into the city's collections.

On December 31, 1945, I was completely broke. I had used whatever money I had to buy Christmas toys. There was a delay in the payment of the mediocre monthly salary allocated to the municipal councilors of Paris. I was living with a girl friend, Ghislaine, on Quai de Conti. I can't remember whether we were fighting or she had other committments. But, for whatever reason, I was alone. I stayed alone for the whole next day, and my food was extremely frugal. It was a good day for reflecting and putting things in order.

Volontés had stopped publication. It had been selling badly. The political parties wanted to get rid of it and sabotaged its distribution. The deficit grew with each issue, and the directors of Ceux de la Résistance had decided to sell it, or at least its stock, but they had not been able to reach any agreement.

Why had the newspaper failed? It was interesting. The editor-in-chief, Michel Collinet, had opened the columns to talented men and women. It was a far-left weekly, but eclectic enough not to be boring. It dealt with all sorts of problems. *Volontés* had spoken against the proletarian revolution and against the notion that the Communists could be outflanked by the left. I had already realized that the proletarian revolution was a chimera. I had argued that proletarian unity was a bait and that any attempt to rectify dogma, returning it to integrity and revising its most contestable points, would be as ineffective as the formation of a sect within the Church. This is an almost physical phenomenon: the body of doctrine, if it is defended by a solid organization that is pitiless toward talents and innovations, never fears minor heresies. It compels recognition through the sole weight of its intolerance, its bureaucratic structure, and its material wealth. The heretics amuse the younger generation by blowing bubbles around an enormous bog. The few schisms that do occur are national phenomena and never destroy the Church.

The Communist Party is destined by its basic principles to have nothing but mediocre leaders. They must be diligent but refuse to enter any new roads, frowning at every venture. Thus the Party reassures the social groups that put their trust in its paltry platform of petty-bourgeois dictatorship and its tactics of one-upmanship. It periodically attracts a few intellectuals fascinated by utopia, but once they have gradually attained the rather simple objectives of the Socialist programs, solely because of the dynamism of middle-class society, they force it to give up any idea of revolution. Or, more exactly, they treat the total chimera of such a revolution as folklore in speeches at commemorative ceremonies. The Party members effectively use the idea to defend and improve their living conditions within the framework of market economy and democracy.

The state officially teaches the Party's doctrine in its university, which assures the training of the intellectuals it needs. On the other hand, the Party gives society political leaders from the working class. The French state, one of the most congealed in the world, is closed to anyone who has not received the "proper" education and is not a member of the professional hierarchy. It is incapable of training industrial leaders and union workers, although it draws the essential part of its resources from them. The Communist Party offers the worker a chance to become a union secretary, a professional politician, a municipal councilman, a senator, or a parliamentary deputy. Just as the industrial leaders use money to break down the tightly padlocked doors of the French mandarins, workers use the electoral mandate they receive from their peers and the renown they acquire in social and political struggles.

The reflections that arose from my unenviable poverty led me to this analysis on December 31, 1945. My thinking was interrupted twice by visits to Ghislaine's grand piano, where I was working on a romance by Gabriel Fauré that my mother used to sing to me in 1913.

My general description of the Communist Party could have applied to the British Labour Party or the German Social-Democratic Party. The originality (if one can put it that way) of the French Communist Party was to its subordination to the interests of the Soviet Union. (Perhaps that was also the source of its strength.) During the last few months of 1945 it launched a violent offensive against General de Gaulle, which was one of the causes for his resignation. Stalin tried to mask his own weakness through endlessly escalating aggressiveness. He took calculated risks of a Third World War, from which he would probably have withdrawn at the very last moment, a few hours before the American planes filled with atomic bombs took off. The relative weakness of the Russians did win the concern of a certain number of intellectuals, who were ready to cede half the world to Stalin's dreadful dictatorship under the pretext that this would reestablish a political balance with the United States.

I felt as though I were watching the last act of a play. Twenty years of efforts by the people, the revolutionary intellectuals, and, particularly, the different leaders who had used the colossal power of national sentiment, of nationalism in the service of the state, had crushed the great reactionary forces stemming from the nineteenth century. This achievement was probably a by-product of the world expansion of capitalism and the disquietingly live force of emancipation contained in merchandise. Consumption, offered everywhere and to everyone, represented the finest, the most complete, the most sophisticated stage of hope. Whether it replaced brutal conquest or the idyllic exchanges of poverty economies, the mercantile system represents absolute progress, in contrast to the bureaucratic distribution proposed by Karl Marx.

Were certain aspects of Marxism all that different from these conquered reactionary forces? The Marxists were indignant at the alienation of the work force, which had been turned into merchandise. But what can you do with your working strength except sell it or use it yourself? And if you have to sell it, isn't the sole issue the matter of getting the best price? Is the individual any different within the Communist Party, the Trotskyite Leagues, the Hitler Youth, the Children of Mary, or the Renault factory? Renault "alienates" the specialized workers for only forty hours a week? That's quite a lot. But the Communist Party, the Hitler Youth, and the Children of Mary achieve a total alienation of the individual. And this will hold true in any *organized* society that imposes its final organization upon man. According to the vow of the Stalinists and Trotskyites, he must be turned into a gear within the social mechanism that operates on behalf of the general interest, that implacable adversary of man. Let us go a bit further: Can man become any different? Isn't he both good and evil, prudish and obscene, peaceful and murderous?

In Ghislaine's studio on that December 31, I was enjoying all the benefits of the formal liberty that the left-wing speakers gloated over whenever they felt obliged to attack democracy. I was free to come and go in a town on holiday. Since I had no money, I couldn't buy anything. So the celebration went on without me. For a moment I imagined life in a Communist society. What would be different for me? Would the state be any less lax in paying my salary? Everything I knew about bureaucracy led to the opposite conclusion. Even if Marx's system of coupons were in effect, the coupons would never be doled out on time. As in Russia, the stores would be empty. Mindless planners would have been unable to supply the capital with turkeys, and other planners would have taken charge of restaurant menus to avoid waste. And if I had complained about receiving a coupon that didn't allow me to acquire the objects I wanted, they would have told me that I had received the value of my work, that I had nothing to carp about. If I had kicked up a row, they would have thrown me into prison as a bad citizen. I wouldn't have been able to invoke the class struggle, capitalist exploitation, or inalienable right to be discontented. I wouldn't have had that right. My reaction would have been considered antisocial, and I would have deserved to be punished like a thief.

On that December 31, I realized that I put liberty of any sort, even purely formal freedom, above everything else. To keep it on the already appreciable level that I experienced during those penniless hours in 1945, we would have to prevent the capitalist system from being destroyed, put a stop to nationalization and collectivization. Marcel Bour's cable works, the Samaritaine department stores, which I could see from the window of Ghislaine's studio, the restaurant on Place Dauphine, where I couldn't go, had to remain private property. They were in the hands of people who could never, in any way, invoke general welfare against me.

Everything I had learned about the "Socialist" countries had proved to me that the type of society they represented was the antithesis of what I wanted out of life, whether these societies were run by the workers themselves or by technocrats who claimed to act in their name. Could attentive and rigorous reasoning have helped me avoid twenty years of illusions? I think not. Ideologies exert a great force of inertia.

In writing these lines, I have in mind not only the production of material goods, the comforts for which "the dictatorship of the proletariat" is challenged, or the personal liberty that Leninism suppressed wherever it took control. I am also thinking of the "immaterial values of wealth." Marx and Engels dealt with that issue, but in absolutely unrealistic terms, limiting themselves to blaming all evils on mercantile economy. In *The History of Economic Doctrines*, which contains reading notes on a work by Henri Storch published in 1823, and whose subtitle is *Intellectual Production* (which may have been added by Kautsky), Marx writes that "capitalist production is hostile to certain immaterial productions such as art and poetry." This peremptory assertion probably goes back to 1861–63. Highly talented poets were still living in England, France, and Germany, and they put up rather well with capitalist production. Its mechanisms brought them both income and a liberty that their predecessors had never known, except when the first manifestations of capitalist production had permitted them to escape the patronage of princes. In 1861 Ingres, Daumier, and Delacroix were famous, and Turner had died just recently; the hundred years to follow could be compared to the greatest periods of mankind in regard to art and poetry.

On the other hand, the intellectual desert of Marxist-inspired societies seems to indicate that there is a remarkable incompatibility between the systems themselves and the production of most of these immaterial riches. Perhaps we could have foreseen in 1930 that the Communist planners, as careful readers of *Das Kapital*, would zealously attempt to drive out nonproductive work, to fit all unproductive activity in the category of services, to outlaw them as an economy move or because of a factitious concern for emancipation (domestics, prostitution). They would act all the more forcefully because the new class of bureaucrats would be consuming all the nonproductive labor. The capitalist economy run by the workers or the planners who arrogate the right to represent them may be derisively labeled Socialism, but it is merely the monstrous and caricatured achievement of a system that Marx described in order to incite the nations to destroy it. The revolution proposed in the *Communist Manifesto* could have no other effect than to annihilate the revolutionaries and subjugate them all to rationing.

In the *Note on Money* I had written in 1929, I had indicated the importance to morality and civilization of the expenditures that rich men make as pure losses. Georges Bataille, in January 1933, published (in *La Critique Sociale*) *The Notion of Spending*, an article that must be one of the major texts of this century. I had read it shortly after Hitler had assured his triumph over the Marxist parties. Although I had never set great store by Bataille's critical writings, this piece obliged me to revise my judgment. I put it aside, somewhat annoyed, and forgot its very existence. But then here, at the dawn of the year 1946, I suddenly recalled that article and felt very eager to read it again. Its arguments (or my idea of them) struck me as the conclusion to that day of heresy.

Ghislaine worked in a bookstore. As soon as she got back, I asked her to dig up issue No. 7 of *La Critique Sociale*. A rereading reinforced both my embarrassment and my admiration: admiration for the inventiveness, the intelligent analysis, but embarrassment at the constant reduction of reasoning to the personal fantasies of the author and at the references to a teleological notion of the class struggle. "Luxury," writes Bataille, "periods of mourning, wars, cults, the building of commemorative monuments, games, spectacles, art, perverse sexual activity (i.e., that diverted from genital finality), are all activities that, at least in their original condition, are an end in themselves. In each case the accent is on *the loss*, which must be as great as possible if the activity is to have a true meaning." Obviously, one cannot hope that the clerks in the Auditing Office will help anyone introduce the idea of unproductive spending into the programs of the state. The same observation can be made about the men who were shocked by the glass of milk that Dali added to a symbolic object.

During the third century, no one tried to become mayor in Gaul's Roman cities. Once elected, the aediles had to ruin themselves to beautify the city and amuse the townspeople. Comrade Gourdeaux, who refused to spend seven million francs (1946 value) for paintings by Bonnard and Matisse, and Comrade Fleury, the municipal councilman of the twentieth arrondissement who objected to the restoration of the house of the Saint-Simonians, would never have been accepted as mayors by Lutetia. Their concepts and methods were reactionary. One could not expect them to agree to the notion that spending has a social value.

André Breton wrote to me as soon as he got back to Paris. He had no telephone. The telephone office couldn't do anything for him for another year. I was happy to rediscover the authority who could give the necessary orders. We celebrated this happy event with a luncheon, but we could not hit upon any reason for working together again, despite the joy we shared. Breton had largely terminated his literary career; I was in the penultimate act of my very mediocre political career. The entire city, the radio, even schoolchildren, were reciting Aragon's poems. We both felt that this success would not make them any better. It was probably a foreshadowing of the attic where such products would join *The Broken Vase* and Voltaire's tragedies. Maurice Thorez was the brains and hope of politics. But this hope, in all honesty, was not that of the nation, and the brains were frail. Thorez was soon to vanish from the political scene.

Breton and I were curious about what each of us could teach the other, and we were disappointed. Perhaps Breton was expecting an evocation of Fourier, some new recipes for action. The only possibility I could offer was my capacity to do something that might relieve a few difficulties and to use the councils to debate administrative problems. Nevertheless, that conversation involved two people who were far from run-of-the-mill. As might be expected, Breton contributed a richness and variety which I was unable to equal. Spiritualism had taken hold of him, less perhaps as a philosophical attitude than as a means of knowledge.

"Have you become a mystic?" I jokingly asked him.

He laughed but did not reply frankly. "I *am* favorable to mysticism, as I am to magic, and I am curious about religions and the religious spirit. But I am not reconciled with the Crucified. Ultimately, I don't care about the intellectual mediocrity of the priests and the poor metaphysics they have preserved since they repudiated Satan and the Golden Legend. I always feel the same aversion to the idea of a fault that can be redeemed through privation, suffering, and sacrifice, and to the apology for resignation, much less the scandalous fantasies that the Church has added to this basic masochism."

"You know," I told him, "that I feel the same way about Christian dogmas. But I've become tolerant. Hitlerism taught me that liberty cannot be sold out. I no longer want to destroy or close the churches or do in the priests. As long as the world is threatened by totalitarian regimes, it may even be important to help preserve every religious or philosophical group that can maintain heterogeneous thinking among men. Furthermore, the Gospel contains the idea of forgiving trespasses, which might do much to discredit the justice of the prince and that of the people, to wreck the concept of the tribunal, the notion of trial and punishment, so that society will be so ashamed that it will keep them on the lowest level. But I no longer believe in the revolution we wished for. Shouldn't we question the very principle of the dialectical method? Benedetto Croce and others have long since shown that in Hegel the contradictory is often confused with the different. This observation puts a lot of dents in the reasoning of the Master of Jena.

I am tempted to raise another objection, which is more serious. Difficult as it may be to define a true contradiction, its presence in a system never leads to a resolution through synthesis. At least, that's what I believe. Contradictions are not resolved; if something is destroyed, its destruction depends on more than the effects of its contrary. If, therefore, in order to prove the dogma right, one pursues the annihilation of the thesis—which can be achieved only through some energy outside the antithesis—the final result will be the creation of a third element, which has none of the features of the synthesis but is more like a surrogate force, intended essentially to prevent the system from collapsing. All the Bolshevik experience is proof of this. Our entire life offers examples. In chemistry, which was so dear to Engels, there is no dialectical process. The famous identity of contraries results merely from a change in perspective. To an outside observer, in certain circumstances, contraries have the same effect. We are satisfied to call this effect a dialectical reversal or a dialectical play. But this has nothing to do with the basic Hegelian mechanism, the triad. Here the synthesis is merely a view of the mind, or one of the two contradictory components as seen from a new angle.

"The proletarian revolution will not take place. Moreover, to safeguard liberty, private capitalism must not be destroyed. Hegelian dialectics is a method of knowledge, one approach among a great many others. You can see that there isn't much left of the faith of my youth."

Breton had never sought to be a specialist in Hegel. He had managed to extract a few of the diamonds that this philosophy contains, but he never got lost in the hodgepodge of subtleties or fantasies that have nourished doctoral dissertations for a hundred years. Hegel's writings, like so many others, are probably very rewarding to anyone who tackles them Surrealistically—that is, disrespectfully, with an avowed interest in distorting them or even in casting them in an absurd light if necessary. Dialectics cannot survive the test to which Marx and Engels submitted it when they put it on feet that it doesn't have. Meant to walk on its head, it can endure a poetic treatment much better than a scientific one. André Breton tore out a few pieces and gave them a new life; by 1946, however, he felt that he wouldn't get anything more out of them. "Do you know Stéphane Lupasco's works?" he asked me. "If not, you ought to read them. You'll find in them a logic of contradiction that eludes the rigid mechanism which Hegel invented."

We agreed that the excessive importance politics had assumed since the French Revolution should be condemned. Previously nourished by ambitions, this trend had become infected with ideologies throughout the nineteenth century. Political parties had come to be like congregations, and then like associations of evildoers. Their slogan should have been: "Illusion and Oppression." At the point we had reached in the West—where the development of productive forces was animated by their own dynamism—all one could talk about was administration. And administration should not be too disorderly. Since both of us thought that governments, whatever they may be, ran the risk of being carried away by a sort of automatism of power, we looked for effective means to defend the governed. I chose the absolute limitation of politics to the handling of things. The study of production and distribution would be carried out electronically, elected assemblies would make and enforce decisions, elected executives would coordinate these activities. Diversity would be the rule. Uniformity and rationalization would never move beyond the area of weights and measures. Breton favored the idea of Estates General: technicians, scientists, educators, artists, and workers, urban and rural, would gather to present lists of grievances and advise the governments. Breton was slightly surprised when I told him that I could subscribe to that outline of a state counseled by sages only if the state wasn't in charge of all property.

The spiritualism of André Breton from 1945 to his death is bound to occasion scholarly studies. Critics will evoke the (probably contradictory) evidence of men and women who were close to him. We can expect that dogmatists will be scandalized, because the logic of the electron is insufficient for explaining or describing a dream. In their panic at the idea of trying to apply the science of dreams to that of particles, they will never depart, in regard to thinking and dreaming, from the gross ideas of nineteenth-century scientists. They will forget that what they fear is the object of a very particular science, pataphysics, whose existence ought to reassure them. On the other hand, there will still be the sectarians of tradition, of the immortality of the soul, and the like. Any evidence can be implied by more cogent evidence. The opposition of life and death may cause individuals endowed with very great pride, such as General de Gaulle, to rally to overly inductive metaphysics. If Breton, in his declining years, more or less furtively believed that the mind can exist outside of time—or, which is not exactly the same thing, that time, like space, is not merely a coordinate of the mind (which is obvious until the disappearance of the source of the mind)— then one must adopt two different approaches to his metaphysical anxiety: one of its aspects is pride, and the other is the transcendence of symbols and rites that can convey and express a spiritual content, even though that expression does not have to be taken as a supernatural thought. *The History of Magic* was never completed, any more than *The Dialectics of Nature.*

Around 1955 I attended a lecture by René Alleau. I sat down next to Breton in the tiny auditorium of the Geographic Society. I was there because of Yvonne, who was fanatically devoted to such "teaching." I knew that she was doomed. The lecturer was as brilliant as he could be, which is no small compliment. Toward the end of his talk, Breton turned to me and said: "These 'initiates' have an extraordinary knack for leaving their audience unsatisfied. At every step of the way, you think they're finally going to say everything. But once they've concluded, you're still no further than before. Maybe there's nothing to learn, but what an intelligent approach to the mystery! Alas, we won't find out anything today!"

I was unwilling to believe in the objective reality of magic and skeptical about the marvels reported by alchemists. But I couldn't simply disregard the path that Breton had taken from the Association of Revolutionary Writers and Artists to René Alleau's lecture. One obvious factor compelled attention: Alleau's intellectual superiority over Fréville, Nizan, and the others. The man who wrote, "All the human sciences are subjective, and it is the lucid and sincere recognition of that basic subjectivity that determines the degree of relative objectivity they can attain," seems more deserving of a chair in Nanterre or Vincennes than the interpreters of Marxism.

The further I veered from some of André Breton's spiritualist preoccupations, the more important they seemed to become. To the extent that I had accepted a political role that could not be justified (and that had not been justified for ten years—except when I took part in combat, where I was useful for defending liberty, the supreme good), I felt concerned about all sorts of subtleties—those of thought, of modes of life, or of the exigencies of birth. The intellectual feels responsible only for his commerce with the sheet of paper or with the ten intellectuals for whom he writes. The politician is responsible for the acts of his supporters, for those of his adversaries, and for the daily life of citizens.

The administration that took office in 1946 not only had all the characteristics of frailty; it was also rife with civil war. A monstrous advantage had been granted to the Stalinist undertaking of cretinization and subjugation which was displaying its audacity and stupidity everywhere. Three parties, all of them thriving on the back of the nation, were colonizing the state. I had endorsed Jacques Baumel's and Georges Izard's arguments in favor of regrouping in a single formation all the non-Communist Resistance movements. The ultimate plan of the Democratic and Socialist Union of the Resistance, of which I was one of the founders, was to bring about a merger with a transformed and rejuvenated Socialist Party. This was out of the question. Gaston Deferre and Mitterand spent seven years trying to break down the doors defended by Guy Mollet. Tedious preliminary talks were started with the radicals. But none of them could lead anywhere, because the participants, with very rare exceptions, concentrated entirely on minor electoral problems that were firmly situated in time and space. Anyone not immediately interested in regaining the Andelys or Lunéville seat was considered an impenitent dreamer.

Nationalism has always been the principal motive force in world history. Its effects have occasionally been reinforced by racism, which was not eradicated by the suicides in the Berlin bunker and which has now reached the nations of color. When Ho Chi Minh came to Fontainebleau, he was received at City Hall like a head of state. One of the principal French negotiators, Max André, was the city councilman. It was extremely funny to see Ho Chi Minh and Francisque Gay in the same room. Physically they looked so much alike that people wondered whether a solution to the Indo-Chinese and French problems might not be to interchange these two men. No one would have noticed!

I chatted at length with a young Annamite who wore the uniform of a French officer, replete with commander's stripes, even though he belonged to the Viet Minh army. The conference seemed to be working out. "And now," said the commander, "France must give us a navy."

I was dumbfounded. "Whatever for! Do you know what a navy costs, in terms of building ships, maintaining them, and training specialists? We have a navy but, fortunately, it has been practically useless for some time now. Why don't we put a dispatch vessel at your disposal, or even a cruiser. We can rent boats and crews. They'll carry out all the police work and surveillance that you assign them to; they'll carry your gendarmes and your customs men."

"We're sovereign. We want our own navy!" Thus hundreds of thousands of new soldiers and generals arose throughout the world, ready for putsches!

The Soviet reconstruction had taken place in terror and slavery. The

workers were attached to the factory as the serfs had once been to
the soil. Michel Collinet reported that "tardiness of even a few minutes was enough to send the delinquent to forced labor." The "people's"
democracies, one by one, became satellites of Stalin's empire after their
former leaders had been massacred. The leprosy spread to Greece, Italy,
and France. People had to learn how to choose so that they could preserve the heterogeneous and contradictory society in which man can
express all his tendencies. There rationalists, alchemists, workers, idlers,
unbelievers, revolutionaries, businessmen, painters, priests, vagabonds,
prostitutes, and chief executives would ultimately get along together.
Later on, when the immediate dangers had been dispelled, I would touch
things up. In 1947, I joined the political organization that General de
Gaulle had finally decided to form. As in 1940, we had to make our
way through an intermediate stage. No one seemed more capable of
maintaining the opposing tensions in relative harmony than the man
who had already twice refused the temptation of dictatorship.

One had to acknowledge that the production, distribution, and ownership of wealth still presented problems. But most of these were
technical, and the mechanisms already in operation took care of them.
The antagonism between capitalism and Socialism is merely the result
of poverty. The point was to save a state that was falling apart and
was threatened with servitude. The next generation would no doubt
decide its fate by looking straight into the face of the social development of man, unmenaced by any bullet from the back and unham-
pered by the hypnosis of dialectics and Christian sexual taboos. One
could then try to rejoin the herd and return to Bakunin, Guénon, and
especially Charles Fourier. Their utopias, which were meant to replace
those of Marx, might possibly give birth to noble motives for revolt
in a world where revolution is an accident.

INDEX